BEYOND BELIEF

BEYOND BELIEF

Two Thousand Years of Bad Faith in the Christian Church

JAMES MCDONALD

BEYOND BELIEF
Two Thousand Years of Bad Faith in the Christian Church

Published by
Garnet Publishing
8 Southern Court
South Street
Reading
RG1 4QS
UK

www.garnetpublishing.co.uk

Copyright © James McDonald, 2011

First Paperback Edition

ISBN: 978-0-86372-345-2

British Library Cataloguing-in-Publication Data
A catalogue record for this book is available from the British Library

Typeset by Samantha Barden
Jacket design by Garnet Publishing

Printed and bound in Lebanon by International Press:
interpress@int-press.com

errata and updates may be found online at
http://www.badnewsaboutchristianity.com/errata/

For Susannah Jones, née Lewis

CONTENTS

✧

ACKNOWLEDGEMENTS

My sincere thanks go to Robert Dinwiddie and to Marcus Williamson for their invaluable suggestions and for their assistance in editing this book.

James McDonald
France, September 2010

INTRODUCTION

And ye shall know the truth, and the truth shall make you free.
John 8:32

To a large extent the history of the Western World over the last 2,000 years is the history of the Christian Church. Without understanding the role of the Church it is not possible to understand the history of Europe, the Middle East, Asia or the Americas. Nor is it possible to understand the development of ideas in such areas as politics, education, medicine, law, sociology and architecture: almost anything in fact from art to astrophysics.

Repercussions from crusades that took place over 900 years ago are still in evidence. The division of the Roman Empire in early Christian times also reverberates to the present day. The border between the eastern and western parts of the Empire re-emerged in the late twentieth century as a fault line in what was then Yugoslavia. That line is now the border between Croatia and Serbia. On the side that used to lie in the Western Empire Croats use the Latin alphabet of the Roman Catholic Church; on the other side, the side that used to lie in the Eastern Empire, Serbs use the Greek alphabet favoured by the Orthodox Church.

Whatever one's own personal beliefs, the Christian Churches provide material for the enquiring mind. Why did Jesus never forsake Judaism if his intention was to found a new religion? Why are there so many different Christian denominations? What do they all believe, and what exactly do they disagree about? Why do the Orthodox Churches claim to be catholic, and why does the Catholic Church claim to be orthodox? Why have long suppressed theories about the role of Magdalene generated such interest in recent times? In the course of looking at the history of the Christian Churches we will find the answers to these and many other questions.

Much of the material here can be confirmed by reference to the Bible, and even some of this will be surprising. Christians are now generally aware that Bible stories are often retellings of stories found in older pagan literature, but many are unaware that numerous gods are mentioned in the Bible, not to mention numerous 'christs'. Almost all will be surprised to discover that for the first few centuries mainstream Christians regarded the Emperor of the Roman Empire as infallible. Addressed as *Your Holiness* and acclaimed as *Pontifex Maximus* and *Bishop of Bishops*, a long line of Emperors were considered incapable of error on a range of matters including faith and morals, long before the concept of a Pope was invented.

The history of the Church is different from the version popularly taught in most European and North American schools. For example, few people, other than Church scholars, are aware that no original text of the Bible, or any part of it, survives. Nor that the texts that do survive are late and contradictory, and bear evidence of tampering (including the late addition of the stories of Jesus' birth and resurrection). Few realise the extent to which forged documents helped Churches to establish doctrine and political power.

Again, most Christians see their system of belief as dating from the earliest times, but this idea becomes difficult to sustain when one looks into when and how key doctrines were established.

This book is likely to contain some big surprises for anyone who is not already a Church scholar, and to explain a few puzzles. The scope is wide, from early history to the present day, from Chinese Nestorian Christians to American Mormons, from ancient Greek philosophical arguments to medieval theology and the rise of science and rationalism.

A NOTE ON SCOPE AND SOURCES

A major difficulty lies in defining exactly what the terms *Church* and *Churches* mean. How does a Church differ from a denomination or a sect? Which organisations count as Christian Churches? Do heretical groups? Do schismatic groups? Do those who deny traditional doctrines, as the Quakers do? Without being pedantic, it is difficult to specify exactly what the terms mean each time they are used. Generally the context will make it clear which denominations are included. There have always been different groups that call themselves Christian while disagreeing with each other on important points of doctrine.

When discussing the early Church, the context will make it clear whether the term Church covers the Jewish Christians, St Paul's group (from which most of today's mainstream Churches have evolved) or the various Gnostic groups.* From the fourth century onwards we are generally talking about St Paul's group, and the context will distinguish between Orthodox Churches (including what is now called the Roman Church) and the many other Churches. From around the time of the Crusades the context will distinguish between the Eastern (or Orthodox) Church and the Western Church (also called the Roman Church or Roman Catholic Church). After the Reformation the context will distinguish between the Western Churches: Roman on one hand and Western Reformed (mainly Protestant – Lutheran and Calvinist) on the other. Later still the context distinguishes between these and a proliferation of nonconformist Churches. The fact is that there have always been so many different factions that it is impractical to indicate in each case exactly which factions are included and which excluded. Any consequent ambiguity is the price of condensing the scope into a

---

* Gnostics are people who believe they possess a secret knowledge of spiritual matters, usually obtained by direct communication with God, or with a god.

single volume. Wherever the term *mainstream Churches* is used, it may be taken as encompassing all but the smallest fringe groups.

It may be helpful to clarify the relationship between the Orthodox Church (or Churches) and the Roman Church. In the first few centuries of the Christian Church, several cities were established as self-governing local centres. Although they were self-governing, they came to regard Constantinople, the new capital of the Roman Empire, as their centre. Greek, the language of the Empire, was also their language. One of the local Churches, the one based in Rome, subsequently split away from the others. Hence it is known as the *Church of Rome* or the *Roman Church*. It adopted Latin in place of the traditional Greek, so it also came to be known as the *Latin Church*. To contrast this Church from the other members of the federation, the other members were referred to collectively as the *Greek Church*.

Both Roman and Greek Churches claimed to encompass the whole of the one true Church and so called themselves catholic (from the Greek for *whole, general* or *comprehensive*). Both also claimed to be orthodox (from the Greek for *right thinking*). In practice, however, the Roman Church is generally referred to as the Catholic Church and the Greek Church as the Orthodox Church, though they are sometimes contrasted as the Western and Eastern Churches.

The Orthodox Church still regards itself as a federation of self-governing Churches, which are thus sometimes referred to as the Greek Orthodox Church, the Russian Orthodox Church, the Bulgarian Orthodox Church, and so on. The Catholic Church, having its head in Rome, is sometimes called the Roman Catholic Church. To sum up:

Western Church = Roman Church = Catholic Church = Roman Catholic Church

Eastern Church = Greek Church = Orthodox Church = Greek Orthodox Church + Russian Orthodox Church etc.

As far as possible footnotes and references are to works that are readily available as well as authoritative, for example to popular English translations of works such as those of early historians like Eusebius of Caesarea (*c*.260–*c*.340) and influential medieval works like *Malleus Maleficarum* (Hammer of Witches). So too, references to Gibbon's *The Decline and Fall of the Roman Empire* are to a popular one-volume edition.

Most readers will not have access to early texts and in any case cannot be expected to be fluent in Hebrew, Greek and Latin. Hence, extensive use has been made of English translations of the Bible. In this way, readers can confirm many of the points made in this book that might appear surprising. In general, quotations from the Bible are from the Authorised Version (also known as the King James Version), except where there is a clear reason not to use it, for example because the meaning is obscured by seventeenth-century English, or because a key word in it was mistranslated. Such cases are always indicated explicitly, and the source of the more recent translation is provided. Modern translations often include useful explanations and footnotes, and two of these have been used extensively – the *New International Version* or NIV (widely used by Protestant Churches) and the *Jerusalem Bible* or JB (widely used by the Roman Church).

1

THE RELIABILITY OF CHRISTIAN AUTHORITIES

THE OLD TESTAMENT

Here is wisdom; this is the royal Law; these are the lively Oracles of God.
Words spoken at the presenting of the Bible
at the British Coronation Service

In this chapter we will review the nature of the Old Testament, and assess some of the claims made for it by Jews and Christians.

The Old Testament is divided into a number of books, most of them originally written in Hebrew, all of them now considered by Jews to have been inspired by God. Some parts of some books were originally written in Aramaic,* some apparently in Syriac or other Middle Eastern languages, but all such texts were rendered into Hebrew. Later these Hebrew scriptures were translated into Greek, Latin and other languages. Some additions to the text were written in Greek and survive only in Greek. The Jews distinguished between three kinds of book within the Old Testament: the *Torah* (Law), *Nebim* (Prophets) and *Ketubim* (Writings). They came to be regarded as divinely inspired in this same chronological order: first the *Torah*, later the *Nebim,* and later still the *Ketubim.*

For centuries the Church taught that God had communicated his word through certain Jewish prophets. There was no doubt about who these prophets were or what they had written, no question that the original text had ever been tampered with, and no possibility that errors had been introduced in authorised translations. Not only was the text

---

* Aramaic was a common language in the Middle East from around 700 BC to AD 700 (and is still spoken today in a few areas).

internally consistent and free from error, but it also contained nothing that was superfluous. Furthermore it was held that the text had been set down in chronological order. Those without learning generally held that the text was to be interpreted literally, but biblical scholars have always used a certain amount of interpretation (they call it exegesis) to help understand the more opaque passages.

Traditionally, Jews believed that the Hebrew text of the Old Testament was the infallible word of God. Orthodox Christians held that the Greek translation called the Septuagint held the same status. For centuries this was the only version used by Christians. The Roman Church later accorded the same status to a fourth-century Latin translation (the Vulgate); and later still Protestants accorded it to their own translations. Many fundamentalist Christians still believe that the Old Testament is the literal and infallible word of God, but over the last 200 years or so virtually all Christian scholars have abandoned such beliefs.

What would we expect of the Old Testament if it were, as claimed, the word of God? We might reasonably expect that there would be no doubt about what constituted the Old Testament. The books in it, called the canon, should be clearly defined. Furthermore this canon should be unchanged from the earliest days of Christianity. We might even expect some sort of divine confirmation of it. We might also expect that the Bible would be original. We would not for example expect to find stories that have been plagiarised from neighbouring cultures or other religions. If the claims made for the Bible were true, then in view of their importance we might expect that the original manuscripts would have been carefully preserved. Failing this, we might expect that various copies would at least agree with each other. We certainly would not expect to find evidence of tampering and later editing. We might also reasonably expect various books to have been written by the authors to whom they are attributed, and in the historical periods claimed for them. Also, if translations were divinely inspired, as the Greek Septuagint, Latin Vulgate, and English Authorised Version have been claimed to be, then we might expect the same standards of them as of the original text. We would not expect to find evidence of deliberate mistranslation. Also, if the Bible represented the infallible word of God, then it might reasonably be expected to be internally consistent and free from factual errors.

These expectations are not unreasonable. Neither are they merely the expectations of modern rationalists. Christians have made all of these claims and in the past have persecuted people for doubting them.

The Canon of the Old Testament

Of making many books there is no end; and much study is a weariness of the flesh.
Ecclesiastes 12:12

There is no evidence that any divine agency ever issued or confirmed an authorised list of contents for anything like a Bible, or even for an Old Testament. Jewish scholars disagreed with each other about what constituted Holy Scripture. When the Jewish historian Josephus (AD 37–c.100) listed books believed to be of divine origin he counted only four amongst what would now be called the Writings.[1] Later Jews (and Christians) would count no fewer than eleven.

By the time of Jesus, the Jews had included some books as scriptural on grounds that are now known to have been flawed. The book of Esther, for example, is a popular romance that does not even mention God. Furthermore, the story in it looks suspiciously like a version of an old Babylonian myth. There was much debate in Jewish circles as to whether Esther should be counted as scripture, and eventually it won hesitating approval, primarily because it justifies the Jewish institution of Purim.* However, the book had to be reduced by half to make it acceptable. The Song of Songs, also called Canticles, is an anthology of love poems, whose place in the canon was also disputed. It won approval on the erroneous ground that its author was Solomon, hence its alternative name, the Song of Solomon. Its explicit sex scenes have long caused unease amongst both Jews and Christians, who have traditionally mollified themselves with the belief that it is some sort of allegory. Ecclesiastes found its way into the canon because it was also mistakenly believed to have been written by Solomon. Uncomfortable material was removed: for example 18 psalms had to be dropped from the book of Psalms.[2] The

---

* Purim is a Jewish holiday that commemorates the deliverance of Persian Jews from a purported plot to exterminate them around the fifth century BC.

[3]

book of Daniel found its way in under false pretences, having been written much later than it purports to have been.

The Jews in Jerusalem were stricter than the Greek-speaking Jews of the Diaspora* in what they regarded as divinely inspired. Greek-speaking Jews included 1 Esdras, Judith, Tobit (Tobias) and the books of the two Maccabees with the histories, and Wisdom of Solomon, Ecclesiasticus (= Ben Sirach) and Baruch and the Prayer of Manasseh with the poetic and prophetic books, while the Song of the Three Holy Children, Susanna and the Elders, and Bel and the Dragon were appended to the book of Daniel. Arguments about what was and what was not genuine scripture prompted Jewish scholars to consider the question around the end of the first century AD. The first attempt at settling a definitive Jewish canon was reputedly made around AD 90 at the Council of Jamnia, where Jewish scholars discussed the validity of various books. If such a council did ever meet,[3] its decisions apparently failed to reach the Jews of the Diaspora, for they continued to accept as scripture works that other scholars had rejected, and indeed they continued to tamper with and supplement what they already had for many years to come.

When early Christians addressed the problem of what to regard as canonical, there was a distinct lack of agreement. No one knows what Jesus would have regarded as canonical. He probably never considered the question, since the question of a canon had not yet arisen. The first Christian known to have assembled a definitive list of Christian writings was Marcion (AD c.85–160), a ship owner and native of Sinope (Sinop in modern Turkey), in the latter half of the second century AD. He had a low opinion of Christianity's Jewish origins and omitted the whole of the Old Testament. Stimulated into action by Marcion, the Church Father Irenaeus (AD c.130–c.200), Bishop of Lyons, compiled his own canon, which did include a version of the Old Testament.

Books that were held to be non-canonical by Jewish scholars continued to be regarded as canonical by the Jews of the Diaspora, and this dichotomy has echoed throughout Christendom to the present day, since Christian scholars generally accepted the Jews as authorities on their own scriptures. Initially the Church accepted the disputed books, at least partly because the Septuagint included them, and the Septuagint

---

* The Jews of the Diaspora were Jews living outside the traditional Bible lands.

was considered to have been divinely inspired. Nevertheless, particularly unconvincing books, such as Esther, were excluded.[4] Leading churchmen were still disputing books like Wisdom and Ecclesiasticus as late as the eighth century,[5] and disagreements continued for centuries to come. When Protestants started reconsidering the canon they rejected the disputed books, falling back into line with the Hebrew texts but printing the disputed ones as an appendix. At the Council of Trent in 1545–7 the Roman Church reconsidered its attachment to the Septuagint and decided to reject from the canon 1 Esdras and the Prayer of Manasseh, along with a late addition, 2 Esdras.[6] The Eastern Churches reached their own compromise in 1672, accepting some disputed books and rejecting others.[7]

So it is that the principal Churches still disagree about the canon of the Old Testament. Roman Catholic versions of the Bible include seven whole books and several further parts of books that are omitted from Anglican and Protestant versions. The material missing from the Anglican versions (listed in Article 6 of the 39 Articles) is included in the Apocrypha, now generally bound as a separate volume.[8] The Apocrypha takes its name from the Greek word *apocryphos* meaning *hidden away*. Works hidden away in the Apocrypha were so unlikely that they have given rise to the word *apocryphal*, meaning fanciful or imaginary. In his German Bible, Martin Luther (1483–1546) excluded 1 and 2 Esdras not only from the canon, but also from the appendix of apocryphal works. To complicate matters further, some books that are not generally considered even apocryphal by modern Churches are considered as fully canonical by some ancient Churches. For example, the Ethiopic Church regards 1 Enoch as canonical. Their case is strengthened by the fact that a New Testament author cites 1 Enoch as though it were valid scripture.[9]

The key point here is not that some biblical works are fanciful but that there is no reliable way of knowing which works possessed God's own authority. Was it the selection of the Jews of Jerusalem or the Jews of the Diaspora? Was it the works chosen by the Eastern Churches or the Western Church, or by the Roman Catholics, the Protestants, or by one of the hundreds of other Christian sects with their own canon? It seems odd that God should have permitted such a lack of clarity and so much disagreement about the contents of his divine revelation. It is also odd that the true word of God is not immediately distinguishable from the work of impostors. No version of the canon was so obviously divine that it could inspire universal agreement. Indeed, Churches typically decide their canons by a majority vote. Furthermore, all the oldest Churches have revised their canons over the centuries. For many people, the implication is that all such canons are not the selections of God at all but of fallible and capricious human beings.

An Original Work?

... Tear down your house, I say, and build a boat. These are the measurements of the barque as you shall build her: let her beam equal her length, let her deck be roofed over like the vault that covers the abyss; then take up into the boat the seed of all living creatures

The Epic of Gilgamesh, c.2500 BC (translation by N. K. Sandars)

If the books of the Old Testament contained God's unique revelation, they might reasonably be expected to be original. If on the other hand they were writings typical of the Middle East between 2,000 and 3,000 years ago, they would be likely to contain material plagiarised from other works and from neighbouring peoples. Which pattern does the Old Testament best fit? Did any biblical stories exist before God revealed them to his chosen people?

The Old Testament is not a single work but a collection of ancient Jewish writings. As a cursory glance shows, it is an amalgamation of laws, genealogies, chronicles (or histories), myths, proverbs, poetry, songs, eroticism, propaganda, prophecy, allegories, morality tales and humorous stories. In the original Hebrew there are numerous folk etymologies, puns and acrostics.* However, nearly all of these are lost in translation.‡ Any good story or choice morsel circulating in the Middle

---

* An acrostic is a poem in which the first letter in each line spells a name or other word.
‡ The original Hebrew is full of folk-etymology puns, along the lines of man ('adam) being created from earth ('adamah), which are lost in translation. Similarly the name Eve is derived from the verb 'to live'. Puns explain many apparently random phrases, for example 'Tell it not in Gath' resonates more in Hebrew, in which the words *tell* and *Gath* sound similar. Examples of acrostics may be found in the first four chapters of Lamentations, also Psalms 25, 34, 37, 111, 112, 119, 145, and Proverbs 31:10–31. In traditional English versions of the Bible, Psalm 119 is still divided up using Hebrew letters as numbers.

East could be included in the anthology, subject to amendments where necessary. The Jewish scholars who compiled the books that now comprise the Old Testament borrowed from the songs, folk tales and myths not only of the Jews themselves, but of their neighbours too. This sort of plagiarism was both widespread and acceptable in the Middle East at the time.

To take a well-known example, the story of Noah's ark (Genesis 6–8) closely parallels the story of a flood given in the *Epic of Gilgamesh*.[10] *Gilgamesh* is an Assyrian work dating from around 2500 BC, almost 2,000 years before the biblical account was written. The story from *Gilgamesh* is the more complete version. In fact the biblical account appears to be an amalgamation of two derivative versions of the Gilgamesh story. Odd details are lost in the biblical account: for example where in Gilgamesh a raven, a dove and a swallow are sent to find dry land, in the biblical version only a raven and a dove are sent. Both stories appear to explain rainbows. In the biblical version Jahveh places his bow in the sky as a reminder of his covenant not to cause such a flood again. In the older version the goddess Ishtar dedicates her spectacular necklace with the 'jewels of Heaven' made by the sky god. The Jews would certainly have known this epic. It was to be found in many Eastern libraries – fragments have been found in Turkey, Syria, Israel and Egypt.[11] A Babylonian version of the story is also known, again older than the biblical version, and again more complete. There is also a well-known Greek version of the story.

The story of Moses' mother hiding her infant son in a basket of rushes caulked with pitch, and entrusting him to the river, is also adapted from an older Middle Eastern story. The original river was the Euphrates, the role of Pharaoh's daughter was played by the goddess Ishtar, and the child grew up to be the Mesopotamian king, Sargon of Akkad. In ancient times rivers were thought of as the embodiment of gods, so in the original tale the mother was entrusting her child to a deity, not abandoning him to the elements. The story of Moses, which may be found in Exodus 2:1–10, dates from about 1,000 years after that of Sargon.

Another well-known story from the Old Testament is that of God giving Moses tablets of stone on which were inscribed God's commandments. But long before then the Babylonian Sun god Shamash had handed stone tablets of the law to Hammurabi, a king during the first dynasty of Babylon, around 4,000 years ago. Again there are clear parallels: Hammurabi received his tablets on top of a ziggurat, while Moses received his on top of a mountain.[12] The laws given to Hammurabi are sophisticated, exceeding 280 in number. They evidently provided the basis not only for the story of divine laws being inscribed on tablets, but also for some of the later Jewish laws. To take an example, the Code of Hammurabi states that:

> If a man shall put out the eye of another, then let his own eye be put out. If a man shall knock out the teeth of another... then let his own teeth be knocked out

The familiar Mosaic Code (Exodus 21:23–4) is more concise:

> ...thou shalt give life for life, eye for eye, tooth for tooth...

Hammurabi predated Moses by many hundreds of years. God seems to have copied the behaviour of other Middle Eastern gods. For example many divinities practised the art of separating the waters, as God did for Moses and his followers fleeing from Egypt.

Other Old Testament events have clear parallels in classical mythologies. For example the story of the Tower of Babel echoes that of the Giant's staircase to Olympus. Samson slaying the lion echoes Hercules slaying the Nemean lion (and also has an older parallel in the saga of Gilgamesh). Again, in Genesis (22:1–13) God tests Abraham by telling him to kill his son Isaac and offer him up as a burnt offering. At the last minute God settles for the sacrifice of a ram instead. This is an adaptation of another old Sumerian legend, tailored to demonstrate God's mercy and benevolence. It also has a classical parallel. When Agamemnon was about to sacrifice his daughter Iphigenia, the goddess Diana, struck by compassion, substituted a goat at the last minute.

Many passages occur in more than one book of the Bible,[13] a reminder of the fact that the Jews considered these books to be quite distinct works, and an illustration of how freely writers would borrow from other writers. Psalms 14 and 53 are the same, except that a Hebrew editor has substituted one divine name (Elohim) for another (Jahveh). Genesis (19:4–8) contains a story of how Lot offered his virgin daughters to the Sodomites in order to appease them. This was a popular Middle Eastern tale. Indeed it was so popular that it appears again in a slightly different form in the book of Judges (19:22–5). The participants are different but the story is much the same. Apparently, different authors have adapted the same basic story for their own purposes, adding different endings to make different points.

The pagan origin of many Old Testament stories has long been known. Sometimes the scribes who did the borrowing did little to disguise their plagiarism, for example failing to amend the text to its new home. Thus, in the Jerusalem Bible, Proverb 22:20 makes reference to 'thirty chapters of advice and knowledge', alluding to the *Wisdom of Amenemophis*, on which, as is confirmed in a footnote, 'this whole passage is based'. Psalm 104 contains material from the *Hymn to the Sun* of the Egyptian Pharaoh Akhenaten, dating from around 1340 BC. Other psalms were originally written in honour of Baal.[14] Again, biblical texts are so similar to older pagan Canaanite texts that it has been possible to explain certain odd-looking Hebrew passages by referring to the Canaanite versions – they turn out to be either mistranslations or mistranscriptions.[15]

Textual Problems

Yet man is born unto trouble, as the sparks fly upward.
Job 5:7 (Authorised Version)

It is man who breeds trouble for himself as surely as eagles fly to the height.
Job 5:7 (Jerusalem Bible)

There is no single original text of the Old Testament, nor is there a single original version of even one book of it. The Jews were remarkably free in early times to edit and re-edit their Hebrew texts. They did not regard their scriptures as a single body, but as separate works. As we have already seen they often copied chunks of one book into another, sometimes changing names and other details to meet the needs of the moment. Impious suggestions were also doctored. For example, it seemed wrong that God should stand before Abraham, so the two swapped places and Abraham now stood before God. There were genuine errors too. A common one was to incorporate marginal notes into the text.

Typically, one scholar would add a note giving his explanation of an opaque passage. A later scholar, copying the manuscript, would interpret the note as a correction and copy it as part of the main text.[16]

In later times (after AD 100) Jewish scribes began to take pains to ensure that texts were accurately copied, for example by checking the number of letters and words in the new manuscripts. The texts then settled down to relative uniformity, although they preserved errors and contradictions originating from earlier editing. Until the twentieth century, the oldest known Hebrew manuscript was only about 1,000 years old. When much older texts were rediscovered, it was possible to confirm what had previously been suspected – that numerous passages had been inserted, duplicated, scrambled or omitted.

A further difficulty was that different Jewish sects each tampered with the scriptures to suit their own teachings. For example the Samaritans had their own version, and so did the Essenes. There were also mainstream variants, and it is now generally accepted that the traditional text, known as the Masoretic Text, is 'only one late and arbitrary line, surviving from an earlier uncontrolled variety'.[17] The texts are only relatively uniform, and surviving manuscripts frequently disagree with each other. The New International Version (NIV) of the Bible gives variant readings in footnotes, showing that Hebrew manuscripts often disagree with each other, and with Greek, Syriac and other texts. Here are extracts from the preface to the NIV explaining how the translators worked:

> For the Old Testament the standard Hebrew text, the Masoretic Text as published in the latest editions of Biblia Hebraica, was used throughout. The Dead Sea Scrolls contain material bearing on an earlier stage of the Hebrew text. They were consulted, as were the Samaritan Pentateuch and the ancient scribal traditions relating to textual changes. Sometimes a variant Hebrew reading in the margin of the Masoretic Text was followed instead of the text itself... The translators also consulted the more important early versions – the Septuagint; Aquila, Symmachus and Theodotion; the Vulgate; the Syriac Peshitta; the Targums; and for the Psalms the Juxta Hebraica of St Jerome (c.340–420). Readings from these versions were occasionally followed where the Masoretic Text seemed doubtful and where accepted principles of textual criticism showed that one or more of these textual witnesses appeared to provide the correct reading.

A recent international committee, considering the text of the Old Testament, identified some 5,000 places where the Hebrew was so puzzling that it might need to be corrected. A few of these are noted in footnotes to modern translations, although different translations handle them in different ways.

Some cases look like simple errors. According to the Masoretic Text corresponding to 1 Samuel 1:24, Sarah took a three-year-old bull to Shiloh, but according to most other manuscripts she took three bulls rather than one. In other cases it appears that the scribes have created rather a mess by deliberate tampering. Take for example the case of the killing of Goliath. Everyone knows that he was killed by David. The Bible says so, at least it does if one reads 1 Samuel 17:49–51. But according to the original text of another passage in 2 Samuel, Elhanan killed him:

> And there was again a battle in Gob with the Philistines, where Elhanan the son of Jaare-oregim, a Bethlehemite, slew Goliath the Gittite, the staff of whose spear was like a weaver's beam.

This is not what is printed in the Authorised Version, however. The translators have inserted the words 'the brother of' before Goliath's name in 2 Samuel 21:19 so that the Authorised Version reads:

> And there was again a battle in Gob with the Philistines, where Elhanan the son of Jaare-oregim, a Bethlehemite, slew *the brother* of Goliath the Gittite, the staff of whose spear was like a weaver's beam.

The words 'the brother of' are italicised in the Authorised Version because they are interpolations – additions made by the translators. They are absent in more accurate recent translations. So why did Christian scholars manipulate the text in this way? In mitigation they could claim that they were merely bringing it into line with a third version of the story in 1 Chronicles 20:5:

> And there was a war again with the Philistines; and Elhanan the son of Jair slew Lahmi the brother of Goliath the Gittite, whose spear staff was like a weaver's beam.

But why then did 2 Samuel and 1 Chronicles contradict each other in the original texts?

What seems to have happened is this: Goliath was killed by Elhanan, and the story, dating from around 950 BC, was recounted in both 1 Chronicles and 2 Samuel. Some 350 years later it was felt that David's reputation needed a boost, so David was made into the hero of the story and this new version was included in 1 Samuel. To cover their tracks the Jewish editors changed the passage in 1 Chronicles by adding the words 'Lahmi the brother of'. They neglected however to change 2 Samuel in the same way, leaving a contradiction which later English translators obligingly tried to cover up using the same technique. The original interpolators made another gaffe, for they used the new David and Goliath story to explain how David came to meet Saul (1 Samuel 17:31–2), neglecting to square it with a different story about how they met, which appears in chapter 16. Early manuscripts contain only one of the two stories, further evidence that the contradictions arose through tampering.[18]

The book of Chronicles routinely tidies up earlier historical accounts. For example in an original story the actions of King Asa were slightly flawed:

> And Asa did that which was right in the eyes of the LORD… But the high places were not removed… (1 Kings 15:11–14)

Asa would have been more impressive if he had removed the (pagan) high places, so in Chronicles we read:

> And Asa did that which was good and right in the eyes of the LORD his God: For he took away the altars of the strange gods, and the high places… (2 Chronicles 14:2–3)

Jewish history was routinely rewritten to show a favourite leader in a good light, or to confirm God's attachment to the Jewish people. Sometimes God was introduced into a story to explain key events. A story in 2 Chronicles 18:31–2 is essentially the same as that in 1 Kings 22:32–3, except that the mechanics of Jehoshaphat's escape is different. In the earlier version he simply calls out to those who are about to attack him:

> And it came to pass, when the captains of the chariots saw Jehoshaphat, that they said, Surely it is the king of Israel. And they

turned aside to fight against him: and Jehoshaphat cried out. And it came to pass, when the captains of the chariots perceived that it was not the king of Israel, that they turned back from pursuing him. (1 Kings 22:32–3)

In the improved version he calls out to God, and God is responsible for his delivery:

And it came to pass, when the captains of the chariots saw Jehoshaphat, that they said, It is the king of Israel. Therefore they compassed about him to fight: but Jehoshaphat cried out, and the LORD helped him; and God moved them to depart from him. For it came to pass, that, when the captains of the chariots perceived that it was not the king of Israel, they turned back again from pursuing him. (2 Chronicles 18:31–2)

Significantly, the original text is not altered, but added to. The later text (Chronicles) is almost identical except that an additional sentence has been inserted.

A man called Jether has different nationalities according to different manuscripts.[19] It appears that it was politically correct for him to become an Israelite, and this was achieved simply by doctoring the text. Did Solomon have a mere 40 stalls for chariot horses, or a much more impressive 4,000,[20] and did Jashobeam kill three men on a single occasion, or was it 30 men, or 300, or even 800 men?[21] There are numerous such inconsistencies, both between different books, and different manuscripts of the same book.[22] Such tampering can be detected only when the editors failed to cover their tracks early enough and well enough. We can never know how many times they covered their tracks successfully.

Like the Jewish scribes who had not always been careful of the truth, neither were Christians. Early Christians tampered with the Septuagint, but this tampering was exposed by comparison with the original Hebrew. Christians then accused Jews of suppressing the truth in their Hebrew versions. But the Jews had largely stopped tampering with their ancient texts by the end of the first century AD and were thus routinely vindicated by the evidence. For example, in the Septuagint, Psalm 96 was amended to include an apparent prophecy about the Lord ruling from the tree (i.e. the cross). The fact that Jewish versions included no such line was explained away by the fact that the perfidious Jews had removed it from the text. In fact it was the Christians who had been responsible for the tampering, a fact easily confirmed by comparing the texts with older copies in both Greek and Hebrew. Christians also inserted a line in Jeremiah to foretell Christ's descent into Hell: 'The Lord God remembered His dead people of Israel who slept in the earth of the grave, and He went down to them to preach to them His salvation.' This fraudulence has been quietly dropped, but the writings of the Church Fathers confirm that they believed it to be genuine and thought that the Jews had tried to suppress it.[23] We will come across a number of other attempts by Christians to insert convenient text – often either retrospective prophecies or justifications for novel doctrines.

Authorship, Order and Dating

Having now shown that every book in the Bible, from Genesis to Judges, is without authenticity, I come to the book of Ruth, an idle, bungling story, foolishly told, nobody knows by whom, about a strolling country-girl creeping slyly to bed with her cousin Boaz. Pretty stuff indeed to be called the word of God!
Thomas Paine (1737–1809), *The Age of Reason*, Part II

Traditionally God was held to have been the author of all books of the Bible, just as Muslims believe Allah to have been the true author of the Koran. In both cases, part of the evidence of divine authorship was the sublime quality of the language used. Many Muslims hold that God must have written the Koran because no human could produce such beautiful prose. Unfortunately its supernatural beauty seems to be discernible only by Muslim speakers of Arabic and remains opaque to other Arabic speakers. The position of the Old Testament is less convincing. Even the most pious Christian scholars found the original text crude and uncouth. St Jerome for example found the language of the prophets 'harsh and barbarous', much preferring the quality of writing of pagan authors such as Cicero and Plautus.

Another problem is that of identifying the human authors. Most books of the Old Testament were not written by the people whose names they bear. Many were written and edited over a long period by unknown hands. Traditional ascriptions are known to be unreliable, and textual analysis reveals some books to be the work of more than one writer. The oldest book whose author is known is an apocryphal book called Ecclesiasticus or Ben Sirach, written by the Jewish scholar Jesus ben Sirach at a surprisingly late date (around 200 BC).

The books of the Law were traditionally believed to have been written by Moses, although this has long been discounted by scholars. No one previously seems to have been unduly concerned that Moses sometimes referred to himself in the third person, as in Numbers 12:3, but writing about his own death and burial (Deuteronomy 34:5–7) raised a few questions. A further give-away was the phrase '...before there reigned any king over the children of Israel' (Genesis 36:31). This could only have been written after there had been a king, which was centuries after the time of Moses. Moses was not the only person traditionally identified as a biblical author to write as historical fact about events that occurred after his death. Samuel, in 1 Samuel 25:1, gives an account of his own death and burial. Again, Joshua (in Joshua 24:31) tells us that '... Israel served the Lord all the days of Joshua, and all the days of the elders that outlived Joshua'.

Scholars generally accept that at least four different hands were responsible for the books traditionally attributed to Moses, and that their contributions have been interwoven by a creative editor (a *redactor*, the scholars call him). The four strands are known as *Yahwist*, *Elohist*, *Deuteronomic* and *Priestly*. These four strands are often identifiable by characteristics in the writing, such as the name the author used for God. For example the *Yahwist* author calls God JHVH or YHWH (spoken as 'Yahweh') while the *Elohist* author calls him Elohim. The *Deuteronomic* author introduced changes by the Levites after the fall of the kingdom of Israel and was responsible for a three-volume work that we now know as Deuteronomy, Joshua and Kings. The *Priestly* author edited these traditions together after the Babylonian Exile. The four traditions are often denoted by the letters J, E, D and P, though J and E were edited together before the others and so are often denoted together as JE. The P strand includes the books of Numbers and Leviticus and also forms the framework into which the earlier books were fitted after the Exile.

Other works are also joint efforts edited together by one or more redactors. The book of Isaiah for example is now generally acknowledged to have been written by three authors, known to scholars for convenience as Isaiah 1, Isaiah 2 and Isaiah 3. Isaiah 2 appears to have been an exponent of the retrospective prophecy. He predicted the coming of Cyrus the Great in the 530s BC after the event, and had his work incorporated into that of Isaiah 1, which dated from 200 years earlier.

Another retrospective prophet is responsible for Zechariah's astonishing prescience, and yet another one for Jeremiah's. Jeremiah's interpolator was caught out by an ancient Greek translation of the original text. Comparing it to the later Hebrew text showed that the Hebrew version had been supplemented by retrospective prophecies.[24] Again, some works are specifically identified as being written by Solomon or David, or other kings or their sons, but these ascriptions are now discounted. As the Jerusalem Bible confirms, the Song of Songs was not written by Solomon but by an unknown author after the Exile, and Ecclesiastes not by a son of David, as it claims, but by an unknown author (possibly a number of unknown authors), again after the Exile.

The Jews took many centuries to agree on a body of scripture. Such a body had crystallised by the time of Rabbi Akiva a few generations after the time of Jesus. As we have already seen, the Jews distinguished three kinds of book:

- The *Torah*, which comprises the first five books of the Bible, i.e. Genesis, Exodus, Leviticus, Numbers and Deuteronomy. The word *Torah* translates as *Teaching*, but these books are generally known in English as the *Law*. The Jews regarded them as being on a higher level than the other books.
- The *Nebim* (English *Prophets*), which comprise Joshua, Judges, 1 and 2 Samuel, 1 and 2 Kings, Isaiah, Jeremiah and Ezekiel along with the 12 minor prophets. In the New Testament reference is sometimes made to 'the Law and Prophets', meaning the *Torah* and the *Nebim*.
- The *Ketubim* (or *Writings*), the remaining books, which have a lower status than the Law and the Prophets.

These categories were ignored by Christians, who came to regard all of the works as equally inspired. In the Christians' Old Testament, the books appear in a different order, with the prophets placed last, so that the final book, Malachi, appears to lead into the New Testament.

Traditionally the order of the books was believed to reflect the chronological order of the events described. Many old versions of the Bible included a chronology, often in a margin parallel to the text, which was regarded as being as free from error as the text itself. However much it was refined, the chronology was flawed by numerous absurdities and contradictions, as demonstrated by the freethinker Thomas Paine (1737–1809) in his book *The Age of Reason*.[25] At the time Paine was accused of blasphemy, as much for querying the chronology as for questioning other aspects of the Bible. No reputable Church now tries to sustain a full traditional biblical chronology.

Perhaps the most infamous case of misdating and misrepresentation is the book of Daniel. It purports to have been written during the Babylonian Exile, but scholars now accept that it was written about 400 years later, between 167 and 164 BC, at least partly in Aramaic. It is propaganda compiled to encourage resistance to the Greek ruler Antiochus Epiphanes, who was then trying to crush the Jewish religion. It tells how Daniel and his associates refused to compromise on matters of faith during the Babylonian Exile, but displays ignorance of the period, and of the Persian succession, and uses Macedonian words that were unknown at the time it was supposedly written.[26] It is a hotchpotch of stories, some in Aramaic, some in Hebrew; some (retrospectively) describing visions, some incorporating known Babylonian tales; some regarded as canonical, some apocryphal.

The most recent Old Testament writings date from around AD 120 – almost a century *after* Jesus lived, which suggests that God continued to refine his old Covenant with the Jews long after he had superseded it with his new one. Divine authorship is also compromised by the parochialism of the text. Whoever wrote the books of the Old Testament knew about nomadic life and tribal warfare in Middle Eastern deserts, but little else. For example locusts are covered exceptionally well, but penguins are badly underrepresented.

Evidence of Tampering

…it is, I believe, impossible to find in any story upon record so many and such glaring absurdities, contradictions and falsehoods as are in these books.
Thomas Paine, *The Age of Reason*, Part II

For many centuries the mainstream Churches denied that there was any evidence of tampering in God's divine word, but this position is no longer tenable, and no mainstream Church now seeks to deny that biblical texts were tampered with. For example the introduction to the Pentateuch in the Jerusalem Bible concludes with the statement that 'Throughout, the hands of the Deuteronomic and Priestly editors are often to be observed, annotating and adapting'.

Sometimes the text has been tampered with in an effort to make sense of it. For example, in 2 Samuel 24:10 David regretted having carried out a census, saying he had 'sinned greatly', even though God had told him to do so. Some 200 years later the story was revised so that it was Satan who instigated the census, but the revisers neglected to revise the original. So it is that a duplicate of the same story appears at 1 Chronicles 21:1, except Satan replaces God.

Sometimes, the disruption of regular patterns betrays the fact that changes have been made either deliberately or accidentally. For example acrostic poems have been broken up, presumably by people who failed to realise that the text formed an acrostic. Psalms 9 and 10 are really a single poem, each verse starting with a Hebrew letter in alphabetical order, but as a note in the Jerusalem Bible puts it 'in the present text there are several letters without their strophes'. Again, in Psalm 145 one of the verses ('Nun') is missing from the Hebrew text and has had to be supplied from Greek texts (see the Jerusalem Bible Psalm 145, note a).

Another give-away arises from taking a passage and inserting it elsewhere without checking the context. Thus for example 2 Samuel 23:9 says that the Philistines were gathered 'there' but gives no indication of where 'there' was. Presumably the passage was picked up from another part of the text where the location of the action had already been established. A parallel passage at 1 Chronicles 11:13 identifies the place as Pas Dammim, and this is frequently substituted in translations of 2 Samuel to cover up the error. Again whoever inserted the text saying that God spoke to Moses 'face to face, as a man speaketh unto his friend' (Exodus 33:11) apparently failed to check that this was consistent with the main narrative, which at verse 20 has God saying to Moses 'Thou canst not see my face'.

If the same fact was stated several times, then a scribe who wanted to tamper with it had to be sure that he changed every incidence. This was often difficult. In the Dead Sea Scrolls and the Septuagint, Jacob is credited with having 75 descendants when his family came to Egypt;

this is also the number quoted by Acts 7:14. But the Masoretic Text gives the number as 70, and this is the figure that appears in biblical versions of Genesis and Exodus.[27]

The Ten Commandments provides a series of examples of the dangers of tampering. The first problem is that there are two versions of the Commandments, at Exodus 20:1–17 and Deuteronomy 5:6–21. The two versions contradict each other by giving different reasons for observing the Sabbath.[28] As a note to the Jerusalem Bible says at Exodus 20: 'This is the Priestly version of the Ten Commandments; another version, the Deuteronomic, is found in Deuteronomy 5, and it is the second which has been adopted by the Church'. But this is only the start, because neither of these versions is the original. The original Ten Commandments, inscribed by Moses at God's dictation, bear little resemblance to either of them, being concerned mainly with religious festivals and taboos (Exodus 34:14–26). It is this list that is explicitly identified in the text as the 'Ten Commandments' and is stated to have been written on the tablets that Moses brought down from Mount Sinai (Exodus 34:27–9). But there is yet another problem, because there are more than ten commandments listed here, which means that this list has been tampered with as well[29] – quite apart from the fact that the whole collection was overtaken by the current Ten Commandments. Furthermore other sets of laws are listed that contradict each other in many details.[30]

Footnotes in the Jerusalem Bible demonstrate all sorts of errors and sometimes how they arose:

'…not always consistent' (Numbers 22b)

Not an accurate figure (1 Kings 20b)

The chronological details cannot be harmonised… (Esther 1c)

…a 'modernisation' by a later hand. (Zechariah 6c)

Different sources have been conflated (Genesis 21b)

…later elaboration… (Genesis 32a)

Two narratives are conflated here… (Joshua 6a)

…contains several traditions put together by an editor;… (Judges 21a)

Editorial comment (Exodus 15a)

Two versions of the institution of the monarchy, a key episode in the history of Israel, are to be found alternating in the five chapters from 1 Samuel 8. One is by an anti-royalist author and the other by a royalist.[31]

Another area particularly subject to both mistakes and deliberate tampering was provided by the numerous genealogies contained in the Old Testament. The New International Version (NIV) identifies dozens of inconsistencies in footnotes, sometimes several in the same genealogy.[32] As an explanation of why two genealogies differ, the Jerusalem Bible (see 1 Chronicles 2 note b) points out that 'Genealogies were often deduced from relationships between clans. This reconstruction of the descendants of Caleb may differ from the list in vv.18–24 because it was made at a date when alliances between clans were different.'

Errors of Translation

Will the unicorn be willing to serve thee, or abide by thy crib?
Job 39:9

Ancient Middle Eastern alphabets contained no vowels. In the earliest biblical texts only the consonants were written down, without punctuation. This provided plenty of scope for misunderstandings, especially as the tense had to be guessed from the context. In many cases the wrong vowels were later inserted, giving the wrong word and the wrong meaning. Again, since there was no equivalent to our quotation marks it is often difficult to identify the end of a speech. There were no gaps between words, and all letters were capitals, so it was sometimes difficult even to tell where one word ended and the next began. Furthermore the Jews did not use separate symbols for numbers, but like the Greeks and the Romans, used letters instead, a practice that opened up further possibilities for confusion. In addition, Hebrew writers often swapped back and forth between first, second and third person personal pronouns, and even when they did not it is not always clear which pronoun referred to which noun. Most translations iron out such ambiguities without comment.

We have seen that the original biblical texts contained errors of various sorts, but further errors have been introduced by translators. Sometimes these errors are deliberate interpolations by translators, performed to tidy up inconvenient or inconsistent passages. In other cases they are genuine mistakes. The following examples include both types.

The Septuagint

Translations of the books of the Old Testament were made during the third and second centuries BC, probably for the library at Alexandria. The translations were made into the common Mediterranean language of the time, which was Greek. This collection is called the Septuagint, which in Latin means seventy, because of a tradition that it was translated by seventy scholars, all of whom were inspired and who independently produced identical translations.[33] The name is sometimes abbreviated as LXX, the Roman numerals for seventy.

In the first century, the New Testament did not exist and authority was believed to reside in the Septuagint and in Jesus' sayings, which circulated orally. At one time both Jews and Christians regarded the Septuagint as divinely inspired, but over the course of time many errors were revealed, and the Jews adopted better translations. The Eastern Church retained its attachment to the Septuagint, while the Western Church adopted a Latin translation instead. The Septuagint was then virtually abandoned within Western Europe. For many centuries the Greek version was regarded there as no more than the book belonging to schismatic Eastern Churches.

The Hebrew and Greek texts differed in many ways, even before Christians started interpolating their own text.[34] In the original text the book of Esther is simply a nationalistic Jewish tract. Christians were not comfortable with the fact that it made no mention of God. Translators therefore inserted references to God into their versions of the Septuagint. From there the additions were transferred to other early translations.

Other additions are more difficult to discover, but are sometimes given away by linguistic features. For example, the story of Susanna and the Elders does not exist in the ancient Hebrew texts, only in the Greek. Had Hebrew editors suppressed it, as Christians claimed? Or had Greek editors added it, as the Jews claimed? As Julius Africanus noted as early as the third century AD, a principal feature of the story is a pun that works only in Greek, and the story therefore seems likely to be an addition to the original Semitic text.

Vulgate

As Jews, Jesus and his disciples would have used Aramaic as their everyday language. In view of their location and their professions, we have no reason to suppose that any of them knew Greek.

Koine, a form of Greek, was the common language of the Mediterranean, and this was the language used by the Pauline Christians. Educated Romans had always spoken Greek rather than Latin, and even up to the third century the language of Roman Christians was Greek. Hippolytus (AD c.170–c.236) was the last Western theologian to write in Greek, and Tertullian (AD c.160–c.225) the first to write in Latin. In Rome, the Eucharist (Communion) continued to be celebrated in Greek up to the time of Pope Damasus (reigned 366–84). Yet in time the Western Church would claim that Latin was the peculiar language of Christianity.

Although the Bible was originally written mainly in Hebrew and Greek, the Western Church ceded primacy to its own translation. St Jerome translated (most of) the Bible into Latin probably between 384 and 404, based on Hebrew and Greek texts, along with earlier Latin translations. His version is the known as the Vulgate, so called because it was written as a new vulgar (i.e. common) edition. At the time it was controversial. There were riots over some of Jerome's translations, which were held to amount to tampering with established traditions.[35] In time it became established not merely as authoritative, but divinely inspired. In 1546 the Council of Trent pronounced the Vulgate to be the only authentic Latin text. It is still considered authoritative on questions of faith and morals by the Roman Catholic Church.[36] How widely it differs from modern translations (such as the Jerusalem Bible) may be seen by the dual numbering system adopted in the Jerusalem Bible.[37] We note a couple of errors for historical interest:

In Exodus 34:29 the Authorised Version records that when he came down from Mount Sinai '...Moses wist not that the skin of his face shone...'. This corrects an error in the Vulgate, which records that when Moses came down from the mountain he knew not that there were horns upon his countenance. The problem was caused by the lack of diacritical marks to represent vowel sounds: in Hebrew the words *qaran*, to shine, and *qeren*, to bear horns, have exactly the same consonants. St Jerome chose the wrong one and translated it with the Latin *cornuta*; so, later, did Luther, who translated it with the German *gehornt*. Because of this mistranslation, many of the most famous depictions of Moses show him with a set of horns. The most spectacular examples are the well-known painting by Rembrandt and the statue by Michelangelo.

When Adam and Eve are being evicted from the Garden of Eden, God promises that snakes and mankind will be enemies: mankind will strike snakes on the head and snakes will strike mankind on the foot. In the original Hebrew of Genesis 3:15 God cursed the snake saying 'it [mankind] shall crush thy head'. This was translated into Greek as 'he [man] shall crush thy head', which Jerome turned into 'she [Mary] shall crush thy head', a mistranslation that has been known for centuries but was held onto by the Church possibly because it helped bolster the claims of Mariologists. According to them Mary will one day crush Satan's head under her immaculate foot. The error was still receiving papal confirmation in the nineteenth century[38] and this is still a favourite theme in the Roman Catholic art of southern Europe. The mistranslation has been admitted by the Roman Church only recently – well within living memory. The Jerusalem Bible has *it* rather than *she*, without so much as a footnote by way of explanation, surprising since this switch reverses the Catholic Church's position on what it traditionally cited as the most important text to justify its Marian doctrines – what it calls a 'proof-text'.

Like other Church leaders of his time St Jerome had a low opinion of sex. In the Vulgate version of the book of Tobit, he made Tobias wait three nights before consummating his marriage (see for example Tobit 8:1–10 in the Douay-Rheims Bible, a Catholic translation of the Vulgate into English). In modern versions, consummation of the marriage has reverted to a single night (Tobit 8:1–9), but the bizarre numbering of the verses in the Jerusalem Bible shows that changes have been made. (For a time the Church tried to enforce three 'Tobias nights' during which newly married couples had to refrain from sexual intercourse, though a dispensation could be bought for a fee.[39])

Another problem was the way Jesus spoke to his mother 'Woman, what have I to do with thee?' (*Gynai, ti emoi kai soi*, in the original Greek, John 2:4). Greek scholars had no doubt that this constituted a stern rebuke.[40] To people like St Jerome who were already in the process of elevating Mary above the rest of womankind, a more opaque translation was needed, and so he translated it as 'Woman, what is that to me and to thee?', which rather takes the edge off it.[41] This softer translation is repeated in the Douay-Rheims Bible (in English), but it is now generally accepted that the original conveys a rebuke.

Authorised Version
Probably the greatest-ever blunder in translation involved the name of God. As already mentioned, in early Hebrew only consonants were written down. There were no letters to fulfil the role of vowels (diacritical marks were sometimes used instead, but not always). One of the Hebrew names of God, written JHVH and probably pronounced something like Yahweh, was regarded from the third century BC as too awful to speak aloud, except in special circumstances. When reading the scriptures aloud, accepted Jewish practice was to substitute the word *Adonai* (Lord) for *Yahweh*. To remind readers about this, the diacritical marks belonging to the word *Adonai* were written along with the name JHVH. The reader would see the name JHVH but say *Adonai*. Not knowing this, European translators in the sixteenth century combined the consonants and diacritics to produce a new name *Jahovah* or *Jehovah*. Some modern versions still use this name; others have reverted to *Yahweh*.

As modern translations admit, many terms used in the Bible are no longer in common use or understood. Among them are some names for animals, flowers, architectural features, clothing, jewellery, and musical instruments. Christians can mostly gloss over these shortcomings – for instance, no one is much worried about what distinguishes the four types of creature mentioned in Joel 1:4. On the other hand, for those who opt to, it must be difficult to follow the Old Testament dietary laws, when no one knows to which animals the prohibitions refer. Some of the traditional translations now seem a little quaint. The Hebrew *re'em* for example was translated into Greek as *monoceros*, and thence into English as *unicorn*. Modern versions translate *re'em* less exotically as *wild ox*.

More serious is the mistranslation of words for doctrinal reasons. For example in Isaiah 14:15 the Hebrew word for a grave (*Sheol*) was translated as Hell – suggesting that the ancient Jews had a concept of an afterlife and eternal punishment. In fact they had neither – these ideas were introduced by Greeks and Egyptians a few generations before Jesus. Again, the continuity of the priesthood from ancient times could ostensibly be confirmed by having the first priest Aaron being invested with a bishop's crown of office rather than some sort of mullah's headgear. So it is that in the Authorised Version, Leviticus 8:9 relates that Aaron wore a *mitre*, while more accurate modern translations render the word as *turban*.

If the translators of the English Bible were divinely inspired, then it is odd that they remained ignorant of some of the hidden information in their texts. When Babylon represented the Jews' greatest enemy it was often impolitic to mention the place by name, so a code word was substituted. The Jews used the Atbash code, a simple substitution cipher that rendered Babylon as *Sheshach* and Chaldea as *Leb-kamai*.[42] The translators of the Bible were apparently unaware that they were writing about Babylon and Chaldea, and simply transcribed the words as Sheshach and Leb-kamai.

In other cases, tampering is designed to disguise the true meaning of the text. The eroticism of the Song of Songs was a little too explicit for most translators. In the Authorised Version the lady in the Song of Songs 5:4 tells us:

> *My beloved put his hand by the hole* of the door, *and my bowels were moved for him.*

The words *of the door* are de-italicised because they do not exist in the original text. Modern translators are even more coy, referring to a latch or latch-opening instead of a hole.

The translators of the Authorised Version did their best to paper over the cracks in the original texts. As we have already seen, they doctored the account of Goliath's death in 2 Samuel. To take another example, they were faced by a contradiction concerning a woman called Michal, a daughter of Saul. According to 2 Samuel 6:23 she remained childless until her death, but according to 2 Samuel 21:8 she had five sons. The Authorised Version disguised this contradiction by implying that she merely brought up these sons for someone else (Adriel). More modern versions of the Bible prefer a method used by a few early manuscripts and replace the name Michal by the name Merab in one of the stories. (The NIV admits the truth in a footnote; the Jerusalem Bible keeps quiet about it.)

According to 1 Samuel 13:1 Saul reigned for one year, but the text then goes on to talk about when he had reigned for two years. The Authorised Version tried to gloss over the problem by some judicious punctuation: 'Saul reigned for one year; and when he had reigned for two years over Israel...'. The NIV abandons the Hebrew in favour of a few late manuscripts of the Septuagint giving a different account: 'Saul was <thirty> years old when he became king, and he reigned over Israel for <forty-> two years'. The Jerusalem Bible avoids the problem by simply missing out the first verse altogether and starting at verse 2.

Often, translators mistranslated the ancient text to reflect the prejudices of their own times. In late medieval times Christians firmly believed that God had cursed women with suffering in childbirth. This idea is not present in the Hebrew, which refers to concept like 'labour', but translators introduced ideas of 'pain' and 'suffering' into European texts, and these ideas became so entrenched that they continue in modern translations of the Bible.[43]

An even more damaging example is that of Hell. By translating different words as *hell*, bibles like the Authorised Version give the impression that the concept of hell dates back to ancient Jewish times, which it does not. Reading an English bible alone it would be impossible to distinguish *Gehenna* in the New Testament from *Sheol* in the Old. Completely different ideas are thus confabulated in English translations, which together seem to confirm the existence of a Satanic realm under the earth. Often a better translation for *Hell* would be *grave*, a different concept altogether.

Witchcraft was a topical issue by the time that the Authorised Version was commissioned in the early seventeenth century, and King James wanted confirmation that the practice of witch killing had divine approval. The names of wrongdoers were therefore now translated as *witch*. For example Exodus 22:18 was translated as 'Thou shalt not suffer a witch to live'. But this was not the most natural translation. The original Hebrew had been *mekashshephah* (magician, diviner, or sorcerer), which had been rendered into Greek as *pharmakos* (druggist, apothecary, maker of potions) and into Latin as *Maleficos* (evil doer, criminal). No one suspected that the term referred to a witch or Devil worshipper, until it became necessary to justify witch persecutions. In modern translations the word is generally rendered as 'sorceress', though there is also a good case for 'poisoner'. Again, the woman consulted by Saul (1 Samuel 28:7) had really been a fortune teller or *ba'alath ob*, a 'mistress of the talisman'. In Latin she became a *mulierem habentem pythonem*, 'a woman possessing an oracular spirit', but in order to conform to the requirements of seventeenth-century England, she became a Devil worshipper as well, the famous witch of Endor.

Other Translations
Translations have always been angled to suit the views of the translators, and not always for doctrinal reasons. As we have just seen, flexibility in

translation can justify activities like witch-hunting. But there have been many other motivations, for example to confirm that kings are divinely appointed. Traditional Christian anti-Semitism has also been accommodated, for example by minimising the Jewishness of important biblical characters. Speaking of his German translation of the Bible, Martin Luther said 'I endeavoured to make Moses so German that no one would suspect he was a Jew'.[44] This was perfectly in line with the traditional techniques employed to make the text conform to current orthodoxy.

Modern translations use a variety of more subtle techniques to manipulate the text. One is to introduce a section heading above a piece of text indicating that the subject matter concerns one thing when it might otherwise be interpreted as concerning something else. Thus for example in the NIV, the real Ten Commandments (Exodus 34:14–26) are not flagged as such, though the text explicitly describes them (verse 28) as the Ten Commandments. By contrast the later laws are so flagged by a heading, though the text does not identify them as the Ten Commandments (Exodus 20). To take another example, the Church has traditionally justified the practice of taxing people through the tithe system by reference to a biblical passage at Deuteronomy 25:4 that does not mention tithes at all. A few versions of the Bible continue an old convention of inserting a heading that mentions tithes and thus helps foster the impression that tithes were justified by scripture.

Again, quotation marks are inserted in places that make the passage conform to Christian requirements, and inverted commas are used to smooth over inconvenient terms. Thus for example the need to deny that there is more than one god is achieved in the NIV by placing the word *gods* (in Psalm 82:1 and 6) in inverted commas, so that Jahveh gives judgement not among the gods, but among the 'gods'. The inverted commas suggest that these gods – who are so clearly identified as such – seem not to be gods at all.

Inconvenient *sons of God* become *children of Israel* in Deuteronomy 32:8. As in earlier translations, the free use of pronouns disguises the number of deities around. For example the following passage looks wrong in the mouth of God 'I overthrew some of you, as God overthrew Sodom and Gomorrah' so it is instead translated as 'I overthrew some of you, as I overthrew Sodom and Gomorrah' (see Amos 4:11 NIV). Capital letters can be used to the same end: *a god* becomes *God* so that

Jahveh ceases to be one god among many (see Deuteronomy 4:33 NIV). Names of gods can be represented as different names for one God. Compare the first two verses of Psalm 91, first according to the Authorised Version, then with the real names of God instead of the conventional translations (key words in italic type):

> He that dwelleth in the secret place of *the most High* shall abide under the shadow of *the Almighty*. I will say of the *LORD*, He is my refuge and my fortress: my *God*; in him will I trust. (Authorised Version)

> He that dwelleth in the secret place of *Elyon* shall abide under the shadow of *Shaddai*. I will say of *Jahveh*, He is my refuge and my fortress: my *Elohim*; in him will I trust. (cf. Jerusalem Bible)

The following table shows how some principal translations deal with the various names of the ancient Jewish gods found in the Old Testament:

Hebrew	Authorised Version	New International Version	Jerusalem Bible	Example
YHWH or Yahveh	LORD	LORD	Yahweh	Passim
YHWH Elohim	LORD God	LORD God	Yahweh God	Genesis 2:4
Adonai	Lord	Lord	Lord	Isaiah 7:14
Adonai YHWH	Lord GOD	Sovereign LORD	Lord Yahweh	Ezekiel 6:11
Shaddai	the Almighty	the Almighty	Shaddai	Psalm 91:1
El Shaddai	the Almighty	the Almighty	El Shaddai	Genesis 49:25
Ja	LORD	LORD	(Allelu)ia	Psalms 149:1 and 150:1
Elyon	the most High	the Most High	the Most High Elyon	Psalm 82:6 Psalm 91:1
El Elyon	the most high God	God Most High	God Most High	Genesis 14:18
Jahveh Sabaoth	LORD of Hosts	LORD Almighty	Yahweh Sabaoth	Malachi 1:10
Eloah (singular)	the Holy One	the Holy One	the Holy One	Habakkuk 3:3
Elohim (plural)	God	God	God	Psalm 91:2

(The names *Jahveh* and *Yaweh* are just variant spellings. Other translators prefer *Yahveh*.)

At least one biblical writer found it necessary to assure readers that Jahveh and El Shaddai were the same god: in Exodus 6:2–3 God explains that he had not used the name Jahveh in earlier times. It is more than likely that Jahveh and El Shaddai were originally separate gods.

Other divinities are melded into one by appropriate punctuation, for example the 'fear of Isaac' in Genesis 31:42 becomes a description of God rather than a separate god. So does the 'God of Abraham' also mentioned in 31:42 and the 'Mighty One of Jacob' mentioned in Genesis 49:24 (NIV). The existence of other divinities is also disguised by judicious mistranslation. The original text of Psalm 110:3 refers to the womb of the goddess of the dawn, but it is not acceptable to mention that the Jews recognised other deities, so the Authorised Version speaks evasively of the womb of the morning. The Jerusalem Bible distorts the passage even further. In this version the womb does not even belong to the morning, let alone a goddess, and it is impossible from the English to deduce that the original author was referring to the womb of a goddess called *Dawn*.

Capital letters are important weapons in the armoury of orthodox Christian translators. By capitalising certain words they can be made into names, and by capitalising phrases it is possible to make them into titles. Thus in the New Testament Jesus is given the title of Son of man, but when the same phrase occurs in the Old Testament referring to someone else (as it is throughout the book of Ezekiel) it is more convenient to render it without capitals as the son of man, so that it is not a title at all. Another example of a name being manipulated is that of the supernatural character called Wisdom. In English translations of the Bible her name is written wisdom, without a capital W, so that it does not look like a name at all. It is possible to read English translations without even suspecting the existence of a character called Wisdom, though she played a major part in Jewish and early Christian theology. By denying her a capital letter, her claim to divinity looks much weaker than it is. The same would be true of the second person of the Trinity if we translated *logos* as *word*, instead of *the Word*. Similarly the *Holy Spirit* would look rather less impressive as a mere *holy spirit*.

Careful translation also avoids the embarrassment to Christians of referring to people other than Jesus as *Christ*. In fact many individuals are referred to in the Old Testament as *Christ* (Hebrew messiah, English 'anointed'). When applied to Jesus in the New Testament the word is always used as a title, but when it is used of kings and high priests in the

Old Testament it is rendered as 'the anointed' (see for example Leviticus 4:5, 4:16 and 6:22). Psalm 105:15 should really be translated as 'Touch not my christs', which does not sound right to orthodox Christian ears. In almost all translations of Isaiah 45:1, God refers to Cyrus the Great as *his anointed*, rather than as *his christ*, which is just as correct.

Inconvenient text can simply be dropped, though missing lines can sometimes be identified by missing verse numbers. Another possibility is to swap the verses around to make the meaning more acceptable, as at Judges 1:19. In the Authorised Version God himself could not drive people from a valley because they had iron chariots.

> *And the LORD was with Judah; and he drave out the inhabitants of the mountain; but could not drive out the inhabitants of the valley, because they had chariots of iron.*

... not very impressive for an omnipotent God. In the Jerusalem Bible the word order is changed and the sense of the account jigged so that God is not involved in the difficulties that occurred in the valley or plain at all, only in the victory in the highlands.

> *19b they could not drive out the inhabitants of the plain, because they had iron chariots*
>
> *19a Yahweh was with Judah, and Judah subdued the highlands.*

... but the game is partially given away by verse 19b preceding 19a.

Contradictions and Inconsistencies

> *Answer not a fool according to his folly, lest thou also be like unto him.*
> **Proverbs 26:4**

> *Answer a fool according to his folly, lest he be wise in his own conceit.*
> **Proverbs 26:5**

God created both man and woman on the sixth day (Genesis 1:27), having already created the plants and animals. But later, after the seventh day, he formed Adam from the dust of the ground (Genesis 2:7), then the plants and animals again, then Eve. In the seventeenth century scholars noted the inconsistencies and deduced that there had been two creations, first of the gentiles then of the Jews. Scholars in the next century realised that the story is composed of two separate accounts, although it took 200 years for this realisation to gain general acceptance. It is now widely accepted to be correct, and biblical scholars concur that the first account was written by the Priestly (P) source and the second by the Yahwist (J) source.

Again, the story of the flood is a confabulation of two versions of the Babylonian story of Gilgamesh, one P, and the other J. In the P version, only one male and one female of each species is saved (Genesis 6:19–20), whereas in the J version, seven (or seven pairs) of each clean animal species and one pair of unclean animal species are saved (Genesis 7:2–3).

Ages and timings are frequently unreliable. Jehoiachin was eight years old when he began his reign according to 2 Chronicles 36:9, but he was eighteen according to 2 Kings 24:8. The two books also disagree about how long he reigned in Jerusalem. Again, Ahaziah was 22 years old when he ascended the throne according to 2 Kings 8:26, but he was 42 years old according to 2 Chronicles 22:2. The first sounds slightly more reasonable since the second would make him two years older than his own father. Other stories in the Bible also stretch the imagination. Enemies of the Jews for example were incredibly tenacious. The Edomites rebelled (2 Kings 8:22) after every male of that race had been killed (1 Kings 11:16). The Midianites were even more impressive. With all their males killed and females captured (Numbers 31:7–9) they somehow managed to defeat the Israelites (Judges 6:1–5). The Amalekites, having been utterly destroyed by Saul (1 Samuel 15:7–20), rose up against David, who left neither man nor woman alive amongst them (1 Samuel 27:9), after which they attacked him yet again (1 Samuel 30:1–17).

There are conflicting versions of what happened when the Assyrian Sennacherib demanded increased tribute from Hezekiah. According to 2 Kings 18:14–16, Hezekiah simply pays up. But, in the subsequent passage, 2 Kings 18:17–19:37, he appears to defy Sennacherib. The angel of the Lord then appears and kills 185,000 of Sennacherib's men during the night so that Sennacherib is obliged to return home defeated. In one place the Old Testament says that Aaron died at Mosera (Deuteronomy 10:6) but in another that he died on Mount Hor (Numbers 20:27–8).

God himself is not always consistent. The modern Ten Commandments say that God will visit the iniquity of the fathers upon the children
(Exodus 20:5 and Deuteronomy 5:9), but Ezekiel 18:20 says that the
son shall not bear the iniquity of the father.[45]

Factual Errors and Anachronisms

*And it came to pass that night, that the angel of the Lord went out, and smote
in the camp of the Assyrians an hundred fourscore and five thousand: and
when they arose early in the morning, behold, they were all dead corpses.*

2 Kings 19:35

Factual errors in the Old Testament are widely (but not universally)
accepted. Like any pre-scientific narrative, the Old Testament makes
assumptions about the nature of the world that are now realised to be
false. For example frequent references are made to the waters under Earth
– waters that many ancient peoples believed in and that gods could use
to flood the world (cf. Genesis 7:11) but are now known not to exist.
Again we know today that stars do not sing (Job 38:7), that Earth does
not have edges or corners (Job 38:13, Psalm 2:8, Ezekiel 7:2), and that
snow and hail are not kept in storehouses (Job 38:22). The Bible also
makes factual errors on subjects like geography, history and etymology,
and assumes the efficacy of traditional folk magic (e.g. Genesis 30:37–43).
Accounts of the creation of the world are clearly incompatible
with what is now known about cosmology and geology. The story of
the creation of Adam and Eve does not square with archaeological or
evolutionary evidence. The animal species known to science, which
include over 4,600 species of mammals alone, could not fit into Noah's
ark, whose dimensions are given in the biblical story.[46] Errors revealed
by science could fill a book; indeed such errors did fill many books
in the nineteenth century when many Christians still believed in the
literal truth of the Bible. Biblical arithmetic is not too reliable either.
In Ezra 2 a list of the men of Israel is given, the total of which is stated
to be 42,360 but which is really 29,818. Nehemiah 7 gives essentially
the same list, but with some changes. This time the total is 31,089,
though it is still stated to be 42,360.

Another class of error in the Old Testament comprises the numerous statements and promises that have proved to be false. For example the earthly punishments promised in Deuteronomy 28:15–68 to those who fail to obey God do not appear to have ever been visited on a single offender. God promised that men and women who follow his laws will never be childless, nor will their cattle; and neither will God's followers ever become ill (Deuteronomy 7:14–15). But none of these promises has been kept. The Jews were told repeatedly that they would not lose their land, but they lost it for many centuries. They were also told repeatedly that they would always have a king to rule over them, but they do not have one today.[47] The Old Testament says that Jerusalem will always be a peaceful abode (Isaiah 33:20), which it has frequently not been; and that the uncircumcised will never enter it again (Isaiah 52:1), though they enter it today, by the thousand. Ezekiel 26 predicts that Nebuchadnezzar will take and destroy Tyre, but he failed to do so and had to be satisfied with Egypt instead.

Old Testament authors often failed to appreciate that times change. They frequently projected titles, rituals and customs from their own time into the distant past. The author of Chronicles (third century BC) did it when writing about the time of David (tenth century BC). The author of Esther (third or fourth century BC) did it when writing about ancient Persia around the fifth century BC, and the author of Daniel (167–164 BC) did it when writing about events 400 years earlier. In each case the author was trying to present his work as being much older than it really was. Like the original authors, later interpolators gave themselves away in various ways. According to Genesis (12:16) Pharaoh gave Abraham a number of animals including camels. The problem here is that camels were not domesticated until some 200 years after the time of Abraham. Since Pharaoh is hardly likely to have provided wild animals as a reward, the passage must be a later interpolation. Again, in Genesis (40:22) Pharaoh has his chief baker hanged. But this form of capital punishment was unknown in Egypt at the time. Again the story seems to have been added later. Aaron placed manna in front of the 'Testimony' or Tablets of the Law – before these Tablets of the Law existed (Exodus 16:34). According to 1 Samuel 17:54, David took Goliath's head back to Jerusalem, but this is hardly likely. Jerusalem was not annexed until years later. Saul's capital at this time was Gibeah in Judah. Genesis 17:11 reports God's supposed commandment:

And ye shall circumcise the flesh of your foreskin, and it shall be a token
of the covenant betwixt me and you.

This is the reason why to this day Jewish males are circumcised. The problem is that when Genesis was purportedly written all Mesopotamian peoples practised circumcision. The custom could be regarded as especially Jewish only much later, when neighbouring peoples no longer practised it. The passage is thought to have been added during the Babylonian Exile, when Jewish leaders were keen to maintain the distinction between their own people and the uncircumcised Babylonians.

THE NEW TESTAMENT

I do indeed think that we can now know almost nothing concerning the life and personality
of Jesus, since the early Christian sources show no interest in either,
are moreover fragmentary and often legendary.
Rudolf Bultmann (1884–1976), *Jesus and the Word*

Christian Churches have generally been successful in fostering the impression that the New Testament represents a divinely inspired, consistent, authoritative, factual account of historical events, dating from the earliest days of the Church and written by those most closely connected with the life of Jesus. In the following sections we shall look at how well these ideas match up with modern scholarship. We shall also look at the books of the New Testament. Has the present selection of books (the 'canon') always been accepted? Alternatively, is the idea of a canon a later and arbitrary concept? Does the canon include questionable material? Does it exclude material that has a better claim to inclusion? Does it contain errors, contradictions or inconsistencies? Does it contain additions or amendments to the original text? Does it contain errors of translation?

The New Testament consists of 27 books: four gospels, The Acts of the Apostles (which is really a sequel to the Gospel of Luke), 21 letters, and the book of Revelation. This much is agreed by all. Hardly anything else is. The following attempts to present the views of the majority of Christian scholars.

In the first century AD there was no New Testament. Authority rested solely in the Greek version of the Old Testament (the Septuagint) and in oral tradition about Jesus. When early Christians referred to scripture they were talking about the Jewish scriptures, not to the writings that we now know as the New Testament. The earliest known fragments of New Testament books date from the second century AD, although these are scraps. The earliest substantial texts are fourth-century copies. The originals were probably written towards the end of the first century AD. All of the books were written in Greek, not the everyday language of Jesus and his immediate followers, which would have been Aramaic. The quality of the Greek is frequently poor.

None of the New Testament gospels is believed by modern scholars to have been written by the man to whom it was traditionally ascribed and whose name it bears. Neither is it likely that any of the authors were eyewitnesses to the events described. Modern scholars are agreed that the gospels were written at different times, in different places and for different audiences, and that they are not attempts at an historically true record, but vehicles for impressing potential converts. They are propaganda to assist in proselytising, often citing supernatural events in an attempt to vindicate their claims. Some of the differences between the gospels may be attributed to the Jewish tradition of free interpretation, others to a simple marketing strategy, tailoring the product to look like what potential converts might want to hear. The John gospel in particular is drama rather than reporting.

Not a single original manuscript of any book of the New Testament survives. In the various copies that exist there are numerous disagreements, and later copies have new chunks of text added by editors. Of the 5,000 or so early manuscripts now known, no two agree exactly. They can however be arranged into families since each copy naturally incorporates all of the changes made to the version from which it was itself copied, as well as the new changes peculiar to itself. Changes can thus be traced through all later copying of the first manuscript to be tampered with. Modern translations are not translations of a single reliable manuscript but composites of a number of different manuscripts, enabling translators to select variant readings (which, cynics claim, frequently happen to agree with the translator's own theology). As the preface to the New International Version (NIV) of the Bible says:

The Greek text used in translating the New Testament was an eclectic one. No other piece of ancient literature has such an abundance of manuscript witnesses as does the New Testament.

As another authority puts it:[48]

> Reconstructing Christian origins from the New Testament depends on establishing a reliable text. None of the original documents is extant, and the oldest existing copies, made by hand before the invention of printing, differ at some points. We know from apocryphal gospels, as well as from statements of orthodox and heretical Christians, that in the second century gospel texts were altered and combined. This was particularly likely to occur in those early days, when the documents were not regarded as authoritative and definitive, and when there was no central organisation to secure and enforce uniformity.

Until the nineteenth century the *textus receptus* (received or accepted authoritative text) was in essence a Byzantine text based on manuscripts whose origins probably date from the third century. Two other families of manuscripts, the Alexandrian and the Western, are earlier than the Byzantine and arguably therefore more authoritative.

The Canon of the New Testament

> *It is reported in the supplement of the Council of Nicæa that the Fathers, being very perplexed to know which were the cryphal or apocryphal books of the Old and New Testaments, put them pell-mell on an altar, and the books to be rejected fell to the ground. It is a pity that this elegant procedure has not survived.*
> **Voltaire (1694–1778), *Philosophical Dictionary***

If the canon of the New Testament were divinely sanctioned then we might expect that it would have been established at an early date, by a competent authority, and have always been universally accepted. The canon would be internally consistent and comprise books 'whose authority was never in doubt in the Church' as Article 6 of the Anglican 39 Articles puts it. On the other hand, without divine sanction, people might well disagree about the canon, and it could take a long time for rival interested parties to reach a compromise. Moreover, the compromise could well incorporate mistakes – for example including books that do not really meet the stated criteria for acceptance, or excluding those that do. We might also expect the original manuscripts to have been lost – not being divinely authorised there would be no reason to take special care of them. We might also expect a certain degree of editorialising in texts, for example tailoring the story to the potential audience, or adding supernatural detail to make the story more impressive. Which pattern best matches the known facts: divine sanction, or human compromise?

The first thing to say is that the current books of the New Testament were not the only contenders for inclusion in the canon when a canon was first proposed (by a man now considered heretical) around 150 years after the crucifixion. There were many contenders, even among the gospels. Indeed the author of the Luke gospel indicates that there were 'many' accounts already in existence before he wrote his (Luke 1:1). It is now known that more than 80 such works existed.

When various writings eventually came to be collected together to decide which were canonical, the existence of numerous incompatible gospels posed uncomfortable problems. Why were there a number of gospels, not just one definitive one? Or if there was one true gospel, which one was it? God could easily have arranged for there to be a single authoritative gospel for the benefit of Christians, but he had not done so. Christians had to select the versions they thought most reliable or that best suited their own beliefs. The Church Fathers who first attempted to assemble the canon of the New Testament soon discovered that the numerous gospels available did not agree with each other. No attempt had been made to ensure consistency between them since each was written for a different audience, and that audience was intended to regard their gospel as *the* gospel.

The four familiar gospels, Matthew, Mark, Luke and John, were the specific gospels of specific factions. For example we know that the Ebionites used Matthew, certain Gnostics used Mark, the Marcionites used a form of Luke, and the Valentinians used John.[49] In some cases gospels may well have been written by and for such factions.

Accepting two or more gospels invited problems because any two of them would contradict each other. The obvious solution was to accept only one gospel into any 'canonical' body of writings. When Marcion had first proposed a version of the New Testament in the second century, he had solved the problem in exactly this way, by adopting the Luke gospel and rejecting the others. Different people adopted different canons. A list called the 'Muratorian Canon', dating from around AD 170, includes some texts now 'lost' and omits a number of books that are now included in the canon.[50] The Church Father Irenaeus produced an alternative list soon after, around AD 180, but individual Churches continued to use whichever books they happened to like. For example, some included a gospel attributed to St Thomas, and some excluded the John gospel. In a pastoral letter of AD 367, Bishop Athanasius of Alexandria specified 27 books to be read in churches. This list eventually came to be generally accepted as the canon of the New Testament, although the matter was not finally settled until the fifth or sixth century, and even then was not accepted by all.

The basic problem was to find a selection that contained all details church leaders wanted to include, while omitting everything they wanted to exclude. But no one gospel contained all the material that was considered acceptable, yet as soon as two or more were brought together they started contradicting each other. The more gospels were accepted, the easier it was to include all the teachings currently approved of, but the more difficult it was to justify the mutual contradictions. Even with four gospels, it was still not possible to include all of the teachings currently approved of. For example, the doctrine of Christ's descent into Hell is not to be found in any of the four canonical gospels. It comes from the non-canonical *Gospel of Nicodemus*. So too, the perpetual virginity of Jesus' mother cannot be established from the canonical gospels, only from apocryphal ones.

In practice there must have been numerous competing pressures affecting the choice of what was and what was not to be regarded as canonical. Writers of later gospels clearly used earlier ones as sources and had few qualms about embellishing them, so that stories became more and more impressive, and events acquired an increasingly supernatural nature. As a result of this trend, some of the later gospels were far too fantastic to be included in the canon. Others were apparently excluded because rival Christian groups, such as the Ebionites or Gnostics, favoured them. Each Christian group had its own favourites. One famous early Christian, the Carthaginian theologian Tertullian, observed that scripture would never convince heretics because they have their own canon.[51] He is himself now considered a heretic.

Here is how an acknowledged authority on the subject, Elaine Pagels, puts it in her book, *The Gnostic Gospels*:

> ... what we call Christianity – and what we identify as Christian tradition – actually represents only a small selection of specific sources, chosen from among dozens of others. Who made that selection, and for what reasons? Why were these other writings excluded and banned as "heresy"? What made them so dangerous?

A brief account of some of the gospel contenders for inclusion in the Christian canon follows, starting with the candidates that proved successful:

The Gospel of St Matthew

This gospel was written, probably between AD 70 and AD 80, in Koine, a form of Greek. The work is traditionally attributed to Matthew, or Levi, a disciple of Jesus who had previously been a tax collector. There is no evidence for this, and almost all biblical scholars now discount it. It is now widely recognised that for centuries Christians were in the habit of attributing their favourite texts to people they believed to have been close to Jesus, in order to give these works an air of spurious authority. As in this case, such attributions were often first made generations after the work was first circulated.

According to tradition the Matthew gospel is the oldest, but most scholars accept that its author used the Mark gospel as a source, which implies that the traditional dating must be reversed (the order of the gospels – Matthew, Mark, Luke, John – represents ancient ideas about their relative ages).[52] The rhyme and rhythm of the Sermon on the Mount shows that at least some of the Matthew gospel was originally phrased in Aramaic. This gospel may well have been adopted from a list of sayings written in a Semitic language and then fitted into a narrative framework.[53] The Jerusalem Bible describes this gospel as a 'dramatic account' in seven acts. It is essentially propaganda for Jewish Christians. Its author may well have been a Palestinian Jew, perhaps representing the views of Jesus' followers in Jerusalem. He repeatedly mentions that Jesus was sent only to the Jews, not to the gentiles, and emphasises Jewish Law. He represents Jesus as a majestic sovereign, descended from an ancient royal line, who comes 'not to bring peace, but a sword'. The author also makes much of Old Testament prophecies and their fulfilment.

The Gospel of St Mark

The Mark gospel is the shortest and almost certainly the oldest of the canonical gospels. It was written in poor koine, probably between AD 60 and 70. The gospel stresses Jesus' humanity – he gets tired and fed up, disappointed and even desperate. It even says explicitly that those close to him tried to take control of him, believing him to be out of his mind (Mark 3:21). The authors of the other gospels used Mark as a principal source, but increasingly toned down Jesus' human weaknesses and developed an increasingly divine persona for him.

According to tradition this gospel was written in Rome by Mark, a companion of the disciple Peter, from Peter's own verbal account. Although it may have been written in Rome, the tradition is otherwise discounted by most biblical scholars. Whoever the author was, he seems to have known little of Jewish life or culture, or of Palestinian geography. He often attributes Roman customs and artefacts to Jesus and his followers. He was writing for a Roman audience, and his narrative is tailored accordingly. He takes pains to explain Jewish customs (e.g. Mark 7:3–4) where he knows about them.

The gospel may have been written as a protest by gentile Christians against the influence of Jewish Christians in Jerusalem. The author consistently denigrates the Jews. Jesus' Jewish followers are made out to be dull, quarrelsome and cowardly. They desert him at the first sign of trouble. The Jewish establishment is presented as trying to trick him and kill him. By contrast the Romans are presented as models of civility and justice. Pontius Pilate, for example, makes every effort not to condemn Jesus, despite Jewish demands. This was a politically correct account during a period when thousands of Jews were being crucified for rebelling against Rome, and it helped earn Pilate his sainthood in the Coptic Church.

The Gospel of St Luke

The author of this gospel is traditionally identified with a Greek physician who accompanied Paul on his travels, though there is no evidence for this, just the customary late attribution. This gospel may have been written at Antioch some time around AD 85. Unlike the other canonical gospels, which were written in koine, this gospel was written in literary Greek. The author, whoever he was, was much more urbane than the authors of the other gospels and other early writers, so it is sometimes possible to see in the original Greek where an editor has incorporated the writing of others. The text contains some parables that are not mentioned by other gospel writers,[54] and the nativity story, added later, may have been translated from an earlier Hebrew text. When translated back into Hebrew it is claimed to resemble typically alliterative Jewish poetry.

This gospel was written for, and angled at, an Hellenic gentile audience. It represents the views of Paul, on his mission to the gentiles, and so omits much of the specifically Jewish material. Here Jesus is represented as a gentle lamb-like teacher of modest birth – the 'Gentle Jesus meek and mild' of childhood prayers. This author has humble shepherds visiting the baby Jesus where the Matthew author has high dignitaries bringing gifts to a new-born king.

The gospel is really only the first volume; the second volume is called *The Acts of the Apostles*. One of the author's chief motivations for writing Luke and Acts was clearly to represent Christianity as a movement that carried all before it. Another important motivation was to stress that it did not constitute a threat to the State.

The Gospel of St John

This gospel is substantially different from the other three canonical gospels. Indeed, apart from the passion story (thought to be a late addition), its presentation bears no relationship at all to them. The few incidents that are common to the other gospels occur at different times, or in different places, and in different circumstances. The other three gospels are together known as the synoptic gospels. (The word *synoptic* means 'seen-together' and is applied to Matthew, Mark and Luke because they share a common point of view.)

The John gospel purports to be an eyewitness account, although most scholars agree that it was the latest of the four canonical gospels, having been written, in koine, between AD 90 and AD 100, several generations after Jesus lived. The author is not identified and there is no reason to believe that he was the apostle John, or even that his name was John at all. The traditional ascriptions seem to have been based on ambiguous passages such as John 19:35 and 21:24 (part of a late addition).

For centuries there was controversy as to whether this gospel should be admitted to the list of canonical books. The Church Father Irenaeus stated that the book had been written to refute the arguments of Cerinthus, a well-known Gnostic who had lived a few years earlier. On the other hand the gospel was itself used by Gnostics – one reason why 'orthodox' Christians wanted to reject it from the canon. Most biblical scholars accept that it represents an interpretation of Jesus that developed late in the first century AD, probably in Ephesus. Its opening verses express ancient Middle Eastern views, personifying the *Word* (*logos*), but they are adapted to a new emerging theology.

The gospel's target audience appears to be educated, middle-class and Hellenic. The author, like the author of the Mark gospel, takes trouble to explain Jewish words, names and attitudes (e.g. 1:41–2 and 4:9). As in other late documents, the gospel is consistently anti-Semitic (the Jewishness of Jesus and his followers is underplayed, even implicitly denied[55] – while his enemies are referred to about sixty times as 'the Jews').

Of the four canonical gospels John stresses Jesus' divinity most strongly and also plays down his human weaknesses most strongly. The miracles are consistently more impressive, and may have been taken from a source in which they served simply as demonstrations of Jesus' power.[56] This gospel has been described as a meditation in dramatic form.

Non-canonical Gospels
It seems natural to us that there should be four gospels, but it was not at all obvious in early times. It took a long time for the four described above to be accepted. One problem was that they contradicted each other on many points. A solution to this problem, adopted by Tatian in the 170s, was to create a new comprehensive gospel, which harmonised them (and reflected the editor's hatred of women). This gospel (the *Diatessaron*, literally 'Fourfold') was widely accepted in the East but did not gain acceptance in the long term.

Incidentally, it was only when the four well-known gospels were considered for acceptance into a New Testament canon that they were ascribed to Matthew, Mark, Luke and John. These second-century guesses sound more homely than say anonymous names like 1, 2, 3 and 4 or A, B, C and D, and give the impression that the authors were known, which they were not.

Today, it is not commonly realised that there were more than just four candidates for inclusion in the canon. There were many others, each of them purporting to be the one true gospel and contending for primacy. The decision to select the four that are now so familiar was largely arbitrary. One of the reasons given by Irenaeus for his selection is that four is a natural number. He cited the four winds and four corners of the Earth as evidence for this.[57]

Other contenders enjoyed various degrees of acceptance in early times, but they ultimately failed to win a place in the orthodox canon. The following are a few of the more interesting failed candidates:

The Gospel of St Thomas

Although manuscripts of the gospel of St Thomas have been in circulation for centuries, their authenticity was doubted until 1946. In that year a fourth-century Coptic manuscript of the gospel was discovered at Nag Hammadi in Egypt.

This gospel is simply a collection of Jesus' sayings. Most, but not all, of these agree with the canonical gospels. The text includes additional storyteller's details omitted from the later gospels but lacks their later allegorical interpretations. Some of the sayings that appear here, but not in the canonical gospels, had been attributed to Jesus by some sections of the early Church. Although the Coptic manuscript of this gospel dates from the fourth century, the text is known to be older, since fragments of a second-century manuscript have also been discovered. It is possible that the canonical gospels were partially created from the Thomas gospel with a generous padding of background detail to make the story more interesting and convincing.

The Thomas gospel was probably omitted from the canon because it was used by Gnostics. Significantly, the gospel gives no special titles to Jesus and is silent about the Resurrection. It was known to the earliest Church Fathers, accepted by the Valentinians, and arguably has a much better claim for inclusion in the canon than the gospel attributed to St John.

The Secret Book of James

This gospel stresses the prime position among the apostles of Jesus' brother, James the Just. James led the Jewish Christians based in Jerusalem, which made him unpopular amongst Pauline Christians. In the canon of the New Testament, James's role is generally played down and Peter's played up, which may well explain why this book was not included. It was allowed by the orthodox to become 'lost', possibly deliberately destroyed, though a copy of the gospel survived in a Coptic text.

The Gospel According to the Hebrews (or the Gospel of the Nazarenes)
This was a work used by Jewish Christians, followers of James the Just, who fled to Syria. It is known only from fragments. It apparently contained material similar to that in the synoptic gospels. St Jerome noted that it was believed by some to have been the original version of what we now know as the Matthew gospel. This may be the same as the Gospel of the Ebionites, according to which it was Jesus' principal aim to stop all sacrificial practices at the Temple at Jerusalem.

The Book of James (or The Protevangelium)
This book is mainly concerned with the life of Mary and the birth of Jesus. It is sometimes called the Infancy Gospel of James. Its account of the birth of Jesus embellishes the account in the Luke gospel. The gospel was accepted as genuine by many of the Church Fathers. It gives an account of Mary remaining *virgo intacta*, after the birth of Jesus, and it is from this source, not the canonical gospels, that the idea of Mary's perpetual virginity developed. Indeed this book was largely responsible for the development of Mariology, and for providing such incidental details as the names of Mary's own parents: Joachim and Anna. This book explained away Jesus' brothers as step-brothers, Joseph's children by an earlier marriage. Among Western Christians, this ensured that the work would be rejected from the canon as the Roman Church was trying to justify the explanation that the brothers were really cousins.

The Secret Gospel of Mark
This was a fuller version of the conventional Mark gospel. No copy of it has survived, though it is referred to in a letter from Clement of Alexandria (AD *c.*150–*c.*215). In 1958 Professor Morton Smith of Columbia University discovered in a monastery near Jerusalem a copy of a letter from Clement, one of the most venerated of the Church Fathers. The letter admitted that the author of the Mark gospel had written material that did not appear in the usual version of the gospel. Clement's correspondent is instructed to lie about the existence of this missing material, even on oath.[58] The letter quotes passages from this lost gospel, including an account of Jesus raising a dead youth. The youth 'loved him and beseeched him that he might be with him'. Wearing nothing but a linen cloth, the youth visited Jesus in the evening, and spent the night with him. The letter reveals that there were rumours current at

the time that Jesus and the youth had been naked together. It appears that one group of Christians (the Carpocratians – regarded as heretics by Clement) knew about this secret information and deduced from it that Christians were granted permission to engage liberally in sexual activity.

The canonical Mark gospel is an expurgated version of this longer gospel.[59] It is not difficult to see why people like Clement might want to promote the edited version as the true one: the fuller version was powerful ammunition not only to the Carpocratians but also to a range of Gnostics.[60] Whatever the reasons for its exclusion, the fact is that the Secret Gospel of Mark had a strong claim to be in the canon in place of the expurgated version.

Other Books

Other gospels, many of which were known to the Church Fathers, include the Gospel of Peter, the Gospel of Matthias (lost), the Gospel of Basilides (lost), the Gospel of the Twelve Apostles, the Gospel of Nicodemus, incorporating the Acts of Pontius Pilate, the Gospel of the Egyptians, and the Gospel of Truth. In addition there are known to have been a number of other Gnostic gospels, but these were sought out and destroyed by upholders of the Pauline line. According to the Secret Book of James 1:7 the 12 disciples each recorded their recollections and organised them into books, yet not a single one seems to have survived.[61]

Gospels were not the only problem. Disagreements raged over other books as well. Different Church leaders favoured different books, and their selection seems to have been largely a matter of personal taste. A number of Churches, for example, admitted the anti-Semitic Epistle of Barnabas. Many of the early Church Fathers regarded the Teaching of the (Twelve) Apostles, or Didache, as scriptural, though it was later omitted from the canon. Likewise, Clement of Alexandria and others admitted the Apocalypse of Peter, which was also later omitted from the canon. Well into the fourth century an influential churchman could include the Wisdom of Solomon amongst the books of the New Testament. On the other hand some books were later admitted that had previously been regarded as non-scriptural. Irenaeus himself had excluded the Third Epistle of John, the Epistle of James and the Second Epistle of Peter, all of which are now included in the canon. Eusebius of Caesarea also declined to classify them with his 'recognised' books and described them as disputed – along with the Second Epistle of John and the Epistle of Jude.[62]

One of the main criteria for acceptance was a direct link with the apostles. So out went the Shepherd of Hermas and an Epistle of Clement to the Corinthians, which had previously been counted as scriptural. The Mark gospel stayed in because of Mark's supposed link with Peter, and the Luke gospel because of Luke's supposed link with Paul. The Epistle to the Hebrews presented a problem. As Eusebius said 'Who wrote the epistle is known to God alone'.[63] Some Church Fathers, notably Clement of Alexandria and Origen of Alexandria (AD c.185–254), had known on stylistic grounds that this letter could not have been written by Paul but were prepared to pretend that it was apostolic in order to allow it into the canon. By the terms of a deal done at the Council of Carthage in 419, it was accepted as being Paul's work. Eastern Churches accepted this conceit, but the Church at Rome refused to, and rejected the epistle on the grounds that it was not apostolic. Rome relented some time in the fifth or sixth century and fell back into line with the Eastern Churches. Modern scholars agree with the original Roman view that the work was not written by Paul.

Many works hung in the balance. The epistles of James and Jude, the Second Epistle of Peter, the Second and Third Epistles of John, and the book of Revelation were disputed but were eventually successful. The book of Revelation, which early Christians had considered the work of a known heretic,[64] was admitted on the grounds that its author was St John the apostle, though later the story was changed and it was attributed to a mysterious St John the Divine.

A number of letters purportedly written by St Paul were excluded from the canon at an early stage – for example the fake Third Epistle to the Corinthians. Fourteen letters were eventually accepted. Of these, it is now widely accepted by scholars that at least four (including Hebrews) were not written by Paul. Some scholars hold that as many as seven of these letters are not his. A comparison of writing styles shows that the three pastoral letters (1 and 2 Timothy and Titus) were all written by the same hand, however that hand was not the one responsible for the other letters.[65] Conversely, textual critics have evidence that at least three genuine letters by St Paul never made it into the canon and have since been lost.[66] Of the letters that did make it into the canon, it is widely accepted that some of them are not original works but edited versions of selected passages from two or three separate writings, fused together.[67]

When we turn to the seven catholic (or general) letters the position is even worse. Not one was written by its supposed author. Furthermore, the Church Fathers excluded a number of similar letters from the canon, although their claim to be included is at least as good as those that were successful. The second letter of Peter is generally accepted to have been written by someone other than the author of the first letter of Peter. Much of it is a reworking of Jude, probably attributed to Peter in order to enhance its status.

Other writings rejected from the canon include Acts of individual apostles: the Acts of John, Acts of Paul, Acts of Peter, Acts of Andrew, and Acts of Thomas; various apocalypses: the Apocalypses of Peter, of Paul, and of Thomas; the Infancy Gospel of James already referred to; and the Epistles of the Apostles, also called the Testament of Our Lord in Galilee. Some well-known 'Bible stories' are not from our present canon, but from these works.[68] Another indication of how uncertain the canon really was may be seen from the Codex Sinaiticus, one of the earliest and most authoritative copies of the books of the New Testament. It includes the Epistle of Barnabas and part of the Shepherd of Hermas.

The works that have been admitted into the canon are not presented in chronological order, though it is still sometimes assumed that they are. The order – gospels, Acts, letters, Revelation – is often taken to mean that the gospels are the earliest documents, though in fact some of the letters were the earliest documents. This is significant because many ideas now considered characteristically Christian were unknown to the authors of these early letters, a fact that is concealed by the failure to list the works in chronological order. The arbitrariness is demonstrated by the order in which the letters are presented. First are those supposedly written by Paul, then those written by others. Those ascribed to Paul are divided into those addressed to Churches (in descending order of length) followed by those addressed to individuals.

Errors

> *No god was ever in advance of the nation that created him.*
> Robert Ingersoll (1833–99), *Oration on the Gods*

Even in mainstream churches, congregations still chant 'This is the word of the Lord' after Bible readings. This view, that God was involved in the production of the New Testament, is undermined by numerous errors in the text. Some are simple errors of fact; others look like interpolations designed to make the text understandable to audiences unfamiliar with the Middle East. Yet others apparently stem from linguistic confusion.

First, simple geographical errors. The original text of Matthew (2:6) speaks of 'Bethlehem, the land of Juda'. The error was corrected by the translators of early English versions who knew that Bethlehem was a town, not a land, so that it reads 'Bethlehem, *in* the land of Juda'. The word *in* is italicised to show that it is an interpolation. The more honest German translation retained the error up to the latter half of the twentieth century. Again, the writer of the Mark gospel is apparently ignorant of Palestinian geography. He says that Gerasa was on the eastern shore of the Sea of Galilee;[69] but Gerasa (modern Jerash) is more than 30 miles away to the south east. The Matthew author must have known that this location was not feasible, so he changed it to Gadara (Matthew 8:28), which was a mere eight miles from the lake. Mark also suggests that Jesus passed through Sidon on his way to the Sea of Galilee from Tyre (Mark 7:31). In fact Sidon is in the opposite direction, and at the time there was no road from Sidon to the Sea of Galilee anyway, though there was one from Tyre.

As in the Old Testament, many errors reflect the author's limited perception of the world. It might have been possible to see all the kingdoms on Earth from a great height if the world really was flat, but climbing a mountain doesn't help much on a spherical planet. Cosmology too reflected contemporary ideas. The third heaven referred to by Paul (2 Corinthians 12:2) only made sense when concentric crystal orbs were believed to circumscribe seven physical heavens. Again, it was not unreasonable for someone to hold seven stars in his hand (Revelation 1:10–16) when the nature of stars was not understood – and gods or angels were thought to steer stars around their appointed courses.

Biblical natural history is also fallible. Paul calls someone a fool for not knowing that a seed must die before it can come to life (1 Corinthians 15:36). Paul is apparently party to a contemporary misunderstanding about seeds, despite his divine inspiration.[70] Throughout the New Testament it is assumed that illness is caused by unclean spirits, prompted by sin. Cures can therefore be effected by forgiving sin and ejecting the unclean spirit. Such beliefs were common in biblical times and remained a central Christian belief well into the nineteenth century, but only a few sects espouse such ideas now, and Churches are ever more embarrassed by their traditional attachment to the practice of exorcism. Again, biblical characters like Simon Magus could be credited with magical powers in early times that now seem more than a little unlikely to most mainstream Christians. Even a person's shadow was believed capable of working miracles (Acts 5:14–16), since shadows were thought to be part of their owner's being in ancient times.

As in the Old Testament there are anachronisms. In Acts 5:36 a famous Jewish teacher called Gamaliel refers to events as though they occurred in the past, when in fact they happened after his death. Again the Jewish Council described in the gospels matches the council after the fall of Jerusalem in AD 70, not the council of Jesus' time. This suggests not merely that the gospels were written after AD 70, but that they were written a sufficiently long time after AD 70 for people to have forgotten that it had ever been different. Sometimes the authors have doctored the text to make it accessible to their target audience. Mark (10:12) quotes Jesus as saying:

> And if a woman shall put away [divorce] her husband, and be married to another, she commiteth adultery.

But the idea of a woman divorcing her husband was unknown to the Jews. The concept simply did not exist. The author of Mark apparently found it necessary to allow for this eventuality when speaking to his Roman audience. Without it the text would appear to prohibit men divorcing their wives, but not wives divorcing their husbands. One might sympathise with the author's dilemma, but the fact remains that he must have added his own words. Again, Luke 5:19 refers to a tiled roof. Such roofs would be familiar to Luke's Hellenic audience, but in Galilee where the story is set the houses would have had thatched roofs.

Sometimes the text disagrees with what is known about Jewish Law.[71] For example, the story of Jesus' trial is flawed in a number of respects. The Sanhedrin is said in the three synoptic gospels to have met during the Passover, but this was not permitted under Judaic law. It is said to have met at night, but again this was not permitted. It was said to have met in a private house, yet it was forbidden to meet outside the precincts of the Temple. Also, it is claimed that the Jews were not permitted to pass the death sentence (John 18:31), but this cannot be true. Earlier, the chief priests had considered putting Lazarus to death (John 12:10) and Jews were responsible for other killings – both formally and informally.[72] The Jews appear to have regarded blasphemy as a capital offence, but only if it involved worshipping idols or using a name of God (and Jesus had not been accused of either). Again, the custom of allowing the people to have a prisoner of their choice released for the Passover festival appears to be a fiction. No such custom existed.[73]

Another sort of error is the misquotation of the Jewish scriptures. Luke 3:36 refers to Sala, 'which was the son of Cainan, which was the son of Arphaxad', but in Genesis 11:12 Sala was the son, not the grandson, of Arphaxad.[74] As we shall see, Old Testament passages were selectively quoted, taken out of context and amended to meet the needs of the New Testament (for example 1 Corinthians 2:9 misquoting Isaiah 64:4).[75] Occasionally it is possible to deduce that an error was made in interpreting an original Aramaic term. Luke 11:39–41 contains a curious injunction by Jesus:

> ...Now do ye Pharisees make clean the outside of the cup and the platter; but your inward part is full of ravening and wickedness. Ye fools, did not he that made that which is without make that which is within also? But rather give alms of such things as ye have; and, behold, all things are clean unto you.

This is saying that one can become clean by giving alms. Interestingly in Aramaic the word meaning to give alms (*zakkau*) is easily confused with the word meaning to cleanse (*dakkau*). Although the New Testament is mainly written in a type of Greek, Jesus himself would have spoken Aramaic so it is apparent that the wrong word has been used. This explanation is supported by a parallel passage in Matthew (23:25–6), which does not mention alms at all, but states that one must clean the inside in order to clean the outside.

As we shall see later, there are many examples of the New Testament misquoting passages from the Old, especially in relation to supposed prophecies. St Paul engaged in some deliberate manipulation, for example substituting the word 'Lord' (i.e. Jesus) for 'LORD' (i.e. God), in order to give the impression that the Old Testament had been talking about Jesus.

Contradictions and Inconsistencies

*If Matthew speaks truth, Luke speaks falsehood, and if Luke speaks truth,
Matthew speaks falsehood; and as there is no authority for believing one
more than the other, there is no authority for believing either...*

Thomas Paine, *The Age of Reason*, Part II

The traditional Christian claim is that the books of the New Testament complement each other to give a unified narrative. In particular the gospels are represented as giving four consistent views of the same events. In this section we shall see how valid this view is. In general, we shall restrict ourselves to the four canonical gospels plus Acts and see if they agree or disagree with each other in describing Jesus' birth, life, death and teachings.

It is now generally accepted that the authors of both Matthew and Luke used the Mark gospel as a primary source. They include many of the same incidents, but change the words to suit their own needs. For example Mark suggests that believers should be prepared to sacrifice their lives for their beliefs, 'let him ... take up his cross, and follow me',[76] but the urbane author of Luke adapts this to suggest that believers should suffer something different, 'let him ... take up his cross daily, and follow me' (Luke 9:23). The insertion of the word *daily* has completely changed the meaning from a nasty death to a persistent inconvenience.

The Matthew and Luke authors give conflicting versions of Jesus' ancestry (Matthew 1:1–16 and Luke 3:23–38). These versions bear virtually no relationship to each other and are irreconcilable. According to the Luke gospel, Jesus had 41 ancestors since David, according to the Matthew gospel only 26. Nearly all the names in the two lists are different. Even the name of Jesus' paternal grandfather is different. According to Matthew he was called Jacob, while according to Luke he was called Heli.

The rest of the nativity stories in the two gospels bear virtually no resemblance to each other, and contradict each other on a number of points. According to Luke, Jesus' family had to travel to Bethlehem for a tax census that took place when Quirinius or Cyrenius was governor of Syria (Luke 2:1–3). This census is stated to have been the first during his governorship (Luke 2:2). Such a census is an historical reality and is known to have been carried out in AD 6 or 7. Furthermore, we may accept that the census was carried out for taxation purposes, since the Romans carried out such censuses for taxation and conscription, and the Jews were exempt from military service.[77] But now the problems start. Luke says that the census was the result of a decree from Caesar Augustus to the whole world, but this must be an error. The real census affected Roman Judæa only. Galilee was not part of Roman Judæa, so Joseph, a Galilaean, would not have been affected. Even if he had been affected, he would not have had to travel to another town. Like the tax it was related to, the census was based on property, so people registered where they lived. The Romans did not care about genealogies, and neither did they require mass migrations. Furthermore, such taxes would have required only Joseph to register – even if a census had been carried out in Nazareth, Mary would not have been required to stir herself, heavily pregnant or not. Luke's story does not hold water. Worse, it cannot be squared with that of Matthew. Matthew does not mention the census at all. According to him Jesus was born before the death of Herod. The only possible Herod is Herod I (Herod the Great) and he died in 4 BC.[78] Thus there is a discrepancy of some ten years between the two stories.

According to the gospels Jesus often contradicted himself. He claimed to uphold the traditional laws unreservedly (Matthew 5:17–19, cf. Luke 16:17). He then addressed a number of questions and in each case overturned the traditional law. These questions concern subjects such as murder, adultery, divorce, swearing, punishment (an eye for an eye), and loving one's enemies. On the question of divorce the accounts in both the Matthew and Mark gospels contradict the traditional laws, under which divorce was a simple matter for men.[79] Not only that, the two gospels are incompatible with each other. Mark 10:9 forbids divorce in any circumstances. Speaking of man and wife Jesus says:

> What therefore God hath joined together, let not man put asunder.

These words are familiar from their use in Christian marriage ceremonies (cf. Luke 16:18). Matthew 19:9 however puts a rather different slant on the matter:

> ...Whosoever shall put away his wife, except it be for fornication, and shall marry commiteth adultery...

This clearly sanctions divorce and remarriage for men whose wives have been unfaithful. But these are not the only versions. Paul had his own quite different ideas. A plain reading of the text shows that he allowed men to divorce ('put away') unbelieving wives and women to leave their unbelieving husbands. The text in question (1 Corinthians 7:10–17) was later to justify the so-called Pauline Privilege, allowing the Church to grant divorces.

God insisted on the death penalty even for such minor misdemeanours as collecting sticks on the Sabbath, but Jesus abrogated this law when his own followers picked ears of wheat on the Sabbath (Mark 2:23–7). According to a passage inserted in later manuscripts at John 8:3–11, he abrogated the law requiring an adulteress to be stoned.

On some occasions Jesus tells his disciples that his message is only for the Jews, on others he says it is also for the gentiles. In Matthew 10:5–6 Jesus tells his disciples not to go among the gentiles, and at Matthew 15:24 he says: '...I am not sent but unto the lost sheep of the house of Israel'. In the next two verses he likens the gentiles to dogs eating crumbs at their master's table. To call anyone a dog in the Middle East at that time was as grave an insult then as it is now. On the other hand at Matthew 28:19 Jesus takes a contradictory view and tells the disciples to 'teach all nations, baptising them in the name of the Father, and of the Son, and of the holy ghost'. (The explanation may well be later tampering. Many scholars regard the end of Mark as a later addition made to the original gospel, which apart from this passage is clearly written by a Jew for a Jewish audience.)

The sermon on the mount related by Matthew differs substantially from its counterpart given in Luke. The one in Luke is similar to that in Matthew, but its text differs in a number of respects. Furthermore it occurs later in the story than it does in Matthew, and is reported as having been given not on a mount, but a plain (see Matthew 5:1–7:27 and Luke 6:17–49). There are other cases where the same story is told more than once, with minor alterations. The story of the feeding of the four thousand (Mark 8:1–10, Matthew 15:29–39) varies only slightly from the same story told elsewhere, when five thousand were fed (Mark 6:30–44, Matthew 14:13–21, Luke 9:10–17, cf. John 6:1–15). That it is really the same story told twice over is confirmed by the fact that on both occasions the disciples cannot imagine how the crowd is going to be fed. If the disciples had already seen the miracle once, then they would hardly be at a complete loss to work out how the second (smaller) crowd might be nourished.

When he lists the commandments, Jesus mentions rather fewer than ten. According to Luke he cites only five. According to Matthew and Mark he cites six, but the extra commandments cited are different and include one (do not defraud) that is not one of the Ten Commandments at all. In summary they are:

Matthew 19:18	Mark 10:19	Luke 18:20
No murder	No murder	No adultery
No adultery	No adultery	No murder
No stealing	No stealing	No stealing
No false testimony	No false testimony	No false testimony
–	No fraud (!)	–
Honour parents	Honour parents	Honour parents
Love thy neighbour	–	–

There are even disagreements over the wording of the Lord's Prayer. Matthew 6:9–13 and Luke 11:2–4 give different versions (neither of which match the version in common use today).

Again, lists of the 12 apostles are not consistent (see Appendix B). Matthew 10:2–4 and Mark 3:16–19 give a list including Thaddaeus; Luke 6:14–16 and Acts 1:13 give a similar list except that it excludes Thaddaeus, and includes a second Judas – Judas son (or brother) of James. Many inconsistencies like this have traditionally been explained by the suggestion that the same person might be known by more than one name. So it is that the Matthew mentioned in the Matthew gospel is traditionally identified with the Levi mentioned in the Mark gospel. Bartholomew is identified with Nathanael in the same way. There remains, however, a suspicion that up to 16 disciples (not counting Judas Iscariot's replacement) may have been condensed in order to arrive at a number with an appropriate Old Testament resonance. It could be mentioned also that the names of individual disciples appear remarkably infrequently; that Jesus is generally seen appointing only four or five disciples; that only those four or five play any significant role; and that the lists of 12 given in the gospels, for example at Matthew 10:2–4 and Luke 6:14–16, are not in the earliest texts.

When he sent out the Twelve (or Sixteen, or however many) Jesus gave contradictory instructions to them according to the gospels. According to Mark 6:8 they were told to take a staff, but according to Matthew 10:10 they were instructed not to take a staff. The gospels frequently disagree about the order of events. According to the Mark gospel Jesus cured Simon's mother-in-law after he called the first disciples at Galilee, but according to the Luke author he did so before he called the disciples. Other minor details are also inconsistent. The John author manages to contradict himself within a chapter. First he claims that Jesus baptises people (John 3:22) then, when Jesus is accused of baptising people, the author of the gospel says that although his disciples do, Jesus himself does not baptise people (John 4:1–2).

When it comes to accounts of Jesus' arrest, trial and death, it is clear that a great deal of creativity has been employed. According to the synoptic gospels Jesus was identified to his captors by a kiss. According to John he simply owned up.[80] The gospels also disagree about the trial – to such an extent that some apologists have been obliged to conclude that there were at least five hearings: before Annas, Caiaphas, Pilate, Herod Antipas, and then Pilate again,[81] but even this is impossible to square with all the gospel details. According to the synoptics a crowd of Jews were there at the main trial before Pilate, according to John they waited outside. Matthew 27:12–14 asserts that Jesus was silent when accused, but John 18:19–37 quotes the words that he used to answer his accusers.

The author of John disagrees with the other three gospel writers about the day on which Jesus was crucified. The John author says that the crucifixion took place on the day of the preparation of the Passover (John 19:14); the others say that the Last Supper was a Passover meal (Matthew 26:17–20; Mark 14:12–17; Luke 22:7–14), which means that the crucifixion must have occurred after the start of Passover. The gospel writers disagree about the time of day that Jesus was crucified. Mark 15:25 says that the crucifixion occurred at the third hour (9 a.m.), while John 19:14 says that sentence was not passed until the sixth hour (12 noon), so that the execution must have taken place in the afternoon. According to Matthew 27:44 both of the malefactors crucified with Jesus reviled him, but according to Luke 23:39–43 only one of them did so, and the second malefactor rebuked the first. According to the synoptic gospels (Matthew 27:32, Mark 15:21, Luke 23:26) Simon of Cyrene was forced to carry Jesus' cross, but according to John 19:17 Jesus carried it himself. All four gospel writers have a different version of what was written on the titulus above it:

The King of the Jews (Mark 15:26)

This is Jesus, the King of the Jews (Matthew 27:37)

This is the King of the Jews (Luke 23:38)

Jesus of Nazareth, The King of the Jews (John 19:19)

According to the Mark author, the veil of the Temple was torn after Jesus died. According to the Luke author it was torn before he died. There are also inconsistencies between the various accounts of Jesus' last words. The Mark and Matthew authors favour a quotation from the beginning of Psalm 22:

My God, My God, why hast thou forsaken me? (Matthew 27:46 and Mark 15:34)

The Luke author prefers these words, which appear to be derived from verse 5 in Psalm 31:

Father, into thy hands I commend my spirit. (Luke 23:46)

The John author is more prosaic:

It is finished. (John 19:30)

Two different accounts are given of the death of Judas. According to Matthew 27:5 he hanged himself, but according to Acts 1:18 he fell headlong, burst asunder in the midst of a field, and all his bowels gushed out. Again, the authors of the gospels give contradictory accounts of the discovery of Jesus' open tomb.

According to Mark 16:1–9, three women visit the tomb just after sunrise: Mary Magdalene, Mary the mother of James, and Salome. They go to anoint the body. There is no mention of any earthquake. The stone has already been rolled away from the entrance to the tomb. No one sees Jesus, but sitting in the tomb the women see a young man in a white robe. He says that Jesus is going on ahead to Galilee (as predicted by Mark 14:28). Terrified, the women say nothing to anyone about what they have seen at the tomb, despite having been instructed to do so by the young man. Of the three Mary Magdalene alone subsequently sees Jesus.

According to Luke 24:1–10, Mary Magdalene, Mary the mother of James, Joanna, and some other women visit the tomb early in the morning, with spices and ointments. There is no mention of any earthquake. The stone has already been rolled away from the tomb. Two men in shining garments suddenly appear (standing). No one sees Jesus. No one mentions that Jesus has gone on to Galilee. The women go off to tell the disciples what they have seen.

According to John (20:1–14), Mary Magdalene visits the tomb alone while it is still dark, for no stated purpose. The stone has been removed from the entrance. There is no mention of any earthquake. She sees no one, but when she returns to the tomb later she sees two angels in white (seated) as well as Jesus (standing). No one mentions Galilee.

According to Matthew (28:1–9), Mary Magdalene and another Mary visit the tomb at dawn. Their purpose is not to anoint the body but to see the tomb. There is a great earthquake. An angel descends from Heaven, rolls back the stone from the tomb, and sits on it. The guards (not mentioned by the others) are badly shaken. No one is seen inside the tomb. The angel tells the women to tell the disciples to go to Galilee. In awe and joy the two women, following the angel's instructions, run to tell the disciples what has happened. Both women encounter Jesus, apparently while on their way back to the disciples.

The four gospels then go on to disagree about who the resurrected Jesus appeared to subsequently – all of them also disagreeing with another account in 1 Corinthians, which does not mention any women at all. Even when the accounts agree about who Jesus appeared to, they disagree about the order in which the appearances happened or where they happened. Did he first appear to the Eleven in Galilee (Matthew) or Jerusalem (John) – or did he appear to Twelve rather than Eleven (1 Corinthians)? Curiously, one of the appearances recounted by the John author is a reworking of the miraculous fishing incident, which according to the Luke author occurred before Jesus' death.[82] Again the Luke author claims that Jesus ascended into Heaven on the day of the Resurrection, but the same author has him appearing to his disciples for 40 days (Acts 1:3).

Whatever mental gymnastics are performed, these contradictory accounts cannot be reconciled (to emphasise the point, some websites critical of Christianity offer substantial cash prizes for anyone who succeeds in reconciling them). It is clear that a few basic facts have been added to in order to make a good story. Significantly the earliest report, the one in Mark, is the most straightforward. The Luke and John authors have introduced suggestions of the supernatural, but the author of Matthew has added a heavy dose of the supernatural. Thus Mark refers to a man dressed in a white garment. Luke refers to two men in glowing garments who appear suddenly. According to John the two are not men but angels. Matthew has only one angel, but he is seen to descend from Heaven and roll away the stone. The story is becoming more impressive with the retelling.

This sort of progressive improvement is common in the gospels, although it is usually John with the trump hand. Miracles for example generally become more impressive in the later gospels. To take an example, Jesus' healing ability improves in later accounts. The Mark author has *all* the sick brought to Jesus and *many* of them cured (Mark 1:32–4). Matthew 8:16 has *many* brought and *all* of them cured. Luke 4:40 has *all* brought, and *all* of them cured. The tale is becoming more impressive all the time. The story of the feeding of the five thousand is similarly an improved version of the feeding of the four thousand. The four thousand were fed with seven loaves and a few fishes, with seven baskets full of leftovers: but the five thousand were fed with only five loaves and two fishes, yet there were 12 baskets full of leftovers. What seems to have happened is that a more modest Old Testament miracle (the feeding of the one hundred with twenty loaves) has been inflated over time: ever fewer loaves, ever more people, ever more leftovers, and the gospels have recorded the story at different stages of its development.[83] (Incidentally, the error of incorporating different instances of the same story provides one of many pieces of evidence that the author cannot have been an eyewitness, since an eyewitness could not have made this sort of mistake.)

In Acts, we find the same stories are frequently told about both Peter and Paul. Some of them are repeated with different details. There are no fewer than three versions of the story of Paul's conversion. In one, Paul's companions see a heavenly light but hear nothing (Acts 22:9). In the second, they hear a voice but see no one (Acts 9:7). In the third (Acts 26:12–14), there is no specific mention of what his companions hear or see, only that they fall to the ground along with Paul. And did Paul take Trophimus with him when he left Miletus for Jerusalem? Acts says he did (Acts 21:29), but this flatly contradicts one of the last few verses of Paul's second Epistle to Timothy, which claims that Paul had left Trophimus at Miletus because he was ill.

Paul's letters (if they are his) also contradict each other. In 1 Corinthians 3:11 Paul says the Church has no foundation other than Christ himself, but in another purported letter (Ephesians 2:20) the apostles and prophets provide the foundation, and Jesus is the cornerstone. Another example concerns the end of the world. Will this come soon, during a period of peace and security 'like a thief in the night' (1 Thessalonians 5:2) or will it come at some later time after, following a rebellion and revelation, and other spectacular signs and wonders (2 Thessalonians 2)?

Amendments to the Original Text

The most reliable early manuscripts and other ancient witnesses do not have Mark 16:9–20.

Note in the New International Version of the Bible

The evidence that early Christians tampered with their holy texts is overwhelming. We have every sort of evidence that it took place.

First, we have the evidence of non-Christians such as Celsus who observed in the second century that the Christians were perpetually correcting and altering their gospels. We also have supporting testimony from influential Christians themselves: the scholar Origen of Alexandria remarks that both Jews and gentiles reject Christianity on the grounds that it was impossible to determine which faction was telling the truth. Origen mentioned explicitly that the factions disagreed not only on minor questions 'but also in the most significant matters of great consequence'.[84]

Second, we have the evidence of Christian sects, who routinely accused each other of such tampering. Each sect, including the one we now regard as orthodox, was inclined to 'correct' existing texts to confirm the orthodoxy of their own views. Christians are known to have rewritten works to suit their own beliefs and prejudices (e.g. Marcion's dislike of Jews and Tatian's dislike of women). We have no reason to believe that the texts favoured by the group now regarded as orthodox were any more reliable than others. It is known, for example, that the Matthew gospel was attacked as unreliable.[85] We know that people saw the need to correct the versions that are now regarded as orthodox.[86] All in all we have ample evidence from early Christians of texts being edited, added to, otherwise manipulated, and in many cases 'lost'. In some cases we know that the 'orthodox' faction accused a 'heretical' faction of tampering with the text, when it was in fact the 'orthodox' faction who had been guilty of tampering.[87]

Third, we have circumstantial evidence concerning the state of mind of early Church leaders. They believed that Jesus was the Messiah, and they believed that the Messiah would satisfy a number of prophecies. It followed that Jesus must have satisfied these prophecies. If there was no evidence of his having done so, it was of little consequence, because the writers knew, or thought they knew, that he must have fulfilled these prophecies. If this meant that gaps had to be filled in, then true believers would happily fill them in. Christians were not exactly lying. In their own minds they were merely supplying missing details. As we shall see, it is sometimes possible to see where the gaps have been filled, for example where the authors were mistaken about the meaning of supposed prophecies. Gospel writers were remarkably free with the concept of truth. Stories could be amended to make them more convincing or more impressive. The John author makes it absolutely clear: 'But these are written, that ye may believe that Jesus is the Christ, the Son of God; ...' (John 20:31). So were other New Testament writers. Paul admits lying quite openly and wonders why people criticise him for it: 'For if the truth of God hath more abounded through my lie unto his glory; why yet am I also judged as a sinner?' (Romans 3:7). What he is suggesting is that it is perfectly acceptable to make up lies if the effect is to make people believe what he believes. Church Fathers shared his views. One of them, Origen, believed that the prime purpose of scripture was to convey spiritual truth, and that the recording of historical events was secondary to this. It was quite acceptable for intelligent Christians to tell white lies to less intelligent Christians. After all, as Origen noted, God had caused the prophet Jeremiah to lie.[88] As we have seen, Clement of Alexandria is known to have suppressed material that he knew to be authentic, and we have no reason to believe that he was less trustworthy than other Church Fathers. Both he and Origen were prepared to pretend that *Hebrews* was written by St Paul, when they knew that it was not.

Texts were frequently edited to bring them into line with current requirements. As doctrines developed, texts were amended to make them comply unambiguously with the latest version of 'orthodoxy'.[89] Biblical writers were clearly aware of the likelihood of their work being tampered with and often took the trouble to give warnings about doing so (e.g. at Revelation 22:18–19).

Fourth, we have the opinion of scholars. Even Christian scholars overwhelmingly accept that there is evidence of editing throughout the texts. Introductions and conclusions were added to existing stories, passages were excised, other passages were inserted, text was added to cover up the joins, key words were altered, and so on. They may be reluctant to advertise the fact, but almost no academic biblical scholars would now dispute any of this. It is often admitted in a roundabout way. Here for example is part of the Introduction to the John gospel in the Jerusalem Bible, skirting around the issue of its authorship:

> It was published not by John himself but by his disciples after his death, and it is possible that in this gospel we have the end-stage of a slow process that has brought together not only component parts of different ages but also corrections, additions and sometimes more than one revision of the same discourse.

Fifth, there is the circumstantial evidence of stories not making sense. Time and again people are surprised at events, even though they ought to be expecting them. As we have seen, the disciples are at a loss to imagine how a crowd of four thousand is to be fed, just a short time after a similar crowd of five thousand has been fed with a few loaves and fishes. Again, Peter is mystified when in a vision God tells him that all foods are clean (Acts 10:13–16), even though Jesus has already told him the same thing (Mark 7:18–19). Later, the disciples are thrown into confusion by the arrest of Jesus, yet they have previously been told several times quite specifically that this will happen. The Mark author spells out the prediction clearly:

> ...Behold, we go up to Jerusalem; and the Son of man shall be delivered unto the chief priests, and unto the scribes; and they shall condemn him to death, and shall deliver him to the Gentiles. (Mark 10:33, cf. Matthew 20:18–19 and Luke 18:31–3)

In each case it appears that editors have inserted a passage, but failed to adapt it to its new environment.

Sixth, there are the many cases where the biblical account ought to be confirmed by independent testimony, but is not. This is particularly common for the nativity and crucifixion stories, which, as we shall see, there are good reasons for regarding as being of dubious provenance. Why should the Romans introduce a bizarre, novel, and inferior method of taking a census, involving mass migrations, without leaving a record of it? Why did no astronomer note the wondrous star in the East, when there were a number who could have done so? Why is there no independent record of such a monstrous act as Herod's massacre of the innocents, especially since the historian Josephus was a keen recorder of Herod's atrocities? Again, why is there no record of the darkness over all the land for three hours on the day of the crucifixion (Matthew 27:45), and why no mention of the earthquake during the crucifixion or the one when the women visited Jesus' tomb (Matthew 27:51 and 28:2)? Also, why is there no independent record of such a wondrous thing as the dead rising from their graves as many supposedly did (Matthew 27:52–3)? Pliny the Elder (AD 23–79) was fascinated by events such as these, yet he seems to have remained entirely ignorant of them, as did Seneca (c.4 BC–AD 65) who was also interested in unusual phenomena. Thomas Paine found it odd that only Matthew mentioned fantastic events like these, especially since the other gospel writers were apparently as ignorant of them as Pliny and Seneca. This was his comment on the dead rising from their graves, given by the Matthew author:

It is an easy thing to tell a lie, but it is difficult to support the lie after it is told. The writer of the book of Matthew should have told us who the saints were that came to life again, and went into the city, and what became of them afterward, and who it was that saw them – for he is not hardy enough to say he saw them himself; whether they came out naked, and all in natural buff, he-saints and she-saints; or whether they came full dressed, and where they got their dresses, whether they went to their former habitations, and reclaimed their wives, their husbands, and their property, and how they were received; whether they entered ejectments for the recovery of their possessions, or brought actions of crim. con. [adultery] against the rival interlopers; whether they remained on earth, and followed their former occupation of preaching or working; or whether they died again, or went back to their graves alive, and buried themselves.[90]

His point is that the story is impressive only if one does not think about it too deeply. As soon as one does think about it, it becomes implausible. Also under this heading we might include incidents that simply do not stack up. They smack of fiction that has not been properly thought through. How were the gospel writers able to quote Jesus' prayer in the garden of Gethsemane, when according to them he was alone? (His followers deserted him before he could have reported his words to them himself.) Again, could the chief priests have been so stupid as to bribe guards to say that they had slept while Jesus' body had been stolen by his disciples (Matthew 28:11–15)? Wouldn't someone have seen the flaw in this – that if the guards had been asleep they would not have known who stole the body? Again, if the priests were so annoyed about Jesus raising Lazarus from the dead, why would they plan to kill him again and provide Jesus with the opportunity to repeat his miracle (John 12:10)?

Seventh, we have both circumstantial and hard textual evidence that alterations took place. When early writers quote New Testament texts they rarely use the exact words with which we are familiar. Sometimes the meaning is significantly different. Sometimes passages have been removed altogether. Worse still, extant early manuscripts simply do not agree with each other, and later manuscripts display more and more alterations. For example Acts exists in two different early versions – one about 10 per cent longer than the other.[91]

Early editors attempted to cover up some of the contradictions between the gospels. For example how could Jesus have been born of the house of David if Joseph were not his father? One not very satisfactory solution was to try to make Mary a member of the house of David too. Luke 2:4 reports that Joseph went to Bethlehem 'because he was of the house and lineage of David', but a few manuscripts were altered to 'because *they were* of the house and lineage of David'. It was a clumsy attempt, and has long since been abandoned, but it illustrates the sort of technique adopted.

Accounts of the Resurrection are especially suspect. The earliest known manuscripts of the gospel attributed to Mark finish before the account of the Resurrection. The Resurrection story is thus the work of a later writer. The important Codex Sinaiticus in the British Museum and the Codex Vaticanus in the Vatican, both dating from the fourth century, lack these passages. Some modern versions of the Bible acknowledge that they are additions – these passages are the ones referred to in the quotation at the head of this section. As well as confirming that the text included in the Bible contained additions, this particular example supports the theory that the story of the Resurrection was invented some time after Jesus' death. Additions appear to have been made to the end of the John gospel as well. Many scholars believe that the original finished at the end of chapter 20, which certainly has the ring of a final paragraph. Also, the Greek of the final chapter is in a noticeably different style from the rest of the text. To clinch matters, the final chapter is missing from a surviving Syriac manuscript.

The story of the woman taken in adultery in John 8:1–11 is also missing from the Codex Vaticanus and the Codex Sinaiticus. It too is the work of a later editor and breaks the flow of the text. In some other manuscripts it occurs not only in the John gospel, but also in the Luke gospel at the end of chapter 21, and may have been plagiarised from the 'lost' Gospel of the Hebrews.[92]

In at least some early manuscripts it was Elisabeth, not Mary, who spoke the words of what is now known as the Magnificat. The manuscripts are lost but Irenaeus himself confirms them, and he is not the only one to do so.[93] Incidentally, the Magnificat (see Luke 1:46–55) is obviously based on the song of Hannah in the Old Testament.[94] That Jesus had 12 disciples might seem clear enough, but as we have seen the question is not at all clear cut. The lists of 12 given in the gospels, for example at Matthew 10:2–4 and Luke 6:14–16, are not in the earliest texts, and their mention in 1 Corinthians is also an interpolation. Why it should have been thought appropriate at some late date to give Jesus exactly 12 disciples is not obvious, though as stated earlier the number does have a satisfying Old Testament resonance. When the idea of the Trinity was being developed, Church leaders must have been curious as to why the concept did not clearly exist in the Bible. No matter, the omission could be remedied. In the Authorised Version, 1 John 5:7 refers to the Holy Trinity:

> For there are three that bear record in heaven, the Father, the Word, and the Holy Ghost: and these three are one.

These words come from the Vulgate, but are not in any early Greek text. The passage is now universally accepted to be an addition. Along with a few other words added to disguise the insertion it is known as the

'Johannine comma'. The Holy Office declared it to be genuine scripture in 1897 and forbade Roman Catholic scholars to say otherwise. Nevertheless it has been quietly dropped from modern translations. It does not warrant so much as a note in the Jerusalem Bible. The reason for its introduction is clear: it confirms the doctrine of the Trinity. Indeed it was once regarded as an essential part of the Church's case against Unitarians. Biblical passages 'proving' Christian doctrine are called prooftexts, and the 'Johannine comma' is still the most frequently cited prooftext for the doctrine of the Trinity, despite the fact that it is universally acknowledged to be bogus.

It is clear that passages from the Old Testament were sometimes used to bolster the story being told in the New. For example the account of Jesus' baptism in Luke 3:22 contains the line '... Thou art my beloved Son...', which is taken from Psalm 2:7. The psalm continues 'this day I have begotten thee', and sure enough, so do some manuscripts of Luke. As in Mark 1:11, Jesus was not born a son of God in the original text of Luke, but was adopted at his baptism. But his adoption was no longer needed once the nativity story had been added to the gospel, so the phrase 'this day I have begotten thee' was no longer needed, and was duly dropped from later versions of the Luke text.

Manuscripts betray a consistent pattern of amending the text to make Jesus less human and more divine. His miraculous birth is played up, while evidence of a normal birth is played down. Passages that claim that Jesus was God are inserted: passages that show him to have human weaknesses are amended. Orthodoxy is affirmed: heterodoxy is eliminated.[95] In many places it is also easy to see why additions or deletions have been made. Sometimes it is to confirm Jesus' status by calling him God (e.g. 1 Timothy 3:16), or by bracketing him with God[96] or to identify him as the son of God.[97] Sometimes angels are introduced to make events more impressive than the original writer had made them.[98] Occasionally we catch someone in the act of matching up events to scripture,[99] or casting the Jews in a bad light (Acts 28:29, which is an addition to the earlier text), or enhancing the status of the apostles (Mark 3:14–15). Uncomfortable uncertainty is removed. The original text of 1 John 2:28, for example, was somewhat vague about the Second Coming 'if he should appear', but later manuscripts are much more positive 'when he shall appear'. Other changes explain Jesus' purpose (Matthew 18:11), or improve the details of a miracle (Luke 8:43), or reduce signs of Jesus' human weakness (Mark 15:39), or make him less dismissive of his mother and family (Matthew 12:47). Sometimes the changes have been made to bring different gospel accounts into line.[100] These and many other discrepancies between manuscripts are confirmed by the NIV, which mentions them in footnotes.[101]

Finally, hard scientific evidence exists of alterations. Infrared photography has revealed numerous examples of the text being changed after it had been first set down. Including simple corrections, there are about 14,500 such changes in the Codex Sinaiticus alone. This is not untypical. And it is therefore not surprising that of the thousands of Greek manuscripts that have survived, no two are identical.[102]

The oldest texts of the gospels date from the fourth century. Christians had already had over 200 years to doctor them and there is currently no way of establishing all the additions, deletions and amendments made. Whatever the original writers set down, probably towards the end of the first century, is irretrievable. What we do have is encrusted with additions designed to make Jesus, his birth, life and death more impressive. All that can be said for certain is that we do not possess a single reliable version of any book of the New Testament.

Errors of Translation

Priests and conjurers are of the same trade.
Thomas Paine, *The Age of Reason*, Part II

Despite their divine inspiration, the versions of the New Testament used by the mainstream Western Churches have always contained errors of translation, sometimes accidental, sometimes not. The Eastern Church does not have this problem because it remains loyal to the original Greek. Yet there is still scope for error. The everyday language of Jesus and his followers was Aramaic, so there is also the possibility of errors of translation between the oral Aramaic and the written Greek, but of course, the evidence for these errors must be circumstantial. For example we have already noted that the Luke gospel appears to reflect someone's confusion over the Aramaic *zakkau* (to give alms) and *dakkau* (to cleanse). Even the Greek is not always straightforward. For example the familiar line from the Lord's Prayer, 'Give us this day our daily bread', is only a guess. The Greek word *epiousion* has been translated as 'daily', but this may not be its real meaning (another guess is 'Give us this day tomorrow's bread', and another possibility is 'extra bread' or 'additional [spiritual] bread').[103] There are literally thousands of words and passages in the Greek text that are uncertain.

The Vulgate

When St Jerome was asked to prepare a new translation of the Bible he was worried about how to reconcile the many different texts that already existed. As he anticipated he was widely and heavily criticised for his work. How much Jerome changed the previously existing texts may be judged by the fact that cultured pagans regarded his translation as readable, whereas the numerous versions before it were regarded as crude and barbarous – a view shared by St Augustine (354–430) and indeed St Jerome himself. Jerome had been criticised for tampering with existing texts, which though flawed had already acquired a gloss of respectability and indeed sacredness. In time the Vulgate acquired a better gloss. For centuries it was held by Western Christians to be the only valid translation of the Bible.

Unfortunately St Jerome had sometimes preferred his own preconceptions to the New Testament Greek. We have already seen how he amended the text of Old Testament passages, and he did the same with the text of the New Testament. For example, Jerome did not care much for the idea that believers could be 'sons of God ... born not of the blood, nor the will of the flesh, nor of the will of man, but of God'. He therefore followed an unreliable tradition for the text of John 1:12–13.[104] He thus made the 'born not of the blood, but of God' description fit not just any believer but only Jesus – as it still does in the Jerusalem Bible.

Some mistranslations have had profound consequences, often influencing doctrine. For example the idea that Mary was 'full of grace' (*gratia plena*) has been developed into a vast body of doctrine, yet it is an error. *Gratia plena* is a mistranslation of *kecharitomene*, a Greek word indicating merely that Mary was pleasing to God, as Erasmus knew,[105] and as modern translations of Luke 1:28 confirm.

Worse still, Jerome's text was altered, either deliberately or by mistake. Various errors and tamperings crept into copies of the Vulgate, so that soon the position was little better than it had been before St Jerome. There were numerous conflicting versions of his work, all purporting to be divinely inspired. The lack of a single authoritative text was a constant problem during the Middle Ages, as copyists multiplied textual variations by a combination of honest error and deliberate tampering.

In the sixteenth century Pope Sixtus V authorised the production of a version of the Vulgate. He grew impatient with progress and took over the work himself, claiming to be the only proper person to do so. His version issued in 1590 was riddled with errors. It contained whimsical additions to the text and omitted entire verses. The Roman Church then had to try to buy back all copies of the pope's disastrous effort. To the delight of Protestants his successors were obliged to issue a corrected edition.

English Versions

God does not seem to have been excessively concerned about ensuring that his divine word was delivered free from error. As well as allowing scribes to add, change and delete text, he allowed printers to make mistakes. Printers responsible for even the most minor errors were fined heavily, and occasionally bankrupted. The following all seem to have been accidental. The so-called *Placemakers' Bible* of 1562 (the Second Edition of the Geneva Bible) says 'Blessed are the placemakers...' instead of 'Blessed are the peacemakers...' (Matthew 5:9). The *Judas Bible* of 1611 refers to Judas instead of Jesus in Matthew 26:36. In the *Printers' Bible* (King James' Version of 1612) David complains that printers have persecuted him, when he should have been complaining about princes (Psalm 119:161). In the *Wicked* or *Adulterous Bible* (The King James' Version of 1631), the word *not* was omitted from one of the commandments making it say 'Thou shalt commit adultery' (Exodus 20:14). The *Sin On Bible* of 1716 instructs a sick man to 'sin on more', instead of to 'sin no more' (John 5:14). In the *Fool Bible* printed during the reign of Charles I, Psalm 14:1 claims that the fool hath said in his heart there is a God, instead of no God. The *Lions Bible* (King James' Version of 1804) referred to 'thy son that shall come forth out of thy lions', instead of 'out of thy loins' (1 Kings 8:19). In the *Camels Bible* (King James' Version of 1823), Rebekah arose with her camels rather than with her damsels (Genesis 24:61). Neither was God much exercised by the divine law appended to Bibles. The *Affinity Bible* of 1923 contains a table of affinity, which asserts that a man may not marry his grandmother's wife. Occasionally errors were made deliberately, for doctrinal reasons. For example, in the *Bad Bible* of 1653 the ordination of deacons was ascribed to the disciples, not to the apostles (Acts 6:6).

The earliest complete translation into English was made by John Wycliffe from the Vulgate around 1384, but the best known is undoubtedly the Authorised Version, so called because it was authorised by King James I of England (VI of Scotland). King James had commissioned it, and for this reason it is sometimes called the King James Bible. It was produced by 47 scholars at the command of the King and published in 1611. It was not based on the Vulgate, but on the original Hebrew and Greek, although the translators drew heavily upon a translation by William Tyndale, as well as other existing English translations including Coverdale's Bible (first printed 1535), Matthew's Bible (1537), and the Bishop's Bible (1568). It is however adapted to the needs of the time. For example the passages that describe kings and their courts are consistently made grander and more impressive, just like God the King and his heavenly court.

Other changes were made to conform to current fashions. Luke relates a story of a woman of Capernaum who washed Jesus' feet as he 'sat at meat' according to the Authorised Version (Luke 7:37). 'Sitting at meat' is a medieval expression meaning 'sitting down to eat'. The original text actually says that he 'lay down at table', which is how people ate meals in the Hellenic world. This sort of editing goes on in the Bible all the time to make things intelligible. Women's nose rings, for example, were routinely converted into earrings before nose rings became fashionable in the West. Other errors are genuine mistakes. In the original Greek, Simon the Zealot (one of Jesus' disciples) is called *kananaios*, a title derived from a Hebrew word *qana* meaning 'zealous'. In the Authorised Version (Matthew 10:4 and Mark 3:18) this is mistakenly translated as Simon the Canaanite.[106] Again, such errors are not very important, except for those who believe that the translations are divinely inspired and thus infallible.

Translations provide the opportunity to take the most orthodox option when there is a choice. It sounds slightly less impressive for the centurion at the crucifixion to say that Jesus was surely *a* son of God, so translators prefer the option *the* Son of God (Matthew 27:54). The change of article, along with a capital *s*, makes a considerable difference. Names are not always translated consistently. Jephthah in Judges 11 is the same as Jephthae in Hebrews 11:32, and one of Jesus' brothers is sometimes Juda (Mark 6:3) and sometimes Judas (Matthew 13:55). All this is innocent enough, but sometimes there is an obvious reason for name changes, for example a judicious name change can be used to disguise inconvenient facts. It was inconvenient to have a woman called Junia being of note among the apostles (Romans 16:7) so she became a man called Junias in later translations.[107] Again, Christian ideas can be reinforced by appropriate translations. Protestant versions of the Bible seem to suggest that saints existed in Old Testament times, as implied by the sentence 'Precious in the sight of the LORD is the death of his saints' (Psalm 116:15, Authorised Version). However, according to Roman Catholics only the Pope can create saints. In some Roman Catholic versions of the Bible it is not *saints* but the *devout* or *faithful* whose death is precious.

Modern translations continue to be selective about how particular words are translated. For example the NIV, written largely for sects that do not have bishops, avoids the word for a bishop. Philippians 1:1 addresses 'overseers and deacons' rather than 'bishops and deacons'. Protestants have no problem about married clergy, so in Protestant versions of the Bible the apostles have 'wives', while in Roman Catholic ones they have female helpers. So too, the Roman Church holds that Mary and Joseph never had sexual intercourse, so instead of Joseph and Mary coming together they merely 'came to live together' (Matthew 1:18). Again, the fact that Jesus and his followers clearly held some Gnostic views that Paul did not share can easily be disguised by translating the word *gnosis* as *knowledge*, instead of rendering it as *Gnosis* (e.g. 1 Corinthians 8ff, 13:2).

Apart from translating words to suit the Church's needs, meanings can be manipulated in numerous ways, as we have already seen. For example when terms are applied to Jesus they are rendered *Christ* and *Son of man*, but when the same terms are applied to other people they are rendered as *anointed* and *son of man* (without capitalisation). Again, capital letters can be used to indicate whether the text is referring to Jesus' father (Joseph) or his Father (God), as in Luke 2:48–9. By translating a word as *Father* instead of *father*, translators can completely change the sense of the text.

OTHER SOURCES

By itself, truth always wins. A lie needs an accomplice.
Epictetus (AD *c.*55–*c.*135)

The Bible says nothing of events that occurred more than a generation after the crucifixion, so there is a huge gap in our knowledge of the development of the Christian Church. When the Bible fails to provide support for a favoured doctrine or practice, Churches often look to other sources to confirm them.

From Constantine onwards it was accepted, at least by the groups whose successors are now called Orthodox and Catholic, that the sole source of authority was the Emperor. The Emperor was a sort of chief bishop, and indeed was styled 'bishop of bishops'. He was accepted as an infallible authority centuries before the idea of a Roman papacy had been conceived.[108] This system, known to historians as caesaropapalism, is something of an embarrassment to modern theologians. Emperors were hailed by Church Councils by titles such as *Pontiff-Emperor* or *Priest and King*, and were invested with infallibility. Giving honour to the Emperor was a form of religious service, as he was God's vice-regent on Earth. His dreams, even incoherent dreams, were interpreted as celestial visions. Later, after it had become an embarrassment, caesaropapalism would be played down to such an extent that few Christians in the mainstream Churches are now aware that it was once central to their religion.*

Almost no one now accepts the principle of a divinely appointed emperor or king, so we will move on to the sources of authority that were developed to fill the void left by the late emperors. There are three principal sources of authority: apostolic tradition (as recorded by early Christians), Church Councils, and for the Roman Church its own head, the Pope. We now look at the reliability of each of these sources.

---

* On the other hand caesaropapalism could always be pulled out of the hat when needed, for example by Holy Roman Emperors in the Middle Ages, or even by Henry VIII to justify himself as the Supreme Head, or Governor of the Church of England, enjoying secret counsel directly from God, just as Constantine had done. Perhaps the last manifestation of the principle was an indecisive attempt by Emperor Franz Joseph of Austria to veto the election of Cardinal Rampolla as Pope in 1903 (someone else was elected anyway).

Apostolic Traditions and the Church Fathers

Hell is paved with the skulls of priests.
St John Chrysostom (*c.*347–407), *Letters*

Since the Bible fails to mention certain doctrines and practices that are now considered characteristically Christian, some branches of Christianity have looked to early traditions to justify them. But the results are disappointing. Few genuine traditions can be justified in this way, and worse still, early authorities often confirm many practices that are now regarded as unacceptable. For example, a return to the earliest practices would mean that no religious icons would be allowed, either pictures or statues. The use of incense would be prohibited as pagan. On the other hand, Christians would hold love feasts, and celebrate the Sabbath on Saturdays. Easter would be celebrated on the 14th day of the Jewish month of Nisan. Infants would not be baptised, and adults would not be baptised except between Easter and Pentecost. Baptisms would then involve the triple immersion of the naked baptismal candidate. There would be no sacrament of confession or penance, or if we accept the earliest (third-century) practices there would be only public penance (*exomologesis*), permitted once after baptism.[109] There would be no priests or bishops, only elders and supervisors, freely elected by the community.

The whole area of 'tradition' is riddled with difficulties. The early Church leader and writer Tertullian, who invented the idea of appealing to tradition, used it to justify the practice of triple immersion at baptism, the requirement that the Eucharist should be taken in the early morning, and the prohibition of kneeling at Easter or on Sundays. There is no doubt about the position of the early Church on these matters and it is for this reason that various reformed Churches have returned to at least some of these ancient practices.

The Roman Church is in a less comfortable position. It purports to give great weight to tradition – the importance of traditions dating back to the apostles was emphasised by the Council of Trent (Session 4). Yet it has persecuted and killed people for the heresies of adhering to apostolic practices – rejecting infant baptism, keeping the Sabbath on Saturday, celebrating Easter on the 14th of Nisan, and so on. Protestant Churches have also persecuted and killed other Christians (e.g. Anabaptists) for such 'heresies'. It is strange enough that apostolic practices are sometimes at variance with mainstream Christian views. Worse is the fact that not a single Church doctrine can be justified by appeal to a reliable apostolic tradition.

In the absence of any first-hand apostolic record, Christian scholars often referred to the Fathers of the Church – early Christians who left a written record of doctrine and practices. The Roman Church purports to ascribe authority to them equal to that accorded to the gospels. But there are problems here as well. In the first place the earliest Fathers knew nothing of doctrines such as the Incarnation or Trinity, and so were liable to make statements that are now heretical. Also, on many matters the Church Fathers contradict each other, and where they unanimously concur they often condemn practices that are now common, for example, the wearing of distinctive clothing by clerics. Often, specific directions by the Fathers are simply ignored. Hippolytus instructed Christians to pray at the third, sixth, and ninth hours of the day, a practice mentioned by many early authorities, such as Tertullian, Origen of Alexandria, and Cyprian, Bishop of Carthage. The practice was inconvenient so it was dropped for those not belonging to religious Orders (though Muslims manage to follow similar rules, taking care to face a certain direction, as Christians once did, and adopting the same posture for prayer as early Christians).

The Fathers held strong views on a wide range of matters. As Gibbon observed:

> In their censures of luxury the fathers were extremely minute and circumstantial; and among the various articles that excite their pious indignation we may enumerate false hair, garments of any colour except white, instruments of music, vases of gold or silver, downy pillows (as Jacob reposed his head on a stone), white bread, foreign wines, public salutations, the use of warm baths, and the practice of shaving the beard, which, according to Tertullian, is a lie against our own faces and an impious attempt to improve the works of the Creator.[110]

In fact the Roman Church's commitment to tradition is widely regarded as questionable. The Church has never attempted to collect together a comprehensive body of tradition, and it is not unknown for Roman Catholic writers to be charged by other Christians with being evasive, and even 'fugitive', on the subject.[111] This is not altogether surprising since numerous Roman doctrines are not evidenced by the Church Fathers, and are universally acknowledged to date from later times (papal infallibility, the Immaculate Conception, and Mary's Assumption, to name but three).

It is difficult to find any Church Fathers who were consistently orthodox by modern standards. Indeed the problem of deciding who counted as a Church Father was much like deciding which books were canonical. People tended to include anyone who agreed with them and to reject anyone who did not. Since there were so few accepted Fathers, broad agreement was eventually reached, though once again there is no definitive list, and Eastern and Western Churches still accord vastly different weights to different Fathers.[112] Since it was difficult, often impossible, to find orthodox writers who confirmed certain doctrines or practices, Churches were driven to accept as authoritative men who had been condemned as heretics. Some of them had been considered heretical even in their own day. Their writings were conveniently 'lost' or tampered with. Many of these early Christians had extremely unfortunate views on sex and punishment, shared extreme anti-Semitic views, and firmly believed a range of absurdities. The most influential were:

- St Ignatius of Antioch (AD *c*.35–*c*.107), an unusually credulous man, given to embellishing stories, and with an unusual personality (he prayed for his own death, preferably by horrific means). He held that only bishops could conduct baptisms and love feasts.[113] He left little else of doctrinal value, and what little he did leave is universally acknowledged to have been radically tampered with by later Christians.

- St Clement of Rome (fl. AD *c*.96), who wrote letters that were initially accepted into but later rejected from the canon of Christian scripture. They deal largely with the great dissent then current within the Church, and suggest that there was no established bishopric at Rome during his lifetime.[114] He seems to have been as credulous as others of his age (he was convinced of the reality of the phoenix). Much of his surviving work is now known to be forged, and little is known of his life, beliefs or death.

- St Justin Martyr (AD *c*.100–*c*.165), a man generally acknowledged to have been of no great intelligence, nor philosophical nor literary skill. He had studied Stoic and Pythagorean philosophy, but had failed to comprehend either and turned instead to Christianity. His writings are of little doctrinal value. He was concerned mainly to refute various charges made against Christians by members of other religions. He has been accused of believing in two Gods, having referred to the *Word* (*logos*) as 'second God'. According to him Christ was worshipped in the 'second rank', and the Holy Spirit in the 'third rank', a view that is now regarded as heretical.[115]

- St Irenaeus of Lyons (AD *c*.130–*c*.200), another exceptionally credulous man, who believed stories that are now accepted to be apocryphal.[116] Like many of his contemporaries, Irenaeus accepted the millenarian heresy, the belief in a 1,000-year period of divine rule following Christ's imminent return to living on Earth. For this reason he was not well regarded by the Eastern Churches. His writings have not been preserved in the original Greek, and Latin translations show evidence of his views having been edited to erase evidence of his heresy.[117] His idea of the Incarnation was that the *Word* (*logos*) was God the Father incarnate in Jesus Christ – a view now considered heretical. He also held that Jesus died as a ransom paid to Satan,[118] a view that might well have come to be regarded as heretical if it had not been almost universal until the eleventh century.

- St Clement of Alexandria (AD *c*.150–*c*.215), who held Gnostic views, denying that Christ had experienced the physical passions of an ordinary man and holding that he had been exempt from human desire.[119] Such views would later be condemned as heretical. Clement is also known to have suppressed authentic gospel material that he wanted kept for an inner élite. He expressed doubts as to whether he even wanted to be associated with those who called themselves orthodox and found it hard to use the word without a half-ironic apology.[120]

- (Quintus Septimus Florens) Tertullian (AD *c*.160–*c*.225), who, like many later Christians, delighted in the prospect of his enemies suffering in Hell. He adopted Montanist views (see page 181), which came to be considered heretical, and held that the orthodox line was the heretical one. He accused bishops of Rome of the Sabellian heresy, the doctrine that Father, Son and Spirit represent different states (or modes or aspects) of a single god at different times (see also pages 181–2). He died fulminating against what is now regarded as orthodoxy.

• St Hippolytus (AD *c*.170–*c*.236), a prolific Greek writer and another supporter of the millenarian heresy, whose works have been 'lost' in the original. Later Latin versions of his *Apostolic Traditions* have clearly been tampered with. He was elected Bishop of Rome in competition with the existing bishop (Callistus), who claimed that Hippolytus believed in two gods. Hippolytus accused two bishops of Rome (Zephyrinus and Callistus) of heresy. Saint Hippolytus is now regarded as the first anti-pope, though he still keeps his sainthood.

• Origen of Alexandria (AD *c*.185–254), a biblical critic, teacher and writer. Most of his works have been lost. Of those that are extant most are known only in translation. He was accused of holding beliefs that would later be regarded as heretical ('Adoptionist'). He held that Jesus Christ was divine, but only in a lesser sense than the Father.[121] He said that Christian worship should be directed solely to the Father and not to Christ, a view that was later to become heretical, as were a number of his other teachings. He also held that all beings will eventually be saved, even Satan himself. Like some of his contemporaries he voluntarily castrated himself to remove a sinful source of temptation. He insisted on observing Jesus' instructions, such as the ones about not carrying an extra coat and not wearing shoes (Matthew 10:10). During his lifetime he was deposed from the priesthood and deprived of his teaching post by the Bishop of Alexandria. He was also condemned by the Bishop of Rome and by a synod of Egyptian bishops. St Jerome held that he had deliberately tried to mislead the orthodox into heresy. Views attributed to him were condemned by further bishops, emperors and councils. To clear up any remnant of doubt, Origen's teachings were condemned by the Second Ecumenical Council of Constantinople in 553.

• Eusebius of Caesarea (*c*.260–*c*.340), who is regarded as the Father of Church history. He was a supporter of the Libyan preacher Arius (*c*.256–336) and his heresy that Jesus Christ was not coequal with the Father, until he was pressured to subscribe to the new official line at the first great Council of the Church. He said that Jesus shared the glory of God, but only in the sense that the saints shared the same glory.[122] Like St Justin Martyr he thought of the Holy

Spirit as being lower than either the Father or the Son, describing it as 'in the third rank', 'a third power', and 'third from the Supreme Cause'.[123] He was accused of adultery, among other things, on the evidence of a prostitute, and was replaced as leader of the moderate party. His history contains statements that still smack of heresy.[124]

- St John Chrysostom (c.347–407), an anti-Semite who interpreted the Bible literally and historically rather than allegorically. He was deposed from his post of Patriarch of Constantinople by the Synod of the Oak in 403, condemned and banished. He was recalled but then banished again and died in exile.

- St Augustine of Hippo (354–430), who was brought up as a Christian but took a mistress and abandoned his religion. He considered the Old Testament to be a collection of old wives' fables, though he himself was unusually gullible, even by the standards of the day.[125] In 374 he converted to a rival religion, Manichæism, and managed to convert some friends as well. But he never managed to graduate as one of the elect. Some nine years after his conversion he became a neoplatonist and then converted back to Christianity, in response to an oracle. He introduced new doctrines into the Church, drawn largely from his Manichæan phase. His views about the evils of sex seem to be due partly to guilt about his mistresses,[126] and partly to his Manichæan training, a fact recognised by at least one of his contemporaries. His views on contraception are not consistent with those of the Roman Church.[127] He was frankly predestinarian (believing people are powerless to change their destiny). He also mentioned the death of the Virgin Mary, not remarkable at the time, but now contrary to Roman dogma. He was also open to charges of a heresy called Sabellianism or Modal Monarchianism (see pages 181–2). His consecration as coadjutor bishop in 395 was illegal, contravening the eighth canon of Nicæa.

- St Jerome (c.342–420), a scholar with a reputation for being offensive to his fellow scholars. He was responsible for creating the version of the Bible called the Vulgate. He surrounded himself by wealthy women in Rome and was involved in a series of scandals there. He left Rome in disgrace, after one of his female acolytes died from the severity of her bodily mortification. He settled in Bethlehem, along with selected women followers.

Other important early theologians, now dismissed as heretics, are nevertheless cited when they agree with the currently acceptable line, especially when they provide the only support for the point in question. Among them are Helvidius (who held that Jesus had brothers); Jovinian (d. *c.*405), a monk who was excommunicated for criticising fasting and celibacy, and for suggesting that Mary lost her virginity in giving birth; and Vigilantius (fl. *c.*400), who deprecated popular devotions, such as vigils and the cultus of the saints, as pagan practices.

It would be fair to say that the most significant thing that the Church Fathers establish is that much Christian doctrine was developed in the fourth century, or afterwards.

Church Councils

> *But why, it will be asked, have so many councils contradicted each other? …Roman Catholics now believe only in councils approved by the Vatican; and the Greek Catholics believe only in those approved in Constantinople.*
> *Protestants deride them both.*
> Voltaire (1694–1778), *Philosophical Dictionary*

Mainstream Churches hold that ecumenical councils embody the true doctrine of the whole Church. Unfortunately they do not agree about which councils are ecumenical and therefore infallible. The Anglican Church usually recognises six:

- Nicæa (AD 325)
- Constantinople I (AD 381)
- Ephesus (AD 431)
- Chalcedon (AD 451)
- Constantinople II (AD 553)
- Constantinople III (AD 680–1)

The Eastern Churches recognise in addition a second Council of Nicæa held in 787. The Roman Church accepts these seven councils along with 14 of its own.

As with other sources of authority, there are big problems in determining validity. How can we know which councils were truly ecumenical and therefore infallible as all mainstream Churches believe? It cannot be a question of who calls the council, for it is not even clear who has the right to convoke a valid council. They have been convoked by all sorts of people. The most important one ever, Nicæa, was called by a Roman emperor. He sent out the invitations. Participants travelled under *his* orders, to *his* council, held at a place and time of *his* choosing. Later, at least in theory, it was the patriarchs* who acted together to convoke councils. This is rather an embarrassment to the Roman Church, which now claims that only the Pope may convoke such councils.

It cannot be a question of who attends. Valid councils have been held without the representation of all the patriarchs. The bishops of Rome played a small part in the councils listed above. In fact the First Ecumenical Council of Constantinople was convoked solely from the East. The Pope (Damasus I) was not even invited. No bishop of the Western Church was present at its meetings, even as an observer. Despite this, the Roman Church now holds that its own college of bishops may form an infallible ecumenical council (code of canon law 749.2).

It cannot be a question of whether or not the council was convened as an ecumenical council. The councils of Ariminum and Seleucia held in 359 were convoked as ecumenical councils, but their rulings on the deity of Christ failed to find universal acceptance. For this reason they ceased to be regarded as ecumenical. Often, grounds are found for disregarding inconvenient councils, and their rulings can then be ignored on the grounds that they were not ecumenical after all. This happened to a council held at Ephesus in 449. The Fourth Ecumenical Council (Chalcedon) in 451 reversed almost all of the decisions made by the council at Ephesus. Now the council held at Ephesus is dismissed as an illegal sham and is called the Robber Council because of the level of intimidation, violence, duress and bribery used to secure its outcome. Yet in truth it was unremarkable compared with other councils in its level of intimidation, violence, duress and bribery. The previous council held in Ephesus in 431, for example, was at least as bad, yet it is still regarded as ecumenical. As so often, the forces that determined which

* The patriarchs were the highest-ranking bishops in the Church, such as the bishops of Alexandria and Antioch.

councils prevailed were political. There is little doubt amongst historians that if the Emperor, Theodosius II, had not died in 450 then the Fourth Ecumenical Council, of Chalcedon, the following year would never have taken place, and the council held in Ephesus in 449 would have continued to be regarded as ecumenical.

It cannot be a question of universal acceptance. As we have seen the Protestant, Roman and Eastern Churches all disagree about which councils should be counted as ecumenical. And there are further difficulties with each of the six that they do all accept. Each of them was rejected by sizeable groups of Christians at the time it was held, in each case causing a schism.

Sometimes, infallible ecumenical councils contradicted previous infallible ecumenical councils in an attempt to heal a schism. For example the decrees of the Fourth Ecumenical Council, at Chalcedon (451), were amended by the Fifth Ecumenical Council at Constantinople (553), with the hope of reuniting the warring schismatic factions. Specifically, a document known as the *Three Chapters* was accepted in 451 but condemned in 553.

In summary there is no clear external criterion by which a council may be judged to be ecumenical or not. This fact is now accepted by at least some orthodox theologians.[128] As so often the practice is the opposite of the theory. Instead of doctrine being determined by valid councils, the validity of a council is determined by the subsequent popularity of its rulings. The assignment of authority is thus circular, and flexible, allowing each Church to make its own selection.

There is a further problem with the councils that are accepted as ecumenical and thus infallible. This is that their solemn statements and requirements are routinely ignored when they cease to suit changing fashions. Thus for example the Ecumenical Council of Nicæa prohibited kneeling on Sundays (canon 20). Other infallible councils prohibited the practice of bishops translating from one See to another, and dozens of other such practices that are now accepted without demur.

Pops

There was a certain rich man, which was clothed in purple
and fine linen, and fared sumptuously every day...
Luke 16:19

Successive popes have informed the world that they are set above the rest of mankind, and enjoy direct communications with the deity. The Holy Spirit guides their election, and their power extends not merely to God's eternal Church, but beyond this world to the next. When speaking *ex cathedra* on faith or morals they are literally infallible.

Despite the theory, it is fair to say that popes have proved their fallibility in all manner of circumstances.[129] Some have contradicted others. Some have contradicted themselves. Some have been guilty of heresy, by departing from what their predecessors and their successors regarded as orthodoxy. The Eastern Churches have condemned Roman popes for a number of heresies – tampering with the creeds, Sabellianism (see page 181), enforcing clerical celibacy, and so on. The first two popes in the third century, Zephyrinus and Callistus, were both accused of heresy[130] by Tertullian and also by St Hippolytus. Marcellinus, who was Bishop of Rome from 296 to 304, offered incense to the pagan gods. For this his name was afterwards omitted from official lists of popes. Three of the next four popes seem to have assisted him, despite being already in Holy Orders, but all of them, including Marcellinus, are now revered as saints. In the middle of the fourth century Pope Liberius condemned Athanasius, the champion of orthodoxy against Arian heretics. This act provided absolute proof that a pope could fall into error. Early in the fifth century Pope Zosimus accepted the Pelagian heresy (see page 181) and changed his mind only when obliged to do so by the Emperor. He then issued a document known as his *Tractoria*, which reversed his earlier position. The fifth-century popes Innocent I and Gelasius I both claimed that babies who died after baptism but before receiving Communion would go straight to Hell. This view was later contradicted and condemned by the Council of Trent, but is now open again since Pope Benedict XVI teaches Original Sin but denies the existence of Purgatory.

Pope Vigilius, in 548, formally condemned the *Three Chapters* already mentioned, which had been formally approved by the Ecumenical

Council of Chalcedon in 451. He subsequently wavered, trying to appease both supporters and opponents, withdrawing his condemnation in 551. He was himself declared a heretic and excommunicated by the Ecumenical Council of Constantinople in 553, which he refused to attend. In exile, but under no duress, except the knowledge that a new pope was to be elected, he wrote a letter admitting that he had been deluded by the wiles of the Devil. He confirmed his error and accepted the decrees of Constantinople. This incident provided proof that a council was superior to a pope.

In the seventh century Pope Honorius I was condemned for a heresy called Monothelitism, the view that Christ had only one will (rather than two – one human and one divine). In 649 Pope Martin I condemned the Monothelete doctrine accepted by Honorius. Subsequently, Honorius was condemned not only by the Sixth General Council, but also by Pope Leo II, who stated that he had tried with profane treachery to subvert the immaculate faith. Subsequent popes were required at their consecration to take an oath condemning Honorius's heresy. In 1046 the Emperor Henry III presided over a synod at Sutri that deposed two popes, secured the abdication of a third, and appointed a fourth (Clement II). The most significant acts of Pope Celestine II in the twelfth century were reversals of decisions made by his predecessor Innocent II. Also in the twelfth century Pope Adrian VI declared Pope Celestine III a heretic for extending the conditions under which marriages could be dissolved. Again, the timeless validity of the bull *Super cathedram*, issued by Pope Boniface VIII in 1301, was somewhat compromised by his blessed successor, Pope Benedict XI, who annulled it because of its unpopularity.

One way out of the problem of fallible popes up to this date is to say that popes were infallible only when addressing the whole Church. The first bull explicitly to do so was Boniface VIII's *Unam sanctam* in 1302. But this opens up the question of why no pope made an infallible statement for over 1250 years, and admits that until that time only councils expressed the mind of the Church – a most uncomfortable admission for the Vatican.

Later, in the fourteenth century, Pope John XXII preached that saints in Heaven are not yet permitted to see God. The Church hierarchy felt this matter to be of the greatest importance. The established teaching was that the saints did see God. John was obliged to reconsider under threat of deposition, and with a gentle reminder that heretics get burned. His reconsideration led him to change his mind. In 1523 Pope Adrian VI summed up the official line on papal infallibility with specific reference to John's heresy:

> If by the Roman Church you mean its head or pontiff, it is beyond question that he can err even in matters touching the faith. He does this when he teaches heresy by his own judgement or decretal. In truth, many Roman Pontiffs were heretics. The last of them was John XXII.[131]

The traditional teaching of the Church has been that embryos do not acquire a soul until 40 days (if they are male) or 80 days (if they are female) after conception. One consequence of this was that abortion could not possibly be homicide if carried out up to 40 days after conception. This view was confirmed on a number of occasions, notably by Gregory XIII in the sixteenth century. However, his successor Sixtus V, in his bull *Effraenatum* of 1588, stated that all abortion amounted to homicide and was punishable by excommunication. His successor Gregory XIV had different ideas and decided that Sixtus's censures were to be disregarded. Modern popes, starting with Pius IX in 1869, have made a third U-turn.

Even the greatest of popes seem to have been surprisingly fallible. Pope Gregory I (St Gregory the Great), for example, taught emphatically that Christ alone was conceived without Original Sin. This indeed was the official line for 1,000 years. Then, after centuries of lobbying on behalf of the Virgin Mary, it was decided that she too had been born without Original Sin (this is the doctrine of the Immaculate Conception). In 1854 Pope Pius IX announced in his bull *Ineffabilis Deus* that 'the doctrine was revealed by God and therefore is to be firmly and steadfastly believed by all the faithful'. Now it was heretical to deny the Immaculate Conception, so the world discovered that Gregory I had been a heretic all along.

In 1963 Pope John XXIII accepted total liberty of conscience, a concept that earlier popes had considered heretical. Gregory XVI had considered it monstrous and absurd, and Pius IX described it as a cardinal error. Popes had made other massive mistakes over many centuries. One after another they affirmed that documents fabricated in the papal chancery were genuine. Whether they knew it or not they were in error.

Even with the benefit of direct communication with God, they were consistently, repeatedly, and unquestionably wrong. They spoke with supreme authority on matters that were pivotal to the faith yet were wrong time and time again. They held that the Bible was the literal word of God, and thus espoused an erroneous cosmology – stating as a fact that Galileo was in error, when they themselves were in error. In an unbroken line from the thirteenth century, more than eighty popes failed to identify any moral difficulties with the operations of the Inquisition. Many rose to power through it, thoroughly approved of it, and extended its power. Many popes, on numerous occasions, confirmed the existence of witches, and the fact that they possessed supernatural powers. After Innocent VIII, it was heretical to deny it.

More than 1,800 years after the time of St Peter it took weeks of debate to decide by a majority vote, and in the face of numerous counter-proofs, that the Pope was infallible. This claim was denied by three of the four ancient patriarchies, by all Protestants, and by many Roman Catholic scholars. Numerous Roman Catholics were unable to accept it and so went into schism. Suddenly, after being a matter of contention, in 1870, acceptance of the principle became necessary for salvation.

For most mainstream Christian sects there is no doubt that an ecumenical council is supreme. But for the Roman Church there is a question as to whether a council is superior to a pope, or a pope to a council. The claim that a pope is superior to a council is badly undermined by the fact that in the past councils have condemned popes and the popes have accepted their condemnation and felt obliged to admit their error (as in the case of Vigilius mentioned above). More embarrassing still is the fact that even in Western Europe councils could be convened validly without the consent of a pope – a spectacular example being the Council of Constance of 1414–18. Convened on an emperor's authority, as the First Ecumenical Council had been, the council deposed a number of rival popes and elected its own pope (Martin V, who is still recognised by the Roman Church as a valid successor to Peter).

SUMMARY

It is the customary fate of new truths to begin as heresies and to end as superstitions.
T. H. Huxley (1825–95), *Collected Essays xii,*
'The Coming of Age of the Origin of Species'

It is increasingly difficult to maintain that any Christian authority enjoys infallibility. We have seen that the Old Testament is unreliable. The New Testament contains no material that purports to have been authorised by Jesus, or that dates from his lifetime, or that was even written in the everyday language of his milieu. The earliest material is from generations later. We know that much bogus material was added, and it not always possible to distinguish it from the rest.

There was a distinct lack of agreement between the early Churches, and between the Church Fathers, as to what should be included in the canon of scripture. We know also that valid material was suppressed. The Western Church took about 600 years to settle its canon, although arguments broke out again when Protestant scholars looked into matters again 900 years later. At about this time the Eastern Churches finally managed to settle their version of the New Testament, although it was still not accepted by all. In fact, full agreement between the Orthodox Churches has not been achieved to this day.

Meanwhile, biblical scholars have shown up flaws in the texts and in attributions, identified editorial tampering, and have shown that valid material has been excluded. Known texts all disagree with each other, and many of the disagreements reveal the hands of people editing the text for their own ends. So do translated texts, even those acclaimed as 'infallible'.

We have looked at other sources of authority in various Churches and at various times. All of the ones we have looked at have been found to be flawed. The fact is that there is no clear reliable authority in the Christian Church, or any of its many branches. Orthodoxy has developed according to the tastes of the dominant factions of the moment. Arguments employed to establish authority and orthodoxy are all circular. Sources are hailed as authorities if they support the views currently in favour. Then these same authorities are quoted to prove the orthodoxy of those views. Orthodoxy was not so much determined by

BEYOND BELIEF

the New Testament. The books of the New Testament were chosen and edited to match the dominant line of orthodoxy. Again, orthodoxy was not confirmed by a band of elect men called the Church Fathers. Men were called Church Fathers because their views differed least from later orthodoxy. Yet again, orthodoxy was not defined by ecumenical councils. Councils were acclaimed as ecumenical because they supported later orthodoxy.

Orthodoxy is thus self-sustaining. Sources that contradict it are simply edited out. Inconvenient gospels are omitted from the canon of the Bible, and labelled apocryphal. Inconvenient early Christian writers are labelled heretics. Inconvenient ecumenical councils are discovered not to have been infallible ecumenical councils after all, merely fraudulent shams promoted by heretics. Inconvenient bishops of Rome have their names removed retrospectively from the list of infallible popes. Despite this selectivity, coherence is still difficult to come by. The gospels contradict each other. Infallible Christian emperors contradict each other. The Church Fathers contradict each other. Ecumenical councils contradict each other. Infallible popes contradict each other, and of course each of the five possible sources (gospels, emperors, Fathers, councils and popes) also contradict each of the other four on numerous points.

Different denominations attempt to minimise the problem in different ways: forget the emperors, ignore the popes, listen to different Fathers, believe only selected gospels, abandon them all in favour of direct personal revelation from God, and so on. To objective outsiders, the hand of God is difficult to discern anywhere in it.

To many outsiders the whole area of authority in Christian teachings looks more than a little suspicious. Why have the earliest Christian writings all been lost? Why have later writings all been tampered with? Why did the Western Church insist for so long that laymen should not own or read bibles? One might have expected the Roman Church to have published at least a summary of all infallible statements made by the popes over the centuries. Yet no such thing exists. No one knows which statements the Church regards as infallible and which it doesn't, because no authoritative list has ever been published. Indeed, there is not even a definitive list of previous popes, so no one can work it out.

Why has there been no attempt to identify and collect together so-called apostolic traditions? Why is it impossible to find unexpurgated versions of what the Church Fathers wrote, or indeed even to obtain a full list of recognised Church Fathers? Why are many of the most influential authorities in early Christianity now regarded as heretics? Why can the Churches not agree about which Church Councils were ecumenical and therefore infallible, and why is it so difficult to obtain translations of exactly what these councils decreed? Original definitions of orthodoxy propounded by these divinely-inspired infallible councils ought to be best sellers amongst Christians worldwide, yet only brief extracts are ever made available to the mass of believers – precisely those extracts that match modern orthodoxy.

If God was as keen to reveal his eternal Truth as many Christians claim, it seems odd that he should reveal so many different and inconsistent versions to so many different people, and equally odd that his revelations are so imprecise, and so unpalatable that they have to be carefully selected for consumption by the Christian public.

NOTES

1   Josephus, *Against Apion*, cited by Eusebius, *The History of the Church*, 3:10.
2   These relegated psalms are now known collectively as 'Psalms of Solomon'.
3   There is some doubt about whether a formal council was convened. In any case the Jews still had no concept of a canon of scripture – their question was whether a text made people unclean if they touched it, and the test of this was whether it included God's name. Neither the Song of Songs nor Ecclesiastes contained the name JHVH, and Esther failed to mention God at all. According to later Jewish tradition the set of books to be regarded as canonical was settled in the fifth century BC, but this is demonstrably untrue.
4   Esther was rejected by important authorities such as Clement of Alexandria (Eusebius, *The History of the Church*, 4:26) and St Jerome.
5   For example John Damascene, *De fide orth*, 4:17.
6   The numbering of the books of Esdras is complicated. The Septuagint contained Esdras A and Esdras B. In the Vulgate Esdras B was split into I Esdras and II Esdras, which we now know as Ezra and Nehemiah. Esdras A became III Esdras (1 Esdras in the modern Apocrypha), and a new Greek work dating from the first or early second century AD became IV Esdras (2 Esdras in the modern Apocrypha). Some manuscripts included an appendix, which is known as V Esdras.
7   Ten books, not present in the Hebrew, are now regarded as Deuterocanonical i.e. Apocryphal, although they were declared to be genuine parts of scripture by the Council of Jassy (1642) and the Council of Jerusalem (1642). Ware, *The Orthodox Church*, p. 208.
8   The Apocrypha includes the disputed books already mentioned plus the rest of the book of Esther and the Epistle of Jeremiah (= Jeremy) sometimes included at the end of Baruch.

9 Jude 1:14 quotes a prophecy from 1 Enoch 1:9.

10 English translations of Gilgamesh are available. For example N. K. Sandars (trans.), *The Epic of Gilgamesh*, Penguin Classics (London, 1987).

11 Romer, *Testament*, p. 30.

12 Hammurabi's Code was rediscovered at Susa in 1902, engraved on a monument. Clay tablets bearing Hammurabi's law code in cuneiform are housed in the Museum of the Ancient Orient in Istanbul.

13 Examples of duplications of passages are 2 Kings 19 and Isaiah 37; Ezra 2 and Nehemiah 7; and 2 Chronicles 36:22–3 and Ezra 1:1–3. In this last example it is clear that 2 Chronicles 36:23 has been cut off part way through. Again, Psalm 70 is a repeat of Psalm 40:13–17.

14 Manfred Barthel, *What The Bible Really Says*, translated by Mark Howson, Souvenir Press (London, 1982), pp. 30 and 141.

15 For example 2 Samuel 1:21 and Psalm 137 both contain scrambled text that can be explained as distorted versions of text discovered at Ugarit. See Romer, *Testament*, pp. 78–9.

16 Several such insertions occur in Jeremiah chapters 25–9 and are indicated in the Jerusalem Bible by being placed in brackets. Some are simple explanations of the text; others are new threats and promises made on behalf of God. The Jerusalem Bible also identifies a couple of cases of inserted marginal digressions in Numbers 21.

17 Robin Lane Fox, *The Unauthorised Version*, p. 101.

18 Robin Lane Fox, *The Unauthorised Version*, pp. 377–8.

19 Jether the Ishmaelite (1 Chronicles 2:17) is none other than Jether the Israelite (2 Samuel 17:25). In some manuscripts he is Jether the Jezreelite. See NIV.

20 1 Kings 4:26 in the Hebrew says that Solomon had 40 stalls, but the Septuagint agrees with 2 Chronicles 9:25, which says that he had 4,000.

21 See the NIV note to 1 Chronicles 11:11, cf. 2 Samuel 23:8. Jashobeam appears to be the same person as Josheb-Basshebeth.

22 For a few further examples see NIV notes to 1 Kings 5:16, 1 Chronicles 4:3 and 2 Chronicles 22:2.

23 St Justin Martyr, *Dialogue with Trypho the Jew*, 72, cf. Irenaeus, *Adversus Omnes Haereses*, III, xx, 4; IV, xxii, 1; IV, xxxiii, 1, 12; V, xxxi, 1.

24 Robin Lane Fox, *The Unauthorised Version*, p. 318.

25 The absurdity of established biblical chronologies was comprehensively demonstrated by Thomas Paine in Part II of *The Age of Reason*.

26 'The historical setting of the story undoubtedly disregards known facts, persons and dates and contains anachronisms in detail; …' – Introduction to the book of Daniel, Jerusalem Bible.

27 Genesis 46:27 and Exodus 1:5.

28 Was the Sabbath instituted because the world was made in seven days (Exodus 20:11) or because the Israelites had been slaves in Egypt (Deuteronomy 5:15)?

29 The issue of the Ten Commandments is discussed, and Wellhausen's reconstruction of the original ten listed, in Dodd, *The Authority of the Bible*, pp. 91–2.

30 Laws specified at Exodus 20–23, Leviticus 11–27 and Deuteronomy 12–26 contradict each other on many points.

31 1 Samuel 8, 10:17–24, 12 is anti-royalist; 1 Samuel 9–10:16 and 11 is royalist.

32 For two spectacular examples see 2 Samuel 23 and 1 Chronicles 1.

33 Irenaeus, cited by Eusebius, *The History of the Church*, 5:8. According to another popular tradition 72 scholars translated it in 72 days.

34 For a few examples where the Masoretic Text varies from the Septuagint see the NIV 1 Samuel 10:1, 2 Samuel 13:34, and Jeremiah 27:1. There are of course thousands of other disagreements.

35 According to St Augustine there were riots in Tripoli over the translation of the Hebrew *qiqqayon* in the book of Jonah as the Latin *hedera* (ivy) instead of *cucurbita* (gourd).

36 According to the Council of Trent, God himself was the true author of all the books of the Bible. This was reaffirmed by the papal encyclical *Providentissimus deus* in 1893.

37 See for example the books of Judith and Jeremiah in the Jerusalem Bible, where significant differences are apparent, and some passages have been moved around.

38 The papal bull *Ineffabilis deus* in 1854 referred to Mary crushing the serpent's head, regarding Jerome's text as authentic, although it was widely known by then to have been a mistranslation.

39 Uta Ranke-Heinemann, *Eunuchs for the Kingdom of Heaven*, p. 8.

40 On the strength of this and other gospel passages, John Chrysostom for example accuses Mary of failing to believe in her son, and also of vainglory. Graef, *Mary*, vol. 1, p. 75.

41 Graef, *Mary*, vol. 1, pp. 19–20.

42 The cipher worked as follows. The letters of the alphabet were written out in two lines, the top line from left to right, and the second line from right to left:

Aleph	Beth	Gimmel	Daleth	He	Waw	Zayin	Cheth	Teth	Yodh	Kaph
א	ב	ג	ד	ה	ו	ז	ח	ט	י	ך
A	B	G	D	H	W	Z	Ch	T	Y	K

Taw	Schin	Resh	Qoph	Tzadhe	Pe	Ayin	Samech	Nun	Mem	Lamed
ת	ש	ר	ק	צ	פ	ע	ס	ן	ם	ל
Th	Sh	R	Q	Tz	P	O	S	N	M	L

To encrypt or decrypt a message each letter was replaced by the one immediately above or below it. (Remember that there are no vowels in ancient Hebrew.) In Hebrew, Babylon is BBL (Babel). Encoding it using the above table, each B becomes a Sh, and L becomes K. BBL therefore encodes to ShShK. When translated into English this becomes Sheshak or Sheshach, as in Jeremiah 51:41 (cf. 25:26). Similarly Chaldea, Hebrew *Kashdim*, transforms to *Leb-kamai* (Jeremiah 51:1).

43 The subject of translators introducing their own ideas of pain and suffering into biblical passages concerning childbirth is treated in detail by Grantly Dick-Read, *Childbirth Without Fear*, Printer & Martin (London, 2004), pp. 90–91.

44 Roland E. Bainton, *Here I Stand, A Biography of Martin Luther* (Penguin, 1995).

45 We might deduce that only daughters bear the iniquity of their fathers, if we did not have examples of God being mollified by the death of sons.

46 The dimensions of Noah's ark are given in Genesis 6:15. It is easy to visualise the volume in question, since St Martin's church in Brighton was built to the same dimensions.

47 See for example Psalms 89:3–4 and 35–7; 2 Chronicles 7:18 and 9:8; 2 Samuel 7:16.

48 Wells, *The Historical Evidence for Jesus*, p. 1.

49 Irenaeus, *Adversus Omnes Haereses*, III, xi, 7.

50 Hebrews, James, 1 and 2 Peter, and 3 John are all missing from the Muratorian Canon, although Wisdom and the Apocalypse of Peter are included. The Muratorian Canon is an eighth-century Latin translation of the second-century list, first published by L. A. Muratori, in 1740.

51 Tertullian, *De Praescriptione Haereticorum*, pp. 17–20.

52 Eusebius, *The History of the Church*, on the relative datings quotes Irenaeus (5:8) and Origen (6:25).

53 Papias is quoted as saying that 'Matthew compiled the Sayings in the Aramaic [i.e. Hebrew] language, and everyone translated them as well as he could'. Eusebius, *The History of the Church*, 3:39:15, cf. 5:8 and 6:25.

54 Examples of parables peculiar to the Luke author may be found at Luke 10:30–37; 13:6–9; 15:3–10 and 16:19–31.

55 Jesus tells Pilate that he (Jesus) has been delivered to the Jews – as though he was not a Jew himself (John 18:36) – and says to his disciples 'as I said unto the Jews…' – as though they were not themselves all Jews (John 13:33).

56 Wells, *The Historical Evidence for Jesus*, p. 133.

57 Irenaeus, *Adversus Omnes Haereses*, III, xi, 7–8.

58 Morton Smith, *The Secret Gospel* (London, 1974), pp. 14–16.

59 For example Mark (10:46) relates that: '… they came to Jericho: and as he went out of Jericho…', which rather looks as though someone has edited out the events in Jericho. Sure enough, according to Clement's letter the Secret Gospel of Mark related that in Jericho '…the sister of the young man whom Jesus loved and his mother and Salome were there, and Jesus received them not'. That the fuller secret gospel is the more reliable is supported by incidental facts. First the author of the John gospel also mentions a man 'whom Jesus loved' (John 19:26–7). Second, the story of a man whom Jesus raised from the dead is otherwise recorded in the John gospel, where the man is named as Lazarus. Also, there is an otherwise inexplicable passage in Mark (14:51–2): 'And there followed him [Jesus] a certain young man, having a linen cloth cast about his naked body; and the young men laid hold on him: And he left the linen cloth, and fled from them naked.' This fits in with the activities described in the Secret Gospel, but makes no sense in the canonical version.

60 The suppressed material referred to gnosis – the secret knowledge that distinguished Gnostic beliefs. It also referred to 'that truth hidden by seven [veils?]', and Clement admitted that it was 'read only to those who are being initiated into the great mysteries'. Distinctly Gnostic ideas are also to be found in the canonical Mark gospel, notably at Mark 4:11–12.

61 St Justin Martyr also refers to the memoirs of the apostles: *First Apology*, 66.3, and *Dialogue with Trypho the Jew*, 101.3, 103.8 and 105.5.

62 Eusebius, *The History of the Church*, 3:25.

63 Eusebius, *The History of the Church*, 6:25.

64 Dionysius, an early bishop of Alexandria, knew of a tradition that the *Book of Revelation* was the work of Cerinthus, the head of a rival sect. Eusebius, *The History of the Church*, 7:25.

65 Wells, *The Historical Evidence for Jesus*, pp. 89ff.

66 2 Corinthians 2:4 for example refers to another letter to the Corinthians, written with many tears, which is unknown to us.

67 For evidence of tampering see Wells, *The Historical Evidence for Jesus*, pp. 8ff.

68 For example the following stories come from these works: Acts of John – Raising of Drusiana; Acts of Paul – story of Thecla; Acts of Peter – Simon Magus and 'Domine, quo vadis?'; Acts of Andrew – his crucifixion; and Acts of Thomas – King Gudaphorus.

69 Mark 5:1. The Authorised Version refers to the country of the Gadarenes.

70 Clement of Alexandria shared a similar, erroneous, view. He offers as 'proof' of the resurrection the fact that seeds decay before somehow multiplying themselves and bringing forth fruit. *First Epistle of Clement to the Corinthians*, 24.

71 There is no reason to suppose that Jewish practices had changed by the time that rabbis wrote about them in AD *c*.200. See Robin Lane Fox, *The Unauthorised Version*, p. 289.

72 Stephen was executed (or perhaps lynched) by the Jews (Acts 7:59–60). James, Jesus' brother was tried, though this time it cost the high priest his job. Josephus, *Jewish Antiquities*, xx, ix, 1. See also Eusebius, *The History of the Church*, 2:23. Other indications are given by the fact that Herod Antipas (a Jew) executed hundreds of Jews, including John the Baptist. According to the Gospels Jesus had run the risk of being stoned by the Jews on several occasions. The famous adulteress who was about to be stoned by the Jews survived thanks to Jesus when he said: '...He that is without sin among you, let him cast the first stone at her...' (it was the custom for the accuser to cast the first stone). Again, after Jesus' death the Sanhedrin had threatened the apostles with death.

73 H. Cohn, *Trial and Death of Jesus*, pp. 97ff and 166ff.

74 Some manuscripts have variant spellings of Sala, possibly attempts to cover up the error. The Authorised Version translates the name in Luke as Sala, the NIV and Jerusalem Bible prefer Shelah, which appears in later manuscripts.

75 Another example of an Old Testament passage taken out of context and amended to meet the needs of the New Testament is John 7:38, either misquoting Zechariah 14:8 or an unknown scripture or making one up.

76 Mark 8:34, cf. Matthew 10:38 and Luke 14:27.

77 For a more detailed account of the conflicts between the Matthew and Luke stories, see Robin Lane Fox, *The Unauthorised Version*, pp. 27ff.

78 Luke cannot be confusing Herod I, King of Judæa (Luke 1:5), also known as Herod the Great, with his son Herod Antipas, because later he correctly identifies the son as tetrarch of Galilee not King of Judæa (Luke 3:1).

79 The existence (and ease) of divorce is confirmed in the Old Testament at Deuteronomy 24:1, Leviticus 21:7, 21:14 and 22:13, and Numbers 30:9.

80 Matthew 26:47–56, Mark 14:43–52, Luke 22:47–53 and John 18:1–12.

81 The hearings were before Annas (John 18:12–23), before Caiaphas (Matthew 26:57–68, Mark 14:53–65, Luke 22:66–71 and John 18:24–8), before Pilate (Luke 23:1–8), before Herod Antipas (Luke 23:8–12), and then before Pilate again (Matthew 27:11–26, Mark 15:2–15, Luke 23:13–25 and John 18:28–40).

82 John 21:1–14, cf. Luke 5:1–11.

83 Elisha fed 100 men with 20 barley loaves and some grain, leaving some leftovers (2 Kings 4:42–4). For a number of other interesting points about the New Testament story see Wells, *The Historical Evidence for Jesus*, pp. 131ff.

84 Joachim Kahl, *The Misery of Christianity* (English translation by N. D. Smith), Penguin Books, pp. 128–9.

85 Eusebius, *The History of the Church*, 6:17.

86 Those who denied the divinity of Jesus for example felt the need to correct the 'orthodox' scriptures: Eusebius, *The History of the Church*, 5:28.

87 A good example is the changing of a key text to refer to Jesus instead of all believers (John 1:13). Tertullian accused the Valentinian Gnostics of having tampered with it to refer to all believers, but the truth was that Tertullian himself, or an 'orthodox' scribe before him, had altered the text to refer to Jesus. See Ehrman, *The Orthodox Corruption of Scripture*, pp. 27 and 59.

88 Origen cited Jeremiah 20:7–12.

89 That texts were amended to make them comply unambiguously with the latest version of 'orthodoxy' is convincingly detailed by Ehrman, *The Orthodox Corruption of Scripture*.

90 Paine, *Age of Reason*, Pt II, p. 154.

91 The Western text is almost 10 per cent longer than the Alexandrian text. It smoothed out a number of difficulties and slanted the text to the detriment of the Jews and in favour of the gentiles. See Wells, *The Historical Evidence for Jesus*, pp. 3ff.

92 Could this story be the one referred to in Eusebius, *The History of the Church*, 3:39? If so, it would not be the only story lifted from the Gospel of the Hebrews and inserted into manuscripts of Luke.

93 Nicetas of Remesiana provides independent evidence that Elisabeth spoke the Magnificat. Giovanni Miegge, *The Virgin Mary* (London, 1955), p. 33.

94 1 Samuel 2:1–10, but with other quotations and allusions. See footnote Luke 1i in the Jerusalem Bible.

95 For numerous examples see Ehrman, *The Orthodox Corruption of Scripture*, pp. 82–99.

96 In Colossians 1:2 Jesus is bracketed with God by an insertion, and in Matthew 24:36 by an omission. In John 13:31–2 God is glorified in Jesus, as Jesus is glorified by God. See the footnotes in the NIV.

97 Mark 1:1 and Acts 8:37 both contain additions referring to the son of God. See the footnotes in the NIV.

98 Luke 22:43–4 and John 5:4 are both additions introducing angels. See the footnotes in the NIV.

99 Matthew 27:35 and Mark 15:27. See the footnotes in the NIV.

100 For example several amendments were made to the Lord's Prayer in Luke 11:2–4 to bring it into line with the version in Matthew 6:9–13. The Matthew version was also added to. The ending 'For thine is the kingdom, and the power, and the glory, for ever' is found only in late manuscripts. Using it was once considered evidence of heresy. It is not included in most versions of the Bible, although it is almost invariably added to the prayer as popularly used. (See footnotes in the NIV for both Matthew and Luke.)

101 For further examples see (in the NIV) Matthew 16:2, 17:21 and 21:44; Mark 10:7 and 14:72; Luke 3:33 and 23:17; and notes.

102 Some 5,366 Greek witnesses are known up to the sixteenth century. Some are more complete than others. The assertion that of the thousands of Greek manuscripts that have survived, no two are identical excludes those witnesses that are tiny fragments. Ehrman, *The Orthodox Corruption of Scripture*, p. 27.

103 The Cathar form of the prayer was, in French translation, 'Donnez-nous notre pain supersubstantiel'. Roquebert, *Les Cathares*, vol. 5, p. 361.

104 Cf. different translations of John 1:12–13:

> But to all who did accept him he gave power to become children of God, to all who believe in the name of *him who was born* not out of human stock or urge of the flesh or will of man but of God himself (Jerusalem Bible, author's italic text).

> Yet to all who received him, to those who believed in his name, he gave the right to become children of God – *children born* not of natural descent, nor of human decision or a husband's will, but born of God (New International Version, author's italic text).

The Jerusalem Bible is undoubtedly better poetry, but the text means something completely different.

The Vulgate (Jerome's translation of the Bible into Latin) gives a similar version to that in the Jerusalem Bible. No Greek manuscript supports Jerome's choice. The only support comes in a single Latin translation.

105 In his commentary on Luke, Erasmus translated the Greek *kecharitomene* into Latin as *gratiosa*, 'being in favour'.

106 Both of the Matthew and Mark authors refer to Simon the Canaanite in the Authorised Version (Matthew 10:4, Mark 3:18). Luke has Simon Zelotes (Luke 6:15, Acts 1:13). In the NIV all are translated as Simon the Zealot.

107 Junia in the Authorised Version becomes Junias in the NIV (and The Jerusalem Bible). No one seems to have been in any doubt that Junia was a woman until the late Middle Ages. See Uta Ranke-Heinemann, *Eunuchs for the Kingdom of Heaven*, p. 109.

108 Ironically a bishop of Rome, now known as Pope Leo, in his famous *Tome* wrote that 'by the Holy Spirit's inspiration the emperor needs no human instruction and is incapable of doctrinal error'.

109 For the views of various Church Fathers see Kelly, *Early Christian Doctrines*, pp. 216–7.

110 Gibbon, *The Decline and Fall of the Roman Empire*, Penguin, p. 286.

111 See for example Evans, *Is Holy Scripture Christian?*, p. 11.

112 For example, probably not one in a thousand adherents of the Western Church could even name all Three Great Hierarchs of the Eastern Churches – Gregory of Nazianus, Basil the Great and John Chrysostom.

113 Ignatius, *Epistle to the Smyrnaeans*, 8.

114 Clement's First Epistle may be found in Andrew Louth (ed.), Maxwell Staniforth (trans.), *Early Christian Writings*, p. 110. His second epistle is no longer believed to be his at all.

115 St Justin Martyr, *Apol.* 13:3.

116 For examples of Irenaeus's credulity, see Eusebius, *The History of the Church*, 5:8.

117 One line of manuscript evidence omits the final chapters of the fifth book of Irenaeus's *Adversus Omnes Haereses*, where he attacks a position now considered more orthodox than his.

118 Irenaeus, *Adversus Omnes Haereses*, V, i, 1.

119 St Clement of Alexandria, *Stromateis*, 3.49.3, 6.71.

120 Chadwick, *The Early Church*, p. 96.

121 Origen held that the Father transcended the Son by at least as much as the Son transcended mankind. *Commentary on the Gospel of John* 13, 25, 151, *Commentary on the Gospel of Matthew* 15, 10.

122 Eusebius, *De eccl. Theol (On the Theology of the Church)*, 3.19, discussing John 10:30. For Eusebius's beliefs see Kelly, *Early Christian Doctrines*, pp. 225–6.

123 Eusebius, *Praeparatio evangelica (Preparation for the Gospel)*, 11.20.

124 The statement that '… on both sides of the Father's supreme power he supplies the secondary beams of light of Christ, and the Holy Spirit' places one person of the Trinity above the other two, and is thus heretical. Eusebius, *The History of the Church*, 10:4.

125 In his *City of God* St Augustine refers to a fountain at Epirus that lights quenched torches and mares in Cappadocia that are impregnated by the wind. He claims to have verified the fact that the antiseptic nature of peacock flesh prevents it from rotting like other flesh.

126 Riddled by guilt over an abandoned mistress and with their son still with him, St Augustine procured another mistress to keep himself occupied while he waited two years for a prospective bride to reach marriageable age. Augustine, *Confessions*, 6.15.

127 The rhythm method of contraception was sanctioned by a synod of Roman Catholic bishops in Rome in 1980 but had been condemned by St Augustine in *De Moribus Manichæorum*, 18.65.

128 Ware, *The Orthodox Church*, p. 257.

129 Most of these examples of papal fallibility (and many other examples) may be found in Kelly, *The Oxford Dictionary of Popes*.

130 Callistus (like other bishops of Rome) was accused of regarding the Father and Son as different manifestations of the same being, a heresy variously known as Sabellianism, Patripassionism, Modalism or Modal Monarchianism.

131 Cited by St Thomas Aquinas in IV, *Scriptum super libros Sententiarum*, *(On the Sentences of Peter Lombard)*; quoted in Viollet, *Papal Infallibility and the Syllabus*, 1908. For a discussion of the possibility of heretical popes, see http://www.romancatholicism.org/duty-resist.htm.

2

THE DEVELOPMENT OF CHRISTIANITY

WHAT DID JESUS BELIEVE HIMSELF TO BE?

...But whom say ye that I am?
Matthew 16:15

Most historians, though not all, accept that Jesus existed.[1] The following represents the sum of what is generally accepted concerning his life:

- He was a Jew, probably born around 2,000 years ago.
- He came from Galilee.
- As an adult he was baptised by a man known as John the Baptist.
- He preached and taught in Palestine, and attracted a group of followers.
- He was involved in a controversy about the Jerusalem Temple.
- He was crucified by the Roman authorities.

There is no historically reliable evidence that Jesus believed himself to be God incarnate, nor that he intended to found a new religion. Such ideas stem partly from the New Testament, which, as we have seen, is not regarded by most Church scholars as a reliable historical account. Even if we do accept the New Testament as a factual account of historical events, matters are still not straightforward, and doubt remains about who Jesus was, and what he thought himself to be. The texts can be, and have been, interpreted in many different ways. In the past, Christian leaders have declared the biblical Jesus to be a model for dictators and for the oppressed; soldiers and pacifists; for capitalists, socialists and communists; and for kings, gentlemen, peasants and revolutionaries. In the last few decades he has been acclaimed as an Essene, a Zealot, a Buddhist, a sorcerer, a homosexual, a space alien, and the product of hallucinogenic mushrooms.

It might seem obvious to the devout that this is all nonsense and that Jesus knew himself to be God incarnate. After all it is well known that according to the gospels he claimed to be Christ, the divine son of God. As a matter of fact he did not make this claim. What he did claim, and what others claimed, and how these various claims were later interpreted is the subject of this section. We will consider the following:

- Jesus the Rabbi
- Jesus the Miracle Worker
- Jesus the Prophet
- Jesus the Messiah
- Jesus the Royal Pretender
- Jesus the Son of Man
- Jesus the Lunatic
- Jesus the Lord
- Jesus the Son of God
- Jesus the Christian
- Jesus the God

Our main purpose is to show which of these attributions are historically realistic, and which support the central Christian belief that he was divine.

Jesus the Rabbi

Rabbi, when camest thou hither?
John 6:25

As a Jewish teacher, Jesus would naturally have been addressed as Rabbi. The title is used in the gospels (e.g. Mark 9:5, 11:21 and 14:45), but it was traditionally translated into English as *Master*. In the John gospel it was left as *Rabbi* (e.g. John 1:38, 1:49, and 6:25).

This form of address was used in the original Greek texts, and we have no reason to doubt its validity.

Jesus the Miracle Worker

*And he could there do no mighty work, save that he laid hands
upon a few sick folk, and healed them.*
Mark 6:5

Jesus' miracles are discounted by many biblical scholars as additions to the original texts, for reasons that we will look at in some detail later. However, even if we accept the miracles, there is still the question of whether they irrefutably establish claims to Jesus' divinity, as is often asserted.

To answer this question we need to compare the reported nature of his miracles. Are they substantially different to the equally well-evidenced miracles attributed to ordinary mortals? The answer has to be 'no'. Historically, miracles have always been relatively commonplace. They are not hard to find in the Old Testament, albeit often performed with divine assistance.* Around the time of Jesus the power to perform miracles was ascribed not only to prophets but also to respected rabbis. For example in the first century BC Honi the Circle-Drawer was credited with the ability to induce rain.[2] In the first century AD Hanina Ben Dosa was credited with healing the sick by divine means and with possessing the miraculous power of withstanding the venom of poisonous snakes.[3] Again Rabbi Simeon ben Yohai and Rabbi Eleazar ben Yose were reported to have cured an emperor's daughter by exorcising a demon.[4] In rabbinic literature a number of Jewish scholars were credited with the power to revive the dead. Pagans also enjoyed extensive miraculous powers. The Roman Emperor Vespasian cured the lame and the blind, while Alexander the Great was credited with emulating Moses' parting of the sea to let his army pass. All these miracles were at least as well attested as those reportedly performed by Jesus.

---

* Aaron caused his staff to turn into a snake (Exodus 7:8–13). Moses produced a miraculous method of preventing people from dying of snake bites (Numbers 21:8–9). Elijah successfully revived the dead son of a widow (1 Kings 17:17–24), and on another occasion incinerated his sacrifice of a bull by means of some sort of divine thunderbolt (1 Kings 18:37–38). Elisha demonstrated that he was a prophet by curing the army commander Naaman of a skin disease (2 Kings 5:1–14). He also restored a dead child to life (2 Kings 4:18–37) and caused an iron axe that had been lost in the Jordan to float so that it could be recovered (2 Kings 6:1–7). Joshua brought down strong city walls by miraculous means (Joshua 6:3–5 and 6:15–20).

On the evidence of the gospels a number of people had the power to cast out devils (Mark 9:38 and Luke 10:17); according to the Matthew author Jesus acknowledged this fact (Matthew 12:27). The New Testament is peppered with examples of Jesus' followers working miracles.* Since New Testament times the ability to work them has been bestowed more liberally still. Irenaeus refers to the raising of the dead by the apostles and by later Christians.[5] A number of saints have been credited with raising the dead: St Dominic and St Francis Xavier to name but two. In the Middle Ages Christian monarchs were regularly credited with miraculous cures. Again many thousands of saints are recognised by the mainstream Christian Churches as having possessed miraculous powers. Even Martin Luther was credited with having performed miraculous cures. Modern Christian groups are even more blessed. In the United States alone there are hundreds of evangelist ministers routinely performing miraculous deeds of healing every day, all verified by grateful believers. Some of these miracles are performed at great distances through the medium of television. Proponents of many other religions perform miraculous deeds that are as well attested as those of Christianity. Muslims ascribe them to Mohammed and to certain Mullahs, Buddhists ascribe them to Guatama and other Buddhas, Hindus ascribe them to Brahmins and Sadhus.

Throughout history thousands of people have been credited with the ability to work miracles, without being regarded as gods. The reported working of miracles by Jesus cannot therefore be regarded as evidence of his divinity, especially since his miracles seem to have depended upon faith in much the same way as those of modern miracle workers. In his

---

* Peter healed the sick and exorcised a number of evil spirits that had possessed people (Acts 5:16). On another occasion he seems to have enjoyed supernatural knowledge and the power to cause people to die through some paranormal effect. Apparently without having been told, Peter knew that a follower, Ananias, who had sold some land, had kept some of the proceeds for himself instead of giving all of it to the apostles. Peter rebuked Ananias and he fell down dead. Later, Ananias's wife Sapphira, not knowing of her husband's death, also was deceitful about the sale proceeds. Peter told her that she would die too, and she promptly did (Acts 5:1–11). Peter also restored a dead woman to life (Acts 9:36–41). Even his shadow was able to work miracles (Acts 5:15). The apostles in general were credited with many unspecified miraculous signs and wonders (Acts 5:12). Paul miraculously blinded the prophet Bar-Jesus in order to impress and convert the proconsul Sergius Paulus (Acts 13:6–12), and was also credited with other miracles. Apparently his miraculous powers even rubbed off onto his handkerchiefs and aprons (Acts 19:11–12).

own time Jesus' miracles were not seen as evidence of divinity, but they might be evidence of the appearance of a new prophet. They were, after all, without exception selected from the standard menu of miracles expected of a prophet at that time.

Jesus the Prophet

A prophet is not without honour, but in his own country,
and among his own kin, and in his own house.

Mark 6:4

Prophets abounded in Old Testament times, and during New Testament times there seems to have been a widespread expectation that some great figure from the past would reappear on Earth. Elijah and Moses were both expected, and even the Queen of Sheba (Luke 11:31). Certainly there was a resurgence of prophetic claimants. The historian Josephus mentions that many false prophets flourished around the time of Jesus,[6] a fact supported by New Testament warnings about them.[7] Some prophets are named in the New Testament. John the Baptist for example was counted a prophet[8] and so was Theudas.[9] A man called Bar-Jesus was another (Acts 13:6). Paul was mistaken by a Roman tribune for a prophet known as *The Egyptian*.[10] Simon Magus, whom Gnostic Samaritans came to regard as the redeemer, was another,[11] as was a man called Agabus (Acts 11:28 and 21:10). Herod Antipas thought that Jesus was John the Baptist come back from the dead (Mark 6:14 and 6:16), but others believed that he was Elias or another prophet (Mark 6:15). That his disciples regarded him as a prophet is confirmed by Luke 24:19. His prophetic status was compared to that of Moses.[12] The masses also recognised him as a prophet (Matthew 21:11 and Matthew 21:46), and Jesus referred to himself as a prophet:

> Nevertheless I must walk today, and tomorrow, and the day following:
> for it cannot be that a prophet perish out of Jerusalem. (Luke 13:33)

By this he meant that he must go to Jerusalem to die because, as a prophet, it would not be fitting for him to die anywhere else. Like other prophets he was expected to perform miracles. The power to perform miracles was regarded as evidence that a man was truly appointed by God. Indeed the fact that Jesus performed miracles led people to conclude that he was a prophet (Luke 7:16, John 6:14 and John 9:1–17). His healing miracles followed traditional patterns, for example using folk medicine and healing waters.[13] On one occasion, after he had failed to work the miracles expected of a prophet, he is reported to have spoken the words quoted at the head of this section 'A prophet is not without honour …'. His failure to perform as a prophet was the source of doubt about him (Luke 7:39) and made him a butt of ridicule after his arrest.[14]

We now tend to regard the foretelling of the future as the principal function of a prophet, an idea reflected in the modern meaning of the term *prophecy*, but the Jewish idea was somewhat different. The ability to foretell aspects of the future was only one of many preternatural powers expected of the later prophets. Any self-respecting prophet was almost routinely expected to heal the sick, cast out demons and raise the dead.

As we have seen, around Jesus' time such miracles were ascribed to false prophets, to Jesus' followers, to devout rabbis, and to other religious figures. Whether or not we ourselves accept that anyone has ever worked a miracle, we may accept that, on the evidence of the New Testament, Jesus was believed by some, during his lifetime, to be a prophet. This is still how Muslims and some Jews regard him.

Jesus the Messiah

And Moses took the anointing oil…
Leviticus 8:10

If Jesus saw himself as a prophet the question naturally arises as to why he is now acclaimed not as a prophet but as the Messiah.

The word *messiah* is of Jewish origin. It means 'the anointed one'. For the Jews, long before the time of Jesus the word was applied to those who had been anointed with oil, as Aaron had been anointed by Moses (Leviticus 8:12). Since the practice of anointing with oil was reserved for high priests and kings, it was high priests and kings that were called messiahs. Cyrus the Great is called a messiah in the Bible, though many translations disguise the fact by referring to him as 'anointed' rather than as a messiah (as at Isaiah 45:1). Again, the Jewish priest-kings from Saul onwards were all messiahs. Even during the Roman occupation of Judæa the Jewish high priest appointed by the Romans was known as the Priest Messiah.[15]

The underlying meaning of the word *messiah* enabled it to be translated into languages that had no corresponding concept – it was just a matter of adapting the word for oil. From a Greek word for oil we have the English word *chrism*, denoting holy oil. A *christ* is simply someone anointed with *chrism*. The word *christ* (Greek *christos*) is thus a literal translation of the Hebrew *messiah*. The earliest Church historian, Eusebius, was well aware of the significance of the word:

> …it was not only those honoured with the high priesthood, anointed with prepared oil for the symbol's sake, who were distinguished among the Hebrews with the name of Christ, but the kings too…

Modern translations of the Bible sometimes retain the Hebrew word *messiah*, sometimes translate it as *christ*, and sometimes use the English equivalent 'anointed'. Selection on doctrinal, rather than linguistic, grounds allows translators to avoid referring to Jewish high priests and others as 'christs' or 'messiahs'. Incidentally, the ancient practice of anointing priests and kings with oil was regarded as so important that it has been carried into modern Christianity. For example chrism is used in bestowing Holy Orders in the Greek and Roman Churches. It is used in the Anglican Church too. The British monarch is anointed with chrism during the coronation service, just as the ancient Jewish kings were.

It might be expected that if Jesus was acclaimed as a christ or messiah, then he must have laid claim to the office of high priest or king (or both). There is no doubt about which claim the Bible emphasises. According to the New Testament Jesus was born of the Royal line of David (Romans 1:3), and the authors of both the Matthew and Luke gospels (or later editors) took the trouble to trace his ancestry back to the old Jewish kings and beyond (Matthew 1:1–16 and Luke 3:23–38). The danger that he might become the King of the Jews was the reason for Herod the Great's interest in having him killed at birth.[17] When he triumphantly entered Jerusalem for the last time he was hailed as the Jewish King: 'Fear not, daughter of Sion: behold thy King cometh'

(John 12:15). He was condemned to death not because he claimed to be the son of God, but because he claimed to be a king, and he was repeatedly referred to as such during his trial.[18] Pilate explicitly mentioned that the Jews themselves called Jesus their king (Mark 15:12). The sign attached to the cross reportedly read *The King of the Jews.** In the gospels Jesus is referred to on two occasions as the King of Israel,[19] and the Luke author also refers to him simply as the King (Luke 19:37–8). He is represented as being expected to restore David's Kingdom (Mark 11:9–10). His claim to the Jewish kingdom was certainly sufficient to qualify him as a messiah.

Around the time of Jesus there was an apparently widespread belief that a new messiah would appear. This belief was not held by all Jews or even, it seems, a majority. Those who did look forward to the coming of a messiah expected a warrior leader who would lead a successful uprising against the Romans. After expelling them he would re-establish a Jewish kingdom with himself as king. The messiah expected by the Jews was to be a human, not a divine leader. It was therefore not a blasphemy to claim to be a messiah. Clearly it would not be reasonable to indict everyone who claimed to be a messiah, since sooner or later, as they supposed, one of the claimants would be genuine. Around Jesus' time there were many who claimed to be messiahs. It is not certain that Jesus himself ever claimed to be one himself. In all of the explicit references in the gospels it is others who use the title. Jesus is evasive about it when asked directly whether he is the Christ, and answers enigmatically in the third person about the Son of man (Matthew 26:63–4, Mark 14:61–2). Hegesippus, in the generation after the apostles, mentioned that some followers had come to believe that Jesus was the Christ, suggesting that this was a novel view.[20] What seems to have happened is that Jesus was known simply as Jesus during his lifetime. Some Jews acknowledged him to be a messiah and styled him *Jesus the messiah* or *Jesus the christ*. Later still someone (possibly St Paul) turned this into *Jesus Christ*, making a name out of an appellation. As a name the first part could be dropped so *Jesus Christ* became *Christ*. Numerous ancient manuscripts capture the transition. In many places the oldest strands talk about *Jesus*, later strands talk about

---

* The four canonical gospels, though they disagree about the other words, are unanimous in ascribing the expression 'King of the Jews' to the sign placed on the cross: Mark 15:26, Matthew 27:37, Luke 23:38 and John 19:19.

Jesus Christ, and later ones still *Christ*. These changes were almost certainly made by 'orthodox' scribes for doctrinal reasons.[21]

In time Jesus Christ would become the second person of the Trinity, and divine. How far the meaning of the title *Christ* has been changed can be illustrated by the application of the term to others who have been anointed. Thus for example it would be etymologically correct to refer to any British monarch as a *Christ*. The apparent blasphemy is attributable to the meaning of the word having been altered, so that most people now imagine that it carries implications of uniqueness and divinity.

In short, Jesus may or may not have thought of himself as a messiah. It is quite possible that he did. In any event, claiming to be a messiah or a christ was far short of claiming to be divine.

Jesus the Royal Pretender

> *A thing is not necessarily true because a man dies for it.*
> **Oscar Wilde (1854–1900)**

However else Jesus might have been seen, the common point of view was that he was a danger to the state. Potentially he might lead a rebellion against the Romans and re-establish a Jewish kingdom. He was, therefore, liable to be seen as a trouble-maker, a revolutionary, a freedom fighter, a royal pretender, or a rightful king, depending upon one's point of view. There is ample evidence from many sources that Jesus was seen in these lights. The Bible itself shows him to have been a danger to the state. His attitude to the Temple for example was clearly subversive. Not only did he disturb the peace, he also threatened the status of the priesthood along with their money-making activities, and thus indirectly the fiscal power of the state.

No empire is likely to welcome an alternative authority, especially one with the traditional characteristics of a ruler (the title of King, a royal lineage, reputed adoption as a son of a god), and especially when he claims to have come to bring not peace but a sword. At one stage Jesus was obliged to flee into the mountains because a mob was getting out of hand and threatening to make him King (John 6:15); his reticence may have been due to their timing rather than their intent. At an early stage of his ministry he did not dare be seen in towns but was obliged to stay in the desert because of the attentions of his supporters (Mark 1:45, cf. Luke 5:15–16). According to the John gospel the Jewish authorities feared that Jesus' miracle working would precipitate a violent Roman reaction that would lead to the destruction of the Temple and the nation (John 11:47–50).

One of Jesus' disciples was Simon the Zealot,[22] a member of a fanatical anti-Roman sect (the Zealots). According to the author of the Luke gospel, Jesus instructed his disciples to buy swords in preparation for what was to come soon before his arrest (Luke 22:36). By the admission of one early Christian writer the apostles were 'ruffians of the deepest dye'.[23] If Jesus was not a terrorist, then he was at least liable to be seen as one. There is indeed a good, though circumstantial, case to be made that Jesus was himself a Zealot.[24] Further supporting evidence for the view that Jesus was seen as revolutionary comes from the fact that he was crucified. This mode of execution was reserved for slaves and those found guilty of treason;* and since Jesus was not a slave, we may deduce that he was condemned for treason. When Paul visited Thessalonica the residents had already heard about people who turned the world upside down, contravened the decrees of Caesar, and said that there was another king called Jesus (Acts 17:6–7).

The early Christians, in their enthusiasm for their own version of orthodoxy, were given to destroying or editing any material that contradicted their beliefs. Consequently it is often difficult to find reliable independent texts concerning Jesus. Scholars are generally agreed for example that mention of him by the historian Josephus has been doctored. The original version was probably one referred to by Origen in the early third century.[25] This denied that Jesus was the Messiah, but no copy of it has survived. At least, no version was believed to have survived. In the nineteenth century a translation in Old Russian dating from around 1260 was discovered.[26] It is known as the Slavonic Josephus. In it Jesus is described as being a political revolutionary, and as a *king who did not reign.*

---

* Slaves were frequently crucified, others more rarely. This gave the punishment a special stigma. The term treason here covers any activity that threatened the stability of the state. As well as rebellion this could cover spying and desertion, and even forgery (which was also a treasonable offence in England for many centuries because it posed such a serious threat to the state).

It is also significant that Galilee was a hotbed of dissent and revolutionary activity directed against the Romans. It had been a hotbed for decades before Jesus' lifetime, and was to remain so for decades afterwards. In fact it was such an established centre for revolutionary activity that the word *Galilæan* came to be synonymous with *rebel*. Many Galilæans had led abortive rebellions against the Romans and their Herodian placemen. A group of Galilæans incited a rebellion in Jerusalem in AD 49.[27] One of the leaders of the First Jewish War against the Romans (AD 66–70) was John the son of Levi from Gischala in upper Galilee, who led a contingent from there.[28] Another trouble-maker was a man called Ezekias, who was executed by Herod around 47 BC for his activities in Upper Galilee.[29] Similar activities were carried on by his son, Judas the Galilæan, a man with royal aspirations who incited revolution and co-founded the Zealot movement, and who is referred to in the New Testament.[30] Two sons of Judas called Jacob and Simon were crucified around AD 47, which suggests that they continued the Galilæan family tradition.[31] A third son, Menahem, captured Masada from the Romans in AD 66. In Jerusalem Menahem entered the Temple wearing royal apparel but was subsequently killed in factional fighting.[32] Another relation, Jairus, is famed as the leader of the group of Zealots who held Masada against the Romans for four years after the fall of Jerusalem.[33] In AD 67, reacting to a widespread rebellion, the Romans advanced on the family's original home, Gamala in Galilee. Thousands of Jews are said to have died fighting, and thousands more committed suicide.

It seems that many rebel leaders saw themselves as messiahs. Certainly each sought to establish himself as the new king. The author of Acts and the historian Josephus both refer to a prophet called Theudas who led a rebellion around the time of Jesus, and who was executed for his efforts.[34] Even foreigners tried their hands. One known as the *Egyptian* planned to attack Jerusalem with a band of Jewish followers.[35] The New Testament suggests that St Paul was mistaken for this same *Egyptian*, the leader of 4,000 assassins (Acts 21:38). The best known of these messianic rebels appeared 100 years or so after Jesus' death. He was Simon Bar Kokhbar, who led the Second Jewish Revolt against the Romans in AD 132–5.[36] His name suggests a claim to messiahship, and Rabbi Akiba acclaimed him as the *king messiah*.[37] As Josephus pointed out, every rebel leader in Judæa was immediately created a king.

When Judæa had come under direct Roman rule in AD 6, it had been thought necessary to crucify more than 3,000 rebels. In Jesus' time the Roman Prefect of Judæa, Pontius Pilate, maintained his headquarters at Caesarea, but made a practice of staying in Jerusalem during the Passover. He did this because the Passover was a particularly sensitive time when Jewish discontent was likely to boil over into violence. The historian Eusebius reported that over 30,000 Jews were crushed to death in Jerusalem in the course of one Passover during the reign of the Emperor Claudius.[38] Jesus could hardly be unaware of the sensitivity of this time. In fact the Bible suggests that some form of uprising did take place while Jesus was in Jerusalem. Writing of prisoners who might be released, Mark 15:7 refers to an 'insurrection':

> And there was one named Barabbas, which lay bound with them that had made insurrection with him, who had committed murder in the insurrection.

It is significant that relatives of Jesus were also executed for sedition or rebellion. According to the historian Josephus, John the Baptist, Jesus' cousin, lost his life not because of his views about marriage, as the New Testament suggests, but because Herod Antipas was alarmed by the likelihood of a revolt inspired by his hold over the people.[39] This explanation fits much better with the fact that Jesus withdrew into Galilee as soon as he heard of the arrest of his cousin (Matthew 4:12 cf. Mark 1:14). Josephus also referred to the execution in AD 62 of James 'the brother of Jesus called the Christ'.[40] A Christian writer says that James suffered martyrdom like the Lord and for the same reason.[41] According to some sources, this was the event that led to the First Jewish Revolt of AD 66.[42]

The Emperor Vespasian issued orders that descendants of David should be rooted out and that no member of the royal house should be left among the Jews.[43] Domitian also gave orders to extirpate David's line. Two great-nephews of Jesus were brought before him because they were of the house of David, but were released because of their insignificance.[44] This pursuit of the descendants of David continued into the reign of Trajan, when an aged cousin of Jesus, Simon son of Clopas, was crucified.[45] This may not have been merely irrational vindictiveness. An early Christian writer indicates that Jesus' relatives took pains to preserve and advertise their ancient genealogies, stretching back to King David and beyond, despite Herod's attempts to destroy them.[46] In passing the writer mentions that these relatives of Jesus referred to themselves as *Desposyni*, a title that can be translated 'Ruling People' and must have invited suspicions of sedition.

The truth seems to be that Jesus was one of a long series of rebels who sought to overthrow Roman rule and establish himself as king. Being of the house of David he was a particularly potent threat. Like many others he failed, and his reward was crucifixion.

Jesus the Son of Man

And the word of the Lord came to me, saying, Son of man, put forth a riddle, and speak a parable unto the house of Israel; ...
Ezekiel 17:1–2

Jesus usually referred to himself as the *son of man*, a locution that in Aramaic was a polite way to refer to oneself. After all a son of man is only another man. Writing it *Son of man* or *Son of Man*, with capital letters, gives the impression that it is a title. Of course there were no capitals in the original text, or rather all letters are capitalised so that the initial letters are in the same style as the others. How the expression *son of man* was used as a title, or indeed whether it was used as a title at all, is still a matter of dispute among scholars. There is some evidence that it was. It had been applied, for example, to the King of Israel (as traditionally ascribed in Psalms 8 and 80) and the prophet Ezekiel reported that a heavenly voice had referred to him as *son of man*.[47]

Jesus might well have had in mind the usage in the book of Daniel 7:13ff where in a vision 'one like the Son of man' is given dominion, glory and a kingdom.[48] If so, then like later Christian apologists, he overlooked the fact that the visionary character was subsequently identified in Daniel not as an individual but as the 'saints of the most high'. An old book of scripture, 1 Enoch, which has been discarded by the modern Church,[49] uses the expression *son of man* extensively, and associates it with a semi-divine character who bears a striking resemblance to later Christian ideas of Jesus. Unfortunately this *son of man* is explicitly identified as Enoch himself, which perhaps explains why some Christians thought of Jesus as Enoch returned, and why others rejected the book of 1 Enoch altogether.

It is interesting that, according to the gospels, Jesus himself almost always used the expression *son of man* when speaking of himself. His disciples never seem to have had any difficulty with its meaning. On the other hand St Paul never used the expression, and the Greek Churches seem to have found the idea it conveyed unpreachable. As the grander titles were introduced the modest ones were abandoned. Thus *son of man* occurs over 60 times in the synoptic gospels, less frequently in the John gospel, and only three times elsewhere. It is not used at all by the authors of any of the New Testament epistles.

Jesus the Lunatic

> ...*people were saying that he was out of his mind.*
> **Mark 3:21 (NEB)**

There is evidence that those close to Jesus believed that he was insane, at least during part of his ministry. On one occasion they attempted to take charge of him, i.e. to lock him up (Mark 3:21). His neighbours did not believe his claims to be a prophet and ridiculed him for failing to work the miracles expected of a genuine prophet. Many Jews said 'He is possessed, he is raving' (John 10:20, New English Bible). Whether or not he was insane is an uncomfortable question for believers, but it is a safe assumption that he did not believe himself to be.

Jesus the Lord

> ... *every tongue should confess that Jesus Christ is Lord...*
> **Philippians 2:11**

Jesus is sometimes addressed as Lord (Greek *kyrios*). This is another ambiguous title. It can be used simply as a respectful form of address, which is how people generally used it of Jesus when they wanted his help.[50] Sometimes it is interchangeable with Master, and once it appears to mean owner (Mark 11:3). At the other extreme God himself was addressed as Lord.[51] In this respect the English closely parallels the Greek: the word *lord* can denote anything from a squire (Lord of the Manor) to God himself (Lord of Heaven).

In the Bible Jesus only once refers to himself unambiguously by the title Lord (John 13:13). Neither this nor any other usage in the New Testament suggests that Jesus was God, though the inherent ambiguity of the word may well have been harnessed in later times to endorse emerging claims to divinity. By interpreting 'Lord' as Christ it was possible to read the Old Testament as referring to Jesus. Writers like Paul helped the process along by substituting the term 'Lord' for a name or title of God when citing ancient scriptures.

It was not merely a matter of identifying Jesus with the God of the Jews. Greek gods were also addressed as lords. Hellenic Christians compared their lord with the lords of various mystery cults, such as Osiris, Serapis and Hermes, and also with Caesar, who significantly was referred to as 'our Lord and God'.[52]

Jesus the Son of God

One of the distinguishing features of ancient Hasidic piety is its habit of alluding to God precisely as 'Father'.

Geza Vermes, Jesus the Jew

In the earliest gospel there is no suggestion of Jesus' divine birth. His relationship with God begins at his baptism when a heavenly voice announces 'Thou art my son' (Mark 1:11). This seems to be a reference to Psalm 2:7: '... Thou art my son; this day I have begotten thee', applied to Jewish kings. These words were probably used during the coronation ceremony, when the king was anointed and adopted as a son of God. The incident of Jesus' adoption as a son of Jehovah is related elsewhere in the New Testament.[53] In some manuscripts of Luke the words 'Thou art my beloved son ...' are supplemented by the rest of the quote from Psalms 'this day I have begotten thee' (Luke 3:22). This fuller form appears in Hebrews 1:5 and is quoted by early Christian writers.[54] The clear suggestion is that an attempt is being made to identify Jesus as a Jewish king by virtue of his adoption by God.

That God adopted sons was recognised as a biblical theme by early Christian writers.[55] Significantly the title Messiah is sometimes yoked to the sonship in New Testament passages, for example: '... Thou art the Messiah, the Son of the living God'.[56] It is also notable that the idea features frequently in passages that scholars recognise to be later additions to the gospels. Whoever added the story of Jesus' birth to the Luke gospel used it twice within a few verses when he retrospectively predicted that Jesus would be called the *Son of the Highest* (Luke 1:31–2) and the *Son of God* (Luke 1:35).

The description *son of God* is known to have been conferred on a number of respected rabbis and charismatics around the time of Jesus. (Remember that the use of a capital letter for 'Son' was a later development.) In the case of the first century Galilaean rabbi Hanina ben Doza, it was even reported that a heavenly voice acclaimed him as *my son*.[57] The term *sons of God* had been used for others too. Sometimes it referred to angels,[58] and sometimes to the people of Israel. Other Jewish sources before and around the time of Jesus identify various beings as *sons of God* or *sons of the Most High* – men, angels, a mysterious pre-eminent (first begotten) angel, and the *Word* (*logos*).[59] According to one biblical work God himself will call any man who acts as 'a father to the fatherless and as a husband to their mother' his son,[60] which means that all step-fathers are entitled to call themselves *sons of God*. Jesus himself reputedly claimed that all peacemakers will be called *children of God* (Matthew 5:9), and Paul asserted that all Christians are *children of God* (Galatians 3:26). It is significant that those who wish to give Jesus a unique status describe him not as *God's son* (too common), nor as *God's **only** son* (untenable[61]), but as *God's **only begotten** son*.

It is sometimes claimed that the fact that Jesus referred to God as *Father* is confirmation that he saw himself as the son of God. It is even alleged that this usage was unique, and indicative of his exalted claims. In fact the New Testament itself tells us that Jesus was to be merely the first born among 'many' brothers (Romans 8:29). Furthermore, many other Jews referred to God as Father (Aramaic *Abba*). Even an Anglican bishop has accepted that Jesus' teaching about the Fatherhood of God is an old familiar doctrine of the rabbis.[62]

Incidentally it was not an offence among the Jews to claim to be a son of God, as is sometimes claimed.[63]

So, did Jesus think of himself as a son of God? If he ever thought of himself as the rightful Jewish king, or as a notable teacher, then the answer may well be that he did. But even if he did, we have no reason to believe that he imagined himself to be divine, any more than we have for the thousands of other sons of God.

Jesus the Christian

There is nothing more negative than the result of the critical study of the life of Jesus. The Jesus of Nazareth who came forward publicly as the Messiah, who preached the ethic of the Kingdom of God, who founded the Kingdom of Heaven upon Earth, and died to give his work final consecration, never had any existence.
Albert Schweitzer, *The Quest for the Historical Jesus*

It rarely occurs to anyone brought up as a Christian to question whether Jesus founded the Christian religion: it seems so obvious that he did. But what if we look for biblical evidence that Jesus was the first Christian, and compare it to the evidence that he was a more or less conventional follower of the Jewish religion?

After almost 2,000 years of Christian development of the story of Jesus it is easy to forget that he was Jewish by descent. In fact Jesus was quite clearly Jewish. He bore a common Jewish name. Animal sacrifices were made by his family to mark his birth in accordance with Jewish custom,[64] purifying the mother and 'redeeming' the son. He was circumcised according to Jewish Law. He accepted the Jewish faith throughout his life. He attended the synagogue, and was familiar with the Jewish scriptures. Indeed he often taught in synagogues (e.g. Mark 1:39, Matthew 9:35, Luke 4:15). On one occasion he even delivered the liturgical sermon after reading the prophetic lesson for the day.[65] As a Jewish teacher his followers naturally addressed him as Rabbi. Many of his teachings were characteristic teachings of the Pharisees, one of the many Jewish sects then popular. After healing a leper Jesus instructed him to go to a Jewish priest and make an offering, as required by Jewish Law.[66] On a number of occasions he indicated that he was interested only in the Jewish people. He is reported as having said:

> I am not sent but unto the lost sheep of the house of Israel. (Matthew 15:24)[67]

Furthermore Jesus specifically forbade his disciples from teaching to the gentiles (Matthew 10:5). He characterised the gentiles as 'dogs' (Matthew 15:26 and Mark 7:27) and as 'swine' (Matthew 7:6). When a man from the gentile city of Gerasa asked to be allowed to join Jesus' followers his offer was declined and he was told to return home (Mark 5:18–19 and Luke 8:38–9). Jesus' teaching was characteristically Jewish. The aspects that are often pointed up as being new and radically different were not at all new, as we shall see later.

Jesus worshipped in the Temple and in synagogues. He never expressed any intention that his followers should do otherwise. He never established a Church in the sense that the word is now used.* After his death his immediate followers continued to worship at the Temple and to attend synagogues. After Paul and his friends proved too troublesome to be accommodated in synagogues, followers worshipped at home. For generations afterwards gentile Christians worshipped in private houses. It was not until later that buildings were specially built or sequestered as churches. Only after this had happened could it occur to anyone to reinterpret the statement 'And I say also unto thee, That thou art Peter [*petros*] and upon this rock [*petros*], I will build my church [*ecclesian*] …' (Matthew 16:18). In the centuries to come, new meanings would be found for this statement, but for the time being it could be used to justify a separate Church and separate Church buildings.

According to the Bible, Jesus never used or heard the word *Christian*. It was not even coined until around AD 42, years after his death, when it was first used in Antioch (Acts 11:26).

Apart from anything else, it would not have made much sense for Jesus to found a religion, because it is clear that he believed the end of the world to be imminent – according to the New Testament he said so on numerous occasions. There would be little point in establishing a Church and its accompanying hierarchy if the world was going to end

---

* In the gospels the word *church* is used to translate the Greek word *ecclesia*. The term denoted a gathering of citizens in a self-governing city state. In the gospels it is apparently used to mean something like fellowship or brotherhood. Jesus' followers constituted a Church only in this sense. There is no question, for example, that Jesus might have intended Church buildings to be constructed.

within a few years at most. The simple fact is that there is no evidence that Jesus ever intended to found a new religion, Christian or otherwise.

Jesus the God

For the Lord is a great God, and a great King above all gods.
Psalm 95:3

The second century philosopher Celsus noted that there were many Palestinian prophets who had claimed to be God, or a son of God or a Holy Spirit.[68] He regarded Jesus as just another one of these, but he may have been wrong. It is possible that Jesus never claimed to be divine. Certainly he never made that claim for himself according to the gospels. Here is one of the most influential Christian scholars of the nineteenth century, Joseph Ernest Renan, discussing the matter in his *Life of Jesus* (1863), chapter 15:

> That Jesus never dreamt of making himself pass for an incarnation of God, is a matter about which there can be no doubt. Such an idea was entirely foreign to the Jewish mind; and there is no trace of it in the synoptic gospels.[i] We only find it indicated in portions of the Gospel of John, which cannot be accepted as expressing the thoughts of Jesus. Sometimes Jesus even seems to take precautions to put down such a doctrine.[ii] The accusation that he made himself God, or equal to God, is presented, even in the Gospel of John, as a calumny of the Jews.[iii] In this last gospel he declares himself less than the Father.[iv] Elsewhere he avows that the Father has not revealed everything to him.[v] He believes himself to be more than an ordinary man, but separated from God by an infinite distance. He is son of God, but all men are, or may become so, in diverse degrees.[vi]...

---

i   'Certain passages, such as Acts 2:22, expressly exclude this idea.'
ii 'Matthew 19:17; Mark 10:18; Luke 13:19 (sic)'.
iii 'John 5:18 ff.; 10:33 ff'.
iv 'John 14:28'.
v   'Mark 13:32'.
vi 'Matthew 5:9, Luke 3:38, 6:35, 20:36, John 1:12–13, 10:34–35'.

How Jesus came to be regarded as a god is not difficult to reconstruct. During his lifetime he was regarded as a rabbi, a prophet and possibly a messiah. He was seen as 'a man approved of God' (Acts 2:22). After his death his title Messiah, with its Jewish associations of military leadership and earthly sovereignty, became untenable. Dead men are not good propositions as earthly kings. *Christos*, the Greek word corresponding to the Hebrew *messiah*, soon acquired a new significance, through the claim that *Christos* had been the son of God. The Greeks and Romans knew well what a son of a god was. They had heard about many of them, and had even seen some of them. Gods frequently coupled with mortals and produced sons that were at least semi-divine. As we shall see, numerous emperors, heroes and even philosophers were acclaimed to have been fathered by divinities. To make any headway, the claims for Jesus would have to be improved. His titles would need to match those of the divine emperors, his chief contenders for a religious following. From the time of Augustus onwards Roman emperors had borne the title *Divi filius*, son of God, so it was not a big step for the title to be ascribed to Jesus. The next step was to improve on the word *kyrios* or lord. In the latest gospel, written around AD 90, the resurrected Jesus is given the title of a deified emperor: *Lord and God* (John 20:28). Other familiar divine titles were adopted too: *sôtêr* for example, the Greek word rendered into English as *saviour*.

The development of Jesus' divinity is apparent in the gospels. In the oldest gospel Jesus is adopted by God at his baptism (Mark 1:11). The Matthew and Luke gospels relate stories of a divine conception and Virgin Birth, which many biblical scholars accept to be later additions to the original. Incongruously, they both retain the adoption by God at Jesus' baptism (Matthew 3:17 and Luke 3:22). Like the author of Mark, neither of these two makes any attempt to represent Jesus as God. The John author, writing about a generation later, has a different story. According to this one, Jesus was the *Word* (*logos*) made flesh: in other words an eternal supernatural being who became incarnate.

Even Paul never made a connection like this. Although he was arguably the founder of Christianity and thoroughly at home in the Græco-Roman world, Paul was still strictly monotheistic. Jesus could be the son of God, but not God himself.[69] Even the John author feels obliged to explain why Jesus could describe himself as a god. When he was threatened with stoning for having claimed to be God, Jesus denied the charge by citing a psalm in which God refers to his audience as *gods*, suggesting that it cannot therefore be blasphemous to use the word *god* for those to whom the word of God is addressed, nor for him to call himself a son of God.[70] His argument was questionable (and did not convince his audience), but the important point is that he did not claim to be God, and indeed denied it.

He is repeatedly shown to be less than God and subject to God (e.g. 1 Corinthians 3:23, 11:3 and 15:25–28). According to the gospels Jesus rebuked people for calling him 'Good Master' on the grounds that only God is good. Again, on the cross he is reported as having asked God why he had forsaken him (Mark 15:34). Such statements only make sense if Jesus did not consider himself to be God.

Reconciling monotheism with Jesus' divinity was impossible for many Jews, and was to prove extremely problematical for Christians in the centuries to come. Many of Jesus' earliest followers denied his divinity. His Jewish followers do not seem to have regarded him as God incarnate. Neither did their successors, who are now referred to as the Ebionites. Neither did a number of other early Christians. According to some of them, not only the apostles but the first 12 bishops of Rome agreed that Jesus was merely human.[71] They said that the official teaching had been tampered with after the time of Zephyrinus, Bishop of Rome (199–217), and the charge seems to be true. Zephyrinus and his successor Callistus were both regarded by progressive contemporary thinkers (like Tertullian and Hippolytus) as holding heretical views, although there is no reason to believe that they had believed anything different from their predecessors. Certainly other contemporary bishops and theologians agreed that Jesus was not God.

Many Christian scholars accept that to his earliest followers Jesus was only a man, however favoured. He became God later, in an Hellenic world where such things were possible, familiar, popular and expected. Throughout the development of early Christianity we shall see the same phenomenon many times over: a minority belief becomes so popular that it becomes 'orthodox' and the old orthodoxy becomes a 'heresy' a few years later.

WHO FOUNDED CHRISTIANITY?

Nothing is so firmly believed as what we know least.
Michel de Montaigne (1533–92)

Although we have hardly any first-hand evidence of what happened after the death of Jesus it is apparent that within a few years his followers had split into a number of camps, each with its own interpretation of his teachings.

The apostles remained in Jerusalem where they continued to practise Judaism. Most of them showed little if any inclination to try to convert gentiles to their faith. Paul, a convert who had never known Jesus while he had been alive, took his own version of Jesus' teachings to the gentiles. A third faction, probably initiated by some of Jesus' Samarian disciples, developed into a loose grouping and came to be known as Gnostics.

At least in the early stages there was considerable overlap between the various factions, but in the course of time distinct groups developed: Jewish Christians (or Nazarenes),[72] Pauline Christians and Gnostics. Having many different opinions, and as yet no New Testament to guide them, they each imagined Jesus to have been something different. For the Jewish Christians Jesus had been a great rabbi, for the Pauline faction he became a son of God, and for the Gnostics he became a divine manifestation.

Nazarenes

How odd of God to choose the Jews.
W. N. Ewer (1885–1976), *How Odd*

There is some evidence that after his own death, Jesus intended his brother James to take over his ministry and lead the remaining Jewish followers. Josephus refers to James taking over, and appears to refer to James as Christ, though the passage is ambiguous.[73] The Gospel of St Thomas refers to Jesus naming James as the disciples' leader after his own departure.[74] In the Secret Book of James, James occupies the dominant role sometimes attributed to Peter in canonical writings.[75] Church Fathers were aware that James had taken over the leadership of the apostles, and he was acknowledged to have been the first Bishop of Jerusalem.[76] Furthermore it is clear from the New Testament that James (recognised by the Church as James the Just) enjoyed primacy over the other disciples.[77] For example James alone makes the final decision about the dietary laws (Acts 15:13–20). A passage in Galatians gives James's name before Peter's, indicating relative rank (Galatians 2:9). Another makes it clear that Peter felt himself subject to James (Galatians 2:11–12).

From the little that the Bible tells us it is apparent that after Jesus' death the disciples continued to live communally. They visited the Temple together every day, gave generously, and were generally well respected (Acts 2:44–7). With the exception of Peter, there is no reason to suppose that any of them left the vicinity of Jerusalem. Nor is there any reason to suppose that they abandoned their Jewish faith.[78] Had this Jewish line survived there is little doubt that it would have had the strongest claim to represent Jesus' intentions. James was executed at the instigation of the Sadducees, in circumstances similar to those surrounding the death of his brother Jesus.[79] James was succeeded by another close relation, a cousin called Simeon (or Symeon),[80] though this succession seems to have caused dissent and schism.[81]

Like James and Simeon, some later leaders, or *bishops of the circumcision* as they were known, were also related to Jesus, suggesting some sort of dynastic succession. Their followers may have precipitated the First Jewish Revolt of AD 66, and certainly suffered from the Roman reaction to it. This faction was virtually wiped out during the Second Jewish Revolt of AD 132. When the Emperor Hadrian banished all Jews from Jerusalem in AD 135 he put an end to this line of 'bishops of the circumcision', a string of Jewish bishops of Jerusalem. The Church historian Eusebius listed the whole line from the first, 'James the Lord's brother', to the fifteenth and last.[82]

After AD 135 only gentiles were permitted to enter the city, and a new bishop was put in charge of those among them who espoused Christianity.[83] Presumably he was a gentile of the Pauline line who brought a new orthodoxy. The *bishops of the circumcision* had lost their throne. A sect of Jewish Christians, known as *Ebionites*, survived for two or three centuries. They retained the Jewish Sabbath, Jewish Law, and other characteristically Jewish practices. Some rejected the doctrine of the Virgin

Birth, others rejected the letters of Paul, regarding him as a renegade from the Jewish Law. Some believed that Jesus had supernatural virtue and power, but all denied that he was the son of God in the sense now usually accepted by mainstream Christianity.[84]

They became isolated from the Pauline branch of the Church and, from the second century, were regarded by them as heretics.[85] The Ebionites disappear from history still repudiating Paul as an apostate. Conveniently for rival factions all but a few records concerning Jewish Christianity are lost to us. The New Testament contains only one work that might be thought to reflect their views, the general letter of James. Luther called it 'A right strawry epistle', though it is possibly the oldest book of the New Testament. Certainly it expresses views on the importance of faith that contrast sharply with those of Paul.

Pauline Christians

*Is it more probable that nature should go out of her course,
or that a man should tell a lie?*

Thomas Paine, *The Age of Reason,* **Part I**

Paul's inspiration was to bring Christianity to the gentiles. This inspiration seems to have come only after the Jews had rejected him. Nevertheless, it has won him a key place in the history of Christianity.

Paul was clearly an unusual and controversial personality. An Hellenic Jew, he seems to have been keen to establish himself amongst Jesus' followers. His writings in the New Testament reveal in him a number of less than admirable qualities: he generally comes over as a trouble-making, complaining, self-seeking misogynist who was clearly out of step with the twelve apostles. Of the many Christians regarded as trouble-makers, the one who caused most trouble was undoubtedly Paul. After his conversion he seems to have developed the knack of creating vast amounts of bad feeling. His visits to towns generally ended up in riots or plots to murder him. The usual picture was that he was at first welcomed into the community and invited to speak in the local synagogues. Sooner or later he stirred up hatred and dissent to such an extent that he was subsequently obliged to flee in order to save his life.

In Damascus he preached in a number of synagogues, and it was some time before anyone set about trying to kill him (Acts 9:20–24). When they did try, he escaped to Jerusalem, where Grecian Jews made another attempt on his life, so he was sent to Tarsus. Later, with Barnabas, he was welcomed into a synagogue in Pisidian Antioch. Before long there was bad blood, and the two of them were expelled from the region (Acts 13:13–52). Off they went to Iconium, where they narrowly escaped death by stoning (Acts 14:1–7). They then fled to Lystra, where Paul was stoned and left for dead (Acts 14:8–20). Later, in Philippi, Paul and Silas were charged with causing an uproar. They escaped a rampaging mob only for magistrates to have them flogged and imprisoned (Acts 16:16–24). Some time after their escape following an earthquake, they went to Thessalonica. Paul spoke in the synagogue there on three Sabbath days before the riots started, and the two of them had to escape to Berea (Acts 17:1–10). Off they went to a local synagogue and before long there was more trouble. Silas stayed behind, but Paul was escorted to distant Athens (Acts 17:10–15). Here the sophisticated citizens seem to have regarded him with bemused contempt, so he was soon on his way again (Acts 17:16–34). When he arrived in Corinth, he spent every Sabbath speaking, and was soon being abused and attacked once again. In Ephesus he spent three months speaking in the synagogue before the derision of the inhabitants defeated him (Acts 19:1–9). He stayed in the area and appears to have provoked a riot (Acts 19:23–41) before deciding to leave (Acts 20:1). He went on to Macedonia and then Greece where there was another Jewish plot against him (Acts 20:3). Later he again narrowly escaped death when the people of Jerusalem tried to kill him (Acts 21:27–36). He owed his salvation to his Roman citizenship (Acts 22:22–30). Next he was transferred to Caesarea in order to avoid an assassination attempt by forty men who, for some unstated reason, had taken a solemn oath to kill him (Acts 23:12–23). He ended up in Rome, where his citizenship failed to save him and he met the death that so many had desired for him.

Why Paul had such an effect on people is not easy to tell. What he said to cause such hatred, we can only guess. To a disinterested reader, however, Paul's personality would seem decidedly odd. He has visions that are suspect in the extreme. He gives three contradictory accounts of his conversion and claims divine intelligence that was denied to the apostles. He likens himself to an angel of God and even to Jesus Christ

(Galatians 4:14). He believes, or at least claims, that he is being crucified along with Jesus (Galatians 2:20), and that he bears the marks to prove it (Galatians 6:17). He refers to an otherwise unknown gospel, which he refers to as 'my gospel' and says will be used by God to judge mankind.[86] He hints, rather heavily, that he has visited Heaven (the third heaven to be precise – 2 Corinthians 12:2–6), and refers repeatedly to his visionary contact with the divine (e.g. Ephesians 3:3 and Colossians 1:25–6). He believes himself able to judge others at a distance, being present in spirit to try them. He can then pass sentence by means of a letter, condemning people to be handed over to Satan for the destruction of the flesh – presumably some form of unlawful killing (1 Corinthians 5:1–5). When Paul is jealous, it is not with normal human jealousy but with 'godly jealousy' (2 Corinthians 11:2).

He seems to know nothing of the gospels, just as they seem to know nothing of him. Paul threatens, abuses and blusters, appointing himself as an additional apostle. He has no qualms about lying if he thinks that he is doing so for the greater glory of God: 'For if the truth of God hath more abounded through my lie unto his glory; why yet am I also judged a sinner?' (Romans 3:7). He also freely admits that he is prepared to become all things to all men in order to achieve his aims (1 Corinthians 9:22–3). His writings are threaded through with repeated assurances that he is telling the truth and attempts to deny implied accusations that he is not. He is known to have been ridiculed by other Christian groups. Some theologians have speculated that Paul was insane. Friedrich Nietzsche (1844–1900) described him as a morbid crank. Whether or not he was, he is by his own admission totally unreliable as a witness.

Paul seems to have known relatively little about the historical Jesus. He does not mention Jesus' place of birth, his parentage, or even when and where he lived. He does not refer to any of Jesus' miracles; neither does he mention any of his parables. There is no mention of Jesus' trial, nor even of the place of the crucifixion. This is probably not too surprising as Paul was writing before the gospels had been set down. He was operating in a vacuum, creating a new religion as his inspiration led him. He was a self-appointed apostle and spent considerable time and effort generating support for his interpretation of Jesus' message. It was Paul who first preached that Jesus was the son of God (Acts 9:20), a claim that in the gospels Jesus had never made for himself. Paul had not met Jesus during his lifetime but claimed to have seen him after the Resurrection (1 Corinthians 15:3–8). Such claims were met with scepticism: when Paul came to Jerusalem the disciples did not believe that he was one of their number (Acts 9:26).

Only after his rejection by his Jewish brethren did Paul offer his version of Jesus' teachings to non-Jews. His first missionary journey introduced a version of Christianity to the gentiles for the first time. This was unpopular among the apostles, not least because Paul appeared to have no qualms about amending teachings in order to make them acceptable to non-Jews. His approach to the Jewish laws provides a prime example of how his teachings differed from those of the living Jesus and of the apostles. Although Paul was a Jew he was an Hellenic Jew. He knew that few gentiles would be willing to accept the Jewish laws, so his solution was simply to drop them. Not being able to claim that Jesus, or any of his disciples, had sanctioned this he was fortunate in being able to state that the gospel he preached had been given to him by divine revelation.[87] God had suddenly decided to change his mind about the ancient laws. Why he should have revealed these changes to Paul but neglected to inform either Jesus or Jesus' disciples is a mystery to which no satisfactory answer has been provided. The disciples were left with an unfortunate burden of cynicism about Paul and his claims. Gibbon sums up the matter. Speaking of the Jewish followers of Jesus he says:

> They affirmed that if the Being who is the same through all eternity had designed to abolish those sacred rites which had served to distinguish his chosen people, the repeal of them would have been no less clear and solemn than their first promulgation; that, instead of those frequent declarations which either suppose or assert the perpetuity of the Mosaic religion, it would have been represented as a provisionary scheme intended to last only till the coming of the Messiah, who should instruct mankind in a more perfect mode of faith and of worship; that the Messiah himself, and his disciples who conversed with him on earth, instead of authorising by their example the most minute observances of the Mosaic law, would have published to the world the abolition of those useless and obsolete ceremonies without suffering Christianity to remain during so many years obscurely confounded among the sects of the Jewish church.[88]

Following his visions St Paul gave assurances that gentile converts did not need to undergo circumcision as prescribed in the Old Testament. Not all Churches accepted this, but the ones that did found it easier to attract converts and in time came to dominate Christianity. Now only the Coptic Church still retains the ancient practice of circumcision (though it also became popular among Victorian Anglicans*). Again, it was Paul who advocated dropping Jewish dietary restrictions, and again only the Coptic Church still retains them. Gentiles were prepared to accept Paul's new form of Christianity, and did so. Other Churches that tried to retain the traditional practices have since died out: a confirmation perhaps of Paul's inspiration.

Paul continued to proselytise and spread his version of Jesus' teachings, despite continuing opposition. He had trouble not only with the Jews, but also with rival Christian groups. It is clear from his letter to the Galatians that he was in dispute with those who insist on circumcision (though he himself had had Timothy circumcised – Acts 16:3). His enmity causes him to become offensive. He goes so far as to claim that Christ will be of no value at all to those who do allow themselves to be circumcised (Galatians 5:2), and expresses the wish that those who favour circumcision should go the whole way and castrate themselves (Galatians 5:12). In the space of a few verses of another letter he characterises them as unruly, vain talkers, deceivers, liars, evil beasts, slow bellies [lazy gluttons], defiled, abominable, disobedient, and reprobate (Titus 1:10–16). The rift seems to have grown wider and wider. He says quite plainly that he does not follow the Twelve in Jerusalem: 'For I suppose I was not a whit behind the very chiefest apostles'.[89] These, the original apostles, apparently preach 'another Jesus'. If we phrase this a little more neutrally we see that on the one hand Paul and on the other hand the twelve apostles were preaching different Jesuses. Later, Paul (or someone writing in his name) refers more dismissively to 'false apostles' (2 Corinthians 11:13), whose Jewishness is specifically mentioned (2 Corinthians 11:22). In short he had fallen out with those who held what was then the orthodox line. Peter, it seems, had difficulties in reconciling the Jewish and Pauline factions. In the New Testament he is

---

* Circumcision was popular among the English upper classes, apparently because Queen Victoria believed that the English were one of the lost ten tribes of Israel and so ought to circumcise in the Jewish manner.

represented as being initially sympathetic to Paul's views, but then changing his mind after emissaries of James have had a discreet word with him (Galatians 2:12).

To the Jewish Christians the Pauline faction was a group of fickle marketeers, changing the unchangeable Mosaic religion to suit gentile preferences. For their part the Pauline Christians keenly felt the need to justify themselves as being the true inheritors of the ancient Jewish faith. This need to justify themselves continued for as long as the Jewish Christians were around and able to demonstrate that they were the orthodox believers. In his *Dialogue with Trypho the Jew* written around AD 160, Justin Martyr was still preoccupied by the need to establish the legitimacy of the Pauline line.

Gnostic Christians

Knowledge itself is power.
Francis Bacon (1561–1626), *Religious Meditations, 'Of Heresies'*

As well as the Jewish and Pauline factions, numerous other groups flourished in the early years. These were principally Gnostic sects, claiming that Jesus' true message was not available to all, but granted only to an inner circle of initiates. Such claims were not unreasonable since the gospels represent Jesus as saying as much himself.* These Gnostic sects seem to have originally been Samarian offshoots of the main Jewish Church,[90] and at least some of them had existed before the time of Jesus, anticipating the coming of a Redeemer. They seem to have competed widely with other forms of Christianity, and in some areas, notably Egypt and eastern Syria, they enjoyed a virtual monopoly.[91]

---

* Jesus sounds distinctly Gnostic when he says that he speaks in parables so that only an elect inner circle will understand him (Mark 4:10–12, Matthew 13:10–13, Luke 8:9–10). Matthew 7:6 (including the famous injunction not to cast pearls before swine) is more convincing as a Gnostic injunction than one about profaning sacred things, which is the usual Christian gloss. Gnostic themes occurs elsewhere e.g. Hebrews 5:11–14. Remember too the characteristically Gnostic secret initiation ceremonies in the Secret Gospel of Mark, information about which was suppressed by Pauline Christians.

Because the Gnostic sects were so numerous and widespread, some of their writings have survived the attentions of later Pauline Christians. Such writings provide interesting background information about the development of early Christianity. Paul himself often made snide and slighting references to Gnostics and Gnosis.[92] As the Pauline line gained predominance, Gnostic views came to be regarded as heretical. Their heresies amounted to holding definite views on matters about which there was little factual evidence, or laying particular stress on one aspect of the religion. Like the Ebionites, some believed that Jesus was a mortal prophet, born by natural conception. Others, called Docetes, denied his humanity. To them it was inconceivable that the son of God could have been executed like the most contemptible criminal. They held therefore that Jesus had been a divine phantom. He had descended from Heaven to the banks of the Jordan in the form of a man. He had had the appearance of flesh and blood, but this was a deception for he was incorporeal and could not therefore suffer. His death on the cross likewise was only an illusion. The Basilides in Egypt and the Valentinians in Rome were both Docete sects. Soon such Docetes were being condemned by the Pauline line as poisonous, and their opinions those of the antichrist.[93] Many such sects were rooted out and destroyed by the Pauline Christians on the grounds of being heretical, and yet the same basic ideas have emerged time and again over the centuries. Each new sect to resurrect the ancient ideas has been in turn persecuted into oblivion. Whether there are any true heirs to this early Gnostic line today is doubtful, though there are certainly claimants.

Further Schismatic Sects

No kingdom has ever suffered as many civil wars as the kingdom of Christ.
Charles, Baron de Montesquieu (1689–1755), Letters

The existence of three distinct groupings among early followers of Jesus is well established, and no reputable scholar now disputes that they existed together during the early centuries. Factions soon emerged within each group, just as in modern Churches. There seem to have been other competing sects too: for example there was a group of followers of John the Baptist (Acts 18:25 and 19:3). Some said that there was no resurrection of the dead (1 Corinthians 15:12), others that the Resurrection was already past (2 Timothy 2:18). Some advocated the renunciation of marriage and abstinence from certain foods (1 Timothy 4:3). Others worshipped angels (Colossians 2:18).

Leading figures in early Christianity criticised and abused those who disagreed with their own opinions. This was a common and well-documented phenomenon, readily discernible from the New Testament and other early writings.

We have already seen that Paul disagreed with other followers of Jesus. He complains of those who preach 'another Jesus' (2 Corinthians 11:4). He, or someone writing in his name, warns of diverse and strange doctrines concerning Jesus (Hebrews 13:9). Elsewhere, in the pastoral letters, the author repeatedly warns of 'false teachers' and heretics (Titus 3:10). Both 1 Timothy and Titus refer to fables, though it is not clear whether or not these are rival Christian fables.

The three letters attributed to John also demonstrate that schisms had arisen at an early stage. He refers to those who have disagreed with him as 'antichrists' and mistakenly believes that their existence signals the 'last time', in other words the end of the world:

> Little children, it is the last time: and as ye have heard that antichrist shall come, even now are there many antichrists; whereby we know that it is the last time. They went out from us, but they were not of us: for if they had been of us, they would no doubt have continued with us: but they went out, that they might be made manifest that they were not all of us. (1 John 2:18–19)

It is apparent from the text that the disagreement referred to concerns the status of Jesus. Seemingly some of Jesus' followers did not regard him as the Messiah or the son of God:

> Who is a liar but he that denieth that Jesus is the Christ? He is antichrist, that denieth the Father and the Son. Whosoever denieth the Son, the same hath not the Father: [but] he that acknowledgeth the Son hath the Father also. (1 John 2:22–23)

The theme runs through all three letters. Indeed, the letters can be understood only against a background of division within the Church. In any case it is also clear that the author's views were poorly regarded by others of Jesus' followers:[94]

> I wrote unto the church: but Diotrephes, who loveth to have the pre-eminence among them, receiveth us not. Wherefore, if I come, I will remember his deeds which he doeth, prating against us with malicious words: and not content therewith, neither doth he himself receive the brethren, and forbiddeth them that would, and casteth them out of the church. (3 John: 9–10)

There is no hint of any doctrinal dispute here, merely a squabble about personal authority. We may safely assume that Diotrephes's version would have been different.

Other biblical writers confirm the general pattern. Jude refers to scoffers following their own passions (Jude v18 NIV). Jude and 2 Peter both criticise 'heretics', by which they mean those who disagree with them. James and Paul disagree over major issues, which have echoed down two millennia. While Paul claims that faith is everything,[95] James insists that faith is nothing without corresponding good works (James 2:14–17). Other contemporary writings confirm the general pattern: Clement of Rome wrote a letter to the Corinthians that was once counted as scripture. In it he indicated the scope of dissension within the Christian community. Recounting the past he wrote that 'Envy and jealousy sprang up, strife and dissension, aggression and rioting, scuffles and kidnappings'.[96] He referred to 'self assertion and braggadocio and stupid quarrelling' and 'odious rivalry'[97] among Christians and to 'dissensions over the title of bishop'.[98] In despair he asked '...why are we rending and tearing the limbs of Christ, and fomenting discord against our own body?'[99]

The early Christian Ignatius of Antioch was famous as the author of a number of letters advertising his own martyrdom. He did nothing to disguise the extent of the dissent within the Church. He referred to fellow Christians as 'a pack of savage animals', and in the next sentence as 'rabid curs' who advocated pernicious teachings.[100] He warned of 'false teachings and antiquated and useless fables'[101] and of 'plausible wolves'.[102] He advocated having no dealings whatever with those who disagreed with his views and instructed the recipients of his letter to 'Abjure all factions'.[103] He referred to 'troublesome ones' who should be brought to order[104] and to 'those who put forward their perverse teachings so plausibly'. He advised his readers to 'Be wary of the devices of sinful men' and to preach publicly against them.[106] These letters were addressed not to one exceptional community but to Christians in a number of major cities.

In brief, the whole Christian movement, from its birth, seems to have been riven by dissent and argument. As one theologian has put it:

> The tensions between Jewish and Gentile Christian churches, between Paul and the Corinthian enthusiasts, between John and early catholicism, are as great as those of our own day. One-sided emphases, fossilised attitudes, fabrications, and contradictory opposites in doctrine, organization and devotional practice are to be found in the ecclesiology of the New Testament no less than among ourselves.[107]

The Triumph of the Pauline Line

He who begins by loving Christianity better than Truth will proceed by loving his own sect or church better than Christianity, and end by loving himself better than all.

Samuel Taylor Coleridge (1772–1834),
Aids to Reflection: Moral and Religious Aphorisms

Despite the great holiness that the Bible accords to early Christians, their contemporaries seem to have regarded them only as trouble-makers. They offended not only the Romans, but also many of their Jewish brethren. Jesus himself was clearly not universally popular, and his enemies were happy to see him crucified. Before long his follower Stephen was stoned to death by the Jews for blasphemy (Acts 6:8–7:60). Other followers in Jerusalem caused such offence that they were scattered throughout Judæa and Samaria.

Already, in AD 66, after the outbreak of the First Jewish Revolt, the Christian community in Jerusalem had withdrawn to Pella, across the Jordan. In AD 70 the Romans destroyed the Temple, which the Jews believed to be divinely protected. Now they were excluded from Jerusalem altogether, beaten and scattered. The Pauline Christians saw the destruction of the Temple as a divine judgement, inaugurating a new dispensation by which sacrifices were abrogated. The further humiliation of the Jews in AD 135, when they were expelled from Judæa, enabled the Pauline faction to consolidate their belief that the Jewish Christians were a deviationist sect rather than the true successors of Jesus. They were dismissed as 'the hypocrites'.[108] As we have already noted, Jewish Christians carried on for a time. Small communities survived in Syria at least until the fourth century, but the balance of power had changed. The great centres of Christianity were now Alexandria, Antioch and Rome – areas where gentile Christianity could flourish.

It is significant that a large proportion of the New Testament is devoted to the doings of Paul, always sympathetically. In the Acts of the Apostles he is always portrayed as the hero of the story, even when he opposes the twelve apostles. We hear of his travels, his visions, his miracles, his suffering, his humility, his authority and even his stigmata. He had established himself, at least to his own followers, as a thirteenth apostle. By the time of the first Church historian he was not merely *an* apostle, but *the* apostle. Almost all surviving sources glorify Paul. On the other hand we hear little of the apostles appointed by Jesus. Most of them disappear from history. Only James (the Great), John, and Peter are more than mere names, and even Peter is portrayed as a hypocrite (Galatians 2:11–14). It is well within the bounds of possibility that the Pauline faction suppressed much of the material concerning the others. In particular, many scholars suspect that inconvenient material concerning James (the Just), the brother and successor of Jesus, has been destroyed. We have only one side of a story that had at least three sides, and possibly many more.

Setting aside New Testament writings, most of the other surviving documents of the early Church also reflect Pauline views, almost certainly because other versions were sought out and destroyed. As Gibbon says:

> The scanty and suspicious materials of ecclesiastical history seldom enable us to dispel the dark cloud that hangs over the first age of the church.[109]

It is known that there were texts that ridiculed Paul, but these have been 'lost'.[110] From the available evidence it would appear that early Christians followed Paul in making a practice of visiting synagogues and expressing their views in such a way as to cause offence. By around AD 85 the Jews had had enough of Christians disrupting their services, and a formal anathema was incorporated into the synagogue liturgy 'May the Nazarenes and the heretics be suddenly destroyed and removed from the book of life'.[111] Nevertheless for a long time Christians continued to disrupt Sabbath services in synagogues. In the third century a Christian called Callistus was charged with brawling in a synagogue on the Sabbath. In his lifetime he was known as a criminal, but his Christian friends saved him from his punishment in the mines of Sardinia. He later become Bishop of Rome, and is now regarded as both a pope and a saint. In many ways he epitomises the triumph of the Pauline line.

HOW OLD ARE CHRISTIAN DOCTRINES
AND WHERE DID THEY COME FROM?

What I tell you three times is true.
Lewis Carroll (1832–98), *The Hunting of the Snark*

Many Christians believe that all essential Christian doctrine is to be found in the Bible. Some denominations explicitly affirm this. The Church of England for example, in the sixth of its 39 Anglican Articles of Religion, asserts that 'Holy scripture containeth all things necessary to salvation'.

In this section we will look at some of the principal doctrines adopted by the main Christian Churches over the centuries. Are they really to be found in holy scripture? If not, how old are they? How did they arise? What authority do they have, and have they ever changed?

First let's look at the creeds, the formal, authoritative statements of Christian doctrine. There have been dozens of creeds, but most have long since been abandoned and some have been 'lost'. By modern standards many are heretical and even blasphemous.[112] On the other hand none of the creeds now in use was known to early Christians. These creeds were formulated mainly from the fourth century onwards. The Western Church in particular continued to tamper with them for centuries afterwards. This tampering was a cause of criticism from the Eastern Churches. The earliest creeds have now all been discarded, and mention of them is to be found only in erudite books on ecclesiastical history. Most modern Christians have never even heard of the Jerusalem Creed or the Old Roman Creed and would probably be surprised that the earliest authoritative statements of Christian belief have been abandoned.

The main creeds that are now used are:

- **The Apostles' Creed:** The name suggests that it was known to the twelve apostles, although there is no evidence at all to support this (and no Church scholar, however conservative, would now make such a claim for it). It seems to have developed from the Old Roman Creed. It was first referred to in a letter of St Ambrose, around the year 390.

- **The Athanasian Creed:** Traditionally attributed to St Athanasius (*c.*296–373), this creed is now generally accepted to date from some time later. It probably dates from the seventh century, since it uses terminology that arose only during contemporary controversies. This creed is still used by the Western Churches, although it has become something of an embarrassment, and is rarely used in Anglican Churches. Since 1867 a number of attempts have been made to remove it from the Book of Common Prayer.

- **The Nicene Creed:** The original Nicene Creed, agreed at the Ecumenical Council of Nicæa in 325, was a heavily edited version of one proposed by a leading bishop (Eusebius). This version is hardly ever used now. It was continually amended over the next century, with successive different versions being adopted as authoritative by successive Church Councils. The creed now usually known as the Nicene Creed actually dates from the Ecumenical Council of Chalcedon in 451[113] (the fact that it is still called the Nicene Creed provides an example of how basic facts in Christianity are often misrepresented to simple believers). Even this 451 version was later tampered with by the Western Church and, as we shall see, a late addition is still to be found in the creed used in Western Churches.

The Eastern Churches accept the Nicene Creed (the AD 451 version), but have never accepted the other two. All three creeds are used by the Roman Church but rejected by some Protestants. The Anglican Church holds that all three 'ought thoroughly to be received and believed: for they may be proved by most certain warrants of holy Scripture'.[114] The following is the Anglican Church's rendering of the Nicene Creed (more accurately known as the Niceno-Constantinopolitan Creed). With the exception of the words in bold type it is accepted by all principal denominations.

> I believe in one God the Father Almighty, Maker of Heaven and earth, And of all things visible and invisible: And in one Lord Jesus Christ, the only begotten Son of God, Begotten of his Father before all worlds, God of God, Light of Light, Very God of Very God, Begotten, not made, Being of one substance with the Father, By whom all things were made: Who for us men and for our salvation came down from Heaven, And was incarnate by the Holy Ghost of the Virgin Mary, and was made man, And was crucified also for us under Pontius Pilate. He suffered and was buried, And the third day he rose again according to the Scriptures, And ascended into Heaven, And sitteth on the right hand of the Father. And he shall come again with glory to judge both the quick and the dead: Whose kingdom shall have no end. And I believe in the Holy Ghost, The Lord and giver of life, Who proceedeth from the Father **and the Son**, Who with the Father and the Son together is worshipped and glorified, Who spake by the Prophets. And I believe in one Catholic and Apostolick Church. I acknowledge one Baptism for the remission of sins. And I look for the resurrection of the dead, And the life of the world to come. Amen.

It would not be practical to print all the variations of all the creeds in use today, but this gives a flavour of their style and content.

We will now look at some of the most widely accepted Christian doctrines, concentrating on those prescribed by the principal creeds.

The Incarnation

> *For the right Faith is, that we believe and confess: that our Lord Jesus Christ,*
> *the Son of God, is God and Man...*
> **The Creed of St Athanasius**

The doctrine of the Incarnation is one of the most fundamental Christian doctrines. It asserts that Christ was both fully God and fully man, with one 'person' but two distinct 'natures'. Yet it is not at all certain that Jesus' earliest followers recognised him as God. Certainly the Ebionites did not, and there is every reason to believe that their views matched those of the apostles more closely than any other faction. Biblical references to Jesus being God are rare and suspicious, and seem to have been added after Jesus had been deified by some of his followers.

Uneducated people in the classical world were familiar with the idea of gods descending to Earth and were unlikely to be interested in a humble Jewish prophet, or even a mere human messenger from a god. The fact that Jesus was already dead would have made it difficult for anyone in the Greek world to take him seriously. Much more promising was the idea of Jesus being the son of God. To the Jews the term signified an angel, a prophet, or a great rabbi; but to the Hellenic world it meant something quite different. The Greeks and Romans knew many examples of earthly sons of gods: super-heroes born as a result of matings between gods and mortals, a number of whom themselves became gods. In most of the stories a male god impregnated a mortal women. Generally she was a virgin. Invariably she conceived a child. Usually the child was a boy. Frequently the boy grew up into a superhuman who was subsequently deified. As we shall see later, many such stories were told, and we have every reason to suppose that the less sophisticated strata of society believed them.

It is against this background that the idea of Jesus being an adopted son of God (i.e. a great rabbi) seems to have developed into the proposition that he was God himself. Exactly what this could mean, if the Jewish principle of one God was to be sustained, was to cause a great deal of trouble in later centuries. The doctrine of the Incarnation developed as follows:

1   Christians divided in the first few centuries into the groups we have already identified: (i) Ebionites and others who believed Jesus to have been a man, (ii) a Pauline faction some of whom believed Jesus to have been superhuman, and (iii) a number of Gnostic sects, most of which believed Jesus to have been divine rather than human.

2   By the fourth century the Pauline faction was dominant and questions arose as to Jesus' superhumanity. The prevailing line seems to have been a set of beliefs now regarded as heretical and now known collectively as Monarchianism. This term embraces a range of beliefs from Dynamic Monarchianism to Modal Monarchianism

(Sabellianism, Patripassionism). Dynamic Monarchianism held that Jesus had been a mere man upon whom the Holy Spirit had descended, as described in the Mark gospel. God had adopted him, so those who believed this are also known as Adoptionists. Modal Monarchianists held a range of views about the relative importance of God the Father, Jesus Christ and the Holy Spirit. The Ecumenical Council of Nicæa in 325 affirmed by a majority vote that Jesus Christ was truly God, a decision that resulted in schisms amongst believers.

3   Questions now arose as to Jesus' humanity. If he was God, could he be wholly man as well? The First Ecumenical Council of Constantinople in 381 affirmed his perfect manhood. The view affirmed by this council contradicted a view favoured by an earlier one at Antioch in 264, which had denied the true humanity of Jesus by saying that he did not have a human soul. Once again, the Church was racked by schism.

4   Many deduced that Jesus must have had some sort of dual personality. He must have had within him a divine 'person' and a human 'person'. Others said that he had only one 'person'. The Alexandrian *one person* party eventually emerged triumphant. It was thus decided that Jesus Christ had only one person, despite being both fully God and fully man. This simply did not make sense to many, and once again the Church fell into schism.

5   Having settled the number of 'persons', the question now arose as to how one 'person' could accommodate both God and man. One solution was that he had two distinct 'natures'. This was affirmed by the Ecumenical Council of Chalcedon in 451, reversing the decision of a previous council held at Ephesus just two years earlier.[115] Once again, those who rejected the new line were sent into schism.

6   The decrees of Chalcedon were amended by the Fifth Ecumenical Council at Constantinople in 553, apparently with the hope of reuniting the warring schismatic factions. Later there was another round of difficulties and dissent over the question how many 'wills' Jesus had possessed.

This is how the doctrine of the Incarnation was settled: by a series of majority votes, carried against significant opposition. As we shall see later the competing ideas were generally inspired by power struggles between Alexandria, Antioch and Constantinople. Decisions were affected by undue influence, duress and even murder. Bribery was used not only to buy votes, but also to manipulate crowds of slaves and the poor in one doctrinal direction or the other. Bands of violent monks were employed to terrorise the opposition and influence the decision. Sometimes the final decisions were contrary to the decisions of previous 'infallible' councils and sometimes they overturned decisions made by an 'infallible' emperor. Bishops walked a fine line between the competing factions. Proterius, Bishop of Alexandria, for example, was literally torn to pieces by his own flock for accepting the decision of the Ecumenical Council of Chalcedon.

The hand of God was not obvious in these decisions, and some modern Christian scholars have speculated that if Nestorius, Bishop of Constantinople, had been richer, less principled, and a better politician, it is more than possible that what is now regarded as the Nestorian heresy would be orthodoxy, and what is now regarded as orthodoxy would be the Cyrilic heresy (see page 187).

The doctrine of the Incarnation as we now know it was never stated before the middle of the fifth century. The Roman Catholic, Eastern Orthodox and Protestant Churches accept it. The second of the 39 Articles of the Anglican Church affirms it. Nevertheless many Christians are not convinced. As we shall see later, many modern Church scholars hold the concept of the Incarnation to be unintelligible, a view shared by most secular philosophers. The doctrine is rejected by Unitarian Churches, Jehovah's Witnesses, and others.

The Holy Ghost (or Holy Spirit)

> *The Holy Ghost is of the Father and of the Son: neither made,*
> *nor created, nor begotten, but proceeding.*
>
> **The Creed of St Athanasius**

The Bible often refers to the Holy Ghost, but nowhere explicitly identifies it with God, except arguably in the *Johannine comma*, an acknowledged addition to the text of the First Epistle of John (see pages 64–5). The creed adopted by the Ecumenical Council of Nicæa failed to mention that the Holy Ghost was divine, let alone a member of the Trinity (it had been referred to in the first draft, but without any suggestion of divinity). The question seems to have arisen in the next few generations. When it did arise, people speculated that the Holy Ghost might be 'force', or a created being, or God; some confessed that they did not know what to call it.[116]

The faction that said it was God eventually triumphed. Those who denied the full divinity came to be known as Macedonians or Pneumatomachians ('Spirit-fighters').[117] The Holy Ghost was declared to be divine by the Second Ecumenical Council, held at Constantinople in 381. The Holy Ghost was accepted as one person of the Trinity, but problems arose as to the relationship between the Holy Ghost and the Father and Son. The Nicene Creed (the one agreed at the Ecumenical Council of Chalcedon in 451) acknowledged the divinity of the Holy Ghost, referring to the 'Holy Ghost ... who proceedeth from the Father'.

In 589 a local council at Toledo added the words 'and the Son' (in Latin *filioque*) to this, an action that was absolutely forbidden by earlier ecumenical councils. In time the whole Western Church adopted these new words. The addition was re-affirmed in 796 by a synod of the Western Church at Fréjus, and soon afterwards it was approved by Charlemagne (*c.*742–814), who seems to have had no understanding whatsoever of the theological implications. Now the *filioque* was Western orthodoxy. For theologians the matter was one of the utmost importance. Adherents of the Western Church accused those in the East of heresy because they omitted the *filioque* from the creed. As the Eastern Churches pointed out it was the Western Church that had fallen into heresy by tampering with the creed without ecumenical authority.[118] This dispute contributed to the great schism between the Eastern Churches and the Western Church. The insertion is still adhered to by the Roman and Protestant Churches. In the Anglican Church it is confirmed in Article 5 of the 39 Articles. Naturally, it is still considered heretical by the Eastern Churches.

The Trinity

So the Father is God, the Son is God, and the Holy Ghost is God.
And yet they are not three Gods, but one God.

The Creed of St Athanasius

The doctrine of the Trinity asserts that God has three *persons*: the Father, Son, and Holy Ghost. It seems to have been introduced into the Church around AD 180 and was first stated explicitly by Tertullian, who is now regarded as a heretic, around the end of the second century.

The doctrine of the Trinity is nowhere mentioned in Greek manuscripts of the Bible, except in passages that are acknowledged as late additions, such as Matthew 28:19, or in ambiguous passages, such as 2 Corinthians 13:14. A clear reference to the doctrine, the *Johannine comma*, was inserted into Latin translations of the New Testament (at 1 John 5:7), from where it found its way into the Authorised Version. Footnotes in modern translations confirm that additions were made to the original text, generally without mentioning the significance of the additions.

The idea of a divine Trinity had been popular in many older religions. The Hindus had, and still have, Brahma, Vishnu and Shiva (Creator, Preserver and Destroyer). The Egyptians had a Trinity comprising Osiris, Isis and Horus (Father, Mother and Son), while the Babylonians had An, Bel and Ea (Heaven, Earth and Underworld). One Roman goddess was worshipped as a triple deity with a similar division of responsibility: Luna, Diana and Hecate (Sky, Earth and Underworld respectively). The Romans also adopted an Etruscan Trinity (Tinia, Uni and Menvra) and converted them into their own threesome: Jupiter, Juno and Minerva. The Greeks divided the Universe between three brothers: Zeus, Poseidon and Hades (Heaven, Sea and Underworld). Even Plato and his followers thought of his three *archical* (i.e. original) principles as three gods. In fact the Greeks had many examples of divine Trinities, some of them regarded as single entities with three aspects. For example, the three Fates were regarded as a single entity. Other triads include the Graia, the Gorgons, the Furies, the Horai, and the Charities or Graces.[119] According to a story related by Hesiod, there were originally three Muses. Moon goddesses were often threefold, their three persons representing different lunar phases. *Hecate*, one of a threesome already mentioned, was associated with places where three roads met, and where statues with three faces were set up. Most significantly of all, Zeus himself was worshipped as a divine Trinity.[120]

The Egyptian threesome of Father, Mother and Son seems to have been the Trinity most favoured by early Christians who sought to fit their theology into a known pattern. They saw the role of Mother in the divine family being played by *Sophia*, the Divine or Holy Wisdom. The Father, his Word and his Wisdom were described explicitly as a Triad, by a late second-century Bishop of Antioch.[121] But the Church Fathers were not keen on women, so Sophia lost her place in the divine family. By the fifth century AD her position in the divine threesome had been taken over by the *Holy Spirit*.[122] So it was that the Christian Trinity consists of Father, Son (= *Word*) and Holy Spirit.

The concept of a Christian Trinity seems to have taken some centuries to develop, slowly accommodating Greek ideas. Some early Christians who knew of the doctrine of the Trinity rejected it as an invention. The Ebionites rejected it, and so did Cerinthus and Carpocrates. Before the Ecumenical Council of Nicæa in 325, God the Father had been supreme. Afterwards the *Word* (*logos*) was co-equal, and later still so was the Holy Ghost. Now God would comprise three co-equal persons. Anyone who preferred the earlier orthodoxy, with the Father being supreme, would not be tolerated. In 386, a Spanish bishop called Priscillian, who held the pre-Nicene line, became the first Christian in Western Europe to be executed for heresy.

With opposition eliminated, the doctrine of the Trinity became established in time in both Eastern and Western Churches. It was adopted by the Anglican Church and appears in the first of the 39 Articles of Religion. To deny the Trinity was for centuries heretical and blasphemous, and therefore punishable by death. Nevertheless learned men did deny it. Some who rejected it came to be known as Unitarians, because they stressed the Unity not the Trinity of God. Many dissenting sects, including some Presbyterians and Congregationalists, are Unitarian. Jehovah's Witnesses consider the doctrine of the Trinity to be an invention of the Devil. Others consider the concept of one God with three 'persons' to be meaningless.

The whole area has become a philosophical quagmire. Many Christians regard as totally meaningless what others consider to be central to their faith. The World Council of Churches has sometimes required member Churches to be Trinitarians: sometimes it has not.

Jesus Visiting Hell

He descended into Hell.
The Apostles' Creed

It is a common Christian belief that Christ descended into Hell after his death and remained there until his resurrection three days later. The idea was that Jesus had gone to Hell to preach to the patriarchs and prophets, and to rescue them from torment. This incident is known as the *Harrowing of Hell*. The story has no biblical foundation. Indeed it clearly contradicts the words of Jesus when he said that one of the men crucified with him would be with him that day in paradise (Luke 23:43).

The visit was presaged by other gods. The Canaanite god Baal, for example, descended into the realm of Mot, the god of death from where the High God El attempted to redeem him. Greek heroes often visited Hades on rescue missions. Theseus had gone there to rescue Persephone; Orpheus had been to retrieve his wife Euridice. Hercules went to capture the three-headed guard dog Cerberus. Perhaps inspired by Greek stories, someone somewhere inserted into biblical texts a mention of the Lord God visiting the dead and preaching to them. Some of the Church Fathers were evidently misled by these insertions, which they took to be genuine.[123] The insertions were later identified as bogus and are omitted from all versions of the Bible now in common use.

The belief that Christ went down to Hell seems to have become popular in the fourth century, especially amongst the Arians, who are now regarded as heretics. The belief caught on in the Western Church, and found its way into the Apostles' Creed. It is accepted by the Anglican Church, specifically in Article 3 of the 39 Articles. Nonconformists are divided about it, sometimes even within the same denomination. For example, British Methodists generally accept it, but American ones do not, and therefore omit mention of it from their version of the Apostles' Creed.

The Resurrection

The third day he rose again from the dead,
He ascended into Heaven,…

The Apostles' Creed

The concept of life after death and resurrection had been unknown to the Jews before they were exposed to Greek influences. This explains why resurrection is mentioned in the Old Testament only in late apocalyptic writings,[124] i.e. around and after the lifetime of Jesus. It also explains why traditionalist Jews such as the Sadducees rejected the concept, as did some early Christians (e.g. 1 Corinthians 15:12).[125] The Greek influence explains why other early Christians adopted the view that resurrected bodies would be spherical: resurrected bodies would be perfect, and Plato had described the sphere as the perfect shape.

There is no explanation of the doctrine of the Resurrection anywhere in scripture, so Church scholars have had to resort to apocryphal backwaters such as 2 Maccabees, 1 Enoch, and 2 Baruch in order to try to make sense of it. The present doctrine is based on the words of St Paul, especially his account in 1 Corinthians 15. As a Greek Jew, Paul would have known that his gentile target audience would be familiar with the idea of the offspring of a god and a mortal being raised from the dead to become immortal. Herakles (Hercules), Dionysus (Bacchus), Æskelepios (Asclepius), Castor and Orion were all credited with having done it. Roman emperors were ascribed divine fathers, and were almost routinely promoted to gods after their own deaths. The concept of a mortal having been raised from the dead as an immortal thus provided an established model for the doctrine of the Resurrection.

That the doctrine was not accepted by all was acknowledged by Paul himself in 1 Corinthians 15:12. At some stage in the early centuries after Jesus' death, resurrection stories were apparently added to the gospels – not all appear in the earliest known (fourth-century) manuscripts. Some early Christians rejected the Resurrection. The Spanish bishop Priscillian, the first Christian in Western Europe to be executed as a heretic, denied both the Resurrection and the Trinity – both of them novel doctrines at the time.

The doctrine of the resurrection is now accepted by all the main denominations. It is affirmed in Article 4 of the 39 Articles of the Anglican Church.

Original Sin

For as in Adam all die, even so in Christ shall all be made alive.
1 Corinthians 15:22

The doctrine of Original Sin asserts that all people since Adam and Eve (with one or two exceptions) have been born sinful. It is based on a passage from Romans:[126]

> Wherefore, as by one man sin entered into the world, and death by sin; and so death passed upon all men, for that all have sinned:

For over three centuries this was interpreted in a number of different ways. Towards the end of the fourth century, St Augustine suggested that it meant that sin was conveyed through the sex act to any child thereby conceived.[127] The idea seems to have been as much a product of Augustine's previous religion, Manichæism, as anything else,[128] but it cannot have helped that he was using a faulty Latin translation of the Bible. The original Greek says that we all die because we all sin, but Augustine's Latin text said that we all die because of Adam, in whom we all sin. So it was that Augustine founded his doctrine of Original Sin on a misunderstanding.

Augustine held that baptism removed the stain of Original Sin. Babies who died unbaptised were thus sinful and destined for Hell. The doctrine was condemned as a novelty by some but accepted by others, and came to be accepted as part of orthodox belief in the Western Church.

Despite its Old Testament justification, the doctrine of Original Sin was accepted neither by the Jews nor later by the Muslims. It was regarded with scepticism in the Eastern Christian Churches, where it was never accepted into orthodoxy. Even in the Western Church it has been argued about by scholars ever since its first exposition. The fate of unbaptised children was particularly troubling, and they were later consigned to a holding area, called *Limbo,* located on the borders of Hell according to the Western theologians, although this place remained unknown to Eastern theologians.*

The biblical passage quoted might be used to support an argument that death is caused by sin, but it does not even hint that sin can be passed from parent to child like a sexually transmitted disease, a premise that lies at the heart of the doctrine. Nevertheless, all the main denominations in the Western Church accept it, and it appears in Article 9 of the 39 Articles of the Anglican Church.

Transubstantiation

This is my body which is given for you:...
Luke 22:19

At the Last Supper Jesus is represented as having told his disciples that the bread was his body and the drink was his blood.

> And as they did eat, Jesus took bread, and blessed, and brake it, and gave to them, and said, Take, eat: this is my body. And he took the cup, and when he had given thanks, he gave it to them: and they all drank of it. And he said unto them, This is my blood of the new testament, which is shed for many. (Mark 14:22–4, cf. Luke 22:19–20 and Matthew 26:26–8)

In Luke 22:19 Jesus tells the apostles that they should remember him when they take and eat bread. It is not clear that this injunction refers to any occasion other than the Last Supper. Wine is not mentioned in the injunction, the other gospels do not mention the injunction at all. Nowhere is it suggested that it applies to anyone except the apostles. To

---

* Even Western theologians were not always fully agreed on the nature of Limbo. St Augustine's teaching was that unbaptised infants burned for all eternity. St Thomas Aquinas said they enjoyed 'natural happiness'. According to Pope Pius X 'they do not enjoy God, but they do not suffer either'. At the time of writing Pope Benedict XVI has tentatively admitted that Limbo might not exist after all, so it is still a mystery where the souls of those dead babies go.

justify these extensions it is necessary to refer to 1 Corinthians 11:23–6, and to John 6, especially 6:47–58.

From early times Christians have eaten bread and drunk wine in remembrance of the Last Supper. As so often, early Christians had a model at hand. Dionysus, the son of Zeus, had been killed and had risen from the dead. His followers drank wine and ate meat to symbolise his blood and his body. Some time after the early Christians began to imitate this practice, their version of it started taking on the characteristic of a solemn rite rather than a meal. The rite is now alternatively known as the Lord's Supper, Eucharist or Mass.

No Father of the Church asserted that the bread and wine became flesh and blood in any real sense. Later Christian scholars affirmed that they did, but none explained fully what this could mean. In the Middle Ages the question of exactly what the words *did* mean was systematically considered by theologians. Were the bread and wine truly converted into flesh and blood, or were they merely tokens, representing flesh and blood? On the one hand most Christians 'knew' that the bread would bleed if a nail were pushed into it, for example by a malicious sceptic. On the other hand bread still tasted like bread, and wine still tasted like wine. The answer, which made sense in the philosophy of the day, was that though the outward appearance remained unchanged, the substance of the bread and wine was transformed into flesh and blood. This view was defined and declared true by the Western Church at the Fourth Lateran Council in 1215. The supposed transformation of the substance is known as transubstantiation.

The Bible gives little if any support for the doctrine of transubstantiation. No Church Father affirmed it, and neither did any other early writer. Nevertheless it is still held by the Roman Church, despite the removal of its medieval philosophical underpinning by later philosophers. The Church of England has been ambivalent. Henry VIII (1491–1547) burned Lutherans for questioning the doctrine. On the other hand, Article 28 of the 39 Articles, agreed in 1562, states that transubstantiation cannot be proved by holy writ and is repugnant to the plain words of scripture. There is no explanation in Article 28 (or any of the others) as to what the words of Jesus do mean.

Incidentally, none of the gospels mentions what was in the cup offered by Jesus to his followers. Views differ. In early times a sect known as Aquarians used only water at the Eucharist. Some Churches use water mixed with wine. Others use wine only. At one time those who used wine adopted the practice of warming it to blood temperature.

The Atonement

…Christ; Who suffered for our salvation:…
The Creed of St Athanasius

Christianity teaches that mankind was reconciled to God through the sacrificial death of Christ. The idea is based on God's known requirement for sacrifices in the Old Testament, and a number of New Testament passages.[129] It also looks like a primitive 'aversion sacrifice'. Jesus' blood keeps the Devil at bay, just as the blood of the paschal lamb kept the angel of death at bay. Unfortunately the exact mechanism for the Atonement has never been explained. As one authority on Christian doctrine says:

> There is no authoritative decision or consensus of teaching which commits the Church to any theory about the details of the method of the Atonement.[130]

The prevailing view among the Church Fathers, and the view generally accepted for 1,000 years, was that the sacrifice was a ransom paid to Satan. St Anselm in the eleventh century saw it as a ransom paid not to Satan but to God, and in time this became the predominant view. Article 31 of the 39 Articles sees it as a propitiation and satisfaction but avoids mentioning to whom it was paid. In recent years many have seen Jesus' death not as a propitiatory sacrifice, but merely as an example to mankind.

A traditional teaching is that Masses constitute further propitiatory sacrifices for mankind, but such ideas were rejected by Protestants and by the Church of England. They are described in Article 31 of the 39 Articles as blasphemous fables and dangerous deceits.

Invocation of the Saints

I believe in ... The Communion of Saints...
The Apostles' Creed

The Invocation of the Saints is the asking of saints in Heaven for their intervention in worldly affairs. There is no mention of this practice in the Bible and no reference to it in Christian writings until the third century. The Invocation of the Saints was common throughout Christendom by the fourth century. Many Christians prayed to the saints just as they had previously prayed to their heathen gods. In fact in many cases Christian saints *were* their old heathen gods with a veneer of Christianity.

To counter charges of polytheism, the Church insisted that saints had no power themselves, they were merely mediators between God and man (as Jesus had been during the early years). Theologians disagreed as to how this might work. The Council of Trent was careful not to be specific. It declared that the Invocation of the Saints was good and useful, that all benefits come from God through the mediation of Jesus Christ, and that all superstition was to be put down (Session 25). The Church of England rejected the Invocation of the Saints as a fond (i.e. foolish) thing vainly invented (Article 22 of the 39 Articles). The Eastern Churches on the other hand permit the invocation not only of saints but also of the dead, an apparent remnant of ancient ancestor worship.

The Virgin Mary

...born of the Virgin Mary...
The Apostles' Creed

The biblical Mary was not particularly notable, especially if we discount the nativity stories as later additions. In the Bible there is no hint of her great merit, or of her being sinless. She is never given any title whatsoever. The only time she is mentioned by the Mark author is when Jesus rebuffs her.

Jesus rejected her along with the rest of his human family. He appeared to hundreds after his resurrection, including a number of women followers, but not to his mother. Biblical authors did not even bother to ensure consistency in naming her (12 Miriams, 7 Marias), and the author of John does not even bother to mention her by name. Other early Christian writers often failed to mention her at all.[131] Those that did were not necessarily complimentary. For example here are the views of some of the most important authorities in early Christianity, summarised by a leading authority on her:

> Irenaeus finds fault with her 'untimely haste' at Cana, and accepts that Christ did reprove her. Tertullian questions whether she believed in him at all. Origen thinks that though she did, her faith wavered at the end. John Chrysostom accuses her of trying to domineer and to 'make herself illustrious through her Son'.[132]

She is far from the modern idea of a living intercessor with God, and even further from her current role of 'Queen of Heaven'. How did she attain her present majestic, semi-divine, heights? We will now consider four doctrines concerning the Virgin Mary:

* her Immaculate Conception
* her virginity
* that she was the mother of God
* her Dormition and Assumption into Heaven

Mary's Immaculate Conception

This is the doctrine that the Virgin Mary was free from Original Sin from the moment of her conception. There is no hint of it in the Bible (the question could not arise until St Augustine had proposed the idea of Original Sin). When the question did arise all authorities agreed. Everyone except Jesus had been born in sin because his or her parents had indulged in sexual intercourse. St Anselm stated the orthodox view in the eleventh century:

> The very virgin from whom His manhood was taken was conceived in iniquities, and in sins did her mother conceive her; and with original sin was she born.[133]

Clearly it would not do to have a sinful woman giving birth to Jesus, so the theory arose that Mary was cleansed of her Original Sin after her own conception but before her birth. This was the line approved by Innocent III (pope 1198–1216) and accepted by all scholars of the thirteenth century. But popular sentiment was against such subtleties. The common people wanted a virgin who had always been without sin, an idea that had been condemned by St Bernard as a presumptuous novelty in the twelfth century.

The Franciscan John Duns Scotus in the fourteenth century became the first theologian of note to support the idea of Mary's sinless conception. St Thomas Aquinas opposed his view.[134] As usual the Franciscans supported Duns Scotus, and the Dominicans, Aquinas. Arguments rumbled on for centuries, both sides producing visionaries to whom the Virgin had appeared in person either to confirm or deny the doctrine according to the visionaries' pre-existing views (Franciscans, yes; Dominicans, no). St Thomas himself appeared in at least one vision to explain that he had not meant what he had written on the subject, and the Franciscans cited this as evidence.[135]

In time the controversy died down. The idea became more and more popular as Marian devotion developed. Eventually the time came to reverse the traditional line, even though there was no evidence, biblical or otherwise, concerning Mary's sinlessness. The doctrine of Mary's Immaculate Conception was defined as a dogma of the Roman Catholic Church by Pope Pius IX in *Ineffabilis deus* issued in 1854. He cited two biblical passages in support of the doctrine, both of which contained serious (and already known) errors of translation.[136]

The Eastern Churches reject the Immaculate Conception, as they reject the doctrine of Original Sin. The Anglican Church also rejects it. The heading to Article 15 of the 39 Articles states that Christ alone was without sin. Mary is not mentioned in the Article, presumably because the doctrine of her Immaculate Conception was not sufficiently well established in 1562 to call for specific repudiation.

Mary's Virginity

The biblical evidence for Mary's virginity is dealt with in detail later (pages 367–75). To summarise: the evidence that she was a virgin before the birth of Jesus is suspicious and contradictory; the evidence that she remained a virgin afterwards is non-existent.

The original impetus for the idea of a Virgin Birth seems to have been a mistranslation in the Septuagint, but the seed found fertile soil in the Hellenic world. Middle Eastern virgin goddesses were common. Among the best known were Hera (Juno), Hestia, Core (Persephone), Artemis, and Aphrodite (Venus). Aphrodite was the counterpart of many Middle Eastern virgin goddesses: Ashera, the consort of El; Ashtaroth; Ishtar; the Sumerian Inana; the Phoenician Astarte; the Canaanite Anath. They all seem to have provided ready prototypes for the Virgin Mary. Sometimes these virgins gave birth. The goddess Hera, the Queen of Heaven, for example gave parthenogenic birth to Typhaon and Aries, and according to some also to Hephæstus.[137] She regularly regained her virginity.[138] Again the goddess Pallas Athene was styled *Parthenos* (virgin) but also *Meter* (Mother).[139] And again, the virgin Core was said to have given birth to Aion.[140] Famous men were credited not only with having been fathered by gods, but sometimes with having been born of virgins. According to legend, Plato was fathered by the god Apollo on Perictione, her husband having been instructed by the god not to consummate his marriage.[141] Simon Magus, one of the false prophets mentioned in the New Testament, claimed that his mother was a virgin.[142]

Virgin births were regarded in the ancient world as only moderately impressive. One reason for this was the widespread belief in parthenogenesis and even the spontaneous creation of life. Also, impregnation was held to be possible by a number of methods that now seem questionable. The wind was thought to be able to impregnate unwary females, and all sorts of things found their way into women's wombs. The Buddha was supposed to have entered his mother's womb in the form of a white elephant while she slept. Happily it was not a full-sized elephant. In Greek mythology Perseus was supposedly born to Danaë after Zeus had seduced her in the form of a shower of gold. Zeus often adopted the form of birds to accomplish copulation, a theme familiar from the legend of Leda and the swan. He adopted the same form to couple with Nemesis, an eagle for Ægina, a quail for Leto, an eagle again for Asteria, a cuckoo on one occasion for Hera, and a pigeon for the nymph Phthia. It is possibly no coincidence therefore that the agent responsible for Mary's impregnation, the Holy Ghost, is traditionally represented in Christian art as another bird. The Holy Ghost is usually represented as a dove, a bird associated with love in ancient times.

Many early Christians rejected the story of the Virgin Birth. Certainly most Ebionites did. So did Cerinthus. The first mention of Mary retaining her virginity after the birth of Jesus occurs in the Book of James (see page 44), which dates from the middle of the second century.

The idea of perpetual virginity was discounted by fourth-century churchmen such as Helvidius, Jovinian and Bonosus, Bishop of Naïssus. It seems to have become popular in the fifth century, helped along by the opinions of St Jerome. Jerome was so keen on the benefits of virginity that he tried to make a case for the perpetual virginity not only of Mary, but of Joseph as well, contradicting the Book of James. Jewish writings of course failed to support the Virgin Birth, and for centuries Christian authorities would sequester and burn Jewish books explicitly for this reason.

Before leaving the subject of Mary's virginity, it is worth considering why it should have acquired such importance. One obvious answer is that it was developed to account for the fact that Mary became pregnant before she was married. Even if Joseph was not the father, there is at least one other earthly candidate, for early Christians were taunted with the charge that Jesus was the son of a Roman soldier called Pantheras.[143] Despite the efforts of the Church, there has been a continuing underground tradition that Jesus' parents were less than perfect. It is interesting that even when the Koran was written it was still thought necessary to deny that Jesus' father was a whore-monger or his mother a harlot (Koran 19:28).

Whatever the truth, there was another practical reason for Mary's virginity being considered so important. This was the attitude of the early Church Fathers to sex. The men who controlled the Church in its formative years had singular ideas about sex. They regarded virginity as the most suitable state for a devout Christian, and sexual intercourse as a regrettable but necessary evil. Also, Christianity in its early years benefited financially from its support for lifelong virginity. Women inherited equally with men under Roman law, and it became customary for powerful families to bring up their sons in the old religion and their daughters in the new one. If these daughters could be induced to accept that virginity was a particularly holy and desirable state, then the Church stood to grow rich by inheriting their worldly goods when they eventually died without heirs. This seems to have been one of the principal sources of finance for the early Church.

Whatever the reasons for the development of the doctrine, liberal churchmen have rejected it. It is quite likely that the majority of Anglican clergymen no longer believe in it. Article 2 of the 39 Articles affirms the Virgin Birth but makes no mention of Mary's perpetual virginity. The Roman Church has fairly consistently followed St Jerome's view. Mary's perpetual virginity was declared a dogma of the Roman Church by Pope Martin I at the First Lateran Council in 649 but fewer and fewer Roman Catholics now accept it, and the Second Vatican Council conspicuously refrained from proclaiming it to be an article of faith in 1964. To the Orthodox Church Mary is still 'Ever-Virgin' (*Aeiparthenos*), as she has been since 553.[144]

Mary, Mother of God

The question as to whether Mary was the mother of God did not arise until it became established that Jesus had been God incarnate. If Jesus was God, then it seemed to follow that Mary was the mother of God. Referring to Mary, Origen had first used the expression *Theotokos*, meaning 'God-Bearer' in the third century. Many Christians rejected the idea, along with the idea that Jesus was truly God. But others were attached to the idea of a Mother goddess.

A Church Council was called at Ephesus (431), the centre of worship of the Mother Goddess Artemis (Diana). After the usual rounds of argument among Church leaders (see pages 186–7) the title *Theotokos* was accepted by the council, and Artemis's great city became Mary's great city instead.

As so often, the council's decision caused a schism. It was reconsidered and confirmed by another council at Chalcedon (in 451), once again followed by schism.

Mary's Dormition and Assumption

There is no suggestion in the Bible and no evidence anywhere else that Mary's life ended in any way other than death. In early centuries there was no doubt about it: Mary had died like other human beings. St Augustine mentioned her death explicitly: 'Mary, born of Adam, died because of sin'.[145] For almost 2,000 years Christian scholars have disputed the site of her grave. Some have favoured Jerusalem, others Ephesus. But there also arose a story that she had fallen asleep in some secret location, and was still hibernating in some hidden corner. This idea, that Mary had not died, seems to have arisen in the fourth century. The earliest, apocryphal, sources date from then. In any case the story became popular in the East and from it developed the doctrine of Mary's Dormition, literally 'Mary's falling asleep'.

Late in the sixth century the Feast of the Dormition arrived in the West. Discarding the apocryphal sources, the real argument for Mary's avoidance of death appears to have been based on St Augustine's link between sex, sin and death. If Mary had been free of the taint of sex and sin, she would not have needed to die, because death is caused by sin. Slowly the story changed so that she was not asleep on Earth. Rather, she had ascended bodily into Heaven. Thus by the ninth century the Dormition was changing into the Assumption.

Protestants originally rejected the Assumption, but some have changed their minds. The feast of the Assumption was dropped from the Book of Common Prayer in 1549 but is observed locally by some Anglicans. That Mary ascended, body and soul into Heaven, was defined as dogma for the Roman Church by Pius XII in his bull *Munificentissimus deus* in 1950. In the bull he referred to eighth-century sources, but not the apocryphal writings on which they were based. His Holiness also omitted to explain how this dogma can be squared with the hundreds of miracle-working bones from Mary's body, preserved in church reliquaries around Europe.

The Eastern Churches still refer to the Dormition, but the doctrine has never been well defined, and many Orthodox Christians now believe in Mary's bodily Assumption into Heaven, though some promptly stopped believing in it when the Roman Church declared it to be dogma in 1950.[146] Many nonconformist sects regard the Assumption as an invention of the Roman Church formulated to support the cult of the Virgin.

Other Doctrines

...daily the trained parrot in the pulpit gravely delivers himself of these ironies,
which he has acquired second-hand and adopted without examination,
to a trained congregation which accepts them without examination...
Mark Twain (1835–1910), Thoughts of God

The examples given by no means exhaust the list of Christian doctrine that lack firm foundations. There is no account in scripture of Confirmation, nor ritual Anointing (Unction) of the Sick, nor the Fall of the evil angels, nor of Purgatory, nor of Limbo,[147] nor even of such a central doctrine as divine grace (which is concerned with the purported favour of God for humankind, especially in regard to salvation). As one authority on the subject says: 'There is no complete system of doctrine on the subject of grace laid down by any authoritative utterance of the whole Church or by an entire consensus of representative teachers'.[148] The list of unreliable doctrines could go on for pages. The shortage of reliable evidence for most doctrines is reflected by the differing views of the Eastern, Roman, Anglican and other Churches, all of which purport to teach the true word of God. Even within the Roman Church the traditional Thomist and Scotist schools differ on so many points of doctrine that they might almost be regarded as different religions.

Often there is no reliable support for doctrine at all. Early writers frequently failed to mention important doctrines, apparently because they were unaware of them. Sometimes they supported doctrines that are now considered heretical and rejected ones that are now considered orthodox. Often they contradicted one another.

The general pattern in the first few centuries is that some Christians adopt a popular pagan theme. It gains popularity and theologians refine it so that it can be accommodated into the body of acceptable Church doctrine. If possible, some sort of biblical justification is found for it, and if not, a suitable piece of text is inserted into the Bible. A Church Council eventually endorses it by a majority vote, and anathematises anyone who denies it. Those who do continue to deny it are condemned as heretics and persecuted into submission or extinction.

It is difficult to find any substantial doctrine that is clearly formulated, has explicit biblical support, and is free of the charge of having been borrowed from contemporary pagan religions. If consistency of teaching is sought as well, then the task appears impossible: not a single doctrine qualifies. An increasing number of Church scholars accept that almost all mainstream Christian doctrine was unknown to the biblical Jesus. It was developed after his death, largely borrowed from other religions, and subject to amendment in later centuries, often looking suspiciously as though it were determined by popular pressure and political expediency.

WHERE DID OTHER CHRISTIAN IDEAS
AND PRACTICES COME FROM?

*Christianity accepted as given a metaphysical system derived from
several already existing and mutually incompatible systems.*
Aldous Huxley (1894–1964), *Grey Eminence*

If we look for possible origins of concepts that we are accustomed to regard as characteristically Christian, we do not need to look far. Jesus and his disciples were all followers of the Jewish faith, so it is not surprising that the early Church drew heavily upon Judaism. The idea of one sacrifice serving to save many is characteristically Jewish. (Jesus seen as an *agnus dei* – a sacrificial lamb of God – is adapted from the story of the Passover where lamb's blood is used to save believers.) Jesus and his followers had worshipped in the Jewish Temple and attended synagogues. When Pauline Christianity subsequently evolved separate church buildings, these buildings were partially modelled on synagogues. The style and content of church services are based on Jewish ones: the reading of the holy scriptures interspersed with interpretation, psalms and prayers. Methods of prayer are Jewish methods. The use of chanting and singing are Jewish, and even Jewish words like *Alleluia* and *Amen* are retained, untranslated from the Hebrew. Christians adopted Jewish scripture, calling it the Old Testament. The practice of baptism is Jewish,[149] so is the use of holy water. The bread and wine of the Christian Eucharist replicate the bread and wine of a Jewish Passover meal, which is of course exactly what the Last Supper was.

The Jews had never believed in the immortality of the soul. There is no hint of it in the Mosaic laws, which promise rewards and threaten punishments only for this life, not for the next one. These ideas came to Judaism from the Hellenic world, where people had developed theories of the soul. To the Stoic philosophers for example the soul (*logos*) was the part of the body responsible for the senses, the power of speech, reproductive capacity, and reason. For other Greek philosophers it was the *psyche*. Although material, the soul (*logos* or *psyche*) survived the death of the rest of the body. Such ideas met opposition from Jewish traditionalists. Of the sects that had arisen by the time of Jesus, the Sadducees held firmly to the traditional line, while the Pharisees entertained the notions of an immortal soul, which would be rewarded or punished in the hereafter. This was a popular belief that became predominant in Judaism and was carried over to early Christianity. So too, in the century or two before Jesus, strong apocalyptic beliefs had developed within Judaism. Jewish literature from this time abounds in predictions about the imminence of the end of the world.

Ideas of God

Man is certainly stark mad; he cannot make a flea,
and yet he will be making gods by dozens.

Montaigne (1533–92)

Greek Gods

Onto its Jewish base Christianity built a structure that would appeal to the civilised world. In practice this meant that the new composite religion had to adopt an Hellenic appearance.

Religions in the classical world were a great deal more sophisticated than modern tales of Greek and Roman myths would have us believe. For one thing the Greek philosophers had long believed that there was but one deity, and that the numerous gods worshipped throughout the known world were merely different manifestations of that one supreme god, whom we usually call Zeus.[150] Romans too spoke of a single God. Edicts issued by the Emperor Diocletian, whom the Christians regarded as a pagan and an enemy, referred to the deity as a single entity.

The Roman counterpart of Zeus was Jupiter, and for centuries Jupiter would be confused and confabulated with the Christian God. Well into the Middle Ages, Dante (1265–1321) could still refer to the Christian God as 'almighty Jupiter',[151] and it is not difficult to find Christian works of art showing God the Father in poses that echo those of Jupiter, for example casting thunderbolts towards earth. At one time it was popular to show Christ in a similar pose hurling divine bolts at those condemned to Hell.

Zeus had originally been a sky god, controlling the weather. He was also addressed by titles such as *Pater*: 'Father', *Basileus*: 'King', and *Sôtêr*: 'Saviour'. Such practices could easily be combined with Christianity while it was still in its formative years. The familiar image of the Almighty sitting on his judgement throne is a straight adoption from conventional representations of Zeus the king. The Greeks conventionally pictured their gods as huge figures dressed all in white, and the Christian God duly adapted himself to these conventions.

The title *Saviour* was not only applied to Zeus. It was also applied to the Sun god Helios, to heroes who attained immortality such as Dionysus, Herakles and Æskelepios, and to others. The title was used in many resurrection cults. It was accorded to vegetation spirits who lived and died, then rose anew and lived again, just as crops and flowers and trees did each year. The Jews applied the title to Yahweh, and the Egyptians applied it to Osiris. The Romans applied it to their emperors: Augustus was on occasion described as Saviour (*Sôtêr*). Augustus was also called 'son of God' (*theou hyios*)[152] as well as simply 'God' (*theos*). Like other emperors he was also called 'Lord' (*kyrios*) so Christians were already familiar with the idea of using all these titles for human beings.

A jealous cruel God who had always favoured the Jews was not likely to be accepted by gentiles. Greek theology had already outgrown parochial tribal deities. Followers of Orpheus for example exalted the supreme god as follows:

> Zeus is the first, Zeus is the last, the god with the dazzling lightning. Zeus is the head, Zeus is the middle, of Zeus all things have their end. Zeus is the foundation of the earth and the starry sky. Zeus is male, Zeus is an immortal woman. Zeus is the breath of all things, Zeus is the sweep of unwearying flame. Zeus is the roots of the sea, Zeus is the Sun and Moon. Zeus is the King, Zeus is the beginner of all things, the god with the dazzling lightning. For he has hidden all things within himself, and brought them forth again, into the joyful light, from his sacred heart, working marvels.[153]

There are many points of interest in this passage. As well as establishing the concept of a supreme deity, it has a tone that appeals to modern ears: particularly the mention of female attributes. Even the concept of a 'sacred heart' is already here. It also shows that the formula concerning the Alpha and the Omega was not an original idea: 'I am the Alpha and the Omega, saith the LORD God, which is and which was and which is to come' (Revelation 1:8, cf. 21:6 and 22:13). Similar concepts are expressed in the *Egyptian Book of the Dead*: 'I am yesterday, today, and tomorrow'; and in Plato's *Laws* (4:7): 'God the beginning and the end'.

Beliefs, practices, customs and conventions were all taken over by the new Christian religion. The letters D.O.M., standing for the formula *Deo Optimo Maximo* (To God the Best and Greatest), may still be found in churches and over church doors. It was originally addressed to Jupiter. The chi-rho monogram, or *labarum*, adopted by early Christians is based on the *labrys*, an ancient cult symbol of Zeus. The Greek letters *chi* and *rho* (χρ, in English *ch* and *r*) had long been an accepted abbreviation of the word *chrēstus*, which means 'auspicious'. They had been used to mark an 'auspicious' passage in pagan texts written on papyri. Now they provided an abbreviation of the word *Christ*. When the Emperor Constantine adopted this *chi-rho* monogram on his imperial standard, it was a symbol of good omen for everyone, non-Christians and Christians alike.

Other popular pagan images were adopted too. The pagan 'Good Shepherd' was one. In the third century Christ was depicted as a traditional Good Shepherd, with a lamb over his shoulder. His physical appearance was amended to the existing pattern – a pattern based on the god Mercury, the guardian of the flocks, who carried a sheep on his shoulders. Thus on carvings in the Vatican Museum Jesus appears as a beardless Roman youth. In some representations he has even acquired a Roman toga. Another acquisition, still sported by bishops, was the shepherd's crook, inherited from Roman, Greek and Egyptian gods such as Mercury, Pan, Apollo and Osiris.

Eastern Gods
Eastern religions also influenced religious thought, notably one founded by Zoroastra.* Between around 550 and 330 BC, Zoroastrianism had been the state religion of Persia (modern Iran). It remained influential for many centuries and survives today.‡ Muslims regard Zoroastrians as one of the *Peoples of the Book*.^ Zoroastrianism influenced other

---

* Zoroastra or Zoroaster is thought to have lived c.600 BC. Zoroaster is the Greek form of the name Zarathustra (as in Nietzsche's 'Thus Spake Zarathustra').
‡ Scattered Zoroastrian groups still survive in Iran. Others were obliged to flee Persia to avoid Muslim persecution in the seventh century AD. Some of them were to become the Parsees of modern India.
^ The Peoples of the Book are those who, Muslims believe, have received divine scriptures from Allah.

religions with which it came into contact, notably Christianity, and was highly respected (according to Church scholars the three magi were Zoroastrians). An offshoot of Zoroastrianism, Manichæism, also influenced Christianity. It was originated by Mani, a Persian born in Babylonia around the year AD 216, who claimed to be the Holy Spirit. Like a number of such innovators, he was not popular among the leaders of the local established religion and was executed for his troubles. Manichæism developed existing Zoroastrian concepts, and it was from here that the idea of heavenly hosts engaged in constant battle with Satan's armies originated, to be adopted by Christianity. In the East the religion reached as far as China where it survived up to the eleventh century. In Western Europe it reached as far as Spain and Gaul. It influenced church leaders in important Christian centres such as Alexandria and Carthage.

Another offshoot of Zoroastrianism, Mithraism, was introduced to the Roman Empire at least two generations before the birth of Jesus, and flourished at the same time that Christianity began to spread. The parallels between Mithraism and Christianity are so close that they are unlikely to be coincidental. Mithra (or Mithras) was the son of the supreme deity. His birth was miraculous and attended by shepherds. His death was sacrificial. He rose again after dying, having descended into Hades in the interim. To his adherents he was 'The Lord', and possessed the usual attributes of a Sun god. He promised resurrection, a final judgement, and eternal life. Rites involved bells, candles, holy water, and a service similar to the Christian Mass, including a sacred meal. Heaven and Hades were strongly contrasted. Sunday was the holy day at a time when Christians were still keeping the Jewish Sabbath day holy. Mithra's birthday was celebrated on 25th December, the common birthday of most Sun gods. An Easter festival was also celebrated to mark his sacrifice and his victory over death. The high priest, addressed as *papa*, sat in a sacred chair in the Mithraic temple on the Vatican Hill. Mithraism was a favourite of Roman soldiers who spread it around the Roman Empire. Had its leaders not made the marketing error of restricting membership to men, it might well have been one of the world's major religions today. Instead, only fragments remain. Temples of Mithras are discovered from time to time – there is one in the City of London. The old sacred chair from the Mithraic temple on the Vatican Hill now resides in the Vatican palace, taken over by another *papa*.

Sun Gods

Philosophers in the Hellenic world had ideas of God that compare with those of modern theologians. However, sophisticated ideas have never been an asset to popular religions. Throughout history the masses have favoured gods who can be seen. Perhaps for this reason Jesus was sometimes identified with Apollo, the Greek and Roman Sun god whose journey across the sky could be seen each day by everyone. Some representations of Jesus are identifiable only because of their associated Christian symbolism. Without these symbols, his representation is identical to Apollo's.

The Romans called their Sun god, a successor to Apollo, *Sol Invictus*, the Unconquered Sun. The religion had come to Rome in the second century from Syria. It was popular in the army, and the Emperor Aurelian adopted it, appointing himself its chief priest or *Pontifex Maximus*. The religion merged with the nascent Christian religion, and soon it was difficult to distinguish between Jesus and *Sol Invictus*. Around AD 200 the Church Father Clement of Alexandria could happily contemplate Christ driving his chariot across the sky like a Sun god. A third-century mosaic discovered under the high altar of St Peter's in Rome shows Jesus as a Sun god riding the solar chariot, pulled by horses, just like Apollo's.

As some commentators have noted, the Sun god transformed himself from Apollo to Sol to Jesus Christ apparently without difficulty. Jesus retained Sol's nimbus, and it can still be seen around his head in Christian art (often referred to as a halo). Sol, like Apollo and Helios, had probably borrowed his nimbus from the Zoroastrian Sun god Ahura Mazda, who seems to have acquired it from Indian gods, who in turn seem to have copied the divine fashion from China.

Christians knelt to the East, the direction of the rising Sun, like followers of other Sun gods. For a while Jesus became a typical Sun god, hardly distinguishable from Apollo. After all, Apollo too was a supreme god, uncreated, eternal, timeless and undeviating. Christian hymns were addressed to *Sol Invictus*.[154] In the fifth century Christians were still reluctant to turn their backs on Sol. They walked backwards up the steps of St Peter's in Rome so that they could remain face-to-face with the Sun god in the early morning. Gildas, the first British historian, described Jesus Christ in the sixth century as 'the true sun', and there were English Christians who thought that Christ was the Sun well into the seventeenth century.[155] The altar in the overwhelming majority of church buildings is still to be found at the east end, and the axis of churches often aligns with the rising Sun on a special day.

Constantine, the Roman emperor conventionally considered responsible for the success of Christianity, had himself represented in the likeness of a Sun god on a porphyry column in his new capital city. He seems to have believed that his deity was a Sun god. Certainly he made little distinction between Sol and Jesus. His coinage continued to depict the Sun god even after his supposed adoption of Christianity. His stated reason for making Sunday a day of rest was respect for the Sun.[156] Christians adopted this new day of rest, when even the law courts were shut. Indeed, so closely did they identify with it that today we do not question why the Christians' special day should fall not on the original Sabbath (Saturday) but on another day, nor why that day is in English called not *God-day* but *Sun-day*.* In the West the birthday of the Sun god, *Die Natalis Invicti Solis*, was 25th December. This same date was also the birthday of other Sun gods.[157] Jesus' birthday on the other hand was in March, or September, or January – there was no general agreement, although 6th January was probably the favourite. Around the middle of the fourth century, 25th December replaced 6th January as Jesus' official birthday in Western Christendom. Presumably it was around the same time that part of the pagan liturgy used on 25th December was adopted into the Christmas celebrations of the Christian Church.[158]

Sunday was central. Not only was the Christians' weekly holy day moved to Sunday, but Easter was moved to a Sunday as well. Easter had originally been celebrated on the 14th of the Jewish month of Nisan: the lunar month starting with the first full Moon after the spring equinox. Western Christians shifted it to the following Sunday, but it still depended upon the lunar cycle, which is why Easter falls at different dates in different years, and why it still causes so much confusion. A complicated set of tables is provided in the Anglican Book of Common Prayer for calculating the date of Easter for each year up to 2299.‡

* In other languages of course Sunday is called the 'Lord's Day', e.g. Spanish *Domenica*, French *Dimanche*, etc.
‡ The calculations, involving mysterious golden numbers, are necessary to ensure that 'ecclesiastical full moons' coincide with 'real full moons'.

Mystery Gods and Hero Gods and Others

Sometimes Jesus was identified with Orpheus, the son of Apollo. Orphism was a mystery religion which taught that, after death, the human soul might obtain eternal bliss; or might be subject to temporary or eternal torment, depending on its behaviour on Earth. Like many other pre-Christian mystery religions, Orphism featured a miraculous birth and resurrection. Religious practices included a sacramental meal of bread and wine, which represented the eating of the god's flesh and the drinking of his blood. The Christian Mass is remarkably similar to this and to related forms of love-magic recorded in ancient papyri. The priest-magician identified himself with a god, then by divine power changed certain approved food and drink into the god's flesh and blood. The priest-magician then offered them to be consumed by those he intended to bind in love.

Jesus possessed similarities not only with Orpheus, but also with many other heroes and gods. Orion for example experienced a miraculous birth. During his life he performed miraculous feats such as walking on water.[159] He died and was resurrected to take his place as a god. Æskelepios, another man who attained immortality, was in the habit of returning to Earth to carry out miracle cures and to foretell the future.[160] The Greek god Dionysus, the son of Zeus, was killed and rose from the dead.

Early Christians seem to have adopted a number of ideas from the Dionysus cult, and from similar mystery religions, but not all survive. Festivals in the god's honour involved riotous behaviour, drinking and sexual indulgence. These festivals were known as *Phallica*, or *Orgia*, or *Bacchanalia*, Bacchus being the Roman equivalent of Dionysus. Early Christians held love feasts, *agapes*, which adopted many orgiastic and bacchic practices. But these parties did not fit well with Church leaders' attitudes. St Paul was already complaining about Christians' drunkenness and misbehaviour (1 Corinthians 11:27–34). Sex was an even bigger problem, and agapes were eventually condemned by the Council of Carthage in 397, having become such scandals that they had to be suppressed altogether.

The Greeks had a concept of deification: the transformation of a human being into a god. Their term for it was *apotheosis*. But the idea was not specifically Greek; indeed it was extremely widespread. In early times kings throughout the known world had been gods. Later kings tended to become gods only after they had died. They were frequently accorded divine parentage: generally a divine father and a mortal mother. There was also generally something special about the conception of the king (or other prominent ruler). For example, after his death Alexander the Great was worshipped as a divinity. According to one story, he had been fathered by a god (apparently Zeus) either in the form of a shaft of lightning or a serpent.[161] According to another story, Romulus, the legendary founder of Rome, was born of a vestal virgin, and fathered by the god Mars.[162] The Emperor Augustus, in whose reign Jesus was born, was thought of as Mercury incarnate, assigned by Jupiter to expiate human guilt.[163] Julius Caesar was spoken of as 'god manifest', offspring of Aries and Aphrodite, and common saviour of human life.[164]

Even Greek philosophers had been credited with divinity. Empedocles claimed himself to be immortal, Epicurus was hailed as a god, and both Pythagoras and Plato were claimed to be of divine parentage.[165] Heroes and demigods were routinely ascribed a divine parent. Æneas was supposedly the son of the mortal Anchises and the goddess Aphrodite.[166] Theseus claimed to be the son of Poseidon and a mortal woman, Aethra.[167] Perseus was the son of Zeus, who impregnated a mortal woman, Danaë, by coming upon her in the form of a shower of gold (this story was known to early Christians and suggested possible parallels for Jesus' divine conception). Herakles was said to be the son of Zeus and a mortal woman, Alkmene.[168] So, according to some, was Dionysus. Æskelepios was believed to be the son of Apollo and the mortal Koronis.[169] Orion was said to be the son of Poseidon and the mortal Euryale.[170] The twins Castor and Pollux were born of Leda, a mortal woman, but fathered by Zeus. Pollux was born immortal, while Castor was born mortal and (like Herakles, Dionysus, Æskelepios, and Orion) was granted immortality after death. Generally these sons of gods lived exceptional lives before winning full deification. Herakles for example worked miracles, overcame evil and established peace throughout the world. He triumphed over death by descending into Hades, and then became a god.

For Roman emperors *apotheosis* took the form of a formal ceremony, authorised by the Senate, at which an eagle was released to carry the dead man's soul to Heaven. Birds were widespread symbols for the soul, and the idea was a popular one. In European art kings are sometimes shown undergoing *apotheosis*. In the church of Sant' Ignazio in Rome, the founder of the Jesuits is depicted in the same way. The pattern was a standard one: a divine birth accompanied by miraculous signs, a virtuous life also attended by miracles, followed by apotheosis. Details were invented to fit the standard pattern. This seems to have been done routinely and quite openly. The orator Menander in the third century AD provided advice to putative praise-poets. In his Orations for Orators he suggests various topics to praise. Amongst them are the subject's birth, for which he suggests inventing a divine portent.

Because Roman emperors expected to undergo apotheosis and become gods when they died, they were not too keen to learn that according to Christian teaching their fate was otherwise. To make their new religion more palatable, a compromise was achieved, by which newly expired Christian emperors became saints. Constantine thus became St Constantine. Not taking any chances, the Senate recorded their gratitude after his death for the 'divine' memory of Constantine, as they were to do for a string of subsequent Christian emperors.

Popular but inconvenient gods were cleared away, generally in one of two ways. Those who were not demoted to demons were promoted to saints. Similarly for goddesses: in Europe alone, thousands of local female divinities transmogrified into the Virgin Mary, a fact that explains why even today she is represented in such conspicuously different ways in different areas of Italy, Spain and Portugal. Even the great Isis was absorbed in this way. The conventional image of the Madonna and child (*Maria lactans*) bears a striking resemblance to older representations of *Isis lactans* – the goddess Isis nursing her holy child, the infant god Horus. This is not too surprising since the conventional depiction of *Isis lactans* was simply adopted by Christians for *Maria lactans*.

Heaven

What man is capable of the insane self-conceit of believing that an
eternity of himself would be tolerable even to himself?
George Bernard Shaw (1856–1950)

The Jews had, at least in the centuries before Jesus, thought of God as a ruler surrounded by lesser gods who gave him counsel. This heavenly court is mentioned in Psalm 82:1 and 6, and described in the opening passages of Job.

In the Roman milieu, Jesus started to be represented as an imperial ruler. When depicted in art he sat on a throne with purple cushions. His head radiated imperial light, later to blossom into crown and nimbus. Like an emperor he had his hand and foot kissed. He reigned from a heavenly imperial court, at which all found a place. Mary became his consort: 'Wearing a crown, clothed with gold-embroidered mantle, she was proclaimed queen of all creation and placed on the right hand of her Son and King.'[171] The apostles joined a heavenly Senate, the angels became heavenly courtiers and heralds, and various saints found themselves in the role of ambassadors, waiting to be ushered into the Presence for an heavenly audience in order to supplicate for their earthly clients. This heavenly court was the centre of a celestial kingdom beyond the clouds, the core of Heaven. The place was much like the home of the Greek gods, described by Homer in the *Odyssey*, 6:42:

> Olympus, the abode of the Gods, stands fast forever. Neither is it shaken by winds nor ever wet with rain, nor does snow fall upon it, but the air is outspread clear and cloudless, and over it hovers a radiant whiteness.

Such ideas were combined with Jewish ideas of the seven Heavens, and synthesised by theologians like St Ambrose to produce a detailed ultra-mundane geography. As well as the seven Heavens there was Hades (a sort of waiting room for the Day of Judgement) and three regions of Hell. The Greeks had concepts of eternal Heaven and Hell, and the various mystery religions all had their own versions of their geography. Descriptions as detailed as Dante's were produced, explaining locations, passageways and gateways between the main areas.

Hell

The infliction of cruelty with a good conscience is a delight to moralists.
That is why they invented hell.
Bertrand Russell (1872–1970), *Sceptical Essays*

In Greek thought Hades was the realm of the dead, located in the under-world. It was populated by shades that carried on an anaemic existence, mere shadows with no real substance, memory or feelings. In later times Hades developed distinct regions. One was a sort of Paradise, the Elysian fields, where heroes lived an active, rather sporty, afterlife. Another was Tarsus, where the especially wicked were punished. It was here that Tantalus spent eternity being *Tantalised* with water and fruit, and Sisyphus spent the rest of time rolling a great stone up a hill. Here too Ixion was bound to an ever-rotating fiery wheel, the daughters of Danaos tried perpetually to fetch water in sieves, and a serpent continually devoured Tityos's liver, or vultures fed on his entrails, depending on which account one favoured. Early Christians identified Hades or Tarsus with the Jewish Sheol. The word *Sheol* appears to mean little more than *grave*, though there is no surviving exposition of mainstream Jewish thought on the nature of the place.[172] The Jews also referred to *Gehenna*, originally the name of a valley on the outskirts of Jerusalem where other gods were worshipped. Later it had become a refuse tip where rubbish, dead animals and executed criminals were burned. The name therefore came to denote an extremely unpleasant place.

Where Jesus apparently refers to Hell in the New Testament, as in Matthew (5:22), the original Greek text uses the word *Gehenna*. When the word Hell appears in the Old Testament it generally corresponds to the Hebrew *Sheol*. The English name *Hell* is of Norse origin. It is a variant of the word *hel*, the name of the underworld, and of the goddess whose domain it was. The domain of *hel* bore little relation to the contemporary ideas of Hell. For one thing everyone, except warrior heroes, went to Hell after their death. The word simply means 'a covered place' and is closely related to the modern English *hall*. It is the same element that occurs in *Valhalla*, literally the 'hall of the slain', which is where those who died in battle were taken by the Valkyries. In northern countries, where people feared the cold, Hell was a place of extreme cold, while its Mediterranean counterpart was to become a place of extreme heat. In English we have taken the Mediterranean concept but given it the northern European name.

The concept of Hell was particularly useful to early Christians. For one thing it provided a stick to contrast with the carrot of Heaven. For another it fitted well with Zoroastrianism, the religion of Persia that influenced much of the Middle East. Zoroaster taught that a constant war is being fought between the forces of light and dark, representing good and evil respectively. The forces of good were led by Ahura Mazda, the god of light (after whom modern Mazda light bulbs are named); the forces of evil were led by Ahriman, an early prototype of Satan. It was the influence of Zoroastrianism that had introduced a personalised Satan into Judaism.[173]

Having adopted a personalised Devil the early Christians needed a concrete image for him. The Jews had been well aware of the Canaanite and Phoenician god *Baal*, a horned god, whose name means something like 'master', 'owner' or 'husband'. Although the Jews never saw him as anything other than what he was, a rival god, he was adopted by Christians as an *alter ego* of Satan, as hundreds of other rival gods were to be similarly adopted in the centuries to come. Like the ancient Persians and Egyptians, Christians liked to personify their image of evil as composite zoomorphic creations – monstrous animal montages. Another early alias was Pan, the Greek god of shepherds. His body resembled that of a satyr, half-human and half-goat. He had horns, a tail and cloven hoofs. Furthermore he had a reputation for lustfulness and an unpleasant habit of inducing fear among innocent passers-by. *Panic* is really *Panic fear*, literally fear inspired by the great god Pan.

Ideas could be picked up from any local religion, and in Rome there were many to choose from. Numerous sects converged on Rome. Anyone synthesising a new religion could choose from Judaism, classical Greek religions, Sun worship, resurrection cults, the worship of Isis and Osiris, and so on. By the Middle Ages Christians had settled on a complex composite Devil. He was large, black, ugly and hairy, with horns, a long tail, cloven hooves, and dragon's wings. He had fangs like a dog, claws like a bear, and a voice like a lion. He also breathed fire. There were many local variations, all reinforced by monks who made liberal use of such figures in mystery and miracle plays.

The idea of a judgement after death came from Egypt. Osiris gave judgement in the hall of the dead, weighing the heart of the newly deceased on a pair of scales against a feather representing truth and justice. Anubis held the scales. Those who passed the test were free to join others in the realm of the gods. Those who failed were eaten by Ahemait, the Devourer, part lion, part hippopotamus and part crocodile. The Græco-Romans adopted the idea of weighing the soul, calling it *psychostasis*, and nominating Hermes (Mercury) for the role of weigher-in-chief. Christians adopted it too. In countless churches throughout the world God is shown weighing the souls of the dead. St Michael has taken the role of Hermes/Anubis in holding the scales. Souls who pass the weighing test are accompanied to Heaven in triumph by angels, while those who fail are dragged into the jaws of a beast-like Devil, who munches them dramatically, just as Ahemait used to do.

Significantly the Devil is described in the Bible as being like a lion looking for people to devour (1 Peter 5:8). No one quite knows what another of his attributed names, Behemoth, means. A leading theory is that the name denotes a hippopotamus, recalling Ahemait. The crocodile also metamorphosed into Satan. A traditional image of the Egyptian god Horus, dressed in Roman military uniform, mounted on a horse, piercing a crocodile with his lance, was lightly Christianised. Horus became St George. He kept his Roman uniform, still sat on his horse, and still wielded his lance, but now used it to skewer a satanic enemy representing evil incarnate – a sort of winged crocodile, which we usually call a dragon.

Old Gods, New Saints

> Vox populi, vox dei *(the voice of the people is the voice of God)*
> **Cited and denied by Alcuin (735–804)**
> **in a letter to Charlemagne**

As the god Ahemait transformed himself into Satan, so other gods found new roles in the Christian hierarchy. The Egyptian Osiris was transmogrified into St Onuphrius, and the god Dionysus (Roman Bacchus) into St Dionysius, St Bacchus, and several other saints. Venus became St Venere; Artemis, St Artemidos; Helios, St Elias; all of whom tend to be mysteriously omitted from modern lists of saints. Others have suffered downsizing. St Charity for example does much the same job as the Greek goddesses known as the three Charities. Sometimes there was cross-borrowing. St Mercourios took over from the god Mercury, and St Michael took over the warlike functions of Mars, but St Michael also took over some of the responsibilities of Mercury, for example the weighing of souls.

Many of the saints recognised by the mainstream Western Christian Churches are ancient gods who have been forcibly recruited into the ranks of the saints. Some were merely heroes. Hippolytus, son of Theseus, who died by being dragged along by horses, became St Hippolytus, who had supposedly been martyred in a similar way. The Irish St Bridget is none other than an ancient Celtic goddess, Brigid, who has slowly been losing her divinity over the centuries. St Vitus was a central European god, as was at least one of the saints called Valentine.

The phenomenon was neither restricted to Europe, nor to early Christianity. Modern depictions of Mexican saints are often indistinguishable from those of Aztec gods. At least one of Mary's multiple personalities is Aztec. In her persona as Our Lady of Guadeloupe, she looks just like a Central American native. In this guise she is a Christianised version of the 'Little Mother' – the Aztec earth goddess Tonantzín. (Believers still leave her votive offerings of corn, just as they did before the coming of Christianity.) New patron saints took over the portfolios of old patron gods. To give a few examples from the many hundreds available:

Greek God	Roman God	Christian Saint	Responsibility
Ares	Mars	Michael	battle
Poseidon	Neptune	Emygdius	earthquakes
Æskelepios	Asclepius	Pantaleon	physicians
Eros	Cupid	Valentine	love
Aphrodite	Venus	Catherine	young women

Just as Middle Eastern nations had angelic princes to protect and look after them, and just as ancient city-states had their own tutelary deities, so Christian countries and cities have patron saints to fulfil the same role. It is the duty of these god-saints to protect their citizens. They watch over their communities and avert famine, war, pestilence and other disasters. Romulus and Remus, divine protectors of Rome, were exchanged for new patrons, Peter and Paul, who took over the joint responsibility for the city. Some patron saints, like St Michael, St James and St George, joined in human battles to help their human charges, just as the ancient Greek gods did. Christian saints still look much like the gods they replaced. They have cults with annual festivals, as the gods once had. They listen to prayers, accept offerings, grant favours and work miracles, as the gods once did. Often they are described as being unnaturally tall or beautiful, or if not their appearance is sometimes exposed as a disguise, and sooner or later they eventually reveal themselves as tall and beautiful. The saints give off sweet smells, emit light from their bodies or faces, and speak in strange awe-inspiring voices, just like traditional gods.

In exchange for little gifts, saints cure illnesses, control the weather and grant other favours, just as the old gods used to do. Altars are dedicated to them, as they were once dedicated to the gods. So are shrines and other holy places, which are decorated with icons and wafted by incense, just like those of pagan gods. Statues of saints are taken, dressed up, crowned and publicly paraded in solemn procession each year, just as previously the statues of gods were removed, dressed up, crowned and publicly paraded in identical annual processions. Devotees keep vigils at their shrines or sleep there in the hope of a miracle or other supernatural experiences ('incubation'), just as the devotees of gods used to do. Crutches, false limbs, and other off-casts of the cured decorate holy healing shrines, just as they once decorated the shrines of healing gods. Eyewitness accounts of miraculous healings are posted up to impress pilgrims, just as they were at pagan shrines.

Demigods and other supernatural beings also found a new home in the Christian hierarchy. Jewish cherubim became Christian cherubs and adopted the Greek form of the companions of the Greek gods Eros and Dionysus – divine but porky toddlers, known to artists as putti. The Jews had not been entirely sure what cherubim looked like. Stories varied from various kinds of hybrid animal to storm clouds (e.g. Psalm 18:10). A figure represented as part man, part lion, part ox, and part eagle was adopted from the Babylonians but this composite proved less popular than naked toddlers. Christian art often retains peripheral clouds whenever naked toddler cherubs are shown.

To the Greeks, angels (*angeloi*) had been lesser gods serving the greater ones, and sometimes visiting the world on their behalf. Christian angels continued to visit people and were likely to be mistaken for ordinary people, just as they had been in earlier times (Hebrews 13:2). Only later would they sprout wings and become immediately recognisable. Christian representations of winged angels are based largely on the Roman goddess Victoria (identified with the Greek goddess Nike and the Egyptian Naphte), though the basic idea seems to have been Babylonian and ultimately Persian. When the Altar of Victory was removed from the Senate House in Rome in 382 because of Christian sensibilities, a statue of

Victoria was left untouched, apparently because she had been adopted as an angel. (Looking at the winged, sword-wielding female figures on top of many British World War II memorials, it is often impossible to determine whether one is looking at the goddess Victoria or a Christian angel.)

The famous statue at the centre of Piccadilly Circus in London is universally called Eros, an indication of how thin the veneer of Christian angels really is, for the statue officially represents the Angel of Christian Charity.

Dæmons, minor Greek divinities, were also enlisted into the Christian pantheon. The original Greek dæmons had been supernatural beings of a nature intermediate between that of gods and men; they were inferior divinities, spirits, or the souls or ghosts of the dead, especially those of deified heroes. To the Romans they were known as *genii*. Everyone had two personal dæmons: one good, one evil. Christian thought changed the good one from a 'guiding genius' into a guardian angel (there is still some doubt about whether these angelic guards are allocated at birth or baptism).[174] The image of diminutive supernatural creatures, one an angel, the other a devil, sitting on one's shoulders and whispering secret advice, is still to be found in modern cartoons, and also in certain old-fashioned theologies.

Other dæmons became demons, malign spirits from Hell, servants of the Devil, soldiers in the satanic hosts under Satan opposed to those in the angelic hosts under the command of Saint Michael.

Inheritances

Originality is the art of concealing your source.
Franklin P. Jones (1853–1935)

As the power of the Roman Empire waned, the power of the Christian Church waxed. The Church, especially the Western Church, adapted the remnants of the Empire for its own purposes. Greek, the language of the gospels and the early Church, was abandoned in favour of Latin, the language of the Western Empire. Bishops adopted the imperial purple, a colour that they wear to this day. They also adopted secular symbols of power like the staff, mitre and pallium.[175] They took to wearing special rings, which people would be expected to kiss. Each took over a *diocese*, which had been the jurisdiction of a Roman governor, previously set up by Diocletian. Similarly, imperial provinces became the jurisdictions of metropolitans.

Church ritual was borrowed from imperial court ritual, and church architecture from imperial architecture. Basilicas were originally secular buildings, large rectangular halls with columns down the side and an apse at one end. The Emperor sat on a throne in the middle of the semicircular apse surrounded by his officials. Similarly a judge would sit in the centre surrounded by assessors. These basilicas were converted into Christian churches, and soon new basilica churches were being purpose built. Now a bishop sat in the apse, his throne (*cathedra*) at the centre of a semicircle of his clergy. The apse of a modern church is a reminder of this arrangement. A modern-day bishop still sits on a throne, called a *cathedra*, and the church in which he keeps his throne is thus known as a *cathedral* church. The thrones are now generally moved to the side, their original position now being occupied by the altar, but the bishop and his subordinates still wear their imperial court robes, a contemporary fashion from 2,000 years ago. In the Western Church clerical robes are modelled on courtly robes from the time of Constantine, while in the Orthodox Churches the vestments worn by bishops are the same as those once worn by the Emperor in church.[176]

The bishops of Rome were particularly good at recycling prestigious remnants of the Empire. They started adopting imperial trappings and practices. Since the emperors had decamped to Constantinople, the bishops of Rome filled a power vacuum. They took to dressing like emperors and adopting a range of imperial styles and titles. While other bishops dressed like wealthy noblemen of the late Empire, the bishops of Rome dressed like emperors. They set themselves up on the Vatican Hill. They adopted the title *Pontifex Maximus* from the Emperor. (The Emperor Aurelius had appointed himself *Pontifex Maximus*, high priest to the Sun god Sol Invictus, and his successors had continued to use the title until 379). This title was applied to the Bishop of Rome originally as a criticism, because of its pagan associations, but that was soon forgotten.[177] Popes also appointed themselves *Bishops of Bishops*, another title borrowed from the Emperor. Constantine himself had once borne it. So too popes decided that they should be addressed as *Your Holiness*, as emperors had been. Since the fourth century they have issued *decretals*, documents with the name and style of imperial edicts. They even invested selected bishops with a fur tippet (or pallium), just as emperors had previously invested their legates.

In early Christianity emperors had been *Vicars of God* or *Vicars of Christ*. In time, bishops of Rome would claim to be *Vicars of St Peter*, and later they too would adopt the imperial titles, purporting to be *Vicars of God* or *Vicars of Christ* or both. Later bishops would claim to be emperors by virtue of their office. They were not only emperors but also monarchs of the world, and they still are. They are still styled *monarch*. They still wear crowns, sit on thrones, add numbers to their names in a royal manner, and are said to *reign*. Until recently they were carried around in a *sedia gestatoria*, a portable chair inherited from imperial Rome. Their old title *Pontifex Maximus* is still used, though usually shortened to *Pontiff*.

Other practices and trappings were adopted from the existing religions of the classical world. As an authority on ecclesiastical history puts it:

> No sooner had Constantine the Great abolished the superstitions of his ancestors than magnificent churches were erected everywhere for Christians. These churches, which were richly adorned with pictures and images, bore a striking resemblance to the Pagan temples, both in their outward and inward form. The rights and institutions by which the Greeks and Romans and other nations had formerly testified their veneration for fictitious deities were now adopted, with some slight alterations, by Christian bishops in the service of the true God. Hence it happened that in the third and fourth centuries the religion of the Greeks and Romans differed very little in its external appearance from that of the Christians. They had both a most pompous and splendid ritual, gorgeous robes, mitres, tiaras, wax-tapers, croziers, processions, lustrations, images, and gold and silver vases; and many such circumstances were equally to be seen in heathen temples and Christian churches.[178]

Bishops adopted not only the shepherd's crook carried by the Egyptian god Osiris but also his crown. This crown was used for example by the Bishop of Rome, and became a prototype papal tiara. Many familiar Christian concepts are pagan ideas only slightly disguised. The clerical tonsure seems to have been borrowed from the priests of Isis.[179] The idea of a conciliatory sacrifice was common to almost all ancient religions, as was the holiness of blood. The word *bless* originally meant to sanctify with blood; it is related to the French verb *blesser*, meaning 'to wound'.

Protestants shied away from the idea of a sacrifice during the Eucharist. To them the Roman Mass was a horrible remnant of paganism with its specific adoption of *sacrifice* at an *altar*, and drinking the *blood* and eating the *flesh* of the sacrificial victim, even referring to it as the *host* (the word *host* comes from the Latin word for a sacrificial victim). Martin Luther considered it as blasphemous, idolatrous and abominable.[180] Protestants replaced the altar with a Communion table and denied that the Communion wine really turned into blood. Nevertheless the etymology of the word Eucharist betrays that it originally denoted a sacrifice.

The laurel twig used to sprinkle holy water in Roman sacrificial rites was replaced in Christian rites by a special brush known as an aspergillum. In pre-Christian times certain women, known as Sibyls, were granted the gift of prophecy by the gods. Christians were initially dismissive, but the technique was useful and popular. Christians soon produced their own Sibyls and their own Sibylline prophecies.

In most places where Christianity became established it took over local pagan sites. This had a number of advantages. For one thing existing veneration for the site was automatically transferred to the new church. For another, Christian priests could prevent those who remained faithful to their old religion from using their old sacred places. The Jews had used this method of eliminating the opposition; now it was practised by the Christian Church, and was actively encouraged by the Church authorities. Throughout the Holy Land ancient holy sites were taken over by one true religion after another. The Jews had acquired them by force from ancient pagans. Now Christians took them from their Jewish owners and turned them into churches. In the centuries to come Muslims would seize many of them from the Christians and turn them into mosques.

St Peter's in Rome was built on the site of a pagan necropolis of the second century AD. This was an ancient holy site, the place where pagan priests had divined the intentions of the gods. The Vatican Hill had even taken its name from these pagan priests – *vaticinators*. The site was also a centre of worship for at least two divinities: the ancient Phrygian goddess Cybele and the more recent Sun god Mithras.

Everywhere, local religions were displaced, often by force, and replaced by Christianity. Temples were destroyed or converted into

Christian churches, pagan icons were replaced by almost identical Christian ones and pagan altars turned into Christian altars.

At Menuthis in Egypt the cult of Isis was replaced by that of local saints Cyrus and John. The Parthenon in Athens had been dedicated to the virgin goddess Athene. In the sixth century it was transferred to a new virgin, St Mary. In the seventh century Pope Boniface IV turned the Pantheon in Rome into a church. Now, instead of serving all the gods it serves St Mary and all the martyrs. St Mary was particularly flexible as a substitute for old gods. Her symbol even replaced the eye of Horus that always used to be painted on the prows of Sicilian fishing boats for protection. Customs and practices associated with ancient holy places were also taken over. Ancient rights of sanctuary, which had been enjoyed by the holiest of pagan temples of Egypt and Rome, were now transferred to the churches that replaced them. We know that the destruction of other peoples' places in England, and later their seizure for use as churches, was deliberate policy because the Venerable Bede recorded correspondence from Pope Gregory the Great that gives instructions to this effect.[181]

Like the structures they replaced, early churches were often aligned with the point at which the Sun rose at the summer solstice. So were graves. Popular sites for churches included existing temples and stone circles. In some places churches were even built inside ancient stone circles.

Like many pagans, the Saxons liked to have the tools of their trade blessed, and the Church happily accommodated them. So it is that even now it is possible to find clergymen blessing ploughs, fishing nets and other tools-of-the-trade. In the last few years they have become reticent about the once widespread practice of blessing instruments of torture, but blessings of hunts and whaling ships are still carried out. Swords, guns, tanks, military aircraft, warships, bombs and other weapons are also still routinely blessed. Such blessings are carried out by Protestant ministers and Roman Catholic priests. Less controversial is the Roman practice of blessing motor cars, apparently a vestige of pagan chariot blessing.[182]

Festivals

> *God rest ye merry, gentlemen,*
> *Let nothing you dismay;*
> *Remember Christ our Saviour,*
> *Was born on Christmas Day;…*

Anonymous Christmas Carol

The tradition of burning a Yule log originated in northern Europe, as did the word *Yule* itself. Yule celebrations were simply changed into Christmas celebrations, the twelve days of Yule becoming the twelve days of Christmas, and a few features from the Roman Saturnalia and from elsewhere were added. The birthday of *Sol Invictus*, 25th December, had been celebrated by cutting green branches and hanging little lights on them, and by giving out presents in Sol's name. December greenery was popular elsewhere too. In 601 Pope Gregory I (St Gregory the Great) wrote to St Augustine at Canterbury, instructing him to copy the custom of using greenery for seasonal decoration. Augustine was told to decorate his churches just as the natives decorated their temples.

Although Christmas trees were late in arriving in England (they were popularised by Prince Albert), an Englishman had originally invented the tradition in the eighth century. Born in Devon as Wynfrith, he became a missionary in Germany and is now remembered as St Boniface, Archbishop of Mainz. He earned fame by decorating a fir tree in compensation for vandalising a pagan holy tree one Yuletide.

The Christmas festival was created from many sources, since most ancient religions held festivals to mark the middle of winter. From Saturnalia (17–24th December) comes the basic celebration and festivity, including school holidays, the making and giving of gifts, as well as much drinking and banqueting. Saturnalia was followed by the Roman Calends, a festival when it was customary to perform pantomimes and put up special decorations. In northern Europe the God Odin would ride out at this time of year. Known as the *Old Gift Bringer* he would visit people in the middle of the night to bring rewards to the virtuous and punishment to the wicked. The later Christian saint Nicholas (Santa Claus) would do much the same thing.

As in most places throughout the known world, the resurrection of a dead fertility deity has been celebrated around Easter since pre-Christian times. The early Church was accused of plagiarism for adopting customs such as those practised in the cult of Cybele, as part of which the resurrection of Attis was celebrated on 25th March. One can see why. Both religions featured public ceremonies, flagellation, and all night vigils with lights and fasting. Both had days of mourning succeeded by days of joy following the day of resurrection. The present Holy Week and Easter are developments of this theme. The Jewish Passover itself may well have been a remnant of a cult such as Cybele's. Early Christians knew of traditions of resurrected gods such as Osiris, Adonis and Tammuz. Tammuz is mentioned in the Old Testament.[183] Such deities were also known in Western Europe. According to Bede, the word *Easter* is derived from *Eostre*, the name of a Saxon goddess whose festival was celebrated at the vernal equinox. Rabbits and eggs, the traditional symbols of Easter, are both fertility symbols from ancient cults.

Almost all Christian festivals were designed to replace existing ones. Thus St Valentine's Day replaced the Roman festival of *Lupercalia*, which Pope Gelasius I tried to suppress late in the fifth century. Candlemas, 2nd February, is really the pagan *Feast of Lights*, when torches and candles were carried in night-time processions. In 701 Pope Sergius I appropriated this day for the feast of the Purification of Mary. In Roman Catholic countries young girls still walk in night-time processions, wearing white veils, and carrying lighted candles, as though still celebrating the pre-Christian *Feast of Lights*. Despite the efforts of the Church, the ancient pagan May Queen has never been fully Christianised in Britain. On mainland Europe the Roman Catholic Church has been more successful and the May Queen has come to be identified with the Virgin Mary. On the first of May each year statues of the Virgin are crowned and bedecked with flowers by ingenuous devotees.

Christian weddings are modelled on ancient Roman ones. The use of wedding rings is attributable to them, as is the wearing of veils by brides. Bridesmaids are also of Roman origin, as is the custom of the man carrying his new bride across the threshold. So is the ancient custom of throwing confetti, rice or grain. Christians also follow the Romans in wearing black for funerals, and Christian symbols of mourning are the same as theirs: the urn, the upturned extinguished torch, and the broken column.

Remnants of ancient Celtic practices also survive in Christian guise. The custom of well dressing, for example, dates from a time when wells were regarded as holy places. Wishing wells are another reminder. The familiar Christmas mistletoe is also a Celtic survivor, the custom of kissing under it being a vestige of its use as a Druidic symbol of fertility.[184] It is probably for this reason that it was always banned from Christian churches (except for York Minster). The date of Hallowe'en was fixed on the date of the Celtic New Year, when the major Celtic festival of Samhain was held, and huge fires were lit to welcome back the spirits of the dead. There are still a few vestiges of this festival kept up at this time of year – open fires, dressing up as ghosts of the dead, children's formalised mischief, and so on. The traditional Hallowe'en pumpkins, designed to look like grotesque human faces, are apparently remnants of Celtic head hunting.

Some Christians still worry about these surviving echoes of Samhain, regarding them as satanic. Each year the national press in Britain reports the continuing efforts of Christians to suppress them. Their concern is not new. Samhain has worried British Christians since the eighth century, and determined efforts have been made ever since to Christianise it. The Celtic Church, for example, celebrated a festival for all of its saints, *All Saints' Day*, on 1st November. Even the name *Hallowe'en* is Christian. It is a contraction of *All Hallows' Eve*, the *Eve of All Hallows*, or the *Eve of All Saints*. After the Celtic Church had been incorporated into the Roman Church, a concession was made to accommodate a further Celtic celebration: in 837, *All Saints' Day* was joined by *All Souls' Day* on 2nd November. All Souls' Day is the Christian version of the ancient *Day of the Dead*, when people used to remember their dead relatives, holding feasts for them as Christians still do in many countries.

In Britain it had long been customary to light huge fires around this time of year. Despite Christian efforts to suppress them, the ancient custom of lighting huge fires has continued in Britain well into modern times. When they could not be suppressed they were instead Christianised. Guy Fawkes provided a convenient excuse for the modern annual bonfire celebration, although Fawkes himself was not executed until several months after the date of his arrest (5th November), and in any case he was not burned but instead hanged, drawn, and quartered. Despite all this, the ancient Celtic fire festival was successfully converted into a Protestant festival against the Roman Catholics held responsible for the treasonable gunpowder plot. In England, 5th November came to be known as 'Pope Day'. It retained this name well into the twentieth century, and effigies of the Pope are still burned in some towns (notably Lewes, in Sussex) on this day. Observation of the day was legally enforceable under James I, and a special annual service was added to the Anglican Book of Common Prayer.[185] Despite all these efforts, in some places in England annual fires are still lit with no tradition of burning Guy Fawkes or the Pope. They continue the ancient Celtic tradition of lighting great fires to celebrate Samhain.

The following table summarises the relationship between on the one hand the four main Celtic festivals (Imbolg, Beltane, Lughnasa, Samhain) and the four main Saxon festivals and on the other eight important Christian festivals. The dates also match the traditional quarter days (on which agricultural rents are still paid). The Celtic festivals correspond to Scottish Quarter Days and the Saxon ones to English Quarter Days.

Date	Pagan Festival	Quarter Days	Date	Christian Festival
Feb 1	Imbolg	Scottish Quarter Day	Feb 2	Candlemas/Purification of Blessed Virgin Mary (BVM)
March 25	**near Spring Equinox** Saxon New Year	English Quarter Day	March 25	Lady Day Annunciation of the BVM
May 1	Beltane		May 1	May Day
May 15	Roman Calends, Flora	Scottish Quarter Day	May 15	Whitsunday
June 21	**Summer Solstice**	English Quarter Day	June 24	St John's Day
Aug 1	Lughnasa	Scottish Quarter Day	Aug 1	Lammas
Sept 29	**Autumn Equinox**	English Quarter Day	Sept 29	Michaelmas
Nov 1	Samhain: Celtic New Year		Nov 1	All Saints Day
Nov 11		Scottish Quarter Day	Nov 11	Martinmas
Dec 22	**Winter Solstice** followed by Yule			
Dec 25	Roman Saturnalia etc.	English Quarter Day	Dec 25	Christmas

Many outdoor Christian ceremonies, adapted from pagan practice, have now been abandoned. These ceremonies were designed to ensure fertility, good weather, or some other divine favour. For example:

...blessing the trees on the 12th Day after Christmas, reading gospels to the springs to make their water purer, and the blessing of corn by the young men and maids after they had received the sacrament on Palm Sunday. The medieval Litanies or Rogations (major on St Mark's Day (25th April), and minor on the three days before Ascension Day) derived from earlier pagan ceremonies, and had been designed to combat war, illness, violent death and other non-agricultural terrors.[186]

Apple trees were blessed by wassailing them, and other crops were encouraged by lighting midsummer fires. A successful corn crop was assured by numerous ceremonies: thinly disguised fertility rites, the making of corn dollies at harvest time, and so on.

From a purely historical viewpoint, Christianity appears to have adopted everything, from its most central doctrines to its organisation and outward trappings, down to the most trivial custom. Most notably, Christian practices and ideas seem to be synthesised from Jewish and Greek ones. A Church is a cross between a synagogue and a basilica. The Eucharist is a cross between a Passover meal and a Greek resurrection meal. Jesus Christ is half Jewish messiah and half Greek hero-god. God the Father is half Jahveh and half Zeus. Indeed, the old accusation that 'Roman Catholicism is Judaism wondrously interlarded with paganism' could equally be levelled at the whole of mainstream Christianity.

The usual Christian explanation for this is that God had already revealed selected elements of his divine truth to Jews and pagans before the time of Jesus, so that the seeds of Christianity already existed in the world concealed in other religions. So for example it was not so much that Christians adopted existing pagan Sun festivals, but that pagan Sun festivals prefigured later Christian ones.

IS THERE SUCH A THING AS ORTHODOX CHRISTIANITY?

Orthodoxy is my doxy; heterodoxy is another man's doxy.
Bishop William Warburton (1698–1779)

A famous fifth-century definition of the one true Christian faith is that which has been believed everywhere, always, and by all.[187] So which is this true faith? Does any faith satisfy the definition? Is there a true one? And how can we tell? Is it the biggest sect, or the one that sticks most closely to biblical teachings, or the one that most resembles the early Church? How can we tell? Many Churches see themselves as representing the one true faith, standing like the trunk of a huge ancient tree, solid, straight and ancient, while other sects have branched off, wispy and insubstantial. They see themselves as different from all the others. For non-Christians, a bramble bush might be a better analogy for the Christian Church. There is not one main stem to this bush, but a number of stems. Some of the oldest stems have died off, and most of the vigorous growth is in the secondary and tertiary offshoots. The bush bears the marks of some forceful pruning over the years, yet it still lacks any main trunk and remains a dense tangle.

Typically, what starts out as a single movement divides into an ever-increasing number of related movements. This phenomenon of division is generally known as schism, from the Greek word *schisma* denoting a split, rent or cleft. Each schismatic faction believes itself to hold the orthodox line. The word *orthodox* is of Greek origin and means simply *right opinion*. Each schismatic group is convinced that it holds the right opinion, and is thus orthodox, representing in its own mind the whole of the true Christian Church, other factions having placed themselves outside it through their heterodox beliefs. It is for this reason that many sects claimed to be *catholic* (i.e. *whole* or *comprehensive*). The word *catholic* is derived from the Greek word *katholikos* meaning universal. The Anglican Church, the Roman Church and the Eastern Churches all claim to be catholic.* Anglicans and many Protestants do not regard their own Churches as dating from the Reformation. They see them as dating back to the earliest Church, although temporarily misled by the Bishop of Rome. As Michael Ramsey, Archbishop of Canterbury put it: 'When an Anglican is asked "where was your Church before the Reformation?", his best answer is to put the counter question "Where was your face before you washed it?" '.

---

* Anglicans concede that by calling themselves *catholic* they mean that they are part of the one true Church, although it is not clear where the rest of this Church is. They regard the Roman Church as having strayed far from the true way. During the Reformation the Church in England considered joining the Eastern Churches, but eventually decided against this.

From the vantage point of any one sect, all others have fallen into error, and their adherents are thus likely to be branded as heretics. In theory a heretical sect has broken away from its parent Church (a fallen branch), while a schismatic sect is still part of the tree (a split trunk). In practice the distinction between schism and heresy is largely political. If the split can be healed by diplomacy, then it is called a schism. But if one side thinks it can eliminate the other by force, then accusations of heresy tend to arise. Wherever possible the branch is chopped off and burned.

Schisms and heresies arise in most religions. The Pharisees, Sadducees and Samaritans mentioned in the New Testament were heretical Jewish sects from the point of view of mainstream Judaism. So were other groups,[188] and so was Christianity when it started to diverge from its Jewish roots. Islam is sometimes regarded as a schismatic offshoot of both Judaism and Christianity. Soon after the death of Mohammed, Islam split into two main groups, the Shi'ites and the Sunni. Soon these too spawned new schismatic sub-sects. In the remainder of this section we will review some of the schisms within Christianity.

The Early Centuries

Jesus' followers divided into a number of opposing factions almost immediately after his death. As we have already seen (pages 125–7), the New Testament mentions a number of these factions, and the Church Fathers and historians tell us of others. The Nazarenes – followers of Jesus who continued within mainstream Judaism – almost certainly represented the nearest approximation to Jesus' own teachings, but this provided no guarantee of supremacy within the wider fellowship. While the Nazarenes continued quietly in Jerusalem, various Gnostic sects flourished in Syria, and St Paul's faction grew fast in the Hellenic world. All suffered further sub-schisms. The Nazarenes for example had problems when Jesus' brother James was executed. As the Church historian Eusebius tells us:

> After James the Just had suffered martyrdom like the Lord and for the same reason Symeon ... was appointed bishop... But Thebuthis, because he was not made bishop, began secretly to corrupt her [the Church] from the seven sects among the people to which he himself belonged: from which came Simon (whence the

Simonians), and Cleobius (whence the Cleobians), and Dositheus (whence the Dositheans), and Gorthaeus (whence the Goratheni), and Masbotheus (whence the Masbothæans). Springing from these the Menandrianists, Marcionists, Carpocratians, Valentinians, Basilidians, and Saturnilians, every man introducing his own opinions in his own particular way ...'[189]

Gnostics seem never to have been a single sect, but a collection of disparate sects, each with its own distinctive ideas, and liable to generate new sub-schisms. Pauline Christians were also subject to sub-schism. Already in his lifetime Paul had cause to reprove Christians in Corinth for dividing into sects. Quarrelling Christians there were claiming to follow different leaders: some St Paul, some Cephas i.e. St Peter, some Apollos, and some Christ (1 Corinthians 1:10–12). Other first-century schismatics include the Cerinthians and Nicolaitans. The Cerinthians, like many others, held that Jesus was born of Mary and Joseph, and that Christ descended on him at his baptism in the form of a dove (cf. Mark 1:10–12).

Pauline Christians are now generally considered to represent the orthodox line, but Paul had many difficulties in dealing with others who were trying to proselytise gentiles, and who held views other than his. On occasion Paul himself gave rise to heterodox ideas. His statement that '... if ye be led of the Spirit, ye are not under the law' (Galatians 5:18) was interpreted as meaning that the ancient laws no longer held for Christians and there was therefore no longer any reason for Christians to control their sexual impulses. Sexual licence became a major problem, and Paul had to tell his followers to stop it.[190] Similar ideas were to resurface in Europe in the sixteenth century when sexual licence again became a popular Christian theme, and the description Antinomian was coined for those who enjoyed themselves more than was thought proper by their Christian neighbours.

In the first and second centuries orthodoxy embraced millenarianism. Millenarians interpreted a biblical passage (Revelation 20:2–4) as meaning that Christ would reign for 1000 years while the Devil was incarcerated. This view has periodically come back into favour, generally with the assumption, based on other New Testament passages, that the end of the world and beginning of Christ's reign were imminent. Such ideas became popular again in the years up to AD 1000, and yet again in the years up to 2000. Millenarianism was adopted by the Anabaptists and others in the seventeenth century and is still taught by Mormons, Irvingites, Adventists, the Plymouth Brethren, and many other denominations.

The Marcionites were followers of Marcion of Sinope who assembled various writings into the earliest version of the New Testament. Marcion, like many other early Christians, believed that Jesus had suddenly appeared in the world as an adult. He and his followers worshipped the god of love, adopted some Gnostic ideas, and appointed women priests and bishops, there being no apparent reason why they should not do so. At the time they were regarded as more or less orthodox except that they received a little too much guidance from the Holy Spirit for their neighbours' tastes. Their gift of prophecy tended to subvert the authority that priests were then establishing for themselves.

Montanists were another Gnostic sect. They followed Montanus, a Phrygian, who believed that he had special divine knowledge not given to the apostles. They sought, as many sects have done since, to return to the beliefs and practices of the primitive Church. For example, they were Quartodecimans, meaning that they kept Easter on the 14th day of the Jewish month of Nisan, as the entire Asian diocese had done.[191] A famous Church Father, Tertullian, became a Montanist around AD 207. Montanists were millenarians and practised speaking in tongues, a facility that is still claimed by Pentecostalist groups. Their keenness on the twin joys of celibacy and martyrdom, along with a willingness of other Christians to oblige them in respect of the latter, ensured their disappearance in the sixth century.

Quintilians were a sub-sect of Montanists, founded by a priestess Quintilia. They used bread and cheese at the Eucharist and also allowed women priests and bishops. Another schismatic sect was the Alogians, who declined to identify Christ as the *Word* referred to at the beginning of the John gospel. This was apparently a reaction to Montanists, who were keen to identify the two as being the same, as modern theologians do.

Sabellians were followers of Sabellius, a Libyan priest. They were Unitarians, holding that Father, Son, and Spirit represented different states (or modes or aspects) of a single god. In later centuries the Eastern Churches were to accuse the Roman Church of Sabellianism and would excommunicate popes for supporting this heresy.[192] Since the time of Jesus there had been a line of followers who believed him to have been merely human, not divine. This view seems to have come to be regarded as heretical towards the end of the second century.[193] Yet there would still be bishops holding these views within the mainstream Church for many years to come, especially those whose sees fell within the patriarchy of Antioch. Eventually, late in 268, a Bishop of Antioch, Paul of Samosata, was removed by the secular power for holding that Jesus was not divine. From then on, bishops had to agree to the 'orthodox' line that Jesus had been divine. Those, like Priscillian, who deviated from the newly established orthodoxy, claiming for example that Jesus was merely an exalted prophet, could expect torture and death.

It was also around this time that Adoptionism first became unacceptable. As we have already seen (pages 109–11), the story that Jesus was not born as the son of God, but had been adopted as a son of God, is related in the earliest gospel (the Mark gospel). The early Christians who preferred this account to the ones developed later were known as Adoptionists. Adoptionism became ever less unacceptable as the doctrine of the Incarnation was developed. The Church Father Origen was posthumously accused of Adoptionism. This early doctrine was never successfully suppressed. In the eighth century at least two Spanish bishops, Elipandus of Toledo and Felix of Urgel, were still Adoptionists. The same Adoptionist 'heresy' has resurfaced repeatedly throughout the history of Christianity.

The third-century Novatians were followers of Novatian, a Roman presbyter. Their sole distinguishing feature was that, in obedience to the Bible (Hebrews 6:4–6), they rejected the re-admission of those who had lapsed into paganism.

By the fourth century one particular Christian group, calling itself catholic, gained the ascendancy. By various means it gained influence over the Emperor Constantine, and used its influence to crush the opposition. Under the influence of this group the Emperor issued an edict announcing the destruction of other denominations:

> Understand now by this present statute, Novatians, Valentinians, Marcionites, Paulinians, you who are called Cataphrygians ... with what a tissue of lies and vanities, with what destructive and venomous errors, your doctrines are inextricably woven! We give you a warning ... Let none of you presume, from this time forward, to meet in congregations. To prevent this, we command that you be deprived of all the houses in which you have been accustomed to meet ... and that these should be handed over immediately to the catholic church.[194]

This was how 'orthodoxy' was established and maintained, by imperial edict. Orthodoxy was whatever the Emperor said it was, so various parties vied for the Emperor's ear, hoping to have their views declared as orthodox. Many sects arose and died out through little more than historical accident. The Donatist heresy, for example, began with the election of rival bishops, Cæcilian and Donatus, at Carthage. Imperial preference, obtained by dubious means, having favoured Cæcilian, the followers of Donatus went into schism, setting themselves up as the one true Church. They were distinguished by their zeal, their hatred of their erstwhile colleagues, and their tendency towards further schism. They persisted for over 300 years, disappearing only when Muslims overran that part of Africa.

Further difficulties were raised by the Arians, followers of Arius, a priest who tried to work out exactly who Christ had been. He held that:[195]

- the Father and Son are distinct beings;
- the Father had created the Son;
- the Son, though divine, is less than the Father;
- the Son existed before his appearance in the world, but not from eternity.

Since there was no single accepted authority to settle such matters, the Emperor Constantine convened a council in 325 to determine the issue. Christians from around the known world travelled to Nicæa (modern Iznik in Turkey). There they considered the nature of Christ. The Arians said that he had been brought into existence to be the incarnate *Word* (*logos*) of God. Their opponents, led by the Archdeacon Athanasius of Alexandria, claimed that this did not go far enough, because it represented Jesus as being a lesser being than God. The matter was settled by Constantine himself. Unbaptised* and only half-Christian, he was well accustomed to the idea of men being gods. He had already had his father Constantius deified and probably expected to be deified himself after death. One danger with the Arian line was that it might countenance other men claiming to be sons of God. The other line accepted the Emperor as the prime focus on Earth of divine power. There was only one divine son of God, and he was already safely back

* Constantine was later baptised into the Christian Church, but not until his last illness.

in Heaven, leaving the Emperor as his personal representative on Earth. This was obviously more appealing to the Emperor.

A formula was drawn up that favoured Athanasius's view, and those present were invited to sign. For those who did sign there was an invitation to Constantine's 20th anniversary celebrations. Those who would not sign faced banishment. Most of those present accepted the formula and the party invitation. Some who signed the creed undoubtedly did so for the sake of church unity. Eusebius of Caesarea for example was clearly embarrassed about it. Afterwards some of the signatories reflected on what they had done and realised its significance. Eusebius of Nicomedia, Maris of Chalcedon, and Theognis of Nicæa wrote to Constantine to express their regrets. Eusebius of Nicomedia summed up their position by admitting that they had committed an impious act by subscribing to a blasphemy out of fear of the Emperor. Ironically, Constantine had probably not understood what the controversy had been about anyway. Gibbon neatly sums up Constantine's views on the matter:

> He [Constantine] attributes the origin of the whole controversy to a trifling and subtle question, concerning an incomprehensible point of the law, that was foolishly asked by the bishop [Alexander of Alexandria] and imprudently resolved by the presbyter [Arius]. He laments that the Christian people, who had the same God, the same religion, and the same worship, should be divided by such inconsiderable distinctions; and he seriously recommends to the clergy of Alexandria the example of the Greek philosophers, who could maintain their arguments without losing their temper and assert their freedom without violating their friendship.[196]

So it was that Christendom adopted as orthodoxy its doctrine about the divinity of Christ, not through the teachings of Jesus, not from the scriptures, but in line with the wishes of a half-pagan self-interested Emperor. After Arius's banishment, orders were made that Arian writings should be burned, and the death sentence was instituted for anyone found in possession of them. Belief in Arian views gradually declined wherever Arians were persecuted. But the story was not yet over, for Constantine subsequently had second thoughts. Arius was recalled from exile and restored to Imperial favour. A series of Church Councils confirmed the Arian line, and as St Jerome noted the whole world now became Arian.[197] As Gibbon says of Arius:

His faith was approved by the Synod of Jerusalem; and the Emperor seemed impatient to repair his injustice by issuing an absolute command that he should be solemnly admitted to the Communion in the cathedral of Constantinople. On the same day, which had been fixed for the triumph of Arius, he expired; and the strange and horrid circumstances of his death might excite a suspicion that the orthodox saints had contributed more efficaciously than by their prayers to deliver the church from the most formidable of her enemies.[198]

Once Arius was dead there was little chance of the decision of the Council of Nicæa being formally overturned. Even though St Athanasius, the champion of what is now considered orthodoxy, was condemned as a heretic by no fewer than six separate Church Councils, even though all the principal leaders of the orthodox faction were deposed and exiled, and even though Constantine was baptised in the last moments of his life by an Arian bishop, nevertheless the established doctrine was retained.

When Macedonius, Bishop of Constantinople expressed ideas similar to those of Arius, he was deposed by a council of Constantinople in 360. His followers, Macedonians, retained their semi-Arian beliefs for years to come. The orthodox line was that Jesus Christ was God and from now on it would be acceptable for Christians to pray to a deity other than God the Father. As a leading modern theologian has put it:

The practice of praying to Christ in the Liturgy, as distinct from praying to God through Christ, appears to have originated among the innovating 'orthodox' opponents of Arianism in the fourth century. It slowly spread, against a good deal of opposition, eventually to produce Christocentric piety and theology.[199]

Disputes have rumbled on to the present day. For many centuries the Arian form of Christianity flourished in Romania, Bulgaria, Spain, Gaul and Lombardy. As a number of theologians have noted, most Western Christians today unwittingly turn out to be Arian when questioned about their beliefs.

Questions about the nature of the Son provided endless material for dispute in early times. Another group, the Apollinarians, supposedly fell into error by opposing Arius. They were followers of Apollinaris, Bishop of Laodicea, who opposed Arianism and denied that Jesus had a human soul. They held that the *Word* (*logos*) fulfilled that role in Jesus' case. The First Council of Constantinople (381) condemned their views as heretical. Other schismatic groups included the Anthropomorphites, who believed that God had a human form; and the Agnoetae, who denied that God was omniscient. The Collyridians offered bread-cakes to the Virgin Mary, worshipping her as Queen of Heaven.[200] The Antidicomarianites denied Mary's continued virginity, affirming that she had had sexual intercourse with Joseph after the birth of Jesus. A Donatist group known as the Circumcellions flourished briefly, propagating violence through North Africa. But they also had a fondness for suicidal martyrdom, and soon died out.

Whichever sect enjoyed the support of the Emperor was the orthodox or catholic faction, and it generally sought to maintain its position by a judicious mix of persecution and politicking. When the Emperor Julian briefly rejected Christianity as the state religion, all sects were suddenly free to persecute each other. Within a year of Julian's accession in 361, numerous Christian sects were at each other's throats. There were no fewer than five bishops in Antioch, each with a mutually hostile following. Since then the number has never again been reduced to one.

The question of whether or not Jesus had been a man continued to be a major point of contention. Many disputes took place as to whether his nature was that of a human being or a God. Nestorius (died c.451), Bishop of Constantinople, proposed a compromise. He suggested that Christ had two distinct natures, one human and one divine, and that Mary was the mother only of his human one. Mary might be *Christotokos*, the mother of Christ, but not *Theotokos*, the mother of God. God could not have been a baby two or three months old, he said. God had always existed. To Nestorius it did not make sense to say that a mother could bear a son older than herself. Furthermore he did not like the implication that if Mary was the mother of God then she must have been a goddess. Cyril, Bishop of Alexandria, made an issue of the matter, apparently to further his position in the political power struggle between the patriarchies of Constantinople and Alexandria.[201] A Church Council was convened at Ephesus in 431, by the emperors Theodosius II and Valentinian III. The council, initially consisting of Cyril's supporters and under his chairmanship, acclaimed the *one person* line. On the same day it condemned and deposed Nestorius, the leader of the *two person* party. When Nestorius's supporters arrived the council was reopened, since Cyril had had no authority to open the earlier session. The decision was now reversed, and Cyril the leader of the *one person* faction was deposed and excommunicated. Later, more of Nestorius's opponents arrived. The matter was reconsidered. Deals were negotiated to induce various parties to agree: Pelagianism (a doctrine concerning free will) was to be condemned as a heresy to satisfy the Western representatives; Cyprus was to be granted ecclesiastical independence (which it still enjoys today), and the Bishop of Jerusalem was to be promoted to patriarch. Cyril encouraged other representatives to agree with him, providing carrots for their support in the form of lavish bribes, and sticks for dissent in the form of a private army of violent monks that terrorised the city. Cyril held a third session, similar to the first one. But the two sides would not even meet, let alone agree. In the end the council had to be dissolved by the Emperor Theodosius without it ever having reached a consensus. The Emperor arrested the leaders of both sides and put them in prison.

A few years later Cyril succeeded in bringing the matter before another council, at Chalcedon in 451, which was more pliant. This council condemned Nestorius, and the inevitable schism soon followed. The Church was once again divided, and a separate Nestorian Church was formed. It flourished in Asia, and boasted enough bishops to rival the ones that are now considered orthodox. Nestorians established a patriarchy at Baghdad, and their influence extended far to the East. At one time there was a Nestorian Archbishop of Cambaluc (modern Peking).* Ghengis Khan was well disposed to Nestorian Christians and married his sons to Nestorian princesses. The Nestorian Church was subsequently reduced by Islam, and all but wiped out around 1400 by the Asian warlord Timur. Small groups of Nestorians, now known as Assyrian Christians,‡ survived in Persia and Turkey up until World War I, during which their numbers were further reduced.

---

* A Nestorian monk from Peking, Rabban Sauma, visited Europe in 1288, apparently without anyone realising that by Western standards he was a heretic. At Bordeaux he gave Communion to King Edward I of England. At Rome he discussed theology with Pope Nicholas IV and celebrated Mass before the cardinals. A few years later a Franciscan, John of Monte Corvino, visited the Khan of Cambaluc (Emperor of Peking) and tried to introduce Western Christianity there, without success.

‡ Nestorians were called Assyrian Christians by Anglican missionaries who thought (mistakenly) that they were descended from the ancient Assyrians.

Eutyches (*c.*380–*c.*456), Archimandrite of Constantinople, held that Jesus had only one nature – a divine nature – after the Incarnation. Eutyches was excommunicated, later reinstated, but then exiled for his beliefs. Nevertheless he attracted many followers. Eventually the Ecumenical Council of Chalcedon (451) decided that Jesus had possessed two natures – one human, one divine. To hold otherwise, as the Eutychians did, was to commit heresy. This meant that many Christians of the time were heretics, since many held that he had been wholly divine. Those who subscribed to Eutyches's view came to be called Monophysites. Alexandria was a major centre for Monophysite beliefs, and the followers of Timothy, the Monophysite Patriarch of Alexandria, came to be regarded as a distinct group known as Timotheans. Alexandrian Monophysites had always retained the Jewish dietary laws and continued to practise circumcision. They have survived in Egypt up to the present time and constitute the Coptic Church, headed by the Patriarch of Alexandria, who is also the nominal head of the Ethiopian (or Abyssinian) Church. Monophysite churches have died out in Nubia, Persia, and what is now the Yemen, but others survive, including the Armenian and Syrian, whose common head is styled the Patriarch of Antioch.

Another major schism was that of the Pelagians in the early fifth century. They were followers of Pelagius, a Welsh monk who moved to Rome around the beginning of the fifth century. Pelagius maintained that people could take the first steps to salvation without the assistance of divine grace. His followers advocated free will, including the ability to accept or reject the gospel, and denied St Augustine's doctrine of Original Sin. The Augustinian faction employed the usual tools of debate: personal influence, under-the-table deals, and bribery in support of their arguments, and finally won the day by the distribution of 80 Numidian stallions to imperial cavalry officers, whose troops enforced Augustine's version of Christian orthodoxy. Few modern theologians are certain that Pelagius should have lost the argument, and fewer still believe that Augustine should have won it.

In the seventh century a schism arose over the question of how many 'wills' had been possessed by Christ, with his one 'person' and two 'natures'. Monotheletes, supported by Honorius the Bishop of Rome, held that he had possessed only one. They went into schism after the Third Council of Constantinople in 680–1 held that he had had two.

The Roman Church was obliged to disown the views of Honorius. So did others. The Maronites of the Lebanon were originally Monothelete Christians, but have been in communion with the Roman Church since 1182 (when a deal was done during the Crusades). They take their name from a Syrian hermit, St Maron, who died in 410.

An argument sometimes advanced by more innocent believers is that the one true Church has always called itself 'orthodox' or has always called itself 'catholic', while mere sects were named after their leaders. This of course, is not a helpful criterion, since almost all sects claim to be both orthodox and catholic. It is also noteworthy that the groups now regarded as orthodox and catholic also had names, just like the groups now regarded as schismatic or heretical. Thus the faction from which the Eastern Orthodox and Roman Catholic churches are both descended was given a dismissive name by the other factions. Members of this sect were called Melkites ('emperor's men') because they allied themselves with the Emperor and depended upon him for their survival. Again, the Eastern Churches refer to Roman Catholics as Azymites, a reference to their 'heretical' practice of using unleavened bread at the Eucharist.

The Great Schism Between East and West

People who believe absurdities will commit atrocities.
Voltaire (1694–1778)

From the fourth century onwards there had been increasing tension between Rome and the other patriarchies. The Church under each of the patriarchies had always been autocephalous, i.e. self-governing and recognising no central authority except the Emperor. This did not entitle patriarchs to change established doctrines and practices.

From the eighth century the Roman patriarchs (whom we now call popes) adopted a number of innovations in Western Christendom that might seem relatively trivial now but at the time were not acceptable to their fellow patriarchs in the East. The Nicene creed was changed to reflect a new understanding of the role of the Holy Spirit, and unleavened bread was used instead of leavened bread for the Eucharist. The popes also encouraged fasting on Saturday and tried to enforce clerical celibacy. Later they would discover Purgatory, a place unknown to other patriarchs. As successive bishops of Rome became ever more wayward in the eyes of their fellow patriarchs, the more incensed those patriarchs became. Periodically the tension became too great, and one or more of them would accuse a pope of heresy and excommunicate him. He would retaliate by declaring them heretic and excommunicating them. The reasons for their irritation were not only those already mentioned: sometimes the Bishop of Rome was claiming new honours for himself, sometimes he was convoking councils of his own, sometimes he was interfering in the jurisdictions of other patriarchs, sometimes he was using forged documents to prove a point. Generally the quarrel would be patched up and sooner or later the mutual excommunications would be withdrawn.

By the eleventh century the position was no longer tenable. The Bishop of Rome was claiming exclusive rights to the title of Pope and pressing for primacy over the whole Church, backed up by the forged *Donation of Constantine*. The Patriarch of Constantinople had had enough, and a serious rift opened up. Attempts at reconciliation failed and in July 1054 anathemas (formal denunciations) were exchanged. The Great Schism between the Eastern Churches and the Western Church is conventionally dated from this time although, as in the previous centuries, relations would continue periodically to warm and chill, and reconciliation was always a possibility. Indeed, at the time the incident was not regarded as a schism, and came to be regarded as one by the Western Church only after 1204. (Rome needed to justify its seizure of Constantinople in that year and did so by retrospectively regarding the exchange of anathemas in 1054 as causing a permanent split in the Church.) The anathemas were eventually withdrawn more than 900 years later, on 7th December 1965.

As the power of the Eastern Churches waned, the Roman Church was successful in picking off a number of isolated religious communities.* To this day, it has allowed these communities to keep their local

---

* Among these groups are the Maronite and Syrian Churches from the Patriarchy of Antioch, the Copts and Ethiopians from the Patriarchy of Alexandria, and the Ukrainian Uniate Church originally from the Orthodox Patriarchy of Constantinople. A small percentage of Armenian Christians (who never got involved in the Monophysite troubles) are also in communion with Rome.

customs, including clerical marriage, even though they are in communion with Rome (which means that they recognise, and are recognised by, the Roman Church).

Later Schisms

For the majority of English people there are only two religions,
Roman Catholic, which is wrong, and the rest, which don't matter
Duff Cooper (1890–1954), *Old Men Forget*

The Middle Ages saw the rise of all manner of dissident sects. They ranged from Adamists, who insisted on conducting their religious rites in the nude, to groups who travelled from place to place working themselves into religious frenzy by techniques such as dancing, chanting or flagellating each other. A major group was that of the Adventists, who affirmed the imminence of the Second Coming. Despite severe persecution Adventist groups have survived into modern times. They still look forward to the imminent Second Coming. Generally they keep to Jewish practices, such as prohibiting the eating of pork, and keeping the Sabbath day as required by the Ten Commandments, rather than Sunday – hence the epithet 'Seventh Day Adventists'.

The corruption and abuses of the Roman Church in the Middle Ages led even its own adherents to question its authority. Peter Waldo of Lyons was originally a conventional Catholic believer who wanted to live like the apostles. He soon attracted followers who came to be known as Waldensians, Waldenses, or Vaudois. He met so much opposition from his own Church that he was effectively driven out. Soon after the movement started, around 1170, Waldo was excommunicated, after which he rejected papal authority. Like others after him, he turned to the gospels and based his theology on them. Waldensians were soon advocating a priesthood of all believers and giving away their wealth. They rejected sacraments not sanctioned by the Bible and condemned practices such as the sale of indulgences and the adoration of saints. Persecution followed, and continued for centuries, with unknown thousands killed, and a few survivors taking refuge in ever more remote places. By the late eighteenth century, depleted survivors had been scattered to the alpine valleys and other remote areas. In the nineteenth century they were assisted financially by Protestants in the United Kingdom and the United States, and many emigrated to Uruguay and Argentina.

Other groups split off from the Church, or were rejected from it. The Beghards for example were essentially orthodox except that they used vernacular translations of the Bible. Eventually they were ejected from the Church and came to be known as Lollards. In England John Wycliffe, a leading Oxford scholar, took the Bible as the sole rule of faith and questioned the Roman sacraments. His followers also came to be known as Lollards and were rejected as unorthodox. Wycliffe's ideas spread throughout Europe and took root in Bohemia. In Prague, Jan Hus adopted them, and his teaching attracted an ever-increasing following. In the fifteenth century, Hussites challenged all rites, institutions and customs not sanctioned by the Bible and questioned the Roman Church's practice of not allowing the Communion cup to the laity. Once again the sect was admonished and then rejected and persecuted.

The rejection of these sects in the twelfth to fifteenth centuries was to prepare the way for much larger schisms within the Western Church at the Reformation. The sixteenth century saw a huge reaction to the corruption and venality of the Roman Church. Orthodoxy was reconsidered, and whole countries defected to new Protestant denominations: Lutheran, Calvinist, and many others. Martin Luther was prepared to admit into worship anything that was not explicitly prohibited by scripture, while John Calvin would admit only that which was expressly allowed by it. Many German states and Scandinavian countries became Lutheran; Holland, Scotland and Huguenot areas of France became Calvinist; while the Anglican Church found a middle ground, purporting to remain Catholic while adopting ever more Protestant ideas. From around the same time, several separate groups arose that are now known as Anabaptists.

The Roman Church has continued to generate schismatic groups into recent times. For example, the declaration of the dogma of papal infallibility in 1870 was unacceptable to many Roman Catholics. Excommunicated, they formed themselves into the Old Catholic Church, and are now in communion with the Church of England. In 1988 Archbishop Marcel LeFebvre formally split with the rest of the Roman Church when he ordained four new bishops. His intention was to continue the one true Church, which he thought had been abandoned by an excessively liberal papacy. His followers now number hundreds of thousands in 30 countries.

Each of the new Protestant Churches started generating new schismatic groups almost as soon as they were established. The Anglican Church gave rise to Puritanism and later to Methodism. John Wesley, the founder of Methodism, was an Anglican priest who died still regarding himself as an Anglican. Animosity from other Anglicans led to the new Methodist group becoming a separate Church. The Methodist Church, like other schismatic groups, behaved much like the early Christians had, and consequently they were regarded much as the early Christians had been by their fellow citizens. Their love feasts were believed to have been orgies. Their fits and convulsions were advertised as the work of God but believed by others to be evidence of demonic possession. Their habit of luring new believers away from their families caused massive resentment, and they were accused of robbing widows and other vulnerable individuals of their savings, just as the early Church had been. The new breakaway Methodist Church soon went into schism and formed half a dozen major sub-sects, followed by many other even smaller ones. Methodism now boasts over 75 million members worldwide. Another schismatic group, the Baptists, claim an estimated 47 million members in the United States alone.

Schismatic sects with a strong Calvinist flavour include Congregationalists and Presbyterians. Some are peculiarly attached to specific countries. For example, the Free Church of Scotland was a schismatic sect of the Church of Scotland, seceding from the latter in 1843. It combined with the United Presbyterian Church in 1900 to form the United Free Church of Scotland. In 1929 this joined up again with the Church of Scotland, apart from a small minority who retained the name of United Free Church. Tens of thousands of schismatic sects – far too many to list here – have arisen from the Western Church. New evangelical churches are created virtually every day.

In the East, the Orthodox Church has also suffered a number of schisms. Before the Great Schism of 1054, there had already been a major schism over the use of icons. Eastern Christendom was riven between those who worshipped icons (iconodules) and those who rejected icons as idols and wanted to destroy them (iconoclasts). Many people were persecuted and killed over this issue.

Often, schisms arose over matters that seem remarkably trivial to non-Christians. The seventeenth century saw an Eastern schism concerning the number of fingers to be used when making the sign of the cross. Was it two, the ancient practice used by the Russian Orthodox Church, or three, an innovation used by the Greek Church? Men were executed for supporting the wrong side. The schism continues to this day, the smaller party ('The Old Believers') having split again between the Popovtsy (with a priesthood) and the Bezpopovtsy (without a priesthood). There are also extensive disagreements within the Church about the calendar. In particular the date of Easter is still problematical, and some groups have been excommunicated for celebrating it on one day rather than another.

The diagram on the following page shows the relationship between the main denominations.

Of the tens of thousands of Christian sects, virtually all purport to be the one true mystical body of Christ and the sole ark of salvation – the Mother Church in a monogamous relationship with God. None has a claim to orthodoxy that, to a disinterested observer, is noticeably superior to the others. Certainly, size is not a reliable guide. Many of the larger denominations have thin claims to orthodoxy, even by their own criteria. It is clear to non-believers that what is now generally called orthodoxy is really whichever line historically came out on top, often by politicking, threats, deception, brute force, or the whim of an emperor.

Any objective assessment would assign orthodoxy to denominations that have been eliminated. The Nazarenes seem to have had the strongest claims. Again, the Donatists were, if anything, ultra-orthodox by the standards of the early Church. After them come the various sects that were universally accepted as 'orthodox' except for beliefs or practices that, though now condemned, are known to have been shared by early Christians. The sole distinguishing feature of the Quartodecimans was that they continued to calculate the date of Easter in the traditional way. The heresy of the Montanists was that they continued to accept the inspiration of the Holy Spirit after the 'orthodox' had changed their views about it. The Marcionites' principal heresy was to regard God as a God of love rather than as a God of fear. Other groups were regarded as heretical because they paid salaries to their clergy – as late as AD 200 the orthodox in Rome and elsewhere regarded this practice as outrageous. The 'heresy' of the Millenarians was to agree with biblical views about the

THE DEVELOPMENT OF CHRISTIAN SECTS IN THE CONTEXT OF RELATED RELIGIONS

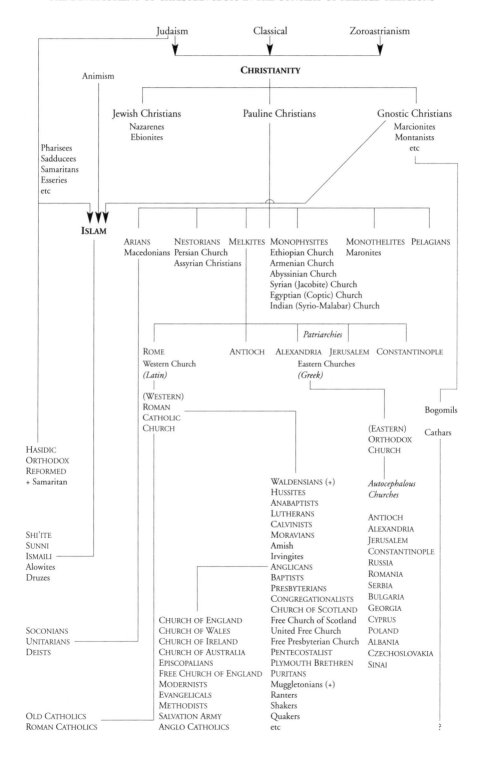

end of the world, while the Collyridians' principal heresy was to worship the Virgin Mary as Queen of Heaven long before other mainstream Christians accepted it as orthodox to do so. The Antidicomarianites on the other hand continued to hold traditional views about Mary after others had abandoned them. They held, for example, that Mary had had a normal marital relationship with Joseph after the birth of Jesus.

The Roman Church developed its own ideas of heresy, often falling into heresy itself by its own earlier standards. For example, it had undoubtedly been heretical to attempt to enforce clerical celibacy before popes tried to enforce it on their own priests. In the Middle Ages the Spiritual Franciscans fell into heresy according to the Roman Church by preaching absolute poverty, copying the example of Jesus as closely as they could. Members of many sects were persecuted as heretics for adhering to the Ten Commandments. Because of the injunction 'Thou shalt not kill', some sects opposed capital punishment, and for this belief they were often executed as heretics by the Christian authorities.[202]

Of the surviving denominations, none has a clear claim to orthodoxy that anyone else considers convincing. If we take as a criterion the extent to which denominations have departed least from biblical teachings (or that least contradict biblical teachings), then we can discount all of the largest denominations, and must look to sects out of the mainstream. There are a few tiny sects that continue to honour the Sabbath rather than Sunday, practise poverty as well as preach it, avoid man-made images of any living thing, refuse to kill, and decline to swear oaths. If anyone has a claim to orthodoxy it seems to be minority groups like these.

The idea that there is a single straight trunk to the great tree of Christianity is untenable. All present-day denominations represent branches, whether young or old, large or small. Generally, it is not difficult to trace back today's offshoots through the older branches from which they grew. To take a simple example, Southern Baptists are an offshoot of the original Baptists, who developed from the Anabaptists, a group of nonconformist Protestant sects that had split off from the Roman Catholics. The Roman Catholic Church itself may be seen as a branch of the Orthodox Church, itself the successor of the Melkites, one of the many outgrowths that vied with each other during the Dark Ages, after the Pauline Christians had pruned back other boughs of the Christian tangle-tree.

It has been remarked that the success or failure of the various early Christian sects was determined not so much by comparative reasonableness or skill in argument (for they practically never converted each other), but by the differences in birth and death rates in the respective populations. Whether or not this is true, it is clear that what we call 'orthodox' is not objectively orthodox, it is 'orthodox' only by convention.

That famous fifth-century definition of the one true Christian faith as that which has been believed everywhere, always, and by all would be convincing if there were such a faith, but there is not, and apparently never has been. The definition was first formulated by an orthodox Roman Catholic monk attacking the novelties of St Augustine – novelties that have now become the pinnacle of orthodoxy in the West. The simple truth is that orthodox belief changes from place to place, from time to time, and from denomination to denomination.

HOW DID THE PRIESTHOOD ARISE?

The theologian may indulge in the pleasing task of describing Religion as she descended from Heaven, arrayed in her native purity. A more melancholy duty is imposed on the historian. He must discover the inevitable mixture of error and corruption which she contracted in a long residence upon earth, among a weak and degenerate race of beings.
Edward Gibbon (1737–94), *The Decline and Fall of the Roman Empire*

The origins of the Church hierarchy are not what most Christians might imagine. Here we shall see how the Church hierarchy originated, how and why it developed as it did, and how well its record matches its claims.

Ecclesiastical Ranks and Titles

Archbishop: A Christian ecclesiastic of a rank superior to that attained by Christ.
H. L. Mencken (1880–1956)

Over the centuries the Christian Churches have developed an elaborate hierarchy of priestly ranks. The following is a summary of some of the main ones.

Deacons

At the lower end of the modern hierarchy are deacons. They are mentioned both in the New Testament and in other early writings. Deaconesses are also mentioned and there is no reason to doubt that in the early Church they were exact counterparts of deacons. It is also notable that appointment as a deacon was apparently for life rather than a probationary stepping stone to higher office. The original duties of a deacon seem to have been the collection and distribution of alms.

Priests

The New Testament does not mention priests except in the sense that all believers are priests;[203] and believers were regarded as priests only in the sense that all Jews had been regarded as priests in the Old Testament (Exodus 19:6). Nowhere in the New Testament is the ministry of Jesus' followers described as a priesthood. Neither is any follower referred to as a priest, except in the general sense that all followers were priests.

Some followers are referred to as *presbyters*. The Greek word *presbyter* means *elder*, and references in the New Testament to presbyters are not to priests but to community elders. Nevertheless, the early Church soon changed its presbyters into priests, borrowing much of the significance from pagan religions where priests were holy men who enjoyed a special relationship with God and made sacrifices to him. A priesthood was thus created without any biblical justification, a fact that may have contributed to the priesthood's reluctance to allow people to read the Bible. When people did read the Bible for themselves and failed to find the word *sacerdos* (priest), only *presbyter* (elder), the result was widespread anger. Indeed, the lack of biblical justification for a priesthood was one of the main complaints of Church dissidents and reformers, and it is for this reason that Presbyterian sects have rejected a priesthood in favour of lay leaders called *elders*. Other Churches suspicious of an official priesthood call their officers *ministers* or *pastors*.

The Roman Church holds that presbyters developed into priests in the early Church with divine approval, and therefore retains them. Anglicans hover between the two extremes – high church priests and low church ministers. Many Anglican priests are more usually referred to by their specific role: rectors ('rulers') or vicars. A vicar is a rector's or a priest's deputy (*vicarius sacerdos*).

Bishops

Bishops are mentioned in the New Testament, but their functions and status bear little similarity to those of modern bishops. The word bishop is derived from the Greek word *episkopos*, which can be translated literally as *overseer* or *supervisor*. In the Septuagint the word is used for minor taskmasters and petty officials. In the Authorised Version of the New Testament the word *bishop* is used to translate both *episkopos* and *presbyter*, but in most modern translations *episkopos* is generally rendered as *overseer*, and *presbyter* as *elder*. Modern translations are strictly more accurate, but the practice of Authorised Version translators is justifiable, since the two Greek words are both used for holders of the same office. Thus for example the same people are sometimes referred to by both titles.[204] In other words there was no separate rank of bishop in the modern sense. *Bishop* was simply an alternative name for a presbyter. This explains why early writings refer to a twofold arrangement of deacons and bishops[205] and why the epistle to the Philippians is addressed only to deacons and bishops. It also explains why the Roman Church technically recognises only two Holy Orders: deacons are in one, priests and bishops together in the other.

Metropolitans, Primates and Archbishops

The bishop of the metropolis of each imperial province came to be styled *metropolitan*. These metropolitans came to dominate their fellow bishops as the bishops had dominated their fellow presbyters. By the canons of the Ecumenical Council of Nicæa (325) they were given certain powers of veto.

The bishop of the primary see in each state came to be styled *primate* ('first' or 'principal'). Outside the Empire the title *primate* was used much as the title *metropolitan* was used within it. In England the bishops of Canterbury and York squabbled for centuries over the primacy, and are now both styled Primate. (The Archbishop of York is Primate of England, and the Archbishop of Canterbury Primate of *All* England.)

In the fourth and fifth centuries the bishops of important sees such as Alexandria and Antioch came to be considered super-bishops and started being styled archbishops. The custom was adopted by metropolitans and has since been extended to other important bishops.

Cardinals

The title *cardinal* was originally applied to any priest permanently attached to a church. Later it was restricted to deacons, priests and local bishops in or near Rome. In practice the title has been used for centuries as a separate rank in the Roman Catholic hierarchy, though cardinals are still properly cardinal deacons, cardinal priests, or cardinal bishops. The observation that 'there were no cardinals at Nicæa' has long been popular amongst those critical of the role of cardinals within the Roman Church.

Popes

In early times the title *pope* was widely used by leading figures in the Church. It is a variation of the Latin word *papa*, Greek *pappas*, English *pa-pa*. Bishops and patriarchs were accorded the title *pope* by those who stood in a filial relationship to them. Thus for example the African bishops addressed their own primate in Carthage as *pope*, but called the Bishop of Rome merely *bishop*. So too, a Patriarch of Alexandria could refer to his predecessor as 'our blessed pope' in the third century.[206] There is no record of a bishop of Rome being accorded the title before the late fourth century, and it was not until the time of Leo the Great (pope 440–61) that the title started to be used by the Western Church specifically of the Bishop of Rome. In fact it was not claimed exclusively by the Bishop of Rome until 1073, and the Orthodox Church has never accepted this claim.

Patriarchs

The first centre of Christianity was Jerusalem. Jerusalem remained the natural centre until the Ebionites were expelled along with other Jews after the uprising in AD 135. Lacking a single focus, Christians from Egypt and Libya looked to Alexandria, those in Asia Minor (modern Turkey) to Antioch, and those in southern Italy to Rome. In the fourth century the heads of the churches in Rome, Alexandria and Antioch were all being accorded the honorific title of patriarch, and the Bishop of Constantinople soon joined them. In the fifth century Christian communities had again grown up around Jerusalem, and the Bishop of Jerusalem was also accorded the title.[207] The title was adopted from the Old Testament[208] and was universally accepted as the highest honorific available. In the East the Patriarch of Constantinople became first among equals and was accorded the style *Ecumenical Patriarch*.

The bishops of Rome, keen to establish themselves as superior to their brother patriarchs, awarded themselves the same title, *Ecumenical Patriarch*, and later appointed their own patriarchs of Constantinople, Alexandria, Antioch and Jerusalem. Founders of religious orders were also called patriarchs.

Modern patriarchs include the heads of the Russian and other Orthodox Churches, along with the heads of various other Churches that have accumulated over the centuries. The head of the Coptic Church, for example, is styled Patriarch of Alexandria, and the head of the Syrian Church, Patriarch of Antioch. There is also a patriarch of the Ethiopian Orthodox Church.

The Biblical Hierarchy

Nowhere in the gospels, the writings of the apostles, or the early Church Fathers is there a hint of the need for metropolitans, primates, archbishops, cardinals, popes or patriarchs. In the earliest times there were not even bishops or priests, merely people who acted as community elders or overseers. The whole edifice of ecclesiastical ranks and titles is a later development. On the other hand the Bible does explicitly mention a hierarchy of appointments sanctioned by God, with seven ranks. First are apostles, second prophets, third teachers, fourth miracle workers and healers, fifth helpers, sixth administrators, and seventh those who can speak in different tongues (1 Corinthians 12:28). For a generation or two this divinely sanctioned hierarchy seems to have operated well enough.[209] Why it disappeared is something of a mystery. There is a possibility that it was suppressed by the bishops, keen to promote their own power. In this respect, it is instructive to remember the 'heretical' Montanists, who reacted against the increasing organisation of the early Church. Like other Gnostic Christians they challenged the authority of priests and bishops and were exterminated.

This new hierarchy (of metropolitans, primates and so on) led to new forms of abuse, as powerful men sought ever more powerful positions. Many of the most famous Christian leaders were rich laymen whose offices were not gained by piety, merit, election, or hard work, but by influence and bribery. Rich families routinely bought Church offices: St Augustine, St Jerome, Origen and Eusebius were just a few of the lucky recipients. St Ambrose was consecrated Bishop of Milan a mere eight days after his baptism.

By the Middle Ages the Church had implemented its own seven-fold hierarchy. Selected boys at the age of around seven started a thirty-year climb up the ladder of Ostiarius (doorkeeper), Exorcist, Lector, Acolyte, Subdeacon, Deacon, and Presbyter (or *sacerdos*, or priest). In the Western Church these positions were developed into minor orders (Ostiarius, Exorcist, Lector, and Acolyte) and major orders (Subdeacon, Deacon, Priest and Bishop). Some of these differed in the Eastern Churches, and some have now been abandoned. The existence of Exorcists for example became something of an embarrassment. In England, the exorcism of infants when they were baptised was dropped from the second Edwardian Prayer Book, and the minor orders, including the office of Exorcist, disappeared from the Ordinal (the book of instructions for daily services) in 1550. The Roman Church suppressed the offices of Ostiarius and Exorcist in 1972.

The Acquisition Of Power By Ecclesiastics

What village parson would not like to be a pope?
Voltaire (1694–1778), *Letters on the English*

There is no suggestion that the earliest elders/overseers went through any sort of ordination or consecration, that they wore special garb, or that they wielded significant power. At some stage leading elders/overseers seem to have monopolised the title *bishop*, and acquired pre-eminence over their fellows. Initially they were merely first among equals, and for centuries to come they would address other presbyters as 'fellow presbyters'. Soon St Ignatius of Antioch (AD *c*.35–*c*.107) was claiming that 'we ought to regard the bishop as the Lord himself'[210] and suggesting that bishops preside in the place of God.[211] The Orthodox Church still holds that a bishop is a living image of God upon Earth,[212] and a 'monarch' in his own diocese.[213] Other clerics also liked the idea, and adapted it to their needs. According to St Benedict, for example, a monk must obey his abbot as Christ himself.

During the second century it came to be accepted that there should be only one bishop in each city, so avoiding conflicts of authority. As time went by bishops laid claim to more and more authority. Already around the end of the first century St Clement of Rome had adopted the idea of apostolic succession.[214] The basic idea had been first developed by Gnostics who listed their teachers, and their teachers' teachers, and *their* teachers, all the way back to Jesus himself. This idea was developed into the proposition that the first bishops were the apostles (or at least were appointed by the apostles), and that all subsequent bishops were authorised by ones already appointed. Thus it should be possible to trace back a succession of bishops from any modern bishop to at least one of the apostles. Bishops became the spiritual heirs of their predecessors, so only bishops could consecrate new bishops. By the 250s apostles and bishops were being equated, and the chain of succession was being used as an explicit argument for authority and obedience.

In theory, this is true of all Churches that claim to be *apostolic*, including Eastern, Roman, and Anglican Churches. The authority of bishops is largely justified on this principle, although few bishops in the Western Churches, if any at all, can reliably trace their succession in this way. Nevertheless, the theoretical link to the apostles has allowed bishops to claim apostolic authority. Imperceptibly, there has been a change from a theme of service and humility to one of authority and command. Bishops were soon pointing out that disobedience to them amounted to disobedience to God. To fail to obey a priest or a judge was deserving of death, and bishops were both priests and judges. They quoted the text of Deuteronomy 17:12: 'And the man that will do presumptuously, and will not hearken unto the priest that standeth to minister there before the Lord thy God, or unto the judge, even that man shall die: and thou shalt put away the evil from Israel'. By the fifth century bishops were important people, expecting others to kiss their hands.

The hierarchy of the Church grew by repeated applications of the principle that the first among equals becomes superior to his fellows. This was how priests had come to be above the common people, and how bishops had come to be placed above priests. It was how metropolitans came to be placed above bishops, and how patriarchs came to be placed above metropolitans. The Patriarch of Constantinople became Ecumenical Patriarch (i.e. universal patriarch) by the same process again. By the beginning of the fourth century it was apparent that ambitious bishops were coveting more powerful bishoprics. By moving to another see they could become a metropolitan or even a patriarch. To put a stop to this, in 325 the Nicene code of canon law forbade bishops moving from one see to another. But the practice continued. Bishops still jockeyed for position, 'translating' from one see to a better one. As a council held at Sardica in 341 noted, the practice of translation was a wicked source of corruption: 'all are aflame with the fires of greed, and are slaves of ambition'. The sale of bishoprics was a scandal within the Church, and remained so for many hundreds of years.

From 451 Christianity was the official religion of the emperors. The Roman Empire, transformed into the Byzantine Empire, became a Christian theocracy. The Emperor was the head of the Christian Church, performing priestly and even semi-divine functions. He exercised supreme authority over the Church. He was responsible for all matters theological, including doctrine. From the time of Constantine, emperors possessed the power to call a Church Council. Constantine himself had called and presided over the Council of Nicæa and dictated its decisions. From his reign onwards the Church was effectively a Department of State advising the Emperor on matters spiritual. Noble families who had previously provided priests for the official pagan religions now provided the priests and bishops for the official Christian Church. Family property was transferred to the Church but kept under the control of the family, thus avoiding taxation on it. Generally, the more powerful the family, the greater the Church office conferred.

The greatest Church officers, the patriarchs, were answerable directly to the Emperor. The Bishop of Rome was one of these patriarchs, and also a duke of the Empire, with control of a duchy and the rights and duties that went with it. When Constantine moved his capital from Rome to Byzantium in 324 he set in motion a train of events that resulted in the division of the Empire in 395, and the deposition of the last Western emperor in 476. After this date the Bishop of Rome was left as the most powerful individual in the old capital, and over the centuries he arrogated to himself more and more worldly power. The Emperor in Constantinople still nominally governed Rome, but papal claims multiplied. Pope Gregory I, who reigned from 590 to 604, increased and consolidated the Western Church's political power. In 756 the Frankish ruler Pepin III, deceived by a papal forgery, allowed the Pope to set up the first Papal State.

The next step was to create a new empire, or at least to annex half of an existing one. Since the Emperor in Constantinople was usually crowned by the Ecumenical Patriarch (the Bishop of Constantinople),

Pope Leo III hit upon the idea of crowning his own emperor. Thus it was that in St Peter's, on Christmas Eve in AD 800, Leo approached Charlemagne from behind while he was praying and, without Charlemagne expecting it, crowned him as Emperor of the Holy Roman Empire. Copying an ancient Roman ceremony, the Pope then prostrated himself in an act of emperor worship. Western Christendom now had its own emperor, sanctified by his own patriarch. The real emperor in Constantinople and his patriarch could only fume impotently. In time popes would make increasingly ambitious claims of temporal power for themselves, notably that God had offered the imperial throne to the papacy, and that the Papal States were inherited from St Peter himself. Popes such as Innocent III claimed to have been given the whole world to rule over by God. Innocent thus considered himself qualified to offer the imperial throne to Otto IV and declared him to be King of the Romans, elected by the grace of God and of the Pope.

As feudalism developed, it permeated Western Christianity. When a vassal paid homage to his lord, he knelt and put his hands together in front of him. His lord then put his hands around the vassal's as the feudal oath was sworn. This position of the vassal is the position still adopted by modern Christians at prayer, offering their hands for their lord to take between his, as though to renew a feudal bond. Ancient Christians had prayed in a quite different manner, standing and with their arms held out, palms upwards. The modern method dates from the flourishing of the feudal system in the twelfth century. Feudal ideas were so strong that they appeared everywhere. Christians even imagined witches paying feudal homage to Satan.

The papacy occupied a pivotal role in the feudal system as intermediary between Heaven and the material world. Serfs owed allegiance to their local lords, who in turn owed their allegiance to barons. Barons owed their allegiance to the great lords. The great lords owed allegiance to the king (or emperor). Kings and emperors owed their allegiance to the Pope, who in turn held the whole world in fief from God. This system paralleled the Western Church hierarchy: believer, priest, bishop, metropolitan, patriarch and pope. Directly or indirectly, everyone in Western Christendom was therefore subordinate, both spiritually and temporally, to the Pope. In theory the rest of the world was too, and still is; but God omitted to mention this important intelligence to anyone outside Christendom.

Feudal hierarchies were more of a network than a pair of distinct hierarchies. For example new bishops and abbots paid feudal homage to the king, swearing feudal fealty like any other feudal tenant. Bishops were royal functionaries. They helped kings to govern, they ran chanceries and exchequers; they were politicians and judges, local potentates and tax collectors, diplomats and royal emissaries. In many respects kings were senior churchmen, often having total control over the Church within their realm. On formal occasions kings dressed like senior bishops, and the ceremony of crowning a European monarch was similar to that of consecrating a bishop. Both involved ritual processions to a cathedral church followed by a formal ceremony. The new king or bishop dressed almost identically. In the course of the ceremony there was the same formal confirmation of religious orthodoxy, followed by the anointing with holy oil, modelled on the ancient Jewish practice of anointing messiahs. The monarch or bishop was then invested with a ring and staff, and the ceremony concluded with a kiss of peace and a Mass.

When the Pope sat at the pinnacle of the feudal pyramid of worldly power, monarchs vied with each other for papal favours. Powerful men applied to the Pope for the title of King, as Alfonso-Henry, Count of Portugal, did when he thought he had earned the right to be King of Portugal. Once they had a crown, kings vied for other honours. Henry VIII of England was famously awarded the title of *Defender of the Faith* by the Pope, before his problems with the Roman Church. The King of France was styled 'His Most Christian Majesty' and the King of Spain was, and still is, 'His Catholic Majesty'. The courts of worldly rulers were seen as reflections of God's divine court. The heavenly king sat on his throne, wearing a gold crown, dressed in ermine-lined robes, holding a bejewelled sceptre and orb, surrounded by courtiers – and so did earthly kings. By copying each other's trappings God and kings validated each other's rights and each other's hierarchies. Popes were especially fond of stressing how their role paralleled that of God. In some late medieval art God was portrayed like a pope. The Eastern Church used a similar technique: in Byzantine art Christ and emperor are often indistinguishable.

God was a bigger and better king than any earthly monarch, but he was still a king. Medieval men followed the same conventions in respect to both earthly and heavenly monarchs. In their presence they took off their hats, bowed their heads and knelt. Kings of Heaven and Earth were treated in the same way because, essentially, they were the same.

The civil crown and the heavenly crown were almost identical. The divinely appointed earthly hierarchy mirrored the divinely appointed heavenly hierarchy. It must have been difficult for many Christians to distinguish fully between the members of these hierarchies, especially when they were all addressed as Lord: *My Lord Earl* and *My Lord Bishop* wielded almost indistinguishable temporal and spiritual swords. They were answerable to *My Lord the King* and *My Lord the Pope*, both on behalf of the *Lord God*.

When they had first appeared as a separate rank in the early Church, bishops had been freely elected by the Christian community. Once the Church hierarchy was in place, senior members of it started to interfere with these free elections and eventually won the right to appoint bishops themselves. The bishops of Rome for example had been elected by the citizens of Rome until the eighth century. Everywhere the franchise was gradually removed from the common people. By the third Lateran Council, called in 1179, lay influence had been eliminated in Western Christianity, and all power was now invested in the clergy. So it was that the whole ecclesiastical hierarchy became self-appointing, though vestiges of the original rights of free election remain in the East to this day.[215] With no accountability to its members, the Church potentates pursued for centuries a policy of self-enrichment. Bishoprics were valuable property, and in the tenth century the office of bishop could be left in wills to near relatives, even to female relatives.[216] Bishops and abbots lived like secular princes. They imposed taxes, sold offices, led armies, dispensed justice, maintained their own prisons, kept concubines, and traded in slaves. On their deaths, their sons often replaced them in the family business.

The Papacy

The Papacy is not other than the Ghost of the deceased Roman Empire,
sitting crowned upon the grave thereof.
Thomas Hobbes (1588–1679), *Leviathan*

The traditional position of the Church is that bishops are called by God, and that they represent him here in the observable world. One might therefore expect that bishops would be, as they have claimed to be, more holy, more wholesome, more moral, more just, and less fallible than those who are not inspired by God. It is not always easy to square these expectations with the historical record. From the third century onwards we find all manner of venality and immoral behaviour. We find bishops leading heresies and schisms, and executing each other. We find every sort of criminal activity from piracy to incest. We find bishops selling Church offices. We find them appointing their sons and other relatives to rich offices. We find them acquiring and misusing power over the secular authorities – their actions frequently driven by political considerations.

We have already seen how the power play between the patriarchies largely determined the development of Christian orthodoxy. The patriarchs jockeyed for position while fighting off threats from their own flock. Their position was precarious, even up to recent times. As one authority noted of the Bishop of Constantinople (the Ecumenical Patriarch), 'Out of 159 patriarchs who have held office between the fifteenth and the twentieth century, the Turks have on 105 occasions driven patriarchs from their throne; there have been 27 abdications, often involuntary; 6 patriarchs have suffered violent deaths by hanging, poisoning, or drowning; and only 21 have died natural deaths while in office'.[217] Offices were often bought and sold. For many centuries after the Turks took Constantinople, the ecumenical patriarchs bought their Offices from the Sultan,[218] bishops bought theirs from patriarchs, priests paid their bishops, and the priests raised the money by taxing the laity.

The position was much the same throughout Christendom at least until the Reformation, but one patriarch excelled his brothers in many respects. The bishops of Rome were over-achievers, needing to match the ecumenical patriarchs in all respects. We have already seen how Pope Leo III created his own emperor, Charlemagne, in Rome to match the real emperor in Constantinople.

We will look more carefully at the Bishop of Rome, not only because as Pope he is the head of the Roman Church, but also because he is one of the five great patriarchs of the undivided Orthodox Church, and is even recognised by the Anglican Church as a valid bishop. We will, however, concentrate on beliefs held by many Roman Catholic adherents. They are:

- that the Pope is the head of the whole Church;
- that Popes have always been elected according to fixed rules, in elections assisted by God;
- that there has been a continuous line of known, canonically appointed popes since St Peter;
- that popes have been uniformly pious, their records being consistent with God's involvement in their selection.

Let's look at some of the evidence that historians have claimed to be at odds with these beliefs. Most of the information concerning the records of the popes can be verified in *The Oxford Dictionary of Popes* by J. N. D. Kelly, which gives a comprehensive list of original sources. Much of the most interesting information comes from records left by authorities such as Bishop Liutprand of Cremona.

Papal Claims to Pre-eminence

Early Christian writers agreed that all bishops were equal. But metropolitans and patriarchs soon established themselves as superior to ordinary bishops. Roman patriarchs were particularly adept at advancing their own status, helped along by the fact that their city had been the capital of the Empire. As other bishops took over the role of governors, the bishops of Rome gradually took over the role of the emperors. They made many claims for themselves. They alone, they said, are entitled to be called Pope. They are above their fellow patriarchs. They are God's deputies on Earth. They are superhuman. They must have not merely their hands, but also their toes kissed by ordinary people. They are infallible. They rule the whole Universe. How did all this come about?

In the earliest years there do not seem to have been any remarkable claims about the position of the Bishop of Rome. Indeed there is no reason to believe that there was a bishop in Rome. The only 'bishop' in early times was the leader of Jesus' followers in Jerusalem. Other bishops were invented in the East generations after Jesus' lifetime. The idea that St Peter had been the first Bishop of Rome seems to have been invented around AD 220. Soon tentative efforts were being made by bishops of Rome to establish themselves as special. In the middle of the same century Pope Stephen I developed an ingenious argument to support his claim to pre-eminence. His argument was later developed by other popes, and is now enshrined in canon law.[219] It may be summarised as follows:

- The apostle Peter had enjoyed pre-eminence among the apostles.
- Peter had been Bishop of Rome.
- Subsequent bishops of Rome were successors to Peter and so enjoyed the same pre-eminence that he had.

All of the elements of this argument are questionable. First, the proposition that *the apostle Peter had enjoyed pre-eminence among the apostles.* The most common view in early times in the Pauline faction of the Church was that all the apostles shared power equally. In the wider Church, if anyone had enjoyed pre-eminence it was undoubtedly Jesus' brother James, who headed the Christian community at Jerusalem, the centre of Christianity. The earliest Church historians refer to the throne of the see at Jerusalem but to no other bishop's throne. It is clear enough that Peter had no special legislative power[220] and that if anything Peter felt himself subordinate to James. Despite the evidence Stephen found support for his claims in the Matthew gospel, where Jesus addresses Peter:

> And I say also unto thee, That thou art Peter, and upon this rock I will build my church; and the gates of hell shall not prevail against it. (Matthew 16:18)

The passage relies heavily upon a pun that works in both Aramaic and Greek (and other languages) in which the name Peter is the same as the word for a rock: Aramaic *Cephas,* Greek *Petros.* Many of the earliest Church Fathers had considered this passage, but none had interpreted it as Stephen did. The next verse of the Matthew gospel was also taken as supporting papal aspirations:

> And I will give unto thee the keys of the kingdom of heaven: and whosoever thou shalt bind on earth shall be bound in heaven: and whatsoever thou shalt loose on earth shall be loosed in heaven. (Matthew 16:19)

The *'power of the keys'* was interpreted as disciplinary power and was enjoyed by all bishops in the early church, and the power to *bind and loose* was not peculiar to Peter either. Jesus granted it to the disciples generally in Matthew 18:18. Roman Catholic apologists have cited Cyprian, Bishop of Carthage, as affirming that Jesus had set up a single bishopric (*unam cathedram*) and had given the primacy to Peter, who enjoyed jurisdiction over the other apostles. But these details are found only in the papal version of the text in question. In the received text these statements are not made. On the other hand the received text states that all of the apostles enjoyed the same authority.[221] It is not known how the papal version came into being, but it may be significant that the idea that the Bishop of Rome enjoyed any special power was a product of forged documents such as the *Capitularies of Benedict the Levite*, included in the *Pseudo-Isidorian Decretals*.

Second, the proposition that *Peter had been Bishop of Rome*. It is not at all certain that the apostles regarded themselves as belonging to any Christian Church. If they did, there is no reason to suppose that they took charge of particular parts of it. Early Christians seem to have thought that the apostles had belonged to the whole Church. As far as is known, no one thought of them as belonging to geographic regions as bishops were later to do. The identification of apostles with specific places seems to have developed over the first few centuries. (Although James had been based in Jerusalem, his authority extended over the whole Christian community, worldwide.) Ironically, one of the earliest geographical identifications was that St Peter had been the head of the Christian community in Antioch, and he was thus referred to as the first Bishop of Antioch.[222] There is not even a hint in the New Testament that Peter was Bishop of Rome. Neither is there any contemporary evidence that he was, or that he took charge of the Christian community there. Indeed Peter seems to have spent only a short time in Rome.[223] His name does not appear amongst those addressed in St Paul's letter to the Christian community there: St Paul sends greetings to many individuals in Rome (Romans 16:1–16), but nowhere mentions Peter. Worse, there is an early record that the first Bishop of Rome was called Linus. His name appeared first on the earliest lists of bishops of Rome, and also in 2 Timothy 4:21, where final greetings are sent to Christian notables in Rome. Again Peter's name did not appear at all. Irenaeus, writing before the year 200, confirms Linus as the first Bishop of Rome, and so did a solemn decree (an Apostolic Constitution) issued in 270. Only later did the convention arise of describing Peter as a bishop of Rome.

Third, the proposition that *subsequent bishops of Rome were successors to Peter and so enjoyed the same pre-eminence that he had.* Even if Peter had been granted some special position by the words reported in Matthew 18, it is still far from clear that they can be applied to anyone else. The passage in question is addressed specifically to Peter. Stephen's argument depends on an extension of the principle of apostolic succession. By virtue of being Bishop of Rome he claimed to inherit St Peter's power. But there is no suggestion in the gospels, or anywhere else, that such power could be inherited. The principle of apostolic succession is no use in itself, for this principle shows only that bishops are successors to the apostles generally. Not one of the great Fathers of the Church recognised any special mode of succession for the bishops of Rome. None refers to them as Peter's successors. There is no suggestion of any special office, or of any inheritance, or of any bishop being identified as a rock like Peter.[224]

Those who conceded that Rome has special rights did so specifically on the grounds that it was the centre of the Empire (which it was until Constantine moved his capital to Byzantium in 324). The claim to special pre-eminence by virtue of a link with Peter had not occurred to earlier bishops of Rome, even when they needed it to bolster their claims. For example, towards the end of the second century, a bishop of Rome (Victor) purported to excommunicate some fellow Christians in Asia for failing to follow his own innovations concerning the date of Easter. He was 'sternly rebuked' by other bishops in the West and was obliged to stop.[225]

Many years were to pass before Stephen developed his argument and asserted his unique authority. His claim carried spectacularly little weight when it was first used. Stephen was trying to establish his authority over Cyprian, the Bishop of Carthage. But Cyprian would have none of it and affirmed the orthodox view (still held by the Orthodox Church) that all bishops were equal.[226] Stephen backed off when another patriarch, Dionysius the Bishop of Alexandria, intervened. It was to be many years before Stephen's claim swayed an argument even within Western Christendom. Constant repetition, the dimming of memories, constructive forgery, and a respectable patina of time seems to have lent authority to it. The Eastern Church has held the same position ever since the claims were first made: it rejects them absolutely. None of the Greek Fathers of the Church mentions, or even suggests, that they considered themselves subject to the Bishop of Rome. No one at all in the whole of the early Church appealed to Rome as final arbiter to settle disputes concerning matters of faith. Indeed parts even of the Western Church rejected the views of the bishops of Rome, as the African Church had done when

Stephen had tried to settle Cyprian's baptismal problem.[227] Of the scores of controversies in the first six centuries of the Christian Church, not a single one was settled by reference to the Bishop of Rome.

It is clear that in early times Rome did not enjoy supremacy over the other patriarchies. Even after the fall of Jerusalem, Rome was no more important than Antioch or Alexandria although, as the capital of the Empire, its name was usually listed first. These great centres did not lay claim to dictate doctrine. Ecumenical councils settled doctrine, and these councils were not called by the bishops of Rome. In fact the bishops of Rome did not even attend many of them, including the most important, the Ecumenical Council of Nicæa in 325. At this council just two presbyters represented the Bishop of Rome. At the next ecumenical council, there were no bishops from Western Christendom present at all.[228]

Eastern bishops always regarded the bishops of Rome as analogous to other patriarchs, and they continued to do so, being successively bemused and outraged by Rome's increasing claims, and the forgeries that were produced to support them. Over the centuries the Roman Church manufactured a large number of forgeries. Even the decisions of the Council of Nicæa were tampered with. For example the sixth canon confirmed that the bishops of Alexandria enjoyed authority similar to that of the bishops of Rome and Antioch. Clerks in the papal chancery added the words 'The Roman Church has always had the primacy'. The faithful in the West believed it, having no way of spotting the imposture, but the Eastern Churches knew better because they had original documents. In time the fraudulent version would be cited at Chalcedon, though it fooled no one, and failed to stop Constantinople being established as the court of appeal from provincial synods.[229]

The claims of Rome continued to multiply. In 343 the synod at Sardica (modern Sofia) had laid down that appeals should be referred to the See of Rome. This convention was set out in the Sardican canons. As papal claims grew, it became expedient to claim this role for Rome not only within Western Christendom, but also throughout the whole Church. In the Roman chancery the Sardican canons were appended to those of the Ecumenical Council of Nicæa, so giving them spurious universal authority. Bishops of Rome then made claim on the strength of them. Zosimus for example tried to impose his rule in Africa on the basis of them, but the Africans obtained a true copy of the Nicæan canons from the East and revealed the imposture.

As the centuries rolled by, the bishops of Rome made grander and grander claims about their rights and abilities. Around 378, Damasus I held a synod that declared he should not be compelled to appear in court. It was Damasus also who started to refer to his fellow bishops as *sons* rather than as *brothers*. Soon, bishop Siricius was self-titling himself 'Pope' and claiming the status of imperial decrees for his edicts. In the fifth century Pope Boniface I made the claim that 'it has never been lawful for what has once been decided by the apostolic see to be reconsidered'.

Further papal claims were bolstered by forged documents. One such was produced by Pope Symmachus, who reigned between 498 and 514. He was charged by the Emperor with celebrating Easter at the wrong time, fornication, and the misuse of Church property. Symmachus's response was to produce what are now called the *Symmachan Forgeries*. This set of documents purported to demonstrate that a pope cannot be judged by mere human beings, no matter what he might have done. For centuries, popes would produce this work of fiction to prove that they were above human justice, sometimes with success. In 664, the argument about the Bishop of Rome being the successor of St Peter scored a major success. Roman representatives at the Council of Whitby convinced members of the Celtic Church that the Bishop of Rome was the successor to St Peter. Since he held the keys to the gates of Heaven, the Celtic Church abandoned its independence and, in effect, joined the Roman Church.

Ever-increasing claims created friction with the other patriarchs. A particular problem was the title of Ecumenical Patriarch accorded to the Bishop of Constantinople. In the sixth century Pope Gregory I had warned his fellow patriarch about using such a proud and sinful title, but without effect. Within a century bishops of Rome were using the title for themselves. By 680, in the reign of Pope Agatho, the Easter synod was confident enough to assert for the first time that Rome enjoyed not merely primacy in the whole Church but supremacy over it. The identification of the Pope with St Peter continued. When in 710 the Pope ordered that the Archbishop of Ravenna be blinded, the verdict was presented as coming from St Peter himself.

St Peter or not, the Pope was still a duke of the Empire. His duchy still belonged to the Emperor, and he still paid taxes accordingly. But by the first half of the eighth century popes felt powerful enough to stop paying. Now they were independent and able to exercise power on their own authority. Their new claims to additional power were supported by more forged documents. The most famous of these was the *Donation of Constantine*. This was a document, supposedly dating from 30th March 315, that purported to confer on the reigning pope, and his successors, primacy over the patriarchs as well as temporal dominion over the West, along with the imperial insignia. It was apparently concocted in the papal chancery around AD 754, and was used by Pope Stephen II (III)* to deceive the Frankish King Pepin III. It was a great success. Not only did Pepin feel obliged to protect Stephen from his enemies, but he also wrote a new document, the *Donation of Pepin*, confirming the claims made in the fabricated *Donation of Constantine*. The *Donation of Pepin* was confirmed in turn by Charlemagne in 774.

Using these documents, a long succession of popes claimed not only seniority over the Eastern patriarchs, but also the exclusive right to judge the clergy, and the right to the imperial crown. As the centuries passed the validity of the *Donation of Constantine* came to be widely accepted. However, the document was so badly fabricated that it was only a matter of time before it was exposed as a fraud. For example, it referred to Byzantium as Constantinople, a name acquired by the city *after* the time when the document was purportedly written. In 1439 a papal aide revealed it as a fraud by highlighting a variety of such blunders, but the truth was suppressed.[230] By the sixteenth century many scholars knew it to be a fraud, but Rome still asserted its authenticity. For centuries one infallible pope after another refused to acknowledge it as the fabrication that it is now universally accepted to be.

The ninth century saw another celebrated set of papal forgeries: the *False Decretals* (or *Pseudo-Isidorian Decretals*). These were attributed to St Isidore of Seville, who had died in 636. They consisted of hundreds of documents, some completely bogus, some genuine but tampered with. Once again they sought to enhance papal claims. They set out precedents defining the rights of bishops and asserting the superior authority of the reigning pope over synods and metropolitans, and indeed the whole Church. It affected all of Western Christendom, including England. As a legal authority puts it:

---

* See page 225 for an explanation of the numbering of popes called Stephen.

The Isidorian forgeries were soon accepted at Rome. The popes profited by documents which taught that ever since the apostolic age the bishops of Rome had been declaring, or even making, law for the universal church. On this rock or on this sand a lofty edifice was reared.[231]

The decretals were invoked by Pope Nicholas I (pope 858–67, now St Nicholas) to support his own claims. They had been compiled in France, probably around AD 850.[232] For centuries scholars have known them to be forgeries, but the Roman Church placed any writing that said so on the Index, its list of prohibited books. It was not until 1789 that Pope Pius VI admitted the truth.

In the eleventh century Pope Gregory VII claimed that he had sole right to the title Pope, an honorific that had been widely used in the early church, and not conferred on the bishops of Rome until the second half of the fourth century. Gregory conceived of the whole world as a divinely established feudal state with himself at its head, in the role of St Peter, Christ's vicar on Earth. In the face of all precedents Gregory required all bishops to take an oath of personal loyalty to him. From that time onwards Roman Catholic bishops took their position not merely by apostolic succession, but by favour of the Pope. He also claimed that the Pope is incapable of making a mistake. In his *Dictatus papae* of 1075, largely based upon forged documents, Gregory spelled out the implications of this. Amongst them were:

- The Pope cannot be judged by any other human being.
- The Roman Church has never erred and never will.
- The Pope alone is entitled to imperial insignia.
- The Pope can depose emperors and kings and can absolve their subjects from allegiance.
- All princes must kiss the Pope's feet.
- By the merits of Peter, a properly elected pope is necessarily a saint.
- His exalted position guaranteed him personal sanctity inherited from Peter and supremacy over all earthly rulers, both spiritual and temporal.

This last claim was undermined when the German King, Henry IV, deposed him.

In 1123 Pope Callistus II became the first pope to convene a Church Council (the First Lateran Council) that was regarded as ecumenical in

Western Christendom, though not of course in the East. The Blessed Eugene III, who ascended the papal throne in 1145, expounded the doctrine that Christ had devolved upon the Pope supreme authority in temporal, as well as spiritual, matters. Popes also expounded on their power in Heaven. For 1,000 years saints had been declared locally, or had simply arisen by common consent. Around 1170 Pope Alexander III tried to reserve to the papacy the power to create saints.

This power was confirmed by Pope Innocent III, who ascended the papal throne in 1198. To his credit, one of his first acts was to root out the nest of forgers operating in the papal chancery. Innocent saw himself not as the *Vicar of St Peter*, but as the *Vicar of Christ*.[233] He claimed to be set midway between God and man, and to have been given not only the Church but also the whole world to govern. He succeeded in extending the papacy's feudal power, acquiring as fiefdoms Portugal, Aragon, Hungary and England, and purporting to reassign important feudal properties of Raimon VI of Toulouse – a precedent that is still mourned to this day. He stated that every cleric must obey the Pope, even if he commands what is evil, for no one may judge the Pope.

Innocent IV (pope 1243–54) confirmed his total dominion over all earthly rulers. Gregory IX (pope 1227–41) declared himself to be the Lord and Master of the whole Universe, not merely of people, or of living creatures, but absolutely everything. Boniface VIII (pope 1294–1303) defined as official doctrine the proposition that every human being must do as the Pope tells him. The pontiff, he said, is the repository and fount of all law. From this he drew the conclusion, in the closing sentence of his bull *Unam sanctum,* that blind submission to his authority was necessary for salvation: '… we declare, state, define and pronounce that for every human creature to be subject to the Roman pope is altogether necessary for salvation'. It was heresy to deny this infallible truth. He also claimed to be the bodily presence of Christ. He would on occasion dress in imperial robes and claim to be Emperor as well.

Papal claims were accompanied by appropriate symbolism. By the eleventh century a coronet had already been added to the rim of the papal tiara. A second was added around 1300, and a third a few years later, so producing the familiar triple crown, which symbolises papal dominion. These claims of dominion have never been rescinded, and popes still sport their triple crown, confirming their absolute rule. Similarly, they took to adopting other super-symbols. Since archbishops carried crosiers with one cross piece, and patriarchs carried crosiers with two cross pieces, the Roman popes adopted one with three cross pieces.

In his bull *Fidem catholicam*, of 1338, Pope Benedict XII proclaimed that imperial authority derives directly from God himself. In fact there seems to have been some confusion between God and the Pope. In the late Middle Ages God was portrayed as the Pope, even wearing the pope's triple crown. Both Van Eyck and Botticelli painted pictures showing God sporting a papal tiara.

Divine claims were at least partly responsible for the Reformation. 'I do not know' wrote Luther 'whether the Christian faith can bear it, that there should be any other head of the universal church on earth than Christ himself'. But papal claims were not to be retracted. Pius V (pope 1566–72) confirmed that he could appoint anyone, including emperors, for any reason and whenever he pleased. He also denied that it could ever be lawful to disobey unjust papal orders. For centuries, one pope after another was to confirm that, by virtue of his office, he enjoyed total dominion, both secular and religious. In 1568 Pius V stated that this was not merely law, but an eternal law.

Popes had exercised absolute power over the Papal States, a large stretch of Italy that had been acquired by the sword, since the Middle Ages. A series of popes made increasingly unlikely claims about them. When Napoleon seized them in the nineteenth century, Pius VII demanded their return on the grounds that 'they are not our personal inheritance, but the inheritance of St Peter who received them from Christ'. By 1870 Garibaldi's army had captured the Papal States and unified Italy. In that year the dogma of papal infallibility was declared. According to this, when speaking *ex cathedra* on faith or morals the Pope is literally infallible.

Leo XIII firmly believed that his power extended over the whole world. In 1900 he dedicated the whole human race to the sacred heart of Jesus. His successor Pius X convinced himself, and others, that he possessed supernatural powers, and was subsequently made a saint on the strength of them. Many papal claims have been replaced by more modest ones, but none has been explicitly abandoned. There may be more claims to come. To this day, Roman Catholic bishops take an oath to maintain, defend, increase and advance the rights, honours, privileges and authority of their lord the Pope.

How Popes were Chosen

Popes have not always been elected in the way they are now. In the earliest times they were elected, like other bishops, by local citizens. Pope Stephen III (IV) curtailed this right in 769. From then on the Roman clergy were, in theory, eligible to elect their bishop. A new system giving control to cardinal bishops was introduced at the Lateran Synod of 1059. Then in 1179 the cardinals won exclusive rights to elect their bishop, who by this time was reserving to himself the title of Pope.

In practice neither the people nor the cardinals or other clergy were always able to elect the candidate they wanted. Sometimes Roman mobs took matters into their own hands. In 896 for example a rioting mob forced the election of Boniface VI, despite his having been twice degraded for immorality and defrocked. More often popes were appointed by whoever exercised the most power at the time. An Ostrogoth king had terrorised the electorate into choosing a Subdeacon, Silverius, as pope in the sixth century. The Empress Theodora wanted a more sympathetic bishop of Rome, so Silverius was arrested and deposed, and the Emperor forced through the election of Pope Vigilius. At the beginning of the tenth century the Western Emperor Otto took a dislike to the rightful pope, Benedict IV. Benedict grovelled at the Emperor's feet, declared himself to be an impostor, and claimed that the Emperor's man was the true pope. So it was that the Emperor's man became Pope Leo V in 903.

At other times popes owed their position to some other European power, or to the influence of a powerful Italian family. Once in power, many popes did their best to keep the papacy in the family. Pope Silverius for example was the son of Pope Hormisdas. Pope Gregory I was directly descended from Felix III (II). Stephen IV (V), Sergius II and Hadrian II all belonged to the same aristocratic family. Alexander IV was the nephew of Gregory IX, himself the nephew of Innocent III, who in turn was the nephew of Pope Clement III. Hadrian V was a nephew of Innocent IV; Pius III of Pius II; Paul II of Eugene IV; Julius II of Sixtus IV, and so on.

For centuries, the papacy was passed around the leading families of Italy and Europe. The Colonnas tried hard for many years to place their man on the papal throne, finally succeeding with Martin V in 1417. Pope Alexander VI, a Borgia, was the nephew of Callistus III. Paul III, previously known as *Cardinal Petticoat*, owed his advancement to his sister who had been the mistress of Alexander. Pius IV in turn owed his position largely to his elder brother, who had married into the family of Paul. Both Leo X and Clement VII were members of the Medici family (they were cousins), and so was Leo XI, nephew of Leo X. The Orsini family managed to place on the papal throne Celestine III, Nicholas III and Benedict XIII.

At the beginning of the tenth century the papacy was controlled by a man called Theophylact and his wife Theodora. This period of dependency is generally known to historians as the *pornocracy of the Holy See*. It extended through the reigns of Popes Sergius III, Anastasius III, Lando, John X, Leo VI, Stephen VII (VIII) and John XI. According to Bishop Liutprand of Cremona, John XI was the illegitimate son of Pope Sergius III and Theodora's 15-year-old daughter. In 935 an influential aristocrat, Alberic II, prompted a revolt against Theophylact's puppet pope, John XI. John was imprisoned and treated like a slave, while Alberic appointed his own pope, Leo VII. Alberic was also responsible for the next pope, Stephen VIII (IX), who tried to exercise a measure of independence and as a result found himself imprisoned, mutilated and murdered. Alberic's next two popes, Marinus II and Agapetus II, were more amenable. Next came Alberic's own illegitimate son, Pope John XII, who was elected in accordance with his father's instructions and in contravention of existing election decrees. Alberic's family (the Alberics of Tusculum) managed to place thirteen of their members on the papal throne over the centuries.

Often, a number of valid popes were alive at the same time. For example, the Emperor Otto appointed Pope Leo VIII to replace Pope John XII after John had been deposed in 963. John subsequently returned to Rome and deposed Leo. After John's death in 964, the Romans elected a new pope, Benedict V. Otto now laid siege to Rome. The citizens handed Benedict over to the Emperor. He was deposed and degraded, stripped of his papal robes, and his papal staff broken over his head by Otto's nominee, Leo, who was then reinstated. John XII, Leo VIII and Benedict V are all now considered to have been valid popes.

After Otto's death in 973, a faction of the Crescentii family tried to get their nominee on the papal throne as Boniface VII. The fact that Otto's nominee Benedict VI still occupied it had to be overcome by Boniface. He instructed a priest called Stephen to strangle Benedict, and the pious Stephen complied. But now another candidate appeared with more powerful backing, so Boniface fled with the papal treasure. The new pope was Benedict VII, another kinsman of Alberic, who enjoyed the support of the Emperor. When Benedict died in 983, the Emperor, Otto II, appointed Pope John XIV apparently without even consulting the people or clergy of Rome. Otto II died in December 983. Without his support John was vulnerable since the new Emperor was only three years old. Boniface VII soon reappeared, and had John imprisoned, deposed and murdered. Boniface himself died in 985, probably the victim of assassination. Pope John XV succeeded him with the approval of the Crescentii family. The period of Crescentii supremacy was turbulent, and by the age of 15 the new emperor, Otto III, felt obliged to visit Rome to attend to matters personally.

The Pope died of a fever before Otto arrived, so Otto was free to appoint one of his own relatives, who became Pope Gregory V. Aged 24 he was Otto's senior by nine years. When Otto returned to Germany the Crescentii family drove Gregory from Rome, and put their own man, John Philagathos, on the papal throne. He lasted only until Otto could reassert his influence, after which Gregory V was restored. John was blinded, and his nose, tongue, lips and hands mutilated, then he was tried, condemned and imprisoned. After the death of Pope Gregory V in 999, Otto appointed a new pope, Sylvester II, who was popularly believed to have made a pact with Satan. Otto died without an heir in 1002 and when Sylvester followed him to the grave the following year, the Crescentii family were again able to put their puppet on the papal throne. The puppet Pope John XVII lasted only a few months and was succeeded by another Crescentii puppet pope, John XVIII. His reign ended in mysterious circumstances in 1009, although he kept his life for the time being. Another Crescentii puppet was then installed as Pope Sergius IV.

In 1012 the house of Tusculum (descended from Theophylact) gained ascendancy over the Crescentii family. The reigning pope, Sergius, and his predecessor, John XVIII, were both murdered. The house of Tusculum placed its man on the papal throne as Pope Benedict VIII. On his death in 1024, his younger brother became Pope John XIX. Not being in Holy Orders, he was elevated from layman to pope in a single day. Such promotion was unusual and called for particularly lavish bribery. After John's death his brother, now head of the family, bribed the electorate and succeeded in getting his own son elected. The son was still a layman, or perhaps lay-child would be a more appropriate term. In the space of a single October day in 1032 this 'mere urchin' became His Holiness Pope Benedict IX. He led a scandalous life, and when his family's fortunes were reversed in 1044 he was obliged to flee Rome.

The Crescentii family regained power and promptly installed their own pope, Sylvester III, early in 1045. Within a few months Benedict's supporters expelled Sylvester, who also fled Rome to the safety of lands under Crescentii control. Benedict was restored as Pope, but within a few months he decided he had had enough of the papacy, and wanted to settle down with an attractive female cousin. He dispensed himself from his obligation of celibacy, and arranged to have himself bought off for over 1,000 lb of gold, though as he pointed out, he was only recovering his father's original expenditure. He then abdicated in favour of the man who bought him off, who happened to be his own godfather, and who now became Pope Gregory VI. Benedict's affection for his attractive female cousin was not reciprocated, so he sought to regain the papal throne. Details of his arrangement with Gregory became public. The German Emperor, Henry III, called a synod over which he presided himself. He assured himself that simony had been committed and deposed both Gregory VI and Benedict IX (and also a surviving Crescentii pope, Sylvester III). He then imposed a new pope, the first of a line of four German popes he was to nominate: Clement II, Damasus II, Leo IX (now a saint), and Victor II. Pope Victor II died in 1057, a year after the Emperor Henry III, while the new Emperor, Henry IV, was still a baby. Seizing their chance, the Romans conducted what seems to have been a fair election, and the product of this remarkable event was Pope Stephen IX (X).

In the thirteenth century the Kings of Sicily managed to get their nominees on the papal throne as Hadrian V, Martin IV and Celestine V. The pope who succeeded Celestine V, Boniface VIII, is reported to have gained his throne in 1294 by taking advantage of Celestine's naïveté. He bored a hole into the wall of Celestine's bedroom at the Castel Nuovo in Naples, then, in the middle of the night, he whispered through the hole a message that Celestine should lay down his office as it was too great a burden for him. In obedience to the Holy Ghost, as he thought, Celestine abdicated, and the perpetrator of the fraud reaped the fruits of his deception by taking his place on the papal throne. Celestine lived out the rest of his life imprisoned by Boniface in a castle tower.

Popes and Anti-popes

In the popular mind there has always been an undoubted line of valid popes in Rome and for a short while also a line of anti-popes, a succession of rivals who set up shop in Avignon in defiance of the true popes. This conception is wrong in almost every respect.

The fact is that often there were two or more papal claimants, and no one knew who the real pope was. This happened countless times, and the city in which the claimants lived was not much of a guide. Many men now considered to have been valid popes never even visited Rome, or Avignon for that matter. What generally happened was that two men would claim to be the rightful pope, each denouncing the other as an impostor. Often they both had as good a claim as each other, having been elected by different groups of electors. Election rules were continually changing, and different factions naturally tended to support sets of rules that favoured their own candidates. On occasion two popes could both claim to have been elected by the same electors. On many occasions one pope was deposed and replaced by another. If the first one was not murdered or imprisoned (as he often was) he would do his best to get himself reinstated. All he needed to do was to rally support from the political factions he was likely to favour if he regained power.

So how did Avignon come into it? The story is this: Pope Boniface VIII annoyed a number of monarchs by his papal claims. Early in the fourteenth century an agent of Philip, King of France, accompanied by the head of the Colonna family, captured Boniface with the intention of trying him for murder, idolatry, sodomy, simony and heresy. Within a month he was dead, but he was posthumously put on trial. His successor Benedict XI failed to appease the king, and soon he too was dead. The cardinals chose as the next pope Clement V, whom they expected to stand up to Philip, but Philip bought him off without too much trouble. Clement was obliged to stay in France for years, before being allowed to move to the safety of Avignon, not then in France, but under the watchful eye of the French King. Once the papacy was in the pocket of the King, there followed a string of French popes, whose election became successively easier as the college of cardinals was packed with Frenchmen: of the 134 cardinals appointed while the papacy was held by Frenchmen, 112 were French.

So it was that a succession of perfectly valid popes never set foot in Rome. Altogether there were seven French popes in a row, all based in

Avignon: Clement V, John XXII, Benedict XII, Clement VI, Innocent VI, Urban V and Gregory XI. This long absence from Rome, extending from 1305 to 1378, is generally known as the *Babylonian Captivity of the Papacy*. The last of these popes in Avignon, Gregory XI, returned to Rome, and when he died in 1378 the Romans let it be known that they wanted a Roman pope, even though there were no realistic candidates. Indeed there were only four Italian cardinals left. Sixteen cardinals met in conclave to elect a new pope, knowing that their lives depended on their decision. They duly elected an Italian, Urban VI, an event that apparently tipped the balance of his mind. The French cardinals immediately made off to safety, where they claimed that they had acted under duress. They denied that Urban was the rightful pope and elected another one, a cousin of the King of France, who took the style Pope Clement VII. As usual, Christendom divided on political lines: the French and their allies Scotland, Spain and Naples supported Clement, while the Italians supported the increasingly insane Urban, as did England and other northern countries, apparently on the grounds that anything was preferable to another French pope. Over the next 30 years there were two lines of popes: Urban VI in Rome was succeeded by Boniface IX, Innocent VII and Gregory XII, while Clement in Avignon was succeeded by Benedict XIII.

In 1409 a council was convoked at Pisa by leading churchmen of the day who felt that this schism had gone on long enough. They solemnly declared that both reigning popes (Gregory XII and Benedict XIII) were heretics and schismatics, and they elected a new pope, Alexander V. Neither Gregory nor Benedict recognised the council, so now there were three popes. Each claimed absolute authority, and each excommunicated the other two. Another council was called at Constance in 1414, this time with more success. In 1415 Gregory abdicated, and Benedict was deposed, as was Alexander's successor, John XXIII. A new pope, Martin V, was elected in 1417, and generally accepted throughout Western Christendom, although a line of successors to Benedict continued for many years, gradually sinking into historical oblivion.

Views as to who was the rightful pope changed as often as the balance of power, as did views as to who had been rightful popes previously. When the appointee of one family became pope, he would often make adjustments to the historical record to reinstate his papal relatives. Over the centuries the same claimant could be regarded as a rightful pope, then as an heretical anti-pope, then as pope again, then as anti-pope, and so on. Evidence of the level of uncertainty about who was, and who was not, a rightful pope is not difficult to find. For example a pope called Stephen, who reigned for three or four days in 752, was not counted as a pope immediately after his death. Later he was recognised as a pope and designated Stephen II. Then, in 1961, he was dropped again, so at the time of writing he is not counted as a pope. The effect of this has been to confuse the numbering of subsequent popes called Stephen. His successor, who also took the name Stephen, was originally designated Stephen II. Later, when the short-lived earlier Stephen was reinstated as Stephen II, his successor had to be upgraded to Stephen III. Now that the first Stephen has been dropped again his successor has gone back to being Stephen II, but to avoid confusion he is generally known as Stephen II (III). Subsequent Stephens are now known as Stephen III (IV), Stephen IV (V) and so on right up to Stephen IX (X). Similar problems occur with popes called Felix.

Another indicator of the confusion is the fact that current lists of past popes have no John XX. It seems that the numerous papal claimants who took the name John led to such a mess that no one even claimed the number XX. Neither was there a John XVI, although there are Johns up to XXIII. Indeed, there have been two John XXIIIs. There had been one in the fifteenth century, but a new pope took the name and style of John XXIII in 1958. There was widespread surprise and puzzlement, since it was well known that there had already been a John XXIII. In fact there is little doubt that the first John XXIII had been the rightful pope, but he had been an acute embarrassment and had been deposed by a council in 1415. (Actually he got off lightly: only 5 of the 54 charges against him were pursued. As Gibbon noted: 'The most scandalous charges were suppressed; the Vicar of Christ was only accused of piracy, murder, rape, sodomy and incest.') In 1958 cathedrals suddenly had to revise their lists, as the fifteenth-century John XXIII was now deemed to be an anti-pope.

Again, according to modern official lists, there was never a valid pope called Alexander V, although there was one with this designation who is now considered an anti-pope and there were also Alexanders VI, VII, and VIII. Neither was there a valid Benedict X, though there have been Benedicts numbered up to Benedict XVI (who became pope in 2005). Another oddity is that some anti-popes are regarded as saints, even by the modern papacy, which simultaneously dismisses them as pretenders to St Peter's throne. For example, St Hippolytus, one of the most important figures in the Western Church in the early third century, was elected as Bishop of Rome in competition to Callistus. Each regarded the other as a heretic. Callistus is now reckoned a true pope and St Hippolytus merely an anti-pope.

It is clear that some properly elected popes are now on the list of anti-popes while many (perhaps most) of the official popes were elected irregularly. One of the most striking examples of a rightful pope being regarded today as an anti-pope is one called Celestine. An old man, he was elected, properly and unanimously, on 15th December 1124. During his installation an armed gang broke in on the ceremony, acclaimed their own man as Pope Honorius II, and attacked Celestine, who died of his injuries soon afterwards. Yet Honorius is now considered a rightful pope, while Celestine is a mere anti-pope.

It is of little relevance to consider which of two contenders reigned as *de facto* pope in Rome. Often the pope now considered the real pope was a powerless exile, while the one considered the anti-pope was happily ensconced in Rome and exercising his office. Pope Victor III, for example, was obliged by rioting mobs to flee from Rome in 1086 before he had even been consecrated. A rival claimant, Clement III, was installed in the Lateran basilica. He was highly regarded, and managed the papal office far better than many others. For example, he was strongly opposed to the simony that had characterised the papacy for so long. He carried out papal functions with success and performed the customary crowning of a new emperor. He also instigated reforms that in time would lead to the founding of the college of cardinals. Victor meanwhile languished in exile. At times he gave up his papal claim and returned to his previous career as an abbot. There is no record that he achieved anything of any significance. Clement exercised the office of pope right through the reign of Victor, and through much of the reign of his successor. Nevertheless we are assured that Clement was an anti-pope, and the blessed Victor was a real pope.

Some claimants are considered popes even though their elections were clearly invalid, and some had little or no experience in the Church. Many had not been bishops, some had not been priests or even deacons before their elevation. Pope Leo VIII was a layman who was rushed through religious orders in a single day. Pope Gregory X, by inclination a warrior rather than a holy man, was ordained as a priest and consecrated as Pope on a single day in March 1271. Hadrian V, who reigned for a few weeks in 1276, was never made Bishop of Rome. The simple fact is that there is no objective way of knowing which of two or more claimants was the rightful pope. Official lists are of little use since they have been changed so often, and might change again tomorrow.

Even after 1,000 years, the truth can easily be massaged. A man who was universally recognised as pope can suddenly be demoted to an anti-pope. Take for example Boniface VII. He became Pope in 974 after having Benedict VI murdered. When the locals turned against him he fled with the papal treasure and was excommunicated. In 980 he returned to Rome and re-established himself, displacing his successor Benedict VII, but fled again when the Emperor turned up with an army. In 984 he returned once again and deposed, imprisoned and murdered his new replacement, Pope John XIV. Boniface himself died suddenly the following year, possibly the victim of a palace conspiracy. His body was stripped and dragged through the streets of Rome, and then left, naked, for public ridicule. Grateful for the opportunity, citizens amused themselves by trampling and stabbing it. None of this is remarkable, and it is easy to find other popes whose reigns were far less illustrious, and whose crimes were far greater. In old official lists he was invariably agreed to have been a valid pope. Nevertheless, it was announced in 1904 that Boniface VII had not been a real pope at all, merely an anti-pope, so God had managed without a personal deputy on Earth for a year, from August 984 to August 985.

Another difficulty with the idea that bishops of Rome owe their appointment to God is that, if this is the case, then God seems to have displayed a certain lack of foresight. He failed to foresee not only the amount of crime and venality that his elect would become involved in but also the fact that in some cases, such as Urban VI and Stephen VI (VII), they might promptly lose their minds. Others had limited lifespans. The Stephen who was elected Pope in 752 suffered a stroke three days after his election and died the day after. Boniface VI died of gout 15 days after his election in April 896. Celestine IV fell ill two days after his election in 1241 and died a few days later, apparently without having performed any official act, or even having been consecrated. Urban VII fell ill with malaria the day after his election on 15th September 1590 and died a few days later, before his coronation. In 1978 'God's candidate'

John Paul I died in his bed just three weeks after his investiture, having achieved none of his planned reforms.

'Papal Crimes' and Popular Opinion

Simony has always been common in Rome. It would be a bold historian who asserted that more popes have gained the throne through merit than by bribery. From the fourth century onwards Roman nobles were exchanging their secular robes for clerical ones, or rather their priestly robes of the old religion for new priestly robes of the new Christian one.

The modern Roman Church was essentially a creation of the Roman nobility. For many centuries the papacy was to be a prize, awarded to the currently most powerful Roman noble family, that enabled the winner to extort vast sums from the whole of Western Christendom. The sale of cardinals' hats and other Church offices has been a bottomless well of treasure. Simony is still commonly known as one of the two *papal crimes*, the other being nepotism. Many popes had illegitimate children, and the convention was to call them nephews. Numerous popes advanced the careers of their nominal nephews, and their real nephews, giving them cardinals' hats, and preparing the way for their succession. The word nepotism was coined to describe this scandal. It is derived from the Latin word for a nephew, *nepos*.

Sergius II, who ascended the papal throne in 844, made his brother a bishop, and the two of them sold bishoprics and other Church offices to the highest bidder. Clement V appointed five close relatives as cardinals and misused the papal treasures to such an extent that his successor instituted legal proceedings against his family to recover some of them. Boniface IX, who ascended the papal throne in 1389, was an outstanding nepotist and simonist – arguably the worst ever. He raised vast amounts of money by auctioning Church offices and marketed indulgences in ways that were considered outrageous even by papal standards.

Pius II created a nephew, the future Pius III, an archbishop and cardinal at the age of 21. The fifteenth-century pope Sixtus IV appointed numerous relatives (three sons and six others) as cardinals, one of them the future Julius II. The chief interest of the Borgia Pope Alexander VI seems to have been the promotion of his family's wealth and influence. Indeed he appears to have aspired to keep the papacy in the family indefinitely. To this end he attempted to crush all potential opposition by murdering members of other leading Roman families and seizing their property. He appointed his own son to several bishoprics at the age of 18 and gave him a cardinal's hat the following year. This reign is generally recognised as marking the high point of papal greed and corruption.

Paul III gave important parts of the Papal States to his son Pierluigi, and gave cardinals' hats to two grandsons aged 14 and 16. His main interest seems to have been to establish his family among the great houses of Italy. Urban VIII was so extravagant a nepotist that his successor Innocent X, who ascended the papal throne in 1644, tried to recover some of the illegal gifts distributed to Urban's relatives. Almost any high Church office could become a sinecure. Such offices were often granted to provide their holders with incomes. Even children could be given them. For example, Pope Leo X, the second son of Lorenzo de' Medici (Lorenzo the Magnificent) was appointed a cardinal at the age of 13, before having the papacy purchased for him by his father.

Far from being elected by their flocks, many popes were positively hated by them. Sabinian, for example, had incurred the hatred of Romans by profiteering during a famine. After his death in 606 they tried to seize and dismember his corpse, and his funeral procession was obliged to pass outside the city walls. In 799 Pope Leo III, an extremely unpopular man, was attacked by a mob, which tried to cut off his tongue and tear out his eyes. Pope Paschal I was given to blinding and beheading his opponents. He was so unpopular that when he died in 824 a public uproar prevented his body being buried in St Peter's. John VIII was poisoned by members of his own entourage in 882, and was then finished off by being clubbed to death. Stephen VI (VII), arguably the most insane of all popes, was deposed by a Roman mob, gaoled, and strangled in 897. The next pope, Romanus, was also deposed after a reign of a few months, and the next one, Theodore II, died of causes unknown after a reign of 20 days. Leo V managed only 30 days as pope before being overthrown by his own clergy in 903 and subsequently murdered.

John XIII, who ascended the papal throne in 965, was widely hated. The citizens of Rome attacked, imprisoned and banished him. They probably regretted that they did not kill him, for he returned with the protection of the Emperor, and punished them with a brutality that was considered remarkable, even by papal standards. Gregory VII was less disliked, but was denounced at the Synod of Brixen in 1080 for having studied magic at Toledo and for having taken up necromancy.

Pope Lucius II, in an attempt to assert his authority over the self-governing commune that had been established in Rome, led an armed force on the Capitol in 1145. Unimpressed by His Holiness, the opposition forces stoned him to death. Alexander III was also obliged to leave Rome, but after his death in 1181 his body was returned for burial. The low opinion of him held by the citizens of Rome was reflected by the insulting graffiti lavished on his tomb. Pope Urban III lived in Verona, since popular hostility in Rome prevented him from living there.

Clement III, who reigned from 1187 to 1191, was the first pope for decades to establish himself safely in Rome, a feat he achieved by the liberal distribution of bribes. Urban IV (pope 1261–64) was so unpopular that he was never able to reside in Rome and never even visited the place. Neither did his successor Clement IV, again because of popular hostility towards him. One of his less endearing acts was to engineer the execution of the popular young prince Conraldin, a ward of the Holy See, whose rights the papacy had sworn to protect. Martin IV, who became pope in 1281, was another who was so unpopular that he was unable to live in Rome.

Urban VI was clearly insane. Because of the circumstances of his election, most of his cardinals deserted him and purported to depose him. Although he appointed new cardinals, they soon became acquainted with his mental incompetence and paranoia, and so started considering a council of regency. Learning of this he had six leading cardinals tortured. Only one escaped with his life. Despite his mental state, Urban reigned for 11 years, at the end of which he died in suspicious circumstances, possibly the victim of poisoning. Who was responsible is difficult to assess, for he was detested not only by the cardinals who had originally elected him under duress, but also by his own new cardinals (such as survived). He was loathed by the clergy at large, the citizens of Rome, many of the monarchs of Europe, and even his own mercenaries.

Innocent VII was exceptionally unpopular and was able to remain in Rome only because of protection from the King of Naples. As a favour to him, one of his nephews had eleven leading citizens murdered. A violent mob stormed the Vatican, and Innocent was lucky to escape with his life. Eugene IV was also the victim of mob violence, and was obliged to leave Rome in disguise. Paul IV, a man of exceeding brutality, had earned his reputation, like many popes-to-be, as head of the Inquisition before ascending the throne in 1555. He had several claims to fame: he was a spectacularly successful simonist, he burned more books than any other pope, and he created the Jewish ghetto. He was feared and hated throughout his four-year reign, but only after his death did the citizens of Rome dare to express their opinion of him. A mob attacked the Inquisition's offices, released its victims, and overturned and mutilated His Holiness's statue on the Capitol.

Pope Sixtus V had already earned a fearful reputation as an inquisitor. As pope he had thousands publicly executed in the Papal States. Loathed by the people of Rome, his statue was torn down from the Capitol by a rioting mob when they learned of his death. Pius IX was yet another extremely unpopular pope. His Prime Minister was murdered, and Pius was obliged to flee Rome in disguise. His reign generated a great deal of anticlerical feeling throughout Europe. When he died in 1878 a Roman mob tried to seize his body and throw it into the Tiber.

It is difficult to find more than a handful of popes who led lives that could be objectively assessed as other than scandalous. Even the most revered seem to have been not quite as they are often portrayed. Pope Gregory I (St Gregory the Great), for example, who is often described as the greatest pope ever, owed his election in 590 to his connections. He belonged to Rome's richest family, the same one as Popes Felix III and Agapetus I. He devoted much time to writing accounts of monstrous births (which he believed to be omens) and other bizarre phenomena. He urged the sequestration of pagan temples and encouraged the bribery of Jews to assist conversion. He expressed delight at the murder of the Emperor in 602, apparently because the Emperor had failed to accept Gregory's claim to primacy over the Eastern Church.

It is true that Gregory stands out as exceptionally competent, but that is only because of the comparisons available. The following selection is not untypical. St Callistus was an embezzler and a bankrupt who had fled his creditors. He became Bishop of Rome in 217. John XII, a 'dissolute boy', became Pope at the age of 16 in 955. The citizens of Rome said that he slept with his mother, that he had turned the Lateran Palace into a brothel, and that he toasted the Devil at the High Altar. His behaviour was so bad that a synod was convoked. A bishop recorded the charges, all confirmed under oath: he was a simonist, he had had sex with numerous women including a relative, he had blinded one cleric and castrated another (a cardinal who had died as a result). Otto I, the Holy Roman Emperor, felt obliged to write to him saying that everyone accused him of homicide, perjury, sacrilege, incest with his relatives, including two of his sisters, and with having invoked Jupiter, Venus and other demons. John refused to answer the charges, so Otto deposed him and a new pope, Leo VIII, was installed. John went into exile until Otto left Rome, then he returned to torture, maim and murder those he felt had not been sufficiently understanding with regard to his behaviour. Leo fled to the imperial court, and in his absence John deposed and excommunicated him. When Otto returned to sort matters out, John fled once again. Soon afterwards, in 964 John was suddenly incapacitated as he lay in bed with a married woman and died a week later. Some said that he had suffered a stroke. Since he was only 24 at the time, the more likely account was that his stroke had been assisted by a hammer blow to the back of the head, delivered by the man whose wife His Holiness had been ministering to at the time.

Stephen VI (VII) was one of the more colourful popes. In 897 he had the body of Formosus, an earlier pope, exhumed. He then had it dressed in pontifical vestments and placed on the papal throne. He presided over a trial of the dead pope, found him guilty, hacked a few fingers off the corpse, and had it thrown into the Tiber. This event is generally known as the *Cadaver Synod*. Stephen was himself deposed by a Roman mob and strangled. What was left of Formosus's rotting body was recovered and allowed to rest peacefully for a few years, until another pope, Sergius III (who had been present at the Cadaver Synod) had it exhumed and condemned again. This time it was beheaded, and a few more fingers were hacked off. Once more it was cast into the Tiber, and once again it was recovered.

Pius II had been a well-known libertine before he ascended the papal throne in 1458. The father of a number of illegitimate children, he was also the author of celebrated erotic works such as *Lucretia and Euryalus* and the comedy *Chrysis*. Julius III (pope 1550–55) was a well-known paedophile. He created a scandal by picking up from the streets a boy called Innocenzo. Unaffected by public opinion he made Innocenzo a cardinal.

The idea that priests have always been expected to be chaste, or even celibate, is severely compromised by the record of the papacy. St Peter (whether one counts him as a pope or not) had been a married man before he became an apostle. Hadrian II had been married before he became Pope in 867. So too had been Clement IV before his election in 1265. He is known to have had two daughters. Many popes were the sons of priests and bishops, and many were married and had children themselves. For example, Felix III (pope 483–92) was the son of a priest and had at least two children of his own. The sixth-century pope, St Agapetus, was also the son of a priest. The next pope, St Silverius, was the son of St Hormisdas (pope 514–23). Theodore I (pope 642–49) was the son of a bishop, as was Boniface VI. The only English pope, Nicholas Breakspear, who became Hadrian IV in 1154, was the son of a monk at St Albans. Other popes were renowned libertines and had impressive broods of illegitimate children. For example, the late fifteenth-century pope Alexander VI had a large but unknown number. The sixteenth-century pope Paul III kept a mistress by whom he is known to have fathered at least four children. Innocent X (pope 1644–55) was unusually dependent upon his sister-in-law and was so close to her that their mutual interests were widely believed to extend well beyond Church matters.

Popes were also murderers in great style. Often they murdered each other. In 366 Damasus had himself proclaimed Bishop of Rome, having hired a gang of thugs to expel Ursicinus, who had just been elected. Damasus's mob climbed onto the roof of the Basilica of Santa Maria Maggiore, where his opponent's supporters were gathered, stripped off the lead tiles, and hurled them down on the congregation below, killing over a hundred. Damasus was later charged with murder but escaped through the intervention of powerful friends. He is now revered as pope and saint. In 537 Pope Silverius was murdered by Pope Vigilius, who in turn was later murdered by Pelagius I. In 653 Martin I was accused of treason, tried, convicted and sentenced to death. He was publicly flogged and his sentence commuted to banishment. Abandoned by his Church and its new pope, he soon died under the harsh conditions to which he was subjected. Both Leo V and the anti-pope Christopher were murdered by Sergius III in 904. Pope Benedict VI was charged with unknown crimes, imprisoned, and strangled on the orders of his successor (Boniface VII), who also had John XIV murdered. John XVIII and Sergius IV were both murdered by Benedict VIII in 1012. Clement II was reputedly poisoned by Benedict IX in 1047. The Borgia Pope Alexander VI enjoys the distinction of being the only pope to have murdered himself. He seems to have intended to poison a cardinal one day in 1503, but somehow the poison was mistakenly given to Alexander and his son instead.

NOTES

1 The historical evidence for Jesus is dealt with by G. A. Wells in *Did Jesus Exist?* and *The Historical Evidence for Jesus*. Much of the subject matter in this chapter is dealt with more fully by Geza Vermes in *Jesus the Jew*.

2 Mishnah, Ta'anith, 3:8, cited by Vermes, *Jesus the Jew*, p. 70.

3 Vermes, *Jesus the Jew*, pp. 72ff.

4 Babylonian Talmud Me'ilah, 17b, cited by Vermes, *Jesus the Jew*, p. 66.

5 Irenaeus, *Adversus Omnes Haereses*, II, xxxi, paragraph 2.

6 Josephus, *Jewish Antiquities*, XX: 167–8.

7 For example Mark 13:22 and Matthew 24:24.

8 Mark 11:32, Matthew 14:5 and Luke 20:6, cf. Josephus, *Jewish Antiquities*, XVIII: 116–19.

9 Acts 5:36. Theudas's claim to be a prophet is recorded by Josephus, *Jewish Antiquities*, XX: 97–8.

10 Acts 21:38. The claims of *The Egyptian* are recorded by Josephus, *Jewish Antiquities*, XX: 169–71.

11 Chadwick, *The Early Church*, p. 37. Simon Magus is mentioned in Acts 8:9–24.

12 Acts 3:22ff and 7:37, cf. Deuteronomy 18:15.

13 At John 9:1ff Jesus uses a traditional remedy for blindness, making a paste with his own spittle, then sends the blind man to wash in the waters of Siloam. Sanctuaries for the sick were often located by such waters, and Jesus performed miracles there in the traditional way, e.g. the sheep pools of Bethesda (John 5:3–9). See Romer, *Testament*, p. 161.

14 Matthew 26:67–8, Mark 14:65 and Luke 22:64.

15 H. Maccoby, *Revolution in Judæa* (London, 1973), p. 99.

16 Eusebius, *The History of the Church*, 1:3.

17 The magi ask Herod where the King of the Jews is to be born, but Herod then asks others where the Messiah (or Christ) is to be born (Matthew 2:2–4).

18 Matthew 27:11, Mark 15:2, 9, 18, and Luke 23:3. In modern translations Jesus explicitly confirms that he is the King of the Jews.

19 Matthew 27:42, Mark 15:32 and John 12:13.

20 Cited by Eusebius, *The History of the Church*, 2:23.

21 The distinction between Jesus and Christ was particularly important to 'Adoptionist' Christians. By changing *Jesus* to *Christ* it became possible for the 'orthodox' faction to refute some of their arguments. See Ehrman, *The Orthodox Corruption of Scripture*, pp. 150–63.

22 In Luke 6:15 and Acts 1:13 Simon is called 'Simon Zelotes', in Mark 3:18 and Matthew 10:4 'Simon the Canaanite'. In modern translations he is consistently 'Simon the Zealot'.

23 *The Epistle of Barnabas*, this translation from Andrew Louth (ed.), Maxwell Staniforth (trans.), *Early Christian Writings*, p. 164.

24 See S. G. F. Brandon, *Jesus and the Zealots*, Manchester University Press (Manchester, 1967).

25 Origen, *Comm. In Matthaeum*, 10:17; also *Contra Celsum*, 1:47.

26 R. Eisler, *Messiah Jesus and John The Baptist*, translated by A. H. Krappe (London, 1932), pp. 167 and 427.

27 Josephus, *Jewish Antiquities*, IV: 120.

28 Josephus, *Jewish War*, XX: 558.

29 Josephus, *Jewish War*, I: 203–4, and *Jewish Antiquities*, XIV: 158–9.

30 Acts 5:37. See also Josephus, *Jewish War*, II: 118, and *Jewish Antiquities*, XVII: 5 (271–2), 18, 1, 1 (4–10) and 18, i, 6 (23).

31 Josephus, *Jewish Antiquities*, XX: 102.

32 Josephus, *Jewish War*, II: 433–48.

33 Josephus, *Jewish War*, VII: 253, 275, 320–410.

34 Acts 5:36. Josephus, *Jewish Antiquities*, XX: 5:1, although the author of Acts has got his chronology wrong. Josephus was also quoted by Eusebius, *The History of the Church*, p. 84.

35 *The Egyptian* is referred to by Josephus, *Jewish War*, II: 259–63, quoted by Eusebius, *The History of the Church*, p. 97.

36 Geza Vermes, *Jesus the Jew*, p. 134, citing Jerusalem Talmud Ta'anith 68d.

37 Y. Yadin, *Bar-Kokhbar*, Weidenfeld & Nicolson (London, 1971), p. 255. *Kokhbar* (or *Kochba*) means star (cf. the star mentioned in Numbers 24:17).

38 Eusebius, *The History of the Church*, 2:19, cf. Josephus, *Jewish War*, p. 144.

39 Josephus, *Jewish Antiquities*, XVIII: v:2, 117–18.

40 Josephus, *Jewish Antiquities*, XX: ix:1, 200–03.

41 Eusebius, *The History of the Church*, 4:22 citing Hegesippus. James is repeatedly referred to as 'James the Righteous' (or 'James the Just' (Hebrew *zaddik*)) by Eusebius and the sources he cites: 2:1 (Eusebius himself), 2:1 (citing Clement of Alexandria *Outlines* Book VI), 2:23 (citing both Hegesippus and Josephus).

42 Eusebius, *The History of the Church*, 2:23 (quoting a lost version of Josephus, which was also cited by Origen, *Contra Celsum*, 1:47, 2:13).

43 Eusebius, *The History of the Church*, 3:12, p. 124, citing Hegesippus.

44 Eusebius, *The History of the Church*, 3:20, pp. 126–27, citing Hegesippus.

45 Eusebius, *The History of the Church*, 3:32, citing Hegesippus. Clopas was Joseph's brother.

46 Eusebius, *The History of the Church*, 1:7, citing Julius Africanus.

47 Ezekiel 2, see also the opening verses of almost all subsequent chapters.

48 In Mark 8:38 Jesus uses the expression *son of man* of someone who will come with his Father's glory and with the holy angels, which could well be based on the passage in Daniel. He seems to use the expression to refer to someone else.

49 1 Enoch was accepted as scripture by the writer of the Epistle of Jude and by many of the Church Fathers. It is still accepted as part of the Old Testament by the Ethiopic Church but was rejected by other Churches and subsequently 'lost' to Western Christendom.

50 Matthew 15:22–7, Mark 7:28; Matthew 8:2, Luke 5:12 (cf. Mark 1:40 which has *Lord* in some old manuscripts), Matthew 17:15, Mark 9:24; Matthew 20:30–1 and Mark 10:51.

51 As it was blasphemy to utter the Hebrew word JHVH, Jews used the word *adonai* instead, which is equivalent to *Lord* in English and *kyrios* in Greek.

52 The styles *Kyrios et Deus noster* and *Dominus et Deus noster* were applied to Roman god-emperors especially from about 40 AD. Vermes, *Jesus the Jew*, p. 106.

53 Matthew 3:17, Luke 3:22 and Hebrews 1:5, cf. 2 Peter 1:17.

54 See for example Clement, *First Epistle to the Corinthians*, 36. '… but of the Son, the Lord declares "You are my son, this very day have I fathered you"'.

55 Eusebius, *The History of the Church*, 7:25.

56 Matthew 16:16, cf. Matthew 26:63 and Mark 14:61. The Authorised Version has *Christ* rather than *messiah*, but the Greek and Hebrew are interchangeable.

57 Vermes, *Jesus the Jew*, pp. 206ff.

58 For example, *son of God* (meaning angel) is used in Daniel 3:25. *Sons of God* is used in Genesis 6:2 and 6:4, Deuteronomy 32:8 (Jerusalem Bible), Job 1:6, 2:1 and 38:7, and Psalm 29:1 (where it is translated in the Authorised Version as *ye mighty*), cf. Psalm 82:6.

59 For a number of examples, including the ideas of Philo, see John Hick (ed.), *The Myth of God Incarnate*, pp. 104–5 and 114.

60 To Roman Catholics this is in the Old Testament: *Ecclesiasticus* (4:10). For others, Ecclesiasticus is called *Ben Sirach* or *Jesus, Son of Sirach*, and is included in the Apocrypha.

61 God's children are mentioned frequently in the Bible: e.g. 'I have said, Ye are gods; and all of you are children of the most High', Psalm 82:6.

62 Montefiore, *Some Elements of the Religious Teaching of Jesus*, Macmillan (1910), p. 93.

63 Rabbi Morris Goldstein, *Jesus in the Jewish Tradition*, Macmillan (New York, 1950), p. 26. 'According to the Mishnah, only misuse of the Tetragram, the sacrosanct name of God, constitutes blasphemy': Vermes, *Jesus the Jew*, p. 35, citing *Mishnah Sanhedrin* 7:5.

64 Luke 2:22–4 referring to an ancient Jewish practice, Leviticus 12:8.

65 Luke 4:16–24. See Vermes, *Jesus the Jew*, p. 27.

66 Matthew 8:1–4, Mark 1:40–5 and Luke 5:12–14. The reference is to Leviticus 14.

67 See also Matthew 10:6. The fact that Jesus healed the servant of a centurion (Matthew 8:5–13 and Luke 7:1–10) is sometimes offered as evidence of his willingness to minister to the gentiles, but there is no reason to believe that the servant was a gentile, in fact Luke 7:3 suggests that he was Jewish.

68 Origen, *Contra Celsum*, 7:9.

69 Paul refers to Jesus as the image of God (2 Corinthians 4:4 and Colossians 1:15) or being in the form of God (Philippians 2:6), or to God's fullness dwelling in him (Colossians 2:9). All these fall short of claiming Jesus to be God. Texts where Jesus is apparently called God are ambiguous, dubiously translated or interpolated (e.g. Romans 9:5, Titus 2:13 and arguably 2 Peter 1:1).

70 John 10:33–38 quoting Psalm 82:6. This quotation did not save Jesus. He was obliged to escape to avoid being stoned. Possibly his audience knew their scriptures well enough to know that in the psalm God was talking to his heavenly court.

71 Hippolytus, *Little Labyrinth*, cited by Eusebius, *The History of the Church*, 5:28.

72 The word Nazarene was used of Jesus himself (John 18:5 and 18:7) and Nazarenes of the sect of which he was the 'ringleader' (Acts 24:5). It is now generally applied specifically to Jesus' Jewish followers who formed a distinctive group after his death.

73 Josephus, *Antiquities*, XX: 9.1, 200–3. The relevant passage could be rendered 'James (the brother of Jesus) who was called the Christ...' or as 'James (the brother of Jesus, who was called the Christ)...'. The first option attributes the title to James, the other attributes it to Jesus.

74 Nag Hammadi, *Gospel of St Thomas*, Logion 12. The following translation is from J. M. Robinson (ed.), *The Nag Hammadi Library*, p. 119: 'The disciples

said to Jesus. We know that you will depart from us. Who is to be our leader? Jesus said to them "Wherever you are, you are to go to James the Righteous...".'

75   The Secret Book of James, see for example passages 1:2, 3:1–2, 3:12, 5:1.

76   Eusebius, *The History of the Church*, 2:23, quoting Hegesippus, refers to James (the Righteous) as the 'first to be elected to the Episcopal throne of the Jerusalem Church'. He (Eusebius) identified James the Righteous with James the Lord's brother who was counted among the apostles (2:1), and who was (according to Clement of Alexandria cited by Eusebius) chosen by his brother Jesus as Bishop of Jerusalem (2:1).

77   See for example Acts 12:17, 15:13 and 21:18.

78   According to writings sympathetic to the Pauline line Peter abandoned the need to eat clean food (Acts 10:14) and avoid contact with gentiles (Acts 11:3), but even if these writings are correct (and there are reasons to suspect that they are retrospective rationalisations) they do not establish the apostles as Christians rather than Jews.

79   Josephus, *Jewish Antiquities*, XX: ix.1, 197–200 says that James was tried by the Sanhedrin, prompted by the high priest Ananus, was found guilty of transgressing the law, and sentenced to be stoned. This James is not to be confused with James the brother of John, who was beheaded on the orders of Herod Agrippa AD *c*.44 (see Acts 12:2).

80   Eusebius, *The History of the Church*, 3:11 and 4:22, cf. John 19:25 (and Luke 24:18).

81   Eusebius, *The History of the Church*, 4:22. Cited by Michael Goulder in (ed. John Hick) *The Myth of God Incarnate*, p. 66, where it is convincingly established that all or most of the schismatics mentioned were Samaritans.

82   Eusebius, *The History of the Church*, 4:5.

83   Eusebius, *The History of the Church*, 4:6.

84   Eusebius, *The History of the Church*, 3:37. Different early Christian authors use the terms Nazarene and Ebionite differently, so it is difficult to be sure of exactly how Nazarenes and Ebionites differed from each other – or even whether they comprised two distinct groups within the Jewish Church. St Justin Martyr (*Dial.* 47) distinguishes the Ebionites as rejecting the Virgin Birth.

85   Ignatius of Antioch (AD 98–117), in his letter to the Magnesians 10, is already becoming hostile in the early second century: 'To profess Jesus Christ while continuing to follow Jewish customs is an absurdity'. In the very next passage he coins the word 'Christianity'.

86   Romans 2:16. See also Romans 16:25 and 2 Timothy 2:8.

87   Referring to the gospel he preached Paul says 'I did not receive it from any man, nor was I taught it; rather, I received it by revelation from Jesus Christ' – Galatians 1:12 (New International Version).

88   Gibbon, *The Decline and Fall of the Roman Empire*, Penguin, pp. 266–7.

89   2 Corinthians 11:5 and 12:11. Sometimes rendered in modern translations as 'arch apostles' or 'super apostles'. The Authorised Version refers to the 'very chiefest apostles'. As modern translations make clear, Paul is claiming in these two passages that he is in no way inferior to the Twelve.

90   'It was the unanimous and confident opinion of the [Church] fathers that the Samaritan teachers had been the first Gnostics' – Michael Goulding in (ed. John Hick) *The Myth of God Incarnate*, 'The two roots of the Christian Myth', p. 67.

Goulding provides a number of references to support this view, the earliest of which is St Justin Martyr, I *Apol.*, 26.

91 W. Bauer, *Orthodoxy and Heresy in Earliest Christianity*, SMC Press (1972), pp. 44–60.

92 Paul is talking about Gnosis for example in 1 Corinthians 8 and again in 13:2. Translations often disguise the true meaning by translating the word *Gnosis* as *knowledge* instead of leaving it in the Greek (and thus suggesting esoteric knowledge).

93 See for example Ignatius, *Epistle to the Trallians* 10 and Polycarp, *Epistle to the Philippians* 7.

94 For a more detailed treatment of the differences mentioned in John's letters see J. L. Houlden, *The Johannine Epistles*, A & C Black (1973).

95 Paul's view that faith is all important is expressed throughout the Pauline writings of the New Testament, e.g. Romans 3:27–8 and 4:3–6.

96 Clement, *First Epistle to the Corinthians* 3.

97 Clement, *First Epistle to the Corinthians* 13 and 14.

98 Clement, *First Epistle to the Corinthians* 44.

99 Clement, *First Epistle to the Corinthians* 45.

100 Ignatius, *Epistle to the Ephesians* 7.

101 Ignatius, *Epistle to the Magnesians* 6.

102 Ignatius, *Epistle to the Philadelphians* 2.

103 Ignatius, *Epistle to the Smyrnaeans* 8.

104 Ignatius, *Epistle to Polycarp* 2.

105 Ignatius, *Epistle to Polycarp* 3.

106 Ignatius, *Epistle to Polycarp* 4.

107 Evans, *Is Holy Scripture Christian?*, p. 87.

108 Jewish Christians were dismissed as hypocrites for example in the *Didache* 8.

109 Gibbon, *The Decline and Fall of the Roman Empire*, Penguin, p. 260.

110 The existence of such a document is mentioned by Eusebius, *The History of the Church*, 4:29.

111 Chadwick, *The Early Church*, p. 21. This official curse was inserted into the synagogue's chief prayer, and authorised by Rabbi Gamaliel II around AD 85. See C. K. Barrett (ed.), *The New Testament Background: Selected Documents* (London, 1974), pp. 166-7.

112 For some of the creeds adopted and discarded by the early Church see Kelly, *Early Christian Doctrines*, pp. 247–8.

113 The Creed adopted at the Ecumenical Council of Chalcedon may have been used earlier at the First Ecumenical Council of Constantinople in AD 381, but this is doubtful. Nevertheless, it is sometimes called the Niceno-Constantinopolitan Creed.

114 Article 8 of the 39 Anglican Articles of Religion.

115 The Council held at Ephesus in 449 is often called the Robber Council, but it was no less flawed through bias or duress than many other councils.

116 Gregory of Nazianzus, *Oration*, 31.5–8.

117 For the views of various Church Fathers, see Kelly, *Early Christian Doctrines*, pp. 258–63.

118 Tampering with the Creed would have been heretical (by the decree of ecumenical councils) even if the Eastern Churches had agreed with the underlying change of

doctrine, which in fact they did not. To them unilateral action by the Western Church constituted a sin against the unity of Christendom or 'moral fratricide'. Furthermore, according to Eastern authorities the theological position of the Western Church is dangerous and heretical (the heresy lying somewhere between semi-Sabellianism and ditheism). Ware, *The Orthodox Church*, pp. 58–9, 67, 236, 218–23.

119 The three Fates were *Klotho, Lachesis* and *Atropos*. Their Greek name *Moirai* means 'part'. Homer speaks of them as a single goddess. [*Iliad* 16.334, refers to 'Moira Krataia'.] Other triads mentioned are the Graia (*Pemphredo, Enyo* and *Deino*); the Gorgons (*Sthenno, Euryale* and *Medousa*); the Furies, or Erinyes, or Maniai or Eumenides (*Allekto, Tisiphone* and *Megaira*); the Horai (*Eunomia, Dike* and *Eirene*); and the Charities or Graces (*Aglaia, Euphrosyne* and *Thalia*).

120 Pausanias, *Periegeta*, 2.2.8.

121 St Theophilus, *Ad. Autol.* 1:7, 2:15, 18.

122 There had been a degree of confusion amongst the faithful regarding God's Son, God's Word, God's Spirit and God's Wisdom. For some Christians, God's Son was an inherent manifestation of God's Word, and God's Spirit was an inherent manifestation of God's Wisdom; but others, like Tertullian, equated God's Wisdom with God's Word. The Council of Sardica in 343 held that God's Son is also his Word, Wisdom and Power. According to the Arians, the Son had not had a human soul, but had had the Word instead.

123 St Justin Martyr, *Dialogue with Trypho the Jew*, 72 mentions the passage. He thought that its absence from some copies of the scripture was due to Jews suppressing it. In fact, its presence in other copies was a Christian imposture. St Irenaeus also seems to have believed the passage to be genuine, though he cited it in several different forms: *Adversus Omnes Haereses,* III, xx, 4; IV, xxii, 1; IV, xxxiii, 1, 12; and V, xxxi, 1.

124 Resurrection is referred to unambiguously only in Daniel 12:2–3 (*c.*164 BC) and Isaiah 26:19 (Isaiah 24–7 being an acknowledged late apocalyptic insertion). Hints of other ideas may be found e.g. Ezekiel 37:12–14 and 1 Samuel 28:7–20.

125 Some early Christians, such as the Docetes, denied that Christ had died on the cross, and consequently denied the doctrine of the resurrection too. Ignatius, *Epistle to the Magnesians* 9, mentions them (or at least some of them). Clement of Rome, in his letter to the Corinthians 23–7, goes to great lengths to convince his readers that there are no grounds for doubting the resurrection, which suggests that others rejected it too, cf. Paul's efforts to the same end, 1 Corinthians 15. Polycarp was also exercised by those (he described them as first-begotten sons of Satan) who asserted that there was no such thing as resurrection or judgement, *Epistle to the Philippians* 7.

126 Romans 5:12, cf. 1 Corinthians 15:21–2 and James 1:15.

127 St Augustine of Hippo, *De magistro* (*The Teacher*), 2.3.381.

128 Augustine's ideas were not entirely original and may for example be found in the writings of Cyprian (d. 258). See Kelly, *Early Christian Doctrines*, p. 176.

129 See for example Mark 10:45, 1 Corinthians 15:3 and Hebrews 9:19–28.

130 Stone, *Outlines of Christian Doctrine*, p. 90.

131 Clement of Rome, Polycarp and Hermas for example all failed to mention Mary.

132 Ashe, *The Virgin*, p. 129.

133 St Anselm, *Cur Deus Homo*, 2, 16.

134 Aquinas said that Mary was sanctified in the womb, but only after 'animation', *Summa Theologiae* III, q. 27, a 1. Animation for female foetuses took place 80 days after conception according to medieval theory.

135 Bernadine of Busti, *Mariale* (1588 edition, vol. 3), Sermon 7 on the Conception.

136 The two critical mistranslations, both from the Vulgate, are 'she shall crush thy head' in Genesis 3:15, and 'full of grace' in Luke 1:28. Both are dealt with in more detail elsewhere in this book.

137 Typhaon: Homer, *Hymnus in Apollinem* 309.
Aries: Ovid, *Fasti* 5.299.
Hephæstus: Hesiod, *Theðgonia*, 928.

138 Hera regained her virginity each year in the spring of Kanathos, near Argos. Pausanias, *Periegeta*, 2.38.2.

139 Pausanias, *Periegeta*, 5.3.2 and Euripides, *Heraclidæ*, 771.

140 Epiphanius, *Panarion*, 51, 22, 3–11, cited by Hugo Rahner, *Greek Myths and Christian Mystery* (London, 1963), p. 138.

141 Origen, *Contra Celsum*, 1:37. Essentially the same legend was recorded by Diogenes Lærtius, *Lives of the Philosophers*, 3, 1, 2. Diogenes cited several other sources.

142 Clement of Alexandria, *Recognitiones* I, 2, 14, cited by E. D. Nourry (Saint Yves d'Alveydre), *Les Vierges-Mères et les Naissances Miraculeuses* (Paris, 1908), p. 258.

143 Origen, *Contra Celsum*, 1:28–32. The relevant accusation was that: 'Mary was turned out by her husband, a carpenter by profession, after she had been convicted of unfaithfulness. Cast off by her spouse, and wandering about in disgrace, in obscurity she gave birth to Jesus by a certain soldier Pantheras.' (Different accounts give slightly different versions of the name.) A detailed exposition of this and other supporting independent sources mentioning Pantheras is given by Rabbi Goldstein, *Jesus in Jewish Tradition*, Macmillan (New York), pp. 35–9.

144 Mary was declared to be *Aeiparthenos* by the General Council held at Constantinople in AD 553.

145 Augustine of Hippo, *Enarratio in Psalmum* 34, 3; quoted by Jean Galot, 'Le Mystère de l'Assomption' in Hubert Manoir de Juaye (ed.), *Maria*, p. 196.

146 Ware, *The Orthodox Church*, p. 264.

147 Limbo has only ever been mentioned in one papal document, the bull *Auctorem fidei* issued in 1794.

148 *Outlines of Christian Dogma*, p. 223.

149 Converts to Judaism were, and are, expected to undergo circumcision and baptism. Such converts are called proselytes in the Authorised Version, as in Acts 2:10. The requirement for baptism before acceptance as Jews caused problems in 1984, after Falashas were air-lifted out of Ethiopia to settle in Israel in 'Operation Moses'.

150 The idea that the gods are of one nature but many names was not novel amongst philosophers. See for example Maximus of Tyre, *Dissertationes*, 39:5. See also Origen, *Contra Celsum*, 5:45.

151 Dante refers to the Christian God as 'almighty Jupiter' in his Divine Comedy: *Purgatory* 6:118.

152 Adolf Deissmann, *Light from the Ancient East* (English Translation L. R. M. Strachan), Hodder & Stoughton (1927).

153 O. Kern, *Orphicorum fragmenta*, 21a. Cited by C. Kerényi, *The Gods of the Greeks*, English translation, Thames and Hutchinson (1979), p. 116.

154 *Verusque sol, inlabere / micans nitore perpeti...*: St Ambrose, in *Splendor paternae gloriae*, quoted by F. J. E. Raby, *A History of Christian Latin Poetry* (Oxford, 1966), p. 35.

155 Thomas, *Religion and the Decline of Magic*, p. 457, citing G. F. Nuttall, *Richard Baxter* (1965), p. 46. When Richard Baxter arrived at his new living in Kidderminster in the mid-seventeenth century he found a number of parishioners who thought that Christ was the Sun (and that the Holy Ghost was the Moon).

156 Constantine's motive was recorded both in statute and inscription, see Chadwick, *The Early Church*, p. 128.

157 25th December was the birthday not only of Sol, but also of Mithras, and of Attis, the Phrygian Sun god.

158 Part of the pagan liturgy used on 25th December was even adopted into the Christmas Office of the Christian Church. Seznec, *The Survival of the Pagan Gods*, p. 43.

159 Hygini, *Astronomica*, 2.34.

160 Origen, *Contra Celsum*, 3.24.

161 Plutarch, *Lives*, Alexander 2–3.

162 Livy, *Annales*, I 4.

163 Horace, *Odes*, I 2. Suetonius identified Augustus's father as the god Apollo.

164 Adolf Deissmann, *Light from the Ancient East*, pp. 342ff, cited in (ed. John Hick) *The Myth of God Incarnate*, p. 98.

165 Pythagoras was said to have been the son of Hermes, and Plato of Apollo. Diogenes Laertius, *Lives of the Philosophers*, 8.2.66. (Empedocles), 3.2.1. (Pythagoras) and 3.1.2. (Plato) respectively.

166 C. Kerényi, *The Gods of the Greeks*, p. 79.

167 Graves, *The Greek Myths*, p. 95.

168 C. Kerényi, *The Gods of the Greeks*, p. 98.

169 Pindarus, *Pythia*, 3.5.

170 Eratosthenes, *Catasterismoi*, 32.

171 John the Geometer, *Life of Mary*, v1, quoted by Graef, *Mary*, vol. 1, p. 197.

172 The scriptures are contradictory on the nature of Sheol cf. Deuteronomy 32:22 (Jerusalem Bible), Psalms 88:12, 94:17 and 30:9, Job 14:13 and Ezekiel 32:27. See also Ethiopian Enoch 22:1–14.

173 Satan as an individual appears for the first time only in the Book of Job and does not acquire his evil aspects until later still.

174 Stone, *Outlines of Christian Dogma*, pp. 281–2. Even the Church of England sings hymns about guardian angels, e.g. hymn 26 in *Hymns Ancient and Modern*. Muslims believe in them too, Koran 13:11.

175 The pallium was a vestment of white wool, draped over the shoulders. Originally it was worn by imperial officials. By the sixth century it was being worn by eastern bishops and a few western ones. The bishop's mitre, like so much else in Christianity, is a synthesis of Judaic and secular Greek practice. In this case it is a fusion of the Jewish priest's head-dress (as worn by Jesus' brother James, and by John) and a sort of Greek crown.

176 Ware, *The Orthodox Church*, p. 253.

177 Tertullian, *De pudicitas*, 1.

178 Whitehead, *Church Law*, p. 266, citing Mosheim, *Ecclesiastical History*, and Rogers, *Ecclesiastical Law*.

179 As so often, Christians seem to have synthesised a number of existing practices. The tonsure was used by pagan priests, but the practice also seems to have been used as part of an old Roman ceremony of adoption. (Trainee priests abandoned their own families and were adopted into the family of their bishops.)

180 'The Mass is the greatest blasphemy of God and the highest idolatry upon earth; an abomination the like of which has never been in Christendom since the time of the Apostles.' Martin Luther, *Table Talk*.

181 A letter from Pope Gregory to Milletus AD 601 cited by the Venerable Bede in his *Ecclesiastical History of the English Nation*, ch. XXX, rescinds an earlier instruction to destroy Anglo-Saxon places of worship and to sequester them instead.

182 At the fiesta di Santa Francesca Romana held in Piazzale del Colosseo in Rome, motor cars are still blessed annually on 9th March.

183 Tammuz is mentioned in Ezekiel 8:14 and referred to obliquely elsewhere (Daniel 11:37, Hosea 4:14, Isaiah 1:29 and 17:10).

184 Mistletoe is the magical *Golden Bough* discussed at length in Sir James Frazier's book of that name.

185 The special annual service for 5th November added to the Anglican Book of Common Prayer was revoked in 1859.

186 Thomas, *Religion and the Decline of Magic*, p. 71.

187 This definition of the catholic faith *Curandum est, ut id teneamus, quod ubique, quod simper, quod ab omnibus creditum est* was put forward by Vincent (died before 450), a monk of Lérins in southern Gaul.

188 In addition to the Pharisees, Sadducees, Samaritans and Essenes, Hegesippus mentions other hostile Jewish groups as Galilæans, Hemerobaptists (who practised daily re-baptism), and Masbothæans (materialists). Eusebius, *The History of the Church*, 4:22.

189 Eusebius, *Ecclesiastical History*, 4:22, quoting Hegesippus. Some of these groups are mentioned both as Jewish and Jewish Christian.

190 Paul complains about sexual licence among his followers in 1 Corinthians 6:12–20.

191 Eusebius, *The History of the Church*, 5:23.

192 One reason why the filioque (the phrase "and the Son") was so controversial was that it appeared to Orthodox Christians to confirm the Roman Church's heresy. If not fully Sabellian, then the Western position was, as one Saint put it, 'some semi-Sabellian monster'. See Ware, *The Orthodox Church*, p. 221.

193 Eusebius ascribed the heresy to one Artemon who had lived around the same time as Irenaeus, although he notes that the holders of Artemon's views claimed that they had been handed down from the apostles. Eusebius, *The History of the Church*, 5:28.

194 The terms of Constantine's restrictions are preserved in Eusebius's *Life of Constantine*, 2, pp. 64–5. The full English text may be found in the Library of the Nicene Fathers, vol. 1.

195 It is difficult to summarise accurately the views of Arius and his followers. For a good unbiased exposition see Kelly, *Early Christian Doctrines*, pp. 226–31.

196 Gibbon, *The Decline and Fall of the Roman Empire*, Penguin, p. 400.

197 Jerome was not sympathetic to the Arian line, 'The whole world groaned and marvelled to find itself Arian' *contra Lucifer* 19.

198 Gibbon, *The Decline and Fall of the Roman Empire*, Penguin, p. 402.

199 John Hick (ed.), *The Myth of God Incarnate*, SCM Press (1977), p. 142. The passage is from Don Cupitt's 'The Christ of Christendom'. The Rev. Cupitt provides a footnote at the end of the first sentence: 'Klauser, *A Short History of the Western Liturgy*, Oxford University Press, 1969, pp. 30ff and notes. See especially A. Jungmann, *The Place of Christ in Liturgical Prayer*, Chapman, 1965'.

200 Such ideas were regarded as heretical by the early Church leaders, who knew of goddesses like Astarte who were regarded as queens of Heaven, and who had cakes made for them (e.g. Jeremiah 7:18). See Ashe, *The Virgin*, pp. 150–1. Roman Catholics now worship Mary and regard her as Queen of Heaven, but this was a late development – a sort of belated vindication of the Collyridian 'heresy'.

201 John Hick (ed.), *The Myth of God Incarnate*, SCM Press (1977). Frances Young, 'a Cloud of Witnesses', p. 28.

202 The Roman Church holds that the civil power has a God-given right to execute certain wrongdoers. It has been held to be heretical to deny this. For example in the Profession of Faith drawn up by Pope Innocent III in 1208, Waldensians were required to profess their belief in the right of the state to inflict capital punishment. Failure to do so constituted proof of heresy.

203 1 Peter 2:9 and 2:5, Revelation 1:6, 5:10 and 20:6.

204 The titles *presbyter* (elder) and *episkopos* (overseer) are used of the same people in Acts 20:17 and 20:28 and again in Titus 1:6 and 1:7 (cf. 1 Timothy 3:2). See the NIV or other modern translations.

205 A New Testament example showing that the ministry was two-fold, not three-fold, is 1 Timothy 3. The two-fold ministry is confirmed by the *Didache* and a letter from St Clement of Rome (fl. *c.*AD 96) to the Corinthians 42.

206 Eusebius, *The History of the Church*, 7:7, citing Dionysius writing about Heraclas.

207 Special honours accorded to the patriarchies were confirmed by Church Councils: Rome, Alexandria and Antioch in canon 6 of the Council of Nicæa (AD 325), Constantinople in canon 3 of the First Ecumenical Council of Constantinople (AD 381), and Jerusalem at the Ecumenical Council of Chalcedon (AD 451).

208 The word patriarch really means head or ruler of a family. It is used in Acts 2:29 and 7:8 of Old Testament characters.

209 Echoes of the original seven-fold ministry may be found in the *Didache*. See Andrew Louth (ed.), Maxwell Staniforth (trans.), *Early Christian Writings*, p. 188.

210 Ignatius, *Epistle to the Ephesians* 6. See Andrew Louth (ed.), Maxwell Staniforth (trans.), *Early Christian Writings*, p. 63. Ignatius also advocated obedience to bishops as though they were Jesus Christ himself, and also held that believers should hold deacons in as great respect as Jesus Christ. Ignatius, *Epistle to the Trallians* 2 and 3. See Andrew Louth (ed.), Maxwell Staniforth (trans.), *Early Christian Writings*, p. 79.

211 Ignatius, *Epistle to the Magnesians* 6. See Andrew Louth (ed.), Maxwell Staniforth (trans.), *Early Christian Writings*, p. 72.

212 Dositheus (Patriarch of Jerusalem 1669 to 1707) asserts in his *Confession* (decree 10) that a bishop is a living image of God upon Earth, and this *Confession* was ratified by the Orthodox Church at the Council of Jerusalem in 1672. Ware, *The Orthodox Church*, pp. 107 and 253.

213 Ware, *The Orthodox Church*, p. 253.

214 St Clement of Rome, *First Epistle to the Corinthians* 44 (see Andrew Louth (ed.), Maxwell Staniforth (trans.), *Early Christian Writings*, p. 41). Ignatius of Antioch gives no hint of the idea of apostolic succession.

215 Modified systems of election survive for example in the Orthodox Churches of Antioch and Cyprus. Ware, *The Orthodox Church*, p. 299.

216 For example the Viscount of Béziers left in his will, as family property, Béziers and Agde, along with their bishoprics, to his wife and daughter in AD 990. Michael Costen, *The Cathars and the Albigensian Crusade*, p. 22.

217 B. J. Kidd, *The Churches of Eastern Christendom* (London, 1927), p. 304.

218 For centuries the Sultan sold to the highest bidder a document called a *berat* to allow them to take office as bishop of Constantinople whenever the position became available.

219 'The office uniquely committed by the Lord to Peter, the first of the Apostles, and to be transmitted to his successors, abides in the Bishop of the Church of Rome...'. Canon 331 of the code of canon law, cf. Canon 330.

220 In passages such as Acts 15:13–19 and Galatians 2:11ff. it is apparent that Peter neither enjoyed nor claimed any special authority.

221 Cyprian, *De Catholicae Ecclesiae Unitatel*, 4. See Kelly, *Early Christian Doctrines*, p. 205.

222 '...Ignatius, the second to be appointed to the bishopric of Antioch in succession to Peter', Eusebius, *The History of the Church*, 3:36. By contrast he says elsewhere that 'After the martyrdom of Paul and Peter, the first man to be appointed Bishop of Rome was Linus'. The first represents Peter as Bishop of Antioch, the second does not represent him as Bishop of Rome, although a passage in 3:4 referring back to the second passage quoted is more ambiguous.

223 Eusebius reported that Peter spent his time preaching to Jews in Pontus, Galatia and Bithyna, Cappadocia and Asia, and that he was tarrying at Rome when he was crucified there. Eusebius, *The History of the Church*, 3:1.

224 Cyprian, Origen, Cyril, Hilary, Jerome, Ambrose and Augustine all considered the words 'Thou art Peter', but none of them applied the words to anyone except Peter.

225 Eusebius, *The History of the Church*, 5:23–25.

226 St Cyprian, *De Catholicae Ecclesiae Unitate* 4: '... to all the apostles after the resurrection he [Jesus Christ] gives his power equally ... The other apostles also were what Peter was, endowed with an equal share both of honour and power; ...'. The Orthodox Church still holds that, as one bishop puts it: 'all bishops are essentially equal, however humble or exalted the city over which each presides. All bishops share equally in the apostolic succession, all have the same sacramental powers, all are divinely appointed teachers of the faith.' Ware, *The Orthodox Church*, p. 35.

227 St Augustine thought that the Africans were right to reject the Pope's view. This is significant because a phrase of Augustine's 'Rome has spoken, the dispute is at an end' is often taken out of context by Roman Catholics apologists to defend Papal claims. (Rome had been the last of a number of authorities to concur, and Augustine thought that that was enough.)

228 The Roman Church, like all mainstream churches, recognises the First Ecumenical Council of Constantinople held in AD 381 as the second Ecumenical (or General) Council of the Church.

229 Chadwick, *The Early Church*, pp. 204–5.

230 That the Donation of Constantine was a forgery was exposed by Lorenzo Valla in a treatise of 1439. He also exposed the letter to King Abagus purportedly written by Jesus, and also the correspondence between Seneca and St Paul. He also pointed out a number of errors in Jerome's Vulgate. He escaped the Inquisition only because he was protected by Alfonso V of Aragon and Naples.

231 Pollock and Maitland, *The History of English Law*, Bk. 1, Ch. 1 (p. 17).

232 The *False decretals* attributed to Isidore Mercator, Bishop of Seville, were actually compiled between 847 and 852 at Le Mans, by a group of clerics who were by contemporary standards very skilful forgers. These decretals were later incorporated into Gratian's *Decretum* and thus into canon law.

233 *Patrogia Latinae cursus completus, series Latina*, 221 vols., ed. J-P Migne (1844–64), Paris, vol. 214:col. 292. Incidentally, in a sense all bishops are vicars of Christ. The term had apparently first been used of St Gelasius I, a bishop of Rome in the late fifth century, but it does not seem to have been adopted as a title, nor invested with the significance that Innocent accorded to it.

3

FACTS AND FICTIONS

MANIPULATION OF THE FACTS

The first law is that the historian shall never dare to set down what is false; the second is that he shall never dare to conceal the truth; the third that there shall be no suspicion in his work of either favouritism or prejudice.
Cicero (106–43 BC)

In looking at the early Church and the development of the priesthood we have already found reasons to doubt its attachment to impartial history in its creation of the Bible. The Bible was not the only set of documents that was manipulated to conform to the requirements of evolving orthodoxy.

In this section we look at the extent to which the Christian Church has manipulated facts by selecting sources, destroying inconvenient evidence, fabricating records, and the use of other methods of hiding the truth that the Church has been accused of, and then at some case studies illustrating these techniques.

METHOD 1: SUPPRESS INCONVENIENT EVIDENCE

The ink of the scholar is more sacred than the blood of a martyr.
Mohammed (c.570–629)

Deliberate attempts have always been made to suppress material that was considered unsuitable by the Church. As already mentioned (page 44), Clement of Alexandria is known to have suppressed gospel material that did not suit him. As he explained in a letter, referring to the Secret Gospel of Mark:

During Peter's stay in Rome he wrote an account of the Lord's doings, not however declaring all of them, nor yet hinting at the secret ones, but selecting those he thought most useful for increasing the faith of those who were being instructed. But when Peter died as a martyr, Mark came over to Alexandria, bringing his own notes and those of Peter, from which he transferred to his former book the things suitable to whatever makes for progress towards gnosis. Thus he composed a more spiritual gospel for the use of those who were being perfected...[1]

Here is confirmation not only that Peter was selective, but also that Mark subsequently tailored the information. What was in the original version of the gospel we may never know. The original was suppressed and its existence denied. Something similar seems to have happened to the story of Barabbas. The name *Barabbas* is composed of the elements *bar* (son of) and *abba* (father). In an early Greek version of Matthew, Barabbas was called *Jesous Barabbas,* which is a transcription of a Hebrew name that translates as *Jesus son of the Father.*[2] Were there two Jesuses, both claiming to be sons of God, and both arrested at the same time? It sounds unlikely. We may never know unless an earlier manuscript turns up. But scholars think it probable that there is more to the story than is related in surviving texts.

Other important historical texts also suffered from tampering. For example Josephus recorded that a Judæan revolt (the First Jewish Revolt of AD 66) had been triggered by the killing of James, the brother of Jesus. The relevant passage does not occur in surviving manuscripts of Josephus, but authoritative Christian sources (both Eusebius and Origen) quote it. It would appear that the passage was edited out of the text by the Pauline line, which had an interest in minimising the importance of James.

We know of many so-called heretics only through the works of their Christian enemies. The works of Helvidius are lost, and we know of them through the writings of St Jerome. Jerome thought that virginity was better than marriage (the line that came to be regarded as orthodox), while Helvidius held that Mary and Joseph had had a normal married life and that Jesus had younger brothers and sisters. As Jerome's line came to be orthodox his ideas are well documented while those of Helvidius are not. Similarly, we know of Gnostic ideas mainly through the writing of their mainstream Christian enemies. Marcion's ideas for example, or a distorted version of them, are known through Tertullian's work *Against Marcion*. Marcion's own writings are 'lost', destroyed by the rival Christian faction that we now call orthodox. When Gnostic writings are recovered, as at Nag Hammadi in Egypt, it frequently turns out that Gnostics did not believe what 'orthodox' critics said they believed. And of course in their writings the roles are reversed. The Gnostics see themselves as holding the true line, while the line that is now held to be orthodox is represented as merely another heretical faction.[3]

As Christian doctrine developed, important early Christian writers came to be regarded as heretical, and their writings were destroyed. In this way the mainstream Church sought to root out any suggestion that its own version of orthodoxy was flawed. For example the book known as 1 Enoch was once regarded as scripture. It failed to be accepted into the biblical canon in the West, and was subsequently 'lost'. In the Ethiopian Church, however, it was accepted as scripture and so survived to be rediscovered by Western Christianity in modern times. Numerous gospels and letters, also 'lost', are referred to in surviving documents. Origen mentioned a Jewish apocryphal work called the Prayer of Joseph, which might have shed considerable light on Jewish ideas about semi-divine men, but it has been 'lost'.[4] Origen was a prolific writer but was himself later condemned as a heretic. Consequently, not one of his scriptural commentaries has survived in full.

Eusebius refers to writings by one Symmachus that cast doubt on the gospel attributed to Matthew[5] – writings that have since been 'lost'. He also mentions the neo-platonist Porphyry, who is known to have written fifteen volumes against the orthodox line, exposing the scriptures as fraudulent (he knew what modern scholars have independently discovered, for example that the book of Daniel could not have been written when it was purported to have been). He also pointed out that the apostles could hardly have been infallible if they quarrelled with each other as the New Testament said. His works were banned as soon as the Empire became Christian, and all fifteen volumes were 'lost'. Writings explicitly opposed to Christianity were also destroyed. The work of Aulus Cornelius Celsus, *Truth Established*, has also been 'lost'. Our knowledge of it comes from Origen's attempt to refute the book's arguments in *Contra Celsum*. Similarly we know of the Emperor Julian's criticisms of Christianity in his treatise *Adversus Christianos* only because of Cyril of Alexandria's attempts to refute them.

Occasionally copies of lost works turn up unexpectedly. The *Epistle to Diognetus* was once 'lost', but a copy was discovered in a fish market in Constantinople. Some works survived for centuries, before someone realised the threat to orthodoxy, or before negligence took its toll. Hegesippus's works were reputedly extant as late as the seventeenth century. They have all since disappeared, including five books of memoirs and a succession list of the earliest bishops of Rome. It is not known whether they were destroyed or hidden away. Other works were tampered with to make them orthodox, or to keep them orthodox. For example the seven letters of Ignatius of Antioch suffered in this way. As one authority puts it:

> Eusebius clearly knew them all. But in their authentic form they became known again only in the seventeenth century, for in the fourth century the Ignatian Correspondence was added to, both by interpolation in authentic epistles and by the addition of spurious ones, and this so-called 'Long Recension'* all but cast into oblivion any witness to the authentic epistles.[6]

Christian authorities have been responsible for the 'loss' of countless invaluable historical and religious records over the last 2,000 years or so: purportedly apostolic and apocryphal writings, Gnostic and Ebionite writings, classical and philosophical writings, Jewish writings and the sacred writings of other religions, all criticism of Christianity, non-compliant histories, anything savouring of heresy or originality. Later we shall see that all manner of other works were also destroyed: science, mathematics, architecture, natural history, medicine, ancient classics – all writings in fact not currently considered orthodox, and in practice this meant everything except officially approved propaganda.

Even the records of Church Councils and ancient biblical texts were mislaid, destroyed or otherwise 'lost'. Many such documents were for example collected for the famous Council of Trent (1546), never to be seen again. Other records have also been lost. For example Church records of trials for witchcraft and heresy are remarkably scanty. Much hard evidence comes from independent contemporary accounts, secret letters and municipal records. Other Church records have also been

---

* The word recension denotes a revised text.

mysteriously lost – records of torture, show trials, interference in politics, and so on. Even recent records are prone to get unaccountably lost. Church records of proceedings against individuals and political groups even in the twentieth century have been mysteriously 'lost'.

METHOD 2: SELECT SOURCES AND ARGUMENTS

Any doctrine that will not bear honest investigation is not a fit tenant
for the mind of an honest man.
Robert Ingersoll (1833–99), *Intellectual Development*

We have already seen that there were disagreements among Christians for many centuries over what material to include in the Bible. We have also seen that important early Christian authorities were prepared to suppress inconvenient material. Christian historians also selected their information. Edward Gibbon said of Eusebius that he 'indirectly confesses that he has related whatever might redound to the glory, and that he has suppressed all that could tend to the disgrace, of religion'. From what we know about the other Church Fathers, we have every reason to believe that Eusebius was typical.

Traditionally Christians have held that the whole of the Bible was divinely inspired. One might therefore expect that all of it would be regarded as equally important, and efforts would be made to under-stand all of it. Critics have frequently pointed out that in practice the overwhelming majority of Christians concentrate on a tiny minority of passages that bolster their own views. Churches simply choose the passages they like and ignore the ones they dislike. For example, congregations often hear the Matthew version of the parable of the talents, a favourite story, but they rarely hear the version in Luke 19:12–27. On the rare occasions that the Luke version is read in church the last verse is almost always left out, presumably because it does not conform to the Church's current version of the type of thing Jesus might say. The verse is:

> But those mine enemies, which would not that I should reign over them, bring hither, and slay them before me.

Unless Christians read the Bible for themselves they are unlikely to hear any but the same few passages over and over again each Sunday. These passages are generally the most inspiring and sympathetic to be found in the Bible. The vast majority of the text is quite different. Much of it seriously offends modern Christian sensibilities: God directing the killing of helpless prisoners or innocent babies, arranging for concubines to be fruitful, punishing people for other people's wrongdoing, or promising to starve parents until they have to eat their own babies. Nor do churchgoers hear much about God's shortcomings, such as that failure to prevail against an enemy equipped with iron chariots (see page 30). In recent years some New Testament stories have been taken off the annual reading rota as well. Churchgoers do not hear nearly as much as they used to about people burning in Hell for eternity, nor about St Paul blinding people, nor about the sudden deaths of those who failed to live up to St Peter's expectations.

As we have seen the 'Church Fathers' are not reliable authorities. Their writings cannot be cited in full because they contain numerous errors, heresies and contradictions. The solution is to select just those passages that suit. As one eminent authority puts it:

> The principal form of the argument from authority became the florilegium or anthology of carefully selected excerpts from orthodox fathers, designed to show that the unchanging orthodox tradition was in accordance with the compiler's convictions. The makers of these collections of excerpts were not always scrupulous about the integrity and authenticity of their texts...[7]

Until the last few years it has been virtually impossible to find full translations of early Christian works. Translations have always been of selected passages, which avoid uncomfortable matters (the acceptability of what are now heresies and unacceptability of what is now orthodoxy). Even influential medieval works were almost impossible to find in translation: one can find selected passages of St Thomas Aquinas for example, but until recently it has been virtually impossible to obtain a full English translation of his most important works, even though he has been the most influential Christian writer since the Dark Ages. When translations do exist, they are often by outsiders. For example Protestant scholars have delighted for centuries in translating early material detrimental to the Roman Church. In the nineteenth century translations of works embarrassing even to Protestants were made by eminent unbelievers. In the twentieth century translations have become available through people such as Geza Vermes (a Jewish scholar) at Oxford, John Allegro (an agnostic) at Manchester, and G. A. Wells (a leading critic of Christianity). Other unexpurgated material comes from the pens of clerics who hover on the fringes of the Protestant Churches, and from priests and teachers who have abandoned the Roman Church.

It was often difficult to find orthodox Fathers to support the compiler's view of orthodoxy, so others were cited by the Church even if they were unreliable. Thus, the most important authorities include Tertullian and Origen, despite the fact that both are now regarded as heretics. It is the same with other authorities. As we have seen, orthodoxy does not depend so much on the rulings of councils, as the status of councils is determined by their agreement with current orthodoxy. From the councils that have always been regarded as authoritative it is still possible to select only those canons that suit current tastes. Papal decretals too were selected as required. For example the infallible views of Pope Celestine III on marriage were edited out of a collection of decretals after a later pope disagreed with them. The New Testament was assembled in the same way. Early Christians wrote dozens of gospels, acts, epistles and apocalypses, some of which became canonical, some of which did not. Inconvenient ones were simply omitted from the canon. Of writings in the canon the most convenient manuscript texts were selected, and the most convenient translations of them adopted.

Roman Catholics and Protestants have been accusing each other for centuries of having deliberately distorted biblical texts. There are some distinct differences between Protestant and Roman Catholic versions of the Bible. For example, in Protestant versions Jesus has brothers, while in Roman Catholic ones he does not. In Protestant versions bishops are required to be married; in Roman Catholic ones they are not. Massive differences in doctrine are reflected in subtly different translations. Are the Greek words in 1 Corinthians 9:5 to be rendered as 'Christian woman' (as in the Jerusalem Bible) or as 'believing wife' (as in the NIV). It seems to depend upon whether the Church to which the translator belongs favours clerical marriage or not. According to one's preconceptions a word can be translated as either *priest* or *elder*; another as either *church* or *congregation*; and yet another as either *penance* or *repentance*. The choice seems to depend upon whether the translator needs to justify an ecclesiastical hierarchy and an official Church, and to recognise penance as a sacrament. Bibles are used to confirm one's own position, and in the past have been commissioned specifically to validate the beliefs of one denomination against those of another. For example, an English version of the Roman Catholic Vulgate Bible (the Douay-Rheims Bible) was written during the Reformation specifically to counter the Protestants' Geneva Bible.

Another selective technique is that of bundling. This can be used to remove embarrassing superfluities. We have already seen the sixteen or more named apostles in the New Testament being converted into the canonical Twelve by making out that some of them had two or more names. Two or three different women were rolled together to give us the familiar Mary Magdalene. Very different places such as Sheol, Gehenna, Abaddon, Hades and Tarsus can all be rolled together to produce Hell. Many Jewish gods can be fused together to provide a single God, and many other supernatural beings combined to give a single Satan.

The same sort of selectivity is applied to the accounts of visionaries. Because visionaries often experience multiple visions, and because some of these contain material that is not acceptable for one reason or another, it is common for their stories to be heavily selected. Thus for example, not everyone was convinced by Jean-Jacques Olier (founder of the seminary of St Sulpice) when he announced that the fifteen-year-old Virgin Mary was occupying his soul. Even those who had heard about these visits were unlikely to know that he had been 'subject to psychological disturbances for several years'.[8] Accounts of Maria d'Agreda's visions often leave out the more questionable claims, and also the fact that her original account had been placed on the Index.[9] After her Miraculous Medal vision in 1830, Catherine Labouré 'suffered from strange periods of amnesia, when she could not remember any details of what she had seen …'[10] When urged by the Archbishop of Paris to appear before an official inquiry in 1836, she declined. Yet millions of faithful admirers are unaware either of this or of the string of unlikely visions that she had experienced before her Miraculous Medal.

It is often repeated that Bernadette Soubirous (the Lourdes visionary) miraculously discovered a spring, but not so many accounts mention the fact that this spring was already well known to local people. The spectacular failure of expected healing miracles is also edited out of most accounts. So is the rather bizarre incident when Bernadette started eating mud and grass. Accounts of the visions at La Salette in 1846 tend to minimise the odder parts of the story as it was later reported – for example that the visionaries (two shepherd children) initially mistook a beautiful transparent lady in medieval court dress, bathed in light and sporting a halo, for a local woman escaping her family. Neither is it mentioned that the Vision might not have been quite as beautiful, transparent, lady-like or awe-inspiring as claimed in these accounts, since it is known that a deranged local woman liked to dress up like the Virgin Mary and parade around the hills. Neither do the faithful hear much about Mary's promises that stones and rocks would turn into wheat, or that the fields would sow themselves with potatoes. Again, the fact that one of the La Salette visionaries (Mélanie Calvat) subsequently abandoned her vocation as a nun is underplayed, and so is the fact that she went on to receive many more exciting visions and revelations. Neither do the faithful often hear that the other visionary, Maximin Giraud, failed to become a priest, went on to market a liqueur called 'Salette', and subsequently admitted that the whole thing had been a fraud.

At Fátima in Portugal, Mary made the mistake of confirming a doctrine that has now become unpopular. She confirmed to the principal visionary, Lucia dos Santos, the reality of traditional hellfire and Purgatory. Lucia 'asked about the fate of two ... children who had died. The lady answered that one of them was in Heaven, but the other was in Purgatory "till the end of the world".' This was once quite acceptable theology, but not anymore, hence in many books this answer has been suppressed.[11] Further problems were presented by the simultaneous appearance of the Holy Child and Christ, who Lucia seems to have thought were two different people. Yet another element to be edited out was the promise that the war then being fought (World War I) would end on 13th October 1917 – wrong by more than a year.

It is common for arguments to be followed only as far as proves convenient. As soon as they start leading to inconvenient conclusions they are abandoned. Thus the Roman Church selectively ignores an argument that justifies divorce when its scope is found to be too wide. *Coitus interruptus* was traditionally prohibited on the grounds that God required semen to be deposited in a vagina. Only then could the Church recognise that valid sexual intercourse had taken place, since the Church required not merely *penetratio* but also *inseminatio*. Thus a couple who had undergone a marriage ceremony but always practised *coitus interruptus* were not legally married, since semen had not been deposited in the required place. It followed that such marriages could be dissolved, as indeed many have been. The use of condoms presented a similar problem. If a condom was used then valid sexual intercourse could not occur, since there was no *inseminatio*. Without *inseminatio* a marriage contract was voidable. It followed that any married couple who had always used condoms should be able to have their marriage annulled, just like couples who had practised *coitus interruptus*. However, presumably because it would make divorce much easier to obtain for ordinary Roman Catholic couples, this argument is not accepted, even though the logic is identical to that used in the case of *coitus interruptus*, and no coherent counter-argument has ever been articulated.

Another old favourite was the 'natural argument'. Things that God was held to approve of were considered natural. Things that he was supposed to disapprove of were labelled unnatural. For example slavery was natural and therefore acceptable, because God approved of it. On the other hand homosexuality was unnatural and therefore sinful, because God disapproved of it. So was atheism, so was democracy, so was the idea of women in positions of authority, and so on. This sort of argument was popular until recent times: if God had wanted us to do something, he would have arranged for it to be 'natural'. Early train passengers were criticised on the grounds that if God had meant us to travel at such speeds he would have provided flat ground, tracks and engines. If God had wanted us to smoke he would have given us chimneys. If he had wanted us to fly he would have given us wings. These arguments always suffered from weaknesses. If God had wanted men to be clean-shaven, he would not have caused hair to grow on their faces (popular with Tertullian, less popular when beards went out of fashion). If God had wanted us to go around without clothes on, he would have caused us to be born naked. That one had to be explained away by reference to the Garden of Eden (God authorised clothes for Adam and Eve after the Fall). If God had wanted us to use buttons he would have provided us with them. That argument was popular when buttons first came into use in Western Christendom, but is now a minority position held onto only by some Mennonites.

Generally the argument was applied only where it led to acceptable conclusions: 'If God had wanted us to live in houses...' was not pursued while 'If God had wanted us to meddle in science...' was, and still is. 'If

God had wanted us to go to the Moon...' was popular in the second half of the twentieth century and can still be heard in the twenty first. Sometimes the arguments are dropped when they are found to lead to the 'wrong' conclusion. For example, until the early twenty-first century it was common to hear Christians claiming that homosexuality was unnatural. God had not created homosexuals, they had made a sinful life-choice. When it turned out that a predisposition to homosexuality has a genetic component one might have expected the argument to switch 180 degrees. If homosexuality is natural after all, because God has created certain genes that cause a disposition towards homosexuality, then there should be mainstream Christians using the following argument in favour of homosexuality: 'God has created homosexuals so we should not condemn homosexuality.' There is, however, a distinct shortage of traditionalist preachers proclaiming that homosexuality is natural and therefore acceptable because God is responsible for it.

Critics have noted that like the 'natural argument', other arguments appear to be designed to justify existing beliefs, and that inconvenient corollaries have to be ignored. A favourite argument, used until recently in almost all Churches and still used by some conservative ones, is that Jesus chose only men to be his disciples so only men could be priests. But this is a dangerous path, since it is necessary to ignore parallel arguments. For example we can use parallel arguments to establish that only married, Aramaic-speaking, circumcised, Middle Eastern, Jewish manual workers should be ordained.

Perhaps the best arguments demonstrating the need for selectivity concern the consumption of alcohol. Any straight reading of the Bible confirms God's approval for drinking alcohol. When God almost exterminated the human race, he kept alive only one family: Noah's, a family of vintners. Jesus himself reputedly turned water into wine for a wedding party. There are many explicit examples of alcohol being recommended in the Bible.[12] Since early times Christians have drunk wine in the belief that they were following Jesus' own instructions. Yet numerous Christian sects opposed to alcohol contrived meanings out of the Bible that are diametrically opposed to the plain reading of the text. While the Bible criticises those who drink to excess, there is nothing advocating abstention – just the opposite: 'Drink no longer water, but use a little wine for thy stomach's sake and thine often infirmities' (1 Timothy 5:23). Yet millions of Puritans, Methodists, Baptists,

Salvationists and other dissenters somehow convinced themselves that the Bible was wholeheartedly opposed to the buying, selling and consumption of alcoholic drinks. Many millions still believe this, though it flies in the face of any honest reading of the text. Temperance campaigners claimed that the wine referred to in the Bible with approval was merely unfermented grape juice (a claim that has no basis and which cannot be reconciled with Mark 2:22).

This sort of unsustainable assertion is not at all unusual. Thousands of Christian sects manage to sustain thousands of contradictory positions on all manner of subjects by the expedient of selecting the texts and interpretations that suit them and dismissing all the others.

METHOD 3: FABRICATE RECORDS

An honest man's the noblest work of God.
Alexander Pope (1688–1744), *An Essay on Man*

An honest God's the noblest work of man.
Samuel Butler (1835–1902), *Further Extracts*

Even by carefully selecting appropriate texts and destroying inconvenient ones, it was still not possible to create a comprehensive body of writing to support Christian orthodoxy. The answer was to fabricate suitable material, which was not difficult for an organisation that exercised a strict monopoly over reading and writing. These texts could then be miraculously discovered. This technique has a venerable history, even among the Jews. For example the book of Deuteronomy had been discovered hidden in the Temple at Jerusalem by King Josiah. This discovery confirmed the King's views during a major doctrinal controversy. It is not now generally regarded as being as miraculous as his supporters thought.

As we have already seen, the early Christians were accused of continuously tampering with their gospels, and the surviving early texts that we have confirm that they did. No two early manuscripts are identical, and scribes felt free to 'improve' the text by deleting, moving or amending chunks of it, or by adding their own. Sects accused each other of tampering, and with good cause. Was Jesus an ordinary man, or was he God incarnate? The gospels could be altered to suit the editor's own views. As one early sect said of another, '...they laid hands unblushingly on the Holy Scriptures, claiming to have corrected them'.[13] It is probably true that not all of the Christians who tampered in this way regarded themselves as dishonest. Perhaps some of them really did think that they were 'correcting' the texts, because it was so obvious to them that the texts should have said what they themselves believed.

Throughout the Christian era scholars have known that the scriptures were extensively tampered with. Here for example is Jean Meslier (1664–1729), a French priest who was also an atheist (sic), discussing this point around the year 1700:

> It is no use saying that the Gospel stories have always been regarded as holy and sacred, and that they have been faithfully preserved without any tampering. It was common practice among the writers who copied these stories to add, delete or alter the text as seemed good to them. The Christians themselves cannot deny this; for St Jerome said explicitly in many places in his Prologues that the text had been corrupted and falsified, having already been through the hands of many people who added and cut out what they pleased; with the result, as he said, that there were as many different readings as there were different texts.[14]

Some unlikely documents were put into circulation, such as correspondence between Jesus and King Abgar V of Edessa.[15] In some versions Jesus promised that the city of Edessa would enjoy freedom from conquest. There were bogus records of Jesus' trial, and several forged versions of a letter supposedly sent by Pilate to the Emperor Tiberius concerning the crucifixion. There was also a host of forged letters from the apostles, from the various Marys, and from other gospel characters. Testimonial letters appeared, purportedly from those miraculously healed by Jesus, for example from a blind man whose sight had been restored.

In the sixth century someone, probably a Monophysite Christian, fabricated theological writings that purported to have been written by Dionysius the Areopagite, who is mentioned in Acts 17:34. These writings were accepted as genuine and had a great influence on both Eastern and Western Churches. They were for many centuries the best 'proof' of Mary's bodily Assumption into Heaven. Another key document justifying the same doctrine is the *Cogitis me*, a document purportedly written by St Jerome but almost certainly fabricated by Paschasius Radbert, a ninth-century Abbot of Corbie (near Soissons in modern France).[16] Claims made by this forgery are still repeated during masses in the Roman Church.[17]

Letters appeared from St Paul to Aristotle. Paul also supposedly wrote six letters to Seneca, and received eight back. All were Christian forgeries. A second-century Christian acting 'out of love of Paul' forged a book, the *Acts of Paul and Thecla*, purporting to describe his activities.[18] Paul himself had been aware of the danger of forgery. He warned his readers against teachings contained in some letters purporting to be from him and made a point of writing the final passages of his letters in his own hand to prove their authenticity (2 Thessalonians 3:17). The *Apostolic Constitutions* are another fabrication. They purport to be written in the name of Jesus' apostles and warn about books falsely claiming to be written in the name of Jesus' apostles. A document called *3 Corinthians* is another known forgery, a fabrication by the same priest who forged the *Acts of Paul and Thecla*. Yet another 'orthodox' forgery was the *Epistula apostolorum*, supposedly written by the eleven disciples remaining after Judas's betrayal.

Bogus lists of bishops were produced to bolster the fiction of apostolic succession for important bishoprics. Bogus accounts of martyrdoms were circulated to bolster the fictions that Christians had been badly persecuted and that they had reacted with great bravery. Given the poor state of Christian scholarship many impositions succeeded for a long time. A popular and influential work concerning the Virgin Mary claimed that she was elected Queen of the Temple Virgins as a young girl, and that bishops came to venerate her.[19] Apparently it did not occur to the author or his readers that there could not have been any bishops at that time. Letters from Mary Magdalene to Lazarus discovered as late as the nineteenth century fooled many Church scholars, despite the fact that they were written in French. A work falsely ascribed to Albertus Magnus (*c.*1193–1280), who became St Albert, was regarded with such awe on account of its supposed authorship that no one noticed until 1952 that it contradicted his known views.[20]

Many of these forgeries should have been easy to detect, even those not written in French. They included anachronisms and other simple mistakes. For example, early Jewish Christians were known as Ebionites from the Hebrew term meaning *the poor*, but Tertullian assumed that they were named after a man called *Ebion*. Soon, Christians were quoting from the writings of the odious Ebion, in order to refute his followers.[21] Letters were exchanged between people who were not contemporaries, or else discussed people who were not yet born, or mentioned cities that were not yet founded. There were letters too from characters such as Prester John, a fictitious Christian ruler in the distant Orient. Since standards of Church scholarship were not high, almost any imposture was likely to succeed.

Not only were new works fabricated, genuine ones were doctored. Passages were inserted into non-Christian works in order to suggest that even non-Christians were impressed by Jesus or by Christianity. A sympathetic reference to Jesus was for example inserted into the writings of the historian Josephus.[22] Writings of other Church Fathers were doctored to suit current tastes. When Irenaeus's tract against heresies was translated into Latin in the early fifth century, the opportunity was taken to omit those parts that by then had themselves come to smack of heresy. When Rufinus of Aquileia translated Origen's *On First Principles* he openly admitted that he had altered the text to make it conform to current orthodox thought. Origen himself had held that it was acceptable to lie to less intelligent Christians, as long as it bolstered belief. Generally it seems that many Christians felt free to manipulate facts in favour of what they perceived as divine truth. Dionysius, Bishop of Corinth (*c*.170), protested that other Christians were changing and forging his letters, just as they had tampered with the scriptures:[23]

> When my fellow Christians invited me to write letters to them I did so. These the devil's apostles have filled with tares, taking away some things and adding others. For them the woe is reserved. Small wonder then if some of them have dared to tamper even with the word of the Lord Himself, when they have conspired to mutilate my own humble efforts.

Cyprian, a Bishop of Carthage (*c*.250) also revealed that Christians had been forging letters in his name.[24] As one authority has pointed out, in the 200 years from around AD 400, false letters were added to the collections of almost every early Christian letter writer.[25] In fact it is impossible to be sure that any single surviving Christian document was written by its purported author and is free from amendment.

Christians practised all manner of fabrication. They even tampered with written records of oracles. Seven volumes of Apolline oracles were edited by a Christian hand around the beginning of the sixth century, and a further four bogus volumes were added to produce the collection called *On True Belief.* They also fabricated verses of the Sibylline Oracles,* complete with chunks of gospel history supposedly seen in visions by sibyls long before New Testament times. By the Middle Ages, twelve of the old pagan sibyls were agreed to have predicted the coming of Christ, and indeed the whole Christian story. The fiction of the sibyls' prescience is still upheld in the Roman Catholic Missal:

Dies irae, dies illa	That day, the day of wrath
Solvet saeclum in favilla	Will turn the universe to ashes
Teste David cum Sibylla[26]	As David foretells, and the Sibyl too

Frauds continued throughout the Middle Ages. A forged *Appeal of the Eastern Emperor* for help in saving the Holy Land was circulated in a successful attempt to whip up enthusiasm for the First Crusade. Material concerning controversial opinions was particularly vulnerable. Thus for example the whole edifice of the Immaculate Conception is built on forgeries and documents wrongly attributed to prestigious authors. According to taste one could follow (pseudo)Jerome or (pseudo)Augustine, or any one of numberless other documents by pseudo-authors. At least one of the sermons of St Bonaventure (d. 1274) – the one dealing with Mary's Assumption – is spurious.[27]

Sometimes the fraud was false attribution. The works of unknown authors were passed off as the work of more prestigious figures. The work of the little-known Saxon Eadmer was passed off as that of his more prestigious master, Anselm. Often the fraud was much greater and more obvious. As we have seen, claims to Church authority were bolstered by a series of major forgeries including the *Symmachan Forgeries*, the *Donation of Constantine*, and the *False (Pseudo-Isidorian) Decretals*. The papal chancery poured out a stream of forgeries for many centuries, and schools of forgers flourished under a long series of popes. One notable

---

* The Sibylline Oracles are a collection of twelve books of prophecies supposedly made by sibyls – women regarded as prophets or oracles by the ancient Greeks and Romans.

culprit was Pope Gregory VII, who in the eleventh century used old and new forgeries to justify his every whim. Under his direction, pliant clerics amended ancient documents, changing their meaning, sometimes to make them say the opposite of what they had originally said. Churchmen created new documents purporting to be old ones and bolstered all manner of papal claims. A huge fabricated superstructure of falsehood was raised, buttressed by earlier forgeries and founded on yet earlier ones.

To any scholars who looked into the matter it would have been clear that many of these authoritative Church documents were crude forgeries. Instead, they were cited in infallible papal bulls by men in personal daily contact with God and incorporated into the *Concordia discordantium canonum*, more popularly known as the *Decretum Gratiani*. This *Decretum* was an authoritative code of canon law compiled in the middle of the twelfth century by a Benedictine monk called Gratian, who included bogus documents in addition to genuine ones. It was through this document that torture was formally justified by the Church as a way of obtaining confessions. Much later theology was based on the *Decretum*, including the work of Thomas Aquinas, whose *Summa Theologica* in turn forms the basis for modern Roman Catholic doctrine. Thus, the authority for this doctrine is compromised, if not completely invalidated.

Pope Gregory I used the *False Decretals* to justify his expanding claims to temporal power. From the fifteenth century, at least, they were widely known to be fake, and yet the Church insisted that they were not.[28] The Italian humanist and educator Lorenzo Valla demonstrated conclusively that the *Donation of Constantine* was also a forgery, as was the famous letter from Jesus to King Abgar – and so too letters from St Paul to Seneca and many other important documents that had been regarded as genuine for centuries. Valla's scholarship was impeccable, but the Church continued to maintain that the forgeries were genuine. It took more than 300 years for the Roman Church to accept, in a roundabout way, that it had been wrong. Some Roman Catholic writers still seem to be unaware that the *Donation of Constantine* is known to be a forgery, repeating its claim that a Roman Emperor ceded his temporal authority to the Church.

Nothing was too sacred to be tampered with. The creeds were amended to make them conform to the requirements of the Western

Church, to the anger and bewilderment of the Eastern Churches. The records of ecumenical councils were tampered with too, when it suited. Thus, records of the Council of Nicæa were doctored to confirm the primacy of the Roman Church. Whenever Eastern scholars brought out a copy of an ancient text to prove a point, Rome would attempt to refute it with a forgery. For centuries the Orthodox Church knew Rome as the home of forgeries. The role of women in the early Church was also something of a problem in later times when the priesthood became a male monopoly. Inconvenient evidence about the role (or even the existence) of women in the early Church was suppressed, so that it became possible to justify women's exclusion from the priesthood by reference to the (fictitious) practices of the early Church. At least partly on the strength of other forged documents women were prevented from serving at the altar in any capacity.[29]

Most people were illiterate in the Middle Ages, but Church art could be used to sustain convenient fictions. Art confirmed the theologians' favourite theories, papering over the fact that these theories had no biblical support. For example, the four evangelists (the purported writers of the gospels of Matthew, Mark, Luke and John) were shown taking dictation from the Holy Ghost, sometimes with an angel guiding their hands. This suggested that the gospels were divinely inspired and authoritative, simultaneously avoiding the uncomfortable facts that they were inconsistent and that their writers had never even met the historical Jesus. When the Bible mentions a messenger (Greek *angelos*), the word was often translated as *angel*. With no effort at all a human messenger was converted into a semi-divine one. In the Bible they had no wings and were likely to be mistaken for ordinary people, but in art they could sprout wings and fly, which looked much more impressive.

It was safer to show fictions in the form of pictures. St Jerome wearing a cardinal's hat suggested that cardinals had existed since early times, which they had not. Joseph was conventionally shown as an extremely old man, which seemed to confirm the story, otherwise unsupported, that he had never engaged in sexual intercourse with Mary. A pope baptising the Emperor Constantine invited all manner of false conclusions: that a pope had existed at that time, that popes were in a position to baptise emperors, that emperors were subordinate to popes, and so on. In fact Constantine was hardly aware of the Bishop of Rome and was known to have been baptised on his deathbed by a

In almost all areas, the truth according to impartial modern historians is less flattering than the traditional accounts taught in schools. In the traditional versions, Christians were on the right side. Deliberate distortions continue. Modern histories of the Church often give the impression that the Churches supported the abolition of capital punishment, penal reform, democracy, human rights and a host of freedoms, when in fact they opposed all of these things. The American Civil War has become a war in which Christianity vanquished a number of un-Christian practices like slavery and established wholesome traditional Christian ideas like liberty, equality and democracy. The truth is exactly the opposite, since it was the South that was supporting the traditional Christian practice of slavery, and the North pursuing the secular principles of the founders of the Constitution. Texts are still being tampered with to make the facts fit the fictions. For example Lincoln's address at Gettysburg made no mention of God, yet when it is cited now the words 'under God' are often added after the words 'this nation'.*

If we had to rely on Church historians we would hear that Christians were almost solid in their opposition to Nazism, which as we shall see later is far from the truth. Almost no textbook will give estimates of the numbers of people killed by Christian Churches or at Christian Churches' behest: pagans, Jews, Muslims, Cathars, supposed witches, heretics, schismatics, rationalists, disabled children, or any other group. Many books confirm the fiction that various reforms were carried out by Christians in the face of fierce opposition from unspecified quarters. Few mention that reform was in almost all cases driven through by popular opinion, led by people outside mainstream Christianity. Key names such as those of Thomas Paine, George Holyoake and Annie Besant are simply omitted from school history books. Other names are omitted too, such as those of the numerous professors who lost their Chairs for accepting scientific facts or for bringing biblical analysis to public attention.

Recent history is adjusted to put the Churches on what is now regarded as the right side. Thus hardly any child leaves school knowing that the Nazi treatment of the Jews was copied point for point from

---

* Most versions available on the internet refer to 'this nation under God', yet the Hay and Nicolay versions kept by the Library of Congress refer simply to 'this nation' and make no reference to God anywhere in the text.

traditional Christian techniques, even from Church statutes. Neither will they have any clue that there had been many Nazi priests and bishops during World War II, both Roman Catholic and Protestant. No criticism of the Church will have been heard. However well established the truth, it simply will not appear in popular books. No school child learns that the Christian Church consistently supported slavery and torture, corporal and capital punishment, and mass killings, or that it opposed almost all social reform. One could visit 1,000 church bookshops without ever finding a single book that betrayed a hint of any of this.

Evidence is being gently massaged as tastes change. One can visit cities such as Rome, Madrid, Avignon, and Toledo and enjoy guided tours of religious buildings without hearing the least hint that they housed ecclesiastical torture chambers. These torture chambers were seen by numerous reliable witnesses (like the prison reformer John Howard) up to the nineteenth century, but now they have apparently vanished. Perhaps they have been destroyed; perhaps they are merely no longer open to visitors. Little by little, all evidence of the uncomfortable past is being eliminated. Coats of arms have been sanitised, to make them more religious and less bellicose. Coronets, swords and crests have been removed from clerical arms. Similarly, hymnals are updated to reflect current tastes. Politically incorrect hymns or verses of hymns have disappeared without trace. In England alone, many hundreds of millions of hymnals were printed with hymns condoning the oppression of women, the acceptance of poverty and the acceptability of racist ideas, yet it is now difficult to find one even in a second-hand bookshop. At the time of writing traditionalist Christians are complaining about the trend for Christmas Carols to be sanitised by removing terms with a feudal and male resonance like Lord and King. It is already difficult to find copies of traditional prayer books containing old services, for example for the expulsion of lepers, formal cursings, and the special Anglican anti-Roman Catholic service for 5th November. How many people have ever seen the text of a service of excommunication, once so popular?

There is also great selectivity in what children and television watchers are told about the beliefs of well-known people. Every Sunday the public media feature television cooks, footballers, singers, and popular entertainers who all avow their deep Christian faith. Unsympathetic philosophers and scientists, and even liberal theologians, are almost never given similar opportunities to express their ideas. The beliefs of well-known people are suppressed and frequently distorted. Few children ever learn that writers such as Shelley, George Eliot, Mark Twain and H. G. Wells were non-believers, nor that intellectual giants like Darwin, Freud, Einstein and Russell all became atheists.[31] Neither are they told that Hitler, Stalin, Franco, Pétain and Mussolini were all Christian believers, most of them benefiting from particularly devout families.[32] Again, reformers like Lord Shaftesbury, Florence Nightingale, and William Wilberforce are falsely portrayed as orthodox Christians, while the most dedicated true reformers, who were non-Christians, such as Thomas Paine, John Stewart Mill and Jeremy Bentham, are almost totally ignored in school history books. It is arguable that the Christian Churches have carried out one of the most successful whitewash jobs in history.

METHOD 4: THE RETROSPECTIVE PROPHECY

Beware of false prophets...
Matthew 7:15

Vaticinia ex eventu – retrospective prophecy – is an ancient technique for gaining credibility. It involves generating a prediction that appears to predate the event that it foretells. The event therefore appears to confirm the miraculous prediction. The trick can be done in several ways. One way is to fabricate a document purportedly written in the past that foretells later events. Biblical scholars generally accept that the Old Testament book of Daniel is an example of this type, written centuries after it was purported to have been written. Another way is to take a genuine old text and look for passages that can be interpreted as foretelling aspects of later times, tweaking facts about later times, up to the present, as required.

It was a fundamental belief of Jews at the time of Jesus that no important event could come to pass unless the scriptures had foretold it. Early followers of Jesus were therefore keen to prove that the main events of his life, or what they believed about his life, had been predicted. If the Old Testament genuinely foretold events in the New, then we might expect that the prophecies would have been clearly acknowledged as prophecies, and in view of their divine provenance they would be free from error. On the other hand, if books of the New Testament were edited to make them appear consistent with supposed Old Testament prophecies, then we might expect a range of human errors. For example, Old Testament passages might be referred to that were not prophetic, or passages might be misquoted, or quoted out of context, or even invented. Again, genuine predictions concerning the life of Jesus would not have been fulfilled already before his time. Since New Testament authors were familiar with the Jewish writings only in Greek translation, anyone fabricating retrospective prophecies might not realise that their Old Testament texts contained mistranslations. Also, since the canon of the Old Testament was not yet fixed, we might find prophecies being quoted from texts that turned out not to be canonical. To see which pattern best matches the facts let's look at some examples.

It seems that it was widely known during his lifetime that Jesus came from Nazareth, in Galilee. This was unfortunate because there was no suitable prophecy in the scriptures about a messiah, or a king, or even a prophet coming from Nazareth. Indeed Nazareth is never even mentioned in the Old Testament. On one occasion, according to the New Testament, the Jews say explicitly that Jesus cannot be the Messiah because he comes from Galilee rather than Bethlehem (John 7:41–2). Biblical authors seem to have known that Bethlehem was the correct place for a messiah to come from because of a passage in the Old Testament:

> But thou, Bethlehem Ephratah, though thou be little among the thousands of Judah, yet out of thee shall come forth unto me that is to be ruler in Israel; whose goings forth have been from of old, from everlasting. (Micah 5:2)

This probably explains why the authors of Matthew and Luke constructed (contradictory) stories to explain how Jesus of Nazareth came to be born not in Nazareth but in Bethlehem. For many Jews it would be unthinkable that God would have neglected to mention Jesus of Nazareth more explicitly in the scriptures if he was indeed who he claimed to be. The Matthew author remedied God's omission by inventing his own prophecy. He relates that Jesus went to live in Nazareth '...that it might be fulfilled which was spoken by the prophets, He shall be called a Nazarene' (Matthew 2:23). There is no such prophecy in any Jewish scripture but, as the writer must have known, it would be almost impossible for his readers to disprove his assertion that there was.[33] Even those who could read did not have access to the scriptures, because they were not available for public reference. Other purported prophecies do not exist either. For example Mark 14:49 and Matthew 26:56 refer to a prophecy concerning Jesus' arrest, but no such prophecy exists.

Early writers were keen to match New Testament events with Old Testament prophecies. This is especially true of the author of Matthew, who was writing for a Jewish audience. He frequently notes that Jesus did things in order to fulfil the scriptures. The fact that he wrote in Greek also provided scope for errors. The Greek version of the Old Testament (the Septuagint) contained errors of translation that could be picked up and incorporated into the New Testament by anyone arranging events to match prophecies. The story of the Virgin Birth, found in Matthew 1:23, as we shall see later, depends upon a mistranslation of Isaiah 7:14. The passage should read:

> Therefore the Lord himself shall give you a sign; Behold, a young woman shall conceive, and bear a son, and shall call his name Immanuel.

But in the Septuagint the word for 'young woman' is mistranslated as 'virgin', and this Greek mistranslation has been picked up in creating a retrospective gospel prophecy. Incidentally there was another difficulty with this prophecy. Mary named her child not *Immanuel*, as required by the prophecy, but *Jesus*. Not to be discouraged, Christians sometimes refer to Jesus as *Immanuel* anyway, especially at Christmas time when the passage from Isaiah is quoted, providing another good example of how events can be manipulated to give the impression that a prophecy has been fulfilled. There is no reason not to suppose that if the prophecy had been about someone called Darren, then Christians could be referring to Jesus as *Darren* with equal facility each Christmas.

In fact, Isaiah's original prophecy had been made to King Ahaz of Judah when he was having some local difficulties with the neighbouring kingdoms of Syria and Israel. What it means is that before a newly conceived child called *Immanuel* (a name meaning 'God is with us') is old enough to distinguish right from wrong, the King's troubles will be over. Sure enough, within a few years the Assyrians conquered the kingdoms of Damascus and northern Israel, thus relieving King Ahaz of his difficulties. The prophecy was thus fulfilled some 732 years before the birth of Jesus.

The familiar line '...Unto us a child is born, unto us a son is given...', recited at Christmas services each year is a quotation from Isaiah 9:6 and refers not to Jesus but to Maher-shalal-hash-baz, a child born in the previous chapter. Again, the author of the Matthew gospel explains that the flight to Egypt fulfils a prophecy.

> ... that it might be fulfilled which was spoken of the Lord by the prophet, saying, Out of Egypt have I called my son. (Matthew 2:15)

The prophecy is to be found in Hosea 11:1:

> When Israel was a child, then I loved him, and called my son out of Egypt.

This prophecy does not refer to the Lord, or to any individual. Moreover, it is phrased in the past tense, and the citation is clearly selective. In fact, the original text refers to the Exodus from Egypt led by Moses, an event that had already happened centuries earlier.

When Jesus entered Jerusalem for the last time he made a point of riding on an ass or a colt. The authors of Matthew and John point out that he did this in fulfilment of a prophecy, which Matthew 21:5 gives as:

> Tell ye the daughter of Sion, Behold, thy King cometh unto thee, meek, and sitting upon an ass, and a colt the foal of an ass.

This is a reference to Zechariah 9:9:

> Rejoice greatly O daughter of Zion; shout, O daughter of Jerusalem: behold thy King cometh unto thee: he is just, and having salvation; lowly, and riding upon an ass, and upon a colt the foal of an ass.

As usual the Matthew author is the most keen to match events to a prophecy, even to the extent that he describes Jesus riding two animals, an ass and a colt. (This passage later led to the observation that Jesus had entered Jerusalem 'like a circus clown on the back of two donkeys', an observation that earned its author nine months' hard labour in 1921–2.[34]) The circus act seems to have arisen because whoever wrote the book of Matthew followed the Greek version of the scriptures too literally. The original Jewish text employed parallelism, a poetic technique using repetition. In other words, the original Hebrew text envisaged only one animal. The Matthew author is thus caught in the act of arranging New Testament events to match his faulty understanding of the Old Testament.* Another important point here is that the prophecy concerns not the heavenly Christ, but an earthly King of the Jews. Also, as usual, the Matthew author's quotation is not exact.

The author of the John gospel was also keen to match events to prophecies. According to John (13:18) Jesus chooses Judas to betray him because of a prophecy:

> I speak not of you all: I know whom I have chosen: but that the scripture may be fulfilled, He that eateth bread with me hath lifted up his heel against me.

This is a reference to Psalm 41:9:

> Yea mine own familiar friend, in whom I trusted, which did eat of my bread, hath lifted up his heel against me.

Interestingly the John gospel continues an error in the original. As modern translations acknowledge, the words 'lifted up his heel against' are wrong and should read 'betrayed' or 'rebelled against'. In Hebrew there is a difference of only one letter, and the mistake may well have been due to a scribal error. It seems odd that Jesus should not have noticed or corrected an error in divine writ.

John (19:33–36) says that the soldiers at the crucifixion did not break Jesus' legs, as they did the legs of the two others who were crucified with him. The author presents this as a fulfilment of a prophecy:

> For these things were done, that the scripture should be fulfilled,
> A bone of him shall not be broken.

This is a reference to Psalm 34:20:

> He keepeth all his bones: not one of them is broken

---

* The other three canonical gospels, which are less concerned with fulfilling prophecy, have Jesus riding on only one animal. See Mark 11:7, Luke 19:35 and John 12:14.

Unfortunately however the psalm is not referring to the Messiah but to righteous men, as the rest of the psalm clearly shows.

All four canonical gospels refer to Jesus' garments being divided amongst the soldiers. Matthew 27:35 says:

> And they crucified him, and parted his garments, casting lots: *that it might be fulfilled which was spoken by the prophet, They parted my garments among them, and upon my vesture did they cast lots.*

The words in italicised text are not found in all manuscripts, only in a few late ones. Someone was clearly trying to embellish the story by adding text, retrospectively citing a 'prophecy' from Psalm 22:18. Many New Testament events are matched with this psalm, though with great selectivity. The psalm incidentally is not intended to be prophetic, but is an account of David's sufferings.

It is relatively easy to select Old Testament passages that seem to predict current events. In fact with the benefit of hindsight it is trivially easy. Theologians developed an intricate web of links between the Old and New Testaments, purportedly showing that the Old prefigured the New: 'The Old Testament is nothing but the New covered with a veil, and the New is nothing but the Old unveiled'.[35] Thus King David prefigured Jesus, the parting of the Red Sea prefigured baptism, Noah's ark prefigured the Christian Church, and so on. Every event was read as prefiguring some aspect of Christianity, and as one commentator has put it, the Old Testament became a book of riddles to which in each case the correct answer was Jesus the Messiah.[36] All this was possible when the answer was already known with absolute certainty, but the correct answer was far from obvious to anyone who did not know what the correct answer had to be. No one, given only the Old Testament, could conceivably predict any of the events of the New except with hindsight – and even with hindsight commentators sometimes experienced difficulty in finding a match. Sometimes the retrospective prefigurations verge on the bizarre. For example the early Church was embarrassed by the fact that there was no prophecy concerning the Resurrection. How could such a central event not have been prefigured? Apart from a dubious passage in Hosea,[37] and some desperate casting around in apocryphal writings, the only other passage from the Old Testament that could be pressed into service came from the book of Jonah, since Jonah spent

[274]

three days in the belly of a great fish.[38] So it was that Christians came to regard Jonah's sojourn in the belly of a fish as prefiguring the Resurrection, simply on the strength that it lasted three days.

To illustrate how easy it is to adapt Old Testament passages, the following paragraphs tell a modern day story with reference to scriptural prophecies. A short perusal of the Old Testament has provided suitable quotations. As in the New Testament, no apologies are made for taking passages out of context, and the use of capital letters is no more misleading than that in English translations of the Bible. The subject matter of this little story, a motorcyclist, is deliberately chosen to make the point that although the quotations fit well enough they could not really have been intended to refer to motorcycling. The quotations are from the Authorised Version:

And it came to pass that Kevin took his motorbike, a Swift, to the local garage to have it serviced. Kevin arrived according to the scriptures 'an hairy man, and girt with a girdle of leather'[39] and 'he had an helmet of brass upon his head'.[40] He said to the chief mechanic that he wanted a good job doing, and the mechanic answered, saying that he could watch the work. He cited the prophets 'be a witness ..... that we might do the service'.[41] The mechanic was learned in the scriptures and, seeing the state of Kevin's dirty trousers, he pointed to them and quoted from the writings of Moses 'what saddle soever he rideth upon ..... shall be unclean'.[42] But Kevin rebuked him with words of scripture 'speak, ye that ride on white asses'.[43]

Kevin beheld an old Triumph motorcycle being refitted in the garage. The chief mechanic told him that it fulfilled the words of scripture that there should be a 'Triumph in the works'.[44] The mechanic, and his apprentice, Sam, then turned to Kevin's Swift. Sam asked the chief mechanic how he should know if there was enough oil in the engine and again the mechanic answered in the words of scripture that he should 'dip his right finger in the oil'.[45] Then the apprentice did as he was bid and, seeing that the oil was too low he topped it up. And the chief mechanic said that it was well, for it was written that Samuel should 'take a vial of oil and pour it'.[46]

Kevin said his motorbike fulfilled the words of the prophet who had spoken of 'the noise of the rattling of the wheels'.[47] Then the chief mechanic looked at the wheels of the motorbike, and he saw that new tyres were needed. The apprentice brought forth a large pile of new tyres. Another mechanic said this must be the 'burden of tyre' of which Isaiah spoke.[48] The chief mechanic answered saying that the apprentice was familiar with tyres because, as the scriptures said 'his father was a man of Tyre'.[49]

Kevin now pointed out that the horn did not work and a new one was needed. A mechanic looked in several drawers and found a small one. Again the chief mechanic said that it was well because the prophets had written 'out of one of them shall come forth a little horn'.[50] And Kevin mentioned that the headlight did not work, so a mechanic put in a new bulb saying to Kevin, in the words of the prophet, that when it was switched on 'then shall thy light break forth as the morning'.[51]

Then said the chief mechanic that all was accomplished. And Kevin asked of him a bill of reckoning. And when he saw it he was much astonished. But the mechanic justified it in the words of scripture 'thou knowest my service which I have done thee'.[52] So Kevin got some money out of his wallet and 'gave it to such as did the work of the service' in fulfilment of the scriptures.[53] Kevin departed from that place, and he gave Sam a lift saying that it was written by the prophet 'We will ride on the Swift'.[54]

And as they rode they were seen by men in blue who were versed in the scriptures and quoted 'Behold, one wheel upon the earth'.[55] And Kevin accelerated away that the men in blue might not catch them. And it came to pass that the men in blue did catch them and they stopped them. The men in blue greeted them thrice. And they spoke in the words of the prophets, saying 'Get up ...... and stand forth with your helmets'.[56] Sam said that their being stopped was in fulfilment of the scriptures, for it is written that 'the race is not to the Swift'.[57]

All of these quotations are genuine, which is more than can be said of the New Testament quotations. Quotation marks are used to show exactly which words are being quoted, as is the practice in modern translations. In a couple of cases, identified in footnotes, tenses have been changed but otherwise the wording is accurate, which again is more than can be said of the New Testament.

Clearly, in retrospect, the gospel authors could have justified whatever they liked by reference to scripture, simply by taking passages out of context, as above. There is little doubt among biblical scholars that that is precisely what they did. As most now acknowledge, the writers of the New Testament found references to Jesus where none was intended.

They copied passages out of context, contradicted their plain meaning, and altered the wording to produce the result they wanted. Not a single prophecy cited in the New Testament is a genuine prophecy quoted in context. Indeed the New Testament authors and interpreters were far from accurate or honest. As Robin Lane Fox put it:

> When Christians quoted those old prophecies, they used Greek translations which were untrue to the Hebrew originals: they ran separate bits of text into one; they twisted the sense and reference of the nouns (Paul, at Galatians 3:8, is a spectacular example); they mistook the speakers and the uses of personal pronouns (John 19:37 or Matthew 27:9); they thought that David or Isaiah had written what they never wrote (Acts 2 or Acts 8:26); they muddled Jeremiah with Zechariah (Matthew 27:9); they reread the literal sense and found non-existent allegory (Paul, to the Galatians at 4:21–3). There are vintage errors in the famous speech which Acts' author gives to Peter at Pentecost: Peter tortures bits of Psalms 16 and 132, mistakes their meaning and context, and quotes them in a poor Greek translation, although Greek was not the historical Peter's mother tongue and most of his supposed audience would not have understood a word of it.[58]

The fact is that the New Testament stories purporting to fulfil Old Testament prophecies fail every test of their veracity.

Incidentally, the retrospective prophecy is not restricted to biblical texts. We have already mentioned (page 262) the Sibylline Oracles, which were retrospectively edited to make them appear to predict the coming of Christianity, and many other works were tampered with in a similar way and for similar motives. Fanciful stories of saints' lives in books such as the *Golden Legend* are often engineered in such a way as to fulfil a prophecy. To take a simple example: a saint's name, according to the *Golden Legend*, almost invariably has an etymology that prophesises the future of the saint (for example, *Christopher* = 'christ-bearer'). This was often cited as evidence of God having arranged the appropriate naming of the infant saint. Unfortunately, the stated etymologies in the *Golden Legend* are almost all factually wrong. They are also often inconsistent. Different etymologies are often given for different saints who share the same name, which rather gives the game away.

METHOD 5:
ATTRIBUTE AMBIGUOUS AUTHORITY TO THE OLD TESTAMENT

Men too often study the scriptures, not so much for the discovery of truth, as to find
support for the prejudices which have already gained possession of their minds.
Thomas Wrightson, *On the Punishment of Death*, 1833

Some Christians, like some Jews, believe that the books of the Old
Testament are the literal word of God, and that as such they should
be followed to the letter. This is a difficult position to sustain, as Laura
Schlessinger, a Canadian radio personality, discovered in 2000. She had
made some comments about homosexuals, based on a literal reading of
the Jewish scriptures. The following is an open letter to her that was
posted on the internet soon afterwards by a listener in the United States:

Dr. Laura,

Thank you for doing so much to educate people regarding God's
Law. I have learned a great deal from your show, and I try to share
that knowledge with as many people as I can. When someone tries
to defend the homosexual lifestyle, for example, I simply remind
him that Leviticus 18:22 clearly states it to be an abomination. End
of debate. I do need some advice from you, however, regarding
some of the specific laws and how to best follow them.

a) When I burn a bull on the altar as a sacrifice, I know it creates
a pleasing odor for the Lord (Lev. 1:9). The problem is my
neighbours. They claim the odor is not pleasing to them. Should
I smite them?

b) I would like to sell my daughter into slavery, as sanctioned in
Exodus 21:7. In this day and age, what do you think would be
a fair price for her?

c) I know that I am allowed no contact with a woman while she is
in her period of menstrual uncleanliness (Lev. 15:19–24). The
problem is, how do I tell? I have tried asking, but most women
take offence.

d) Lev. 25:44 states that I may indeed possess slaves, both male
and female, provided they are purchased from neighbouring
nations. A friend of mine claims that this applies to Mexicans,
but not Canadians. Can you clarify? Why can't I own Canadians?

e) I have a neighbour who insists on working on the Sabbath. Exodus 35:2 clearly states he should be put to death. Am I morally obligated to kill him myself?

f) A friend of mine feels that even though eating shellfish is an abomination (Lev. 11:10), it is a lesser abomination than homosexuality. I don't agree. Can you settle this?

g) Lev. 21:20 states that I may not approach the altar of God if I have a defect in my sight. I have to admit that I wear reading glasses. Does my vision have to be 20/20, or is there some wiggle room here?

h) Most of my male friends get their hair trimmed, including the hair around their temples, even though this is expressly forbidden by Lev.19:27. How should they die?

i) I know from Lev. 11:6–8 that touching the skin of a dead pig makes me unclean, but may I still play football if I wear gloves?

j) My uncle has a farm. He violates Lev. 19:19 by planting two different crops in the same field, as does his wife by wearing garments made of two different kinds of thread (cotton/polyester blend). He also tends to curse and blaspheme a lot. Is it really necessary that we go to all the trouble of getting the whole town together to stone them (Lev. 24:10–16)? Couldn't we just stone them to death at a private family affair like we do with people who sleep with their in-laws (Lev. 20:14)?

I know you have studied these things extensively, so I am confident you can help. Thank you again for reminding us that God's word is eternal and unchanging.

Your devoted disciple and adoring fan, Franc Mosbaugh

Mr Mosbaugh was presenting Laura Schlessinger with some of the modern problems that arise if the Jewish scriptures are interpreted literally and regarded as unchanging. Similar problems have arisen for centuries, even before the birth of Christ. But we are interested here only in the ones that have affected Christianity. For Christians, the question boils down to one of whether or not the faithful are bound by the regulations and prohibitions of the Old Testament. The authority of these regulations and prohibitions has been a constant problem for Christians. The position of the Church of England illustrates the difficulty in trying to define its authority:

> ...Although the Law given from God by Moses, as touching
> Ceremonies and Rites, do not bind Christian men, nor the civil
> precepts thereof ought of necessity to be received in any common-
> wealth, yet not withstanding, no Christian man whatsoever is free
> from the obedience of the Commandments which are called Moral.
> (Article 7 of the 39 Articles of the Anglican Church)

On the one hand the Old Testament was held to be divinely inspired.
Much Christian teaching was founded on it, and Jesus was recorded as
having made numerous references to it. Indeed, he was keen to emphasise
that it was no part of his mission to overthrow the ancient laws contained
in the Old Testament. The author of the Matthew gospel quotes him
as saying:

> Think not that I am come to destroy the law, or the prophets: I am
> not come to destroy, but to fulfill. For verily I say unto you, Till
> heaven and earth pass, one jot or one tittle shall in no wise pass
> from the law, till all be fulfilled. (Matthew 5:17–18)

Moreover, there were many things in the Old Testament that the
Church wanted to retain. The New Testament did not explicitly sanction
popular Christian practices such as killing witches, extorting tithes,
slavery or genocide, all of which Christians justified by reference to the
Old Testament. Again, Jesus had failed to cite all Ten Commandments
in the New Testament,[59] so the full list had to be quoted from the Old.
On the other hand the Old Testament said many things that conflicted
with the New Testament. For example, Jesus discarded the old law about
taking an eye for an eye, a tooth for a tooth.[60] In such cases Christians
have regarded Jesus as having repealed the old law and given them a
new dispensation. Consistently applied there should be little difficulty
here. If Jesus did not override the existing law then it should stand. If he
did, then his statements should supersede it. One might think that the
position would be clear enough, but there are still a number of problems,
for example:

- There were cases where Jesus overrode Old Testament laws implicitly
  but not explicitly. Did this mean that the laws were no longer
  applicable?
- There were cases where people other than Jesus purported to overturn
  the ancient laws. Paul for example felt himself qualified to abrogate

eternal laws. Such laws did not apparently apply to people like St Paul, who enjoyed direct communications with the deity. As he said 'But if ye be led of the Spirit, ye are not under the law' (Galatians 5:18). Were such people to be believed?

- There were cases where the New Testament (though not Jesus himself) implicitly accepted Old Testament laws. Did this mean that the laws should stand even if they seemed undesirable?

- The simple rule that existing laws stood unless overturned by Jesus produced unacceptable results, endorsing unpopular practices and failing to endorse popular ones. In some cases Jesus implicitly accepted Old Testament laws that seemed undesirable. What was to be done in these circumstances?

To complicate matters the New Testament contradicted itself on some important questions, such as divorce. We shall now look at examples of these various problem areas, to see how consistent the answers have been in practice:

Adultery

This is an example where Jesus implicitly overrode Old Testament laws. If we accept the authenticity of John 8:1–11 then it is clear that Jesus taught by example that we should not punish adulterers. The adulteress brought before Jesus was simply forgiven, yet Christians have frequently preferred the traditional Old Testament view. When the Church had control over such matters, adultery remained a serious offence, sometimes a capital offence as it had been in the Old Testament.

Blood Taboos

This is an example where New Testament characters implicitly accepted Old Testament laws. According to the Old Testament women remained unclean for 40 days after the delivery of a baby boy and for 80 after the delivery of a girl.[61] God required animal sacrifices as burnt offerings and sin offerings to purge the uncleanness of women after childbirth (Leviticus 12:6–8). Such a sacrifice was made by Jesus' mother after his birth (Luke 2:24). But blood sacrifice was already going out of fashion in Jesus' time and soon it died out altogether amongst Jews and Christians.

[281]

The purging sacrifice was converted into a Christian ceremony now known as the Churching of Women. After giving birth, a woman was regarded as being in a state of sin and had to be reconciled to the Church through this ceremony. In the Roman Catholic Church such a woman had to behave like a public penitent – if not she could be refused Communion, barred from the baptism of her own child, and refused a Christian burial when she died. All this was justified by the Old Testament purification rights. In some places un-Churched women were being barred from their own children's baptisms up to the 1960s.[62]

The Anglican Church has for centuries been keen to play down the original purpose of Churching. The Book of Common Prayer for example refers to the Anglican ceremony as 'the thanksgiving of women after childbirth commonly called the churching of women'. Still, the elements of ritual impurity were obvious enough. The ceremony was regarded as obligatory. Echoes of the ritual uncleanness persisted for many centuries. New mothers were expected to wear a veil as though ashamed of some sin, and were often required to sit in a special seat.

There were other blood taboos. The Old Testament God regarded menstrual blood as unclean, requiring sacrifices to purge the uncleanness (Leviticus 15:19–33). Menstrual blood was not quite as bad as blood shed during childbirth, but in the Eastern Church it was sufficient to bar women from Communion. Some clergymen in the Western Church shared this view. Such ideas of impurity also helped exclude women from Holy Orders. It was at least partially for this reason that women and post pubescent girls were excluded from the vicinity of the altar for so long, but this too became politically incorrect towards the end of the twentieth century.

Other blood taboos were abandoned early on by the mainstream Churches, if they were sufficiently unpopular, even when explicitly confirmed. The New Testament confirms clearly that the consumption of blood is prohibited (Acts 15:28–9), yet it is extremely rare to find Christian activists attempting to ban the sale of blood-containing foods such as black puddings. On the other hand members of some Christian sects refuse to take part in medical treatments such as blood transfusions, citing both Old and New Testaments (Leviticus 17:10–12 and Acts 15:28–9) though both refer to eating the blood of slaughtered animals.

Dietary Laws

The 12 apostles, who like Jesus were all Jews, obeyed the Jewish dietary regulations set out in Leviticus 11. Gentiles were not at all keen on such restrictions and were reluctant to convert to a religion that required such behaviour. Happily Paul and Peter received divine intelligence informing them that the ancient restrictions were no longer to be enforced. The dietary laws were thus rescinded in the gentile sections of the Church. It now became necessary to explain away the extensive prohibitions on eating various animals laid out in the scriptures. Here is a short extract from an early Christian authority explaining what the old dietary laws laid down by Moses *really* mean.

> Among other things, he also says, 'you are not to eat of the hare' by which he means you are not to debauch young boys, or become like those who do; because the hare grows a fresh orifice in its backside every year, and has as many of these holes as the years of its life. And 'You are not to eat the hyena' signifies that you are to be no lecher or libertine, or copy their ways; for that creature changes its sex annually and is a male at one time and a female at another. The weasel, too, he speaks of with abhorrence, and not without good reason; his implication being that you are not to imitate those who, we are told, are filthy enough to use their mouths for the practice of vice, nor to frequent the abandoned women who do the same – since it is through the mouth that this animal is impregnated.[63]

This interpretation is apparently no longer regarded as orthodox, though it is not clear exactly when it ceased to be so.

Circumcision and Sacrifice

Circumcision was abandoned, apparently for reasons similar to those for dietary restrictions: potential male converts were put off by it. This time the old requirement could be explained as a requirement to circumcise not the penis, but the ears, in some figurative sort of way.[64] Almost any requirement could be rationalised away in this manner. Thus, the animal sacrifices required by the God of the Old Testament were commuted into the Mass, a ceremony represented as a sort of reformed blood sacrifice. Many Christians have since wondered why Jesus obeyed Jewish dietary laws, and never suggested that his followers should do otherwise, and why he was himself circumcised like any other Jew, yet never troubled to point out that genital surgery was after all unnecessary.

Judgement

Christians encouraged God to judge cases by oracle. A popular method was the casting of lots, which had been used extensively in the Old Testament[65] and confirmed by Proverbs 16:33. This method was also used by the apostles after Judas's death: the remaining eleven used it to select Matthias (Acts 1:23–6) to make their number back up to twelve. The Church used lotteries for many purposes, the apportioning of patronage by cathedral chapters, allocating church pews, deciding which Church benefices to augment. Between 1665 and 1676 juries in Britain were allowed to cast lots when they could not reach a unanimous decision. After mutinies and similar offences it was common to execute a proportion of the offenders (generally one in ten), chosen by lot – only those selecting lottery tickets marked with words such as 'life given by God' escaped execution. After John Wesley died in 1791 a Methodist conference tackled the question of whether Methodist preachers had the spiritual authority to administer Communion. The matter was determined by prayer, followed by the drawing of lots.[66] Although such practices continued for a long time, all mainstream Churches abandoned the technique of drawing lots. Instead, they regarded lotteries as inherently sinful, or at least they did for most of the twentieth century. Churches campaigned against the introduction of a national lottery in Britain – until they recognised the opportunity to benefit themselves. Since receiving lottery funding they have stopped campaigning and have gone very quiet about their doctrinal objections, so perhaps are returning to the biblical approach.

Shaving

Problems frequently arise when no-one in the New Testament gainsays the Old Testament, especially when the Church Fathers are known to have accepted Old Testament views. For example God's views on shaving may be found in Leviticus 19:27:

> *Ye shall not round the corners of your heads, neither shalt thou mar the corners of thy beard.*

In other words you must not shave your hair from side to side, neither must you shave the edge of your beard. It is because of this regulation that Orthodox Jewish men wear distinctive side-locks. The early Church had similarly strong views about shaving. Tertullian held that it was an insult to God, and even today Orthodox priests are never found without beards. In early times all priests wore beards, but after several centuries they had become unacceptable for clerics in the Western Church, while to Western Christians the beards of Eastern priests were taken as evidence of their Church's degeneracy. On the other hand, fashions changed from time to time and from place to place: some clerics within the Western Church grew beards in the sixteenth century, and clerical pilgrims to the Holy Land were often expected to grow one. Missionaries were generally excused for growing them, as were, for no obvious reason, French priests. The matter became one of fashion, and the Old Testament injunction quietly forgotten.

Tattoos

Leviticus 19:28 prohibits the practice of tattooing. Until recent years this passage was often cited against sailors and other travellers who had their bodies tattooed, but now most mainstream Churches seem to have abandoned God's teaching on this matter.

Shoes

In Exodus 3:5 God states that shoes must be taken off at holy places, and this is confirmed in Joshua 5:15. Most Christians and Jews simply ignore this injunction, although Muslims still obey it.

Genital Injuries

The Old Testament states that men with genital injuries are not permitted to enter into the congregation of the Lord (Deuteronomy 23:1). For centuries such men were thus barred from entering a church. Then some popes took a liking to castrati and installed them in the choir of the Sistine Chapel. Christendom was shocked, but in time everyone seems to have forgotten what the Bible had to say on the matter. In theory, men wounded in the testicles or having undergone, say, surgical removal of the penis or a testicle, should still be debarred from the congregation of the Lord. Once again, this regulation is ignored by most Christians, although some denominations still obey it, as do the Jews.[67] The mainstream Churches now content themselves with excluding such men from the priesthood and from sainthood.

Bastardy

Another regulation affects nearly everyone:

> A bastard shall not enter into the congregation of the Lord; even to his tenth generation shall he not enter into the congregation of the Lord. (Deuteronomy 23:2)

This should mean that anyone who is illegitimate, or has any ancestor within ten generations who was illegitimate, may not be a member of the Church. Human nature being what it is (and given that everyone has around 2000 ancestors, going back to the tenth generation), this would statistically rule out almost everyone now alive. It would be interesting to know how many bishops, priests and moral reformers are able to show that they satisfy this condition and are thus entitled to be members of God's Holy Church: quite possibly none at all. In practice mainstream Churches have contented themselves with denying Church offices to those born out of wedlock, which is rather less than what the Bible requires.

Death Penalties

Until the Middle Ages, Christians were still executing criminals for witchcraft, blasphemy and a range of sexual activities. In each case the justification was to be found in the Old Testament. Even with agreement that a crime was deserving of death there were further problems. For example, Christians often executed people for blasphemy, citing Leviticus 24:16, but they generally failed to use the method of execution specified, which was stoning. Some particularly devout English judges and magistrates pointed out exactly this discrepancy, and advocated a change to English law to bring it into line with God's law, but Parliament never got around to legislating on the matter. Other Old Testament capital laws were applied throughout Christendom.

> If an ox gore a man or a woman, that they die: then the ox shall be surely stoned, and his flesh shall not be eaten; but the owner of the ox shall be quit. (Exodus 21:28)

Ecclesiastical law not only accepted this principle but also extended it to other animals. During the Middle Ages many animals were solemnly tried and executed for murder. As soon as such attitudes became unacceptable because of growing rationalism, they were simply dropped. What had long been regarded as a divine duty suddenly wasn't a divine duty at all.

Polygamy

Polygamy is acceptable throughout the Old Testament (see for example Exodus 21:10) and by implication also in the New (except for bishops who are permitted only one wife: 1 Timothy 3:2 and Titus 1:6).

The usual excuse here is that polygamy was merely tolerated in the Old Testament, but this is simply not true. It was regarded as perfectly acceptable. God has no problems at all with polygamy. Many of the patriarchs had numerous wives. Solomon, praised by God for his wisdom, had 700 of them (1 Kings 11:3). Polygamy was still practised, on a smaller scale, in Jesus' time, yet he never troubled to criticise the practice. Some sects have taken this as implicit confirmation of the acceptability of polygamy. Most have ignored the Bible and sought to justify their beliefs by other means.

When conditions suited, the Church was always prepared to turn a blind eye to polygamous marriages. For example when it was politically convenient for the Church for the Grand Duke of Kiev to marry the Byzantine Emperor's daughter in 987, the bishops diplomatically ignored the fact that he already had four wives and numerous concubines. More usually, the Church has tried to disguise the fact that the biblical God had approved of polygamy. One explicit reason for not allowing Native Americans to learn Latin and refusing vernacular translations was that if they could read the Bible, they would realise that polygamy was not prohibited, and would return to traditional polygamous practices. For almost 2,000 years the mainstream Churches have been trying to stop polygamy wherever they encountered it, frequently among sects that took the Bible literally. Adherents of the Latter-day Saint (Mormon) movement, for example, practised polygamy legally in Utah until the federal government of the United States put pressure on them to stop it. The largest group within the movement, the Mormon Church (Church of Jesus Christ of Latter-day Saints) officially renounced polygamy in 1890, though it is still practised by some schismatic sects. Outside the United States, the Catholic Church is still understanding when it needs to be. President Mwai Kibaki of Kenya, a devout practising Catholic, like many of his peers, is well known to be in a polygamous union, but no one in his Church seems to consider it worth mentioning, let alone criticising.

Concubinage and Slavery

God approves of concubinage: Solomon had 300 concubines as well as his 700 wives according to 1 Kings 11:3. Furthermore, God expects maidservants to satisfy their masters' sexual requirements. Abraham, for example, fulfilled God's covenant by getting his maidservant, Hagar, pregnant (Genesis 16:4). Jacob was married to two sisters Leah and Rachel, both of whom gave their maidservants to him so that he could father children on them (Genesis 29:15–30:13). Again, slavery was perfectly acceptable in the Old Testament. Jesus mentioned the practice but failed to criticise it. His silence provided supporters of slavery with a strong enough case to keep the practice popular among upright Christians well into the nineteenth century. As they repeatedly pointed out, if Jesus had regarded slavery as wrong he would undoubtedly have said so.

The Leverite Law

On one occasion Jesus was asked about the Leverite law by which, according to the Old Testament, a man was obliged to marry his sister-in-law if his married brother died childless. Jesus failed to criticise the practice or to indicate that the ancient law had been abrogated. Christians nevertheless chose to abandon the practice, regarding it as incestuous, although the case was still arguable in the sixteenth century.

Cursing

Jesus himself quoted the legal requirement that anyone who curses his father or mother must be put to death, apparently criticising the scribes and Pharisees for not enforcing it,[68] but this requirement has not been popular for a while, and has also been quietly abandoned.

Usury

A classic example of how views have changed is the law about usury. The Old Testament explicitly discourages lending, or at least making a profit from it (Exodus 22:25, Leviticus 25:36–7 and Deuteronomy 23:19–20). Jews, Christians and Muslims alike were therefore debarred from conventional banking. Devout Muslims still abide by this rule, and so did the Christian Church in the Middle Ages. Commercial banking between Christians was contrary to the word of God. To deny this was sinful and heretical, and likely to excite the interest of the Inquisition (though exceptions were made for those close to the Pope[69]).

Calvin found an easy way out, claiming that the biblical provisions applied only to Jews. His followers were soon claiming that charging interest was not only permitted, it was actually necessary for salvation. But Roman Catholics and Lutherans continued to attack the lending of money at interest well into the seventeenth century. Lutherans abandoned this particular word of God when it became obvious that it was restricting commercial expansion, but the Roman Church held fast. Up to the nineteenth century, popes consistently condemned the taking of interest on loans in any circumstances. The Church has still not withdrawn its condemnation, although by the twentieth century this position had become untenable, following the establishment of the Vatican's own bank, which charges interest on loans like any other bank.

The Second Commandment

Representational art is unconditionally prohibited by the second of the Ten Commandments:

> Thou shalt not make unto thee any graven image, or any likeness of any thing that is in heaven above, or that is in the earth beneath, or that is in the water under the earth. (Exodus 20:4)

This is clear enough: all artificial representations are prohibited. In earlier times Jews, Christians and Muslims all accepted and obeyed this

commandment. This is why Muslim art traditionally avoids any naturalistic images and depends heavily upon abstract patterns and calligraphy.
The early Christian Church was also strict. Icons, whether pictures or
statues, were absolutely proscribed. So it is that few early pictures of Jesus
exist, and those that do were generally produced by Gnostics. Eusebius
summed up the position that held until the fourth century when he said
that Christian art does not exist and cannot exist.[70]

As it happened many Christians in the Hellenic world rather
liked icons, so in the course of time, and to the fury of traditionalists,
the rule about them was abandoned.[71] Typically such transitions take place
gradually, as this one did. First, naturalistic representations of inanimate
objects were permitted, then of plants and animals, then of historical
characters, then of living people, then of supernatural beings, then
parts of God (such as a hand), then God in his full glory.[72] In Western
Christendom this was not too controversial. In the East it was. The
controversy culminated when the Byzantine Emperor Constantine V
called a council in 753 that denounced the use of all icons. Offenders
were to be punished as heretics. This was not universally popular and for
the next 100 years or so iconodule (icon-worshipping) and iconoclast
(icon-destroying) Christians felt obliged to kill each other to emphasise
the justice of their causes.

Eventually a compromise was achieved: pictures were allowed, but
statues were not. This is roughly still the position in the Greek Orthodox
Church. Strictly, God himself could not be portrayed until the sixteenth
century, when images of him appeared in Moscow under Western
influence. Coincidentally around the same time in Western Europe, the
Puritans became keen supporters of the second commandment. They
did their best to destroy Christian art that had accumulated in the
West. As they pointed out, their views were exactly in line with those
of the Bible and the earliest Christians.

The purpose of the original biblical injunction had been to rule
out the possibility of superstitious worship of icons. As the injunction
was relaxed, certain practices arose that looked to many to amount
to exactly this. By the time of the Reformation the charge that
Christians were worshipping images was widespread. Article 22 of the
39 Articles of the Anglican Church describes the 'Romish Doctrine
concerning ... Worshipping and Adoration ... of Images' as a 'fond
thing, vainly invented, and grounded upon no warranty of Scripture,

but rather repugnant to the Word of God'. The 'Homily Against Peril of Idolatry' (a standard sermon dating from the Reformation) declares that 'by God's word, and the sentences of the ancient Doctors, and judgement of the Primitive Church, that all images, as well ours, as the idols of the Gentiles, be forbidden and unlawful, namely in Churches and Temples'. Images of saints were ordered to be removed from all churches in 1548. The mere presence of religious images in English churches was forbidden by statute law, although a number of legal cases have since relaxed the effects of this provision.[73] Even the Roman Church has hesitated to support images of God absolutely. The Council of Trent, for example, defended images of saints and Christ (Session XXV, 3rd and 4th December 1563) but remained silent on images of God the Father.

Beyond question, the current practices of all mainstream Churches would have been unanimously regarded as blasphemous and heretical by the ancient Church, on the grounds that they breach the second commandment.

The Fourth Commandment

The fourth commandment states quite clearly that the Sabbath day is to be kept holy. God himself stated explicitly that keeping the Sabbath is an eternal covenant (Exodus 31:16). Without question the commandment refers to the Jewish Sabbath, sunset on Friday to sunset on Saturday. No one suggests that it ever referred to Sundays. Yet most Christians ignore this commandment and behave as though God had really been talking about Sundays. In England, anyone who suggested that the Sabbath should be observed on Saturdays rather than Sundays was liable to punishment as late as the seventeenth century.[74]

Seventh Day Adventists and a few other sects are exceptions to the general pattern, recognising the Jewish Sabbath rather than Sunday.

The Sixth Commandment

The sixth commandment *Thou Shalt Not Kill* (Exodus 20:13) is absolute and unconditional (although it was always taken for granted that the commandment did not apply to animals). Sometimes the commandment is translated as *Thou shalt not do murder*, which looks more straightforward. Christians could not kill fellow human beings. But was a slave

[291]

a human being? Was a foetus a human being? Were non-Europeans human beings? Was a disabled child a human being? In each of these four cases, the Churches gave different answers at different times. Also, was the injunction absolute? Could Christians kill in self-defence? Could they fight in wars? Could they inflict capital punishment?

There have always been arguments about killing in self-defence. As we shall see later, the mainstream Christian position on killing in war has gone through 270°. In early times Christians were not allowed to enlist in armies at all. Later Christians were not merely allowed but obliged to enlist. Conscientious objectors were regarded as heretics. Now many Churches are half way back to their original position – priests and bishops, for example, no longer take an active part in warfare.

The main Western Churches and particularly the Jesuits advocated the murder of their enemies, especially rich and influential enemies. Protestant leaders could therefore be assassinated with impunity. This was seen as merely an extension of the idea of killing in war, which by this time all Christians had concluded was perfectly acceptable. The Churches also needed to rid themselves of other enemies. They thus accepted another exception to the commandment. It became acceptable to kill people after due process of law. And of course the law could be moulded so that it was possible to kill anyone who offended the Church. As soon as Christians achieved political power in the Roman Empire, they started executing their political enemies.[75] It became quite acceptable to kill people because they did not fully accept the current line of Christian belief: millions of Jews, Muslims, followers of other religions, dissenters and apostates were killed. Few of them would now be regarded as warranting even a small fine in modern ecclesiastical courts. Senior Churchmen, including popes, also conspired to murder political enemies, the most famous example being the attempted murder of two Medici brothers in a Cathedral Church as the celebrant raised the Host during a Sunday Mass. The would-be murders were priests acting under orders of an Archbishop with papal knowledge.[76]

Long after the Church had ceased to execute people for offending it, it still supported the right of the State to impose the death penalty. Judicial killing was acceptable to all major denominations. The papacy carried out its own secret executions into the nineteenth century, and the Church of England validated capital punishment in Britain right up to its abolition in the twentieth century.[77] As for so many traditional beliefs, the Church justified its position by reference to scripture: for example the justification for executing murderers was derived from biblical passages such as 'Whoso sheddeth man's blood, by man shall his blood be shed' (Genesis 9:6) and 'the land cannot be cleansed of the blood that is shed therein, but by the blood of him that shed it' (Numbers 35:33). Such biblical prooftexts were frequently cited by churchmen and Christian judges to justify capital punishment. Judgement of death, they repeated, was decreed by God. The Old Testament sanctioned the death penalty, and since there was no criticism of the practice in the New Testament, it was clearly acceptable. Time and time again proponents cited the silence of the gospels as endorsing the practice. Clergymen claimed that it would be sinful to go against God's wishes by failing to inflict capital punishment when it was so explicitly required by God in the Old Testament. Jesus' words in Luke 19:27 'But those mine enemies, which would not that I should reign over them, bring hither, and slay them before me' could also be used to prove that he was perfectly happy with the concept of capital punishment – even without a trial.

When public opinion changed, the Churches followed. From overwhelming support of capital punishment in 1955, the Church of England had moved to overwhelming opposition by 1965.[78] With the customary delay, the Roman Church followed some time later. It was only in early 1999 that a pope stated for the first time that the death penalty was wrong in principle – directly contradicting earlier papal statements on the subject. In the strongly Christian United States opinion is slowly shifting too. At the time of writing both Christian advocates of capital punishment and Christian opponents of capital punishment bolster their loud public arguments by citing the sixth commandment.

* * *

The fact is that the status of the Old Testament is ill-defined in all mainstream churches. Some Christians cite it as justification for banning homosexuality, adultery, blasphemy, and so on, while others cheerfully dismiss it as obsolete. This ambivalence permits Christians to pick and choose the parts that appeal to them and ignore the others. When the occasion suits, the Old Testament can be cited to justify various practices and doctrine, and when it does not, then it can be disregarded. Different sects select different passages to formulate doctrine according to taste. Even the mainstream Churches change their views about it with remarkable ease. When it was politically expedient to condemn Joan of Arc, she could be charged with transvestism, which was prohibited in the Old Testament. When it was politically expedient to rehabilitate her, this particular crime could be ignored on the grounds that Old Testament restrictions had been abrogated. To many the Old Testament looks like a sort of religious supermarket, where customers are free to select the items they like the look of, and leave the items that do not appeal to them.

METHOD 6:
IGNORE OR DISTORT NEW TESTAMENT INJUNCTIONS AND EXAMPLES

There was never anything by the wit of man devised, or so sure established,
which in continuance of time hath not been corrupted.
Preface to the *Book of Common Prayer*

The Bible contains many rules and regulations. Unfortunately it is not always clear for whom they are intended. The Jews always imagined that the scriptures were meant for them, and so did the earliest followers of Jesus, which is not surprising since Jesus and his followers were all practising Jews. As we have seen, later gentile Christians were able to select the rules and regulations they liked by attributing ambiguous authority to the Old Testament. One might expect there to be less scope for such selectivity in the New.

In this section we will concentrate on New Testament passages that give directions about how to live: laws, injunctions and examples. In many cases a few sects follow the teaching, while mainstream churches do not. In other cases the mainstream Churches once followed the teaching but have now abandoned it, or they have traditionally rejected it and later adopted it.

For many centuries churchmen taught that laughter was evil and sinful. Roman Catholic, Protestant and Puritan alike could all quote Luke 6:25 '...Woe unto you that laugh now! for ye shall mourn and weep'. As they pointed out, there is not a single example of Jesus laughing or even smiling in the Bible. This sort of interpretation is no longer popular, and the passage from Luke is rarely heard today.

Reputable Church leaders sometimes teach the exact opposite of what the New Testament says. For example, the reason almost invariably given for Jesus' use of parables is that he was trying to make it easy for everyone to understand his message. In fact the gospels quote him as saying that the reason he uses them is exactly the opposite – so that only certain people will understand, and others will not be able to. According to Luke 8:9–10 Jesus was asked by his followers about the parable of the Sower:

> And he said, Unto you it is given to know the mysteries of the kingdom of God: but to others in parables; that seeing they might not see, and hearing they might not understand.

The wording is different, but the meaning the same, in Matthew 13:10–13 and Mark 4:10–12. Parables were not used to help people understand, they were used to prevent people from understanding.

No matter how explicit the text, Churches feel free to adopt teachings directly contrary to it. For example Hebrews 6:4–6 says quite clearly that God will not forgive apostates, but the mainstream Churches knew better and accepted them back into the fold. Not only that, but these same Churches actually persecuted as heretics a third-century sect, the Novatians, whose heresy was to agree with the Bible about the readmission of apostates.

Biblical injunctions are also ignored on grounds of fashion. According to 1 Timothy 2:9 women should not braid their hair or wear gold or pearls, nor expensive clothes. Yet this is routinely ignored. Today bouncers are employed in Southern Europe to stop women going into some churches wearing shorts or with bare arms – which are not banned by the Bible – yet they allow in women with braided hair, gold brooches, pearl earrings, and expensive clothes, all of which are banned by the Bible.

Again, the teachings of the Eastern Orthodox, Roman Catholic, Anglican and Protestant Churches on married bishops all defy the New Testament:

> A bishop then must be blameless, the husband of one wife...
> (1 Timothy 3:2, cf. Titus 1:6)

The Orthodox and Roman Catholic Churches contravene it by insisting on episcopal celibacy: Anglicans and Protestants contravene it by permitting episcopal celibacy. Once again, the meaning of the passage is ignored.[79] It does not seem to matter how clearly a teaching is stated, or how often, or whether it is confirmed by both Old and New Testaments. If it is inconvenient, it will be quietly ignored. Perhaps most surprisingly, the very words reportedly uttered by Jesus are widely ignored. The following are a few notable examples of injunctions not taken up, rules not applied, examples not followed, Jesus' words disregarded because they did not suit:

Poverty

Jesus was definite about the importance of poverty:

> It is easier for a camel to go through the eye of a needle, than for a rich man to enter the kingdom of God. (Mark 10:25 cf. Matthew 19:24)

Even if he actually said *rope* rather than *camel* in the original Aramaic, the meaning is much the same. Jesus said that it is not enough merely to keep the Commandments. To get to Heaven one must sell everything one has (Mark 10:17–25, Luke 18:18–25, cf. Matthew 19:16–24).

In the Middle Ages, when the Church had become the richest organisation in the world, and its leaders extremely wealthy, this teaching became an embarrassment. Medieval Church leaders therefore invented a more acceptable interpretation. The story they invented was that a narrow gate in the walls of Jerusalem was known as the *Needle's Eye*. According to this story a camel might experience a little trouble in passing through this gate, but not enough to cause concern to the rich. There is no evidence that any such gate ever existed, yet the fiction is still repeated today.

For a while, a group of Franciscans did try to follow Jesus' teaching and advocated absolute poverty. Known as Spiritual Franciscans, they were declared heretical in 1323 for holding that Jesus and the apostles had not owned any property. Pope John XXII, the richest man in the world at the time, handed over more than 100 of them to the Inquisition to be burned. The rest were persecuted into oblivion.

Even today it is rare to find Christians giving away *all* their wealth, though it is easy enough to find Churches and various leaders and other personages associated with the Church amassing it. The Anglican Church is still one of the greatest landowners in Britain, and it is an unusual American televangelist who is not a millionaire. Recent popes have ignored the biblical injunction to disperse their wealth just as easily as their predecessors. As the head of the Vatican (which has massive investments in assets such as property, gold, and shares in multinationals), each successive incumbent pope becomes one of the richest men in the world. Pope Pius XII had gold door handles fitted to his American Cadillac. Pope John Paul II managed to find funds for his swimming pool at Castelgandolfo, his palatial summer retreat, from where he occasionally blessed the poor. There is no reason to believe that the present Pope, Benedict XVI, is about to change all this. Yet without even a trace of irony, on 1st June 2006, he told his weekly general audience that Christians should renounce power and wealth and should choose instead to serve others with Christ's humility.

Families

Throughout his life Jesus had little time for families if we are to believe the gospels. At the age of twelve he failed to return home with his family from the Passover feast at Jerusalem. He was found in the Jerusalem Temple three days later by his sorrowing parents, who had returned from Nazareth to look for him (Luke 2:42–8) – not very thoughtful behaviour on the part of the son of God towards his mother one might think. Jesus was routinely dismissive of his mother and her feelings. Mariologists have long been embarrassed by the way he spoke to her, for example 'Woman, what have I to do with thee?' (John 2:4). The usual explanation is that translators unwittingly introduced an element of curtness, but this is simply not true. In any case, Jesus rejected his family more than once. When they asked for him when he was addressing a multitude, he denied his mother and brothers, and said that those listening to him at the time were his mother and brothers (Mark 3:31–5 cf. Matthew 12:46–9 and Luke 8:19–21).

As the gospels clearly state, Jesus had no qualms about taking his disciples away from their families. The brothers James and John abandoned their father, leaving him to manage as best he could with the fishing nets they had been preparing.[80] Jesus gave a clear instruction that his followers should 'call no man your father upon the earth' on the grounds that they had only one father and that was the one in Heaven (Matthew 23:9). According to some, Peter abandoned his wife and family to follow Jesus.[81] On one occasion a disciple asked permission to go and bury his dead father:

> But Jesus said unto him, Follow me; and let the dead bury their dead. (Matthew 8:22 cf. Luke 9:60)

Jesus then refused another potential follower who asked permission to say goodbye to his family before abandoning them (Luke 9:61–2). We learn that this attitude was entirely in line with Jesus' purpose:

> For I am come to set a man at variance against his father, and the daughter against her mother, and the daughter-in-law against her mother-in-law. (Matthew 10:35)

Jesus consistently taught that his followers should abandon and despise their families. Everlasting life is promised to those who leave their present homes and families (Matthew 19:29, Mark 10:29–30 and Luke 18:29–30). The Luke author gives Jesus' summary of his views on family life:

> If any man come to me, and hate not his father, and mother, and wife, and children, and brethren, and sisters, yea, and his own life also, he cannot be my disciple. (Luke 14:26)

A similar sentiment is expressed in the non-canonical Gospel of St Thomas.[82] Indeed, this gospel goes further: 'Whoever recognises his father and mother will be called the son of a whore'.[83]

The Church's traditional attitude towards family life has been consistent with Jesus' views until recent times. The pinnacle of achievement was to remain a virgin and so not have a family at all. Converts were expected to abandon their families if their families declined to become Christians as well. Polygamists were required to abandon all but one wife. Priests were required to abandon their wives and families, just as the apostles and early Church Fathers had done. St Alexis won his sainthood by abandoning his new bride on his wedding day. Christianity was responsible for an untold number of abandoned wives, divided families, and disinherited children. Later we will revisit this subject, but for the moment the key point is that in the last few decades it has become fashionable to support family values. Since the 1960s the Churches have found it expedient to portray themselves in exactly the opposite light to that in which they have traditionally basked. As a leading liberal churchman has noted:

> The idealisation of the family is a modern cultural creation, which the Churches have validated, and now no modern bishop would dream of publicly endorsing Jesus' views about the family.[84]

Once again the Church has reversed its traditional teaching to agree with modern opinion. Much creative imagination now goes into the pretence that the gospels do not mean what they plainly say: that followers of Jesus must hate their families. Except for a few men and women who do abandon their families to become hermits, anchorites, missionaries, Roman Catholic priests, monks or nuns, there are now virtually no Christians who follow Jesus' teaching about family life.

Food and Clothing

Jesus said that his followers did not need to work. God, knowing their needs, would clothe and feed them (Matthew 6:25–32 and Luke 12:22–30). In view of the thousands of Christians who die of exposure and starvation every year, a non-believer might be sceptical about this, but Christians do not have the option of scepticism. The overwhelming majority wilfully defy the words of Jesus by working to provide for themselves and their families.

Giving Judgement

Jesus is reported to have taught that we should not judge others: 'Judge not, that ye be not judged' (Matthew 7:1 cf. Luke 6:37). Yet few Christians take this seriously. Christian countries still establish courts of law. Christian judges have no qualms about judging others. Mainstream Churches even have their own ecclesiastical courts – in which, in the past, they have prosecuted and condemned Quakers for following New

Testament injunctions. It may be argued that to do away with the courts would be impractical. And this may or may not be true, but the practicality of it is irrelevant. The fact is that according to the gospels Jesus told his followers not to pass judgement. His directive covered all courts and all of his followers.

Turning the Other Cheek

Jesus' teaching on this matter is well known:

> But I say unto you, That ye resist not evil: but whosoever shall smite thee on thy right cheek, turn to him the other also. (Matthew 5:39 cf. Luke 6:29)

Hardly anyone follows this teaching when it affects themselves. Christians have been happy enough not to resist evil when the evil has been done to others, but rarely when it has been done to them. Christians say all manner of things about the depth and beauty of Jesus' injunction, but few ever attempt to put it into practice. Throughout history Christian Churches have carried out a great deal of smiting, but it is difficult to find examples of cheek turning when there was an alternative course of action. Critics of Christianity routinely receive death-threats from the more devout followers of Jesus.

Again, Jesus is reported to have said:

> Give to him that asketh thee, and from him that would borrow of thee turn not thou away. (Matthew 5:42)

He also said not to try to recover stolen goods (Luke 6:30). There are few Christians who give whatever is asked, or lend whatever is asked, or fail to try to recover property stolen when they know who stole it. Many probably do not realise that they are expected to do these things, because no one has ever mentioned it to them.

If Thine Eye Offend Thee...

There is no reason to believe that Jesus was speaking metaphorically when he recommended cutting off limbs and plucking out eyes that have caused sin (Mark 9:43–7). On the contrary, the choice is clearly between physical pain now, and everlasting torment in the fires of Hell. Believing in this straight choice, some early Christians castrated themselves,[85] arguing that their genitals caused lust, and lust was sinful.

In line with this idea, for centuries severe mortification of the flesh was held to be highly praiseworthy. Now mortification of flesh is generally recognised as thinly disguised sadomasochism, and is therefore practised in secret by the devout. One can imagine the outcry if a modern bishop were publicly to recommend a wholesome round of dismemberment and self-mutilation for sinners. Yet if he did so he would be doing no more than echo the words of Jesus and of his followers up until the nineteenth century.

Swearing Oaths

According to the 1983 Roman code of canon law, 'an oath is the invocation of the divine name as witness to the truth' (canon 1199), and most denominations would agree with this definition. Jesus said explicitly that his followers should not swear oaths:

> But I say unto you, Swear not at all; ... But let your communication be, Yea, yea; Nay, nay; for whatsoever is more than these cometh of evil. (Matthew 5:34–7)

Early Christians accepted this and refused to swear oaths in any circumstances, even though they were liable to be executed for their refusal.[86] Most sects now ignore the prohibition, and do not bother themselves about the fact that by swearing oaths they are inviting damnation, which is the penalty promised in the Bible (James 5:12). Some Churches have adopted a position diametrically opposed to that of the Bible. Since 1184, when Pope Lucius III published *Ad abolendum*, the refusal to take an oath has been automatic confirmation of heresy in the Roman Church. Pope Innocent III confirmed that those who took Jesus' teaching on this matter literally were heretics, and that they deserved to die. Later, in the Church of England, it became an article of faith that Jesus had not meant what he said, for the last of the 39 Articles of the Anglican Church asserts that a man may swear when a magistrate requires it. It claims that Jesus and James had only forbidden vain and rash swearing, but that is patently not true. All swearing was forbidden.

Following Jesus' words, the Quakers refused to swear oaths. They were persecuted and imprisoned for refusing to take oaths such as the Oaths of Supremacy and Allegiance. They knew, as anyone who read the Bible would know, that all swearing of oaths is forbidden. Any Christian who swears an oath as a witness in court, or on signing a deposition, or on taking up public office, or for any other reason, is promised damnation to eternal hellfire. Baptists and Quakers still interpret this passage as forbidding *all* oaths, including those oaths traditionally taken in courts of law, which is of course exactly what its wording implies. Nearly all other Christians routinely ignore Jesus' clear teachings as set out in the gospels.

METHOD 7:
INVENT, AMEND AND DISCARD TEACHINGS AND PRACTICES

Man is a pliable animal, a being who gets accustomed to everything.
Fëdor Dostoevsky (1821–81), *The House of the Dead*

We have seen how material from the Bible has been manipulated in the past, but many Christian teachings and practices are not mentioned in either the Old or the New Testaments. The Church has traditionally justified these teachings and practices as God-given, absolute, binding and immutable. In this section we assess how well this claim stands up against the alternative theory that the Church has adopted and discarded practices as a matter of convenience.

We have already seen that some of the most important doctrines date from the third or fourth centuries – for example the doctrines of the Incarnation, the Trinity, the Harrowing of Hell, Original Sin, and Mary's perpetual virginity. Some doctrines were hammered out only in the Middle Ages – for example transubstantiation and the sacraments. And many of these were abandoned by Protestants, whose own doctrines were fluid for centuries. Some teachings have been recognised as dogma by the Roman Church only in recent times. Examples are the Immaculate Conception (1854), papal infallibility (1870), and the bodily Assumption of Mary into Heaven (1950). The lack of a firm historical basis is often reflected in the disparate views of different modern Churches.

Churches even disagree over the number of grades of the Christian ministry ('Major Orders' or 'Holy Orders'): Eastern Churches 3, traditional Western Churches 2, some Methodists 1, other nonconformists 0. Some doctrines have never been fully defined, for example the Atonement, grace, and whether or not the human soul and the spirit are identical or separate. Nevertheless, it must be said that the Eastern Churches have changed their views much less frequently than the Western ones over the last millennium, and this section therefore concentrates on the Western Churches. The following are examples of other teachings and practices that have changed, or are still in the process of changing.

The Status of the Bible

As we have already seen, the Western Church regarded its own Latin translation of the Bible as divinely inspired and infallible, despite its known errors. In early times vernacular translations were also used, often to help missionary activity, but as doctrines diverged more and more from the biblical texts, it became expedient to permit translations of only selected parts (for example the psalms). After the reign of John VIII (pope 872–82) the use of local languages was banned so that all Church business, including services, was to be conducted in Latin, the language approved by God. The Vulgate was the only permitted version of the Bible, and only clerics were permitted to read it. Western Church Councils forbade the laity from possessing bibles, especially vernacular versions. Reading the Bible for a layman was contrary to the faith, and thus an invitation to the Inquisition of the day. Following the Reformation all this changed: it became acceptable for anyone to read the Bible, and more accurate translations were made into English, French, German and many other languages. Today, translations can be made into any language and even into dialects: there is one in Yorkshire dialect and another in the dialect of Harlem in New York. Inexplicably, the Catholic Church no longer seeks the death sentence for the translators or even seeks to condemn them at all.

Following the Church Fathers, the Church taught that the Bible was written by God and was therefore infallible.[87] The Roman Church confirmed at the Council of Trent that God was the true author of the Bible (Session 4), and so did Pope Leo XIII in the encyclical *Providentissimus Deus* of 1893. According to Leo, every part of the Bible was written under the inspiration of the Holy Spirit, and this precluded all possibility of error, since God must be incapable of teaching error. Until recent times a number of translations were held by various Churches, Protestant as well as Roman Catholic, to be the divine word of God. Each Church claimed that its version was free from error and that it was to be interpreted literally.

Under pressure from scholars, historians and scientists, this position became untenable during the course of the nineteenth and twentieth centuries. One by one, the mainstream Churches were obliged to abandon their positions. Now only edenists, or fundamentalists as they have come to be known, hold to the traditional teachings. Others talk about the divine inspiration of the human authors, but the stark fact is that the mainstream Churches have all shifted their ground. They no longer interpret the Bible literally, just as they no longer burn lay people alive for reading it for themselves.

Hell

Belief in eternal hellfire was taught by Jesus and was once universal among Christians. Those who denied the reality of hellfire, or doubted whether it was eternal, were heretics. As the infallible Second Council of Constantinople put it in 553, 'Whosoever says or thinks that the punishment of demons and of the wicked will not be eternal, that it will have an end … let him be anathema'. The only questions concerned matters such as the range of punishments available there, and whether the damned shed real tears.

For centuries children and peasants were terrorised by the promise of eternal damnation. Theologians assured them that they would be crushed in giant wine presses, torn to pieces by wild animals, fed with the gall of dragons, burned for eternity, tortured by demons, and so on. As Cardinal Newman pointed out, belief in Hell was central to Christian theology, it was 'the critical doctrine – you can't get rid of it – it is the very characteristic of Christianity'. The existence of God was held to prove the reality of eternal hellfire, so denial of eternal hellfire amounted to denial of God. The reality of Hell was simply not open to question. Well into the twentieth century children were encouraged to read works such as that of Father Furniss, a Roman Catholic priest known as the 'children's apostle'. He, like his contemporaries, had no doubt about the reality of eternal damnation. Here he is describing a boy in Hell:

> His eyes are burning like two burning coals. Two long flames come out of his ears... Sometimes he opens his mouth, and breath of blazing fire rolls out of it. But listen! There is a sound just like that of a kettle boiling. Is it really a kettle which is boiling? No; then what is it? Hear what it is. The blood is boiling in the scalding veins of that boy. The brain is boiling and bubbling in his head. The marrow is boiling in his bones![88]

And again:

> The little child is in the red-hot oven. Hear how it screams to come out; see how it turns and twists itself about in the fire. It beats its head against the roof of the oven. It stamps its little feet on the floor... God was very good to this little child. Very likely God saw it would get worse and worse and never repent, and so it would have been punished more severely in Hell. So God in his mercy called it out of the world in early childhood.

This booklet is full of descriptions like this. It was not the product of a maverick. It represented mainstream Roman Catholic thought and sold over 4,000,000 copies. Here is the text of the approbation on the inside cover:

> I have carefully read over this *Little Volume for Children* and have found nothing whatever in it contrary to the doctrines of Holy Faith; but, on the contrary, a great deal to charm, instruct, and edify our youthful classes, for whose benefit it has been written. (William Meagher, Vicar General, Dublin, 14th December, 1855)

The horrors of Hell were taught to countless generations as the literal truth, Roman Catholic, Protestant and nonconformist alike. Now belief in Hell seems to be no longer necessary. Certainly the Church of England does not require it. The Privy Council decided many years ago that belief in it is optional.[89] Theologians have now started to redefine Hell. In fact, according to the Church of England's Doctrine Commission, traditional teachings of hellfire and eternal torment are 'appalling theologies which made God into a sadistic monster and left searing scars on many'.[90]

According to recent theories Hell is not a place at all. It is, as the heretic Origen suggested, a condition of being distant from God. Alternatively, if it does exist it is probably empty! This solution attempts to reconcile the traditional doctrine of the reality of Hell with the requirement for a modern, caring, God. It is a classic example of the way in which teachings change when doctrine starts to become unteachable because of widespread disbelief. The Church cannot bring itself to agree explicitly with the atheist Lucretius (*c.*96–55 BC) and admit that 'There is no murky pit of Hell awaiting anyone',[91] but that is really what churchmen have come around to after 2,000 years.

Purgatory and Indulgences

The idea of Purgatory has no foundation in scripture.[92] It has never been well defined, especially in the Eastern Churches. The Western Church developed the doctrine and confirmed it at the Council of Trent. According to Roman Catholic doctrine, Purgatory was a place where the dead atoned for their venial (pardonable) sins, though they were sometimes permitted to return to the world of the living, where they appeared as ghosts. An individual's suffering in Purgatory could be reduced by the actions of the living. The theory underlying it is that the Pope had the power to redistribute the merit of the saints in Heaven to those less worthy. It was once common practice in the Roman Church to sell or exchange this merit in the form of indulgences. In practice it was a sort of contract: a simple Christian would pay money or perform some service in exchange for a piece of paper letting his or her soul off some of the punishment due to it after death. Pope Boniface XI is said to have instituted an indulgence, *Boniface's Cup*, for those who drank a toast to his health after grace.

It was common practice for the building of cathedrals to be financed by the sale of indulgences, and this practice became a scandal in the Middle Ages. Professional fund-raisers (Pardoners) were employed on commission to sell indulgences, much like travelling salesmen. These indulgences (or pardons) from the Pope were hot property to Chaucer's Pardoner:

> His walet, biforn him in his lappe,
> Bretful of pardoun, comen from Rome al hoot[93]

Indulgences were also used to benefit the Papacy financially in other ways. For example one condition inserted into indulgences after 1462 was that they were invalid for anyone importing Turkish alum (as the Pope was trying to establish a monopoly within Christendom for his own newly discovered alum deposits at Tolfa).[94]

Matters came to a head in the sixteenth century when a Dominican called Johann Tetzel (*c*.1465–1519) undertook a sales tour of Germany, hawking indulgences. Proceeds were to be used partially to pay for the building of St Peter's in Rome and partly to discharge debts incurred by the Archbishop of Mainz. As soon as a coin rang in the bottom of Tetzel's coffer so soon was a soul released for Heaven, or so he said. Better still, Tetzel sold the right to sin in the future. It was this sales tour that so outraged Martin Luther, lighting the touch-paper of the Reformation.

Protestants reject the doctrine of Purgatory, holding that the dead proceed immediately to Heaven or Hell. The Church of England is scathing about it. The 22nd of the 39 Articles of Religion for example says:

> The Romish Doctrine concerning Purgatory … is a fond [i.e. foolish] thing vainly invented, and grounded upon no warranty of Scripture, but rather repugnant to the Word of God.

The Roman Church has also backed off recently. For centuries it had set tariffs for certain virtuous actions. Specific pilgrimages, relics, prayers or gifts to the Church bought specific reductions in one's sentence. It was possible to read off the reduction of suffering against specified acts: so many days for a certain prayer, so many days for a certain pilgrimage, so many days for joining a crusade, so many days for acquiring a holy relic, and so on. Pope Leo X calculated that a pious German who collected over 17,000 holy relics had saved himself 694,779,550.5 days in Purgatory. More recently, in 1991, one considerate believer organised a campaign to induce 200,000 people to say a certain prayer five times a day for a year. He pointed out that St Gertrude the Great had been told by Our Lord nearly 700 years ago that this prayer would release 1000 souls from Purgatory. It was thus believed that 365,000,000,000 souls could be released each year. The challenge was to empty Purgatory altogether.

After many centuries of acceptability the authorities are now embarrassed by this sort of thought, and tariffs have generally been abolished. The sale of indulgences is now universally regarded as corrupt and inimical to Christianity. No longer is it possible to tick off the days of one's sentence in Purgatory as one collects holy relics.

Clerical Dress

The earliest priests wore the same clothes as everyone else. Then they took to wearing white, imitating the garb of priests of pagan religions. Later their dress became more and more colourful and distinctive. In 428 Pope Celestine I censured bishops in southern Gaul for wearing distinctive costumes. Bishops and other clergymen found a way to circumvent such prohibitions. They did not adopt new costumes; they simply continued to wear old ones after they had fallen out of fashion. Nearly all modern clerical vestments are remnants of antique upper class secular Roman dress. The traditional Eucharistic vestments of amice, alb, girdle, maniple, stole, and chasuble are all secular clothing of the second century. Cassocks were ordinary everyday clothes up to the sixth century. Much later, they came to be colour-coded to show ecclesiastical rank: currently black for priests, purple for bishops, red for cardinals, white for popes.

During the Reformation, Protestants rejected the wearing of distinctive costume and made it illegal for clergymen to wear the chasuble, alb, tunicle, biretta, girdle and stole. English clergy were required to wear a simple surplice, though even this offended Puritans. Over the years, various gorgeous vestments have crept back into the Anglican Church, but are clearly unlawful. Decisions of the Privy Council have confirmed that it is even illegal for an Anglican bishop to wear a mitre and carry a pastoral staff.[95] Nevertheless, they are now standard equipment. Nonconformists also rejected special vestments, and for the same reason as the Anglicans had done, but all this did was to reset the clock. The Moderator of the Free Church of Scotland, for example, wears clothing that was fashionable in late eighteenth-century Scotland.

Women Priests

In the earliest days of the Church women played a full role: '...there is neither male nor female: for ye are all one in Christ Jesus' (Galatians 3:28). There were *helpers in Jesus Christ* such as Priscilla (Romans 16:3), whose designation was indicative of official authority, but who are never given a formal title in translations. Again, Phebe had been a Christian teacher. Had she been a man she would probably have been regarded as a bishop on the strength of Romans 16:2, but because she was a woman she became a mere *deaconess* (Jerusalem Bible) or *servant of the church* (Authorised Version). Similarly, at some time in the Middle Ages, a person with a woman's name, Junia (Romans 16:7), acquired a man's name, Junias (Jerusalem Bible), though earlier authorities unanimously regarded her as a woman.[96] She had been counted among the apostles, but the Church did not want to know about female apostles, so her name and her gender were changed.

When a system of Holy Orders and a hierarchy of bishops, priests and deacons were established, deaconesses were accepted into Holy Orders. There were no fewer than 40 of them on the staff of the Church of the Holy Wisdom in Constantinople in the year 612. In time the hierarchy decided that it could do without them. Deaconesses disappeared in the Western Church in the fifth century and in the Eastern Church in the twelfth century. Women were excluded from lesser functions as well. They were prevented from serving at the altar and even debarred from church choirs. For centuries it would have been heretical to claim that women could be priests or deaconesses.

In recent times women have once again demanded, and have gradually been granted, a greater role in Church affairs. Girls have been accepted into Church choirs and given minor official roles. The office of deaconess was restored, although initially without Holy Orders. The first Protestant deaconess was appointed in 1836, the first Anglican one in 1861, and the first Methodist one in 1888.

The position is similar with regard to the ordination of women as priests. Not long ago the mainstream Churches universally held that women could not be ordained, indeed such an idea was plainly heretical. But public opinion shifted during the twentieth century. Anglican, Lutheran and other Protestant Churches changed their minds and now ordain women priests. Some have consecrated women bishops. As soon as the *volte-face* was complete in 1991, the Archbishop of Canterbury announced that 'The idea that only a male can represent Christ at the altar is a most serious heresy.'[97] Yesterday's heresy was today's orthodoxy, and yesterday's orthodoxy was today's heresy.

As popular opinion continues to change, more Churches may follow. In North America and parts of Europe there is already significant pressure within the Roman Catholic Church. At the time of writing it is still likely to be many years before the pressure becomes strong enough for women priests to be accepted in all denominations.[98] Whether or not there are more changes to come, there have already been enough to compromise any claim to constancy.

Marriage

Christian teachings on marriage have changed continually since the time of Jesus. In its early years the Church simply followed Roman law, which was based on the maxim *consent constitutes matrimony*. If a couple declared to each other that they were married, then they *were* married. They did not require witnesses, or a priest to officiate. Such marriages were described as 'clandestine' but there was never any question about their validity.

Marriage was essentially a civil contract, *sponsalia*, which in medieval England generally took place at the church porch (*in facie ecclesiæ*). Chaucer's wife of Bath makes reference to this practice in her *Prologue* (l.6) when she says 'Five husbands have I had at the church door.' There was no great religious significance to this; the local church was simply the social centre of the village and the natural meeting place for people to negotiate various kinds of personal business and conclude contracts. The couple would simply plight their troth with a ring outside the church, after which they might or might not enter the church for a nuptial Mass. Often the priest's role was confined to blessing the marriage bed. There was an ecclesiastical counterpart of marriage, called *matrimony*, but this was optional. *Sponsalia* created a legal bond, even before consummation.

The Western Church started to secure control of marriage ceremonies at the Fourth Lateran Council in 1215, but it was not until 1563, at the Council of Trent, that an obligatory form for matrimony was introduced. Suddenly, a priest and two witnesses were indispensable conditions of a valid marriage.[99] The Council of Trent also declared matrimony to be a sacrament. It had not previously been a sacrament but now it was. Later, Anglicans decided that matrimony was not a sacrament after all, as Article 25 of the 39 Articles of the Anglican Church confirms. In Protestant countries civil marriages continued to be recognised. Courts would uphold *sponsalia* in preference to holy matrimony if, for example, one party subsequently married someone else in Church.[100] In England these civil marriages were valid up until Lord Hardwicke's Act in 1753. In Scotland they continued until 1940.[101] They live on in the popular imagination as 'common law' marriages.

The whole topic of marriage is a confusion of changing views and regulations. For centuries the Church argued with itself about whether marriage was a contract authenticated by a ceremony, or whether sexual intercourse was required to consummate it. At different times the Western Church reached different conclusions, although in the end it was decided that sexual intercourse was required. In 1982 a priest refused to marry a man suffering from muscular dystrophy and his visually impaired fiancée until they could prove that they were able to have children.[102]

Another area of confusion is the marriage of Christians and members of other faiths. As soon as it could do so, the Church had prohibited marriage between Christians and Jews, making such a marriage a capital offence. For centuries the marriage of a Christian to one of another faith was treated as a crime. Similar feelings were expressed after the Reformation about marriages between Roman Catholics and Protestants (or between members of any two sects opposed to each other). Now mixed marriages are not such a great tragedy, and Churches no longer insist on capital punishment for those who 'marry out'. Some Churches now even recognise same-sex marriages.

The Sacraments

Different denominations recognise different numbers of sacraments. To cite just a few examples – the Salvation Army 0, the Church of England 2, Roman Catholics 7. Eastern Churches have *mysteries* instead of *sacraments* and their number has varied between 2 and 10, and is still not fixed.[103] That there are seven sacraments was first suggested in the twelfth century.[104] There was still disagreement as to what they were. Some held an oath to be a sacrament, others the Incarnation, others holy scripture.

The list of seven now accepted by the Roman Church (baptism, Confirmation, the Eucharist, penance, Holy Orders, matrimony, and anointing of the sick or last rites) was first recorded by Peter Lombard in the second half of the twelfth century, and received papal sanction in 1439.[105] The Eastern Churches accepted the list at a Council of Constantinople in 1642 but in practice disagree on a number of points. Protestant Churches rejected the list as lacking biblical authority. The

Church of England accepts only two sacraments, baptism and the Eucharist, although there is some ambiguity on the matter in the wording of Article 25 of the 39 Articles.

The Eucharist, Communion, or Mass has proved particularly problematic. We have already seen the difficulties associated with the doctrine of transubstantiation, but there is more. When Jesus invited his followers to remember him as they ate bread or drank, he seems to have envisaged them doing so at ordinary meals, as in their own homes. The Church was soon turning these meals of remembrance into rituals, and insisting that priests conduct them. The ancient Church provided both bread and wine at the Mass, apparently as part of a full meal. The full meal seems to have disappeared during the first few centuries, leaving just the bread and wine.

After a further 1,000 years, by the thirteenth century, the Roman Church took to reserving the wine for priests only. This practice had no biblical authority and was rejected by the Eastern Churches and later by Protestant Churches. Offering wine to the laity contributed to the appeal of Protestantism and so to its popularity. In an attempt to stop the slide into Protestantism in the sixteenth century, Pope Pius IV authorised the Communion of both kinds (i.e. both bread and wine) to the Roman Catholic laity in Germany, Austria and other regions. Once the Protestant threat had passed, the faithful were soon back to bread only. To Christians it is a matter of the greatest importance whether or not they should be permitted to share fully in the Lord's Supper, and yet the Roman Church changed its mind for political rather than doctrinal reasons. In recent times there has been a widespread recognition that there is no real reason for denying the wine, and since the Second Vatican Council it has become common for both bread and wine to be given to communicants in the Roman Church.

Other sacraments have been just as variable. For many centuries only a bishop could give absolution. Confession (penance) took place only once, just before death. Then it could be made after any grave sin, then once a year[106] (on Shrove Tuesday), then once a week. Now confession can be made more or less at will. Baptism originally required immersion in cold running water. Total submersion in warm water or still water was permitted only if cold or running water was not available.[107] For the Eastern Churches and for Western Baptists immersion is still required. Other Western Churches offended the orthodox by abandoning the practice of total submersion. At one time total submersion was required not merely once, but three times, and in the earliest times the practice was for candidates to be baptised in the nude. St Augustine was baptised naked by St Ambrose as late as 387. Again, baptism was once routinely preceded by an exorcism. At the Church door the priest would blow in the child's face and instruct the 'unclean spirit' to leave it. During the baptism the North Door of the Church was (and sometimes still is) left open to allow the Devil or the unclean spirit to leave the building. The formal exorcism however was dropped from the second Edwardian Prayer Book of 1552.

Sacraments have varied enormously over the centuries, which tends to suggest that they are merely human constructs. This suggestion is supported by the differences between the practices of different denominations today.

Church Festivals
There is no evidence that the early Church celebrated any of the festivals that are now such an integral part of the religion. Important observances such as Pentecost, Ascension Day, Lent, Holy Week and Christmas were unknown before the fourth century. They are all accretions that have acquired a patina of antiquity in the course of centuries. Once a date was fixed for Christmas it was possible to create a number of other annual festivals. For example the Annunciation must have taken place nine months before Christmas Day (25th March); the Feast of the Circumcision seven days after Christmas Day (1st January), and Epiphany, when the magi were supposed to have arrived, a few days later[108] (6th January). The only festival that is likely to date back much earlier than the fourth century is Easter.

The Churches of Asia Minor preserved the oldest method of calculating Easter. They simply used the date of the Passover, the 14th of the Jewish month of Nisan. Alexandrian Christians chose to hold their celebrations on the Sunday immediately after the Passover. No one seems to have minded about this innovation. The Alexandrian Church was autocephalous and entitled to decide such matters for itself. Around AD 160 an annual Easter festival was adopted at Rome, and the Alexandrian practice was adopted there. Within 30 years the Bishop of Rome was claiming that everyone should adopt this method of reckoning

Easter. Since the date of the festival was arbitrary, and the Bishop of Rome was the Patriarch of the West, many in the West did so, though others did not. The Celtic Church was less than enthusiastic, but eventually decided to fall into line with the rest of the Western Church at the Council of Whitby in 664. As we have seen, those in Asia who kept to the old ways – *Quartodecimans* as they were nicknamed – came to be regarded as heretics. If the date of Easter seems a minor matter it is well to remember that people have been executed in the past as heretics for disputing it.

Burials

Since early times Churches have taught that dead Christians will be bodily resurrected on the Day of Judgement. In anticipation of this, Christians have traditionally striven to ensure that their bodies are buried in one piece. They have apparently wanted to make God's job that much easier when the great day arrives.* Some Christians still retain amputated limbs and surgically removed internal organs, and even extracted teeth, so that they can be buried along with the rest of their bodies, to be reassembled later by God. So too, eunuchs were buried with their severed genitals in the hopeful expectation of a bodily reunion. All good Christians were encouraged to keep their bodies as intact as possible for burial, in anticipation of their bodily resurrection. Criminals on the other hand could not expect Christian society to help them in this respect and thus were publicly gibbeted or dissected. As late as 1752 a British Act of Parliament stated that 'in no case whatsoever the Body of any Murderer shall be suffered to be buried'.[109] So too heretics were traditionally burned, and their ashes scattered into a river.

Good Christians had to be buried, preferably in sacred ground, along with their fellow good Christians. In the Middle Ages the requirement about burial became inconvenient. In times of plague the requirement to bury bodies ensured that virtually everyone came into contact with a

---

* That it was necessary to keep the body of the deceased together did not stand up to intellectual enquiry. What about the righteous whose bodies were dismembered and scattered by their enemies? Would God be unable to reassemble them? Educated people were happy to have their hearts and other pieces of their bodies removed after death, to be buried separately.

deadly disease. A theological excuse was therefore found to change the rules, and cremation suddenly became an acceptable alternative, in direct contradiction to previous ideas. Many survivors were convinced that their dead relatives had missed the chance of eventual resurrection. Once the plague had passed, burial became obligatory again.

It was not until 1884 that cremation was permanently permitted in England, against the wishes of bishops of the Church of England. The Roman Church has permitted cremation only since 1965. It still earnestly recommends that the pious custom of burial be retained, and seems to imagine that people might be cremated for 'anti-Christian motives'.[110] Greek Orthodox Christians, as well as Muslims and Orthodox Jews, still prohibit cremation.

The Church once found it enormously important to ensure that certain sinners were not buried in consecrated ground. The motivation seems to have been to make God's job of separating the sheep from the goats on the Day of Judgement a little easier. Mothers and babies who died in childbirth were sometimes denied a Christian burial because of the sin associated with conception. Such practices would cause outrage now, and so have been completely abandoned and almost totally forgotten.

Suicides

Many martyrs of the early Church were really suicides, since they sought and welcomed their own deaths. (Whole sects were wiped out because of this.) Later, suicide was discouraged and came to be regarded as a mortal sin. Up until 1824, suicides in England were buried on a highway (often a crossroads) with a stake through the body (usually through the heart). Since 1882, the Anglican practice has been merely to deny to suicides a Christian burial service,[111] unless the suicide was found to have taken his or her own life while of unsound mind. Such conventions could always be ignored when they did not suit. Thus, in 1988 a host of Anglican bishops and priests officiated at the funeral service of the Rev. Gareth Bennett, an Oxford don who had committed suicide after being revealed as the author of an anonymous attack on the Archbishop of Canterbury. The same flexibility is evident in the Catholic Church. In 1981 Catholic priests found no doctrinal difficulties in offering communion, absolution, final unction, and funeral masses to ten convicted prisoners who starved themselves to death in jail in Northern Ireland.

These prisoners were explicitly committing suicide as a form of protest because they did not like being treated as common criminals, regarding themselves as political prisoners and therefore entitled to privileges such as not having to wear standard prison clothes. Again, when Fr Sean Fortune committed suicide in 2003, having been accused of multiple sex crimes against children over many years, his bishop, the Bishop of Ferns, Dr Brendan Comiskey, found no difficulty in delivering the main homily at the funeral.[112] Immutable rules proved sufficiently elastic to accommodate changing mores and personal preferences of the Church hierarchy.

Diet

Jesus and his disciples followed the traditional Jewish dietary laws. The following foods, amongst others, were prohibited: pig, camel, hare, shellfish, ostrich, various owls, cormorants, pelicans, storks, herons, hoopoes, bats, and most arthropods except locusts, crickets, and grasshoppers. Also banned are weasels, mice, geckos, chameleons and other lizards.[113] These rules were soon abandoned by gentile Christians, and in time were replaced by entirely different rules about eating. For many centuries Roman Catholics were not permitted to eat meat on certain days. To do so invited a visit from the Inquisition. Roman Catholics generally ate fish on Fridays. Rather disingenuously, a number of animals were conveniently classified as fish. The Barnacle Goose, for example, was regarded as fish on the erroneous grounds that it developed from a goose barnacle. Beaver's tail was regarded as fish for no better reason than it was hairless.

Pope Pius XII did away with the need for such deceptions in 1953 when he announced that Roman Catholics could eat meat on Fridays after all. Fast days in the Roman Church are now reduced from well over 100 to a mere two (Ash Wednesday and Good Friday). Fast days were mentioned in the 1969 canons of the Church of England, but no one seems to know what is required for their observance.

How can the rules be so uncertain and flexible if fasting is so important to God? And if it is not important to God, why were people tried and executed for failing to follow arbitrary temporary rules?

Natural Phenomena

For many centuries the Churches taught that God was responsible for natural phenomena. He caused earthquakes, floods and volcanic eruptions. In the seventeenth century, and later, many thought it heresy to deny God's personal involvement in such phenomena, since they were known to be signs of divine disapproval against a sinful world. God controlled the weather too. It was for this reason that Christians opposed the innovation of fitting lightning rods to church buildings: if God wanted to burn down his own churches, it was no business of ours to stop him.

Celestial phenomena such as comets and eclipses were known to be divine warnings, a belief that was still common, even among educated classes, when a comet was observed in 1677. It was also necessary to believe that (with God's permission) witches and demons were active in disturbing the weather. Church bells were routinely rung to frighten off the demons that caused storms. To deny the existence of witches or demons was an attack on Christianity itself and was treated first as heretical and later as atheistic.

Churchmen verified for many centuries the idea that God actively managed events on Earth and in the skies. Today such ideas are generally regarded as primitive (although insurance companies still refer to natural disasters as 'Acts of God'). Having spent so long controlling every aspect of all natural phenomena, God is now relegated to the role of disinterested observer. The 180° shift has taken place without the least visible trace of embarrassment.

Excommunication

In earlier centuries whole communities were excommunicated. Pope Adrian IV excommunicated Rome in 1155, and Pope Innocent III excommunicated the whole of England in 1208. To carry out such an excommunication now would be seen as absurd. Again, prayers of cursing were once quite acceptable. Curses and anathemas were distributed liberally. They were laid upon those who disregarded the decrees of Church Councils, or read the contents of papal letters, those who failed to pay their tithes, those who stole, those who committed murder, and indeed all enemies of the Church. Now they are watered down to anodyne services of commination. Can it really be that those excommunicated in the past for failing to pay tithes will burn in Hell for eternity, while those who fail to pay them now will not?

Church Architecture and Furniture

Jesus' early followers worshipped in the Jewish Temple and attended synagogues, as Jesus had done. Gentile Christians met in ordinary houses. The first Christian buildings to adopt a distinctive architectural style seem to have first appeared in the fourth century. In an attempt to return to ancient simplicity, various sects have rejected the use of church buildings. George Fox dismissively called them *steeple houses*, and Quakers still prefer their own *meeting houses* to *steeple houses*. One of the fastest growing sects towards the end of the twentieth century was the house church movement, which holds its meetings in ordinary houses, just as Christians did for the first few centuries.

The use of candles, and other Church props, also dates from the fourth century or later times. Incense was used in many religions to mask the smell of burned sacrifices. Its use was severely prohibited in the early Church, but like many pagan practices it was popular. By the fifth century it was being used in Christian places of worship. Because it had been banned in the early Church, its use at services of the Church of England and other Protestant Churches was made unlawful at the Reformation. Altars, also inherited from religions that practised sacrifice, were employed in Christian Churches because masses were sacrificial in nature. This idea too was rejected at the Reformation. Stone altars were physically destroyed, and replaced by wooden Communion tables. Other traditional Church furniture, such as pulpits, appears to have been introduced only in the Middle Ages. Confessional boxes were introduced later and pews later still. Pews are still rarely found in Orthodox churches, and congregations are expected to stand throughout the service, as they did previously in Western churches.

Churches routinely ignore the canons of ecumenical councils, which are believed to be divinely inspired and thus infallible. Canon XX of the First Ecumenical Council, for example, forbids people from kneeling on Sundays or on any of the 50 days between Easter and Pentecost, yet this canon is disregarded by the Western Church and increasingly disregarded in the East. Ideas as to the acceptability of Church music have also changed from time to time. In early times singing was always unaccompanied, as it still is in traditional Eastern Churches. Western Churches have varied their practices many times. At one time harps were favoured (there were supposed to be harps in Heaven, but the rest of the orchestra was condemned to Hell). At other times all manner of instruments have been permitted, but in recent centuries they all gave way to organs. Many in the West came to imagine that organs in Churches dated from biblical times. When guitars and other instruments were introduced in the 1960s, many Christians complained that almost 2000 years of tradition were being overturned.

Conventions as to who may enter churches have also changed. People are no longer allowed to set up shop in churches, as they did in medieval times, and dogs no longer roam freely inside the naves as they once did. Changing moral concepts are highlighted by the bouncers at St Peter's in Rome, who refuse admission to women with bare arms, despite the fact that inside are numerous nude female statues, including a famous one of a papal mistress (now fitted with a discreet metal corset).

* * *

Few, if any, practices have been consistently upheld since apostolic times, just as few, if any, doctrines have been consistently taught since those times. There would be nothing remarkable about an ordinary organisation changing its teachings and practices to suit current conditions. In the case of the Christian Church, however, such changes are remarkable because they undermine the Churches' claims to represent a perfect, infallible and unchanging God here in an otherwise imperfect, flawed and ever-changing world.

It is difficult to believe that Churches were right to execute thousands of people in the past for their opinions, while they make no effort now to punish people with identical opinions – and have even adopted some of those opinions themselves.

METHOD 8: MANIPULATE LANGUAGE

*What can be said at all can be said clearly; and whereof one
cannot speak thereof one must be silent.*
Ludwig Wittgenstein (1889–1951),
Tractatus Logico-Philosophicus

In this section we will look at some aspects of language, and how it has been used to support religious claims.

Linguistic Deceits

*'When I use a word', Humpty Dumpty said, in rather a scornful tone, 'it means
just what I choose it to mean – neither more nor less'.*
Lewis Carroll (1832–98), *Alice Through the Looking-Glass*

Words are not always as straightforward as they appear. To take a simple example, descriptive names are not always accurate. As Voltaire (1694–1778) observed, the Holy Roman Empire was neither holy, nor Roman, nor an empire. Again, the Edict of Milan was not an edict, and neither was it issued at Milan. Sometimes a name can be deliberately misleading: George Orwell's Ministries of Truth, Peace, Plenty and Love are classic examples. Sometimes the accuracy of the name is a matter of belief. Christian Scientists presumably regard their faith as scientific. Roman Catholics regard their Church as catholic. Jehovah's Witnesses believe that they bear true witness to Jehovah. In each case members regard the name as an accurate description, while non-members may not.

Much confusion arises from the fact that different people interpret the same words in different ways. In some cases this happens naturally, for example because words change their meaning over time. The Holy Ghost has recently become known as the Holy Spirit. The reason is that the word *ghost*, which originally meant much the same as *spirit*, has acquired new meanings similar to *spectre* or *apparition*. This change is understandable. Words do change their meanings, and to retain clarity it is sometimes necessary to rephrase sentences to retain their original meanings. More worrying is the deliberate changing of a word's meaning, in order to meet one's own ends. Theologians sometimes do this to keep scripture credible after it has been shown to be in error. For example, the Bible says that the world was made in six days, but in the nineteenth century it became widely accepted that it took many millions of years for Earth to form. To reconcile these contradictory facts theologians proposed that the biblical *day* was not an earthly day of 24 hours, but a heavenly day, which could conveniently be equated with millions of Earth years.[114] This simple device allows the same words to be used, but the meaning to be completely changed. Using this technique, churchmen never need to acknowledge that they have been wrong.

The Jesuits spent much time and effort developing a doctrine called *equivocation*. The basic idea is that in certain circumstances it is desirable to mislead people by saying something that will be understood one way by the listener but means something else to the speaker. The doctrine effectively permits lying even under oath, as long as it is possible to construe the words as accurate in some sense, however tortuous. Equivocation was popular in England when the authorities were threatened by Catholic terrorist attacks like the Gunpowder Plot. Some priests and fervent Catholics plotted, and more were suspected of treason. Those accused used equivocation to allay suspicion. Thus a priest wishing to conceal his identity might say that he is 'no priest', meaning in his own mind that he is not Apollo's priest at Delphos. If asked if he had ever been beyond the seas he might answer no, meaning in his own mind that he had not been beyond the Indian seas, even if in truth he had sailed to foreign countries for treasonable purposes. The doctrine may sound absurd, but it was adopted, justified and used for centuries. The two examples given are real ones, both used by a certain Father Ward around the time of the Gunpowder Plot in 1605.[115] Another priest, Father Garnet, wrote a treatise on the subject around the same time, giving practical examples of how to equivocate, and pointing out that Jesus himself had employed the technique.* With a little imagination it is clearly possible to justify any untruth using equivocation. A modern Jesuit might say that he believes in the Virgin Birth, while in

---

* Father Garnet's examples included Jesus claiming not to know when the end of the world would be (Matthew 24:36 and Mark 13:32), and Jesus saying that Jairus's dead daughter was not dead (Mark 5 and Luke 8).

fact he believes no such thing – in his own mind he might believe it in a figurative mythical sort of way, or he might believe in the phenomenon of parthenogenesis, or something else equally irrelevant. The trick has been used in the twenty-first century by a Catholic bishop to conceal information about child abuse in the Church.

Inconvenient teachings can be adjusted in a similar way, by changing a word's definition. For many centuries the Church taught that 'There is no salvation outside the Church'. This was universally accepted as meaning that only those who belonged to the sole denomination favoured by God had a chance of going to Heaven. Protestants held that only Protestants could go to Heaven. Baptists held that only Baptists could go to Heaven. Roman Catholics held that only members of the Roman Church could go to Heaven, and so on. This idea of there being no salvation outside the Church is increasingly unacceptable to modern theologians, who find it difficult to accept that members of other denominations, and indeed most of humankind, can be damned without a chance. As one professor of theology has written of this doctrine:[116]

> Is not such an idea excessively parochial, presenting God in effect as the tribal deity of the predominantly Christian West? And so theologians have recently been developing a mass of small print to the old theology, providing that devout men of other faiths may be Christians without knowing it, or may be anonymous Christians, or may belong to the invisible church, or may have implicit faith and receive baptism by desire, and so on. These rather artificial theories are all attempts to square an inadequate theology with the facts of God's world. They are thoroughly well intentioned and are to be welcomed as such. But in the end they are an anachronistic clinging to the husk of the old doctrine after its substance has crumbled.

According to the Church of England's current position, 'It is incompatible with the essential Christian affirmation that God is love, to say that God brings millions into the world to damn them' and 'We can see empirically that people are enabled to lead better lives through loyally following other faiths, and this must mean that God is at work in these faiths'.[117] In plain terms the Church of England (like many other denominations) no longer teaches that 'there is no salvation outside the Church'.

But how can any Church abandon one of its central tenets without admitting a massive mistake? The answer is to keep the same words, but change their meaning. In this case the trick is to change the meaning of the word *Church*. As attitudes became more ecumenical and Christians started to accept that members of other denominations might be saved, the word Church was reinterpreted to mean not merely one particular denomination, but the community of all good Christians. Thus for example Roman Catholics could suddenly accept that Protestants could be saved. More recently it has became popular to believe that any good person might be saved, even a Jew, Muslim, Buddhist, indeed even an atheist. The word *Church* has had to be reinterpreted again to include this wider group. So now it means a special community of worthy people suitable for admission to Heaven. The *Church* is a sort of invisible community known only to God. Certain people belong to it, Christian and non-Christian alike, but no one knows who they are. Now the statement 'there is no salvation outside the Church' means something quite different. What has happened is that theologians have reversed their position, for they are now asserting that non-Christians *can* be saved. They are in fact teaching that there *is* salvation outside the Church.

By changing the meaning of a key word, they have been able to continue to use the ancient maxim and thus claim that their position is unchanged. Indeed by switching the meaning of the word *Church* from one occasion to another, clergymen can enjoy the best of all possible worlds, matching the doctrine to the needs of the moment. Priests will sometimes affirm the original doctrine, and sometimes deny it, without abandoning the wording, simply by redefining the term *Church* according to the needs of the moment.

Similar reinterpretations are used to explain away all manner of inconvenient material. The Bible prohibits the practice of usury. The word *usury* means simply taking interest on loans. For centuries that was how it was universally interpreted. The prohibition became untenable as capitalism developed, so the word was redefined. Suddenly *usury* denoted not merely the charging of interest, but specifically the charging of unreasonable interest. Now the Church can claim that it has always disapproved of usury, and in a sense this is true, even though it has completely changed its views on the practice of charging interest. In November 2005, Benedict XVI was quoted as condemning the 'social plague' of usury, saying that it should be combated through prevention, solidarity and education.

Other words were similarly redefined, and sometimes even changed. The purported reason for altering a word is that the new word conveys better the original meaning, just as the *Holy Ghost* became the *Holy Spirit*. So it is that biblical *slaves* became *helpers*, clerical *wives* became *female relatives*, and *concubines* became *maidservants*. Inconveniently, historians have no doubt that the words slave, wife, and concubine still best represent the true meaning. The words *helper*, *relative* and *maidservant* are really euphemisms, intended to detract from the full impact of the original term. We have already seen this technique in use for biblical translations. For sects that believe in the Virgin Birth, Jesus' *brothers* and *sisters* become '*cousins*', and for sects that do not permit clerical marriage, *bishops* become '*elders*'. According to requirements *presbyteroi* can be presbyters, priests, elders or even old-timers. Again, the *Word* (*logos*) can be rendered as word, idea, message, doctrine, system, book or pre-existent being. By using the same word for several different things it is easy to produce specious arguments. The technique is common. Witnesses turn into victims of persecution simply by changing the meaning of the word *martyr*. Thousands of early Christian have been acclaimed as martyrs, simply because they were witnesses, i.e. believers.

Another popular technique is to invoke human limitations of understanding of the meaning of words. For example God is often claimed to be all-merciful. This does not square easily with his biblical persona. How can an all-merciful God commit genocide, or encourage the killing of children, or punish people for the sins of others? The usual solution to this difficulty is to say that God is indeed all-merciful, it is just that our puny human understanding is inadequate when it comes to comprehending attributes such as divine mercy. It is beyond us. Other inconvenient theological contradictions can be handled in the same way. A perfect God who makes mistakes in creation, leading to suffering, is explained by our failure to understand divine perfection. An all-powerful God who is sometimes unable to perform is explained by our failure to understand divine omnipotence. An all-knowing God who is sometimes ignorant of worldly events is explained by our failure to understand divine omniscience. Our standards are not comparable to those of God, and it is presumptuous of us, even impious, to pretend that they are.

To a non-Christian what is happening here is that God is being invested with lots of qualities that humans consider desirable: benevolence, perfection, omnipotence, omniscience – all of them concepts defined by human standards. The words are used to convey the idea that God possesses properties that we consider desirable. But as soon as we start asking uncomfortable questions we are told that these words do not mean what they normally mean – they mean something completely different, but we do not know what. Many people suspect that theologians are trying to have it both ways. The words bear the ordinary meanings when it suits them and mean something else when it doesn't. *Divine benevolence* sounds well enough, but if it means something different from *human benevolence*, we might be excused for asking what it is. At worst *divine benevolence* might equate to something like *human cruelty*. This is not merely cynicism, for as the theologians point out, we have no way of knowing what *divine benevolence* might mean. And these theologians are in no position to help. Like any other human being, as they themselves admit, their understanding is totally inadequate to comprehend God's attributes.

We have only one concept of benevolence and that is the human one. If theologians want to apply that attribute to God then they ought to have reasons for doing so. If they want to invoke a different concept of *divine benevolence*, then they should have the honesty to admit that since they know nothing about it, there is no reason to suppose that it bears any similarity to *human benevolence*. In that case it is misleading to use the word *benevolence* at all, because people naturally assume that the sort of benevolence being talked about is the ordinary, familiar kind. Incidentally, many philosophers believe that theologians know perfectly well what they are doing when they use verbal tricks of this kind. Theologians often get away with it because unsophisticated audiences fail to realise that a key word is being given a new meaning part way through an argument.

A further source of confusion arises from the use of words that can bear more than one meaning. Consider the assertion that 'God is perfect: therefore God is'. Here, the first *is* means *possesses the attribute*, the second *is* means *exists*. The assertion is really 'God possesses the attribute "perfect". Therefore God exists'. Suddenly, the argument has evaporated. The assertion that 'God is perfect. Therefore God is' can be seen as a trick with words. One might equally well deduce that *God is just* from the statement that *God is just a human invention* – this variation on the trick clearly depends upon two different meanings of the word *just*. Similar games are played with the word *know*. If we know

God, then God must exist in order for us to know him. But the word *know* has two distinct functions in English. It means both *to comprehend* and *to be personally acquainted with*. If one were personally acquainted with God, one would have grounds for believing in his existence. If one merely understood the concept of God, one would not. These tricks are dependent on the language in which they are presented. Other languages have different words for the two meanings of the English word *know*, for example, French distinguishes *savoir* (to comprehend) and *connaître* (to be acquainted with). German makes the same distinction between *wissen* and *kennen*. The argument therefore is obvious nonsense if expressed in these languages.

Another venerable technique is the *non sequitur*. Desired conclusions are represented as being the logical consequences of foregoing statements, though in fact they do not follow at all. Here is an example of St Paul, a master of the non sequitur, in action, with his arguments on the appropriateness of men and women covering or uncovering the head when praying (1 Corinthians 11:3–15). This translation is from the NIV:

> Now I want you to realise that the head of every man is Christ, and the head of the woman is man, and the head of Christ is God. Every man who prays or prophesies with his head covered dishonours his head. And every woman who prays or prophesies with her head uncovered dishonours her head – it is just as though her head were shaved. If a woman does not cover her head, she should have her hair cut off; and if it is a disgrace for a woman to have her hair cut or shaved off, she should cover her head. A man ought not to cover his head, since he is the image and glory of God; but the woman is the glory of man. For man did not come from woman, but woman from man; neither was man created for woman, but woman for man. For this reason, and because of the angels, the woman ought to have a sign of authority on her head.... Does not the very nature of things teach you that if a man has long hair, it is a disgrace to him, but that if a woman has long hair, it is her glory? For long hair is given to her as a covering.

As most theologians would now concede, Paul is simply stating a number of personal preferences, conditioned by his own cultural milieu. But he uses a string of non sequiturs to make out that there is a better justification for his ideas. Evidently his first argument did not convince even himself, for he eventually appeals to *the angels* to justify his ideas, and then to the very nature of things. It does not seem to occur to him that 'long hair is given' to men as well as to women. If men have short hair, it is only because they get it cut.

It is sometimes assumed that all statements formulated in English convey meaning. That this is a mistaken assumption is easily illustrated by a sentence created specifically to demonstrate the point. An example is the assertion that *colourless green ideas sleep furiously*. The individual words all appear meaningful, and the syntax is unimpeachable, yet the sentence as a whole is nonsense. Unfortunately, it is not always as easy to see that statements are meaningless. Pseudo-scientists and some politicians make a living from the production of plausible sounding assertions and arguments that are entirely devoid of meaning. Mere words can easily give an illusion that matters of substance are under consideration, especially if learned terms are used. The eminent philosopher A. J. Ayer formed the opinion that Christians routinely seek to deceive themselves and each other in this way: 'I think it is a very reprehensible form of cheating for someone to utter sentences to which no meaning is attached, and then pretend that he has said something frightfully important ...'[118]

Yet another form of cheating, as many philosophers see it, is to refuse to accept the usual rules of logic whenever they lead to unwanted results. An example is as follows. Christians traditionally maintain that God is both omnipotent and benevolent. The question then arises as to why evil exists in the world (this is known as the Problem of Evil). How for example could God permit such enormities as the Nazi death camps during World War II? We may assume that he is aware of such things because he is also held to be omniscient, so the possibilities are that either God has no power to prevent evil, or else he does have the power but chooses not to exercise it. If he has no power to prevent it then he is not omnipotent. On the other hand if he chooses not to prevent it then he is not wholly benevolent. The conclusion is that God cannot be both omnipotent and benevolent after all.

When results like this are obtained, theologians often refuse to accept the normal conclusion – that at least one of the assumptions is wrong. Instead the contradiction is dismissed as a 'mystery'. Thomas Paine identified the problem over 200 years ago:

> When men, whether from policy or pious fraud, set up systems of religion incompatible with the word or works of God in the creation,

and not only above, but repugnant to human comprehension, they are under the necessity of inventing or adopting a word that should serve as a bar to all questions, inquiries and speculation. The word mystery answered this purpose, and thus it has happened that religion, which is itself without mystery, has been corrupted into a fog of mysteries.[119]

Forewarned, we now address the question as to whether important assertions made by Christian Churches are meaningful.

The Incarnation

The doctrine of the Incarnation asserts, amongst other things, that Christ was both fully God and fully man. Since the Ecumenical Council of Chalcedon in 451, orthodox Christians have tried to justify the doctrine of the Incarnation. Ordinary Christians who trouble to think about the problem often arrive at explanations that are technically heretical. The ancient Nestorian heresy, that God and man coexisted in Christ as two persons, can be characterised as a Clark Kent/Superman type dichotomy. Theologians claim that explanations such as this are simplistic, but they have never themselves been able to formulate explanations convincing to objective outsiders.

A major problem is that of how one person can be wholly God and wholly man, when on the one hand God is all-powerful, all-knowing, transcendent and incapable of sin, and on the other man is limited in power, restricted in knowledge, fleshy and sinful. It is a common criticism that theologians' explanations only ever seem to convince those who already accept the doctrine of the Incarnation as a matter of faith. To many disinterested observers, theologians have succeeded in weaving an ever more intricate web of linguistic confusion. Even eminent theologians now ask whether the doctrine is meaningful. As a Regius Professor of Divinity at Oxford has written '...it seems to me that throughout the long history of attempts to present a reasoned account of Christ as both fully human and fully divine, the church has never succeeded in offering a consistent or convincing picture'.[120] The same author has asked 'Are we sure that the concept of an incarnate being, one who is fully God and fully man, is after all an intelligible concept?'[121]

Theologians took the approach that a single object can possess two separate properties. Moreover it can possess them both wholly, and at the same time. We may, for example, easily conceive of a coin that is both round and metallic. The fact that it is perfectly round does not make it less metallic, nor does the fact that it is made of metal mean that it cannot be round. This is true, but misleading, for this argument concerns properties that are unrelated. If we look at properties that are mutually exclusive, the picture is different. Few people, for example, would be likely to accept the existence of a coin that is made of 100 per cent gold and also 100 per cent iron. The concept is meaningless. We can conceive of alloys in any proportion of gold to iron that we might desire, but no alloy can be simultaneously both pure gold and pure iron. The hub of the matter is whether the possession of one perfect *nature* allows the possibility of another. Common sense declares that it does not. Even fictional characters like Dr Jekyll & Mr Hyde (who are provided with one *person* but two *natures*) have to share their time between the two *natures*, for their creators know that the fiction would be meaningless if they exhibited the two natures simultaneously. The fact is that in order for any statement of the doctrine of the Incarnation to be preserved, words like *person* and *nature* have to be supplied with such contrived meanings that they cease to be intelligible. Certainly, modern philosophers have difficulty with them, and many have inferred that they are designed to obscure rather than enlighten. If we phrase questions in straightforward English it becomes much easier to provide straightforward answers. How could Christ be fully infallible God if he was as fallible as he often showed himself to be in the gospels? And how could he be wholly mortal man if he was immortal? The only rational answers are that he could neither be wholly man, nor wholly God, much less could he be both.

As Paine pointed out, the usual response to straightforward conclusions like these, arrived at by the application of reason, is that it is not for us to question these things; this is a most profound mystery. In practice any mention of profound mysteries tends to conclude discussions on such matters. Theologians feel that the word *mystery* supplies them with a triumphant ace, while philosophers regard the same word as a coded admission of defeat, another contribution to the 'fog of mysteries'.

The Trinity

The doctrine that God has three *persons* (Father, Son, and Holy Ghost) arose through a series of deductions based on the teachings of St Paul and his followers. For example, if we accept the premise that Christ was divine, along with the premise that there is only one God, we are driven to the conclusion that Christ and God are in some way the same. A similar argument concerning the Holy Ghost, applied at a later date, led to the conclusion that the Holy Ghost and God were also the same. There are a number of ways in which these conclusions could be accommodated.

The obvious conclusion is that God, Christ and the Holy Ghost are identical. In other words *Father, Son* and *Holy Ghost* are alternative names for the same being. This conclusion was rejected, apparently because the Bible shows the Father, Son and Holy Ghost to have different physical manifestations, to fulfil separate functions, and to have different levels of understanding. A second possible explanation is that God reveals himself in one of three different ways at different times. Some Christians adopted this explanation, but others rejected it. Those who accepted it (Sabellians, Patripassions, or Modal Monarchianists) were persecuted out of existence in the fifth century, although the Eastern Churches would accuse the Western Church of Sabellian heresies for centuries to come. A related idea was that the three persons of the Trinity represented three different aspects of God. For example Pierre Abélard identified the Father, Son and Holy Ghost as Power, Wisdom and Goodness respectively. A third solution is to reject one of the premises. Either there was more than one God, or Christ was only a man after all and whatever the Holy Ghost was, it was not divine. Some people adopted these explanations. Tritheists, who believed in three separate Gods, were eliminated by the sixth century. Arians, who believed that Christ was not as exalted as the Father, were enormously influential in the fourth century and almost became the principal (i.e. orthodox) line, but were eventually defeated. Macedonians denied the godhead of the Holy Ghost and were also eliminated.

The compromise eventually adopted was that God has one *substance* but three *persons*. Whether or not this statement actually means anything is open to doubt. Certainly it is difficult to see what the word *person* means in this usage. And the position was no better in the original formulation of the doctrine in Greek. Fierce arguments raged for centuries over the minute differences between alternative Greek words used in early formulations of the doctrine.*

---

* The Arian dispute boiled down to whether to use the word *homoousion* (of one substance with) or *homoiusion* (of like substance to) to describe the relationship between the Son and the Father. Thus the gibe that 'Christendom was convulsed by a diphthong'.

Like so much Christian doctrine the concept of the Trinity seems to be unintelligible to anyone who does not already believe in it (and indeed it seems to be unintelligible to many who do). It is not at all clear what it can possibly mean for the Trinity to represent a single godhead. The statement that *God has one substance but three persons* looks superficially like a meaningful statement, but until someone succeeds in expounding this meaning we have no reason to suppose that it signifies any more than the assertion that *colourless green ideas sleep furiously*.

It is as though there are really three separate gods, but in order to maintain a fiction of monotheism, they are said to represent a single godhead. By analogy it would be possible to contend that the gods of, say, ancient Greece were really representations of a single deity. The fact that each so-called god had a separate manifestation, a separate role, and a separate intelligence, would be of no consequence. They would be, as the argument might run, simply different aspects of a single natural universal force, in other words different facets of the same god. Clearly it would be possible to apply a similar argument to any religion and prove it to be monotheistic. Indeed some ancient Greek philosophers did argue that their religion was monotheistic, despite its extensive pantheon. Some modern Hindus make similar claims for their religion, again despite its extensive pantheon. Such arguments would be as satisfactory, or unsatisfactory, as the one presented to support Christianity's claim to monotheism, at least so far as the Trinity is concerned.

For many philosophers it is tempting to conclude that the concept of a three-in-one deity is no more than a linguistic deceit, devised to reconcile the fact that Christianity makes contradictory claims. These claims are that on the one hand there is only one God, and on the other that there are three Gods: God the Father, God the Son, and God the Holy Spirit. This contradiction is another *mystery*.

Transubstantiation

The doctrine of transubstantiation originates from a description of Jesus' actions and words at the Last Supper (the gospels disagree about his exact words):

> And as they were eating, Jesus took bread, and blessed it, and brake it, and gave it to the disciples, and said, Take, eat; this is my body. And he took the cup, and gave thanks, and gave it to them, saying,

> Drink ye all of it; For this is my blood of the new testament, which is shed for many for the remission of sins. (Matthew 26:26–8, cf. Mark 14:22–4, Luke 22:19–20)

This phraseology appears to suggest that, at least at that particular meal, the bread and wine changed into Jesus' flesh and blood.* However, this seems unlikely in view of the fact that Jesus was still there at the meal, and presumably still clothed in his human flesh. A possible explanation is that in most Middle Eastern languages (notably Aramaic) there is no easy way of distinguishing between the statements 'A is B' and 'A is like B' or 'A represents B'. So, even assuming that Jesus did utter the words reported, it seems likely that he intended a figurative interpretation. In any case, one might have thought that the correct interpretation could be discovered easily enough for later re-enactments of the Last Supper: if at the Eucharist the bread and wine was transformed so that it looked and tasted like flesh and blood then a conversion had taken place. If it continued to look and taste like bread and wine, then these items were merely tokens, and the act purely symbolic. No chemical change has ever been shown to take place, so the obvious conclusion is that they are indeed mere tokens, and the words are to be interpreted figuratively. Medieval Christian scholars chose to ignore this conclusion and formulated a theory that depended upon concepts used by Aristotle and other ancient Greek philosophers.

A distinction was made between on the one hand the *substance* of the bread and wine, which they said was changed into flesh and blood, and on the other the so-called *accidents* (or outward appearance), which they said remained unchanged. This encapsulates the doctrine of transubstantiation as declared by the Fourth Lateran Council in 1215. Unfortunately, later philosophers pulled the rug from under this doctrine, for the distinction between *accidents* and *substance* was recognised as illusory and unhelpful. At the Reformation the Protestant Churches took the pragmatic view that the Eucharist was purely symbolic. The doctrine of transubstantiation was rejected by most Protestants and by

---

* Some scholars believe that these words were added to texts at a relatively late date, and that the whole idea is copied from contemporary religions. For present purposes we are only interested in the meaning of the words, whenever they were written, whoever wrote them, and for whatever reason.

the Church of England (see Article 28 of the 39 Articles of the Anglican Church). The Orthodox Churches have skirted around it. Lutherans and some other Christians tried for a compromise, asserting that the substance of the bread coexisted with Christ's flesh, and the substance of the wine coexisted with his blood. This idea is called consubstantiation. It is open to much the same criticism as transubstantiation, in that it depends upon philosophical concepts that are no longer respectable.

The Roman Catholic Church is still committed to its position of 1215 – a position that philosophers and semiologists regard with some bemusement. It is rather as if a man were to claim that his pet rabbit had been transformed into a fish. He freely concedes that it still looks and behaves like a rabbit. It still breathes air and would drown in water. It is fond of lettuce and carrots. It will breed with other rabbits. Its skeleton is like that of other rabbits. No conceivable test will reveal it to be anything other than a rabbit, even if its molecular structure is examined in the finest detail. Yet the man persists in claiming that it is really a fish, and he holds that only its outward appearance is that of a rabbit. He concedes that the animal looks like a rabbit, but asserts that at some deeper level it is really a fish. What he is doing is disregarding what it means to be called a rabbit. He is ignoring the accepted meaning of the word *rabbit*, for *rabbit* is the noun applied to animals with certain characteristics, just as *fish* is the noun applied to animals with certain other characteristics. He is either unwittingly deceiving himself or consciously trying to deceive others. Either way, he is relying upon an elementary trick with words and would be unlikely to convince many ordinary people that his pet had merely the appearance of a rabbit and that its real, but mysteriously hidden, nature was that of a fish.

The Atonement
The doctrine of the atonement asserts that Christ's death reconciled humankind to God. The idea is that Original Sin, and other sin, is an insult to God. Any crime against God is so serious that it deserves eternal punishment. Guilt for such crimes is so great that it cannot be expiated by human beings themselves. To wash away this guilt requires that God himself (in Christ) must suffer and die through sacrifice, and this expiation is not merely sufficient, but more than sufficient to redeem humanity.

In the Middle Ages, at a time when the law frequently required compensation to be paid to expiate a crime, theologians saw the atonement as a sort of compensation paid to God.* Today, the sacrifice is often seen merely as an example to mankind. For our purpose the important point is that theologians almost invariably refer to the Atonement as though there were some sort of conventional causal relationship: 'Christ died *in order to* save us', 'We are saved *through* the blood of Christ', 'We are redeemed *because* Christ was crucified', and so on. These formulations link two statements of the essential meaning 'Christ was killed' and 'We are saved'. If they did so with a conjunction such as *'and'* there would be no problem because both elements stand alone, the first part as a matter of fact, and the second a matter of faith. By employing the word *'therefore'* instead of *'and'* the position is changed completely. 'Christ was killed, *therefore* we are saved' appears to confirm a matter of faith by reference to a matter of fact. To take an example that shows up the flaw more clearly: if we were reliably informed that Mr Smith had died, and if we accept that cabbages are green, we could accurately state that *cabbages are green and Mr Smith is dead* but we should be unwise to formulate the proposition that *cabbages are green therefore Mr Smith is dead*. Only if we could establish a causal link would we be justified in making such a statement.

Of course, none of this establishes that there might not be a causal relationship in propositions about the Atonement but, if there were, we might reasonably expect to hear about this causal relationship. If Christian theologians elect to give their teachings the form of rational arguments, then we expect to hear a clear formulation of their reasoning. As it is, we have only disjointed statements that mimic the form of rational arguments, and, to make matters worse, appear to contradict everyday experience. It is difficult to see exactly what was achieved by the death of Jesus, for the world seems to have been much the same after the crucifixion as it was before. If Jesus came to eliminate sin, he does not seem to have been altogether successful. Also, if self-sacrifice is so potent, why do other voluntary sacrifices have so little effect? Many men and women have sacrificed their lives in much more testing circumstances than those experienced by Jesus. Moreover they have often done so to save a single child, or a friend, or even a stranger. Why are their sacrifices not more

---

* If Christ's sacrifice provided superabundant restitution, it is not clear why anyone should ever be condemned to Hell since the crucifixion – but this is a different problem.

potent? Objectively, they are more impressive than that of Jesus, for the people involved have no certainty of eternal life as we are told Jesus had. Indeed, many are quite convinced that their sacrifice will mean the total and absolute end of their existence. No doubt the fact that Christ was also God incarnate was a significant factor, but its relevance has never been explained. Without an explanation, one could reasonably deduce that linking statements together in such a way as to suggest a causal link is another form of what A. J. Ayer called *cheating*.

The misuse of conjunctions such as *because, therefore, so* and *consequently* is common in sermons, hymns and theological discourses. Such words may sometimes be seen as vehicles for misleading the unwary into drawing invalid conclusions from premises, even when these premises are themselves valid.

The New Theology

My dear child, you must believe in God in spite of what the clergy tell you.
Benjamin Jowett (1817–93), quoted in
Margo Asquith's autobiography

For many hundreds of years there was no doubt at all that Christian doctrines were to be interpreted literally, just as the Bible was to be interpreted literally. To suggest otherwise was blasphemous and heretical. Christian doctrines were not allegories, they were strict literal truth, and anyone who denied this central truth was a criminal. The Anglican Church, when it was established, adopted the traditional line and its Articles of Religion were explicit about the matter. They were prefaced by a declaration by the King, the Supreme Governor of the Anglican Church, insisting that the articles were to be accepted in full and read in their ordinary senses. For each he required that

> ... no man hereafter shall either print, or preach, to draw the Article aside any way, but shall submit to it in the plain and full meaning thereof: and shall not put his own sense or comment to be the meaning of the Article, but shall take it in the literal and grammatical sense.

Belief in the literal truth of all manner of things (the infallibility of the Bible, the Virgin Birth, the Resurrection, etc.) were all once absolutely necessary to the faith. Anyone who did not believe them could not possibly be a Christian. Today, however, they are widely disputed, even in relatively conservative quarters.

The problem is that for many people the texts, if read literally, are simply unbelievable. Generally the solution is to abandon the literal interpretation and to find an alternative interpretation. Thus for example, God has changed from a supernatural being who looked like Zeus – a gigantic old man, sporting a long white beard, dressed in white and sitting on a throne in the sky – into an increasingly vague abstraction. For critics, the problem with increasingly abstract concepts is that they do not provide good targets, and the suspicion is that God has become more and more abstract for exactly this reason – the old man in the sky was too easy a target. Here is Sigmund Freud's opinion on the state of God's transition in 1927, when theologians were still considered to be philosophers:

> Where questions of religion are concerned people are guilty of every possible kind of insincerity and intellectual misdemeanour. Philosophers stretch the meaning of words until they retain scarcely anything of their original sense; by calling 'God' some vague abstraction which they have created for themselves, they pose as deists, as believers, before the world; they may even pride themselves on having attained a higher and purer idea of God, although their God is nothing but an insubstantial shadow and no longer the mighty personality of religious doctrine.[122]

During the second half of the twentieth century God became more abstract still. Now he/she is asexual and defined as the 'ground of our being', the 'depth of our life', the 'ultimate reality', or even the 'one in whom existence is completely transparent to essence'. God is not unintelligible but 'superintelligible'. The terms sound grand but are, as far as disinterested observers can tell, entirely devoid of meaning. No one seems to be able to explain what any of these descriptions mean, though they are now the common currency of theologians.[123] As one observer has noted of the more general problem of religious beliefs, 'If postulates are to be unquestionable, it is important that they be incomprehensible.'[124]

The Devil, like God, has also become increasingly abstract. Few people in Europe believe in a personal Devil, and theologians now say that the concept is only a sort of analogy, personifying evil. It therefore came as rather a shock to many of the faithful, and indeed made newspaper headlines, when Pope John Paul II announced in the 1990s that he still believed in such a being. Fifty years earlier the Pope would merely have been confirming what all Christians knew. By the 1990s his traditionalist views of Satan and his realm seemed unusual. Many Christians had abandoned the idea of his Satanic Majesty ruling over a kingdom of eternal torture. The idea of a God of infinite mercy allowing such a thing did not fit modern tastes. It turns out that making God into a sadistic monster responsible for Satan and Hell was not merely mistaken but, according to Anglicans, it was blasphemous.[125] Again it turns out that the soul is not to be understood in the traditional way, but as the 'information-bearing pattern of the body', which might be held in the mind of God after death. Again, Christians always used to know that religious doubt pointed the road to certain damnation: 'He that doubteth is damned' (Romans 14:23). Now bishops and archbishops assure us that doubt is not only permissible, it is an essential part of faith! By redefining words like *devil, Hell, faith* and *damnation* it is possible to make traditional texts mean exactly the opposite of what they originally meant.

Traditional affirmations of belief are routinely ignored. The fourth of the 39 Articles of the Anglican Church asserts that Christ ascended 'with flesh and bones' and that he is now sitting in Heaven, yet the Archbishop of Canterbury's Commission on Doctrine declared in 1962 that such descriptions are 'to be interpreted symbolically'. In the past it was universally held that the Bible was literally infallible. A few Christians still believe this, but most have long abandoned such beliefs. On the other hand, if the word infallible can be redefined so that it means something new and sufficiently abstract, even modern scholars can agree that the Bible is infallible. Here is an extract from the preface of the NIV:

> ...the translators were united in their commitment to the authority and infallibility of the Bible as God's Word in written form.

Taken at face value this statement is wholly inconsistent with the footnotes that these same translators have provided to their translation, so the word *infallible* is presumably to be understood in some mysterious, figurative way. This seems to be another case of manipulating words to paper over controversial cracks. It sounds as though the translators are faithful to the traditional line, accepting the infallibility of the Bible, which keeps the masses happy. In truth they share the scholarly consensus, and their statement means something quite different. We cannot know exactly what they do mean because we cannot know what the word *infallible* means in this context – whatever it means it does not preclude the translators noting hundreds of imperfections in 'God's Word'.

When the Bible was read literally, Christians knew that they could be healed of any illness. The Bible promised it:

> Is any sick among you? Let him call for elders of the church; and let him pray over him, anointing him with oil in the name of the Lord: And the prayer of faith shall save the sick, and the Lord shall raise him up; and if he have committed sins, they shall be forgiven him. (James 5:14–15)

Prayer would effect a cure, the patient would get up out of bed, and if the illness were caused by sin (rather than by demons) then the sin would be forgiven. But how to explain the fact that many sick people died, however much praying went on? Evidently the assurance was false, or priests and bishops did not qualify as genuine Church elders. However, if we re-interpret the words, we do not have to make such an admission. By assigning new meanings to 'save the sick' and 'raise him up' it is possible to make the sentence mean something completely different – nothing at all to do with healing the sick, but rather a matter of spiritual salvation. The passage cited above is the justification for the 'extreme unction' (last rites) given by the Roman Church to those believed to be dying. Almost all of those believed to be dying do indeed die soon afterwards, and no one notices that this contradicts the original meaning of the biblical assurance, because it is now taken to mean something else.

The biblical account of the Second Coming is now something of an embarrassment. Certainly a straightforward, literal interpretation is unacceptable to many. The Bible says repeatedly that Jesus will descend from the skies, surrounded by clouds, and that everyone will see him, just as people saw him ascend into Heaven. Here for example is one assurance:

For the Lord himself shall descend from heaven with a shout, with the voice of the archangel, and with the trump of God: and the dead in Christ shall rise first: Then we which are alive and remain shall be caught up together with them in the clouds, to meet the Lord in the air... (1 Thessalonians 4:16–17)

According to the Church of England such passages 'are not intended to provide literal depictions of the event, as though Jesus were a space traveller returning to Earth. They refer, in the far more profound language of biblical imagery, to the manifestation in this world of that which is already true of Jesus Christ in Heaven'.[126] This 'profound language of biblical imagery' seems to have escaped earlier believers. All Christian authorities agreed for almost two millennia that Jesus would physically reappear descending from the sky.

The root of the problem is that educated churchmen generally have beliefs far in advance of their flocks. They cannot admit to these views because the faithful masses will not understand and will be left angry and alienated if they were to learn what their priests really believe.[127] Professor Rudolf Bultmann, an early advocate of mythical interpretation of scripture, expressed this clearly when writing about the co-author of his book in 1954:

He is as convinced as I am that a corpse cannot come back to life or rise from the grave, that there are no demons and no magic causality. But how am I, in my capacity as pastor, to explain in my sermons and classes, texts dealing with the resurrection of Jesus in the flesh, with demons, or with magic causality.[128]

This dilemma has been a serious problem for the mainstream Churches since the middle of the nineteenth century. Some clergymen have abandoned their Churches, others have been thrown out for voicing their views. In the more authoritarian Churches clergymen are denied licences to teach, or authority to publish, or even permission to speak out. The more usual solution is for theologians to find a form of words to express their views, which certain people will understand and other people will not. The ones who will understand are generally educated liberals, the ones who will not are the conservative literalists. In this way traditional dogma is not abandoned, it is merely reinterpreted. Statements are no longer literally true, but are valid as somehow 'expressing the faith'.

Christian myths are claimed to embody important truths that cannot otherwise be put into words. This permits Christian Churches to embrace a vast range of views, from those who still believe in the inerrancy of the Bible and literal truth of the Virgin Birth and the Resurrection, to those who regard virtually all supposedly historical aspects as mythological. As one Roman Catholic priest famously put it in 2002, 'Everything in the Bible is true, except the facts'. Usually theologians are more circumspect. Here is an example of scholarly language being used to soften what is really being said. Scholars have long doubted that Jesus claimed many of the titles now attributed to him (King, Saviour, Messiah, God, etc.). Indeed, it is doubtful that he even heard most of them, but it would not do to say so directly. So how can this be admitted without upsetting the faithful? A Christian New Testament scholar who has assessed the significance of Jesus' titles concluded,

> '(a) that the titles and concepts were there to be used before the early Christians adopted them – that is, they can be found in non-Christian documents and with non-Christian interpretations;
>
> (b) that by their application to Jesus they were filled with new content, and new interpretations became inevitable as a new combination of once distinct concepts was made;
>
> (c) the combination was probably the result of believers searching for categories in which to express their response to Jesus, rather than Jesus claiming to be these particular figures; and
>
> (d) each block of writings in the New Testament has its own emphases and combinations, that is, its own christological picture...'[129]

The book from which this is taken was extremely controversial when it was written, but not as controversial as it might have been without the theology-speak. A plain English version might be:

> The titles commonly attributed to Jesus are largely unwarranted. They were appropriated by his early followers from other contemporary uses and their meanings were changed in different ways by different factions to suit their own ends.

Clergymen cannot tell this to their flocks. They would be offended and upset. Many priests therefore join an unofficial conspiracy of silence. In all mainstream Churches there is a convention that priests and ministers do not talk too much about the views of Church scholars, at least not sympathetically. It is not unusual for theologians to proclaim the traditional literalist view when speaking to the faithful masses, and another when speaking to other theologians, who like themselves believe almost no literal truths at all. It is for example common for senior theologians to affirm the Virgin Birth in public, and to deny it (and even ridicule it) in private. The phenomenon is not new. In the early fifth century a respected philosopher called Synesius was chosen as Bishop of Alexandria. He accepted on condition that he might 'speak in myths' in church, and that he would still be free to 'think like a philosopher' in private. Synesius was not even a Christian.

How far modern theology has moved away from the straightforward literal language of early Christians is demonstrated by a theological parody, which puts the words of modern theologians into the mouth of an apostle:

> Jesus said to them 'But whom say ye that I am?'. And Peter answereth and saith unto him 'Thou art the eschatological manifestation of the ground of our being, in the kerygma of which we find the ultimate meaning in our interpersonal relationships'. (cf. Mark 8:29)

The greatest irony is that the position of modern theologians is similar to that of Greek and Roman priests before the birth of Jesus. Those priests generally came from prestigious families and were well educated. They did not believe literally what their religion taught, but could not say so openly. The priesthood saw religious stories as myths that embodied great truths and were not to be understood literally. They too joined an unofficial conspiracy of silence. The educated elite who staffed the pagan priesthood developed theological ideas remarkably similar to those of modern theologians. Cato wondered that two of them could look each other in the face without laughing.[130]

CASE STUDY A: RE-BRANDING A SKY GOD

Beware the man whose god is in the skies.
George Bernard Shaw, *Man and Superman, Maxims for Revolutionists*

When facts contradict one's favourite beliefs, the choices are stark: one must change one's mind, find some sort of rationalisation, or deny the facts. In this section we will take a single example of a case where Christians are faced with just such a problem. The problem is that God is presented today as wise, kind, gentle, merciful, all-powerful, and all-knowing. Yet the God of the Old Testament is not at all like this. Worse still, he seems to belong to a once-popular class of gods called sky gods, whose characteristics appear controversial from a modern moral perspective. How can this be reconciled? First we look at the evidence.

Primitive societies often invented stories to explain aspects of the world that seemed mysterious to them. Indeed, almost all cultures have generated such stories. The ones most familiar to Europeans are those of Classical Greece and Rome, and to a lesser extent those of northern Europe. Their myths sought to explain things such as the origin of mankind, the reason for the existence of evil and suffering, the meaning of natural phenomena, and the origin of language. Invariably these myths called upon gods for explanations.

One of these gods, according to many ancient peoples, was a particularly powerful sky god, responsible for many natural phenomena. Familiar European sky gods include the Greek Zeus, the Roman Jupiter and the Teutonic Tew. Such gods lived in the sky beyond the clouds or on mountain tops. They demanded respect and expected blood sacrifice from humankind. When angry they caused floods, earthquakes or volcanic eruptions. They controlled the weather: they brought the sun and the rain, they concealed themselves behind clouds, their breath was the wind, and their voices thunder. Their weapons were thunderbolts. Despite such great powers, these gods behaved much like human beings. They took human forms, possessed human weaknesses and exhibited human failings. They displayed human duplicity, gullibility, capriciousness, spite and blood lust, and of course they had the same outlook and prejudices as those who invented them.

So which paradigm does the God of the Bible match? Is he a sky god, or is he the beneficent, all-powerful, all-knowing supreme deity of modern theologians? The rest of this section looks a little closer at the God of the Old Testament, with a view to establishing whether he is really a sky god. In particular we will look at the propositions that will help establish his identity, namely that he:

- has a human form and experiences human emotion;
- causes natural phenomena;
- is fallible – neither omnipotent nor omniscient;
- is spectacularly unmerciful;
- appreciates blood sacrifice.

In doing this we will rely on the Bible itself, not because it can be regarded as historically true, but because it reveals the beliefs of the people who wrote it, and also because the evidence adduced can easily be checked. For those who regard the Bible as literally true, the case made will be even stronger.

God Has a Human Form and Experiences Human Emotions

On a number of occasions the Old Testament impresses on us that God has a human form. He is sometimes mistaken for a man, for example in Genesis 18:1–3 and 32:24–32. He is referred to explicitly as a 'man of war' (Exodus 15:3). Old Testament writers refer to his arms, face, nostrils, mouth, lips and eyes. He walks (Genesis 3:8), wrestles (Genesis 32:24–32) and enjoys certain smells (Genesis 8:20–1, Leviticus 1:9, 13 and 17). For fundamentalist Christians none of this is surprising, since man was made in God's image (Genesis 1:27). Neither is it surprising to anthropologists, since sky gods are invariably made in man's image.

In the Bible, God suffers a range of human emotions including love and hate. He experiences pleasure (Leviticus 1 ff.), remorse (Genesis 6:6, Exodus 32:14, 1 Samuel 15:35), grief (Genesis 6:6), anger (Deuteronomy 3:26, 2 Samuel 6:7), and jealousy: '… the Lord, whose name *is* Jealous, *is* a jealous God' (Exodus 34:14). He is also vengeful, even in the New Testament (Romans 12:19).

God Causes Natural Phenomena

God walks Earth's high places and creates the wind (Amos 4:13). He causes other natural phenomena too. In Psalm 18 God is called upon for assistance and makes his presence felt just like Zeus, Jupiter or Tew:

> ...the earth shook and trembled... There went up a smoke out of his nostrils, and fire out of his mouth ...yea, he did fly upon the wings of the wind... The LORD also thundered in the heavens... Yea he sent out his arrows, and scattered them; and he shot out lightnings...

He was responsible for mighty winds, earthquakes and fires (1 Kings 19:11–12). He also caused the flood that killed everyone in the world except a single family. He set his rainbow in the sky and brought the clouds (Genesis 9:13–14). Rays flash from his hand; he scatters mountains and makes the ground tremble (Habakkuk 3:6–10). He lives in the heavens, and tends to make his appearances veiled in clouds and on mountain tops. He kills people by hurling large hailstones down from the sky (Joshua 10:11). When he appears on Earth at ground level, he is generally said to *come down* to it, often from a mountain.[131] One of his biblical names, *Shaddai*, is that of a rain-making mountain god.

That God personally controls the weather is still popularly believed. Christians frequently offer prayers in times of drought or tempest. Even the Anglican Book of Common Prayer still contains prayers for rain and fair weather.

God is Fallible

According to the book of Genesis, God told Adam not to eat of the tree of knowledge of good and evil because 'in the day that thou eatest thereof thou shalt surely die' (Genesis 2:17). This promised not just death, but immediate death. Adam did eat of the tree, yet he did not die that day. He went on to have three sons and lived for 800 years after the birth of the third of them (Genesis 5:4–5). Either God lied, or else he was mistaken. When he wrestled with Jacob (Genesis 32:24–30) God 'prevailed not against him', which is unimpressive for an omnipotent deity. On another occasion he was unable to drive off inhabitants of a valley 'because they had chariots of iron' (Judges 1:19). He was wrong when he said that David had kept his statutes and commandments (1 Kings 11:38), for he should have known that David had broken at least three commandments (he had coveted and seduced the wife of Uriah the Hittite, born false witness, and conspired in causing Uriah to be killed in battle as told in 2 Samuel).

Like any tribal sky god he is also partisan. He is *Yahweh Sabaoth*, the *Lord of Hosts* or *God of Armies*. He fights for Israel. No biblical writer suggests that Israel ought to be fighting for him. Neither are God's plans immutable. By a bit of judicious haggling Abraham induced him to change his mind a number of times (Genesis 18:20–33). Sometimes he is irrational. When Ahab grovels for forgiveness, God decides not to punish him but instead punishes his house (i.e. his family) in the next generation (1 Kings 21:27–9). He also errs. His errors are the only possible reasons for his regret and repentance (e.g. Genesis 6:6, and Exodus 32:14). As a result of Saul's failure to carry out God's genocidal instructions, God repented that he had set up Saul to be king (1 Samuel 15:11).

Neither is the God of the Old Testament omniscient. He called out to Adam to ask where he was (Genesis 3:9). He did not have first-hand knowledge of what was happening in Sodom and Gomorrah, having heard only reports about it (Genesis 18:20–1). He had to 'go down' to see for himself whether the reports were true. In Deuteronomy 8:2, God had to test the Israelites to find out what was in their hearts.

God is Spectacularly Unmerciful

The God of the Old Testament takes an active part in battle. On occasion he kills more of the enemy than the Jews themselves (Joshua 10:11). He killed 185,000 Assyrians in a single night (2 Kings 19:35). He encouraged murder and even genocide. In Numbers 31 for example Midianite married women and male children were slaughtered in accordance with his wishes. Helpless captives, they were killed on the orders of Moses, acting on God's instructions. God arranged for Joshua to kill all that lived in the city of Ai, 12,000 men and women (Joshua 8:1–29). Earlier, he had arranged for Joshua to take Jericho, and on this occasion had wanted absolutely everything destroyed. Joshua therefore killed men and women, young and old, cattle, sheep and donkeys (Joshua 6:15–21). At Dabir, Joshua 'utterly destroyed all that breathed, as the LORD God of Israel commanded' (Joshua 10:40). Generally, when a city was taken, God wanted all the men killed and the women, children, and animals taken as plunder, but in the case of the Hittites, Amorites, Canaanites, Perizzites, Hivites and Jesubites everything that breathed had to be destroyed completely (Deuteronomy 20:10–17).

According to the Bible God killed more than 2,270,971 people, many of them innocent of any wrongdoing, considerably more than the 10 killings attributed to Satan.[132] (God's tally does not count the large but unspecified numbers such as the Flood and Sodom and Gomorrah, nor Satan's 10 for which he was given permission by God).

God often forbids his followers to show pity or mercy (e.g. Deuteronomy 7:2, Ezekiel 9:5–6). Sometimes, God undertakes the mass killing of children himself (Exodus 12:29). Indeed, children have a particularly hard time of it. Not only are they punished for the crimes of their ancestors, but they are also victims of family cannibalism. To people who fail to meet God's requirements he promises that, amongst many other tribulations, they will have to eat their own children (Leviticus 26:29 and Deuteronomy 28:53).

In 1 Samuel 15 God instructs Samuel to tell Saul to wipe out all of the Amalekites. Saul makes the mistake of leaving their king, Agag, alive. God is not pleased by this act of mercy and Samuel has to complete the job as instructed. Although Agag was now a helpless captive 'Samuel hewed Agag in pieces before the LORD...' On another occasion 70,000 innocent people were killed by God for the unlikely reason that David had taken a census of fighting men (2 Samuel 24:1–15, cf. 1 Chronicles 21:1–14). God's punishments are astonishingly vicious. When a group of boys made fun of Elisha's baldness, Elisha cursed them in the name of God, and immediately 42 of them were torn to pieces savaged by bears (2 Kings 2:23–4).The author of the psalm that begins 'By the rivers of Babylon ...' entertained no doubt that God will be happy for his chosen people to dash enemy babies against the rocks (Psalm 137:7–9).

Actions that would seem to most people to be justified may incur severe penalties. For example, a woman who tries to help her husband in a fight by grabbing his opponent by the genitals is to have her hand cut off (Deuteronomy 25:11–12). Muslim-style mutilations are not only permissible, but also mandatory according to the biblical God. He also has some curious scatological tendencies. According to Ezekiel 4:12 God instructed Israelites to bake their food with human excrement, though this was later commuted to cow dung. Malachi 2:3 quotes God as saying 'Behold, I will corrupt your seed, and spread dung upon your faces...'[133]

God also finds it quite acceptable to punish the innocent. He says as part of the second commandment that he will punish the children, grandchildren, and great grandchildren of those who offend him (Exodus 20:4–5 and Deuteronomy 5:8–9, confirmed in Exodus 34:7). And he does so too. A famine caused by God because Saul had killed the Gibeonites was lifted only after seven of Saul's descendants had been handed over and executed by Gibeonite survivors (2 Samuel 21:1–14). Again it is not David, but David's sons who die for a crime of their father's (contriving the death of Uriah). Killing children for the sins of their fathers is perfectly acceptable to God – 'Prepare slaughter for his children for the iniquity of their fathers...' (Isaiah 14:21). God seems to have no concept of justice as we now understand it. For example, he kills Uzzah on the spot, merely for taking hold of the ark of the covenant, even though Uzzah apparently did so for the most innocent of reasons (the oxen pulling it had stumbled – 2 Samuel 6:6–7).

God requires the death penalty for a range of offences. Among them:

- blasphemy (i.e. profaning the divine name) (Leviticus 24:16)
- bestiality (both parties) (Exodus 22:19, Leviticus 20:15)
- homosexuality (Leviticus 20:13)
- pre-marital sex (women only) (Deuteronomy 22:20–1)
- adultery (Deuteronomy 22:22 and Leviticus 20:10)
- wizardry (Leviticus 20:27)
- witchcraft (or poisoning or making potions, depending on the translation) (Exodus 22:18)
- spiritualism (Leviticus 20:27)
- making sacrifices to other gods (Exodus 22:20)
- worshipping other gods, or heavenly objects (Deuteronomy 17:2–5)
- cursing one's parents (Exodus 21:17, Leviticus 20:9)
- being a stubborn and rebellious son (Deuteronomy 21:18–21)
- desecrating the Sabbath (Exodus 31:14)

Moses hesitated when a man was brought to him for gathering sticks on the Sabbath, but God had no doubt about what should happen to him. He instructed Moses to have the man stoned to death (Numbers

15:32–6). By Jesus' time, many Jews already regarded this as barbarous, and the law was widely considered to have been somehow repealed, but this does not change what the Bible says about God.

God Appreciates Blood Sacrifice

It is clear from the Old Testament that God expects blood sacrifices. That he prefers animal sacrifice to agricultural sacrifices is clear from the story of Cain and Abel (Genesis 4:1–8). God was pleased with Abel's animal sacrifice but not with Cain's crop sacrifice. This was the reason for Cain's jealousy, which led him to murder his brother.

As in many primitive religions, God wanted blood. Blood was far more important than the flesh. It was the life force, the seat of life itself (Genesis 9:4, Leviticus 17:11). Anyone might eat the flesh but the blood belonged to God himself. It was for this reason that the Jews thought it wrong to drink blood or to consume it with the flesh. Great efforts were (and still are) made to drain the blood from animals killed for food.

The point that God prefers animal sacrifices is reinforced when God lists the types of animal that are suitable as sacrificial offerings (Leviticus 1–2). He confirms his position again:

> And the Lord called unto Moses, and spake unto him out of the tabernacle of the congregation, saying, Speak unto the children of Israel, and say unto them, If any man of you bring an offering unto the Lord, ye shall bring your offering of the cattle, even of the herd, and of the flock. (Leviticus 1:1–2)

The details given are rather gory, involving killing, sprinkling blood, disembowelling, dismemberment, and then burning the remains. God repeatedly makes the point that this must be done in front of him, and that he likes the smell of the burned flesh. Referring to Noah's mass animal sacrifice, Genesis 8:20–2 tells us that 'the LORD smelled the pleasing odour'. On occasion God took an active part in sacrifices. In 1 Kings 18:17–40 Elijah calls upon God to show his power by sending down lightning to consume a sacrificial bull and a huge libation. God obliges and, in triumph, Elijah causes 450 rival prophets of Baal to be slaughtered.

Although he generally expected animal sacrifices, God did not seem to be averse to the occasional human one. Human sacrifice does not seem to be unequivocally prohibited anywhere in the Old Testament.[134] According to the book of Judges, Jephthah killed his only child in fulfilment of a promise made to God (Judges 11:29–40). As the narrative points out God was taking a personal interest in Jephthah at the time yet he did not attempt to stop him. Nor was Jephthah regarded as acting excessively. He was well regarded as a judge and was mentioned with approval in the New Testament.[135]

Some biblical passages look as though they have been mistranslated to disguise their true meaning. Leviticus 27:29 for example appears rather cryptic: 'None devoted, which shall be devoted of men, shall be redeemed; but shall surely be put to death'. The Hebrew word translated as *devoted* here really denotes the irrevocable giving over to God, generally by complete destruction. When the word is applied to animals it combines the concepts of sacrifice and total annihilation, but here it is being applied to both animals and humans. Exodus 22:29–30 (cf. 13:1–13 and 34:19–20) seems to leave no doubt:

> ...The firstborn of thy sons shalt thou give unto me. Likewise shalt thou do with thine oxen, and with thy sheep...

An episode described in Exodus 4:19–26 may suggest that circumcision is a substitute for human sacrifice, but the meaning is not at all clear. Even when God declined a human sacrifice as a burned offering he seemed to need an appropriate substitute such as a ram, as in the case of Abraham and Isaac (Genesis 22:13).

Biblical characters certainly understood that God had required human sacrifice, though they were not sure exactly why, or in what circumstances.[136] As society progressed, people were puzzled as to why God had required human sacrifice and developed stories as to how the requirement could be commuted. Thus for firstborn children and for firstborn unclean animals, one is expected to pay a ransom or redemption fee of five shekels instead of killing them (Numbers 18:15–16). (The Christian Church later found an alternative interpretation, namely that people ought to give their first or second born child to the service of the Church.)

It now seems primitive and absurd that God might require human sacrifice, but the idea was well accepted in medieval times. Heretics were burned as 'a fiery offering and propitiation to God' as one chronicler put it.[137] Priests and Flagellants encouraged the extermination of Jews specifically to placate God and avert the Black Death. As late as the eighteenth century, Christians were executing their enemies as sacrifices to God. The great Lisbon earthquake, for example, was followed by a burst of ecclesiastically inspired executions intended to appease him. It was this human sacrifice, as much as the earthquake itself, that inspired Voltaire to write *Candide*.

* * *

In summary, the God of the Old Testament behaves much like a human being. He has a human form, suffers human weaknesses and displays human failings. He lives in remote high places and controls the elements. He is astonishingly partisan and brutal by modern standards, with a taste for blood sacrifice. He is capricious, spiteful, bloodthirsty, and he had the same outlook and prejudices as Jews who lived 3,000 to 2,500 years ago. We might also note that he has no objection to capital or corporal punishment, genocide, mutilation, polygamy, concubinage, slavery or racism. Indeed he encourages all of them. By modern standards he veers between the immoral and amoral, and bears no resemblance at all to the merciful, omniscient and omnipotent God favoured by modern theologians. All in all, the God of the Old Testament is a perfect example of an ancient tribal sky god.

How do Christians reconcile their merciful, omniscient and omnipotent God with this monster depicted in the Old Testament? One solution is simply to ditch the Old Testament, as many early Christians did, and more recent deists have done. Another solution is to claim that the God of the Old Testament who created the world is not a supreme god, but a flawed subsidiary god – this was the solution adopted by Gnostics, Manichæans, Cathars and Jehovah's Witnesses. A third is to claim that God showed to humankind a face that matched their stage of human development, but this is not a satisfactory solution when the pagan Greeks were far in advance of God's chosen people in their understanding of ethics, morality, philosophy and so on. Another problem for this last explanation is that human mental abilities have changed little in the last 5,000 years, so ancient peoples were as capable as modern Christians of appreciating the God of the modern theologians.

The remaining option is to ignore the facts. The offending passages are not read in church, God's many failings are not taught to children, and awkward questions are dismissed with the answer that it is a divine mystery. The same carefully selected passages are cited over and over again to portray an acceptable picture of God. So it is that most Christians have not the slightest inkling that their God was ever anything like the one depicted in the Old Testament.

CASE STUDY B: MAKING ONE GOD OUT OF MANY

All men have need of gods.
Homer (*c*.900 BC), *Odyssey*

Some early Christians believed in more than one god. Some believed in two, some in three, some in thirty, some in 365, and some in even more.[138] In time the orthodox view came to be that there was only one god. The others had to be tidied away.

Like its close relatives Judaism and Islam, Christianity experienced some difficulty in tidying away its supernumerary gods. It may seem obvious that the clean up was completed long ago, and that the question has now been settled. In fact, matters are not quite so simple. It is indisputable that Christianity has claimed since the early centuries that it is monotheistic. But the fact that a religion purports to be monotheistic is no guarantee that it is. Mainstream Christian Churches accept the existence of a range of superhuman beings who might be regarded as candidates for godhead. The following is a brief review of some of them.

God the Father
It is an uncomfortable fact for Jews and Christians alike that the God of the Old Testament is not a single god, but an amalgam of many gods. This is reflected in the large number of names attributed to him (see page 28), most of which are glossed over in translations of the Bible. The most common name, *Yahweh*, probably means something like *he who is*, or *he who calls into being*, but it is possible that the name was adapted from that of a Samarian goddess. An error in translation of this

word gave us the name Jehovah. A related form, *Jah*, is also found in biblical poetry. *Hallelu Jah*, or *hallelujah*, means literally *praise Jah*.

Another divine name found in the original Hebrew is *El*, meaning *the powerful one, the ruler*, or *god*. It is found as part of many biblical names, for example *Israel* (who sees El), *Gabriel* (might of El), *Emmanuel* (El with us), *Michael* (who is like El), *Samuel* (asked of El) and *Daniel* (judgement of El). The name *Elijah* (Jah is my god) incorporates both *Jah* and *El*. *El* was originally the name of a Phoenician and Canaanite god, the father of other gods, including Baal. Etymologically the name is related to the Arabic name for God, *Allah*.

Eloah is the name for God used in the book of Job. In a different form, *Elohim*, it occurs elsewhere in the Bible some 3,000 times. The *-im* ending is a masculine plural. In other words this is the name not of a single god, but at least two. Elsewhere God reportedly refers to himself in the plural. When he decided to make human beings he said 'Let us make man in our image, after our likeness...' (Genesis 1:26). After Adam ate the forbidden fruit God said 'Behold, the man is become as one of us...' (Genesis 3:22), which suggests that he is addressing at least one other god. Again, in Psalm 95:3 he is described as a great King above all gods. Elsewhere he says 'Thou shalt not revile the gods' (Exodus 22:28).

The name *Shaddai* is used over 300 times in the Bible. It originally denoted a sky god. The name meant something like *he who lives on the mountain tops* or *rain-maker*. *Elyon* was the name of another god, a name that had previously been used of an ancient Canaanite deity. *Sabaoth* is yet another one, usually found in the compound *Yahweh-Sabaoth*, meaning *Lord of Hosts*, which is how it is usually translated. It signifies a great military leader and protector in war. On occasion a divinity appears as the *captain of the hosts of the Lord* (see Joshua 5:13–15), and there are yet other divine characters conventionally identified with God in order to reduce the number of divinities around: the *Ancient of Days* for example in Daniel 7:13. The *angel of the Lord* is sometimes identified with God (Judges 6:11–24) but is sometimes distinct (Genesis 24:7). Occasionally the fact that various divine characters are distinct is made explicit. For example according to Habakkuk 3:3 *Eloah* was coming from Teman as the *Holy One* was coming from Mount Paran.

The fact that God is really a confabulation of many gods is usually explained away by saying that there is only one God with a number of different titles. The plural forms are explained either by invoking a hypothesis that God spoke of himself in a manner akin to the royal *We* – which also requires that he was in the habit of talking to himself – or alternatively that it was God the father talking to the other two persons of the Trinity. Neither explanation confronts the explicit mention of other gods.

God the Son

Christians seem to have had difficulty in convincing non-Christians that they believed in only one god. Early Christians felt obliged to answer charges of polytheism. As one philosopher observed:

> If these men worshipped no other God but one, perhaps they would have a valid argument against the others. But in fact they worship to an extravagant degree this man who appeared recently.[139]

The doctrines of the Incarnation and the Trinity were developed specifically to explain how two or three gods could be regarded as one, but the explanation did not satisfy all Christians in the fourth century, when they were developed, and do not satisfy all Christians today.

Christians asked how Christ could be co-equal and co-eternal with the Father when the Bible provided clear evidence to the contrary. The Bible referred to the Father alone as God: 'And this is life eternal, that they might know thee the only true God, and Jesus Christ, whom thou hast sent' (John 17:3). It is clear that the Father and Son are quite separate and that the Father had created the Son.[140] Contrary to modern dogma, Christ was clearly described as inferior to the Father: '... for my Father is greater than I' (John 14:28). Specifically, the Son does not know everything that God the Father knows (Matthew 24:36). Again, the Son is fallible. He could not even work a minor miracle on one occasion. He needed help when tempted. He grew in wisdom, which means that he cannot always have been all-wise, as the Father was. He said that he did not know when the world would end, this information being available only to the Father (Mark 13:32). He suffered un-godlike passions, being tired and thirsty at the well in Samaria and weeping at Lazarus's tomb. Also, the Son has a separate physical manifestation: in Heaven he sits at the right hand of the Father. Elsewhere in the Bible, the Father has authority in commanding the Son, and the Son even prays to the Father.

Such considerations led many Christians to conclude that Jesus Christ could not have been divine. Others held that he was divine, but inferior to the Father. The line that eventually triumphed simply ignored the Bible texts and held that the Son was co-equal with the Father. To many this looked like the Father and Son were two gods.

A further complication was how to accommodate the concept of the *Word* (*logos*). The stoic idea of each human being having a *logos* (soul) could easily be extended so that Jesus possessed not just any old *logos* but the divine *logos*, the 'Word of God'. By the time of Jesus, the idea of a divine *logos* was familiar to both Jews and Stoic philosophers. Some Christians thought that the divine *Word* (*logos*) occupied the role of Jesus' soul, though this line was later to be condemned as heretical. A different view eventually became orthodox, that Jesus Christ was the *Word* (*logos*) incarnate. This idea is characteristic of the gospel ascribed to John: 'In the beginning was the Word, and the Word was with God, and the Word was God' (John 1:1), which incidentally could also be rendered 'In the beginning was the *logos*. The *logos* accompanied a god, and the *logos* was a god'.

For present purposes we will ignore the difficulties implicit in the orthodox conception of the person of Christ, but the distinction between *God the Father* and *God the Son* is a more significant problem.

The Holy Ghost

The Holy Ghost is not mentioned in the Old Testament, but plays a large part in the New. Little is known about the nature of it (or *him*, or *her*).

The John gospel also refers to a *Paraclete*, a word that is generally translated as *Comforter* or *Counsellor*, and this is identified with the Holy Ghost (John 14:26). The status of the Holy Ghost posed a problem for centuries. If it was a god then Christianity could be accused of having three gods, as indeed it was. The solution that emerged was that God the Father, God the Son, and God the Holy Ghost are all the same God, of one substance but three persons. As we have already seen (pages 136–7) the meaningfulness of the concept of the Trinity is open to doubt. Some Christians, many Muslims, most philosophers, Unitarians and Deists, and almost all non-believers regard the doctrine as a thin disguise for polytheism.

Divine Personifications

It is not unusual for attributes of gods to be personified as semi-independent divinities in their own right: the 'power of god', the 'energy of god', the 'idea of god', the 'glory of god', the 'wisdom of god'. The Egyptians had long accepted such ideas:

> To Thoth was ascribed the mental powers of Ra, and, indeed, the dicta of Ra seem to have come from his lips. He was the Divine Speech personified.[141]

Such personifications were popular in the Middle East and several of them were adapted into Christianity. As we have just seen, the *logos* or *Word of God*, was personified as the *Word*, and the *spirit of God* was personified as the *Holy Spirit*. Both were incorporated into the Christian Trinity. The *Might of God* became a lesser being, the angel whom we know as *Gabriel*. There were others too: for example the *Power of God*, the *Energy of God*, the *Grace of God*, the *Wisdom of God* and the *Prudence of God*.

> I Wisdom dwell with Prudence, and find out knowledge of witty inventions (Proverbs 8:12, AV, but with names capitalised as in modern translations)

In Jewish writing Wisdom was personified in the manner of a goddess. This is most striking in Proverbs 3:19 and 8:22ff, which were cited to show that Wisdom had existed since the beginning of time. Indeed, she helped God to create the world (Proverbs 8:22 and Wisdom of Solomon 7:22–8:1). She was known as the *Holy Wisdom*, just as God's spirit was known as the *Holy Spirit*. She came within a hair's breadth of acknowledged Godhead by the same route as God's word and God's spirit. As Sophia (Greek for wisdom) Gnostics regarded her as a divine emanation, but the faction now considered orthodox was confused about her. Some represented her as incarnate in Christ. St Paul, for example, described Jesus by her title, the *wisdom of God* (1 Corinthians 1:24), and other writers explicitly identified her by what came to be Jesus Christ's title, the *Word of God*. Yet others identified her as the Holy Spirit, the *spirit of God*. She featured in early attempts to define a Christian Trinity, but was eventually dropped, possibly because of her sex.

However she was seen, she was enormously important. For over 900 years, until the Muslims took it in 1453, the greatest church in

Christendom was the Church of the Holy Wisdom in Constantinople. Now Wisdom is something of an embarrassment, especially in the Western Church. She even has her name spelled with a small w. Often her name is kept in Greek: *Hagia Sophia* or translated as *Sancta Sophia*, so that most Western Christians who have heard of her assume her to be merely St Sophia. Stories were created in the Middle Ages to explain why Sophia had been canonised. According to the *Golden Legend* she was a woman who won her sainthood by witnessing the martyrdom of her three daughters, saints Faith, Hope and Charity.

The Devil

The Devil was a relatively late entrant into Jewish theology, from where he was incorporated into Christianity. Our concept of the Devil is essentially the one originally borrowed by the Jews from Zoroastrianism. He seems to have been adopted as a personal entity during the Babylonian Exile. As Satan he was first introduced into Judaism as a supernatural being in the first two chapters of the book of Job, where he appears to be on good terms with God. Christians saw him as a sort of henchman for the divinity. King James I described him as 'God's hangman'.[142]

The name *Satan* derives from the Hebrew word for *adversary*. In the New Testament the word was sometimes translated by the Greek word *diabolos*, meaning accuser or calumniator. English translations of the Bible generally retain the Hebrew word *Satan* but render *diabolos* into English as *Devil*. The Old Testament uses only the name *Satan*. The New Testament, written in Greek but drawing upon the Old Testament, uses both names. The English term *accuser* is also applied as a title (Revelation 12:10).

The identification of a personalised Satan with Lucifer is much later, and founded upon a mistake. The mistake arises from a passage in Isaiah:

> How art thou fallen from heaven, O Lucifer, son of the morning! how art thou cut down to the ground, which didst weaken the nations! (Isaiah 14:12)

The original Hebrew refers not to Lucifer but to a daystar. This is most likely to be the planet we now call Venus, though it might have been the

Moon. The Romans called Venus and the Moon *Lucifer* and *Lucifera* respectively. The Jews seem to have shared the Roman view that Lucifer was the son of Aurora, the goddess of the dawn.

Venus was known as the morning star because it is often visible in the morning sky after other planets and stars have faded. The Greeks knew it as *Phosphorus*, the 'light bringer' or harbinger of dawn, and the Romans' name *Lucifer* has the same meaning. The writer in Isaiah seems to be talking about the morning star, used as a metaphor for a king's diminishing power. The word *Lucifer* means simply 'light bringer', which is why it was used in Victorian times as a name for what we now call safety matches. By applying a little imagination and generous interpretations of other biblical passages (notably Luke 10:18 and Revelation 9:1–11) later commentators managed to identify Lucifer with the Devil. The fact that early Christians made no such connection is apparent in the free use of Lucifer as a forename. A famous fourth-century Bishop of Calaris in Sardinia was named Lucifer.

Other unrelated characters are introduced elsewhere in the Bible and identified with Satan. Among them are rival gods such as *Baal* or *Baalim*, *Molech*, *Beelzebub* and *Belial*.[143] Satan is identified with the serpent in the Garden of Eden, largely as a result of a connection made by St Paul.[144] As in many ancient cultures it is probable that the serpent originally represented wisdom or knowledge, as it still did in New Testament times: 'Be ye therefore wise as serpents...' (Matthew 10:16). Nevertheless, following other New Testament writings, Satan is now firmly identified with a serpent or a dragon (Revelation 12:7 and 20:2). Isaiah calls a sea serpent *leviathan* (Isaiah 27:1), and this association, because of the much later serpent connection, seems to be responsible for the term *leviathan* also being applied to Satan. Satan has also been identified with *Asmodaeus*, a character from the Apocrypha (Tobit 3:8 and 17).

The Christian conception of Satan is largely developed from the New Testament. Here he is identified with the *prince of the devils* (Matthew 12:24), the *tempter* (Matthew 4:3 and 1 Thessalonians 3:5), the *evil* or *wicked one*,[145] the *prince of this world* (John 12:31 and 16:11), the *prince of the power of the air* (Ephesians 2:2), and the *angel of the bottomless pit*, known in Hebrew as *Abaddon* and in Greek as *Apollyon* (Revelation 9:11). These Hebrew and Greek names both mean *destroyer*, a word that is also used as one of his titles in Wisdom of Solomon 18:25.

The supposed existence of a number of powerful supernatural evil forces is damaging to the Christian case for monotheism, even if they could all be shown to be subject to a single satanic being, or even to be manifestations of the same satanic being.

Other Old Testament Gods
As the Jews became monotheistic they generally abandoned their traditional gods, but occasionally the old gods lingered on with a reduction in rank. The Sun, Moon and stars were almost universally regarded as gods in ancient times. Now, to emphasise their subordination to the Jewish God they were made to praise him (Psalm 148:3). They are still instructed to do so in modern hymns:

> Praise the LORD! ye heavens, adore Him,
> Praise Him, Angels, in the height;
> Sun and moon, rejoice before Him,
> Praise Him, all ye stars and light:
> (*Hymns Ancient and Modern*: 292)

And even more striking 'Sun and moon bow down before Him' (hymn 298 in *Hymns Ancient and Modern*). Ancient peoples also imagined that the planets were really gods, a fact recalled by our names for them. Later these gods were demoted to angels, although one was especially favoured – Venus, the bright star of dawn, or daystar. It had been Lucifer: now it was Christ (Revelation 22:16).

The angel of the Lord in Genesis 16:7–14 was a god according to verse 13, but various translations gloss over this in various ways without so much as a footnote. Translators of the Bible have written some other divinities out of the script: Lucifer's mother Aurora, goddess of the dawn, for example. The original Hebrew text of Psalm 110:3 refers to the womb of Dawn just as the Greeks would have spoken of the womb of the goddess Aurora, but as we have seen earlier (page 29) some modern translations fudge the words so that the goddess Dawn does not appear. Similarly the Queen of Heaven, Asherah, the consort of El, had her name translated as *grove*, so that anyone reading the Vulgate or the Authorised Version could not guess that a goddess was being worshipped in the Jerusalem Temple:

...where the women wove hangings for the grove. (2 Kings 23:7, Authorised Version)

...where women did weaving for Asherah. (2 Kings 23:7, NIV, cf. Jerusalem Bible)

Rival gods are also mentioned in the Old Testament. In addition to those already mentioned, such as *Baal* or *Bel*, others include *Ashtaroth*, *Dagon* and *Nebo*. There seems to have been no doubt that they were real gods and not merely idols. Two of them, *Bel* and *Nebo*, crouched and cringed together helplessly as their idols were carted off by the servants of Yahweh (Isaiah 46:1–2).

The Virgin Mary

To many Protestant eyes, Roman Catholics worship Mary as a thinly disguised goddess. The reaction of the Roman Catholic Church has been to emphasise a distinction between the types of worship that are due to God and to Mary. God alone is entitled to *latria* (adoration), and Mary alone is entitled to *hyperdulia* (hyper-veneration). The Orthodox Church makes a similar distinction. Whether or not the difference is merely a semantic one is a matter of opinion. To many the distinction appears artificial. Roman Catholics sometimes point to a critical distinction between the worship of God and Mary. Only God has the power to answer prayers. Mary acts merely as a mediator, or rather mediatrice. She does not answer prayers herself as a goddess would, but only brings the matter to the attention of God in the person of Christ, the sole source of salvation.

According to Roman Catholic belief, Mary's powers of mediation are sovereign: Christ, her son, cannot refuse his mother. The question then arises as to whether there is any real difference between Mary answering prayers herself and having her answers metaphorically rubber-stamped by a higher authority. Many see the rubber-stamping as a conceit designed to maintain the appearance of a monotheistic religion. Indeed, the concept of Mary as mediatrice was largely developed to rebut accusations that she was worshipped as a goddess. The familiar *Ave Maria* or *Hail Mary* has been amended over the centuries to reflect this more acceptable line. Thus the closing words 'Pray for us sinners, now and at the hour of our death' were added to the prayer specifically to emphasise God's sovereignty, in response to Lutheran criticism in the sixteenth century. Other prayers, the forms of which were settled before the Protestant accusations of polytheism, show Mary as possessing independent powers. The following example, from the *Sub tuum praesidium*, is at least 1,000 years old, although a fragment from the third or fourth centuries suggests that it is much older:

> We seek refuge under the protection of your mercies, Mother of God; do not reject our supplication in need, but deliver us from perdition, you who are alone blessed.[146]

Moreover, it used to be perfectly orthodox to claim that Mary 'ordered' or 'commanded' God, and that he 'obeyed' her,[147] but these claims are ever more muted, precisely because of the implications. So too, the claim that Mary's intercession is all-powerful can be explained away by saying that 'she invariably intercedes in accordance with God's will'.[148] Many will find this explanation less than convincing, since it implies that Mary only ever asks for things that God has already decided to grant, so reducing her role as intercessor to nothing. Theologians who are regarded as perfectly orthodox have claimed that Mary can direct and guide our destinies as she wills; that no one can be saved except through her; that she reigns along with her son and is praised by angels, and that nothing can resist her. Indeed, she is omnipotent. She heals Hell, treads demons underfoot, saves mankind and restores fallen angels. She is above the angels. She is 'another Paraclete', i.e. another Holy Spirit. She is the cause of our redemption. She is our 'saviour'. Indeed salvation is impossible without her. She has the same 'glory' as the second person of the Trinity. She is the 'complement of the Trinity'. She is even called the 'Spouse of the Father', 'Spouse of the Holy Spirit', and most frequently 'Spouse of Christ'. All three have been described as her lovers (*amatores*). It is even ventured that she is co-creatress (*symplástes*) with God. Theologians can start prayers to her with the words 'Our Mother who art in heaven ...'. She is acclaimed as Queen of Mercy as God is King of Justice. She is in some respects superior to God himself and exercised power over him. Theologians ask her to over-rule God (e.g. to free them from Hell if Christ should condemn them to it). She 'stops the arm of God's justice, power and revenge by the force of her mercy and love'.[149]

Her cult came too late for her to be admitted to the divine Trinity, but there had been an obvious need for a feminine influence ever since the demotion of *Sophia*. This helps explain Mary's promotion into the divine Imperial Family (*Mother of God*, *Bride of Christ*, and *Mater Sapientiae* 'Mother of Sophia'). Her titles reflect her growing divinity. She acquired the title *Theotokos*, Mother of God, in the fourth century, and her first known feasts date from the fifth century. She was given the title *Notre Dame*, Our Lady, in the twelfth century, after which she collected titles at an ever accelerating rate. She is, amongst many other things: Mother of Mercy, Empress of Angels and Empress of Heaven, Bower of Divinity, Mistress of the World, Queen of Queens and Holy of Holies. She took over the title of the virgin goddess Hera in 1954 when Pope Pius XII proclaimed her *Queen of Heaven*. In 1964 Mary was awarded yet another title: *Mater Ecclesiæ*, Mother of the Church.

Marian devotion is particularly strong in southern Europe, where it is clear to any observer that the distinctions of Roman Catholic theologians mean little to many Marian worshippers. They know that she is assigned a place above the highest angels and act accordingly. They pray to Mary, Queen of Heaven, and expect her to answer their prayers, just as 2,000 years ago their ancestors prayed to the goddess Juno, Queen of Heaven. To any objective observer there can be little doubt that Mary represents an updated melange of popular mother goddesses, among them the Greek Diana, the Egyptian Isis, the Phrygian Kybele, and the Middle Eastern Ashtaroth. For each sky god, King of Heaven, there is generally a *Magna Mater* as Queen. The titles Queen of Heaven and Mother of God are both liable to lead ordinary believers into thinking of Mary as a goddess. As one authority says of the title Mother of God (Greek *Theotokos*):

> Theotokos – in Latin *Dei Genitrix* – is hardly used; not, however, on theological grounds, but for the simple reason that it might give rise to misunderstandings on account of the pagan worship of Kybele, the Mother of Gods.[150]

Whether this is ingenuous or disingenuous we need not concern ourselves. For us, the question is whether the Christians who regard Mary as a goddess are a small aberrant group, or a mainstream group protected by purpose-designed word play.

Angelic Beings

Hellenic philosophers around the time of Jesus regarded gods as lesser beings in a divine hierarchy subordinate to one supreme god. The Jews also had a hierarchy of heavenly beings subordinate to their one supreme god, namely the angels. It is clear, as theologians have long accepted, that angels are the discarded gods of polytheism.[151] This sort of belief, henotheism, is typical of the transition from polytheism to monotheism.

Jewish and Christian literature refers to a number of different types of angelic being. They are traditionally ranked in three circles, each of three orders, and feature much more heavily in Christian hymns than in biblical writings. Authorities differ as to their names and relative ranks, but usually cite nine from the following list: seraphim, cherubim, orphanim, thrones, virtues, dominions or authorities, princes or principalities, powers, archangels, and angels. Modern writings tend to ignore the various angelic ranks, but they feature in dogma, even in Anglican dogma.[152] Orthodox Christians pray to angels just as they pray to saints. Prayers to guardian angels are especially popular, and the Roman Church favours such prayers as well.[153]

The word *angel* is derived from the Greek *angelos* meaning messenger, a word used to translate a wide range of Hebrew expressions including ones denoting *men, sons of God* or *sons of gods, sons of the mighty, mighty ones, holy ones, keepers, watchers,* and *armies of God*.[154] In the earliest books of the Bible they are represented as men, as is God himself (Genesis 18). Indeed, God is sometimes regarded as a sort of pre-eminent angel (e.g. Genesis 48:15–16 and Judges 6:11–24). In early Christian writings, before Jesus had been promoted to the divine Trinity, he too also seems to have been regarded for a while as a pre-eminent angel, apparently identified with the Archangel Michael.[155]

Demons

The Old Testament refers to a number of demons. Rahab, for example, was a demon personifying water (Psalm 89:10), while the female demon Lilith is mentioned as living in the desolation of Edom (Isaiah 34:14, Jerusalem Bible). Of the two goats selected as offerings by the Jews, one was sacrificed to Yahweh, the other, the scapegoat, was sent into the desert to the demon Azazel (Leviticus 16:8–10, Jerusalem Bible). Such demons were minor gods to whom sacrifices were made (Deuteronomy 32:17 and Psalm 106:37).

When the New Testament refers to *devils* it generally means demons. That they are supposed to be actual beings, not merely false idols, is confirmed by James 2:19.

Unclean Spirits

Unclean spirits are mentioned several times in the Bible. They caused various illnesses. Their exact nature is never made clear, but it is apparent that they enjoyed supernatural powers. Jesus had conversations with, and exorcised, a number of them.

Saints

Many saints are recycled pagan gods. According to Roman Catholic teachings they are entitled to a type of worship called *dulia* (veneration). The question arises as to whether this, like the *hyperdulia* accorded to Mary, is much different from the type of worship due to God.

The role of the saints, like that of Mary, is now conceived as one of intercession. In effect Christian believers supposedly direct their requests to God through the saints: they do not pray to the saints for their direct intervention. The line is a fine one, and it is apparent that it is not universally recognised by the faithful. Take for example St Christopher, the traditional protector of travellers. Many tens of millions of Christians carry around St Christopher talismans. They may be seen on neck chains and on car dashboards throughout the world. They are often called *charms* because they are believed to act as magical charms to ward off danger. There can be no doubt that many of those who rely upon St Christopher talismans believe that their efficacy comes from St Christopher. His charms often bear the inscription 'behold St Christopher and go thy way in safety'. Whatever the official line on such matters, and whether or not St Christopher ever existed, it is clear that millions believe that a supernatural being other than God is able to provide them with supernatural protection.

To many non-Christians, and some Christians, it is difficult to see the difference between the Christian St Christopher and the Greek god Hermes or the Roman god Mercury, both of whom were supernatural patron protectors of travellers. It is also notable that until this sort of criticism was raised against the role of saints it was held that the saints could work miracles themselves, not merely by applying to God. As scholars pointed out, St Peter could kill with a rebuke, without any need for superior assistance.[156]

In Russia, Orthodox Christians address prayers both to Christ and to St Nicholas. Outside the Orthodox and Roman Catholic Churches, Christians are less susceptible to charges that they worship saints.

Emperors and Popes

In the early church, the Emperor was universally accepted as being infallible, having been appointed by God as head of the Christian Church. Since 1870 bishops of Rome have also claimed infallibility, and Roman Catholics are required to believe this as a matter of dogma.

The clear implication is that emperors possessed, and the Pope still possesses, abilities denied to ordinary human beings, in other words supernatural powers. As pope, Innocent III claimed to be set midway between God and man. Since subsequent popes have never denied this claim, it would seem that it is still upheld. For many it is difficult to see what the difference is between a demigod and an infallible being with supernatural powers.

Christians

Eastern Orthodox Christians believe that they will attain *theosis* or deification at some stage in the future.[157] They will then share the substance of God, as do the three persons of the Trinity. Whether or not this will make new gods is a question parallel to the question of whether the concept of the Trinity is meaningful.

The Dead

The invocation of the dead is a remnant of ancestor worship still practised in Eastern Churches. The living frequently ask their dead ancestors to pray for them.[158] Arguments for polytheism are similar to those concerning saints.

Icons

Icons are also worshipped. For example the *adoratio crucis*, liturgical worship of the cross (by kiss and genuflexion) has been practised since the dedication of the Church of the Holy Sepulchre in 335. The Second Council of Nicæa in 787 made the veneration of images lawful. Henceforth *proskunesis* (reverence) might be paid to them, but not *latria* (worship).

* * *

Our problem centres on the definition of a god. According to Chambers Dictionary, a *god* is 'a superhuman being, an object of worship'. This definition and similar ones in other dictionaries accord well with our general understanding of the word's meaning. Of the entities discussed so far, all are claimed to be superhuman, except for icons and for living Orthodox Christians, who will become superhuman only in the future.

The only question then is whether the various remaining super-human beings are worshipped. On this criterion it is possible to acquit Wisdom, demoted Old Testament gods, unclean spirits and living popes. Demons can be let off on the grounds that they have not been worshipped recently. In the interest of brevity, we shall leave on file questions arising from the fact that God and Satan are both confabulations, likewise the implications of the invocation of the dead.

Our best candidate for the title of another god is Satan. There is no doubt that he is seen as a powerful supernatural force. Until recent times baptismal catechisms included the lines 'Forsakest thou the devil? And all devil worship'. Christians affirm that Satanists still worship the Devil, so there can be no argument about his being worshipped. The fact that Christians themselves do not worship him is not sufficient to disqualify his claim. The fact that certain ancient Greeks worshipped only, say, Apollo is not an argument that Apollo was a monotheistic god. He was part of a system of belief in which other people worshipped other gods, so he was a member of a pantheon. A parallel argument holds here for Satan. In any case the New Testament refers quite specifically to Satan as *the god of this world*.[159]

The next best candidates are the second and third persons of the Trinity. We have already seen that the concept of the Trinity is questionable.

To many, including many who call themselves Christians, it is unintelligible. If it is no more than a linguistic deceit then we are left with three gods masquerading as one.

Perhaps the next best candidate, in the Roman Catholic Church at least, is Mary. The claim that she is merely a powerless intermediary is a difficult one to sustain. First, the idea of the role of intermediary seems to have been developed specifically to refute charges of idolatry, and is hardly recognised at all by many of the faithful. Second, the system of intercession is difficult to reconcile with God's supposed omniscience, omni-benevolence and omnipotence. Why should God's decisions be affected by information channelled through figures such as Mary, when he already knows such information? Any intermediary is superfluous. Third, even if it is accepted that Mary is herself powerless, and able to act only as an agent of God, this does not debar her from being regarded as a goddess. Many polytheistic religions recognise that subordinate gods may not be free to act without leave from a superior one. Homer and Virgil tell us that lesser gods were constrained by Zeus during and after the Trojan War. According to Homer, Zeus himself was subject to those most ancient divinities, the Fates (Iliad 8.68).

Arguments for the divinity of others are almost as powerful. Saints and angelic beings worshipped in the Eastern Orthodox and Roman Catholic Churches are good candidates. The argument is identical to that for Mary.

In brief, the number of gods recognised by Christianity depends on our definitions. If we accept that the concept of the Trinity is meaningful, and that the distinction between different forms of worship is valid, then mainstream Christians still have at least two gods: God and Satan. If the Trinity is only a linguistic deceit, then they have at least four: the Father, Son, Holy Ghost, and Satan. If the distinction between the words *latria* (adoration) and *hyperdulia* (hyper-veneration) is illusory then the Roman Church has at least five gods: the Father, Son, Holy Ghost, Satan, and Mary. If the distinction between *latria* and *dulia* (veneration) is illusory then it has many thousands.

The principal point here is that there is a case to be answered, and few Christians are aware that there is a case at all. Familiar techniques are used to cover up the problems: different gods are bundled together and presented as one God with different titles. Others are translated away into oblivion, or deprived of the capital letters that would otherwise identify them as supernatural beings. Biblical passages that fit the case for monotheism are quoted extensively, while those that compromise it are ignored. Teachings are changed when they become indefensible, although without any admission that the earlier teachings were wrong. Words change their meanings as required. For many, there is a suspicion that linguistic deceits have been employed specifically to obscure uncomfortable truths and to maintain a claim to monotheism.

CASE STUDY C: HOW THE VIRGIN MARY STAYS A VIRGIN

Where the virgins are soft as the roses they twine,
And all, save the spirit of man, is divine?
George Gordon, Lord Byron (1788–1824), *The Bride of Abydos*

The Virgin Birth is mentioned in New Testament passages, but there are grounds for regarding these mentions as unreliable additions, a fact well known to all theologians, but not generally passed on to the faithful. Different Christian denominations have different understandings of Mary's virginity. Orthodox Churches refer to her as *aeiparthenos* (ever-virgin). Roman Catholics and some others state specifically that she remained *virgo intacta* throughout her life, even during the birth of Jesus.[160] Others believe that she remained a virgin throughout her life in the sense that she never engaged in sexual intercourse with a man. Almost all accept that she was a virgin at the time of Jesus' conception. For clarity we will look separately at the claims to virginity after, during, and before the birth of Jesus.

After the Birth of Jesus

We pick out a text here and there to make it serve our turn; whereas if we take it all
together, and consider what went before and what followed after,
we should find it meant no such thing.
John Selden (1584–1654), *Table Talk, 'Bible Scripture'*

The claim that Mary remained a virgin after the birth of Jesus is difficult to sustain. For one thing the gospels strongly imply that sexual intercourse took place between Mary and Joseph. The author of Matthew, for example, says 'then Joseph ... took unto him his wife: and knew her not till she had brought forth her firstborn son...' (Matthew 1:24–5). Earlier in his account, the same author refers to a time 'before they came together...' (Matthew 1:18). (In modern translations the euphemisms *knew* and *came together* are sometimes replaced by other euphemisms such as *came to live together*, *having union*, or by explicit references to *intercourse*.)

More damaging still are the numerous references throughout the New Testament to Jesus' brothers and sisters. One of his brothers is called James,[161] explicitly identified as the brother of Jesus in Galatians 1:19. Jude (or Juda or Judas) is referred to as James's brother in Jude 1:1. Both James and Jude, and others named Joses and Simon along with unspecified sisters, are mentioned in the Matthew gospel. Jesus' brothers are also mentioned in Matthew 12:46, Mark 3:31, John 2:12, Acts 1:14 and 1 Corinthians 9:5. Elsewhere the historian Josephus mentions Jesus' brothers.[162] Again, in the non-canonical Gospel of the Hebrews Jesus specifically addresses James (James the Righteous) as 'my brother'.

Such facts are difficult to reconcile with the concept of Mary's eternal virginity. In an attempt to reconcile the contradictions, it has been pointed out that Middle Eastern languages do not always distinguish between close relations such as siblings and cousins, and that Jesus' brothers and sisters could really be cousins. Since the gospels were not written in a Semitic language, but in Greek, and supposedly by people close to the events, this argument is of doubtful value. Both Mark and Luke use the word *adelphoi*, which means *brothers*, rather than *anepsioi* or other alternatives, which might have meant 'close relations' (and similarly for *adelphai*, sisters).

Another difficulty for the close relation theory is that some of the brothers are specifically identified as sons of Mary. First, Matthew 13:55–6 introduces the family group:

> Is not this the carpenter's son? is not his mother called Mary? and his brethren, James, and Joses, and Simon, and Judas? And his sisters, are they not with us?...

A parallel passage in Mark 6:3 gives a similar list (with Juda instead of Judas). Critically, the Mark author identifies Mary as the mother of James, Joses, and perhaps one of the sisters (Mark 15:40). Rather tenaciously, theologians have sought to explain this away by suggesting that Mary had a sister who was also called Mary or, when that theory became too difficult to sustain, that she had two sisters, both of them also called Mary.[163] Many consider these theories to be contrived, and of little value against the straightforward interpretation that the same Mary was the mother of Jesus, James, Joses (or Joseph), Simon, Judas (or Juda, or Jude), and at least two sisters.

Different Churches tried to explain away Jesus' siblings in different ways, attributing weight to dubious early writings according to whether they supported their favoured line. They became Mary's nephews and nieces in the West, but another explanation was favoured in the East. According to Eastern Churches Mary's other children were step-children, Joseph's sons and daughters by an earlier marriage. There is not a scintilla of evidence for either contention. The truth is that any straightforward reading of the New Testament suggests nothing other than that, after the birth of Jesus, Joseph and Mary settled down to an ordinary married life, and that Mary bore Joseph a number of children. This is the interpretation given in Protestant versions of the Bible, and also seems to have been the prevailing view of the earliest Christians.[164]

During the Birth of Jesus

It is one of the superstitions of the human mind to have imagined that virginity could be a virtue.
Voltaire (1694–1778), *Notebooks*

What exactly it can mean to remain a virgin during birth has been the subject of much speculation. For present purposes we shall adopt the meaning favoured by the Roman Catholic Church, that the hymen remains intact during birth.

There is no evidence, not even a suggestion, in the canonical gospels of Mary's hymen having remained intact during the birth of Jesus. Early Christian writers accepted that Mary did lose her virginity during the birth of Jesus.[165] The earliest sources that suggest otherwise, dating from the second century AD, are Gnostic,[166] and would now be discounted as heretical if they had not been the only straws to clutch at for those who liked the idea of Mary remaining *virgo intacta*. Some later Church

Fathers had also clutched at those straws, and the Roman Church now cites these Fathers as authorities on the matter. The earliest and most respected Fathers either did not consider the question or else rejected the idea of Mary remaining *virgo intacta* during the birth. The same applied to other important figures well into the fourth century, including the champions of orthodoxy.[167]

Possible mechanisms by which Mary could have remained *virgo intacta* have exercised the minds of theologians since the fourth century. During the Middle Ages, it was widely believed that Mary had conceived by being inseminated by the Holy Ghost through her ear,[168] a belief that resulted in female ears being treated with the utmost modesty for a time. However, an ear would hardly serve for the delivery. One possibility was that Jesus had exited Mary's womb through a sort of door in her abdomen,[169] or through her side, or that he emerged as a ray of light from her intact vagina, or that he dematerialised in the womb and then re-materialised again outside of Mary's body. One Church Father claimed that he came through Mary like water through a pipe.[170] However it was done, traditional teaching has been that it involved no labour pains and no afterbirth – known to theologians as *sordes*, or filth.

The tradition that Mary had retained her virginity arose at the same time as, and is just as reliable as, a range of other pious traditions that have now been abandoned: for example that the baby was weightless, never cried, never needed cleaning, and was born with adult intelligence. The canonical gospels make no suggestion that the birth was carried out in any but the usual way, and imply that parturition was perfectly normal. After all, purification was required under Jewish Law for women after childbirth primarily because of the blood involved; and Mary undoubtedly underwent purification.[171] Furthermore the gospels confirm in so many words that Jesus was born in the conventional manner:

> And when the days of her purification according to the law of Moses were accomplished, they brought him [Jesus] to Jerusalem, to present him to the Lord (As it is written in the law of the Lord, Every male that openeth the womb shall be called holy to the Lord;) (Luke 2:22–3)

'Openeth the womb' is as specific a term for conventional childbirth as one could hope for. In the absence of any other contemporary evidence it is difficult to reach any conclusion other than that the mechanics of the birth of Jesus were perfectly conventional. For an objective scholar there is no reason to doubt that they involved not only the normal orifice, but also normal labour and normal afterbirth.

Before the Birth of Jesus

> *Now has come the last age according to the oracle at Cumæ…*
> *Now too, the virgin goddess returns.*
> **Virgil (70–19 bc),** *Eclogues,* **4, 1.4**

That Mary was a virgin before the birth of Jesus is at least supported by the gospels. Luke for example reports that she claimed to be a virgin at the time of the conception:

> Then said Mary unto the angel, How shall this be, seeing I know not a man? (Luke 1:34)

Also she is referred to as a virgin on a number of occasions. The case therefore looks reasonably good, until we look into the matter a little more deeply. First it is notable that the oldest New Testament writings refer to Jesus as being born of a *woman* rather than of a *virgin*.[172] His human ancestry on the male side is assumed in Galatians 3 (see particularly verse 16). St Paul makes no mention of the Virgin Birth anywhere in his copious writings. Also, the earliest gospel, Mark, offers no nativity story at all. In fact the nativity story occurs only in two gospels, Matthew and Luke, and the versions are different and often contradictory. The older of the two, the Matthew gospel, makes little of Mary's virginity. He mentions it only once and then indirectly:

> Now all this was done, that it might be fulfilled which was spoken of the Lord by the prophet, saying, Behold, a virgin shall be with child, and shall bring forth a son, and they shall call his name Emmanuel, which being interpreted is, God with us. (Matthew 1:22–3)

This is a reference to a passage in the Old Testament:

> Therefore the Lord himself shall give you a sign; behold a virgin shall conceive, and bear a son and shall call his name Immanuel[173] (Isaiah 7:14)

A critical point is that in the original Hebrew the word translated as virgin in Isaiah is *'almah*, and *'almah* does not mean 'virgin' but 'nubile young woman', which is a different concept altogether. Elsewhere in the Old Testament the word *'almah* is applied to harem girls and to young widows.[174] If the Hebrew text had meant to convey the idea of virginity, a more explicit word like *bethulah* could have been used.[175] The confusion apparently arose because the word *'almah* had been inaccurately translated into Greek in the Septuagint as *parthenos*, which does mean 'virgin', rather than an alternative word for a girl such as *neanis*. So *parthenos* was the term that the Matthew author would have found in the Septuagint. This, therefore was the term he used as well, apparently unaware of the error in the original translation. Matthew's error has long been known. A Jew named Trypho pointed it out in the second century AD.[176]

What all this seems to suggest is that some Greek speakers invented the Virgin Birth in order to match a prophecy that they had misunderstood. It begins to look as though the virginity aspect was introduced to improve the match between a supposed Old Testament prophecy and Jesus' life story. As we have seen (pages 269–77), a number of the details mentioned by the Matthew author seem to have been invented to fit in with real or imagined prophecies. Incidentally, the Orthodox Church, aware of this embarrassing situation, has found an explanation. It claims that the mistranslation in the Septuagint was made deliberately under the influence of the Holy Spirit as part of God's continuing revelation.[177]

The only other canonical gospel to mention Mary's virginity is the Luke gospel. The author of this gospel is universally accepted as having drawn upon the Matthew gospel, and it is more than possible that he took the virginity story from there. Neither in the Matthew nor Luke gospels are the events of the nativity referred to again after the initial story. Neither is the nativity mentioned anywhere else in the New Testament. Sometimes the nativity stories are plainly at variance with the rest of the text. For example, after searching for three days Mary and Joseph found Jesus in the Temple:

And when they saw him, they were amazed: and his mother said unto him, Son, why hast thou thus dealt with us? behold, thy father and I have sought thee sorrowing. And he said unto them, How is it that ye sought me? wist ye not that I must be about my Father's business? And they understood not the saying which he spake unto them. (Luke 2:48–50)

Mary and Joseph's failure to understand would be relatively unremarkable if they had thought Mary to be the ordinary mother of an ordinary child with an ordinary father. It is not however consistent with the knowledge with which the nativity stories credit them. Even after 12 years, one might suppose that a mother would not forget the words of angels, much less the fact that her child's father was God himself. What can be the explanation for this? Is the text reliable? The answer to this question has to be 'no'. The two nativity stories are widely acknowledged by Bible scholars to have been additions to the texts of the Matthew and Luke gospels. Moreover, a number of textual variants reveal the hands of interpolators. For example the genealogy of the Matthew writer is altered in different ways in different manuscripts, apparently to avoid naming Joseph explicitly as the father of Jesus.[178] Significantly, the earliest surviving Semitic version of Matthew, the Old Syriac Gospel, retains Joseph as the father.[179] Surviving manuscripts betray a range of amendments, not only in the genealogies but also throughout the texts, clearly made to avoid mentioning that Joseph was the real father. Indeed, there are so many that they provide a good academic case study in how 'orthodox' Christians have deliberately corrupted their own scripture.[180]

There is no suggestion of Jesus being born the son of God in the Mark gospel. Instead he seems to have been adopted as a son of God at his baptism (Mark 1:9–12). Echoes of this event are still to be found in the other gospels, providing another set of inconsistencies.

If we discount the nativity stories as later additions, many anomalies are automatically removed from the New Testament. The author of Matthew, for example, had taken great trouble to trace Jesus' ancestry through Joseph to King David and ultimately to Abraham,[181] which would hardly be appropriate if Joseph was not his father. Elsewhere Jesus claims to be descended from David (Revelation 22:16). He is referred to as 'the seed of David according to the flesh' (Romans 1:3–4) and as being descended from the patriarchs (Romans 9:5 Jerusalem Bible). Mary and Joseph are explicitly mentioned as Jesus' 'parents' (Luke 2:41), and as cited above Mary refers to Joseph as Jesus' 'father' after finding him in the Temple. Jesus is also explicitly identified as the son of Joseph in John 1:45 and 6:42. The nearest any early writings come to attributing divine fatherhood to Jesus is in a passage by Ignatius of Antioch, who died around AD 107. In a letter to the community at Ephesus he introduced a divine influence into an otherwise conventional human conception: 'Jesus Christ our God was conceived by Mary of the seed of David and of the spirit of God...',[182] and in another letter he referred to Jesus as being 'truly of David's line in his manhood, yet Son of God by Divine will and power'.[183]

If we look at the beliefs of others that were in a position to know, such as the Jewish Christians known as Ebionites, we find that they denied the Virgin Birth, regarding Jesus as 'the child of a normal union between a man and Mary'.[184] So did other early sects (like the Carpocratians), and so did important early Church figures like Jovinian. According to early non-believers, Jesus' real father was a Roman centurion named Pantheras,[185] an accusation that is supported by Jewish documents.

If the two gospel nativity stories are unreliable, there is no basis for the belief in the Virgin Birth. On the other hand there are many reasons for doubting it. We know that the Jews never expected the Messiah to be born of a virgin, and it is clear enough that the Matthew author did only because of a mistranslation. We know that the Matthew author liked to arrange matters to match Old Testament prophecies. Elsewhere, Jesus' human ancestry is assumed, and in some instances, which escaped the attentions of editors, Joseph is named as the father. We even have evidence of editors erasing mention of Jesus' human father from the text. All in all, the case for doubting the story of the Virgin Birth is a strong one.

Perpetual Virginity

It is undesirable to believe a proposition when there
is no ground whatever for supposing it true.
Bertrand Russell, *Sceptical Essays*

On the evidence Mary did not remain a virgin after the birth of Jesus. There is no reason at all to suppose that she remained *virgo intacta* during the birth of Jesus, and the evidence for her having been a virgin before the birth is questionable.

It is not difficult to see how the Virgin Birth story might have arisen. Early Christians were embarrassed that their leader was reputed to have been illegitimate. In the Hellenic world, where gods often impregnated human women, an obvious solution for any illegitimate putative leader was that a deity was the father. This had the dual advantage of explaining the illegitimacy and introducing an element of the divine. An Old Testament passage about a birth to a virgin apparently provided the key to the solution, or it would have done, had not the passage contained a critical mistranslation.

Many modern theologians accept that the story of the Virgin Birth is a myth designed to emphasise Mary's purity. It follows an established pattern, and may well have been based on existing stories. For example the mother of the Buddha was believed to have conceived without the aid of her husband. The infant emerged not by normal means but through his mother's side. She died soon afterwards 'because it is not fitting that she who bears a Peerless One should afterwards indulge in love' (Mahavastu 21).

Despite all the evidence Mary still purports to retain her virginity. The trick is done by tampering with the original texts, retaining known errors of translation, inserting suitable confirmatory material into sacred texts, rejecting the plain meaning of words in favour of contrived meanings, and glossing over contradictions and inconsistencies. All this is an open secret. No Church scholar of any standing denies it. But then none openly advertises it either, so the faithful masses remain in ignorance.

CASE STUDY D: HOW THE NATIVITY STORY WAS CREATED

I count religion but a childish toy,
And hold there is no sin but ignorance.
Christopher Marlowe (1564–93), *The Jew of Malta, Prologue*

Biblical inconsistencies are smoothed out and covered up so well by theologians that many Christians believe that the Bible tells a reliable and consistent story. Take for example the nativity story that is told each

Christmas with the aid of selected gospel passages. Many Christians believe that the four canonical gospels contain consistent versions of the story of Jesus' birth, as re-enacted by millions of school children each year. A summary of it is as follows:

> The angel Gabriel appears to Mary and Joseph with the news that Mary, a virgin, is pregnant and will give birth to Jesus. Before the birth Joseph and Mary travel from Nazareth to Bethlehem, Joseph's home town, for a census and to be taxed. When they get to Bethlehem they can find no room at the inn and are obliged to stay in a stable. There, on 25th December in AD 0, accompanied by an ox and an ass, Mary gives birth to Jesus. Lacking suitable facilities the new parents use the animals' manger (feeding trough) as a crib for their new-born child. A host of angels appears to shepherds watching over their flocks in fields nearby and directs them to the site of the birth. Meanwhile, a star appears in the sky. This star leads three kings, Gaspar, Melchior, and Balthasar to the site. Mounted on camels they follow the star, taking with them three gifts: gold, frankincense and myrrh. On the way the three kings let Herod the Great, King of Judea, know the purpose of their journey. Now aware that a King of Israel has been born, Herod orders the murder of all male children under the age of two. Having been warned of this by the angel Gabriel, Joseph and Mary escape to Egypt with their baby, until it is safe to return to Nazareth.

Familiar though this story is, it appears nowhere in the Bible. It is a confabulation. Only two of the four canonical gospels give an account of the nativity at all. The two narratives give different and often contradictory accounts of the circumstances of Jesus' birth. Many of the subsidiary details are not mentioned in the gospels at all, nor anywhere else in the New Testament. Taking a few details one by one illustrates these points.

Gabriel
According to Matthew the news of Mary's pregnancy was conveyed to Joseph in a dream (Matthew 1:20). According to Luke the angel Gabriel appeared not to Joseph but to Mary and not in a dream, but in person (Luke 1:26–38).

Mary's Virginity
Both the Matthew and Luke gospels agree about this but, as we have seen in the previous section, the Virgin Birth seems to have been introduced

as the result of an unsuccessful attempt to match the nativity story with an Old Testament prophecy.

Bethlehem
Both authors place the birth in Bethlehem. However, according to Luke, the family originally lived in Nazareth and went to Bethlehem for a census (Luke 2:4–7), whereas according to Matthew the family settled in Nazareth only after their return from Egypt (this is evident from Matthew 2:23).

The Census
As we have seen (pages 51–2), the story of the census is not credible. Apart from contradicting known facts it gives a date for the birth of Jesus that is incompatible with the dates of the reign of Herod the Great.

The Time of Year
The date is not mentioned in the Bible. There is no reason to suppose that the birth took place in December. Indeed the fact that sheep were in the fields at the time makes it unlikely. As most Christian scholars now acknowledge the date was selected simply to coincide with the popular festivities that marked the winter solstice. The year of birth is not known either. The year was calculated in the sixth century by a monk, Dionysius Exiguus, who fixed AD 1 as 754 AUC (*Anno Urbis Conditae* = years after the founding of the city of Rome). It was subsequently realised that Herod the Great had died four years earlier than this, so a recalculation was made and the purported year of birth moved back to 750 AUC, or 4 BC. (There is no year AD 0 or 0 BC: the year preceding AD 1 was 1 BC.)

Kings
Neither Matthew nor Luke mentions kings visiting the new-born child. No one does. Matthew mentions an unspecified number of wise men or magi, by which he probably meant Zoroastrian priests. Luke mentions neither kings nor magi. Tertullian was the first to suggest that these magi were kings. The idea seems to have come from unrelated passages in the Old Testament:

> Because of thy temple at Jerusalem shall kings bring presents unto thee. (Psalm 68:29)

> The kings of Tarshish and of the isles shall bring presents: the kings of Sheba and Seba shall offer gifts. Yea all kings shall fall down before him: all nations shall serve him (Psalm 72:10–11)

The numbers of wise men, or kings, purported to have visited Jesus has varied over time. In early Christian art there were two, four or six. According to Eastern traditions there were 12. Other sources say 'many'. The number three seems to have chosen because the Matthew author mentions three gifts. The names Gaspar, Melchior and Balthasar occur nowhere in the Bible, and different Churches give the magi/kings different names: for example according to the Syrian Church they were called Larvandad, Hormisdas and Gushnasaph.

Camels

The camels come from another unrelated Old Testament passage (Isaiah 60:3–6):

> And the Gentiles shall come to thy light, and kings to the brightness of thy rising... The multitude of camels shall cover thee, the dromedaries of Midian and Ephah; all they from Sheba shall come: they shall bring gold and incense; and they shall shew forth the praises of the LORD.

Shepherds

Luke has an unspecified number of shepherds coming to see the baby. Matthew does not mention them at all.

The Star

According to Matthew the magi, having seen a star in the East, went to Jerusalem, which was the wrong place to go. Only after Herod had directed them to Bethlehem did the star reappear to lead them to the right place (Matthew 2:1–9). Stars were common portents in the ancient world, and the births and deaths of kings were frequently marked by such celestial events. Nevertheless, the author of Luke does not mention the star at all.

It is clear that the star story was continuously being exaggerated and embellished over time. For example, the star was soon being described as being miraculously brilliant,[186] and according to Ignatius of Antioch, all the rest of the stars along with the Sun and Moon gathered around this new star, which nevertheless outshone them all.[187]

The Inn
In the original Greek none of the gospels mentions an inn. The Matthew author refers to mother and child in a house (Matthew 2:11). The Luke author uses the word *katalemna* meaning a temporary shelter and this was badly translated into English as *inn* (Luke 2:7). Elsewhere in the Bible *katalemna* was translated by the word tabernacle (as in 2 Samuel 7:6 for example).

The Manger
No manger is mentioned by the Matthew author. The word used in the original Greek by the Luke author is *thaten*, a word that has a range of meanings, including a baby's crib and an animal's feeding trough. Obviously the meaning here is baby's crib, not manger.

The Stable
Neither Matthew nor Luke mentions a stable. The idea that one is involved apparently stems from the erroneous translation of *thaten* as manger. Other sources, such as the non-canonical Gospel of James, locate the birth in a cave. So do many of the Church Fathers.[188] The Koran (19:17–22), possibly repeating another ancient tradition, locates the birth by a palm tree in a far off place.

The Ox and Ass
Neither Mark nor Luke mentions these animals. Their inclusion in the story is apparently attributable to later Christian scholars who picked up the idea from an unrelated Old Testament passage.

> The ox knoweth his owner, and the ass his master's crib (Isaiah 1:3)

Significantly in the Septuagint the word corresponding to crib is *thaten*, the same word translated as manger in the Luke author's nativity story. The ox and ass in the Christmas story first make their appearance in an apocryphal gospel (pseudo-Matthew) probably dating from the eighth century. St Francis of Assisi apparently set up the first model Christmas crib, with accompanying ox and ass, in the thirteenth century.

Herod's Massacre of the Innocents
The author of Matthew mentions this, but the author of Luke does not. One might have supposed that such a draconian measure would have

been recorded elsewhere, as were less significant historical events. The mass murder of the infants has no historical corroboration, and is probably no more than an imaginative way of bringing both Bethlehem and Nazareth into the story. Indeed this massacre cannot have taken place as described, otherwise Jesus' second cousin and contemporary, John the Baptist, would have been killed, yet John survived to reappear later in the story. Once again it looks as though a story has been retrospectively added to the gospel, without thinking through all the consequences.

This sort of story was far from unknown in the ancient world. In the usual myth a king tries to kill a baby who, according to a prophecy, is destined to occupy his own throne. The king fails, though he does not know it, and years later he is supplanted by the child, now an adult, in accordance with prophecy. It is probably best known with some embellishments as the Greek story of Oedipus, but the same basic tale was also familiar in the Middle East. An earlier King of Media (where the magi came from) had ordered the murder of his own grandchild, because of a prophecy that the infant would grow up to overthrow him.[189] Like the infant Jesus, this child also escaped death to fulfil his destiny.

Matthew could not quote a suitable prophecy about a baby surviving an attempt to kill him, later to become king, because none exists in the Old Testament. Instead, Matthew cited a passage that he must have thought could be stretched to cover a massacre of children:

> Then was fulfilled that which was spoken by Jeremy the Prophet, saying, In Rama was there a voice heard, lamentation, and weeping, and great mourning, Rachel weeping for her children, and would not be comforted, because they are not. (Matthew 2:17–18, referring to Jeremiah 31:15)

As is the case in most of the prophecies cited by Matthew, the connection is tenuous and unconvincing. Wrong people, wrong place, wrong tense, and not a single child death. Matthew neglects to mention that, in the next verse of Jeremiah, God says that these children will return from an enemy country.

The Flight to Egypt
Luke does not mention the flight into Egypt at all. Matthew does, apparently, as we have already seen (page 272), so that he can cite another prophecy.

* * *

No independent historical records support either Matthew or Luke's story where they might be expected to: not the need to migrate for a census, nor the appearance of a new star, nor the massacre of the children. What seems to have happened is that both authors have improvised. Matthew has invented a story to fit Old Testament prophecies. Throughout the Matthew gospel references are made to current events fulfilling scriptural prophecies. These references are clearly intended to lend credibility to the stories and to impress readers. The prophecies, like those that we looked at earlier, are generally taken out of context, and in most cases they are not really prophecies at all in the sense that we now understand the term.

Luke has tried to give his story historical background. He seems to have heard, possibly from reports of the Matthew gospel, that Mary was a virgin, that her husband was called Joseph, and that Jesus was born in Bethlehem, though it was widely known that he came from Nazareth. Apart from that there is no agreement at all. The two stories contradict each other on matters such as Joseph's ancestry, whether or not he came from Nazareth or went there only after Jesus' birth, and the appearances of Gabriel. They disagree about the year, the flight into Egypt, the appearance of the star, the shepherds and the magi.

Neither of these authors mentions three kings (or kings at all, or three of anyone for that matter), nor camels, nor a stable, nor oxen or asses, nor the time of year. As a final indictment, it also seems that the stories were continuously being tampered with for generations. Surviving manuscripts show a range of alterations of varying subtlety and intention. No Father of the Church cites the birth stories exactly as we now know them in the gospels until Irenaeus in the last quarter of the second century.

According to an ancient tradition (acknowledged in the Jerusalem Bible), the original version of the Matthew gospel was written 'in the Hebrew tongue'. This version is likely to have been the gospel used by the Ebionites. One of the interesting things known about this Ebionite gospel was that it was shorter than the Greek version. One reason for this was that the opening verses about Jesus' miraculous birth were absent. If this Ebionite gospel was indeed the original version of Matthew, then the nativity story must be a later Greek addition, which is exactly what many scholars independently suspect from other evidence. It is also significant that we know of early versions of the Luke gospel that also lacked the nativity story.[190]

Even the most conservative Christian scholars now regard the stories of Jesus' miraculous birth as being historically unreliable.[191]

CASE STUDY E: TEXTUAL PROBLEMS

When I was a child, I spake as a child, I understood as a child, I thought as a child: but when I became a man, I put away childish things.
Corinthians 13:12

This case study is a little different. Here we will look at how the mainstream Churches have changed their views, and why they have changed their views, on the reliability of the Bible.

Porphyry (*c.*232–*c.*303) demonstrated that the book of Daniel could not have been written when Jews and Christians claimed it was. His works were later condemned and burned, and facts he had unearthed were denied, then forgotten. Christian writings attempting to refute his works were also burned, as even these works were too compromising. Again, early Christians had been well aware that the scriptures contradicted each other, but this too was denied. Anyone who could read could see the contradictions for themselves. For a long time laymen were not permitted to learn to read, so there was little danger of them finding out the truth. Those who let out the secret were dealt with. Those outside the Church could expect death. Those inside could expect the same, unless they were already respected scholars. Pierre Abélard is perhaps the best known example. In the eleventh century he was sentenced to life imprisonment for listing church contradictions in a work entitled *Sic et Non* (*Yes and No*).

When humanist scholars returned to Hebrew and Greek texts of the Bible, they discovered that many passages had been badly mis-interpreted. The authority of many medieval accretions was destroyed, and this created a wave of reaction against the Church. Humanists ridiculed the Church in works such as Sebastian Brandt's *Narrenschiff* (*Ship of Fools*) of 1494, and Erasmus's *Moriae Encomium* (*In Praise of Folly*) of 1509. Written soon after the introduction of printing, such works became best sellers, and their widespread popularity ensured the life and liberty of their authors. Humanism and the revival of learning would fuel the Reformation.

When Protestant Churches came into being, the Bible became available to all, even in vernacular translations. Now it was not only scholars who were aware of discrepancies and textual irregularities in the Bible. By the seventeenth century men of learning were starting to air the existence of contradictions publicly. In his *Leviathan*, published in 1651, Hobbes gave cogent reasons why Moses could not possibly have written the whole of the Pentateuch. He risked his life in doing so. A few years later, in 1679, a student at Edinburgh University made the same assertion, along with other similar ones, and was hanged for it. Baruch Spinoza (1632–77) risked persecution by Jews and Christians when he pointed out biblical mistakes, inconsistencies and impossibilities, thus denying the infallibility of scripture. Newton doubted the authenticity of the New Testament but chose to keep his views to himself.

In an academic study of 1711 a German minister, H. B. Witter, disclosed his discovery that the Bible's account of the creation was really two interwoven stories, written by different authors and at different times (see pages 30–1). In the 1720s Thomas Woolston was put under house arrest for life, for voicing doubts about the Resurrection and other biblical miracles. In 1753 Jean d'Astruc, a physician to Louis XV, took Witter's ideas a stage further, revealing in an anonymous booklet that different hands could be seen in the book of Genesis. By the simple method of stripping out the text in which the author referred to God as *Jahveh*, and the text in which the author referred to him as *Elohim*, is was possible to identify coherent strands that had been edited together. Suddenly the duplication – two creations, two accounts of the flood, and so on – made sense. Witter's ideas rapidly gained acceptance among scholars.

A few years later Thomas Paine popularised the right to doubt in England. In *The Age of Reason* he established that the Old Testament books could not have been written by the authors ascribed to them, that their chronologies were absurd, that they contradicted themselves on many points, and that many of the claims traditionally made for them were untenable. He purported to show that the story of Jesus was false and that the canonical gospels had not been written by their ascribed authors. He said that the biblical story of Jesus had every mark of fraud and imposition stamped upon the face of it. At the time Paine's findings were denied, and he was considered a blasphemous atheist. But now the facts were available to all, not just a closed circle of scholars. People were teaching themselves to read specifically so that they could read Paine's works for themselves.

Protestants

By the end of the seventeenth century the genie was well and truly out of the bottle. Protestant scholars were pioneering new forms of biblical criticism, particularly in Germany, where the biblical scholarship was not under Church control as it was elsewhere in Europe. H. S. Reimarus, Professor of Hebrew and Oriental Languages at Hamburg, rejected the biblical miracle stories, held that Jesus was a failed revolutionary, and deduced that biblical authors were fraudulent. Such opinions were highly controversial, and would have cost Reimarus his job if they had been published during his lifetime. Scholars started wondering who had written the Pentateuch if it had not been Moses. J. G. Eichorn (1752–1827), a German Old Testament scholar, confirmed d'Astruc's view that there are two distinct strands in Genesis, a J strand where God is called *Jahveh*, and an E strand where he is referred to as *Elohim*. There were thus at least two authors. Eichorn's work was fiercely rejected by theologians, and attempts to have it translated into English were frustrated by Church and university authorities. It was finally translated only in the twentieth century.

By the end of the eighteenth century scholarly scepticism was gathering pace, though scholars were still paying a high price for their integrity. W. M. L. De Wette, a Berlin professor in the first part of the nineteenth century, doubted biblical miracles and regarded the stories of Jesus' birth and the Resurrection as mythical. He was deprived of his professorial chair. Around the same time F. C. Baur founded the Tübingen School, which held that the New Testament was largely a second-century synthesis of ideas from Jewish followers of Peter and gentile followers of Paul. In 1835 the first part of D. F. Strauss's *Leben Jesu* (*Life of Jesus*) was published. Comparing the gospel accounts, Strauss deduced that the miracle stories were mythical, and that the gospel stories were not eyewitness accounts, but later confabulations of garbled traditions. He was dismissed from his post at Tübingen University. His colleagues, though sympathetic, dared not speak out for fear of their own positions.

No matter how many teachers were dismissed, or professors deprived of their chairs, the movement was now unstoppable. In the same year the Berlin philologist Karl Lachmann argued that contrary to Church teaching, the Mark gospel was an earlier work than the Matthew gospel, a view that is now almost universally accepted. By the 1880s Julius Wellhausen had identified the four main strands running through the Pentateuch.

Closely related to textual analysis of the Bible was modernism. Modernists accepted the fallibility not only of the Bible, but also of other authorities, including tradition, councils and popes. Modernists were however still sincere Christians. Attempting to salvage something from the consequences of their own scholarship they advocated the reinterpretation of Church teachings. They held that Christianity must be continuously revised in the light of contemporary requirements and advances in scientific opinion. As time went on, and scholarship became more refined, positions veered ever further from traditional teaching. Albert Schweitzer (1875–1965) believed Jesus to have been a badly mistaken man whose crucifixion came as rather a nasty shock to him. Rudolf Bultmann, Professor at Marburg between 1921 and 1951, saw almost the whole of the New Testament as mythical. German Protestants had to accommodate themselves to an entirely new theology where the Bible was at best figurative rather than literal, and at worst a mish-mash of various people's fantasies. Many scholars, like D. F. Strauss, ended their lives no longer Christians at all.

Anglicans

The position of the Church of England had been crystallised soon after the Reformation. Its position on any matter of doctrine that might have been in doubt was stated explicitly in the 39 Articles of Religion. The King's Declaration prefixing the Articles specifically prohibited 'the least difference from the said Articles' and took pride that clergymen 'all agree in the true, usual, literal meaning of the said Articles'. Nevertheless, scepticism grew within the Church of England. Many educated people, including at least one Archbishop of Canterbury, had harboured doubts about the Trinity even in the seventeenth century, but most kept their views to themselves.[192] By the early eighteenth century Anthony Collins was able to point out discrepancies between Old Testament prophecies and their supposed fulfilment in the New.[193] Widespread doubts were becoming publicly visible in the late eighteenth century as more and more people read Thomas Paine.

By the nineteenth century a school of Modernists known as Neologians flourished in Oxford. They survived through influential support and a relatively liberal atmosphere. Even so, many clerics felt obliged to leave the Church, even though it meant giving up their university positions. Notable losses included Arthur Hugh Clough (1848), J. A. Froude (1849) and Sir Leslie Stephen (1862). The Professor of Theology at King's College, London lost his chair in 1853 for making observations about eternity that now seem particularly unremarkable.[194]

Neologians, or Broad Churchmen as they came to be known, became ever more vocal. Their views seemed particularly threatening after Darwin published *The Origin of Species* in 1859. In 1860 a collection of *Essays and Reviews* by Broad Churchmen raised a storm of controversy, and two of its authors were tried for heresy: one for denying the inspiration of scripture, the other for denying eternal punishment. Five counts were upheld in the ecclesiastical court (the Court of Arches), and sentence passed, but the verdicts were overturned on appeal to the Judicial Committee of the Privy Council. At around the same time the Bishop of Natal in South Africa was also tried for heresy for pointing out biblical contradictions, denying accepted authorship and doubting eternal punishment. He was condemned, deprived and excommunicated, but then acquitted on appeal to the Privy Council.

The requirements of His Majesty's declaration had become untenable. In 1865 an Act of Parliament, the *Clerical Subscription Act*, decreed that the clergy were not to be bound by every word of the 39 Articles, but that they should assent to their general tone and meaning. The Church approved this in the following year. It opened the door to questioning all of the Articles openly, although the implicit understanding was that theologians should do so only amongst themselves. It was a sort of open secret among the educated classes that science had discredited traditional teachings and that they could no longer be interpreted literally. Yet it was not permissible to admit such a thing openly. In the 1880s an eminent Scottish professor, William Robertson Smith, was tried for contributing articles to the *Encyclopaedia Britannica* that discussed Wellhausen's discoveries and suggested the Bible could be analysed scientifically. Smith won his case but lost his chair at Aberdeen University.

The fallibility of traditional Church teaching was still a sort of open secret, and scholars were still expected to keep quiet about certain matters in public. In the twentieth century a number of leading churchmen caused uproar in the Church by breaking this convention, for example by openly rejecting the Virgin Birth, denying the Resurrection, and questioning whether Christ had instituted the Eucharist at the Last Supper. Among them have been E. W. Barnes, the Bishop of Birmingham, in 1947; and J. A. T. Robinson, the Bishop of Woolwich, with his book *Honest To God* in 1963. Robinson felt safe enough to concede that 'God is intellectually superfluous, emotionally dispensable and morally intolerable'. Later, numerous theologians contributed to *The Myth of God Incarnate* in 1977; and David Jenkins, Prince Bishop of Durham, made various pronouncements throughout the 1980s on subjects such as his scepticism about Jesus' physical Resurrection. In his 1998 book *Why Christianity Must Change or Die*, John Spong, Episcopal bishop of Newark, New Jersey, dismissed the idea that Jesus was divine and pointed out that the God that most traditional Christians believe in is an ogre. Richard Holloway, Archbishop of Edinburgh, published a book called *Godless Morality* in 1999, destroying the myth that morality is a specifically Christian characteristic. Each time there were excited calls for resignations, defrockings and heresy trials. The furore was not so much over the ideas, which were increasingly widely shared, but over the breaking of the convention that the faithful masses should not be told about scholarly opinion within the Church.

Roman Catholics

The experience of the Roman Church was somewhat different. It was wary of allowing its scholars access to the opinions of others because so many had so often defected in the past. A number of crusaders, for example, had joined the Eastern Churches, or converted to Islam, and preachers sent to convert heretics were themselves frequently converted. Even senior churchmen defected, most notably Bernardino Ochino (1487–1564). Ochino, who had been head of the Capuchin Order, had been granted permission to study Protestant books in order to refute them. In the course of his studies he converted to Protestantism. A safer reaction to the views of non-Catholics was to ignore them. Such views were heretical, and no good could come from studying them. The best safeguard was ignorance.

Pope Clement XI, in his constitution *Unigenitus* of 1713, insisted that the reading of the holy scriptures was not for everyone. Open debate was not for Roman Catholics. No matter that the genie had been long gone, the Roman Church still hoped to force the stopper back into the bottle. Cardinal Newman, who regarded anyone who questioned the infallibility of the Bible as being wicked at heart, kept his copy of Paine's *The Age of Reason* locked up in a safe to protect his students.

Late in the nineteenth century Roman Catholic theologians became aware of the spectacular progress in understanding of the origins of the Bible that had been made by German Protestants. Catholic scholars were being left far behind, as the Germans' critical approach was almost universally accepted in academic circles outside the Roman Church. The then Pope, Leo XIII, relented. He permitted new research because he wanted Roman Catholic scholars to be able to refute the views of Protestant ones. His hopes misfired, for the more his theologians studied the Bible scientifically, the less easy they found it to accommodate themselves to Roman dogma.

A Roman Catholic Modernist movement soon created difficulties throughout Europe. In England the Modernist George Tyrrell was obliged to retire to the countryside after writing about Hell in 1899. He was later expelled from the Jesuit order and excommunicated. In France the threat to orthodoxy grew ever greater. Theological books by Lucien Laberthonnière in 1903 and 1904 were placed on the Index. Pierre Batiffol, who was associated with the Modernists, was forced to resign as Rector of the Institut Catholique at Toulouse in 1905, and his book on the Eucharist was placed on the Index in 1911. Alfred Loisy, one of the leaders of Roman Catholic Modernism in France, published works that acknowledged that, far from being divine and infallible, the Bible is full of errors. He doubted the Virgin Birth and the authenticity of the John gospel. Five of his works were placed on the Index in 1903–4, he lost his chair at the Institut Catholique in Paris, and he was excommunicated in 1907, along with Tyrrell.

Modernism was in danger of running away with orthodoxy, and had to be stopped. Pope Pius X condemned the Modernist movement in the decree *Lamentabili*, as part of his attack on theological novelties in 1907. He treated progress as something akin to heresy. Soon afterwards a papal encyclical, *Pascendi dominici gregis*, envisaged a massive conspiracy, inspired by Protestants, to undermine the Roman Church. The Pope was particularly opposed to the heresy of Americanism – a species of Modernism that upheld democracy, progress, secular education and unfettered reason. In 1910 Pius authorised a strong anti-Modernist oath to be taken by all ministers and teachers. More writers were excommunicated, and the Church was cleansed. Modernism apparently disappeared from the Roman Church, and Roman Catholic teaching was back in the Middle Ages. *A Handbook of Heresies*, published some 20 years later and bearing the Roman Catholic imprimatur, states the position as follows:

> In the Catholic Church, true to the dogmatic principle taught by the living Voice, Modernism could retain no foothold. Outside the Unity it was far otherwise: in all sects, but especially the Anglican Establishment, owing to her boast of comprehensiveness, and to her purposely ambiguous formulas, modernism has triumphed. One by one the old creeds, the old doctrines are restated, re-interpreted, rejected. To-day there is no sect in Europe of any size or standing that dares insist on the acceptance of any dogma whatever – in its literal meaning – as a condition of membership or even ministry. The Catholic Church alone stands today as she has ever stood, judging – not judged by – modern thought...[195]

The position is not really quite so straightforward. For one thing popes are still finding it necessary to censor clerical opinion. Hans Küng, Edward Schillebeeckx and Leonardo Boff have all been silenced for voicing opinions that differ from the Pope's. The first woman to hold a chair of Roman Catholic theology (Uta Ranke-Heinemann) had her teaching licence withdrawn in 1987, after she questioned the Virgin Birth. On the other hand, during the twentieth century the Roman Church has slowly been doing what it always said it would *never* do, reconciling itself to progress. Around the beginning of the 1980s, Pope John Paul II finally acknowledged what Eichorn had known well over a century before, that there are two distinct strands in Genesis, a J strand where God is called *Jahveh*, and an E strand where God is referred to as *Elohim*.[196] If John Paul II had said this when he was a young priest, he would never have been allowed a licence to teach theology, and could have been excommunicated as a Modernist heretic. If he had said it a few centuries earlier he would have been burned at the stake. The fact is that the Roman Church shifts ground just like the more liberal Churches – it is just that it moves so slowly that not everybody notices.

Many biblical scholars now agree with Thomas Paine that the biblical story of Jesus has every mark of fraud and imposition stamped upon the face of it, and they may not have to wait long before a pope agrees, although his wording may be a little more diplomatic.

New Scriptural Texts

He who will not reason is a bigot; he who cannot is a fool,
and he who dare not is a slave.

George Gordon, Lord Byron (1788–1824)

There are still a few sensitive areas where Churches will try to defeat science and scholarship by the traditional techniques of interpreting and 'losing' important evidence. We have seen that traditionally the Church would destroy inconvenient writings and replace them with its own forgeries. It cannot hope to get away with forgeries in the twenty-first century, but there is still scope for traditional methods of manipulation. One such case in which the Roman Church has been involved is that of the Dead Sea Scrolls, which have been described as the most important archaeological discovery ever.[197]

In 1948 a number of ancient scrolls were discovered in a cave in the Judæan hills, at a place called Qumran. More scrolls were discovered buried in nearby caves. The scrolls dated from before AD 70, most of them Old Testament biblical texts at least 1,000 years older than other known copies. There were also other texts, previously unknown. The excavation of these scrolls was overseen by Father Roland de Vaux, a Roman Catholic priest, who taught at the Ecole Biblique et Archéologique, a French Catholic Theological School in Jerusalem. This institution was run by Dominicans, and had been established in 1890, in accordance with the Church's then policy of using biblical and archaeological studies to strengthen the faith.

Some of the scrolls disappeared, but others ended up in the Rockefeller Museum, the Palestine Archaeological Museum in East Jerusalem. A group of scholars was assembled to study the scrolls under the leadership of de Vaux, almost all Christians, and with a heavy concentration of Roman Catholics nominated by the Ecole. No Jews were included, ostensibly for political reasons, although the scrolls were clearly Jewish, and needed a Jewish historian to set them in context. No atheists were included, although one agnostic, John Allegro, was allowed access to selected texts. De Vaux continued to refuse to allow any Jews to work on the scrolls in the Rockefeller, even after Jerusalem came under Israeli control in 1967.

It was soon apparent that the scrolls contained information that did not fit well with Christian orthodoxy. In particular the scrolls revealed that whoever occupied Qumran, they had their own Davidic messiah, whom they regarded as a 'son of God' and as begotten of God. This text was not officially published, although details were leaked and published in the Biblical Archaeology Review in 1990.[198] In other inconvenient texts, the word *messiah* is translated as 'thine anointed' apparently in order to disguise its full import – exactly as earlier translators had done with biblical texts. Also it came to light that the Qumran community practised baptism, recognised 12 leaders based in Jerusalem, and shared goods in common (cf. Acts 2:44–6). They also used many phrases now regarded as characteristically Christian (such as 'followers of the Way' and 'poor in spirit'). They also recognised a *Teacher of Righteousness*, echoing a title accorded to Jesus' brother James and perhaps to Jesus himself.[199] They ate meals together, a priest blessing the bread and wine.

> And when they gather for the Community table ... and mix the wine for drinking, let no man stretch forth his hand on the first of the bread or the wine before the priest, for it is he who will bless the first fruits of bread and wine... And afterwards, the Messiah of Israel shall stretch out his hands upon the bread...[200]

Some passages link together and explain early Christian texts, but these too were not published. Despite many striking similarities between the community at Qumran and early Christianity, the Roman Catholic Church scholars insisted that they were completely different. De Vaux consistently misinterpreted evidence – archaeological, numismatic, textual and palaeographological in order to make the facts fit his preconceptions. Despite the evidence he continued to hold that the site was occupied by a peace-loving Essene community, and that it dated from a century or two before Christian times. In fact there is good evidence that Zealots occupied the site during and after the time of Jesus. De Vaux and his fellow priests not only advocated their own (objectively untenable) theory, but they also did their best to discredit anyone who made alternative suggestions about interpretation, virulently denouncing scholars like John Allegro, Robert Eisenman and Edmund Wilson who pointed out that de Vaux's team had interpreted the texts to suit their own religious beliefs. Sometimes the team found it necessary to minimise the importance of texts that do not conform to Roman Catholic preconceptions. In a particularly striking example, de Vaux dismissed one scroll (the important 'copper scroll') as a mere fantasy, claiming that it was of interest to historians of folk-lore, and dismissing it as 'a whimsical product of a deranged mind'.

A suspicious level of control was exercised in the allocation of material, and some of it was kept secret. All fragments were brought first to de Vaux or another Ecole nominee (Milik), and complete secrecy was kept until they had had the opportunity to study them.[201] By the mid-1950s a gulf was opening up between John Allegro and other members of the team. Allegro's objective assessments were not at all to the liking of his Christian colleagues.

In 1956 de Vaux was appointed to the Pontifical Biblical Commission, providing a direct chain of control from the Vatican. Since 1956 every director of the Ecole Biblique has also been a member of the Pontifical Biblical Commission. The Church seemed to be tightening its grip. By the end of 1957 Allegro realised that 'the non-Catholic members of the team are being removed as quickly as possible...'[202] Later he claimed that '... de Vaux will stop at nothing to control the scrolls material' and 'I am convinced that if something does turn up which affects Roman Catholic dogma, the world will never see it. De Vaux will scrape the money out of some other barrel and send the lot to the Vatican to be hidden or destroyed...'[203] Since the Catholic faction exerted total control, there is no way of knowing whether Allegro was right. Many suspect that inconvenient material was suppressed, in much the same way that inconvenient material has been suppressed in previous centuries.

Access to the scrolls was allowed only to those who could be trusted to promote the approved Church line. This seems to have been one reason why Jewish scholars were denied access, despite the fact that the scrolls were Jewish documents, written by Jews for Jews. Ignorance of Judaism was no bar to being involved, and dislike of Judaism appears to have been acceptable. John Strugnell, who became head of the Qumran team in 1987, published almost nothing of the mass of materials available to him. He was unusually open about his views on Judaism, even if badly mistaken about his facts. In a widely reported interview he disclosed that Judaism is 'a horrible religion. It's a Christian heresy, and we deal with our heretics in different ways.'[204] Apart from any other implications, this did little to inspire confidence in his scholarship, and particularly his understanding of the relationship between Judaism and Christianity.

In the opinion of many, the secrecy surrounding the Dead Sea Scrolls is an outrage.[205] The scrolls were kept secret for decades by men with strong religious convictions and a strong interest in maintaining Roman Catholic orthodoxy whatever the objective evidence might be. De Vaux never published a final report of the original excavations. There has never been a full inventory of all the scrolls and fragments, and some of the more interesting texts were published after forty years only because they had been leaked. After half a century, Allegro, the sole agnostic, was still the only scholar to have published all of the material in his care. The failure of the others is widely recognised as scandalous. Morton Smith, Professor Emeritus of Religion at Columbia University, has described the failure to publish the scrolls as 'too disgusting' even to talk about. Geza Vermes, Reader in Jewish Studies at Oxford University, has called the secrecy about and excessive control over the scrolls 'the academic scandal *par excellence* of the twentieth century'.

SUMMARY

A great deal of intellectual dishonesty is evidenced in the history of Christianity. This dishonesty seems to have continued from the earliest times to the present day. Why should any organisation have engaged in such extensive forgery, destruction and manipulation? Why have honest scholars been persecuted for 2,000 years whenever they have pointed out a problem? And why has it been necessary to shift ground so radically – so radically that bishops and popes now hold beliefs that were previously so heretical that people were burned alive for holding them?

NOTES

1 Toy, *What are Apocryphal Writings?*, p. 19. For more on this see Morton Smith, *The Secret Gospel* (London, 1974).

2 In the *Novum Testamentum Graece et Latine*, by Augustinus Merk, edited in 1933 for the *Istituto Biblico Pontificio*, Matthew 27:16 is given as '...And they had then a notable prisoner, Jesus called Barabbas...', which at least introduces the name Jesus, even if it leaves *Barabbas* untranslated.

3 Ehrman, *The Orthodox Corruption of Scripture*, gives examples at pp. 9, 15, note 8 on p. 166.

4 John Hick (ed.), *The Myth of God Incarnate*, p. 113 citing Origen, *Comm. In Joh.*, 2.31.

5 Eusebius, *The History of the Church*, 6:17.

6 Andrew Louth (ed.), Maxwell Staniforth (trans.), *Early Christian Writings*, p. 55.

7 Chadwick, *The Early Church*, p. 207.

8 Graef, *Mary*, vol. 2, p. 35.

9 Graef, *Mary*, vol. 2, p. 55. Maria d'Agreda's original account had been placed on the Index because it was so unlikely (until the King of Spain insisted that it be taken off). It was placed on the Index again in 1704 but removed again the following year.

10 Graef, *Mary*, vol. 2, p. 87.

11 Graef, *Mary*, vol. 2, p. 137.

12 Wine is mentioned favourably for example in Psalm 104:15, Song of Songs 7:9, and 1 Timothy 5:23.

13 Eusebius, *The History of the Church*, 5:28. The particular passage quoted is by a member of the divine-Jesus faction against the human-Jesus faction.

14 Jean Meslier, *Mon Testament*, extracts published by Voltaire, *Extrait du Testament de J. Meslier*, 1762 (Ch. 1, 2) and cited in translation by Knight, *Humanist Anthology*, p. 24.

15 Quoted by Eusebius, *The History of the Church*, 1:13. The text of the correspondence cited differs from the surviving Syriac text.

16 Graef, *Mary*, vol. 1, pp. 176–8.

17 'Mary is "the Virgin who alone has destroyed all the wickedness of the heresies", a saying which, carrying the authority of St Jerome, is still recited in the Tract of the Roman Mass of the Common of the Blessed Virgin in Lent and in certain Offices' – Graef, *Mary*, vol. 1, p. 178.

18 Tertullian, *De baptismo*, 17 reveals that the *Acts of Paul* were forged by a priest.

19 *Vita Beatae Virginis Mariae et Salvatoris Rhythmica*, pp. 881ff.

20 The work in question is the *Mariale Super Misses Est*. See Graef, *Mary*, vol. 1, pp. 266–71.

21 Both Tertullian and Hippolytus thought that the sect was named after a man called Ebion. (Tertullian, *De Praescriptione Haereticorum*, 33, Hippolytus, *Philosophumena* (or the *Refutation of all Heresies*) 7.35.i.)

22 Different texts of Josephus disagree significantly on passages that mention Jesus or his brother James. For example the passage quoted in Eusebius's *Ecclesiastical History* 23 (also known to Origen) is not in surviving known manuscripts. See also the note in Feldman's translation of Josephus, *Antiquities* XVIII: iii.3, 63–4.

23 Eusebius, *The History of the Church*, 4:23:12.
24 Cyprian, *Epistles*, 9.2.
25 R. M. Grant, *Journal of Theological Studies* (1962), vol. 13.
26 *Order of Mass for the Dead*, 'Sequentia' (often called *Dies Irae*), 1.1.
27 St Bonaventure, *Commentary on the Sentences*, Sermon 6. See Graef, *Mary*, vol. 1, pp. 281 and 288ff.
28 For example Nicholas of Cusa and John Torquemada both knew them to be forgeries in the fifteenth century, so did Renaissance scholars, including Erasmus.
29 The Second Pseudo-Isidorian Decretal, a blatant forgery, criticised the practice of allowing women to touch sacred vessels or linen. It was cited as papal authority for centuries.
30 H. Thurston, *Catholic Encyclopedia*, under 'rosary'.
31 Although it was well known that Einstein had abandoned his faith at the age of twelve, for many years religious apologists claimed that Einstein must have believed in God (because he sometimes used the word God – as in 'I don't believe that God plays dice'). The apologists' claim was destroyed by the discovery in 2008 of a letter, written in German by Einstein to the philosopher Eric Gutkind in 1954 just a year before his death in which he described all religions as 'childish superstitions'. See http://www.telegraph.co.uk/news/1951333/Einstein-thought-religions-were-childish.html.
32 There have been a number of attempts to portray Hitler as not being a Roman Catholic or even Christian. (The topic is hotly contested by editors of Wikipedia.) For a thorough treatment of the extensive evidence that he remained a Catholic throughout his adult life (including his own writings, speeches, use of biblical quotations, use of Church precedents, reports from friends, Nazi artefacts, photographs, etc) see http://www.nobeliefs.com/Hitler1.htm. Stalin remained an Orthodox believer even as his regime discouraged religious belief. His original vocation had been as a priest and he had studied at the Tiflis (now Tblisi) Theological Seminary.
33 Alternatively, the Matthew author might have misrepresented Isaiah 1:11, which talks about a *shoot*. In Hebrew the word for a shoot is N-Tz-R. By supplying his own vowel sounds the author could contort it into Nazarene. See Wells, *Religious Postures*, pp. 236–7, note 17 citing Howard C. Kee, *Miracle in the Early Christian World*, Yale University Press (New Haven and London, 1983), p. 186n.
34 John William Gott was convicted in 1921, the last man to be imprisoned for blasphemy in Britain. A man in his sixties when he was sent to prison, he died soon after completing his sentence.
35 St Augustine, *City of God*, 16, 26.
36 'Thomas Paine, The Age of Reason' in *The Life and Works of Thomas Paine*, ed. William M. Van der Weyde, vol. 8, *The Age of Reason* (New Rochelle, New York: Thomas Paine National Historical Association, 1925), 6.
37 The best that churchmen could find was Hosea 6:2, 'After two days he will revive us: in the third day he will raise us up, and we shall live in his sight'. But the raising up has nothing to do with death. What it is really saying is that God will restore Israel – a meaning which is perfectly clear from the text.
38 Matthew 12:40 cf. Jonah 1:17.
39 2 Kings 1:8.
40 1 Samuel 17:5.

41 Joshua 22:27.
42 Leviticus 15:9.
43 Judges 5:10.
44 Psalm 92:4.
45 Leviticus 14:16.
46 1 Samuel 10:1, tense changed.
47 Nahum 3:2.
48 Isaiah 23:1.
49 1 Kings 7:14, actually referring to the city of Tyre.
50 Daniel 8:9, tense changed.
51 Isaiah 58:8.
52 Genesis 29:27.
53 2 Chronicles 24:12.
54 Isaiah 30:16.
55 Ezekiel 1:15.
56 Jeremiah 46:4.
57 Ecclesiastes 9:11.
58 Robin Lane Fox, *The Unauthorised Version*, pp. 339–40.
59 Different versions of Jesus' list of commandments are given at Matthew 19:18, Mark 10:19 and Luke 18:20.
60 Matthew 5:38–9, referring to Exodus 21:24, Leviticus 24:20 and Deuteronomy 19:21.
61 The relevant Jewish law may be found in chapter 12 of the book of Leviticus. It is clear from the text that the purification was required because of the blood involved. An interval of ritual uncleanness followed menstruation for similar reasons, although these intervals were necessarily rather shorter.
62 Uta Ranke-Heinemann, *Eunuchs for the Kingdom of Heaven*, pp. 16–17.
63 The Epistle of Barnabas 10.
64 The Epistle of Barnabas 9, making reference apparently to Jeremiah 6:10.
65 God gave judgement through lots on numerous occasions, e.g. condemning Jonah (Jonah 1:7) and Jonathan (1 Samuel 14:41–2).
66 Thomas, *Religion and the Decline of Magic*, p. 142.
67 A man with injured genitals in Israel is, for example, barred from marrying a legitimate born Jewess (though he may marry bastards and converts to Judaism).
68 Matthew 15:4, citing Exodus 21:17 and Leviticus 20:9.
69 For examples of pre-Renaissance cardinals holding a 'discrezione' – i.e. an interest-bearing bank account – see Strathern, *The Medici*, p. 40.
70 For examples of the horror in which early Church leaders held Christian images, see John Hick (ed.), *The Myth of God Incarnate*, p. 138.
71 Don Cupitt notes the rage of Church leaders when Church art first appeared. See John Hick (ed.), *The Myth of God Incarnate*, p. 138. For an account of later developments see pp. 138–45. See also Chadwick, *The Early Church*, pp. 277–84.
72 The same transition may be observed today in Muslim countries. Islamic art traditionally relied heavily upon calligraphy and abstract patterns, because of this commandment, but more and more living things are being portrayed. Muslim rulers' heads now appear on coins, paper currency and stamps. In some Muslim countries pictures of Mohammed himself are now freely available, where a few years

ago they would have been considered blasphemous. At the time of writing Muslims still do not permit representations of God. The Jews are following the same path.

73 B. Whitehead, *Church Law*, 'Images', pp. 165–6.

74 The English Puritan Theophilus Brabourne, for example, was imprisoned for 18 months for publishing a pamphlet in 1631 which pointed out that the Sabbath should fall on Saturday, not Sunday.

75 Eusebius, *The History of the Church*, 9:11.

76 Strathern, *The Medici*, Chapter 13. The murder plot (the 'Pazzi Conspiracy') was hatched by Francesco de' Pazzi and Francesco Salviati, Archbishop of Pisa, and supported by Pope Sixtus IV. In the event Giuliano de' Medici was murdered but his brother Lorenzo escaped. The attempt took place on Sunday 26th April 1478.

77 Convocation called for an end to capital punishment for the first time in 1961 (Lower House) and 1962 (Upper House).

78 Potter, *Hanging in Judgement*, especially pp. 187, 193, 198–9, 202, similarly for other Anglicans p. 254 note 6.

79 At the time 1 Timothy was written there may not have been any distinction between priests (elders) and bishops (overseers). But this only opens up the possibility that all priests should be married to one woman, not just bishops. Rather disingenuously the Jerusalem Bible uses the word 'elder', pleading in a footnote that the Greek word *episkopos* had not yet acquired the meaning of 'bishop' when this was written.

80 Different versions of the disciples abandoning their fishing nets are given at Matthew 4:21–2, Mark 1:19–20 and Luke 5:10–11.

81 That (Simon) Peter was married is shown by reference to his mother-in-law (Matthew 8:14, Mark 1:29–30 and Luke 4:38). According to Protestant versions of the Bible Peter (= Cephas) took his wife with him on his travels, but in Catholic versions he did not (1 Corinthians 9:5).

82 The Gospel of St Thomas, Saying 55.

83 The Gospel of St Thomas, Saying 103. (*The Secret Teachings of Jesus*, p. 37, gives a politically correct gender-free version.) Elsewhere Jesus announces that he has come to bring domestic conflict, as well as fire, sword and war, Saying 16.

84 Don Cupitt, in (ed. John Hick), *The Myth of God Incarnate*, pp. 133–4.

85 Statutes in the time of Hadrian made castration without official permission a capital offence, presumably because of its unacceptable popularity. St Justin Martyr in his *1st Apology* refers with approval to a young man who wanted to be castrated. Origen of course castrated himself.

86 Eusebius for example mentions with approval one Basilides who was martyred having 'insisted that he was unable to swear an oath in any circumstances'. Eusebius, *The History of the Church*, 6:5.

87 Irenaeus, *Adversus Omnes Haereses*, II, xxviii, 1, St Jerome, C. *Ruff* 2,27, *Praef in Paral*, St Thomas Aquinas, *Summa Theologica* 1,1,10. For further confirmation see Stone, *Outlines of Christian Dogma*, p. 310.

88 Father John Furniss, *The Sight of Hell*, 1855. Extracts quoted are from XXVII The Fourth Dungeon and XXVIII The Fifth Dungeon. The Catholic Encyclopaedia notes that 'He was a wonderful story-teller, seldom moving to laughter but often to tears. He spent his spare time writing books for children which, though written with the utmost simplicity of language, are models of good English.' It

also says that he sold over four million booklets in English-speaking countries alone.

89 It may seem curious that the Privy Council could decide matters of doctrine, but the Church of England is an established Church, and Parliament is its ultimate authority. The Judicial Committee of the Privy Council was the ultimate court of appeal for cases heard in the Ecclesiastical Courts. In this case the decision was reached around the turn of the nineteenth century, against the will of both English archbishops.

90 Quoted from the report of the Doctrine Commission of the Church of England, *The Mystery of Salvation* by *The Independent*, 11th January 1996.

91 Lucretius, *De Rerum Natura*, Bk. 3a.

92 The best evidence for Purgatory that has been adduced are Jesus' statement that a certain sin will be forgiven 'neither in this world, neither in the world to come' (Matthew 12:32). See also 2 Maccabees 12:39–45 regarding an apparent offering made in remission of sin.

93 Geoffrey Chaucer (*c*.1343–1400), *The Canterbury Tales* 'General Prologue', l. 686.

94 Strathern, *The Medici*, p. 136.

95 Whitehead, *Church Law*, see 'Mitre' and 'Pastoral Staff'.

96 St John Chrysostom in the fourth century, for example, seems to have no doubt that Junia was a woman. 'How enlightened and capable a woman she must have been to be deemed worthy of the title apostle' (*In Epistolam ad Ramanos homilia*, 31, 12).

97 Dr Carey was quoted in an interview for the March 1991 edition of the *Reader's Digest*. Cited in an editorial in *The Independent* newspaper, 28th February 1991.

98 Ironically the Roman Church can claim one of the first female priests in recent times, since a man in Holy Orders underwent a sex change operation in the mid-1980s. Since the Church holds that a priest remains a priest forever it is clear that it already has at least one female priest, although it has not been too vocal in its boasting. 'Beyond the Aisle', *The Economist*, p. 57, 3rd October 1987.

99 There were, however, exceptions – until the publication of *Ne Temere* in 1908 when the requirement was extended to everyone.

100 That sponsalia was recognised in preference to later matrimony was established by the Buntings Case (Bunting v Lepingwell) in 1585. See J. H. Baker, *An Introduction to English Legal History*, p. 256.

101 Restrictions were introduced for Scottish marriages in 1856, but the services of a clergyman were not required until 1940.

102 *Westdeutsche Allgemeine Zeitung*, 3rd December 1982, cited by Uta Ranke-Heinemann, *Eunuchs for the Kingdom of Heaven*, pp. 224–5. Actually the question should not have been whether the couple could have had children, but whether the man was able to sustain an erection (since 1977 the Roman Church has held that an impotent man cannot marry, even if he *is* able to father children).

103 Ware, *The Orthodox Church*, p. 282. Seven mysteries are currently recognised primarily for 'convenience in teaching'.

104 Gregory of Bergamo, *On the Reality of the Body of Christ*, 14.

105 *Outlines of Christian Doctrine*, pp. 151 and 318.

106 Fourth Lateran Council, canon 21. The name *Shrove Tuesday* reveals its nature: it was the day on which the faithful were *shriven*.

107 *Didache* 2:7.

108 The fourth-century Western festival of Epiphany seems to have been adopted from the Eastern Churches, which had celebrated Jesus' baptism since the third century.

109 26 Geo. II, c. 37, cited by Potter, *Hanging in Judgement*, p. 8.

110 The Roman Catholic *code of canon law*, canons 1176.3 and 1184.1.2.

111 45 and 56 Vict. C. 19 (Internments (Felo de se) Act, 1882).

112 http://www.rte.ie/news/2002/0320/abuse.html. Bishop Comiskey later resigned when it was revealed that he had known of Father Fortune's crimes as early as 1984 but had failed to remove him from parish work in rural Wexford, where he had regular contact with young boys.

113 This list is taken from the *Soncino Chumash*. The Authorised Version of the Bible (Leviticus 11) has a different list including rabbits, beetles, tortoises, ferrets, snails and moles because of mistranslations. Modern translations such as the NIV frankly admit in a footnote that the precise identification of some animals is uncertain.

114 No biblical justification could be found for equating a day with millions of years. The best available was 'For a thousand years in thy sight are but as yesterday when it is past, and as a watch in the night', Psalm 90:4.

115 Fraser, *The Gunpowder Plot*, p. 242.

116 John Hick, Professor of Theology at Birmingham University, in (ed. Hick) *The Myth of God Incarnate*, p. 180.

117 Quoted from the report of the Doctrine Commission of the Church of England, *The Mystery of Salvation*, by *The Independent*, 11th January 1996.

118 Sir Alfred Ayer, quoted by Gerald Priestland in *The Case Against God*, p. 84.

119 Paine, *The Age of Reason*, Pt I, p. 63.

120 Maurice Wiles in (ed. John Hick) *The Myth of God Incarnate*, p. 4.

121 Maurice Wiles in (ed. John Hick) *The Myth of God Incarnate*, p. 5.

122 Sigmund Freud, *The Future of an Illusion* (Hogarth Press, 1927), Ch. VI (translation by W. D. Robson-Scott).

123 For a comprehensive exposé of various attempts by theologians to reinterpret traditional Christian teachings see Wells, *Religious Postures*, especially Chapters 3, 4 and 5.

124 Roy A. Rappaport, *Ecology, Meaning and Religion*, North Atlantic Books (Richmond, California, 1979), p. 165.

125 *The Mystery of Salvation*, published in January 1996 by the Church of England's Doctrine Commission.

126 *The Mystery of Salvation*, published in January 1996 by the Church of England's Doctrine Commission. Reported in *The Independent*, 11th January 1996.

127 In a survey of over 500 Anglican clergymen carried out by Gallup in 1984 the following questions were asked:

Was Jesus raised bodily from the dead, three days after his crucifixion, or did he make his personality and presence known to his disciples in a spiritual, not bodily, way? Only 77 per cent of full-time clergy agreed that he had been raised bodily.

Do you believe that gospel miracles are mostly historical facts, mostly gospel writers' interpretations, or mostly legends? Only 62 per cent of full-time clergy agreed that they were historical facts.

Do you believe that the Virgin Birth is an historical fact or a legend? Only 68 per cent of full-time clergy (and only 67 per cent of suffragen and assistant bishops) believed that it was an historical fact.

The clergymen were selected at random from Crockford's Clerical Directory. Not enough bishops were willing to participate for their results to be statistically significant, and their views were not therefore reported. See *The Times*, 10th December, 1984. Church of England clergy are now discouraged from participating in such polls – apparently because many churchgoers are unhappy about the results.

128 Rudolf Bultmann and Karl Jaspers, *Zur Frage de Entmythologisierung* (*Myth and Christianity*), translated by Norbert Guterman (New York, The Noonday Press, 1958), pp. 60–61.
129 Frances Young in (ed. John Hick) *The Myth of God Incarnate*, p. 15.
130 Cicero, himself an Augur, cited with approval Cato's comment. Cato was referring to haruspices (diviners). Cicero *De Divinatione*, ii, 51, cf. *De Deorum Natura*, i, 71–2.
131 See for example Habakkuk 3:3.
132 For a detailed list of people killed by God see http://forums.macnn.com/95/political-war-lounge/305843/who-killed-more-people/ For those killed by Satan see the Book of Job.
133 This is from the Authorised Version. The Jerusalem Bible has God threatening to throw dung in priests' faces. The NIV has him threatening to spread offal on their faces.
134 Deuteronomy 18:10 is sometimes cited as a prohibition against human sacrifice but (a) it applies only to one's own sons and daughters (b) it may refer to sacrifices to other gods, and (c) it may not refer to sacrifices at all. The Hebrew word translated as *sacrifice* could equally well be translated as '*pass through*' (see footnote in the NIV).
135 Hebrews 11:32–4. In the Authorised Version the name is spelled *Jephthae*, but it is the same person. Modern translations confirm the man referred to is *Jephthah*.
136 For various interpretations see Ezekiel 20:26, Isaiah 14:21 and 2 Kings 21:6. God told others that he required sacrifices for other reasons too. The two sons of Hiel mentioned in 1 Kings 16:34 (see NIV) seem to have been killed as foundation sacrifices (an ancient practice which continued into Medieval Europe).
137 Alberic of Trois-Fontaines, *Chronica*, pp. 944–5, referring to the 183 Bulgarians sent to the stake at Mont-Aime in 1239.
138 Ehrman, *The Orthodox Corruption of Scripture*, p. 3.
139 Origen, *Contra Celsum*, 8:12.
140 The Bible repeatedly affirms that God created Jesus Christ and made him what he was: 'God hath made that same Jesus, whom ye have crucified, both Lord and Christ' (Acts 2:36). Jesus is described as '...the firstborn among many brethren' (Romans 8:29) and 'the firstborn of every creature' i.e. the firstborn of creation (Colossians 1:15). Jesus was also 'faithful to him that appointed him' (Hebrews 3:2).

141 Lewis Spence, *Egypt*, Senate (London, 1994), p. 106.

142 James I (of England, VI of Scotland), *Daemonologie* (Edinburgh, 1697), 'To the Reader'.

143 *Baal* or *Baalim*: Judges 2:11, 2:13, 3:7, 8:33, 10:10, 1 Samuel 12:10, 1 Kings 18:18 and Jeremiah 11:13; *Molech*: Leviticus 18:21; *Beelzebub*: Matthew 12:24 and 27, 10:25; *Belial*: 2 Corinthians 6:15.

144 Romans 16:20. The connection is probably based on Apocryphal and Old Testament passages, notably Wisdom 2:24.

145 Matthew 13:19, John 17:15, Ephesians 6:16, 1 John 2:13f, 3:12 and 5:18f.

146 See Graef, *Mary*, vol. 1, pp. 48 and 221, also Marina Warner, *Alone of All Her Sex*, p. 287, citing Dom. F. Mercenier, *Le Muséon*, 52 (1939): pp. 29–33, and Ashe, *The Virgin*, pp. 170–1. As Hilda Graef points out the key word translated as 'deliver' (*rysai*) is the same word used in the Lord's Prayer. So Mary, like God the Father, can deliver us (from perdition/danger/evil).

147 Germanus of Constantinople (d. 733): '...God obeys [peitharchei] you [Mary] through, and in, all things', G. Perrone, *De Immaculato Beatae Virginis Mariae Conceptu* (1847), 98; 352A. Guibert of Nogent (d. 1124): '... as a good son in this world so respects his mother's authority that she commands rather than asks, so he [Christ], who undoubtedly was once subject to her, cannot, I am sure, refuse her anything; and what (I speak humanly) she demands, not by asking but by commanding, will surely come to pass, cited by Graef, *Mary*, vol. 1, p. 225. See also p. 226. Godfrey of Admont (d. 1165) said that Christ can refuse Mary nothing, Graef, *Mary*, vol. 1, p. 248. Richard of St Laurent says that she can command [imperare] Christ by her maternal authority, Graef, *Mary*, vol. 1, p. 269. See also vol. 2, p. 20. Vincent Contenson, '...she has dominion and power over Christ', vol. 2, p. 46. John Baptist van Ketwigh: she 'orders' and 'commands' Christ, vol. 2, p. 68.

148 Graef, *Mary*, vol. 1, p. 147.

149 These epithets are cited in Graef, *Mary*, which gives comprehensive references (and many more examples). The following are references to that work. Mary can direct and guide our destinies as she wills (Andrew of Crete, vol. 1 p. 157). She can grant us 'the blessedness to come' (Andrew of Crete, vol. 1, p. 158). No one can be saved except through her (Ambrose Autpert, vol. 1, p. 167). She reigns along with her son, and is praised by angels (Hincmar, Archbishop of Rheims, vol. 1, pp. 180–1). Nothing can resist her (Euthymius, vol. 1, p. 196). She is omnipotent (Richard of St Laurent, vol. 1, p. 269, cf. Bérullle, vol. 2, p. 39, John Baptist van Ketwigh, vol. 2, p. 69). Whatever is asked of Christ will be received quicker through the intercession of Mary (Fulbert of Chartres, vol. 1, p. 206, Eadmar, vol. 1, p. 216, John Baptist van Ketwigh, vol. 2, p. 70). If he [Christ] refused her he would be breaking his own law (Guibert of Nogent, vol. 1, p. 225). She heals Hell, treads demons underfoot, saves mankind and restores fallen angels (Anselm, vol. 1, p. 212). She is above the angels (Bérullle, vol. 2, p. 32, Contenson vol. 2, p. 45). She is 'another paraclete' (John the Geometer, vol. 1, p. 198). She is the cause of our redemption (Godfrey of Amont, vol. 1, p. 248). She is our 'saviour' (salvatricem – Guibert of Nogent, vol. 1, p. 225; salvatrix – St Bridget, vol. 1, p. 309). Salvation is impossible without her (Alphonsus Ligupri, vol. 2, p. 74). She has the same 'glory' as the second person of the Trinity (Arnold of Bonneval, vol. 1, p. 244, cf. Engelebert of Admont, vol. 1,

p. 297). She is the 'complement of the Trinity' (Contenson, vol. 2, p. 45). She is called the 'Spouse of the Father' (Rupert of Deutz, vol. 1, p. 228), 'Spouse of the Holy Spirit' (Swords, vol. 1, p. 307). All three members have been described as her lovers [amatores] (Godfrey of Admont, vol. 1, p. 248). It is even ventured that she is co-creatress [symplástes] with God (Isidore Glabas, vol. 1, p. 345). 'Our Mother who art in heaven …' (Richard of St Laurent, vol. 1, p. 266). She is Queen of Mercy as God is King of Justice (Pseudo St Bonaventure, vol. 1, p. 289). She prevents God from striking sinners (Conrad of Saxony, vol. 1, p. 291, cf. Alphonsus Ligupri, vol. 2, p. 75, confirmed by the visionaries of La Sallette, vol. 2, p. 100). It is possible to appeal from God's tribunal of justice to Mary's tribunal of Mercy (John Baptist van Ketwigh, vol. 2, p. 70). She is in some respects superior to God himself (Bernadine of Sienna, vol. 1, pp. 315–18). She exercised power over him (Grignion de Montfort, vol. 2, p. 59). Theologians ask her to over-rule God (Eadmar, vol. 1, p. 220). She 'binds the power of Jesus Christ to prevent the evil he would do to the guilty' (Bérullle, vol. 2, p. 39). She 'stops the arm of God's justice, power and revenge by the force of her mercy and love' (Bérullle, vol. 2, p. 39).

150 Graef, *Mary*, vol. 1, p. 100.

151 C. H. Dodd, *The Authority of the Bible*, p. 171.

152 Stone, *An Outline of Christian Dogma*, pp. 34–41.

153 After the recital of the Angelus on 12th December 1962 Pope John XXIII declared 'Our desire is to expand the worship of guardian angels, the heavenly companions given to us by God.'

154 Genesis 32:4, Deuteronomy 2:26, Judges 6:35, Isaiah 33:7, and Malachi 1:1 all refer in the original Hebrew to *mal'akh*, which is translated as *angel*, although human beings are being referred to. 'Sons of God', *bene 'elohim*, occurs in Genesis 6:2–4 (cf. Daniel 3:25). 'Sons of the Mighty', *bene 'elim*, occurs in Psalms 29:1 and 89:7. 'Mighty ones', *gibborim*, occurs in Joel 3:11. 'The Holy Ones', *qedoshim*, occurs in Zechariah 14:5. 'Keepers', *Shomerim*, occurs in Isaiah 62:6. 'Watchers', *'irim*, occurs in Daniel 4:13. Joshua 5:14 refers to *zeba' Yahweh*, 'the host of Yahweh'; Isaiah 24:21 to *zeba' marom*, 'the host of the height'; and Deuteronomy 17:3 to *zeba' shamaim*, 'the host of heaven'.

155 Kelly, *Early Christian Doctrines*, pp. 94–5.

156 See for example Kramer, *Malleus Maleficarum*, Pt I, q2.

157 Ware, *The Orthodox Church*, pp. 236–42.

158 Ware, *The Orthodox Church*, pp. 258–61.

159 2 Corinthians 4:4. Some modern translations give the title as *the god of this age* rather than *the god of this world*, but for the present discussion it is sufficient that the word *god* is used at all.

160 In 451, at the Ecumenical Council of Chalcedon, Mary was given the title *aeiparthenos* (ever-virgin). In 649 at the first Lateran Council Pope Martin I declared Mary's perpetual virginity a dogma of the church. The catechism of the Council of Trent (AD 1563) upheld the virginity of Mary even during and after Jesus' birth. The Second Vatican Council of 1964 chose not to declare such a belief to be an article of faith. Nevertheless a number of people have been excommunicated for expressing doubts about her virginity *in partu* and *post partum*, most notably Jovinian.

161 There are several Jameses amongst Jesus' followers, and it is not always clear which is which. James the great was the brother of the disciple called John. It is unclear whether James, the brother of Jesus, might be the same person as James the

less (Mark 15:40) and/or James son of Alphaeus (Mark 3:18). It is very possible that the latter two Jameses were the same person.

162 Josephus, *Antiquities*, XX: 9.1, 200–3.

163 According to the *Golden Legend: Nativity of Our Lady*, the three Marys were daughters of St Anne by three different husbands: Joachim, father of the Mary who married Joseph; Clopas, father of the Mary who married Alphaeus (father of James the less, Joses (Joseph the Just), Simon and Jude (= Juda = Judas)); and Salome, father (sic) of the Mary who married Zebedee (father of James the Great and John the Evangelist).

164 We have already mentioned the views of the Ebionites and other early Christians. Their ideas seem to have been shared by others, even after the Church started to suppress them. See Graef, *Mary*, vol. 1, pp. 38–48 (as late as *inter alia* Tertullian, *De Carne Christi*, 23, 2, and Origen, *Homily* 14). John of Damascus, who died around 750, mentions that people say 'she is the mother of many children' (cited by Graef, *Mary*, vol. 1, p. 156).

165 Most notably Tertullian, *De Carne Christi*, 20.

166 The earliest documents to discuss the miraculous birth were the *Ascension of Isaiah* (early second century) and the *Odes of Solomon* (mid-second century). The latter dates from around the same time as the Protevangelium of James.

167 For example Epiphanius rejected the idea in *Panarion* 77, 8. Athanasius, the great champion of orthodoxy in the fourth century, also rejected it: *Letter to Epictetus*, 5.

168 The theologian John of Damascus seems to have been one of the first to espouse this idea. See Graef, *Mary*, vol. 1, p. 154. A hymn with the line 'the virgin conceived through her ear' is apparently still sung to this day. It may be found, in its Latin form, in *The Oxford Book of Latin Verse*, edited by H. W. Garrod (Oxford, 1921), pp. 23–4.

169 Statues of Mary with the whole Trinity snuggled behind an opening door in her belly were once popular objects of devotion. Characterised in this way Mary was known as the *vierge ouvrante*.

170 Irenaeus, *Adversus Omnes Haereses*, I, vii, 2.

171 The sacrifice of two birds after Jesus' birth (Luke 2:24) fulfils the purification requirements set out in Leviticus 12.

172 Jesus is said to have been 'made of a woman' in Galatians 4:4, which is generally accepted by scholars as predating the gospels.

173 The spelling of Immanuel rather than Emmanuel follows the Authorised Version.

174 From the context it is clear that the word *'almah* is applied in the Song of Solomon 6:8 to harem girls (they are mentioned along with queens and concubines). The word is also applied to a widow in Joel 1:8: 'Lament like a virgin girded with sackcloth for the husband of her youth'. English translations of the Bible still generally use the word virgin in Isaiah. *The Revised Standard Edition* is an exception, translating *'almah* more honestly as 'young woman'.

175 Jewish proselytes have been pointing out since very early times that Isaiah was talking about a young woman and not a virgin. See Eusebius, *The History of the Church*, 5:8.

176 St Justin Martyr, *Dialogue with Trypho the Jew*, 43ff., 67.

177 Ware, *The Orthodox Church*, p. 208.

178 For a discussion on Jesus as the son of Joseph, and how different manuscripts have been doctored, see Vermes, *Jesus the Jew*, pp. 215–8.

179 Vermes, *Jesus the Jew*, p. 216; see also Ashe, *The Virgin*, pp. 52–5.

180 See for example Ehrman, *The Orthodox Corruption of Scripture*, pp. 54ff.

181 Jesus' paternal ancestry is given in Matthew 1:1–17. Luke gives an ancestry for Joseph, though it is wildly incompatible with Matthew's version. The Luke author tries for the best of both worlds by citing Joseph's prestigious Royal ancestry, but then disclaiming it because of Jesus' divine origin.

182 Ignatius, *Epistle to the Ephesians* 18.2, cf. *Epistle to the Romans* 7 where Jesus is merely 'the seed of David' and *Epistle to the Romans* 9 where he is 'of David's line'.

183 Ignatius, *Epistle to the Smyrnæans*, 1.1.

184 Eusebius, *The History of the Church*, 3:27.

185 Origen, *Contra Celsum*, 1:28–32. For a fuller discussion see Warner, *Alone of All Her Sex*, pp. 35 and 367 notes 3 and 4.

186 See for example *Protevangelium of James* 21:2 and Clement of Alexandria's *Excerpta ex Theodoto*, 74.

187 Ignatius, *Epistle to the Ephesians*, 19.

188 Among the early authorities who mention the birth in a cave are St Justin Martyr, *Dialogue with Trypho the Jew*, 78; Origen, *Contra Celsum*, 1:51; and St Jerome, *Letter 58* to Paulinus.

189 The king was Astyages, his grandson was Cyrus the Great. Herodotus (1:109–129).

190 The Docetist Marcion for example used a version of the Luke gospel that lacked the nativity story.

191 For the views of some leading Christian scholars see Wells, *Religious Postures*, Ch. 3.

192 Redwood, *Reason, Ridicule and Religion*, Ch. 7.

193 Anthony Collins, *Discourse of the Grounds and Reasons of the Christian Religion*, 1724.

194 This was Frederick Denison Maurice, whose *Theological Essays* was published that year.

195 Cozens, *A Handbook of Heresies*, p. 85.

196 Pope John Paul II's mention of the E and J strands was made during his Wednesday addresses on love and sexuality between 5th August 1979 and 21st May 1980.

197 Harrington, *Wisdom Texts from Qumran*, p. 92.

198 The text is catalogued as 4Q246, *Biblical Archaeology Review*, March/April 1990, p. 24, cited in Baigent and Leigh, *The Dead Sea Scrolls Deception*, pp. 98 and 111.

199 *Zaddik* (The 'Righteous One' or the 'Just One') occurs repeatedly in the Dead Sea Scrolls. For the title Zaddik applied to James see Eusebius, *The History of the Church*, 2:1 and 2:23 citing Clement of Alexandria, Hegesippus and Josephus. For the same title used by Stephen (presumably referring to Jesus) see Acts 7:52.

200 *The Rule of the Congregation*, ii, 11–22.

201 Letter from John Allegro to Muilenburg, 24th December 1957, cited in Baigent and Leigh, *The Dead Sea Scrolls Deception*, p. 101.

202 Letter from John Allegro to Muilenburg, 24th December 1957, cited in Baigent and Leigh, *The Dead Sea Scrolls Deception*, p. 101.

203 Letter from John Allegro to Awni Dajani, 10th January 1959, cited in Baigent and Leigh, *The Dead Sea Scrolls Deception*, p. 101.

204 *New York Times*, 12th December 1990.

205 Much has been written about the academic scandal par excellence of the twentieth century, notably by John Allegro and Geza Vermes (both non-Catholic scholars in the field). A more populist work explains the scandal to a more general readership: Michael Baigent and Richard Leigh, *The Dead Sea Scrolls Deception*, Corgi (1992).

4

SCIENCE AND CHRISTIANITY

In this section we look at areas where Christianity and science have overlapped. First to be considered are some areas where science has found itself in conflict with Christian teaching. This is followed by an examination of continuing skirmishes.

TRADITIONAL CHRISTIAN BATTLEGROUNDS

The ancient Greeks were outstanding mathematicians, philosophers and scientists. One of them, Empedocles, showed that air is a material substance (and not just a void), experimented with centrifugal force, knew about sex in plants, proposed a theory of evolution, speculated that light travels at a finite speed, and was aware that solar eclipses are caused by alignments of the Sun, Moon and Earth. Knowledge of astronomy was advanced. Hipparchus accurately determined the distance between Earth and the Moon,[1] estimated the length of the lunar month to within a second, and discovered the precession of the equinoxes. Some of the achievements of the ancient Greeks are astonishing. Heron of Alexandria invented an internal combustion engine. Thales of Miletus, who lived around six centuries before the birth of Jesus, was familiar with static electricity. By Roman times elementary batteries had been invented, although no uses for them appear to have been exploited.

The outlook of Christians was fundamentally different from that of the ancient Greeks. According to Christians, God revealed himself through the Bible and the Church. As Tertullian explained, scientific research became superfluous once the gospel of Jesus Christ was available. The Church taught that it knew all there was to be known. Christian knowledge was comprehensive and unquestionable. Rational investigation was therefore unnecessary. Existing learning was not merely superfluous, but positively harmful. Theologians were convinced that God had defined strict limits on the knowledge that human beings might acquire. As St Augustine of Hippo put it, 'Hell was made for the inquisitive'. To seek to discover more was a sin and therefore also a crime, the crime of *curiositas*.

Christianity brought the Dark Ages to Europe, a period when scientific endeavour was abandoned and learning of all kinds was rooted out and destroyed. With the exception of military technology, the Church was to oppose advances in virtually every scientific discipline for many hundreds of years. Philosophers were persecuted and their books burned. Such was the persecution that men of learning were driven to destroy their own libraries rather than risk a volume being seen by a Christian informer. Efforts were made to destroy evidence of Greek successes. We can never know how much was lost forever. Some Greek learning was preserved because Christian heretics, notably Nestorians, took it east with them when they fled the wrath of the orthodox Church. These refugees flourished under Zoroastrian and Muslim rulers in centres like Damascus, Cairo, Baghdad and Gondeshapur in Persia. There they translated surviving works into Syriac, Hebrew and Arabic.

It was later re-translations of these works, mainly from Arabic into Latin, that fuelled humanism and the development of the scientific method in Western Europe almost a millennium after Christian orthodoxy had begun its intellectual holocaust. Conquests of Constantinople by crusaders in 1204 and then by the Turks in 1453 both resulted in the flight of Greek scholars to Western Europe. They brought remnants of more ancient works that had been preserved in the East. These influxes encouraged the revival of Greek learning, leading to an intellectual rebirth that we know as the European Renaissance.

Having produced no distinctive philosophy of its own, the early Church had adopted the philosophical ideas of Plato. For centuries Plato was honoured as a sort of quasi-Christian. Among the works brought back from the East were the writings of his pupil Aristotle. Aristotle appealed to medieval Christians even more than Plato, but some of his ideas seemed incompatible with theirs. Thomas Aquinas attempted to reconcile Aristotelian thought with Christianity, and for a while it was accepted that he had succeeded. Aristotle was now credited with almost divine authority, and it became as difficult to overturn his ideas as it was biblical ones. Time after time the Church would seek to suppress scientific discoveries by reference either to the Bible or to Aristotle.

Ignatius Loyola summed up the traditional Christian view when he said, 'We sacrifice the intellect to God' and Martin Luther was even more direct in expressing the view that 'Reason is the Devil's harlot'. At the end of the seventeenth century, churchmen – even Anglican churchmen – were still claiming that the Christian religion was the only real source of knowledge,[2] and the Bible was still regarded as an infallible and comprehensive encyclopædia. It provided information on the origins, history and nature of the Universe, Earth, animals and mankind. How such ideas came to be abandoned by most Christians is the history of Western science. We will now look at a few examples of what happened when new scientific truths contradicted old religious ones, beginning with the most famous case of all.

Cosmology

...I humbly begged His Holiness to agree to give him the opportunity to justify himself.
Then His Holiness answered that in these matters of the Holy Office the procedure
was simply to arrive at a censure and then call the defendant to recant.

Letter from Francesco Niccolini to Andrea Cioli, about Galileo,
dated 5th September 1632

For religious reasons it was necessary for Christian scholars to place Earth at the centre of all creation. God had created the Universe for humans, so it was natural that he should build it around them. Accepted Church doctrine in early times was that our world was flat and circular, and sat immobile at the centre of the cosmos.[3] The vault of the sky was a solid structure, a huge dome rather like a gigantic planetarium. Stars were physically moved around its inner surface by angels. Anyone adventurous and blasphemous enough could conceivably break through the firmament at the edge of the world into the hidden heavenly realms beyond.

Within the dome, theologians imagined a number of concentric hemispheres separating a series of holy regions – the seven heavens that appear in Jewish, Christian and Muslim literature.[4] Churchmen knew exactly where the centre of their circumscribed world was. It was Jerusalem, as medieval maps confirm. Indeed the precise spot within Jerusalem could be identified, for it was where Jesus had been crucified. It is supposedly located in the Church of the Holy Sepulchre. The site of the crucifixion thus marked the radial centre of the hemispherical firmament – the exact centre of the Universe.

According to later theologians the heavens were fully spherical and rotated about a stationary spherical Earth suspended in space. These heavens were made of transparent crystal, which explained why they could not be seen. The Earth lay at divine rest at the centre of all creation, just as God did in his heaven. This second spherical theory was certainly an advance on what had been believed before, but it was still well behind the ancient Greeks, who had known that Earth is spherical almost 2,000 years earlier. Parmenides of Elea recognised it to be so in the fifth century BC. Pythagoreans found proof that Earth was round: they noted that our planet cast a curved shadow on the surface of the Moon during lunar eclipses. Other Greeks spoke of the opposite side of the world where the Sun shone while it was their night. Eratosthenes of Alexandria (275–194 BC) calculated Earth's size and arrived at a circumference of 252,000 stades, which is thought to correspond to 39,690 km (24,663 miles) – only a little short of the correct figure for the polar circumference, which is 40,008 km (24,860 miles). Eratosthenes also developed the system of latitude and longitude. That Earth was spherical was so well established by Roman times that emperors carried an orb to signify their sovereignty over the whole world.

In the sixth century BC, Thales of Miletus learned from the Babylonians how to predict the motion of heavenly bodies. He was able to anticipate a solar eclipse in 585 BC. Anaxagoras of Clazomenœ, who was born around 500 BC, held the Sun to be an incandescent mass of hot stone – as near to the truth as he could have got. He also said that the Moon shone merely because of the Sun's reflected light, as indeed it does. Pythagoras seems to have speculated in the sixth century BC that Earth went round the Sun, not the Sun round Earth. Aristotle mentions Pythagoreans who regarded Earth as a planet – a heavenly body circling around the Sun, the central fire that created night and day. Towards the middle of the third century BC, Aristarchus of Samos further developed the Pythagorean theory that Earth was in motion about the Sun. Other philosophers wondered why, if the Pythagorean theory were right, the fixed stars did not appear to change position as Earth moved. But Aristarchus had an explanation for this. He pointed out that it could be accounted for by the vast distances to the fixed stars, a theory that was to be vindicated in the nineteenth century.

The ancient Pythagorean view was revived by Nicolaus Copernicus early in the sixteenth century, over 2,000 years after it had first been put forward. Copernicus did not dare to publish his ideas on the matter, because the Church was certain that Earth lay at the centre of everything. He kept his book, *De Revolutionibus Orbium Cœlestium*, secret for 36 years. It was published only after his death. The Inquisition would later condemn his cosmology as 'that false Pythagorean doctrine utterly contrary to the Holy Scriptures'. Their scriptural prooftext included Ecclesiastes 1:5, which talks about the Sun rising and setting, and Psalm 104:5 which says that Earth can never be moved. The Church knew beyond all doubt that the Sun rotated about Earth because on one occasion God had made it stand still in the sky (Joshua 10:12–13). According to the greatest Church authorities it was not possible to believe in the Pythagorean/Copernican system and still remain a Christian. Even Martin Luther agreed that this cosmology was incompatible with Christian faith.

The Church taught that sin and imperfection existed only at the centre of the Universe – on Earth and as far above its surface as the Moon. God's abode, the heavens, beyond the lunar orbit, were perfect. On Earth were imperfection and decay, and natural motion was in a straight line; in Heaven was perfection and constancy, and natural motion was perfectly circular. All celestial orbits were thus circular, and in particular the Sun moved around Earth in a circle. Apart from being wrong about which body revolves around which, the Church was also mistaken about the shape of celestial orbits. If heavenly bodies revolved around Earth in circular orbits then they would have constant apparent brightnesses. But the apparent brightnesses of planets vary, an observation that had led ancient Greeks to deduce, correctly, that the distances between

Earth and various other planets were not constant. In fact, Earth and the other planets all orbit the Sun, and their orbits do not have the shapes of circles but rather ellipses, albeit ellipses that (for Earth and most of the other planets) closely resemble circles. In an impressive piece of mathematics, the German astronomer Johannes Kepler calculated the laws of motion for the elliptical orbits of the planets around the Sun. His book *The New Astronomy* effectively proved Copernicus' heliocentric theory. It was placed on the Index in 1609.

Another error of the Church was its denial that Earth spins on its own axis. Heraclides of Pontus had realised in the fourth century BC that Earth rotates once every 24 hours. A little later Aristarchus of Samos (*c*.310–230) had advanced a complete Copernican hypothesis. He said that all planets including Earth orbit the Sun, and that Earth itself rotates on its axis. By the early 1600s, Copernicus and Kepler had vindicated Aristarchus, but the Roman Church could not accept that he had been right, much less that it had been wrong.

The greatest scientist of his day, Galileo Galilei, was fascinated by the evidence, and saw that the model proposed by Aristarchus and Copernicus was better than the one taught by the Church. Galileo was censured for teaching Copernican cosmology in 1616. Suddenly, the full implications of this cosmology were appreciated. Copernicus was posthumously declared a heretic and his cosmological treatise placed on the Index.

Galileo could no longer teach the theory, but with papal approval he continued to discuss it. His discussions did not favour the Church's theory, so he found himself in trouble again. In 1633 Pope Urban VIII had him arraigned on a charge of heresy. He was found guilty. His sentence contained the following statements:

> ...by order of His Holiness and Most Eminent and Most Reverend Lord Cardinals of this Supreme and Universal Inquisition, the Assessor Theologians assessed the two propositions of the Sun's stability and the earth's motion as follows:

> That the Sun is the centre of the universe and motionless is a proposition which is philosophically absurd and false, and formally heretical, for being explicitly contrary to Holy Scripture;

> That the earth is neither the centre of the universe nor motionless but moves even with diurnal rotation is philosophically equally absurd and false, and theologically at least erroneous in the Faith.[5]

Galileo recanted under threats of torture by the Inquisition. He was obliged to say that it was the Sun and not Earth that moved, and to abjure his heretical depravity in claiming otherwise. He may have been tortured – we would not know because victims of the Inquisition were obliged to take an oath not to divulge what had happened to them. In any case he would have before his mind the image of Giordano Bruno, another great thinker of the age. Bruno had also considered possibilities denied by the Church. He said that stars were really distant suns, and that there could be inhabited planets orbiting them. He rejected the idea of a solid firmament. He thought the Universe infinite and denied that Earth was at its centre.[6] In 1600 he had been publicly burned at the stake in Rome for his heresies.

Old and sick, and well aware of Bruno's fate, Galileo now knelt in penitence before the inquisitors. His writing on the subject, the *Dialogue Concerning the Two Chief World Systems*, was placed on the Index. He was sentenced to life imprisonment. In fact he spent the rest of his life under house arrest, a mercy almost certainly attributable to the fact that he was a personal friend of the reigning Pope.

Galileo's Copernican ideas had not been the first to create difficulties. He had made many scientific discoveries, a number of which had contradicted Church teachings. He had looked through his early telescope at the Moon and realised that it was not at all like the theologians said. It had mountains, just as the Greek philosopher Anaxagoras had said 2,000 years earlier (anyone with normal eyesight and an open mind can see their shadows), and these mountains were interspersed with plains. Few theologians would look through his telescope to confirm his findings, for they already knew for a fact that the Moon had a smooth polished surface. Those who did look said that the shadows they saw must be blemishes in the telescope lenses. They did not test this hypothesis by rotating the telescope, or by using another telescope. There was no point – again because they knew for a fact that the surface was smooth. Galileo found other difficulties with Church orthodoxy. Following Aristotle, the Church taught that natural motion on Earth was always in a straight line, but Galileo showed that projectiles describe parabolic curves. Aristotle said that a heavy object will naturally fall to the ground faster than a light one. Galileo showed that all objects fall at identical rates under gravity (unless some other force, like air resistance, acts on them). Since the Church had adopted Aristotle's teaching as its own, it was wrong every time he was.

The Church also disputed the existence of the moons of Jupiter. With his telescope Galileo had seen four moons in 1610, but churchmen said they did not exist. They could not exist because all heavenly bodies rotated around Earth. The existence of sunspots was another inconvenience. These were first studied seriously from around 1610 by Galileo and a German Jesuit priest, Christoph Scheiner (among others). Scheiner had to publish his findings under a pseudonym, because of Church opposition. The familiar argument was that the Sun, being a heavenly creation of God, must be perfect. Therefore its face could not suffer any form of blemish. The existence of sunspots thus continued to be disputed by theologians long after their discovery, even though they could (and can) sometimes be clearly seen with the naked eye around sunset. Comets provided yet another difficulty. On the one hand they were recognised as destructible, which meant that they must exist within the imperfect region bounded by the Moon; on the other hand it was realised in the seventeenth century that they orbit the Sun – which meant that they must lie beyond the Moon's orbit. Once again theological cosmology contradicted scientific cosmology. Whether they existed within or without the lunar orbit, the Church deemed that comets must have a purpose, and that purpose could only be to act as divine portents. Theologians explained how angels created them as the need arose and dismantled them when they were no longer needed.[7]

There was more. When Galileo turned his telescope on Venus he noticed that it had phases like the Moon. These phases had been predicted by the heliocentric theory, and provided another problem for the Church. Yet another difficulty was that through his telescope Galileo could see thousands of stars that were too dim to be seen with the naked eye. The problem here was that the Church taught that the stars, like everything else, existed only for the benefit of mankind. To devout churchmen it did not make sense for God to place anything in the firmament unless it visibly shed light, or was of some other practical use to people on Earth.

For similar reasons the Church stayed in the age of astrology while people were pioneering modern astronomy. Theologians knew for certain that devils were given to molesting people at certain phases of the Moon.[8] Even popes used the services of astrologers. For example, Julius II chose the date of his coronation on astrological calculations, and Paul III chose the time of each consistory (meeting of the college of cardinals) on a similar basis.[9] Leo X founded a chair of astrology. Astrology might be useful, but astronomy was not, because the Church already knew everything to be known about the mechanics of the Universe from God's infallible handbook. Even the men who pioneered astronomy spent their time trying to reconcile Church teachings to the real world. The consequence was that great minds were held back by fruitless attempts to match theology and observation. Scholars tried to explain planetary orbits as epicycles (i.e. compound circular motions) for a long time, because circles would be less offensive to orthodox religious ideas. Galileo himself spent time trying to accommodate the biblical account of the Sun standing still. Kepler might have made further important discoveries if he had not been constrained by the belief that planets are guided by angels. So might later cosmologists if they had not required God to wind up their mechanical universe like a giant clockwork toy. Such ideas affected even Isaac Newton. By the 1680s, Newton had deduced the same results concerning planetary motion as Kepler had arrived at, using his new theory of gravitation. He still imagined God nudging the planets back into line from time to time, which invited a degree of teasing from Leibnitz who wondered why God failed to get it right first time. Despite this, Newton's theory marked a turning point. Even if it was conceded that supernatural forces were needed for occasional fine-tuning, theologians were horrified by the idea of forces that acted without physical contact. If gravity could explain basic planetary motions, then supernatural explanations might soon become superfluous altogether – those guiding angels would become redundant. Newton was criticised for presuming to intrude into forbidden territory. As Edmund Halley put it, Newton had penetrated the secret mansions of the gods. Churchmen had imagined that they held all the keys to God's heavenly mansions and did not like trespassers, especially trespassers like Newton who could open doors that remained closed to them.

Edmund Halley is best remembered for giving his surname to a famous comet. He realised that various comets recorded in history were in fact the same comet reappearing every 76 years. This undermined the idea that comets were divine portents. It also suggested that theologians had been wrong about angels constructing and dismantling them as the need arose. The Anglican Church did not like trespassers any more than the Roman Catholic Church did, especially if their religious views were less than orthodox. Halley's views were less than orthodox. He believed that the world would continue forever, an idea that contradicted the doctrine of the Second Coming of Christ. Halley was suspected of atheism, and because of this he failed to win the Savilian Chair of Astronomy at Oxford in 1691–2. Its gift lay with the Anglican Church. Halley's was a petty affair in comparison to Galileo's, but the principle was the same. Churches did not want to hear theories that contradicted their own, and they did not want other people to hear them either.

Galileo's *Dialogue Concerning the Two Chief World Systems* stayed on the Index until 1835, an annually increasing embarrassment for educated Roman Catholic believers. By that time the divine role had been reduced to nothing. The French mathematician Pierre-Simon Laplace had established that those oddities that Newton had identified in the planetary orbits did not after all require gods or angels to correct them. They were, he showed, self-correcting. When Napoleon asked him where God came into celestial mechanics, Laplace replied 'I have no need for that hypothesis'.

By now it was clear to many that the theologians and their infallible truths had been comprehensively wrong. There is no solid firmament. Earth is not at the centre of the Universe, and nor is it stationary. Neither the Sun nor the planets revolve around it. Celestial orbits are not circular, and neither in general is motion in Earth's gravitational field a straight line. The Moon is not a perfect silver disk, nor is the Sun a perfect gold one.

In educated circles people would soon be noting that all significant advances in astronomy had been made since the Church lost its grip on cosmology in the seventeenth century. Churchmen who tried to hold the traditional line would find themselves distanced ever further from educated opinion. Nevertheless, senior clergymen continued to believe that angels were responsible for planetary movement and other phenomena well into the nineteenth century.[10] Some Christians still do, but they are now a small minority. Mainstream Churches have generally accommodated themselves to scientific discoveries, although without ever admitting earlier errors explicitly. The Vatican reviewed Galileo's case during the 1980s. After a ten-year enquiry the Roman Church exonerated itself and justified its earlier actions, an outcome that met with a degree of surprise in the wider world.[11] Cardinal Ratzinger speaking at La Sapienza University in Rome (and quoting Paul Feyerabend) described the Church's position as 'reasonable and just'. This explains why, after he became Pope Benedict XVI, professors and students alike complained about his planned visit to the University in 2008, causing him to call it off.[12]

Bruno's case has not yet been reconsidered, and most of the evidence has apparently now mysteriously disappeared while in the custody of the Vatican.

Mathematics and Physics

Hypatia was devoted to her magic, astrolabes, and instruments of music ...
She beguiled many people through her satanic wiles.

Bishop John of Nikiu, 4th century

One might imagine that pure mathematics could not pose too much of a threat to Christianity. Not so. Mathematics was tantamount to enquiring into God's mind, and such presumption could not be permitted. Churchmen declared geometry to be the work of the Devil, and accused mathematicians of being the authors of all heresies. Ancient thinkers like Pythagoras were regarded as having been dangerous magicians. Living mathematicians were regarded in much the same way. Hypatia, a famous woman mathematician and head of the library at Alexandria in the fifth century, was seen as a major threat by Christians. She is thought to have invented the astrolabe, an astronomical instrument, but Christians made no distinction between science and magic.

> In those days there appeared in Alexandria a female philosopher, a pagan named Hypatia, and she was devoted at all times to magic, astrolabes and instruments of music, and she beguiled many people through Satanic wiles.[13]

In 415 she was seized by monks and other followers of Cyril, the local bishop. They stripped her and dragged her naked through the streets to a church. They cut off chunks of her flesh with sharp sea-shells until she was dead, and then burned what was left of her body. Pagans were horrified, Christians delighted. For them Cyril was a hero. They dubbed him *Theophilus* or 'Lover of God'. He is now St Cyril.

Another great saint, St Augustine of Hippo, often referred to as the Father of the Inquisition, shared the opinion of his fellow saint and all right thinking Christians:

> The good Christian should beware of mathematicians and all those who make empty prophecies. The danger already exists that mathematicians have made a covenant with the Devil to darken the spirit and confine man in the bonds of Hell.[14]

Because of such hostility, mathematics progressed only a little beyond that of Euclid for many centuries. Indeed, the end of the flowering of mathematics in the ancient world is usually dated from the murder of Hypatia. How little progress was made after her time is demonstrated by the continued use of Greek textbooks. Euclid's *Elements* was still in common use in Christian schools into the twentieth century. Astrolabes are still in use today.

The Church had its own use for mathematics. In the Middle Ages almost all mathematical effort was directed towards calculating the date of Easter, a matter that the Church believed to be of the utmost importance. Complicated tables concerning so-called golden numbers and the movements of imaginary moons, called ecclesiastical moons, are still included in the Book of Common Prayer for this purpose. Real mathematics was still a form of diabolical magic. When the concept of zero was introduced from the East it was seen not as what it is – the most important advance since ancient times – but, in the words of William of Malmsbury, as 'dangerous Mohammedan magic'. Late medieval popes led an extended battle against the alien and heretical concept.

When religious reformers cleaned up Oxford University they destroyed mathematical manuscripts believing them to be conjuring books.[15] It was almost certainly at this time that the great collection of fourteenth-century works of the school of astronomers based at Merton College disappeared. In Tudor times mathematics was still a form of black magic, and the terms *conjure* and *calculate* were used as synonyms. Astrologers, conjurors and mathematicians were regarded as being the same.[16] In 1614 a Dominican preacher, Tommaso Caccini, could lampoon Galileo and all mathematicians as magicians and enemies of the faith.

Even in the eighteenth century scientists had to be wary of offending churchmen. Newton's theory of fluxions, now generally called differential calculus, the gateway to modern higher mathematics, was thought to be a threat. Bishop Berkeley tried to refute Newton's ideas, seeing them as incompatible with Christianity. Berkeley could still complain about 'heathen zeros'. The only reason Newton did not come under greater attack was that he concealed his true beliefs about Christianity and made a point of stating that he hoped his work would be useful to Christian apologists. His greatest work, the *Principia*, was deliberately written in an abstract style so that only mathematicians would understand the implications of it.

Christians were also opposed to atomic theory, largely because the Greek philosophers who had first proposed it had been atheists. These philosophers had held that the world came into existence through the natural interaction of atoms, and that life had developed out of a primeval slime. Leucippus had first developed an atomic theory, and it had been espoused by Democritus, Epicurus of Samos and the Roman philosopher Lucretius. They held that there is no purpose to the Universe and that everything is composed of physically indivisible atoms, with empty space between them. How else, they asked, could a knife cut an apple? If the apple were solid matter such a thing would be impossible.

Atoms were indestructible and were in perpetual motion, cannoning off each other when they collided, or sometimes combining if they interlocked. There were an enormous number of them, differing in size, shape and heat, and governed by mechanical laws. When men like Thomas Hobbes started to resurrect atomic theories in the seventeenth century, Christians were alarmed by the revival of this ancient horror. They were convinced that godlessness was a necessary corollary of atomism.[17] Perhaps they were right. The overwhelming majority of physicists today are both atomists and atheists.

Biology

The religion that is afraid of science dishonours God and commits suicide.
Ralph Waldo Emerson, *Journals*

Animals were an ever-increasing source of embarrassment to Christians. For one thing it became difficult to believe that they had all fitted into Noah's ark. As more and more species were discovered it became more and more difficult to reconcile the facts. Where was all the fodder stored, and what had the carnivores eaten during the voyage? How were the tropical animals kept warm, and the Arctic ones cold? How did Noah collect them all, and how did they all get back home afterwards? Finally, why were so many animals not mentioned in the Bible, God's infallible and comprehensive encyclopaedia?

Another problem was the question of why animals suffered, since they had never sinned like Adam and Eve and incurred God's wrath. One answer to this was that, despite appearances, they did not suffer. They were mere soulless automatons, so it did not matter what was done to them. This view has survived in the Roman Church to this day. But if animals did not have souls, how could they live at all? The answer to this was that they had a sort of lesser soul, or spirit, or 'vital force' much inferior to a man's and even to a woman's, but indivisible just like theirs.[18] It was this spirit that animated them, just as souls animated human beings. In the eighteenth century this theory came under suspicion when it was discovered that movement persisted in the hearts of animals after death. How was this movement possible without an animating spirit? Again, muscle tissue, even when removed from the body, would contract if pricked. But how could tissue move without an animating spirit? Thinking people started to suspect that life was not spiritual at all, but merely mechanical. Such people were called materialists and were branded by the Church as atheists.

The questions remained and indeed multiplied. If the human personality was the outward manifestation of the human soul, why was it affected by disease, or drugs, or food and drink? For that matter why was it affected by age, or temperature, or climate? Then in the 1740s Abraham Trembley discovered that a freshwater polyp, or hydra, could regenerate itself when cut into pieces. Did each piece have a spirit? If animal spirits were divisible after all, why not human souls? For the time being the question had to be left open, for inquisitive Christians had still not yet succeeded in identifying the seat of the soul. As soon as its physical location could be established, Christian truth could be proved once and for all and the materialists confounded. So far the search has been unsuccessful. The Churches seem to have given up hope of identifying a biological soul, and now deny that there is such a thing. Biologists long ago switched to more productive areas of research.

Earth Science

Had I been present at the Creation, I would have given some useful hints for the better ordering of the Universe.
Attributed to Alfonso 'the Wise', king of Castile (1221–84)

Leonardo da Vinci had suggested that Earth's past could be explained by natural forces, but this suggestion was at odds with the Christian view. God had made the world, and neither it nor its inhabitants were mutable. Any theory that contradicted this view was not to be countenanced. In the seventeenth century the Bible was still the infallible source of all knowledge:

> No one seeking to enquire into rocks or minerals, into Earth history or the formation of Earth's configuration could afford to ignore or deny the value of his primary source, the Bible.[19]

The immutability of Earth and its biology was to remain the established view up to the nineteenth century. One factor that constrained many pathways of thought was the chronology of Earth and the Universe. The Jews had held that the world had been created around 4000 BC (a belief that is still repeated at every Rosh Hashanah and every Jewish wedding ceremony). Because of an arithmetical error by a monk, it became accepted Church doctrine that it had actually been created in 4004 BC. In the sixteenth century Dr John Lightfoot, Vice-chancellor of Cambridge University, had even worked out the date and time: God started his creation at 9 am on 23rd October 4004 BC. Bishop Ussher's estimate in the mid-seventeenth century differed by 3 hours. He placed the time of creation at noon on the same day.[20] A detailed chronology was worked out for the whole of the Bible, with dates attributed to every event. Such chronologies were accorded respect comparable to the biblical text itself. When Thomas Paine pointed out the absurdities and contradictions in the Bible in *The Age of Reason*, he laid considerable stress on the absurdities of the received chronology. Both he and his readers believed that an attack on these chronologies was an attack on Christianity itself. Their common view was that if the biblical chronologies were wrong, then Christianity itself was discredited.

The position that accepted biblical chronology could not be wrong precluded any understanding of Earth sciences, or indeed any possibility of initiating such sciences. That geological processes took millions of years to shape Earth was unthinkable, as it was unthinkable that evolution had been responsible for the diversity of life on Earth. God did not make mistakes or change his mind about his creation. Animal life was immutable. Mankind had existed from the formation of Earth in 4004 BC, and so had the various animal species. The rose red city of Petra was not merely poetically half as old as time, but literally half as old as time. Climate and geography were the same as they had always been. God had created perfect animals, and allowed imperfect ones like snakes, frogs and mice, to be made by demons or to arise spontaneously from the process of putrefaction.[21]

Once again the Church was entirely mistaken, and by contrast ancient Greek thinkers had been on the right track. Anaximander, a Greek born over 600 years before Jesus, had had an inkling about evolution. He said that land animals had developed from aquatic ones and that mankind was descended from a different species. He reasoned that human beings have such long infancies that they could not always have survived as they do now. To Christians such ideas were blasphemous. God's creation was immutable. There was no possibility of change. Species could not evolve any more than they could die out. God had ordained their existence, and God did not make mistakes. All manner of explanations were found for the existence of fossils. The ones still popularly known as devil's toenails were believed to be demonic nail parings (they are actually the remains of bivalve molluscs of the genus *Gryphaea*). Belemnites were the remnants of God's thunderbolts. Ammonites were coiled snakes that had been turned to stone by an obliging local saint, such as St Hilda. The fact that they had no heads was conveniently rectified by carving heads on, so that they could be sold to pilgrims as proof of the saint's remarkable power. Fossils of ancient marine life found inland were explained by Noah's flood which had supposedly washed them there.

In the seventeenth century skeletal remains of mammoths were discovered in England. These remains were also attributed to the flood, but not everyone saw the explanation as wholly satisfactory. Another possibility was that they were the remains of elephants that had been brought over by the Romans, but this was not viable either, and neither was the theory that they were the bones of giants ('There were giants in the earth in those days...' (Genesis 6:4)). Other discoveries contributed to the confusion. Fossils found in Germany in 1696 had to be dismissed as a 'sport of nature', which was hardly a satisfactory explanation.

As early as the 1740s the Swedish taxonomist Linnaeus had realised that the 5,600 species he had named could not possibly have been accommodated by Noah's ark. In the second half of the century Robert Hooke theorised that species were mutable and liable to extinction.[22] He and others who took an interest in geology incurred the antagonism of churchmen for such ideas. The systematic cataloguing of fossils gave support to Hooke's views, for it became increasingly obvious that species had indeed become extinct. Christian teaching was also undermined by animal remains found in places with currently unsuitable climates.

Theologians had always claimed that their divine encyclopædia was not only infallible but also comprehensive. It contained all world knowledge. This belief was sustained for centuries in the face of unforeseen discoveries. It even survived the unexpected discovery of the Americas but was dealt a fatal blow by the discovery of Australasia. In the eighteenth century, Christians were at a loss to explain how the existence of a whole continent could have been omitted from their comprehensive encyclopædia.* Particularly embarrassing was the fact that earlier Christians had executed men for affirming that there existed undiscovered habitable lands on the other side of the world. Persecutors had justified themselves by reference to the Bible's infallibility and comprehensiveness. Now it was clear that they had been wrong, and the heretics had been right. For a while, the devout searched for explanations, loopholes, anything to reconcile the contradictions. None was convincing, and ever more geological discoveries were being made. By the nineteenth century the Church's traditional teachings had become untenable, but geologists and other academics were still being deprived of their careers for mentioning it.

---

* It was a long time before America was known for certain to be a separate continent. In the meanwhile its existence could be considered consistent with the second book of Esdras, which was interpreted as saying that there was only one continent.

Chemistry

Do you really believe that the sciences would ever have originated and grown if the way had not been prepared by magicians, alchemists, astrologers and witches ...
Friedrich Wilhelm Nietzsche (1844–1900), *The Gay Science*

Once Aristotle had found favour with the Christian Church, his theory that earthly matter was composed of four elements – earth, air, water and fire – was adapted and clung to despite its flaws. Any real investigation into the chemical properties of matter was suppressed. Those who tried were branded as alchemists and risked the censure of the Church authorities, although the possibility of transmuting lead into gold seems to have been too much of an attraction for many churchmen. Some employed professional alchemists: others practised alchemy themselves.

Alchemists are sometimes dismissed as little more than conjurers, but the fact is that, until chemistry emerged as a science in the wake of the Enlightenment, it was alchemists who made whatever progress was made in the field of chemistry. Alchemists were familiar with elements such as sulphur, arsenic, antimony, mercury, gold, silver and other metals. They knew that arsenic was poisonous, despite the fact that it promotes growth and increases appetite. If conventional Christian physicians had known as much, quite a few people over the centuries might have enjoyed longer lives. Alchemists created compounds from elements, for example cinnabar (mercuric sulphide). They knew about acids such as vitriol (sulphuric acid), aqua fortis (nitric acid) and aqua regia (a mixture of nitric and hydrochloric acids). They used these acids, and other methods, to refine metals. They employed techniques such as distillation to produce aqua vitæ, alcohol distilled to a high proof. They used saltpetre (potassium nitrate) to make gunpowder. One of them, Böttger (*c*.1682–1719) discovered how to make porcelain. They developed scientific theories about chemical reactions. The specialist equipment they developed can still be identified in modern laboratories.

It was alchemists who originated the theory that combustion involved phlogiston. In this case they were wrong, but they had formulated a scientifically testable theory, and in testing it the element oxygen was discovered. The alchemist Theophrastus Bombastus von Hohenheim (1493–1541) alone arguably did more for medicine than all approved

Church physicians put together over one and a half millennia. Aware of his own abilities he called himself Paracelsus because he believed himself to have surpassed Celsus, the early anti-Christian polymath. Paracelsus started the battle between scientific medicine and the atrophied Church version of Galenic medicine. The Church regarded him as an enemy, and the feeling was reciprocated (Paracelsus likened Luther and the Pope to two whores discussing chastity). Iron and other elements, copper sulphate and potassium sulphate were added to pharmacopœia through Paracelsus, and he was the first to realise a connection between goitre and cretinism. He made advances on many fronts, learning from herbalists and wise-women. He rejected the idea of panaceas in favour of specific medical treatments.

Alchemy was proto-chemistry, and as such attracted the attention of distinguished scientists. Although Robert Boyle publicly discredited alchemy he believed in its fundamental objective, transmutation, and wrote at least two treatises on the subject. Newton suspected that Boyle's role in repealing a statute against alchemy had been inspired by his own transmutation experiments.[23] Newton was himself an advocate of alchemy, and was widely criticised for it. At every step alchemists and proto-chemists faced opposition from the Church and its physicians. Chemistry emerged as a separate scientific discipline only in the nineteenth century, just after the Church had lost its power to prohibit independent research.

Pharmacy and Medicine

And the prayer of faith shall save the sick...
James 5:14–15

Herbalists had existed since ancient times, and herbalism was known everywhere. The Mesopotamians, for example, knew about hellebore, hyoscyamus, mandrake and opium. Such knowledge was scorned by the Church, as were herbalists themselves. Like alchemists, they were often accused of practising witchcraft. Had churchmen taken a more positive interest they might have learned that witches' sabbats owed their existence more to hallucinogens such as hyoscine than to Satan. They might also have learned that naturally occurring compounds can be used as antibiotics and anaesthetics. Mandrake, hemp and poppy were all alkaloids traditionally used as anaesthetics. As well as hyoscine (scopolamine), modern drugs such as picrotoxin, serpasil and cocaine were all documented in ancient pharmacopœias.

Frazier's famous *Golden Bough*, mistletoe, also known as *all-heal*, was used for remedies throughout Europe. The Church shunned it because of its pagan connotations. Ivy too was used for medicinal purposes, being a diaphoretic and cathartic. Willow bark provided an early version of aspirin for fevers and headaches.[24] Again, herbalists had known for centuries that dried foxglove leaves could be used to treat heart conditions, but it was not until 1775 that a botanist, William Withering, having learned the use of foxgloves (*Digitalis purpurea*) for treating dropsy from an old woman, introduced digitalis into orthodox medicine.

For many centuries the Church clung to the theory of signatures. Theologians taught that God had created certain plants with magical medicinal properties and that he had left clues to these properties. Thus a yellow blossom would cure jaundice, and a red one could improve the blood. A root shaped like a foot would relieve gout. Like so many other beliefs of the Church, this one was utterly mistaken and served only to hold up progress. Objective research was pointless because the Church already knew the answers. Pharmacy therefore remained static, confined in a straitjacket of error.

The Church retarded and even regressed other areas of medicine, rejecting sophisticated rational ideas of ancient times. Ancient peoples had practised surgery, including cataract operations, brain surgery and plastic surgery. They used ligatures. They were aware of the importance of public health and personal hygiene. Followers of Hippocrates held that every illness has a natural cause. Christianity rejected all of this. In their view illness was indisputably caused by sin, diabolical possession, witchcraft and other satanic forces. To deny it was to invite the attentions of the Inquisition. Those who carried out medical research were therefore constantly at risk. Men such as Leonardo da Vinci were obliged to carry out research in secret. Any publicity was dangerous. The man who recognised mental illness as the explanation for diabolical possession was persecuted and obliged to flee for his life. Anyone who adopted Hippocratic techniques was regarded as a heretic. Medical assistance was an attempt to confound the will of God. A professor of medicine at

Bologna who used skin grafts for plastic surgery was charged with impiety. Powerful churchmen forbade vaccination during smallpox epidemics because it was 'against the natural law'. Anaesthesia was prohibited on the grounds that if God meant us to suffer, then we ought to accept the suffering and not seek to ameliorate it. It was better that a woman with an ectopic pregnancy should die, in accordance with God's will, than that an operation should be performed. Christian morality informed official medicine. So it was that Christian physicians adopted the view that sexual activity was responsible for all manner of physical ills, a view that even minimal scientific research could have discredited centuries ago.

Philology

And Noah was five hundred years old: and Noah begat Shem, Ham, and Japheth.
Genesis 5:32

The Church taught that human language was a gift from God, and the fact that there were many languages was explained by reference to the Bible – that infallible encyclopædia of all world knowledge. The story was that for a while after the flood all people spoke the same language (Genesis 11:1). When people attempted to build a tower reaching up to Heaven, God confounded their plan by making them speak different languages. The story of this tower, the so-called Tower of Babel, thus accounted for the world's different languages. No better explanation was possible until the Church lost its absolute control on the subject.

The first important steps in philology were taken by Johann Herder, a student of Immanuel Kant, in an essay published in 1772. For the first time the topic was approached rationally, and the origin and development of languages investigated. Still, it was always politic to mantle advances in biblical lore. A convenient and enduring story was that three important language groups were derived from Noah's three sons: Ham, Shem and Japheth. It had long been held that they had given rise to the populations of Africa, Asia and Europe respectively. With a little development this idea could be adopted to label the known family groups. Ham's descendants spoke Hamitic, a North African family of languages including Egyptian and Berber. Shem's descendants spoke

Semitic, a Middle Eastern family including Hebrew and Arabic, and Japheth's spoke Japhetic, a group now usually known as the Indo-European family of languages. Relationships within the Indo-European family were identified and explained by William Jones in the eighteenth century.

The Greeks and Romans had been aware of similarities between various languages. Stoics and Alexandrian philosophers had theorised about the origins of language and developed the study of comparative linguistics. Without the coming of Christianity they might well have carried out important comparative studies, for example identifying the principal language groups, and perhaps making discoveries that are now impossible. Knowledge of languages such as Hittite, Etruscan, Gothic and Pictish is now lost, probably forever. As in so many areas of science, it is quite possible that the Greeks or Romans did carry out important work, and that it was destroyed by later Christians because it contradicted their own biblical explanation.

Philosophy

Philosophy for philosophers, religion for the rest
Averroës (1126–98)

Philosophy is another discipline that flourished in the ancient world. Christians did not like it, mainly because philosophers often arrived at conclusions inimical to the Christian faith. Some Greek and Roman philosophers saw the gods as human inventions and religion as an unnecessary evil. Diagoras of Melos, Lucian, Socrates, Anaxagoras and Seneca were all religious doubters. Leucippus held the belief (anathema to later Christians) that there were natural laws in the Universe. Democritus, anticipating the modern anthropologist's discovery of sky gods, suggested that religion was just a primitive personification of natural phenomena like thunder and lightning. Others noted that important beneficial things tended to be deified – things like fire and water, or the Sun and Moon. One surviving fragment of text suggests that the gods were a deliberate human intervention introduced to encourage good behaviour.[25] Epicurus of Samos (*c*.341–270 BC) saw good and evil as human conceptions and regarded religion as an unnecessary cause of fear. His primary motivation for studying nature was to rid the world of its superstition. Lucretius, a Roman philosopher, advocated morality without religion in his great poetic work *De Rerum Natura*. All of these ideas find echoes in modern thought.

Greek philosophers such as Xenophanes and Parmenides took the view that there was only one god. It was also clear to them that to be true, a religion must be equally available to all people. It was a commonplace idea in the fourth century BC that the gods were all one. Like modern Christian theologians, educated people in the Hellenic world interpreted their religion in terms of sophisticated myths and timeless psychological truths. Platonic philosophers thought about the nature of God and speculated that it might be the cosmos, masquerading under another name. The similarity with modern pantheistic ideas of God is striking. As Lucan wrote when Christianity was still an obscure Jewish sect:

> Is the abode of God anywhere but in the earth, and sea, and sky, and air, and virtue? Why do we seek heavenly ones beyond? Whatever you see, and whatever you touch, that is Jupiter.[26]

Early Christians, lacking any philosopher of note, initially attached themselves to the Neo-Platonic school but contributed little of value. Christians knew that there was only one path to truth, and that it was theirs. Philosophy was therefore at best mistaken and at worst positively evil. According to one Christian theory, philosophy was not even a human enterprise. It was the product of fallen angels, wickedly sharing the secrets of Heaven with the ungodly. So it was that philosophers were persecuted, and philosophy abandoned.

In the twelfth century Western Christendom rediscovered Aristotle. The problem was that he seemed to be right about so many things, yet some of them appeared to contradict known biblical truths. Plato was abandoned and attempts were made to reconcile Christianity with Aristotelian thought. These attempts appeared to have succeeded for a while in the thirteenth century when Thomas Aquinas synthesised Aristotelian reason and Christian faith. Philosophical investigations were now reduced to the sort of speculation popularly characterised by questions such as how many angels could dance on the point of a needle, and whether the damned shed real tears in Hell. This sort of speculation characterised a type of philosophy called scholasticism. It was as near as theologians ever came to anything like ancient or modern philosophy. Even at the time, it was recognised as absurd. Thomas More described scholastic theology as milking a billygoat into a sieve. It is no mere chance that a leading medieval Christian philosopher, Duns Scotus, a genuinely intelligent man, has had his name turned into the word *dunce*.

Aquinas's carefully constructed synthesis was soon being weakened by the facts, an inconvenient phenomenon since it was recognised that 'truth cannot contradict truth'. Within a generation his synthesis was fatally undermined by William of Occam, but a façade was propped up until its Aristotelian foundations were demolished by Galileo and Kepler and the whole edifice was consigned to history's rubble tip. The philosophical theories of the Roman Church thus became untenable, yet have never been formally abandoned.[27] Apart from the work of William of Occam, it is fair to say that virtually no significant advances were made during the many centuries that scholastic theology dominated philosophy under the Christian Church. In fact many philosophers would say that no substantial advance was made between the time of Aristotle and the eighteenth century. Any churchman who looked as though he might make a useful contribution was silenced. Men like William of Occam, Pierre Abélard, Roger Bacon, Nicolaus Copernicus, Giordano Bruno and Michael Servetus were declared heretic and either obliged to flee for their lives or else burned alive.*

Sir Francis Bacon (1561–1626) pioneered the scientific inductive method of inferring general laws from the observation of phenomena. Soon, men like Hobbes and Spinoza revived genuine philosophy outside the Church. In the coming centuries sceptics like Voltaire, Locke, Hume and J. S. Mill would turn it back into a genuine academic discipline. The Enlightenment would end the period of domination of philosophy

---

* An interesting experiment is to take any objective source of information about great world developments in the arts and sciences arranged chronologically (there are many books and websites arranged like this) – discard those advances that originated outside traditional Christendom. What you are left with is a pattern of steady advance up until the Christian era, then a tiny trickle of advances through the 1300 years or so of Christian hegemony, then a gradual increase of new discoveries following the Renaissance followed by an explosion at the Enlightenment when the Church lost its grip on power. Now go back to that tiny trickle during the Christian period and take a look at how many of them were the work of 'heretics'. Depending on the source you will probably arrive at a figure between 95% and 100%.

by the Church's scholasticism. Once again, competing schools would flourish, as they had done 2,000 years earlier under the ancient Greeks.

The Church dominated philosophy for centuries and produced almost nothing that modern philosophers would recognise as useful or even meaningful. By contrast, the works of the ancient Greeks are still studied intensively and feature in university courses. So do the works of Spinoza, Locke and Hume. Their intellectual successors, Bertrand Russell and G. E. Moore, developed an analytical philosophy that encompassed contemporary work at Oxford, Cambridge and Vienna and is now the world's largest philosophical movement. The works of Voltaire and Hobbes are long-term best sellers. Scholasticism on the other hand is now barely recognised as philosophy at all, except by some theologians. Otherwise it is of interest only to historians.

RECENT CHRISTIAN BATTLEGROUNDS

The man who never alters his opinion is like standing water,
and breeds reptiles of the mind.
William Blake, *The Marriage of Heaven and Hell*

Most of the important battles in which religion attacked science were lost centuries ago, but one in particular dominated the nineteenth century, and skirmishes have continued into the twenty-first century.

Evolution and Genetics

Extinguished theologians lie about the cradle of every science
as the strangled snakes beside the cradle of Hercules.
T. H. Huxley

During the first half of the nineteenth century new discoveries continued to chip away at theological certainties. By the 1830s the geologist Charles Lyell had realised that for geology to become a respectable science it was necessary to accept that the forces that had sculpted Earth's surface in the past were just the same as those that operate now. The problem was that this implied hugely extended timescales. Lyell doubted the story of Noah's flood and felt obliged to resign his chair at King's College London in 1833. There were biological problems too. If species were immutable then the intestinal worm must have existed since the creation. Yet Adam and Eve lived in perfection until their fruity disobedience. So how did the intestinal worm survive between the creation and the expulsion from the Garden of Eden? This question presented a serious problem for the theologians. They eventually deduced that worm eggs must have existed before the fall, but were not hatched until after it.

In England at least, the questions of Natural History were answered by Natural Theology, as developed in the work of William Paley, a fellow of Christ's College, Cambridge. Arguments were brought to bear to prove that various aspects of nature provided proof of the conscious work of a benign God. How thoughtful he had been to provide stomach linings to protect us from our own stomach acids. How clever to provide lions with big teeth. How wise to place polar bears in the Arctic instead of sun-dried deserts. How considerate to provide rabbits with conspicuous white tails, so that they would be easier to shoot. How imaginative to provide so many harmful creatures to chastise us and so remind us of our sinfulness. Such explanations convinced many, but evidence continued to accumulate to show that species were not immutable. And there were other problems too. Why had God omitted to mention Australasian marsupials in his infallible book of all world knowledge?

The whole question of the mutability of species was resolved by Charles Darwin and Alfred Wallace. Darwin had originally been destined for the Church, and had attended Paley's old college at Cambridge. In the 1830s he sailed on board the *Beagle* as ship's naturalist. He was an outstanding observer, and widely read. Amongst other works he had read Malthus on population growth, and he took Lyell's *Principles of Geology* with him on the *Beagle*. He had also been exposed to some revolutionary ideas. His own grandfather, Erasmus Darwin, had speculated about evolution. When Charles came to prepare his journal for publication after his voyage he started to question his belief in the permanence of species. As one authority says:

> Darwin was struck by a number of facts observed during his voyage
> which seemed at odds with the view that each species had been

individually created. The organic life and fossils he studied so intensively and collected with such assiduity seemed littered with clues, odd similarities, and juxtapositions. Why did closely allied animals replace one another as one travelled southwards? Why did extinct fossil species show such close structural relation to living animals? Above all, why, in the Galapagos Islands did the finches and the giant tortoises show slight variations from island to island, so that the local inhabitants could always tell from which island a tortoise had come? The more closely different species resembled each other in adjacent areas or in different epochs in the same area, the more likely did it seem that those species might share a common ancestor, and the less plausible seemed the hypothesis of a separate creation of each separate species.[28]

The horror was that Darwin and Wallace proposed a mechanism (natural selection) by which new animal species could have come into existence. Worse still, it explained how complex organs – like eyes – could have come about without the need for divine assistance. This was a severe blow to the Church because, for the first time, there was a credible alternative explanation for the existence of mankind, although Darwin himself was careful to play this down.

Clergymen in nineteenth-century England were often keen naturalists. Country parsons studied flora and fauna, and found in their studies repeated confirmation of God's creation. They knew the ways of nature, its complexity, its intricacy, its interrelationships and its curiosities. It had all been seen as evidence of a great design. But now Darwin and Wallace had blown a great hole in this bastion of certainty. Darwin himself, once a prospective candidate for the clergy, lost his Christian faith and in time came to regard Christian teaching as a 'damnable doctrine'.[29] As he said: 'The old argument of design in Nature, as given by Paley, which formerly seemed to me so conclusive, fails, now that the law of natural selection has been discovered'.[30]

Those country parsons knew too much about natural history to dismiss Darwin's theory, as uneducated fundamentalists could. As amateur naturalists they might themselves have wondered why God should have created the upland goose with webbed feet if it had never needed to swim. Why did vestigial organs exist? Why had God given to the bee a less than ideal defence – a sting that killed the bee itself if it was ever used? Why were there apparent family resemblances between horse and donkey, dog and wolf, rabbit and hare, sheep and goat, and so on? Like Darwin, amateur naturalists may well also have been horrified to think that their all-merciful God could have created something like the ichneumon wasps, whose parasitic larvae feed upon caterpillars from within their living bodies. As Darwin put it, 'What a book a devil's chaplain might write on the clumsy, wasteful, blundering, low, and horridly cruel works of nature!'[31]

Only the ignorant could ignore Darwin's discovery. His work was a bombshell that shook the Church of England and all other mainstream Churches to their foundations. Some clergymen left the Church. Others fought a rearguard action and tried to refute the theory. Some possible fronts had been foreseen by Darwin himself. For example, he had noted that any animal feature that existed for the benefit of another species, but did not confer any benefit on its own, would be fatal for his theory. Churchmen looked for such features, and some are still looking. No such feature has so far been found. Another possibility was to find an example of some feature that could not possibly be explained by evolution. This seemed a promising area, since many features had always been assumed to have been created by God purely for the delight of mankind. In Darwin's time there were quite a few possibilities, but they provided perfect scope for further research. (In investigating apparent anomalies scientists were to refine their understanding of evolution, for example identifying the gene and not the organism as the primary driver of evolution,[32] and understanding the role of sexual selection, competitive evolutionary races, and parasitism.[33]) Another argument used was that Darwin's theory failed to explain the development of complex organs, the classic example being the eye. As it turned out the eye provides a good case study showing how complex organs can evolve, since eyes have evolved many times over and there are living examples to illustrate each major stage of development.[34]

In June 1860 Thomas Huxley faced Bishop Samuel Wilberforce in a public debate at Oxford. This is generally held to mark a turning point in the influence of the Church in England, but it would take a long time for its power to wane significantly. In 1864 it was still possible to muster almost 11,000 clergymen to sign a declaration that the whole of the Bible was the word of God. Academics who accepted the new ideas had to be careful if they wanted to keep their jobs. Inconvenient fossils were now explained away as tests of faith planted deliberately by God. The idea was that the discoveries concerning fossils would affect only those with inadequate faith and thus weed them out from true believers. Alternatively, perhaps some species had become extinct after all, but all this meant was that God had made a few 'providential adjustments' for his own reasons to his perfect creation. Or perhaps there had been several separate creations. Perhaps the present one was only the last in a series of them, and only this one was described in the Bible.

Professors who spoke out for science put their chairs at risk, as Lyell had done. In America the geologist Alexander Winchell lost his position at Vanderbilt University in 1878 for informing his students that they were descended from organisms that lived before the time of Adam. Such sackings continue even now, where the Church still exercises power. For example George Coyne was removed from his position as Director of the Vatican Observatory by Pope Benedict XVI in 2006, apparently for voicing his scientific views on evolution and doubting the so-called 'intelligent design' hypothesis favoured by His Holiness.[35] Even so there are signs of movement. Well into the twentieth century the Roman Church held to the line that the creation story in Genesis was strictly historical but they and most other mainstream Churches have gone quiet on this question. Those chronologies of events alongside the text of Bibles could still be found into the twentieth century, but have now been abandoned.

As Darwin and Wallace were developing their ideas, the science of genetics was independently being pioneered by Gregor Mendel, an Augustinian monk, later Abbot of his monastery in Moravia. His work, published in 1866, was frowned upon by his superiors, even though its implications were not foreseen at the time. The significance of his work, and its relationship to that of Darwin, was not appreciated until the twentieth century. Nevertheless Mendel was consistently discouraged from pursuing his researches. In spite of this he made some of the most important biological breakthroughs of his age, although the full scope of his discoveries will never be known. The abbot who succeeded him was a conventional churchman with traditional Christian views of science, and so caused Mendel's scientific papers to be burned. Fortunately Mendel had already had some papers published. His work was rediscovered in the twentieth century, and provided a key step in unravelling the physical mechanism by which heredity and evolution operate. Mendel's discoveries were synthesised with Darwin's only in the 1930s, setting the scene for the discovery of the structure of DNA in 1953.

Creation Science

Nothing is more dangerous than an idea, when you have only one idea.
Alain (Émile-Auguste Chartier) (1868–1951),
Propos sur la religion (1938), no. 74

After a long series of defeats, mainstream Christians have given up the battle over evolution and retreated to more ethereal territory, whose existence is unknown to science. Relatively few crusaders are still prepared to sally forth to attack infidel scientists on solid ground, but some do. Skirmishes are still taking place, and Christian books are still being published that purport to disprove the theory of evolution.

Most Christians in developed countries now accept the *Theory of Evolution* as being as much a fact as the *Theory of Gravitation* or the *Germ Theory of Disease*. More liberal denominations have accepted it as a fact since the 1870s, and others have gradually been catching up. In 1996 Pope John Paul II recognised that evolution was 'more than a hypothesis'.[36] On the other hand his successor seems to favour so-called 'intelligent design'. Some 65% of people in the United States still believe that human beings were created directly by God, and that apparently does not include those who believe in 'intelligent design'.[37]

Anglican churchmen embrace Darwin's theory with enthusiasm, claiming that it demonstrates the glory of God. This position was more credible when it was widely thought that mankind stood at the pinnacle of the evolutionary tree, for it could then be claimed that evolution had been God's vehicle for creating a being worthy to worship its creator. Unfortunately no evolutionary scientist now believes mankind to hold a special place in evolution. There is no pinnacle of evolution. We are at the end of one branch and there is nothing at all special about that branch. Furthermore like all other living branches, the one we occupy is still developing. We have not reached perfection, nor are we even evolving towards perfection. Like all living creatures on Earth we are evolving to best fit our changing environment. Another shock to those who sought to place humanity high aloft at the pinnacle of creation came when it was discovered that more than 98.5 per cent of human DNA is shared with chimpanzees, and over 50% with bananas.

One reaction to such facts is simple denial. Fundamentalist Christians can still be found who deny a wide range of scientific discoveries, including the evidence that Earth is more than 6,000 years old. To do this it is necessary to reject the validity of carbon dating and similar techniques with other isotopes. They deny the reality of genetic mutation despite the fact that certain viruses (like the influenza virus) are known to mutate every year. They deny the power of selection, despite the power of artificial selection, as demonstrated, for example, by the wide variation in breeds of cats and dogs (which is attributable to selection by humans). They deny the significance of common skeletal forms and shared DNA patterns. They also refuse to accept that since the nineteenth century extensive fossil series have been discovered showing the development of a number of species. They dismiss the parallel taxonomies obtained by physical and genetic analysis. They find excuses for inconvenient bits of anatomy like the human coccyx. They also ignore the correspondence between embryonic development (ontogeny) and the evolution of the species (phylogeny), such as the gills developed by the human foetus in its early stages of development, a reminder of those of our ancient aquatic ancestors. Why do human foetuses grow a coat of hair and then lose it again at five months? Why do baleen whale foetuses grow sets of teeth that are later reabsorbed into the body? For most of us it is because ontology recapitulates phylogeny but for biblical literalists it is yet another great mystery, to set beside the mystery of why God arranged for around 99% of all species that he ever created to die out.

Some apologists repeat old arguments that have long been refuted. For example, the argument that evolution fails to explain the development of complex organs, such as the eye. This argument is still used by fundamentalists who ignore its repeated refutation. Since there is no evidence to reject evolutionary theory, fundamentalist authors are often obliged to fall back on falsehoods and half-truths.[38] Apparently unaware of the state of modern science, even mainstream churchmen are still using arguments that display ignorance of the subject. The Bishop of Birmingham, Hugh Montefiore, has employed what has been called the Argument from Personal Incredulity. It may be summarised as follows: I can't think of a reason why X should evolve, therefore there is no evolutionary reason. Consequently God must be responsible for it.

To take a specific example: I can't think of a reason why polar bears should evolve with white fur, therefore there is no evolutionary reason. Consequently God must be responsible for it. Apart from the obvious flaw in the argument, the bishop was apparently unaware that evolutionary scientists have a perfectly good explanation for the polar bear's white fur.[39]

One of the main arguments against evolution put forward by creationists is Paley's long discredited argument that the world is too complex to have occurred 'by chance' and so must have been designed by an intelligent entity. This argument betrays a misunderstanding of how evolution by natural selection operates. Although randomly-occurring genetic mutations play a part in evolution, the primary driver of the whole mechanism, natural selection, is the antithesis of a random or chance process: it is by definition *selective* i.e. non-random, non-chance. To continue trying to use Paley's argument therefore betrays not just a misunderstanding of evolution, but a wilful insistence on misunderstanding evolution.

Elsewhere, even stranger ideas survived. In 1980 a judge in Georgia stated that the teaching of evolution was a direct cause of adultery and incest. In the next decade fundamentalists in the United States enjoyed a resurgence. Taking the word *theory* to mean what it does colloquially (a guess) rather than what it does scientifically (a rigorously tested hypothesis), they concluded that evolutionary theory was no more reliable than their creationist theory. Here was another example of the linguistic deceit in action, for the whole point about scientific theories is that they can be rationally tested, and a prime characteristic of religious beliefs is that they cannot. Despite this, the ploy was partially successful. Proponents put forward the claim that creationism deserves equal scientific status, and equal time in school curriculums. In Texas, guidelines were issued stating that evolution should be presented as *only a theory*.

Attempts were made to dress creationist arguments in secular clothes. Creationism, now presented as 'intelligent design' was acclaimed by fundamentalist Christians as an alternative scientific theory, deserving of equal respect. In Kansas the School Board passed a resolution that alternative theories ('intelligent design' and evolution) should be given equal time on the scientific curriculum. This position became untenable when a third theory, that of the Church of the Flying Spaghetti Monster, was introduced to the fray with a similar request for equal time.[40] Having attracted the derision of the entire Western world, the fundamentalist

Christian members of the board were roundly defeated in the next election and this line of purporting to give equal time to all 'theories' was abandoned.

Origins of Life

I sometimes think that God, in creating man, overestimated his ability.
Oscar Wilde (1854–1900)

The failure of science to explain the diversity of life can no longer be adduced as evidence for divine creation. But the origin of life was another matter. The failure of science to explain the origin of life could still be cited as evidence for divine creation. For the argument to work it was necessary to find something special about life, something that could be explained only by recourse to God.

By the end of the eighteenth century the argument took the form that only living organisms could generate organic chemicals, and they did so because of some mysterious life force. Scientists could try to synthesise organic chemicals, but they would always fail because only God could do it. This doctrine was called *vitalism*. It was abandoned after Friedrich Wöhler showed how to synthesise an organic compound, urea, from ammonia and cyanic acid in 1828.

After regrouping, the next theological offensive was to claim that, even though scientists could synthesise organic chemicals, they could not explain how the building blocks of life could have come into being. In 1952–3, Stanley Miller and Harold Urey demonstrated that an electric charge passed through an atmosphere of simple inorganic gases could produce amino acids and nitrogenous bases. It was now clear that complex organic compounds, the building blocks of life, could be made under natural conditions from a mixture of naturally occurring gases such as ammonia, nitrogen, methane, oxides of carbon and water vapour. Another line was looking untenable, so an alternative was required.

The best alternative argument was that, however clever scientists were, they could not explain how Mendelian inheritance worked. The mechanisms were a divine secret. But not for long. Crick and Watson discovered the structure of DNA within months of Miller and Urey's experiments. Now the work of Darwin and Mendel fitted even more firmly into place.

The next line was that however clever scientists were, they could not create life itself. The giving of life was the province of God alone, and he would not permit mere humans to usurp his prerogatives. But then scientists started to do exactly that. Complex self-replicating molecules have been developed in a number of laboratories, and even if these discoveries are discounted (on the grounds that the environment is artificial, or life is more than molecular replication) there are other ways of creating life. Animals were cloned, hybrids created artificially, and human babies fertilised in a test tube. The human genome has been deciphered so that the only remaining constraints on creating human life are ethical ones. The Churches no longer assert that scientists will never be able to create life. On the contrary, many complain that they already can and do. Ardent Christians in various countries now campaign for ever tighter laws to stop them.

Consequences

> *When enough people share a delusion, it loses its status as a psychosis and gets a religious tax exemption instead.*
> **Ronald DeSousa**

For traditional Christianity, science was sinful. The Bible contained the answers to all questions. Consequently almost no progress in human knowledge occurred while the Church controlled learning. It impeded and regressed progress in all fields, except scientific warfare, for hundreds of years. It tried to extinguish the learning of the ancient world, and persecuted proto-scientists within its own dominions – herbalists, midwives, alchemists and others. Only in the late Middle Ages did people start to realise how much they had lost, and were then obliged to comb the known world for items of ancient knowledge that their Christian forbears had failed to destroy. When Europeans began to explore the world in the fifteenth century, they had to re-learn the arts of map-making and navigation from Ptolemy's *Almegast*, a compendium of Alexandrian learning dating from around AD 150, shortly before Christians took over power in the Roman Empire.

If Christians had encouraged the sort of theoretical enquiry permitted in ancient times, our knowledge today would certainly be much greater than it is. Without the restraints on free thought and suppression of contrary opinions, the theory of evolution might have been proposed centuries earlier than it was. If genuine rational enquiry had been encouraged, there is no other reason why technology should not have developed much earlier. Hypatia, or someone like her, might have developed advanced scientific methods. Electricity and magnetism might have been harnessed during the Dark Ages. Non-Euclidean geometry, the theory of relativity, non-standard algebras, atomic physics, modern technologies, and a host of other developments could have taken place 1,000 years ago. People then were essentially no different from people now. Their mental abilities were the same. The only difference was the influence of the Church.

Arguably, one of the greatest crimes of the Church was to divert great minds into vapid speculation when those minds might have helped mankind in medical research or in a thousand other useful ways. Men like Aquinas and Duns Scotus spent their time speculating about the location of Hell; the Jesuit Athanasius Kircher spent his time working out how Noah's ark was constructed. Kircher was one of the greatest ever minds of conventional Christendom. As a scientist he might have made important contributions to the world. As it is he is remembered by a few for his religiosity, his 'vomiting machine', his eaves-dropping statues, his cabalistic studies and a sort of musical instrument powered by screeching cats.

Such men (and countless unknown women) might have rivalled Leonardo da Vinci or Galileo if the Church had not trammelled their minds. Who knows how far society might have advanced if Galileo had not been constrained by the orthodox view that planetary orbits must be circular, or Kepler by the view that angels kept the planets moving? How much more might Newton have achieved if he had not spent so much time attempting to decipher the Bible's hidden secrets, or Darwin as a young putative clergyman if he had spent less time puzzling over bogus prophecies in the book of Daniel?

Christianity has always made an enemy of science, although science has only ever made an enemy of ignorance. The Church declared war on science, and used every weapon it had: coercion, censorship, suppression, persecution, torture, imprisonment and the stake. The Church had God on its side in every battle, yet it lost every one, generally to a handful of independent and often self-financing freethinking eccentrics – always after a prolonged struggle. Christianity's book of all world knowledge, the Bible, was shown to be badly flawed in many ways. The Christian Churches, depending upon it, were consistently wrong. They were wrong about the age of the cosmos and of Earth. They were wrong about the length of time mankind had existed. They were wrong about geographic and climatic stability. They were wrong about the immutability of species and the occurrence of mass extinctions. Christians thought that they were right beyond all doubt and asserted that they were voicing God's eternal truths, as God himself confirmed to them from time to time, yet they were consistently and comprehensively wrong.

As they retreated, the Church fought rearguard actions. As it withdrew it was left with ever-smaller patches of territory. The God who once ruled everywhere became the God of the Gaps, as Einstein called him. Christianity now occupied gaps in scientific knowledge where science had not yet advanced. The God of the Gaps became ever less credible as the gaps became smaller and fewer. Protestants have learned to retreat ever more gracefully, and now rarely pick new fights. Roman Catholics generally hold out until faced with mass desertions by the faithful, then abandon territory as quietly as possible, and then claim that they never held that particular territory anyway. Fundamentalists imagine that they still hold territory that everyone else agrees was lost many years ago. At the other extreme liberal theologians are careful not to claim any territory at all that they might conceivably have to relinquish at any stage in the future and, to make doubly sure, have developed their own language comprehensible only to themselves and impenetrable to everyone else.

Now the areas of conflict arise for different reasons, for example because academic disciplines have taken an interest in Christianity and its belief system. Archaeologists have uncovered acts of vandalism; chemists have revealed the frequency with which documents were forged; biologists and physicists have exposed miracle-working relics as frauds; historians have shown where and when doctrines originated; psychologists have identified factors that predispose people to Christian belief; psychiatrists have revealed the nature of sadomasochistic and other sexual fantasies so popular in traditional Christianity; anthropologists have shown Christianity to be much the same as other religions in function and development; philosophers have discredited Christianity's 'proofs' of God's existence, and indeed the whole of scholastic philosophy, just as astronomers comprehensively discredited the Church's cosmology. Scientific revelations are sometimes seen by the devout as unfair, and sometimes even as fabrications – as though scientists were attacking Christian belief, rather than exposing the truth.

Christians are still generally antipathetic to scientific endeavour. Studies during the twentieth century revealed for example that Christians are vastly under-represented among American scientists. In one study Roman Catholics accounted for less than 1 per cent of the scientists surveyed, although they accounted for over 26 per cent of the population at large. Non-Christians on the other hand were vastly over-represented. Some 77 per cent of scientists were neither Protestant nor Roman Catholic, yet only 7 per cent of the population fell into this category.[41] Christian graduates saw a serious conflict between science and Church teachings.[42] A study concentrating on differences between academic disciplines revealed that fewer than 14 per cent of distinguished psychologists believed in God. No figures were available for philosophers, apparently because they found the concept meaningless, or at least inadequately defined.[43] Other studies revealed that the more eminent scientists were, the less likely they were to believe in God,[44] and another that the strength of religious belief is inversely related to scientific productivity.[45] Another study showed that the strength of religious belief is related to authoritarianism and inversely related to creativity.[46]

NOTES

1   Hipparchus estimated the distance to the Moon (which on average is about 385,000 km or 240,000 miles) to within 5 per cent of the correct figure. Ptolemy estimated the average distance of the Moon from Earth at 29.5 times Earth's diameter. The correct figure is about 30.2.

2   Even senior academics thought that religion was the only source of knowledge. One notable one was the Master of Christ's College, Cambridge, Ralph Cudworth, author of *The True Intellectual System of the Universe* (1678).

3   Revelation 7:1 clearly refers to Earth's four corners. It is not obvious how there could be four corners if Earth was circular and flat, but orthodoxy nevertheless held that there were.

4   See for example 2 Corinthians 12:2, and more explicitly the Koran 41:10–13 and 67:4–6.

5 Inquisitors' sentence dated 22nd June 1633, quoted by Finocchiaro, *The Galileo Affair*, p. 288. [I have taken the liberty of changing the word *world* to *universe*, as this better conveys the intended meaning, without going into detail about Finocchiaro's usage of the word *world* – which is of course in any case a translation into English – JM].

6 Giordano Bruno, *On the Infinite Universe and Worlds* (London, 1584).

7 Kramer and Sprenger, *Malleus Maleficarum*, Pt I, q5.

8 Kramer and Sprenger, *Malleus Maleficarum*, Pt I, q5.

9 Seznec, *The Survival of Pagan Gods*, p. 57.

10 'The angels are the real cause of movement, light, life and the elementary principles which are offered to our senses in different combinations, and thus suggest the idea of cause and effect and what we call the laws of nature.' Cardinal Newman, *Apologia pro Vita Sua*, 1864, p. 152.

11 *The Times*, 10th May 1983. See also 'Inquisition in the Clear over Galileo', *The Independent on Sunday*, 11th November 1992.

12 John Paul II was loudly heckled when he spoke at La Sapienza University in 1991, but Cardinal Ratzinger was even less liked. For the 2008 cancellation see 'Galileo protest halts pope's visit', http://www.cnn.com/2008/WORLD/europe/01/15/pope.protest/index.html and 'Papal visit scuppered by scholars', http://news.bbc.co.uk/2/hi/europe/7188860.stm.

13 The quotation is from John, Bishop of Nikiu, from his *Chronicle* 84.87–103. For a full translation of his account of Hypatia's murder, see http://www.badsnewsaboutchristianity.com.

14 St Augustine, *De Genesi ad Litteram*, II, xvii, 37. This English translation is from Morris Kline, *Mathematics in Western Culture*, Oxford University Press (New York, 1953). The original Latin reads: 'Quapropter bono christiano, sive mathematici, sive quilibet impie divinantium, maxime dicentes vera, cavendi sunt, ne consortio daemoniorum animam deceptam, pacto quodam societatis irretiant.'

15 John Aubrey, *Brief Lives*, p. 29, cited by Peter J. Zetterberg, 'The Mistaking of "The Mathematics" for Magic in Tudor and Stuart England', *Sixteenth Century Journal*, v11 (1980), p. 85.

16 John Aubrey, *Brief Lives*, p. 167.

17 Redwood, *Reason, Ridicule and Religion*, pp. 109–10 and 216.

18 Alternatively, all living things had spirits, but humans had souls in addition to their spirits (cf. 1 Thessalonians 5:23).

19 Redwood, *Reason, Ridicule and Religion*, p. 116.

20 For a sympathetic assessment of Ussher's chronology see Stephen J. Gould, *Eight Little Piggies*, Jonathan Cape (London, 1993), Chapter 12 ('Fall in the House of Ussher'). The French, following the Jesuit Petavius, placed the creation on Monday 26th October, 21 years later than Ussher.

21 Kramer and Sprenger, *Malleus Maleficarum*, Pt II, q1, c8.

22 Robert Hooke, *The Posthumous Works* (London, 1705).

23 H. W. Turnbull (ed.), *The Correspondence of Isaac Newton* (Cambridge, 1941), iii, p. 217.

24 Willow bark and other barks and plants provided salicylic acid, the structure and properties of which are almost identical to those of aspirin (acetylsalicylic acid).

25 Critas, *Sysyphus*, fragment 25.

26 Lucan (AD 39–65), *Pharsalia*, I, 128.

27 For example the Church theory of 'Universals' proved to be a dead end, and the distinction between 'substance' and 'accidents' a positive embarrassment, which the Roman Church is still stuck with because the concept of Transubstantiation depends upon it.

28 John Burrow, in his Editor's Introduction to the Penguin edition of Darwin's *Origin of Species*.

29 Charles Darwin, *Autobiography* (1958 edition), cited by Knight, *Humanist Anthology*, p. 61. It is not absolutely clear from the text whether Darwin was referring to Christianity in general, or to the Christian doctrine of eternal punishment in particular:

'Thus disbelief crept over me at a very slow rate, but was at last complete. The rate was so slow that I felt no distress, and have never since doubted even for a single second that my conclusion was correct. I can indeed hardly see how anyone ought to wish Christianity to be true; for if so the plain language of the text seems to show that the men who do not believe, and this would include my Father, Brother almost all my best friends, will be everlastingly punished. And this is a damnable doctrine.'

30 Charles Darwin, *Autobiography* (1958 edition), cited by Knight, *Humanist Anthology*, p. 61.

31 Charles Darwin (1809–82), Letter to J. D. Hooker, 13th July 1856 (in Correspondence of Charles Darwin vol. 6 (1990)).

32 See for example Richard Dawkins, *The Selfish Gene*, new ed., Oxford University Press (New York, 1989).

33 See for example Matt Ridley, *The Red Queen*, Penguin (London, 1994).

34 See for example Richard Dawkins, *River Out of Eden*, pp. 88ff. for a simple explanation, also *The Blind Watchmaker* by the same author.

35 'Pope Sacks Astronomer Over Evolution Debate', *Daily Mail*, 23rd August 2006. http://www.dailymail.co.uk/news/article-401950/Pope-sacks-astronomer-evolution-debate.html

36 'Message delivered to the Pontifical Academy of Sciences', 22nd October 1996. See http://www.ewtn.com/library/PAPALDOC/JP961022.HTM for the full text in English.

37 Wolpert, *Six Impossible Things Before Breakfast*, p. 212 reports oddly that 'Some 65 per cent of Americans believe that human beings were directly created by God, while only 22% per cent believe in Darwinian evolution and intelligent design'. American scientists are more in line with their peers in Western Europe: over 90% of scientists belonging to the National Academy of Science in the United States are non-believers (p. 214).

38 A spectacular example of a book opposed to evolutionary theory that relies heavily on falsehoods and invalid reasoning is *Life – How Did It Get Here? By Evolution or Creation?* published by the Watchtower Bible and Tract Society Of New York, Inc. International Bible Students Association, Brooklyn, New York, United States (1985).

39 Richard Dawkins, *The Blind Watchmaker*, pp. 37–41, deals with the bishop's Argument from Personal Incredulity and in particular the whiteness of polar bears.

40 The *Church of the Flying Spaghetti Monster* is still flourishing. See http://www.venganza.org/about/open-letter.

41 F. Bello, 'The Young Scientists', *Fortune*, 49, (1954), pp. 142–3.
42 G. E. Lenski, *The Religious Factor*, revised edition, Doubleday (New York, 1963).
43 J. H. Leuba (1934), 'Religious beliefs of American Scientists', *Harper's*, 169, p. 297.
44 Several studies showing an inverse relationship between Christian belief and scientific eminence are cited by Argyle and Beit-Hallahmi in *The Social Psychology of Religion*, p. 88.
45 P. Heist *et al* (1961), 'Personality and Scholarship', *Science*, 133, pp. 362–7.
46 Several studies showing an inverse relationship between creativity and author-itarianism, and religious belief are cited by Argyle and Beit-Hallahmi in *The Social Psychology of Religion*, pp. 94–5.

5

RELIGION TODAY AND TOMORROW

*God is dead: but considering the state the species Man is in, there will
perhaps be caves, for ages yet, in which his shadow will be shown.*
Friedrich Wilhelm Nietzsche (1844–1900), *Die Fröhliche Wissenschaft*

Our review of Christianity has revealed a story that is different from
the one preferred by Christian Churches, Christian schools and Christian
history books.

In this section we look at some of the ways in which Christianity
continues to affect society, and ways in which it may affect it in the future.

First we take a look at the question of religious discrimination in
the world today, with examples from religions other than Christianity,
before turning to Christianity itself.

RELIGIOUS DISCRIMINATION

*We must respect the other fellow's religion, but only in the sense and to the extent
that we respect his theory that his wife is beautiful and his children smart.*
H. L. Mencken, Notebooks, *'Minority Report'*

One of the most obvious problems caused by allowing special legal rights
to members of one religion is that it gives others cause for complaint.
In Britain, Muslims, Jews, Hindus and others are outraged to find that
their faith is not protected by the law of blasphemy as the Christian
faith is. If the law discriminates in favour of one group then it must
equally discriminate against those who do not belong to that group.
To take another example, British law requires that animals should be

rendered unconscious before slaughter, but exceptions are made for certain religious groups. Jews for example may slaughter conscious animals (*shechita*), in order for the meat to be considered kosher. Similarly, Muslims slaughter animals in conditions that many people consider unacceptable so that the meat may be *halal*. Ordinary farmers on the other hand would commit a criminal offence if they killed their own beasts in the same way. The Free Church of Country Sports is a religion that considers fox-hunting a religious duty.[1] One is at a loss to explain why this Church does not benefit from articles 9 and 14 of the 1998 Human Rights Act which allows organisations to manifest their religious beliefs and not be discriminated against because of those beliefs. Why does the law permit ritual killing for Muslims and Jews, but not for members of the Free Church of Country Sports?

Here is another British example. Sikh men are exempted from having to wear motorcycle crash helmets because of a mistaken belief that they have a religious duty to wear turbans.* Anyone who refuses to wear a motorcycle crash helmet for other reasons, whether religious or not, commits an offence.

In some countries religious leaders enjoy a legal exemption permitting them to take drugs that are otherwise illegal. For example, in India Hindu Sadhus are not prosecuted for smoking marijuana. Other countries are less understanding. In Britain, Rastafarians claim that smoking marijuana (ganja) is essential to their religion, yet no exemption is made for them. Similarly, in the United States members of the Native American Church are prevented from using traditional psychotropic drugs. The fact is that wherever we draw the line some religions will feel aggrieved. Christians in the United States were shocked to find that under the American Constitution witchcraft was as legitimate a religion as their own.[2] If there were any Satanists in the world, it is difficult to see why Satanism should not also enjoy formal recognition as well. Clearly it is impractical to extend immunities to all of the requirements of all religions. If this were done, we might expect to see for example the introduction or reintroduction of all manner of religious practices: Hindu *suttee* (widows immolating themselves on their husbands' funeral

---

* There is a Sikh religious duty concerning the cutting of hair. Wearing the turban is a cultural convention.

pyres), Celtic head hunting, Saxon stranglings, annual human sacrifices to the Sun, ritual mutilations, the burning of heretics, and so on.

In other cases the law is not enforced against selected religious groups – apparently depending on how vocal the group chooses to be. Since the Satanic Verses affair in 1988 a number of Muslim clerics have made death threats against Salman Rushdie, Jewish people, Americans, and others.[3] Further spates of death threats were made following the events of 11 September 2001 and again after October 2005 when a Danish newspaper published cartoons featuring the person of the prophet Mohammed. If any secular person had made such threats they would have been arrested, tried and almost certainly gaoled. Unofficial exemptions generate ill feeling because they undermine the principle of equality before the law. So it is that Muslims question why churches are allowed to ring bells to call the faithful to prayer, while their muezzins are not allowed to fit loudspeakers on their minarets for the same purpose. On the other hand Christians in London question why police sniffer dogs are allowed in churches but not into the religious areas of mosques. Animal lovers wonder why practitioners of Voodoo seem to be free to break the bones of conscious animals before sacrificing them. Few, if any, prosecutions are brought for animal cruelty, though prosecutions of farmers and pet owners are common enough for less cruel activities.

In the United States, religious groups are exempt from prosecution for denying medical attention to their children. Again in the United States, there are sects who handle poisonous snakes, relying on Jesus' promises of immunity to believers, as described in Luke 10:19 and Mark 16:18. Many adherents die of the bites they sustain. No statistics are available on the number of children killed in this way and we can only speculate on the likely success of a murder charge in such circumstances, because none has ever been brought. The law is applied selectively elsewhere too. In some countries it is unacceptable for Moonies to indoctrinate children and young adults, yet it is acceptable for Christian, Jewish and Muslim schools, seminaries and madrassas to indoctrinate children in the same way.

In many countries male genital mutilation (circumcision) is lawful, but female genital mutilation (clitoridectomy) is not. There is no medical justification for either practice and the legal acceptance of one but not the other is essentially a form of cultural and religious discrimination.

It is not only the law that discriminates. Employers also discriminate, often citing cultural sensitivity. Here is a revealing letter from a Dr Harry

Baker to a national newspaper in the United Kingdom, published in 2007:

> I hear doctors may be allowed to extend the range of procedures they can opt out of on religious or conscience grounds, and some Muslim medical students are refusing to attend lectures relating to sexually transmitted diseases or diseases caused by alcohol abuse. Now you report Sainsbury's has agreed that Muslims should be able to opt out of selling alcohol... What about Jews selling pork, Christians not selling books by Richard Dawkins or Christopher Hitchens, atheists not selling bibles, vegetarians not selling meat, antivivisectionists not selling anything in most chemists shops? Why are Muslims so privileged?[4]

Dr Baker seems unaware that Roman Catholic physicians and pharmacists already enjoy exemptions allowing them to opt not to give family planning advice and not to provide contraceptives, but his broader point is valid. Religious discrimination creates more problems than it solves.

Few liberal thinkers would wish to deny others the right to believe whatever they want. All beliefs must be respected equally, however bizarre or odious. But can there ever be a justification for the State giving support to any set of religious beliefs? If there is, how should we decide which set (or sets) of beliefs merit such support? Certainly there is no objective way of distinguishing a true religion from a false one, or a true sect from a false one. By all objective tests Christianity fails to distinguish itself from other mainstream religions. Similarly, within Christianity no sect stands out as more genuine than any other. From any objective viewpoint all religions and sects appear to be equally valid or equally invalid. Clearly we cannot permit all religions to enjoy the special privileges that they would like – not least because the requirements of one group would cause offence to other groups. Providing privileges and exemptions to one group is guaranteed to cause trouble. If Christians can have state-funded schools, why cannot Muslims? If Muslims, why not Jehovah's Witnesses? If Jehovah's Witnesses, why not Jedi?[5]

Many non-Christians find Christian traditional worship offensive. For example, the idea of worshipping a dead man, and claiming to eat his raw flesh and drink his cold blood, is horrifying to some. Encouraging, or forcing, children to join in such behaviour is arguably a form of cruelty amounting to child abuse. Many children are obliged to look at representations of dreadful martyrdoms and other such horrors, and are told in great detail about the tortures of Hell, often with obvious sadomasochist overtones. Gory depictions of the crucifixion on classroom walls in Bavaria led to at least one child being made to feel ill, and ultimately to a court case over the matter in 1996. If gory, cruel and often fictitious Christian depictions can be allowed, why not a wide range of other sadomasochistic images belonging to other religions and interest groups.

Once again, the issue here is that of equality before the law. Why should one set of beliefs ever be officially favoured over another? If the law can exempt Sikhs from wearing motorcycle crash helmets, why can it not exempt Rastafarians from the law prohibiting the smoking of marijuana? And why should religious views merit rights denied to other views? For example what about eccentrics who decline to wear motorcycle crash helmets on political grounds? Are religious beliefs more worthy than political ones, or ethical ones, or philosophical ones?

In fact there is a simple solution to all these problems. The solution is to treat all religious groups in the same way as each other, and as any secular group. If none enjoyed special rights, privileges or exemptions, then no one would feel discriminated against. This would hardly revolutionise the world, but it would end anachronistic discrimination and equalise obligations. This solution is obvious, equitable and simple – and has so far been adopted nowhere in the civilised world.

CHRISTIAN DISCRIMINATION

A corrupt tree bringeth forth evil fruit.
Matthew 7:17

The Church still holds on to vestiges of inequality, with no evidence of embarrassment. For example, on the one hand modern clergymen decry sexual discrimination in Britain, while their Churches practise it, enjoying one of the few exemptions from Equal Opportunities legislation. Similarly they acclaim Human Rights legislation although their sole contribution to it was to negotiate exemptions for themselves. Such concessions are common around the world. European Community legislation upholds the practices of Orthodox monks on the Mount Athos Peninsula. Even today females are not permitted to defile the peninsula by their presence – not even female animals.

In 2003 the European Union passed laws prohibiting discrimination on religious grounds, making exceptions for organisations with a religious ethos. The idea was to allow for jobs, such as Christian priests, for which at least some Christian belief might be reasonably expected in the less liberal Churches. Christian groups in the United Kingdom immediately started planning ways to exploit this loophole to encompass a wide range of jobs, from science teachers to cleaners. All an organisation needed to do was draw up a suitable document confirming its religious ethos, and it would be able to dismiss non-Christians and replace them with Christians. A number of Christian charities including the YMCA sponsored a set of guidelines to allow schools and other organisations to exploit the new legislation to weed out non-believers and recruit believers while staying within the new law.[6]

Churches in Britain enjoy many special rights – tax exemptions, exemptions from civil duties, exemption from planning laws, over-representation in Parliament, a separate court system, and so on. Other laws are designed to protect Christianity. Blasphemy laws protect Christian beliefs but not others. Section 2 of the *Ecclesiastical Courts Jurisdiction Act* of 1860 gives special powers to stifle dissent.[7] Under this Act it is illegal publicly to contradict a Christian preacher while it is not illegal to contradict a non-Christian preacher, or any other orator.

The founding fathers of the United States were keen not to allow religion any special place in the government of the country, as reflected in the first and sixth amendments to the constitution. James Madison, the author of these amendments, was against appointing chaplains. Here for example is his view on constitutional chaplains: 'The establishment of the chaplainship to Congress is a palpable violation of equal rights as well as Constitutional principles'.[8] Nevertheless, today Americans fund chaplains not only in the two Houses, but elsewhere, for example in prisons and the armed forces.

Many aspects of American law favour religion in general and Christianity in particular. For example the offence of blasphemy still exists in some states. In Massachusetts it is illegal to expose to ridicule 'the holy word of God contained in the holy scriptures'.[9] A man called Ruggles was prosecuted in New York State for blasphemy in 1810. He appealed on the grounds that there was no law of blasphemy for him to be convicted under. The Chief Justice, James Kent, stated that English common law was part of American law. Since blasphemy was an English common law offence it carried over to American law, and still does. It is thus legal in the United States to revile atheism but not Christianity: the clearest possible example of discrimination on religious grounds.

Religious discrimination takes other forms in the United States. Churches are exempt from taxes. Church schools are funded from public money. Religious pledges and songs are common in schools, despite the provisions of the Constitution. Rationalist and scientific books are commonly removed from library shelves at the behest of Christian pressure groups. Humanists are prohibited from handing out literature door-to-door (as Christian sects do) by Christian-initiated zoning laws. Pagans can be dismissed from their employment for wearing jewellery (a gold pentagram say), but no Christian could be dismissed for wearing a gold crucifix. Again, it has been almost impossible to obtain exemption from military service as a Conscientious Objector on purely philosophical grounds, yet comparatively easy on religious grounds. When the United States introduced conscription for its military presence in Vietnam, the authorities would not consider granting exemption without a supporting letter from a priest or minister. This made it impossible for atheists to gain exemption, even though studies consistently show atheists to have a greater moral abhorrence of war than mainstream Christians.

Judges frequently make rulings that favour fundamentalist Christians. One of the most curious was a judgement made by Judge Brevard Hand, a federal judge in Mobile, Alabama. In a 1987 ruling, described by the *Washington Post* as 'profoundly and irremediably wacko', he banned more than 40 school textbooks because of their secular humanist content. A keen Christian, he seems to have been under the impression that humanism was some sort of rival religion.[10] President George H. W. Bush probably spoke for many American Christians when he famously declared in the same year '… I don't know that atheists should be considered as citizens, nor should they be considered as patriots. This is one nation under God.'[11] In the United States, hardly anyone outside the atheist community bothered to challenge him on this sentiment, though it scandalised the developed World.

MORAL DANGERS OF RELIGION

*If we're absolutely sure that our beliefs are right, and those of others wrong; that
we are motivated by good, and others by evil; that the King of the Universe
speaks to us, and not to the adherents of very different faiths; that it is wicked
to challenge conventional doctrines or to ask searching questions; that our
main job is to believe and obey – then the witch mania will recur
in its infinite variations down to the time of the last man.*

Carl Sagan, *The Demon-Haunted World*

The following are some of the dangers that arise as a result of Christian
morality.

Unbalanced Views

Belief is generally regarded as at least as important as meritorious
conduct – in most Protestant sects faith is all important and all forms
of meritorious conduct ('good deeds') are irrelevant to salvation. It does
not matter what we do if our salvation depends on what we believe. This
tends to lead Christians to spend their lives in contemplation rather
than action. Moreover, action that is taken sometimes appears to be
cosmetic, as though done to gain divine merit points. Much Christian
aid to the third world has been criticised as superficial and short term,
and has arguably been responsible for more harm than good in the long
term – for example destroying local economies, breeding dependency,
and causing overpopulation. A distorted moral outlook always led to
distorted moral actions. Here is Bertrand Russell on the subject:

> The medieval conception of virtue, as one sees in their pictures,
> was of something wishy-washy, feeble, and sentimental. The most
> virtuous man was the man who retired from the world; the only
> men of action who were regarded as saints were those who wasted
> the lives and substance of their subjects in fighting the Turks, like
> St. Louis. The church would never regard a man as a saint because
> he reformed the finances, or the criminal law, or the judiciary. Such
> mere contributions to human welfare would be regarded as of
> no importance. I do not believe there is a single saint in the whole
> calendar whose saintship is due to work of public utility.[12]

Making medical advances, advancing social reform, and developing life-saving technology was, and still is for mainstream Christianity, far less impressive than performing conjuring-style miracles such as levitating or surviving being cut in half.

Personal Responsibility

In traditional Christianity moral precepts are linked to a system of supernatural rewards and punishments. This sometimes leads Christians to believe that they can avoid the consequences of their actions. Many believers imagine that they can wipe clean some sort of divine slate by confession, penitence or prayer. The danger is that people will commit serious wrongs without compunction if they imagine that God will forgive them on request. There is for example more than a suspicion that organisations like the IRA and the Italian Mafia retain priests as members to give absolution to murderers and other criminals. Churchmen and other ardent believers cheer on their fellow Christians who murder doctors for carrying out legal abortions. If a priest or minister has forgiven them on behalf of God then the murderer's conscience will be clear. Other Christians, believing what they have frequently heard preached, are under the impression that they can sin with impunity, imagining that God hates the sin, but not the sinner.

Fatalism

Traditional Christianity has encouraged a fatalistic attitude, now more popular in the East than the West. The reasoning behind it seems to be something like this: God is all-knowing, he is aware of everything that will happen until the end of time. There is therefore no point in my trying to do anything since my future, like the future of everything else in the Universe, is already determined and already known to God. There is therefore no point in my trying to avoid the plague or a traffic accident. If God has ordained that I am to die today, then there is nothing I can do to stay alive, and if he has ordained that I live, then I cannot die, however recklessly I behave. There is therefore no point in struggling to avoid or overcome disease, no point in avoiding overtaking on blind bends, and no point trying to improve my lot, or the lot of my fellow creatures. There is no point trying to eradicate poverty because

Jesus said that the poor would always be with us. This fatalism may account for the fact that Christians have played so little part in reform movements whether social, scientific, political, economic, medical, philosophical, penal, legal or constitutional, and on the contrary have generally opposed reform movements on the grounds that trying to improve life for people subverted the divine natural order, 'playing God' and 'flying in the face of the Almighty'.

Sex

The Churches seem to many to be preoccupied by sex and suffering, and continue to confuse sex with morality. Concepts of morality where sex is so important lead to conclusions at odds with mainstream opinion (Churches are now increasingly embarrassed by their traditional position that masturbation was a greater wrong than murder, and *coitus interruptus* more serious than rape).

This preoccupation with sex has led many Christians to reject contraceptive practices. In certain branches of Christianity the problems of overpopulation are simply ignored. Outside these denominations, overpopulation is widely accepted to be one of the greatest dangers facing the world today. Among the dangers are the exhaustion of natural resources, guaranteed periodic famines, an increased danger of contagious diseases, plant and animal species driven to extinction, reduced quality of life for all, a degraded environment, more industrialisation and more pollution. All this is of no consequence to those who know that God wants us to go forth and multiply.

Traditionally, gonorrhoea and syphilis were regarded by Christians as God's punishment for fornication (though it has never been explained why the punishment extended to the innocent wives and husbands of infected sinners). Dangers associated with sexually transmitted diseases are still exacerbated by Christian attitudes: examples are the Catholic Church preventing the use of condoms where they would reduce the incidence of HIV and Christian politicians and schools resisting vaccination programs against the human papillomavirus virus (which causes cervical cancer) on the grounds that sexually transmitted diseases like this provide an impediment to premarital sex.[13] Traditional Christian attitudes are reflected in the fact that gonorrhoea among teenagers is now seventy times greater in the overwhelmingly religious United States than it is in more secular countries like Holland and France.[14] Thousands, perhaps millions, of people throughout the world suffer and die unnecessarily because of Christian attitudes to sex.

Economic Development

The history of northern Europe goes back no further than that of southern Europe, nor does that of North America go further back than that of South America. The question arises as to why in each case the North should be relatively affluent.

Traditional teachings on lending money at interest (usury) stifled economic development for many centuries, until first Protestants and later Catholics decided to abandon this particular doctrine. The delay appears to partially explain why until the twentieth century at least, the largely Protestant North was relatively affluent, inventive, clean and stable, with a well-educated population, while the Catholic South was relatively poor, superstitious, squalid and politically unstable, with a large peasant population.

Is it a coincidence that these areas correspond to traditionally Protestant and Roman Catholic spheres of influence respectively? If we look elsewhere around the world the correlation is similar. One possible explanation is that Roman Catholicism is responsible directly or indirectly for authoritarianism, ignorance, overpopulation and poverty. The disparity, confirmed by objective studies, cannot be explained by geographical location, natural resources, or historical factors other than religion.

Attitudes to Truth

The religious outlook is fundamentally different from the secular humanist outlook. Secular thinkers are interested in pursuing the truth wherever it might lead: Christians are often interested in truth only when it leads to desired conclusions. Christianity has therefore always subordinated rational truth to religious dogma. The consequences of this include book burning, scientist burning, obscurantism, suppression of evidence, rewriting history, linguistic deceits, and hostility to scientific advances. Churchmen are still suppressing or manipulating other information – about the Bible, about the Dead Sea Scrolls, about ecclesiastical forgeries, and so on. As has been frequently observed, eminent scientists have rarely been typical of the religious traditions in which they grew up. Religious dogma made Christianity the enemy of science and free enquiry, and the hostility continues. Having lost medical battles over vaccination, anaesthetics and sexual health, leading churchmen are still fighting rearguard actions, for example trying to prohibit research on embryonic stem cells.

CONTINUED ABUSE OF POWER

And shame it is to see – let priests take heed – A shitten shepherd and a clean sheep
Geoffrey Chaucer (c.1340–1400), *Canterbury Tales, General Prologue*

Christian Churches continue to exert political power. This takes many forms, from Roman Catholic bishops in Ireland instructing their diminishing flocks on how to vote in State referenda, to US Baptist ministers fund-raising for extreme right-wing politicians; from English bishops sitting in Parliament to European Christian Democrats keeping Turkey out of the European Union explicitly because it is not a Christian country. Christian Churches are still active throughout the world, fomenting dissent against governments. By attributing their own political views to God, they are able to justify any form of illegality. To subvert an elected government might be treason against the state, but to fail to do so would be treason against God. Those who believe themselves to be guided by God inevitably believe that their divine inspiration supplies a higher authority than any man-made law. God's law over-rides all others. So it is that Churches ignore national laws that do not suit them. They smuggle illegal books into dozens of countries. They continue the long tradition of vandalising non-Christian religious icons. They defy court orders in Asia, Europe and the Americas. They protect war criminals, child molesters and other criminals from the secular law. They perform illegal ceremonies and hold illegal meetings. Around the world a stream of adults and children die through so-called exorcisms and other privations sanctioned by fringe and mainstream Churches alike.[15]

Despite their unlawful behaviour, Christian Churches continue to enjoy significant privileges in countries around the world. Churches are often state-funded, they run state schools, and sometimes state universities, they operate their own courts, and they are exempt from numerous taxes and from certain laws. In Britain, clergymen enjoy personal privileges such as exemption from conscription and from jury service. Bishops still sit in the House of Lords, even after parliamentary reforms made in 2000. By favouring a minority in this way other people are penalised: those others pay more taxes and shoulder a greater burden of civic responsibility while being under-represented in the legislature.

School children are often taught religious opinions as though they were established facts, often by schoolmasters who have been selected for their religious orthodoxy. In Britain schools are legally obliged to teach school children hundreds of hours of religion, yet most children leave school without ever having spent five minutes studying the elements of law, medicine, economics, politics or philosophy. In the United States they might never learn any science and leave school without understanding, or even ever having heard about, the most important ever discovery in biology. Many will leave school believing the Bible to be the literal word of God, unaware that hardly any modern theologians share this discredited view.

Another area of concern is the Church's commitment to stopping child abuse in its ranks, or lack of it. Widespread child abuse is now acknowledged in many Churches mainly in English-speaking countries where the matter has been investigated by secular authorities. Churchmen have acknowledged that paedophiles will be attracted to Holy Orders by the prospect of easy pickings and that it is impossible to identify a genuine vocation from predatory opportunism. Widespread abuse has been revealed in every country where it has been properly investigated. It is curious therefore that no Church seems to have thought to carry out its own global investigations, so that perhaps millions of children are still being sexually abused around the world in the countries where the secular authorities are not powerful enough or not willing to instigate investigations.

State funding of sectarian schools in many countries is widely seen as another source of scandal – leading in Northern Ireland for example to the perpetuation of ancient religious conflicts. The so-called Troubles in Northern Ireland only make sense when seen as the last vestige of the Wars of Religion that raged throughout Europe in the fifteenth and sixteenth centuries, and the unique sectarian school system in Northern

Ireland explains why this vestige has survived in modern times from one generation to the next.

As Richard Dawkins has pointed out, we allow parents to turn their children into Christian (or Muslim, or Hindu, etc.) children, but would not contemplate parents imposing other personal preferences and beliefs in the same way. Some people now regard religion as a form of child abuse.[16] Even in technically secular countries regressive religious ideas still hold sway – denying legislative, social, medical and scientific advances and promoting ignorance. Many people in secular societies are mystified and frightened by the effects of Christianity especially in the United States where, even in the twenty-first century, surveys reveal the continuing strength of fundamentalist religious beliefs that contradict facts. Over half the population reject the Theory of Evolution and believe the world to be less than 10,000 years old – including some 25% of school teachers. Around 20% of Americans still believe that the sun orbits the Earth.

Higher up the academic ladder, theologians are over-represented, particularly in the older universities where anachronistic professorial chairs are reserved for them. In many countries Churches retain a stranglehold on certain disciplines. For example, there are really two distinct sets of university philosophers – the ordinary university academics and the theologians. In some countries the theologians enjoy a monopoly in philosophy departments, a vestige of medieval times when scholasticism, a long discredited form of theological philosophy, enjoyed a similar monopoly. In other countries there are parallel structures of theologians and academic philosophers. In either case theologians are appointed to university chairs for their orthodoxy, not for their intellectual ability. To appreciate how bizarre this it, it is rather as though universities continued to fund pre-scientific disciplines like alchemy or astrology, and to appoint professors of these subjects on the strength of their Christian belief.

The grip of the Church is still powerful in other fields. Around the world Christian laws still limit what other people can do, especially on Sundays and other Christian festivals. Different countries suffer different restrictions, but the pattern is similar, always limiting people's freedom to have fun and to do what they want to do: restrictions on drinking alcohol; restrictions on singing and dancing; restrictions on games, sports and gambling; restrictions on buying and selling; restrictions on art galleries, exhibitions, music, theatre, cinema, concerts, circuses and other public performances. In some places it is still almost impossible to travel by public transport on a Sunday.

Perhaps most worrying is the phenomenon of End-Timers in the United States. End-Timers represent a reappearance of an early Christian movement that imagined that it could help trigger the end of the world by promoting events that would presage the Second Coming of Jesus Christ. Reading works such as the book of Revelation they set themselves to destroy the Roman Empire. This was the motivation for their repeated acts of arson, but their ultimate goals were wars around the world and civil breakdown everywhere. Just like these early Christians, modern End-Timers believe the end of the world to be imminent, and imagine that they can accelerate its arrival by arranging to come to pass the same events that those early Christians looked forward to: world war and civil breakdown. The parallels are precise, with the European Community (created by the Treaty of Rome) playing the role of the Roman Empire. We have no idea how many End-Timers are currently seeking political office in the United States – certainly dozens, possibly hundreds or thousands. They represent a real threat to world peace – potentially occupying high offices in government and the armed forces. Any internet search will reveal large numbers of websites promoted by End-Timer Christians of various degrees of virulence, many working to 'hasten the inevitable', anticipating a Third World War and the Second Coming.

PRESENT DANGERS

Theological religion is the source of all imaginable follies and disturbances: it is the parent of fanaticism and evil discord. It is the enemy of mankind.
Voltaire (1694–1778), ***Philosophical Dictionary of Religion***

For the first three centuries the Church was relatively powerless and did little harm. It taught brotherhood, tolerance, peace, love, justice, mercy, and so on, to the extent of encouraging Christian soldiers to desert the Imperial armies. For the next 1,500 years it was extremely powerful and harmful throughout Europe. It caused division, persecution, war, hatred, and injustice, and practised the most spectacular viciousness and brutality. The Church, in its numerous guises, has a less than enviable record on a wide range of social issues. It has befriended and supported totalitarian, authoritarian, and extreme right-wing regimes. It has abused its power and opposed legal, political and educational reform. It has also opposed liberties and human rights. It has opposed science and rational medicine and taught a wide range of nonsense, insisting that illness was caused by evil spirits, witchcraft and sin. For many centuries the Church maintained its position by a combination of fraud and terror, opposing advances in learning and suppressing the truth. Where Christian dogma has been strongest, so has poverty, misery and ignorance. Christian Churches were wholly responsible for the deaths of millions whose only crime was to dissent from their current version of orthodoxy.

In its heyday the Christian Churches practised routine persecution. They tortured, mutilated, branded, dismembered and killed as a matter of course. They condemned to death any who questioned their dogmas. They burned Jews, heretics, apostates and pagans in large numbers. They imagined enemies everywhere and had them exterminated. Among their countless victims were women whose chief crimes seem to have been living alone, looking old, keeping pets, and knowing something about herbs and midwifery. Christians even persecuted their fellow believers. It is sobering to reflect that over almost 2000 years Christians have never been persecuted by any of their supposed enemies as viciously as they have been persecuted by fellow Christians.

Over the last 200 years the Churches have been losing power and have become relatively harmless again in proportion to their diminishing influence outside the United States. They have sought to obliterate the evidence of their behaviour, substituting sympathetic histories with their members as heroes. In this they have been largely successful. Most people in the developed world, even non-Christians, have a largely positive view of Christianity and its historical record.

Once again Churches preach brotherhood, tolerance, peace, love, justice and mercy. One is reminded of a dangerous recidivist criminal. When in custody he is mild, reasonable, plausible and friendly. But as soon as he is at liberty he commits the same crimes again and again. At the moment he is in the custody of secular society, but he is looking forward to his next parole. At all times and in all parts of the world, mainstream Churches have oppressed people exactly to the extent that they have been able to. This pattern could continue in the future. There is no reason to doubt that it will.

NOTES

1 'Hunt enthusiasts call faithful to Free Church of Country Sports', *The Telegraph*, 23rd May 2004. See also http://news.bbc.co.uk/1/hi/uk/3687340.stm

2 Witchcraft was recognised as a legitimate religion in *Dettmer v Landon*, a case heard in the state of Virginia in 1985. In the following year a Federal Appeal Court confirmed that witchcraft (the Church of Wicca) was protected under the First Amendment.

3 Letters inciting murder, and other clear evidence of incitement to murder Salman Rushdie, were printed in British broadsheet newspapers during December 1989 (for example *The Independent*, 20th December 1989).

4 Letter from Dr Harry Baker of Meldreth, Cambridgeshire to the *Sunday Times* published on 7th October 2007. On the same day, the same newspaper reported cases of religious medical students refusing to treat alcohol related medical conditions of even to examine members of the opposite sex, 'Muslim Medics turn refusnik over alcohol'.

5 The Jedi are already asking for rights comparable to those enjoyed by other religions. See http://www.jedimasters.info.

6 'Christian groups "plan job purge of unbelievers"', *The Times*, 30th August 2003.

7 Peter Tatchell was prosecuted under this Act in 1998 for disrupting a sermon by the Archbishop of Canterbury. See the *New Humanist*, vol. 114, no. 4, December 1998.

8 James Madison, *Detached Memoranda*, ca. 1817. For the full text see http://press-pubs.uchicago.edu/founders/documents/amendI_religions64.html

9 Here is the current Massachusetts law: 'Whoever wilfully blasphemes the holy name of God by denying, cursing or contumeliously reproaching God, his creation, government or final judging of the world, or by cursing or contumeliously reproaching Jesus Christ or the Holy Ghost, or by cursing or contumeliously reproaching or exposing to contempt and ridicule, the holy word of God contained in the holy scriptures shall be punished by imprisonment in jail for not more than one year or by a fine of not more than three hundred dollars, and may also be bound to good behaviour.' The General Laws Of Massachusetts, Part IV. Crimes, Punishments And Proceedings in Criminal Cases, Title I. Crimes And Punishments, Chapter 272. Crimes Against Chastity, Morality, Decency And Good Order, Section 36. Blasphemy. See http://mass.gov/legis/laws/mgl/272-36.htm.

10 'Humanist Textbooks Banned on Religious Grounds', *The Times Educational Supplement*, 20th March 1987.

11 For a full account of this incident see http://www.positiveatheism.org/writ/ghwbush.htm.

12 Bertrand Russell, *Has Religion Made Useful Contributions to Civilization?*, 1930.

13 'Forbidden Vaccine' (editorial), *The New York Times*, 30th December, 2005.

14 N. D. Kristof, 'Bush's Sex Scandal', *The New York Times*, 16th February, 2005.

15 It is not only the Roman Catholic Church that still sanctions exorcism. Reports of children being tortured to death during exorcisms sanctioned by various Churches in Britain appear regularly in national newspapers in the early twenty-first century. Exorcisms are also common in the Orthodox Church – many of the faithful were horrified by the case of a Romanian priest, Daniel Petru Corogeanu, and four nuns sentenced in 2007 for killing a fifth nun during an exorcism. She had been chained to a cross and denied food and water for days then suffocated. The outrage was not at the priest's exorcism – perfectly normal in the Orthodox Church – but at his arrest, trial and conviction, a unique event in the Orthodox Church. For more see http://www.cbsnews.com/stories/2007/02/19/world/ap/main2492368.shtml and http://news.bbc.co.uk/2/hi/europe/6376211.stm.

16 Hitchens, *God Is Not Great*, Chapter Sixteen ('Is Religion Child Abuse?').

APPENDICES

APPENDIX A: JESUS' FAMILY

Mark 6:3	Mark 15:40	Matthew 13:55–6	Matthew 27:56
Children of Mary Siblings of Jesus the carpenter	Children of Mary (who may or may not be Mary the mother of Jesus)	Children of the carpenter and Mary Siblings of Jesus	Children of Mary (who may or may not be Mary the mother of Jesus)
James	James the less	James	James
Joses	Joses	Joses	Joses
Juda		Judas	
Simon		Simon	
Unnamed sisters	Possibly, Salome	Unnamed sisters	

Luke 24:10 refers to Mary the mother of James, who may or may not be Mary the mother of Jesus. Galatians 1:19 refers to James, the Lord's brother. Jude 1 refers to Jude the brother of James.

Jesus' brothers (brethren) are referred to in John 7:3, Acts 1:14, and 1 Corinthians 9:5.

Joses = Joseph = Joset

Jude = Judah = Judas = Judaeus

APPENDIX B: THE APOSTLES

Matthew 10:2–4	Mark 3:16–19	Luke 6:14–16	John 1 and 21	Acts 1:13 and 26
Simon (Peter)	Simon (Peter)	Simon (Peter)	Cephas = Simon Peter[1]	Peter
Andrew	Andrew	Andrew	Andrew	Andrew
John	John	John		John
James son of Zebedee	James son of Zebedee	James		James
Philip	Philip	Philip	Philip	Philip
Thomas	Thomas	Thomas	Thomas[2]	Thomas
Bartholomew	Bartholomew	Bartholomew	**Nathanael**[3]	Bartholomew
Matthew	Matthew	Matthew		Matthew
James son of Alphaeus	James son of Alphaeus	James son of Alphaeus		James son of Alphaeus
Simon the Canaanite	Simon the Canaanite	Simon the Zealot		Simon the Zealot
Lebbaeus whose surname was Thaddaeus	Thaddaeus	**Judas the brother (or son) of James**	**Judas**[4]	**Judas the brother (or son) of James**
Judas Iscariot	Judas Iscariot	Judas Iscariot		Matthias (in place of Judas Iscariot)
	Levi the son of Alphaeus[5] **(2:14)**	**Levi** (5:27)		
James,[6] the Lord's brother (13:55)	**James**, the Lord's brother (6:3)			
13	14	13	6	12

Simon Peter and Andrew were brothers (John 1:40)

John was the brother of James, son of Zebedee, they were known as the sons of thunder (Boanerges) (Mark 3:17)

James son of Zebedee = James the great

James son of Alphaeus is generally identified with James the less, although Mark 15:40 suggests that James the brother of Jesus may be James the less, if the Mary referred to here is Jesus's mother.

Altogether there are no fewer than 16 names given to apostles (the 12 listed in Matthew 10:2–4 plus the four in bold text), excluding Judas Iscariot's replacement, Matthias.

NOTES

1 Cephas is Aramaic for Peter.
2 Thomas was also called Thomas Didymus. Thomas means twin in Aramaic, as does Didymus in Greek.
3 Nathanael from Cana in Galilee, John 21
4 John 14:22 refers to a Judas other than Judas Iscariot.
5 Levi, the son of Alphaeus, is conventionally identified with Matthew.
6 James the Lord's brother is mentioned elsewhere and specifically identified as one of the apostles (Galatians 1:19). He is also known as James the Righteous (or Just). He is sometimes identified with James the less (Mark 15:40), although the title James the less is generally accorded to another James, the son of Alphaeus. He cannot be the James known as James the Great, since he is mentioned as still living after the death of James the Great (Acts 12:2 and 12:17). In any case James the Great was stated to be the son of Zebedee.

APPENDIX C: POSTBURIAL EVENTS

Who Visited Jesus' Tomb?

Matthew 28:1	Mark 16:1–9	Luke 24:1–11	John 20:1–14	1 Corinthians 15:5–8
Mary Magdalene	Mary Magdalene	Mary Magdalene	Mary Magdalene	
the other Mary	Mary mother of James	Mary mother of James		
	Salome	Joanna		
		other women		

Who did Jesus appear to after the Resurrection?

Matthew 28:9–20	Mark 16:9–14	Luke 24:1–33	John 20:14–29	1 Corinthians 15:5–8
Mary Magdalene	Mary Magdalene	-	Mary Magdalene	-
'the other' Mary	Two others	Cleopas One other	-	-
-	-	Simon (Peter)	-	Peter
The Eleven	The Eleven	The Eleven	The disciples	The Twelve
-	-	-	-	> 500 men
-	-	-	-	James
-	-	-	Thomas + disciples	-
-	-	-	The disciples	All the apostles
-	-	-	-	Paul

BIBLIOGRAPHY

Ackerknecht, Erwin H., *A Short History of Medicine* (London: Johns Hopkins University Press, 1982).

Argyle, Michael and Beit-Hallahmi, Benjamin, *The Social Psychology of Religion* (London: RKP, 1975).

Armstrong, Karen, *A History of God* (London: Mandarin, 1993).

Ashe, Geoffrey, *The Virgin* (London: Arkana, 1988).

Augustine, St, *City of God* (London: Penguin, 1984), (English translation by Henry Bettenson).

Baigent, Michael and Leigh, Richard, *The Dead Sea Scrolls Deception* (London: Corgi, 1991).

Baker, J. H., *An Introduction to English Legal History* (London: Butterworths, 1971).

Barber, Malcolm, *The Trial of the Templars* (Cambridge University Press, 1998).

Barkow, Jerome *et al* (eds.), *The Adapted Mind* (Oxford University Press, 1997).

Barraclough, Geoffrey, *The Medieval Papacy* (London: Thames and Hudson, 1992).

Berman, David, *A History of Atheism in Britain* (London: Routledge, 1990).

Bocock, Robert and Thompson, Kenneth, *Religion and Ideology* (Manchester: Manchester University Press, 1985).

Boyer, Carl B. and Merzbach, Uta C., *A History of Mathematics* (New York: John Wiley and Sons, 1989).

Bradford, Ernle, *The Shield and the Sword* (London: Fontana, 1974).

Brenon, Anne, *Les Cathares* (Paris: Jacques Granger, 1997).

Brooke, John Hedley, *Science and Religion: Some Historical Perspectives* (Cambridge University Press, 1991).

Chadwick, Henry, *The Early Church* (London: Pelican, 1967).

Christie-Murray, David, *A History of Heresy* (Oxford University Press, 1989).

Clark, Sir George, *Science and Social Welfare in the Age of Newton* (Oxford University Press, 1949).

The Code of Canon Law (London: Collins, 1983). (English translation.)

Cohen, A. (ed.), *The Soncino Chumash* (London: Soncino Press, 1974).

Confucius, *The Analects* (London: Penguin, 1979). (English translation by D. C. Lau.)

Costen, Michael, *The Cathars and the Albigensian Crusade* (Manchester: Manchester University Press, 1997).

Coudert, Allison, *Alchemy, The Philosopher's Stone* (London: Wildwood House, 1980).

Cozens, M. L., *A Handbook of Heresies* (London: Sheed and Ward, 1974).

Curtis, Vesta Sarkhosh, *Persian Myths* (London: British Museum Press, 1993).

Dalrymple, William, *From the Holy Mountain* (London: Flamingo, 1998).

Daniell, Christopher, *Death and Burial in Medieval England 1066–1550* (London: Routledge, 1997).

Darwin, Charles, *The Origin of Species* (London: Penguin, 1968).

Davies, R. Trevor, *Four Centuries of Witch-Beliefs* (London: Methuen, 1947).

Davis, C. S. L., *Peace, Print & Protestantism 1450–1558* (St Albans: Paladin, 1977).

Dawkins, Richard, *The Selfish Gene* (London: Penguin, 1976).

——, *The Blind Watchmaker* (London: Penguin, 1986).

——, *River out of Eden* (London: Phoenix, 1996).

Deanesly, Margaret, *A History of the Medieval Church* (London: Routledge, 1972).

Dennett, Daniel C., *Breaking the Spell, Religion as a Natural Phenomenon* (London: Penguin, 2006).

——, *Consciousness Explained* (London: Penguin, 1991).

——, *Darwin's Dangerous Idea* (London: Penguin, 1998).

Early Christian Writings (London: Penguin, 1987). (Translation by Maxwell Staniforth, edited by Andrew Louth.)

Ehrman, Bart D., *The Orthodox Corruption of Scripture* (Oxford University Press, 1993).

The Epic of Gilgamesh (London: Penguin, 1972). (English translation by N. K. Sandars.)

Eusebius, *The History of the Church* (London: Penguin, 1965). (English translation by G. A. Williamson.)

Evans, Christopher, *Is Holy Scripture Christian?* (London: SCM Press, 1971).

Finocchiaro, Maurice A., *The Galileo Affair: A Documentary History* (London: University of California Press, 1989).

Flew, Antony, *An Introduction to Western Philosophy* (London: Thames and Hudson, 1989).

Foucault, Michel, *Madness and Civilization* (London: Routledge, 1995). (English translation by Richard Howard.)

Fox, Robin Lane, *The Unauthorised Version* (London: Viking, 1991).

——, *Pagans and Christians* (London: Penguin, 1988).

Fraser, Lady Antonia, *The Gunpowder Plot: Terror and Faith in 1605* (London: Arrow, 1999).

Frayling, Christopher, *Vampyres* (London: Faber and Faber, 1991).

Frazer, James G., *The Golden Bough* (London: Macmillan, 1957).

Freud, Sigmund, *Totem and Taboo* (London: Pelican Books, 1938).

Gibbon, Edward, *The Decline and Fall of the Roman Empire* (London: Penguin, 1987).

Graves, Robert, *The Greek Myths* (2 vols.) (London: Pelican Books, 1960).

——, *The White Goddess* (London: Faber and Faber, 1961).

Harrington, Daniel J., *Wisdom Texts from Qumran* (London: Routledge, 1996).

Harris, Sam, *Letter to a Christian Nation* (London: Bantam Press, 2007).

Herrick, Jim, *Against the Faith* (London: Glover & Blair, 1985).

Hibbert, Christopher, *The Roots of Evil* (London: Penguin, 1966).

Hick, John (ed.), *The Myth of God Incarnate* (London: SCM Press, 1977).

Hitchens, Christopher, *God Is Not Great* (London: Atlantic Books, 2007).

Humphreys, Margaret, *Empty Cradles* (London: Corgi Books, 1995).

Jahoda, Gustav, *The Psychology of Superstition* (London: Pelican, 1970).

Johnson, Paul, *A History of Christianity* (London: Penguin, 1976).

Johnson, Steven, *Emergence* (London: Penguin, 2001).

Josephus, *Jewish Antiquities* (London: Harvard University Press, 1996). (English translation.)

Kahl, Joachim, *The Misery of Christianity* (London: Penguin Books, 1971). (English translation by N. D. Smith.)

Kamen, Henry, *The Spanish Inquisition* (London: The Folio Society, 1998).

Kelly, J. N. D., *Early Christian Doctrines* (London: A & C Black, 1968).

——, *The Oxford Dictionary of Popes* (Oxford University Press, 1986).

Kerényi, C., *The Gods Of The Greeks* (London: Thames and Hudson, 1974). (English translation by Norman Cameron.)

Kidd, B. J., *Documents Illustrative of the History of the Church* (2 vols.). (London: SPCK, 1932).

Knight, Margaret (ed.), *Humanist Anthology* (London: RPA, 1967).

The Koran (London: Penguin, 1974). (English translation by N. J. Dawood.)

Kramer, Heinrich and Sprenger, James, *Malleus Maleficarum* (London: Arrow, 1971). (English translation by Montague Summers.)

——, *A History of the Inquisition of the Middle Ages* (3 vols.). (London, 1888).

Le Roy Ladurie, Emmanuel, *Montaillou, village occitan de 1294 à 1324* (Paris: Editions Gallimard, 1978).

——, *Montaillou* (Abridged English Version) (London: Penguin, 1978).

Lloyd G. E. R., *The Revolutions of Wisdom* (London: University of California Press, 1989).

Lucretius, *On the Nature of the Universe (De Rerum Natura)* (London: Penguin, 1951). (English translation by R. E. Latham.)

MacKay, Charles, *Extraordinary Popular Delusions and the Madness of Crowds* (London: Random House, 1980). (Originally published in 1841 under the title *Memoirs of Extraordinary Popular Delusions*.)

McKay, John P., et al, *A History of Western Society* (Boston: Houghton Mifflin, 1991).

Marsh, John, *Saint John* (Commentary). (London: Pelican, 1968).

Meyer, Marvin W. (translator), *The Secret Teachings of Jesus, Four Gnostic Gospels* (New York: Random House, 1986).

Murray, Gilbert, *Five Stages of Greek Religion* (London: Watts & Co, 1935).

——, *Humanist Essays* (London: Unwin, 1964).

Nelli, René, *Les Cathares du Languedoc* (Paris: Hachette, 1995).

Nineham, D. E., *Saint Mark* (Commentary). (London: Pelican, 1969).

Norton, David, *A History of the Bible as Literature* (2 vols.). (Cambridge University Press, 1993).

Norwich, John Julius, *Byzantium The Early Centuries* (London: Penguin, 1992).

——, *Byzantium The Apogee* (London: Penguin, 1993).

——, *Byzantium The Decline and Fall* (London: Penguin, 1996).

O'Shea, Stephen, *The Perfect Heresy* (London: Profile Books Ltd, 2000).

Obianyido, Anene, *Christ or Devil?* (Nigeria: Delta, 1988).

Pagels, Elaine, *The Gnostic Gospels* (London: Orion, 2006).

Paine, Thomas, *The Age of Reason* (New York: Prometheus, 1984).

Peterson, Michael, et al, *Reason & Religious Belief, An Introduction to the Philosophy of Religion* (Oxford University Press, 1991).

Pollock, Sir Frederick and Maitland, Frederic William, *The History of English Law* (Vol. 1). (Cambridge University Press, 1968).

Potter, Harry, *Hanging in Judgement* (London: SCM Press, 1993).

Ranke-Heinemann, Uta, *Eunuchs for the Kingdom of Heaven* (London: Andre Deutsch, 1990). (English translation by John Brownjohn.)

Redwood, John, *Reason, Ridicule and Religion* (London: Thames and Hudson, 1976).

Richards, Jeffrey, *Sex, Dissidence and Damnation: Minority Groups in the Middle Ages* (London: Routledge, 1995).

Ridley, Matt, *The Red Queen* (London: Penguin, 1994).

Riley-Smith, Jonathan, *The Atlas of the Crusades* (London: Times Books, 1991).

Robinson, James M. (General Editor), *The Nag Hammadi Library* (London: Harper Collins, 1990).

Roquebert, Michel, *L'Épopée Cathare* (5 vols.). (Privat; v1 1970, v2 1977, v3 1986, v4 1989, v5 1998).

Romer, John, *Testament: The Bible and History* (London: Michael O'Mara, 1988).

Runciman, Sir Steven, *A History of the Crusades* (3 vols.). (London: Penguin, 1971).

——, *Byzantine Style and Civilization* (London: Penguin, 1990).

Russell, Bertrand, *Why I Am Not a Christian* (London: Unwin Hyman, 1979).

——, *A History of Western Philosophy* (London: Routledge, 1991).

Sagan, Carl, *The Demon-Haunted World* (London: Headline, 1997).

Sale, Kirkpatrick, *The Conquest of Paradise* (London: Hodder & Stoughton, 1991).

Scholder, Klaus, *A Requiem for Hitler* (London: SCM Press, 1989).

Scott, George Riley, *A History of Torture* (London: Senate, 1995).

Seznec, Jean, *The Survival of the Pagan Gods* (Princeton University Press, 1972). (English translation by Barbara F. Sessions.)

Slack, Kenneth, *The British Churches Today* (London: SCM Press, 1961).

Smith, George H., *Atheism: The Case Against God* (New York: Prometheus, 1979).

Staniforth, Maxwell (ed.), *Early Christian Writings* (London: Penguin, 1987).

Stone, Darwell, *Outlines of Christian Dogma* (London: Longmans, 1927).

Strathern, Paul, *The Medici* (London: Pimlico, 2005).

Tacitus, *The Annals of Imperial Rome* (London: Penguin, 1971). (English translation by Michael Grant.)

Tannahill, Reay, *Sex in History* (London: Abacus, 1981).

Thomas, Keith, *Religion and the Decline of Magic* (London: Penguin, 1991).

Toy, John, *What Are Apocryphal Writings* (York: The Vicar's Press, 1991).

Trevelyan, G. M., *Illustrated English Social History* (4 vols.). (London: Pelican, 1964).

Tribe, David, *100 Years of Freethought* (London: Elek, 1967).

Tyerman, Christopher, *God's War, A New History of the Crusade* (London: Penguin, 2007).

Vermes, Geza, *Jesus The Jew* (London: SCM Press, 1983).

de Voragine, Jacobus, *The Golden Legend* (2 vols.). (Princeton: Princeton University Press, 1993). (English translation by William Granger Ryan.)

de Waal, Frans, *Good Natured. The Origins of Right and Wrong in Humans and other Animals* (Harvard University Press, 1996).

Walter, Nicholas, *Blasphemy Ancient and Modern* (London: Rationalist Press, 1990).

Walvin, James, *Black Ivory, A History of British Slavery* (London: Harper Collins, 1992).

Ware, Timothy, *The Orthodox Church* (London: Penguin, 1991).

Warner, Marina, *Alone of All Her Sex* (London: Picador, 1967).

Wells, G. A., *Religious Postures* (La Salle: Open Court, 1967).

——, *The Historical Evidence for Jesus* (New York: Prometheus, 1967).

Whitehead, Benjamin, *Church Law* (London: Stevens & Sons, 1911).

Wilson, A. N. *Jesus* (London: Flamingo, 1993).

Wilson, Bryan, *Religion in Sociological Perspective* (Oxford University Press, 1982).

Wolpert, Lewis, *Six Impossible Things Before Breakfast, The Evolutionary Origins Of Belief* (London: Faber & Faber, 2006).

Yallop, David, *In God's Name* (London: Corgi, 1988).

Young, Frances, *The Making of the Creeds* (London: SCM Press, 1996).

INDEX

sacrifices, 283, 347, 348
Sadduccees, 117, 139, 152, 179, 242n188
Sadhus, 446
saints, 165, 167, 265, 266, 306, 362, 363,
364, 366
patron, 166
see also individual saints by name
Sala, 50, 91n74
Salome, 56, 403n163
Salvation Army, 311
Salvationists, 258
Samaria, 353
Samarian, 123
Samaritans, 10, 179, 237n90, 242n188
Samhain, 175, 176
Samson, 8
Samuel
1 Book of, 11, 12, 15, 16, 20, 25, 26,
31, 33
2 Book of, 12, 16, 18, 25
Samuel, 346
Sanhedrin, 49, 91n72, 237n79
Sant' Ignazio, church, 160
Santa Claus, 173
Santos, Lucia dos, 255
Sapphira, 98n
Sardica, synod, 213
Sargon of Akkad, 7
Satan, 18, 23, 75, 76, 120, 156, 164, 168,
205, 221, 239n125, 241n173, 254,
346, 356, 357, 365, 366, 400n132,
423
see also Lucifer, Devil
Saturnalia, 173
Saul, 12, 25, 26, 31, 33, 345, 346, 347
Saviour, as title, 154
Saxons, 172
Scheiner, Christoph, 412
Schillebeeckx, Edward, 389
schisms, 178, 191, 192, 193, 194, 208
see also Great Schism
Schlessinger, Laura, 278, 279
scholasticism, 428, 429, 441, 458
Schweitzer, Albert, 385
Scotist school, 151
scribes, 288
Sea of Galilee, 48
Second Coming, 65, 191, 338, 414, 459

Second Council of Constantinople (553)
see Council of Constantinople (553)
Second Council of Nicaea (787)
see Council of Nicaea (787)
Second Ecumenical Council of
Constantinople
see Council of Constantinople (553)
Second Jewish Revolt, 105, 117
Second Lateran Council, 149
Second Pseudo-Isidorian Decretals, 395n29
Second Vatican Council, 312, 402n160
Secret Book of James, 43, 45, 116, 237n75
Secret Gospel of Mark, 44, 45, 90n59,
123n, 247
sects, 179, 180, 181, 182, 183, 185, 186,
187, 188, 189, 190, 191, 192, 194,
195
Senate, Rome, 160, 161, 167
Seneca, 62, 245n230, 260, 263, 426
Sennacherib, 31
Septuagint, 2, 4, 5, 10, 13, 18, 21, 25, 35,
87n6, 88n20, 89n34, 199, 271, 372,
379
Serbia, xi
serfs, 205
Sergius I, pope, 174
Sergius II, pope, 219, 228
Sergius III, pope, 220, 232, 233
Sergius IV, pope, 221, 233
Sergius Paulus, 98n
Sermon on the Mount, 39, 53
Servetus, Michael, 428
sex, 45, 77, 454, 455
sex crimes, 316
Shaddai, 344, 352
Shamash, Babylonian sun god, 7
shaving, 284, 285
Shem, 425
Sheol, 163, 241n172
Shepherd of Hermas, 46, 47
shepherds, 378
shoes, 285
Shrove Tuesday, 312, 399n106
Sibylline oracles, 262, 277
Sibyls, 171
Sicily, kings of, 222
Sidon, 48
Sikhs, 446, 449